A FAREWELL
TO JUSTICE

Other Books by Joan Mellen

Big Bad Wolves: Masculinity in the American Film
Bob Knight: His Own Man
A Film Guide to the Battle of Algiers
*Hellman and Hammett: The Legendary Passion of Lillian Hellman
and Dashiell Hammett*
In the Realm of the Senses
Kay Boyle: Author of Herself
Literary Masterpieces: One Hundred Years of Solitude
Literary Masters: Gabriel García Márquez
Literary Topics: Magic Realism
Marilyn Monroe
Natural Tendencies: A Novel
Privilege: The Enigma of Sasha Bruce
Seven Samurai
Voices from the Japanese Cinema
The Waves at Genji's Door: Japan Through Its Cinema
Women and Their Sexuality in the New Film
The World of Luis Buñuel: Essays in Criticism

A FAREWELL TO JUSTICE

Jim Garrison, JFK's Assassination, and the Case That Should Have Changed History

JOAN MELLEN

Potomac Books, Inc.

WASHINGTON, D.C.

Potomac Books, Inc. Copyright © 2005 by Joan Mellen.

Library of Congress Cataloging-in-Publication Data

Mellen, Joan.
   A farewell to justice: Jim Garrison, JFK's assassination, and the case that should have changed history / Joan Mellen. —1st ed.
      p. cm.
   Includes bibliographical references and index.
   ISBN 1-57488-973-7 (hardcopy : alk. paper)
   1.   Kennedy, John F. (John Fitzgerald), 1917-1963—Assassination.
   2.   Garrison, Jim, 1921-   I. Title.
   E842.9.M443 2005
   973.922—dc22

2005012425

(alk. paper)

Printed in the United States of America on acid-free paper that meets the American National Standards Institute Z39-48 Standard.

Potomac Books, Inc.
22841 Quicksilver Drive
Dulles, Virginia 20166

First Edition

10 9 8 7 6 5 4 3 2 1

For Robert Buras

"He has abandoned his life to understanding that moment in Dallas, the seven seconds that broke the back of the American century."
Don DeLillo, *Libra*

CONTENTS

ACKNOWLEDGMENTS

F OR HER COMMITMENT TO this project, I would like to thank most my agent, Ellen Levine. The platonic ideal of a literary agent, she has been a beacon of light and inspiration, no less of courage and integrity. I am grateful.

Rick Russell, my editor at Potomac Books, has manifested an intellectual courage rare among publishers. For his confidence in this project, his resolute objectivity, and the broad range of his wisdom as a professional historian, I am also grateful. I would like to express my appreciation as well to Jehanne Moharram for her tireless efforts and ready imagination.

Michie Shaw approached the production of this book with a rare standard of excellence and commitment.

A very special thank you for his generosity and many kindnesses to Malcolm Blunt, that most brilliant navigator of the National Archives. James H. Lesar of the Assassination Archives and Research Center in Washington, DC, was a source of encouragement from the beginning to the end of this project. I'm grateful as well to Dan Alcorn for reading the manuscript and for his suggestions. Special gratitude goes as well to Teresa Neaves, who worked with Don Lee Keith on an investigation of the murder of Mary Sherman. The hospitality of Gordon Winslow in Miami is much appreciated.

I owe as well special thanks to those who stood by with encouragement and support. When I looked up, they were there: Christopher Sharrett; Gary Aguilar; Larry Hancock; Andy Winiarczyk; Donald V. Organ and Joan Bovan Organ; Zachary Sklar; Peter Whitmey; Marlene Mancuso; Gaeton Fonzi; and Stuart Wexler. And especially for his faith in this project, Lyon ("Snapper") Garrison. A particular thank you goes to James Rubino, to Marianne Fisher-Giorlando, Gregory Parker, and Larry Haapanen.

In New Orleans, Numa Bertel, John Volz and Robert Buras understood the nature of this task. For their patience, generosity and wisdom I am particularly grateful.

And a special thanks to Dr. Frank and Cathy Martello.

I am grateful to Temple University for its generosity in offering me a study leave and a summer research grant to complete this project; to Professor Robert Caserio, now the chair of the Department of English at Penn State University, for his help and interest; his departure is Temple's overwhelming loss; to Professor Alan Singer, director of the graduate program in creative writing during the years of this project, for his generosity and friendship; to Marina Angel, professor at the Temple University School of Law, for her graciousness and the loan of her own research assistants who worked on Jim Garrison's opinions for the Court of Appeal of Louisiana, Fourth Circuit; Professor Justin Vitiello did simultaneous translation from the Italian; Professor Emerita Maria Luisa Caputo-Mayr translated from the German.

The transcendent liberality of spirit and open-mindedness of all these people are herewith acknowledged; if Jim Garrison had ever suffered public attack for his investigation of the murder of John F. Kennedy, you would not have known it from them.

The following people contributed to my understanding of Jim Garrison, of Louisiana politics or of Jim Garrison's investigation. I am grateful to them all: William Alford; Anselmo Aliegro; Joseph E. Allain; Mark Allen; Smiley Anders; Richard Angelico; Thomas Angers; Trent Angers; Edward I. Arthur; Gerald P. Aurillo; Michael H. Bagot; F. Lee Bailey; Peggie Baker; Wilma Baker; Judge Denis A. Barry; Herbert Barton; Alvin Beauboeuf; Eddie Becker; Tammy Beckham; Thomas Edward Beckham; Jack Benjamin; Sally Boyce Benjamin; Barbara Bennett; Col. Esteban Benuvides; Pierre Bezou; Richard N. Billings; Gary Bizal; Christopher Blake; Don Bohning; Steve Bordelon; Isidro Borja; Joseph Bosco; Jeffrey Bowman; Carol Boyd; Edgar Eugene Bradley; Jim Bradshaw; Sheila Breaux; H. John Bremermann; Mickey Bremermann; Milton E. Brener; Tyler Bridges; the late Linda Brigette; Carlos Bringuier; Eric J. Brock; Betty Brown; Jordan Brown; Morris Brownlee; Vincent J. Bruno; Jay Bryant; Carl Bunch; Van H. Burns; Clay Calhoun; Debra Calhoun; Allen Campbell; Daniel Campbell; Martin Xavier Casey; Lawrence J. Centola Jr.; Loraine Chadwick; Patricia Chandler; the late Judge Lawrence Chehardy; Dan Christensen; John Ciravolo;

Ramsey Clark; John Clemmer; the late Corrie Collins; James A. Comiskey; Raymond Comstock; Harry Connick; Dr. Dimitri L. Contostavlos; Jean Franco Corsini; Curtis Crafard; Edward Craford; Louis Crovetto; Jorge Navarro Custin; Martin F. Dardis; Howard K. Davis; Warren de Brueys; L. J. Delsa; Bill DeMar; the late Irene Dempsey; the late Jack Dempsey; Dr. Doug Desalles; Bernard Diedtrich; John J. Dolan; Michael Dolan; Julius N. Draznin; Thomas Duffy Jr.; Judge Adrian Duplantier; Clarence O. Dupuy; George Dureau; Judge Thomas A. Early Jr.; Paul Eberle; Lolis Elie; Samuel Exnicios; Wayne Fairchild; the late Mary Ferrell; Diane Fernandez; Silvio Fernandez; Phillip Foto; Alberto Antonio Fowler; George Fowler; Charles W. Frank Jr.; Donald Freed; Richard Gaille; Warren Garfunkel; Eberhard Garrison; Elizabeth Garrison; Jasper Garrison; Mrs. Liz Garrison; Max Gartenberg; Pat Gartenberg; Edwin H. Gebhardt; Seymour Gelber; the late Walter Gemeinhardt; Darrow Gervais; the late Vance Gilmer; K. Eric Gisleson; Earl Patton Gore; Fred Gore; Alvin Gottschaull; Morgan Goudeau; C. Jackson Grayson Jr.; Carla Grayson; Elizabeth Grayson; Lawrence Guchereau; Judge James C. Gulotta; Joy Gulotta; H. Jeremy Gunn; Edwin Guthman; David Halberstam; the late Walter Hammer; Margaret Palmer Harvey; John Haygood; the late Dr. Robert Heath; Bob Heller; Gerald Patrick Hemming; Sharon Herkes; Matt Herron; Don Howell; Mary Howell; Merryl Hudson; Mrs. Nora Ibert; Louis Ivon; Dr. Bernard Jacobs; Stephen Jaffe; Rosemary James; Steve Jennings; Roger E. Johnston Jr.; the late Don Lee Keith; Iris Kelso; Maxine Kemp; Angelo Kennedy; Arthur Kinoy; Phillip Kitchen; Burton Klein; Judge William F. Kline; Helen Kohlman; the late Herman Kohlman; Allen B. Koltun; Louise Korns; Gail Kramer; Phyllis Kritikos; Irene Lacost; Elizabeth Landry; Rob Landry; Mark Lane; Jose Antonio Lanuza; Judge Rene Lehmann; Professor Henry Lesnick; Mary Lesnick; Dr. Harold Lief; Sheriff Elmer Litchfield; Marcie Ann Little; Judge Marcel Livaudais; William Livesay; Lt. Col. Lawrence E. Lowry; Irvin L. Magri Jr.; Scott Malone; Michael Marcades; Victor Marchetti; Ray Marcus; Vince Marino; David Marston; the late Layton Martens; Dr. Robert N. McClelland; Edwin Lea McGehee; Ray McGuire; the late Emory Carl McNabb; James McPherson; Lou Merhige; the late Frank Meloche; the late Gene Miller; Dr. Frank Minyard; Van Morgan; Jefferson Morley; Pat Morvant; Hugh Murray; Antonio Navarro; John Newman (New Orleans); Nicholas Noriea; Donold P. Norton; Gordon Novel; Joseph A. Oster; Lester Otillio Jr.; Dr. Martin Palmer; Salvatore Panzeca; Andy Partee; Jack Peebles; William Pepper; Paulette Perrien; Morris

Phillips; Shawn Phillips; Rosemary Pillow; Joseph W. Pitts; Monique Poirrier; William Porteous, III; Bill Preston; the late Colonel L. Fletcher Prouty; Carlos Quiroga; Brucie Rafferty; John R. Rarick; Joseph Rault Jr.; Ellen Ray; Gary Raymond; Karlem (Ducky) Reiss; Dr. Randy Robertson; Suzanne Robbins; Dr. Luis Fernandez-Rocha; Rolando Masferrer Rojas; Clark Rowley; Juan Salvat; Verla Bell Sample; Martha Ann Samuel; Dr. Monroe Samuels; Stephanie Brett Samuel; Edward Sapir; James Savage; Jack Sawyer; Ross Scaccia; Russell J. Schonekas; Danielle Schott; Donald G. Scheuler; G. Harrison Scott; Dr. C.B. Scrignar; Mike Seghers; Julie Serera; Ralph Slovenko; Courtney Smith; the late Sergio Arcacha Smith; Sanford Socolow; Michael F. Starr; Oliver Stone; Jefferson Sulzer; Victoria Sulzer; Anthony Summers; Elizabeth Swanson; the late Joseph T. Sylvester Jr.; Robert K. Tanenbaum; John Tarver; Angie Teasdel; Jay Teasdel; Wilmer Thomas; Stuart Timmons; Joseph J. Trento; William W. Turner; Stephen Tyler; Roland Wall; William Walter; Bruce Waltzer; Barbara Ward; Lenore Ward; Dr. Cyril Wecht; Ralph Whalen; Gus Weill; Judge Tom C. Wicker; Judge David R.M. Williams; Fred Williams; John D. Wilson; Christine Wiltz; Fritz Windhorst; Maj. Gen. Erbon W. Wise; Louis E. Wolfson; David Wolkowsky; Gaby Wood; Joyce Wood; Aline Woodside; Ross Yockey; Billy Zachary.

For hospitality in the state of Louisiana, I am grateful to the late Dr. Frank Silva and Debbie Silva, whose rare kindness can never be repaid; to Anne Butler of the Butler-Greenwood Plantation; to Anne Hundley Dischler, for her great generosity to me; and in Los Angeles, to Shirley Magidson.

I have been greatly helped by the historians who came before, some in large ways and some in small: Thank you everybody: Debra Conway; Stephen Roy; Jim DiEugenio; Gary Mack; Jim Marrs; Peter Dale Scott; Romney Stubbs; the late Harold Weisberg; Len Osanic; Martin Shackelford; Joe Biles; Michael Kurtz; Vincent Salandria; Gus Russo; Clayton Ogilvie; Kathy Strang; Steve Jones; John Kelin; the late Richard Popkin; Gary Shaw; Jim Olivier; Ed Sherry; with a special note of gratitude to Jerry Shinley. For his research help, I would also like to acknowledge Peter Vea, who worked tirelessly on behalf of this project. Julie Luongo was an able and committed assistant.

These friends were there: Michael and Elena Wood; Ruth Prawer Jhabvala and C.R.S. Jhabvala; Judge Richard A. Posner; Dorothea Straus; Richard Kluger; and Alan Wilde.

My former students helped out graciously: Adrian Khactu; Jeffrey Reichman; Andrew McCann; Rob Schmitt; Ian Flamm; Jimmy J. Pack; Jonathan Hall; and Ian Mount, who made the discovery at Tulane University that the FBI had come in and eviscerated the papers of Hale Boggs . . . and my gratitude to the dining group that drove out to the country: Hugh Rosen, Virginia Nalencz, Debra Leigh-Scott, Joanne Daume, and Jim Quinn. And a special thank you for her generosity of spirit and help to Sonia Vora.

My gratitude to Martha Wagner Murphy of the JFK Collection of the National Archives: lucid, competent, always helpful, a superb research librarian. Thanks, too, to James R. Mathis for his courtesy and assistance.

I am grateful always to the Mercer County Library, Hopewell Branch, for their courtesy and help, in particular to its director Ed Hoag, and to Hope Sulow.

I am particularly grateful to Irene Wainwright at the Louisiana Division/City Archives of the New Orleans Public Library; Pat Ferguson at LSU–Shreveport; Laura B. Street, archivist, Louisiana State University–Shreveport; Noel Library Archives; Louisiana State University Library, Special Collections: Emily Robison; Bruce Petronio, Mercer County Library, Lawrenceville Branch.

The following librarians also offered generous assistance: Brian A. Stiglmeier of the Supreme Court of the United States library; William Meneray, Curator of Special Collections, Tulane University; Wayne Everard, Archivist, New Orleans Public Library; Alvin Bethard, University Libraries, University of Louisiana, Lafayette; Scott Taylor, Georgetown University Library; Professor Sarah Brown of Florida Atlantic University; Ann Kerr of the Mercer County Library, Lawrence Branch; First Lieutenant Larry D. Pool, Department of the Army, United States Army Field Artillery Training Center, Fort Sill, Oklahoma.

Thanks to the staff at Fort Sill for their assistance. University of Iowa Special Collections: Ethel Bloesch and Kathy Hodson; Norelius Community Library, Dennison, Iowa; Doug Parker, photo librarian at the *Times-Picayune* newspaper; Mary Linn Wernet, Curator of Special Collections, Watson Memorial Library, Cammie G. Henry Research Center, Northwestern State University of Louisiana at Natchitoches; Bob Aquilina, historian, U.S. Marine Corps, Marine Corps Historical Center.

Thanks, too, to the Florida Thoroughbred Breeders and Owners Association of Ocala, Florida.

The late Lynn Pelham—one of the greats—was extraordinarily generous. The cover photograph is his work.

No book on the Kennedy assassination can be written today without use of the records made available at the National Archives. All historians of this subject owe an enormous debt of gratitude to film director Oliver Stone for lobbying successfully, with passion and integrity, for these records to be made public. Were it not for Stone's efforts, this book could not have been written, nor would any of the books written after 1992 about this period of American history have been possible.

The staff of the Windsor Court Hotel in New Orleans were kind to me in every way during my many visits. In particular, I would like to thank Jacqueline Doise for her unfailing courtesy and generosity.

Had it not been for Ralph Schoenman, this book would not have come into being; his friendship, devotion and understanding have been without parallel.

PREFACE

I BEGAN WITH A BIOGRAPHY of Jim Garrison, flamboyant district attorney of Orleans Parish, Louisiana, a Don Quixote in a three-piece suit, and emerged with my own investigation into the murder of President John F. Kennedy. As a DA, Garrison was daring, a reform democrat and civil libertarian. What catapulted him onto the stage of history, however, was not his liberal approach to crime, but his discovery that the planning and a good part of the implementation of the assassination of the president occurred not in Dallas, Texas, but in Louisiana. The cover-up began in the tiny rural towns of Clinton and Jackson, north of Baton Rouge.

The release in the 1990s of thousands of documents, most from the CIA and FBI, has established the truth of Garrison's lone cry in the wilderness. To the moment of his death in 1992, Garrison was persuaded that the CIA, the same team that had overthrown President Arbenz of Guatemala in 1954, among them Lawrence Houston, Richard Helms and David Atlee Phillips, had planned the assassination, and then, with the assistance of the FBI, attempted to cover its traces, not always successfully. Kerry Thornley, the Marine Corps buddy of Lee Harvey Oswald, who told the Warren Commission that Oswald was a Marxist, turned out himself to have been a CIA employee trained, according to a CIA document, in Washington, D.C., in chemical and biological warfare.

Garrison's chief suspect, Clay Shaw, was a CIA operative, who, as a director of the Centro Mondiale Commerciale in Rome, joined fellow agents, like Ferenc Nagy, who since 1948 had worked for the CIA under the direction of Assistant Director of Central Intelligence, Frank Wisner. Despite his denials, Shaw knew Oswald's mentor David Ferrie so well that he cosigned a loan for him a week before the assassination so that Ferrie could rent a plane and fly to Dallas.

When Ferrie denied he had been in Dallas for eight to ten years, the FBI turned a blind eye to his well-documented acquaintance with Oswald. Ferrie was never called before the Warren Commission.

Oswald not only was set up as a scapegoat, but there were alternative scapegoats trained should he not fulfill the job, among them Thomas Edward Beckham, whom the CIA protected in Omaha. As for Oswald, not only was he an FBI informant and a CIA employee working for Counter Intelligence, but he was also an operative for United States Customs, a dual role shared by customs officers in Miami.

I met Jim Garrison in New Orleans in May of 1969, where he registered my husband and me as "Mr. and Mrs. Lyndon Baines Johnson." My husband had sent Garrison a series of articles from an Italian newspaper called *Paese Sera*, which revealed that Garrison suspect Shaw had been on the board of directors of what had been a CIA front. That Garrison's arrest of Shaw coincided with the publication of the articles was a coincidence of history.

Jim Garrison arrived, a very tall, heavyset man with a smooth, rosy complexion. You did not look at him—you listened to his deep, sonorous baritone, because he did not stop talking. He spoke not about Clay Shaw's trial, which had concluded three months earlier with Shaw's acquittal, but about the assassination. He did not mention that he was running for reelection as district attorney. He did not even suggest that he presently was district attorney. He did not mention his wife or his children. He spoke only of what had befallen President Kennedy.

Dinner was at Moran La Louisiane. Garrison had us seated in the center of the red brocade-walled room, directly under the crystal chandelier. After dinner, he lit a cigar. He was not downcast and you would not know that he had lost anything. The next day he talked of how Earl Cabell, the mayor of Dallas, was the brother of Major General Charles Cabell, who had left the CIA when John Kennedy fired Allen Dulles after the Bay of Pigs invasion.

In later conversations we discussed his novel manuscript. My husband sold *The Star-Spangled Contract* for him to McGraw-Hill for a quarter of a million dollars. Jim was broke then, and grateful. Ralph was not a literary agent and didn't want to take any commission, but Jim insisted. Then he refused to sign the contract unless Ralph agreed to be paid.

I saw Garrison for the last time in the spring of 1989. He mentioned that a film was to be made about his investigation, that his memoir, *On the Trail of the Assassins,* was a best seller. But all that really mattered were the facts of the assassination. He spoke ill of no one, blamed no one for the harsh turns his life had taken. Instead he wanted to discuss the changing of John F. Kennedy's Dallas parade route, one more time.

What began as the chronicle of a man I once knew, a sardonic ironist, who would talk for hours about the assassination, became a biography of his investigation. Interviewing over a thousand people, I was able to demonstrate the specifics of how the FBI and CIA, led by National Security Agency, FBI and CIA veteran Walter Sheridan, attempted to destroy Garrison's effort, not least by bribing his witnesses.

The decades-long campaign to silence Jim Garrison included the participation even of "Deep Throat" himself. Hardly interested in the "truth," as those who laud him for providing guidance to Bob Woodward suggest, Mark Felt on the matter of the Kennedy assassination is revealed in documents to have been an open enemy of free inquiry, no less than a convicted felon specializing in FBI "black-bag jobs."

W. Mark Felt was high among those in the government attempting to sabotage Jim Garrison's investigation. An FBI document of March 2, 1967, the day after Jim Garrison arrested Clay Shaw, has an investigator named H.L. Edwards reporting to Felt on scurrilous rumors that might be enlisted to undermine Garrison and his evidence. Edwards is obviously replying to an assignment from Felt to find a way to stop Garrison. He quotes Frank Manning, chief investigator for Louisiana Attorney General Jack P. F. Gremillion, who calls Garrison a "psychopath" and accuses Garrison of shaking down "hundreds of sex deviates in the New Orleans French Quarter."

Manning confided to Edwards that "Garrison might himself be a sex deviate, or at least he is a participant in some deviate activities with other homosexuals." None of this was true. But Edwards' focus is revealed in his writing for the record that "Garrison has absolutely no basis for his present publicity stunt in claiming that he has reason to believe Oswald acted as a part of a conspiracy in the assassination." Edwards knew that Felt was interested, not in Garrison's prosecutorial foibles as a district attorney, but in destroying his credibility, the better to subvert his challenge to the Warren Commission. Edwards recommends to Felt that the New Orleans field office contact Manning directly so that they might dig into cases where, hopefully, they can "discover" that money was paid to Garrison to have cases against these "sex deviates" disappear.

William C. Sullivan, who would be Felt's rival in assuming the leadership of the FBI after J. Edgar Hoover's day was done, only to be shot in an "accident" where, standing on his porch, he was mistaken for a deer (!), read the document addressed to Felt. Then he urged that the FBI "move with prudence."

Less circumspect voices prevailed and the FBI's General Investigative Division wrote to Felt recommending that the information in Edwards' memo be made available to the White House and the attorney general in what was patently a conspiracy to silence Jim Garrison. Four days later, Felt obliged.

If I believed Garrison, who was so persuasive a talker that he won wily reporter Jack Anderson over to his side, it is the overwhelming documentary evidence that has vindicated his effort since the CIA had trained its sights on an independent president. Its involvement in President Kennedy's assassination has been an open secret for these forty years. The mainstream media have persisted in granting credence to the by now thoroughly discredited Warren Commission Report, a document based on a scant and arbitrary pseudo-investigation, in actuality on no investigation at all.

On the fortieth anniversary of John F. Kennedy's death, a Gallup poll recorded that twice as many people believed that the CIA had masterminded the assassination as were persuaded that Lee Harvey Oswald, a man without a motive, had acted alone in the dastardly deed.

Reader, you decide.

CAST OF CHARACTERS

The District Attorney's Office, Orleans Parish
Jim Garrison, District Attorney

Assistants
James Alcock
William Alford
Denis A. Barry
Numa Bertel
Milton E. Brener
Richard Burnes
William Martin
Alvin Oser
Ross Scaccia
Andrew (Moo Moo) Sciambra
Ralph Slovenko
John P. Volz
Charles Ward
D'alton Williams

Investigators
Raymond Beck
Steve Bordelon
Raymond Comstock
Pershing Gervais
Louis Ivon
Frank Meloche
Lester Otillio

Staff
Tom Bethell
Sharon Herkes
Joyce Wood

The Garrison Family
Mrs. Jane Garrison Gardiner, mother
Mrs. Leah (Liz) Garrison, first wife
Phyllis Weinert Kritikos, second wife
Children: Jasper, Virginia, Lyon (Snapper), Elizabeth, Eberhard

The Shaw Defense Team
F. Irvin Dymond
Salvatore Panzeca
Edward F. Wegmann
William Wegmann

Louisiana Politicians
Hale Boggs, Representative to Congress
Jack P. F. Gremillion, Attorney General
Aaron Kohn, Metropolitan Crime Commission
Earl Long, Governor
Russell B. Long, Senator
John McKeithen, Governor
Frank Minyard, Coroner of Orleans Parish
Chep Morrison, Mayor

New Orleans Police
Robert Buras
L. J. Delsa
Frank Hayward
Richard Hunter
Norman Knaps
James Kruebbe
Francis Martello
Edward O'Donnell
Robert Townsend
Major Presley Trosclair, police intelligence

Louisiana State Police
Colonel Thomas Burbank

Francis Fruge
Captain Ben Morgan

Guy Banister's Office
Guy Banister, former FBI Special Agent in Charge, ONI, CIA asset,
    "detective"
Helen Louise Brengel, secretary
William Dalzell, CIA
Vernon Gerdes
Lawrence Guchereau, detective
Jack Martin, CIA
Joe Newbrough, CIA
I. P. Nitschke, former FBI agent
Delphine Roberts, lover and secretary

Banister's Infiltrators
Tommy Baumler
Allen Campbell
Daniel Campbell
George Higginbotham

The New Orleans Bar
Edward Baldwin
Burton Klein
Stephen B. Lemann
Jim McPherson
Lou Merhige
Donald V. Organ
Louis P. Trent
Sam (Monk) Zelden

Suspects
Thomas Edward Beckham, Banister courier and country singer
Edgar Eugene Bradley, assistant to the Reverend Carl McIntire,
    falsely charged
David Ferrie, police informant, ex-Eastern Airlines pilot,
    CIA contract pilot
Loran Hall, CIA mercenary
Lawrence Howard, CIA mercenary
Clay Shaw, managing director, International Trade Mart
Kerry Thornley, Oswald Marine Corps cohort and author of a
    book about Oswald

Friends of David Ferrie

Alvin Beaubouef, traveled to Houston and Galveston with Ferrie the weekend of the assassination; Ferrie's heir

Bob Boylston, Civil Air Patrol

Morris Brownlee, named Ferrie his "godfather" during his conversion to Catholicism

Melvin Coffey, traveled to Houston and Galveston with Ferrie and Beaubouef

G. Wray Gill, Ferrie's attorney

Jimmy Johnson, Ferrie acolyte and informant for Jim Garrison

James Lewallen

Layton Martens, indicted by Jim Garrison for perjury

Benton Wilson

John Wilson

Friends of Clay Shaw

Patricia Chandler, wife of David Chandler

Jack Sawyer, news director, WVUE-TV

Donald G. Schueler, professor

Jefferson Sulzer, professor

Nina Sulzer

The International Trade Mart

David G. Baldwin, public relations

Theodore Brent, first managing director

Lloyd J. Cobb, founder in 1946 and president from 1962 and during the Shaw trial

Jesse Core, public relations

J. B. Dauenhauer, Shaw assistant

Witnesses

Dean Andrews, attorney telephoned by "Clay Bertrand"

Dago Garner, Dallas roustabout

The Reverend Clyde Johnson

Jack Martin, once and present CIA operative

Julia Ann Mercer, saw Ruby at Dealey Plaza on the morning of November 22

Richard Case Nagell, CIA operative; warned FBI of the November Dallas conspiracy involving Oswald and two right-wing Cubans

Donold P. Norton, CIA courier

The FBI

John Edgar Hoover, Director

Cartha DeLoach ("Deke"), third in command at headquarters after Hoover and Clyde Tolson

Regis Kennedy, Special Agent, New Orleans field office

Warren de Brueys, Special Agent, New Orleans field office

William Walter, clerk, New Orleans field office

Elmer Litchfield, Baton Rouge resident agent

Department of Justice

Ramsey Clark, Acting Attorney General

Herbert J. Miller Jr., Department of Justice attorney and CIA liaison

Fred Vinson, Assistant Attorney General

Walter P. Yeagley, Assistant Attorney General, Internal Security Division

The CIA

James Angleton, Chief of Counter Intelligence

Major General Charles Cabell, Dulles' assistant, forced to resign when Dulles was fired

Allen Dulles, Director of Central Intelligence, fired by John F. Kennedy after the Bay of Pigs fiasco

Desmond Fitzgerald, JMWAVE

Richard Helms, DDP (Deputy Director, Plans), chief of clandestine services on November 22, 1963

Lawrence Houston, Chief Counsel

Hunter Leake, second in command, New Orleans

John McCone, Director of Central Intelligence on November 22, 1963

David Atlee Phillips, Chief of Western Hemisphere, COG (Cuban Operations Group), Chief of Cuban Operations at the Mexico City Station in 1963; at his retirement in 1975, he was Chief of Latin American and Caribbean Operations

Lloyd N. Ray, chief, New Orleans field office

Raymond Rocca, nicknamed "The Rock" by James Angleton; head of Counter Intelligence's research and analysis division (R&A).

Jack Rogers, attorney, Louisiana Agency asset, and Chief Counsel for the Louisiana Un-American Activities Committee

Walter Sheridan, Department of Justice attorney and intelligence operative sent to New Orleans as an NBC producer to destroy Jim Garrison's case

Clinton Witnesses

Verla Bell, CORE activist

Corrie Collins, Chairman, East Feliciana CORE

Anne Dischler and Francis Fruge, investigators for Jim Garrison

William Dunn, CORE activist

Merryl Hudson, secretary, personnel office, East Louisiana State Hospital at Jackson

Maxine Kemp, staff, East Louisiana State Hospital

Edwin Lea McGehee, barber, Jackson, Louisiana

Reeves Morgan, State Representative, East Feliciana Parish

John Manchester, Town Marshal

Henry Earl Palmer, Registrar of Voters, East Feliciana Parish

John R. Rarick, District Court judge during the summer of 1963 and former congressman

Dr. Frank Silva, medical director, East Louisiana State Hospital during the summer of 1963

Cubans

Frank Bartes, CIA asset, second cousin of Dr. Frank Silva, and contract pilot

Carlos Bringuier, arrested with Lee Harvey Oswald on Canal Street

Eladio del Valle, David Ferrie's CIA handler in Florida

Bernardo de Torres, CIA and FBI asset and plant in Garrison investigation

Alberto Fowler, veteran of Bay of Pigs and Garrison investigator

Orestes Peña, operator of the Habana Bar and FBI informant

Carlos Quiroga, assistant to Sergio Arcacha Smith

Sergio Arcacha Smith, New Orleans Cuban Revolutionary Council

Juan Valdes, close associate of Lee Harvey Oswald, International Trade Mart employee, suspect in Mary Sherman murder

Soldiers of Fortune

Howard Kenneth Davis

Loran Hall

Gerald Patrick Hemming

Lawrence Howard

E. Carl McNabb ("Jim Rose"): CIA contract pilot and Garrison investigator

FBI Informants on the Garrison Case

Hugh Aynesworth, *Newsweek,* formerly with the *Dallas Morning News*

Sam Depino, New Orleans television

Gordon Novel

Joe Oster, former partner of Guy Banister and founder of Southern Research

Orestes Peña, proprietor of Habana bar

James Phelan, *Saturday Evening Post*

Arnesto Rodriguez, language school, and Oswald contact

Lawrence Schiller, author

The Fourth Estate

Hugh Aynesworth, *Dallas Morning News* and *Newsweek*

Richard N. Billings, *Life* magazine editor

Donald Dean Bohning, CIA asset as AMCARBON-3, *Miami Herald*

David Chandler, *Life* magazine stringer

Jack Dempsey, *States-Item*, broke the Garrison case

Sam Depino, FBI informant, New Orleans, Channel 12

Rosemary James, *States-Item*

Iris Kelso, *States-Item*

James Phelan, *Saturday Evening Post* writer and FBI/CIA asset

David Snyder, *States-Item*

William Stuckey, CIA asset writing for *States-Item*

Richard Townley, WDSU, assistant to Walter Sheridan

AN ARTICLE IN *ESQUIRE* MAGAZINE 1

I guess part of me still thought I was living in the country I was born in.
—Jim Garrison

IN MARCH OF 1965, with Governor John McKeithen barred by law from succeeding himself, Orleans Parish district attorney Jim Garrison decided to run for governor of Louisiana. On a rainy morning, he flew to Shreveport with his favorite assistant John Volz, two very tall, black-haired, handsome, politically ambitious men. While Garrison addressed a convention of dentists, Volz was to distribute a press release to the local radio stations. Ever late, Garrison rushed to board the return flight, his raincoat flapping over his arm, a copy of *Esquire* magazine in his hand.

"Read this!" Garrison told Volz, pointing to an article by Dwight Macdonald, reviewing the *Report of the President's Commission Investigating the Assassination of John F. Kennedy*. The Warren Report, Macdonald wrote, was a work of fantasy and literary imagination, an American "anti-*Iliad*"; it bore no resemblance to a murder investigation. Perceiving that the Warren Commission's task was one of "exorcism," not a search for truth, Macdonald wondered how FBI and CIA involvement in the assassination, which seemed obvious to any disinterested observer, came in "motive-wise." "Officials of a feather stick together," Macdonald concluded, regretting that neither Sherlock Holmes nor Earl Stanley Gardner had been on the scene. On the orders of FBI director J. Edgar Hoover and President Lyndon Johnson, a Justice Department lawyer close to the CIA, Herbert J. Miller Jr., had rushed to Texas to forbid the Dallas police from doing any investigating on its own.

At the end of March, Jim Garrison found himself in Washington, D.C., in the company of Louisiana congressman Hale Boggs, who had been a member of the Warren Commission. Garrison expressed his doubts. Boggs then confided to Garrison that during a closed January 22, 1964, session of the Commission, Oswald's FBI number and FBI wages had been examined. "I would hope none of these records are circulated to anybody," Boggs had told Earl Warren and the former CIA director fired by John F. Kennedy, Allen Dulles.

Then he revealed what had been said to Jim Garrison. From his own experiences as a hunter alone, Boggs believed, one man could not have fired those shots. Boggs told Garrison that no notes, no transcription had been made of the hours of interrogation of Oswald by the Dallas police, which also claimed to have no record of the calls received and made by Oswald while he was in custody.

It was Hale Boggs who nurtured Jim Garrison's doubts about the Warren Report and encouraged his investigation. Later, Jim Garrison would insist that it was Senator Russell Long who had motivated him to investigate the Kennedy assassination, but it wasn't so. That Garrison was guilty of saying too much to the press would be another myth perpetrated by his detractors. To the day of his death, he protected Hale Boggs' role in inspiring his investigation into the murder of John F. Kennedy.

John McKeithen, an iron pragmatist with a soft-spoken demeanor, jammed a bill through the legislature allowing him to succeed himself, a feat accomplished not even by Earl Long. Jim Garrison moved on to what was in fact a reinvestigation. Four days after the assassination, he had interviewed a disgraced Eastern Airlines pilot named David W. Ferrie about his relationship with the accused assassin Lee Harvey Oswald. The tip had come from an ex-CIA agent out of Louisville named Jack Martin, who had broadcast it all around New Orleans that Ferrie knew Oswald and had been enlisted to fly the assassins out of Dallas.

Garrison, "a somewhat messianic district attorney," as Ferrie would later describe him, turned David Ferrie over to the Secret Service and the FBI, who let him go. Now Garrison began to study the twenty-six volumes published by the Warren Commission. He would become the sole law enforcement official to investigate the assassination, a quest, messianic indeed, that would cost him his political career. He was the father of four children, with a fifth and last, Eberhard Darrow, to be born in 1966, and the husband of a woman with conventional political ambitions. Garrison forged ahead nonetheless.

"It was my jurisdiction," Garrison would explain. "Should I leave well enough alone and disregard the apparent possibility that the men who planned the terrible murder are among us today? Should I say that the death of John Kennedy is not my affair?"

Jim Garrison was born Earling Carothers Garrison in Denison, Iowa, on November 21, 1921. Imagination and curiosity were a birthright. His forebears were rebels and free thinkers, among them the abolitionist William Lloyd Garrison, a family reprobate, as one Judge Thomas Garrison Stansbury would write: "He was a talented man, but rather eccentric in his views with regard to the African race in America."

Jim Garrison grew up to be six feet six inches tall, courtesy of his mother's side, the Robinsons. His two irreverent seven-foot Robinson uncles one day joined a circus. When people asked how the weather was, the Robinson boys would spit and say it was raining. Further back there were Irish rebels, one of whom fought in the American Revolution.

At the age of two, while his mother Jane was distracted by a telephone call, Garrison escaped from the bathtub, only to be found at Cushman's, a local store, stark naked but for his mother's picture hat. A babysitter on another day was alarmed to discover that little Carothers had disappeared; he was found hiding in the oven. By four he could read. At five, he was in kindergarten when one day Jane Garrison arrived to collect him. Stern and square-jawed, six feet three inches tall, Jane demanded of the teacher, "Where's my Earling?"

"There is no Earling in my class," the teacher said. Brushing past her, Jane strode into the room. Soon she spied her son.

"Oh, you mean Jimmy!" the teacher said. Earling Carothers Garrison had changed his name, borrowing "Jimmy" from the newspaper boy. So he would be "James Carothers" until, in politics, he changed his name legally to "Jim."

Jane left her alcoholic husband, with Jimmy and his sister Judy in tow. Soon Earling Garrison, a feckless younger son, kidnapped Jimmy back to Iowa. But Jane had her way, hiring a private investigator to kidnap her son back. She moved from Chicago to Vincennes to Evansville, Indiana, surviving the Depression by supporting herself and her children with jobs, from selling corsets to real estate to brokering oil leases. Jane Garrison ended up at that dead end for those fleeing the mid-West, the Port of New Orleans.

There her fatherless son grew up solitary, a poor child unable to afford a bicycle. He amused himself by reading, or drawing pictures, for which he had considerable talent. "You're putting too much blue on the man," his elementary school seat mate, Walter Gemeinhardt, observed of the tall boy whose oversized foot stuck out in the aisle.

Jimmy kept silent. He was shy, and at Alcee Fortier High School, he invariably ate lunch by himself. "I don't relate to real easy," he remarked later. But if he got to know you, you might become the butt of his practical jokes, like Alvin Gottschaull, who found himself arrested for twenty-one nonexistent parking violations before a laughing district attorney confessed.

He developed his lifelong appreciation for the Big Bands, his favorite, Glenn Miller, and fell in love with Peggie Baker, whose home became his, although he was too poor to take her to the movies or to dances at the Roosevelt Hotel. Jimmy was the most intellectual of his group of friends, talking about religion and politics. "Everybody's a Unitarian," Jimmy said one day, "everyone interprets the Bible just the way they want to." He was contemptuous of Governor Huey Long.

Before the United States entered World War II, he joined the Army to escape from his overly possessive mother. Not to be denied, Jane followed him to Fort Sill, Oklahoma. For the Army Air Force, unarmed but for a .45 pistol, Jim Garrison flew thirty-five reconnaissance missions in France and Germany. Enlisting his childhood talent for drawing, he painted the Flying Tiger insignia on his tiny "Grasshopper" plane. He named his plane: "Roger The Dodger." On April 30, 1945, Jim Garrison, armed with a small camera, entered the Dachau concentration camp one day after its liberation. "What I saw there has haunted me ever since," Garrison told *Playboy* in 1967. The photographs he took at Dachau, including a grisly one of a decapitated head, he was to keep in a home-made album close by his side until his death.

He had become a man who kept his feelings to himself, so that his Tulane law school classmate and lifelong friend Jimmy Gulotta concluded he was afraid of people. He never mentioned to his Jewish classmates at law school that he had even been at Dachau. Instead, at law school he developed a zest for king making, an escape from boredom. Making Law Review, he declined the honor as too much trouble. His most imaginative scheme was an attempt to have elected as class president Wilmer Thomas, the class buffoon, and a practical joker himself. Wilmer's mischief included stealing one book a day from the school library, to begin, he said, his own collection, a peccadillo he made up for in later years as the most generous of benefactors to the Tulane School of Law.

"I'll take the class renegade and I bet I can get him elected student body president," Garrison said. He ran Wilmer on the "Nazi ticket," a mockery of the Louisiana political system where at that time you could not run for office unless someone put you on their "ticket." "Hotsy-totsy, I'm a Nazi," became the chant of these mostly World War II veterans whose patriotism was unquestionable.

Garrison constructed the "Wilmer board," on which were soon posted Garrison-authored telegrams from Eleanor Roosevelt, J. Edgar Hoover, Joe Stalin, General Franco and Hitler himself. "Lay off my younger brother," John L. Lewis ostensibly wrote as Garrison needled one of Wilmer's rivals, Floyd Lewis, among the school's humorless elite. A message to the Wilmer board arrived referring to a professor named Neighbors who taught oil and gas law: "We'll can Neighbors' ass/In oil and gas." The authorities made them take that one down. Its author was indubitably Jim Garrison, who called his close friend Nigel Rafferty "Duck Butt," because Rafferty was only about five feet four inches tall to Garrison's six six.

Wilmer won in the first primary, only to lose in the run-off by a scant seven votes.

Among the devastating events of Jim Garrison's post–law school years was that Peggie Baker, whom he had assumed would become his wife, married another man. With Peggie married, no one else would ever matter in the same way and no one could take her place. Twenty years later, on a Delta Airlines flight in the early 1970s, Jim Garrison, by now a national celebrity, received a note from one of the flight attendants. "I'm Peggie Baker's daughter, Mindy," it read. The district attorney grabbed the startled air hostess and pulled her onto his lap. Tears streamed down his cheeks.

He received a master's degree, joined the law firm of Eberhard Deutsch, then spent a desultory few months as an FBI agent in the Pacific Northwest. He took six months off to pursue his lifelong ambition, writing. One of his short stories of that time, "The Assassin," was eerily prescient: Gomez attempts to uncover the killer of a politician, suspecting "the loyal bodyguards," while a man named Zapato is falsely accused. All Gomez can do is wait and see which of the bodyguards will rise to power, following the criterion of *cui bono* (who profits?), a criterion Jim Garrison would enlist in his investigation of the Kennedy assassination.

He consulted a New York literary agent named A. L. Fierst, who told him the stories were "decidedly promising." He "handle[d] language well" and had a "fresh imagination." "Give your work your best efforts, please," Fierst wrote, "I believe you will hit the mark in not too long a time."

Jim Garrison kept a complete set of Shakespeare (whom he preferred to the Greeks) on his office desk in later years. He had written a modernization of *"The Taming of the Shrew"* for WDSU-TV's live drama program, "Theatre 6." His Petruchio wears "blue denim trousers, a wrinkled sweat-shirt" and a "baseball cap or denim hat" with fishing flies pinned to it. The script didn't sell, and he moved on. Whoever publishes first, Jim Garrison bet his friends, Jack Grayson and Jay Teasdel, will buy the others dinner at Antoine's. Only a few years before his death, Jim Garrison was insisting he had won, having inscribed his 1976 novel *The Star-Spangled Contract*, his second book, "to my old friend Jay Teasdel, America's most distinguished unpublished author."

He became a lawyer because he could not earn his living as a writer and returned to the firm where Eberhard Deutsch introduced his young disciple Jim Garrison to Mayor Chep Morrison. So Garrison's political career began. In 1952 he became deputy safety commissioner, handling a backlog of more than 200,000 unpaid traffic tickets, including one belonging to his friend Jack Bremermann's wife, Mickey. "Ask Jim, he'll fix it," Mickey said.

"Yes, I'll help Mickey," Jim said. He paused. "I'll get her to the head of the line." Yet when Morrison offered to appoint him as a traffic court judge, Jim Garrison turned him down. "I don't want to be a traffic court judge," he said. "I want to be district attorney one day." As an assistant district attorney, uniquely, he allowed police reporters like Herman Kohlman to view his files. "Just close the door when you're finished," he said.

He continued to write. In the summer of 1956 at the Practicing Law Institute in New York for a month, bored with the lectures, he outlined a story he called "The Witness" or "The Juror." It would be about "one man's dramatic involvement in a situation," as once more he predicted his fate.

Then he was ensnared in corrupt Louisiana politics as legal adviser to the grand jury. Malfeasance charges had been brought against Mayor Chep Morrison and police superintendent Provosty A. Dayries. Garrison, on Morrison's instructions, paid an overnight visit to New York where he collected the police report of an arrest at a gay party of grand jury foreman Marc Antony. The best efforts of self-styled chairman of the Metropolitan Crime Commission Aaron

Kohn, who had orchestrated the charges against Morrison and Dayries and who numbered Marc Antony among his string of informants, had been in vain.

Garrison bided his time and when in 1964 Morrison ran for governor for the third time, he threw his considerable support to John McKeithen. He had taken to keeping a little black book and if you had done something to him that he deemed unfair, your name would go down. But because he was a forgiving man, it was easy to get your name erased.

He began to run for office. He ran for assessor, an effort so futile that on election day he overslept, not bothering to get out of bed by six A.M., the deadline for posters to be put up. "If I had only listened to your suggestion that I post additional signs," he told fellow assistant Milton Brener, "I would have won." Later Garrison remarked to his friend Robert Haik, "Posters don't vote." His presence was dynamic, and he would ever after rely on television, on which he appeared to be even handsomer than he was, earnest, intellectual, and sincere, his wandering eye not apparent.

In 1960, back to practicing law, he ran against criminal court Judge George A. Platt. Platt was known to frequent the racetrack, always firmly in his seat in time for the first race. Platt "may be a sitting judge, but he is not sitting in the court room," Garrison quipped.

He lost, but he would not lose another election for thirteen years. He was a liberal and as assistant city attorney, a plum Chep Morrison had thrown his way, he refused to prosecute civil rights demonstrators charged with disturbing the peace and loitering.

One Friday afternoon in 1961, five young attorneys, dubbing themselves the "Nothing Group" because they possessed neither money nor favor, sat drinking the twenty-five-cent martinis at Brennan's. Jim Garrison and his law partner Denis Barry were among them as they discussed the vulnerability of district attorney Richard Dowling, whose office was known to sell cases "like crazy."

Soon Jim Garrison was a candidate, enlisting his verbal facility as his best weapon. When Dowling bragged of having two hundred and twenty-five narcotics convictions, "more than the whole state of Louisiana," Garrison quipped, "That's just like saying a Plaquemines Parish fisherman catches more oysters than the whole state of Arizona." Haik tried to secure Mayor Victor Schiro's endorsement for Jim Garrison, but Schiro had made a deal with Dowling that they not oppose each other; Schiro's name now went down in Jim Garrison's black book.

For a television debate among the candidates, prominent attor-

7 ◀

ney F. Irvin Dymond, fresh from a cocktail party and half-drunk, slouched in his chair and puffed away on a cigarette. No, he would not be a full-time district attorney, he declared: "If the people of New Orleans want a $17,500 per year man as their district attorney, I'm not their boy!" Back at the cocktail party, Dymond's supporters gasped, knowing the only issue that remained was the timing of Dymond's withdrawal. Jim Garrison would become the first district attorney in Orleans Parish to run without being on a ticket, but as an independent, beholden to no faction.

"We will do no favors," he told his newly assembled staff. He saw New Orleans as mired in "tolerance of the status quo" and the "smog" of its dubious ethics. Louisiana is "one of the few states which treats defendants with . . . little regard," Garrison found. Under his regime, no one would be above the law. Lottery operators were charged. "This time," he said, "it was not Parish Prison but the pen." Dowling had run his office like a "Chinese whorehouse in a hurricane," Garrison said, as he searched for more than a hundred missing files.

He renovated the office and built himself a private elevator. It was big enough only for one person—himself—and led directly to his private bathroom. He had the law books removed from his office: "A good lawyer doesn't need law books," he said. He kept only "Criminal Procedure."

Cherishing his time in the military, he ran his office like the field artillery unit he had served, he the "commanding officer," delegating the details. The staff was on call twenty-four hours a day and there was no overtime. His executive officer was Frank Klein, who hung a gruesome picture of the electric chair behind his desk, where he kept a model of the guillotine.

Garrison himself was cheerful. In the office, they called him Giant. Sometimes, ungainly and unathletic as he was, he swung a hula hoop around his hips. Office administrator D'alton Williams was inefficient, and one night Garrison emptied all the trash cans himself, putting the refuse in Williams' office. "I really appreciate your keeping the office so neat. Thank you," he told Williams. He was sensitive and indirect, and he would not embarrass you if he could help it.

"Just another day at Tulane and Broad," was his mantra, no matter what happened. He didn't like being called "The Jolly Green Giant," but when someone hung a poster of the green giant on secretary Joyce Wood's door, he eyed it sardonically. "I see you have my photograph on your door," he said.

A young lawyer named Ross Scaccia wrote asking for a job. He had no connections and never pressured for any. "I'm trying to do it on merit," he said.

"You're hired," Garrison wrote back. He hired the first woman assistant district attorney in New Orleans history, Louise Korns, who had been first in her class at Tulane, and entrusted most of the research to her. Lacking any desire for notoriety, he surprised Korns by allowing her to do oral arguments for the office before the U.S. Supreme Court. Personal ambition was alien to him, Korns noted. Jim Garrison did enjoy dispensing patronage. "Those who support us in the first primary get the jobs," Governor Earl Long said, famously. "Those who support us in the run-off get good government," a double entendre since "good government" was the name of an anti-Long political faction. Dealing in favors was a refined Louisiana pastime.

Garrison's was the first office to employ full-time police investigators, among them Louis Ivon—tough, taciturn, fair-minded, and "Buck" to his boss until the day of Garrison's death. Lean, hard-eyed Raymond Comstock signed on because Dowling had not prosecuted Frances Welch, the abortionist he had arrested who had committed a murder. Comstock had made an anonymous call to candidate Garrison, who then went on television excoriating Dowling for not prosecuting Welch. If Dowling is reelected, I would rather ride a horse in City Park than be a police officer, Comstock thought.

Garrison dressed nattily in three-piece suits and he was not corrupt, rejecting the Napoleonic premise that political office was a form of private property. John McKeithen offered him a bank charter, which would at once have made him rich. Garrison turned him down. "I don't have time," he said. That charter was given to a New Orleans insurance man named Marshall Brown, who dabbled in politics and made it as far as the state board of education. Brown went on to sell the charter for $750,000. McKeithen suggested that Garrison open a law office to which business would flow from the governor and the state, and where Garrison could repair once he was no longer district attorney. He rejected that, too. Money meant nothing to him, and his desk drawer invariably included uncashed National Guard paychecks.

A gambler named Jules Crovetto from St. Bernard Parish ("The Parish") down river on the east bank of the Mississippi began to pay off a Garrison assistant. On Fridays, he sent five prime porterhouse steaks to Mayor Chep Morrison, along with the requisite cash. He was close to Felix Bonoura, the "chicken man," owner of Magnolia Broilers, and as much a purveyor of fowl as Carlos Marcello was the "tomato salesman" FBI agent Regis Kennedy dubbed him. Crovetto thought that for insurance, should the police arrest any of his lottery vendors on illegal gambling charges, he had better bribe Garrison as well. Surely Jim Garrison could be bought.

Chief of detectives Ray Scheuering made the introduction at the Roosevelt Hotel. Soon it became apparent. Jim Garrison did not take bribes. The assistant whom Crovetto was paying off disappeared from the district attorney's office. Garrison eliminated the corrupting practice of paying bail bondsmen on the installment plan, and offered, to "Special Assistant" Denis Barry's distress, too much access to Aaron Kohn. "Any file in this office is available for inspection by you," Garrison told Kohn.

Soon, led by Denis Barry, the office began the most persistent crackdown of Bourbon Street abuses on record. Bars, which encouraged B-drinking where girls lured unsuspecting tourists into buying expensive bottles of champagne, were padlocked. "B-drinking" meant, literally, "drinking for the bar," because for every drink a tourist bought, the girl got her cut, usually one-third for each drink, with two-thirds going to the bar.

A girl persuaded an unsuspecting hayseed into buying expensive bottles of champagne, which, as the evening dwindled, were more often than not a cheap sauterne with club soda. The girl put her swizzle stick—it bore her own particular mark so she could collect later—into her champagne cocktail, which was invariably ginger ale and lemon. Or she would spit her own champagne into a plastic red-frosted "water glass," half-filled with ice.

Promising to meet the John out front later, she fled out the back door. Or she might pour a knock-out drop into his drink and escape. The drunk tourist would then be gentled back to his hotel by the police, who sometimes covered for the clubs.

A (B)ust-out booth was at the back, and there a girl like "Hot Water Sue" might be accomplishing a hot-water enhanced blow job, or a John might be kissing a girl's breasts only, when the police arrived, for the bartender to press a buzzer and the girl "bust out" of the booth and disappear. A (B)uy-out meant a customer could buy a girl for the entire night for two or three hundred dollars, but this did not include sexual intercourse, only her company, and, as former police officer Robert Buras remembers, "a hand job or head job in the back booth."

Many of these bars were now padlocked.

In the 1960s this district attorney was a unique Louisiana citizen; the word "nigger" never passed his lips. If a relative of someone charged gained Jim Garrison's ear, the charges more often than not would be reduced. He had, his assistant William Alford says, "a heart of gold." William Porteous, another assistant, said Garrison would invariably temper justice with mercy. If he had to let someone go, Alford says, he found him a better job elsewhere. Garrison was a prosecutor who opposed the death penalty, and the longer you sat in his office, the better your chances that the prosecutor would recommend no jail time at all.

The driver in an armed robbery case was serving nine years at Angola, the state penitentiary, while his confederates had pled guilty and received probation. Garrison and the man's lawyer, Ray McGuire, signed a joint motion for a new trial. When the police sent in a report on the wrong man in another case, Garrison picked up the telephone. "Are you sure this is the man you wanted?" Saving face meant nothing to him.

The police arrested some actors for public nudity at La Mise En Scène, a French Quarter theatre. Ever a supporter of the first amendment, Garrison disdained obscenity charges. "You have to prosecute them. They broke the law," John Volz told him. "Well, I don't believe in that law," Garrison said. "I don't want them charged."

At crimes against nature, Garrison scoffed. "I'd have to put my whole staff on trial," he joked. If an act was between consenting adults, he told Alford, "it shouldn't be a crime." Then, to underline the point, he broke into a chorus of "On the Road to Mandalay." For a year he had the office experiment: no one would be charged with a sex crime; you had to find some other charge, or not. He refused to charge a Tulane medical school professor set up on his yacht on Lake Pontchartrain by a cop. "The only crime against nature is a hurricane, a cyclone or an earthquake," Garrison said.

To priests involved in sexual misconduct, whether with children or adults, he granted no favors, and the Catholic church became his enemy. He didn't care. Alford prosecuted these wayward priests, who in the old days enjoyed the privilege of private visits with Judges Tom Brahney and Bernard Bagert: the priest would plead guilty and escape with a small fine and unsupervised probation.

Garrison punished police officers for the use of excessive force against blacks, another unheard-of action. "We won't tolerate this," he said, bringing police officers before the grand jury and earning the enmity of many.

Yet, in contradiction to all of this, as his chief investigator he hired a disgraced ex-policeman whom he had known in his army days named Pershing Gervais, long known as one of the best safe crackers in New Orleans, and a person with no regard whatsoever for the law. His parents were deaf mutes and he grew up a connoisseur of survival—clever, virulent, and dangerous. Gervais was a heavyset man with broad shoulders, thin lips and a bulbous nose, his prodigious physical strength matching his penchant for violence. His long belly hung over his belt, a cigarette dangled from his lips, and he would disarm you with witticisms, among which were confessions of his own wrong-doing. He was an older man, a quasi-father figure for Jim Garrison, and utterly amoral. John Volz calls Gervais "the devil incarnate."

Pershing shook down the bars, collecting tribute from card games at the Gaslight, the Cover, the Spot, and the Music Box. The Canal Street Steam Bath also paid off. He took money to make cases go away, and kept dossiers on everyone he knew. Comstock bit his lip. Gervais is to Garrison as Professor Moriarty was to Sherlock Holmes, he concluded. Raymond Comstock, Robert Buras thought, would have made a far better chief investigator. The day Jim Garrison hired Pershing Gervais the whole town knew: the office would never be entirely honest.

"Why does everybody holler about my being chief investigator?" Pershing demanded. "If you want to catch a crook, what you do, you get a better crook." He had been an informant for Aaron Kohn before he took the job with Jim Garrison, and remained so afterward, informing on Garrison to the FBI as well.

If a lawyer balked, Pershing had a ready reply: "Those who have money, get a *nolle prosequi* (a refusal to prosecute even if the grand jury produced evidence); those who want justice, get a trial." His former partner, Sal Marchese, was his bag man, collecting a thousand dollars a week from the lottery owners alone. Confronted by one of the officers attached to Garrison's office, Pershing faced him down. "I didn't know Marchese was collecting that much," Pershing smirked. For three years, behind Jim Garrison's back, Gervais went on fixing cases.

Only the clubs that gave Pershing payoffs escaped the Bourbon Street crackdown, not those with connections to mob boss Carlos Marcello. Marcello associate Frank Caracci's 500 Club, Old French Opera House and Third Sister Hideaway were all hit. Carlo Montalbano escaped prosecution because he had been instrumental in helping Jim Garrison get elected by offering evidence that he had been shaken down by Richard Dowling's staff.

Everyone feared Pershing Gervais as he ruled over Garrison's police investigators. On his desk sat an electric chair skull cap, said to have been used in the electrocution of five men at Angola. He brought a mynah bird with him into the office, and it sang the "Star-Spangled Banner" in a voice sharp and clear, "Sonny Boy" in the voice of Al Jolson, and a tune appropriate to his residence at Tulane and Broad: "The old red flannel drawers/That Maggie wore/She hung them on the line . . ." Pershing taught "Mr. Bird" to irritate those he didn't trust, those, like Lou Ivon, whose loyalty was to Jim Garrison and not to him. When one day Ivon hung an elegant sport coat on a rack close to Mr. Bird's cage, the mynah flew over to express his disapproval. Ivon was irate:

"Fuck you, Louie!" Mr. Bird said.

With his cynicism ("a man that don't take money can't be trusted"), Pershing seemed the opposite of idealistic Jim Garrison. Yet Garrison found him streetwise, humorous, bawdy, and intelligent and kept him on. Denis Barry balked, but Garrison argued that Pershing had testified voluntarily in federal court about graft being paid to the police. You had to know the streets to catch criminals. Lou Ivon thought it was just like Garrison to give someone like Pershing a break, and compared his hiring to Garrison's helping lawyers even when their licenses were suspended, paying them to do "research."

Gervais, a character even Damon Runyon could not have invented, who bragged to Comstock, "I lead Garrison around by the nose," amused him, and the assistants as well. One day Pershing stood at an open window during a lightning storm: "If there's a God, let him strike me dead!" he cried. The chief psychiatrist at Tulane University, Robert Heath, had talked about experimenting with electrode implants to give people orgiastic pleasure. "I could get a girl from the French Quarter to do that without an implant," Pershing laughed. At Norma Wallace's high-toned whorehouse, Pershing was said to have sold *his* formidable favors for as much as $1500.

"Without him, I would be a square on Bourbon Street," Garrison said, believing he could control Pershing. He couldn't. His weakness for Pershing Gervais pointed to another aspect of Jim Garrison's temperament, that aloofness that led to a profound naïveté about people, rendering him vulnerable to deception. It takes him "a long time to recognize the real character and purposes of people," assistant D'alton Williams confided to Aaron Kohn. In his novel *The Star-Spangled Contract*, in an implied final word on the subject of

Pershing, Garrison rejects the fallacy of viewing people as all black or all white. His villain, Quillier, talks about a "fundamental American flaw, a failure to entertain ironies, contradictions, complications. You want it all apple-pie easy—the good guys and the bad guys."

Of all Pershing's scams the ugliest was his framing of a bail bondsman named Hardy Davis, who was corrupt, but no more so than many. Pershing had learned Davis had gossiped about his son, who had been arrested on a narcotics violation, and he vowed to get even. Among Pershing's many French Quarter informants was a tough, hot-tempered ex-Marine amateur heavyweight boxer named William Livesay. His forearms were as big as Popeye's, his hands huge and beefy, his violence reflexive.

Livesay was a waiter at The Court of Two Sisters restaurant, and shared with Pershing a girlfriend who was a stripper at the Circus Club. He knew Hardy Davis, who had helped him on a knifing charge. On that matter, Livesay had consulted Eugene Davis (no relation to Hardy), the night manager. Young men busted for charges and in trouble with the law turned often for help to Eugene Davis.

When Livesay asked Eugene Davis for the name of a lawyer, Davis suggested "Dean Andrews," a local jive-talking, roly-poly lawyer who took his clients where he found them, and who would figure profoundly in Jim Garrison's investigation of the murder of President Kennedy. Among Andrews' clients during the summer of 1963 would be Lee Harvey Oswald.

"Tell him 'Mr. Bertrand' sent you," Davis said. "Bertrand" was the name you used if you were a young male in trouble in the Quarter, and it was clear to Livesay that Davis was not referring to himself when he used the name "Mr. Bertrand." It would be a "Clay Bertrand" who would telephone Andrews on the Saturday after President Kennedy was shot, requesting that Andrews go to Dallas to represent Oswald.

As a favor to Pershing, Livesay lured Hardy Davis, who was homosexual, to the Gaslight Bar, in which Pershing had an interest. Livesay proposed that they talk at an apartment on Dauphine Street.

The police had drilled peepholes in the bathroom door, and stood poised with a movie camera. A tape recorder whirred quietly under the bed. Just as Livesay had his penis in Davis' mouth, the police converged.

"You guys busted in too quick!" Livesay quipped. "What was the hurry? There were about nine inches of my dick (give or take a couple of inches) swabbing his tonsils," Livesay says.

This chain of events would result in Livesay's accidentally killing a man named Perry Tettenburn, whom he feared had been sent to harm him in retaliation by Hardy Davis. Now, while Davis was booked at the First District station on a "crime against nature" charge, Livesay was driven to Tulane and Broad to type a statement. It was a Saturday. As Livesay wrote that Davis had solicited him for sexual purposes, he heard excited voices outside.

"Quick! Someone hide him! The boss is here! Don't let him see him!" Jim Garrison had chosen to make one of his Saturday appearances at the office. Even as Jim Garrison did not know in advance of Pershing's setting up of Davis, he later was compelled to take responsibility for this "Gervais operation," as Louis Ivon calls it. When Livesay was convicted of murder, Garrison opposed a reduction in his life sentence for what was an involuntary manslaughter case at best. He never prosecuted Hardy Davis on the crime against nature charge. Running for reelection in 1965, Garrison admitted that his investigators had "clearly violated" Davis' constitutional rights.

Louisiana corruption seeped. In May of 1965 two assistants, John Shea and Edgar Mouras, who handled the complaint desk, a venue brimming with opportunities for graft, resigned in what the *States-Item* called a "shakeup." Another Garrison former army buddy who worked for the office undercover, Max Gonzales, told an FBI informant a case could be dropped for $2,000. A prostitute named Kay Roberts, also an FBI informant, reported she heard that for $10,000 a prostitute would not be prosecuted. A Garrison assistant, Al Oser, a chronic gambler ("he would bet on two roaches running across the floor," Volz says), borrowed money from a Marcello operative, Nick Christiana. Garrison demoted Oser, but kept him on.

For Jim Garrison, being district attorney had already lost its shine. "Our situation is not unlike that of a man who is paddling upstream in a leaky boat," he admitted. "If he stops rowing so as to bail out the water, then he starts slipping downstream. If he stops bailing out the water so as to row, then the boat begins to sink." Then he enlisted the theme song of the civil rights movement: "We Shall Overcome."

Jim Garrison enjoyed the small prerogatives of the office: free dinners at La Louisiane (owner Jimmy Moran gave up sending him the bills that went unpaid) and the elegant suits, bills paid at a snail's pace, from Terry and Juden's. None of these was enough to keep him interested in being district attorney of Orleans Parish. Politics, finally, bored him. "Never learned to slap a stranger on the back or pretend to remember a strange face and never will," he was to admit.

THE MAFIA, SACRED COWS, THE CUPID DOLL AND A SPY LEFT OUT IN THE COLD

2

There is no final answer. There is only an honest striving toward the unattainable.
                    —Jim Garrison

SIX MONTHS AFTER GARRISON read Dwight Macdonald's *Esquire* article, a New Orleans billboard read, "Vote for Jim Garrison." It specified no particular office. But in the autumn of 1965, just before he began his investigation of the Kennedy assassination, Jim Garrison ran, not for mayor against Victor Schiro as had been rumored, but for reelection as district attorney. His opponent was Malcolm O'Hara, son of William O'Hara, who three years earlier had been one of eight criminal court judges suing Garrison for defamation.

The issue had been control of the pot of bail bond forfeiture money and fines paid by petty criminals, money Garrison used to finance the Bourbon Street raids. Furious with this interference, Garrison attacked the judges, who had their own hands in the till, and who now insisted that only the police department could investigate crime, whether or not it was doing it.

That these judges were corrupt could be amply demonstrated. Edward A. Haggerty, later to play a prominent role in Jim Garrison's Kennedy investigation, was an alcoholic and roustabout, ever in fear of being arrested for gambling and whoremongering. Haggerty was likely to grab a file out of the hand of an assistant district attorney, glance at it, then advise the defense, "Don't plead. They don't have shit on you." Judge Platt was at the racetrack. Judge Cocke had run the corrupt Dowling office. Judge Schulingkamp was an open racist. On one occasion, with the same crime committed under similar circumstances, he gave a black defendant one year and a white man three. "The white man should know better," Judge Schulingkamp said.

Garrison attacked the judges for laziness, and for taking more than two hundred holidays, "not counting the legal holidays like All Saint's Day, Long's Birthday and St. Winterbottom's Day." Yet they carried on unimpeded, like "the sacred cows of India." Worse, they were subject to "racketeer influences." Judge Haggerty was close to Francis Giordano, a Marcello associate. Judge Brahney's heavy-stakes card game partner was Frank Caracci.

Jim Garrison himself, despite J. Edgar Hoover's later strategy of undermining his Kennedy investigation by spreading the rumor that he was close to the Mafia, had no Marcello connections. Carlos Marcello confided to Governor McKeithen, who *was* beholden to him, that he wanted Jim Garrison out of office. Garrison was unreliable, Marcello complained. The judges felt the same way.

The prosecutor in the case against Garrison would be Louisiana attorney general Jack P. F. Gremillion, not much of a lawyer. "If you want to hide anything from my attorney general," Governor Earl Long had once confided, "just put it in a law book." Gremillion's chief investigator, Frank Manning, concocted that file against Jim Garrison, "proving" that Garrison was "shaking down" hundreds of sex deviates, and "might be a sex deviate or at least he is a participant in some deviate activities with other homosexuals"—the gossip that had found its way into the hands of Mark ("Deep Throat") Felt—no matter that Garrison did not believe in charging people with victimless sex crimes. Garrison was defended by a masterful attorney named Donald V. Organ, who constructed the defense on first amendment grounds.

In court, as each judge testified, Garrison sat writing a three thousand-word parody of Shakespeare's *Richard the Third*, titled "King James the First." In a forest, Lord Bernardo (J. Bernard Cocke) and seven dukes denounce James. They fear that "our lives, families, holidays are in jeopardy and may not last the year." Platt is afraid of losing "our lawful claim to lay witness to the daily double." Bernardo hates this "upstart king" who has surrounded himself with "silken drapes and chartreuse rugs," a reference to the color of Garrison's new office carpet.

"What of our Fridays?" Sir Oliver (Schulingkamp) demands; the criminal court judges rarely sat on Fridays. Garrison calls himself a "long-legged jack-a-napes, this raggedy-ass James," and ridicules the criticism that he sought power and would be "saint" as well as "king." The judges repair to their "en banc discourse," as Lord Bernardo, the leader, in art as in life, threatens "woe upon him whose tragic fate is sealed by our vote of five out of eight."

In court, among the facts emerging was that Judge Platt had lied about his mother owning a lottery business. Judge Schulingkamp had paroled people for Frank Costello, who had brought big-time gambling to New Orleans. But this was Louisiana and Garrison lost, and lost again on his appeal to the Louisiana Supreme Court. When the U.S. Supreme Court agreed to review the case, he dismissed Don Organ and allowed Eberhard Deutsch, ever eager for notoriety, to argue for him. He told Organ that Deutsch would be refunding five thousand dollars of his expenses, and Organ wondered what expenses those might be since he had not been paid.

Deutsch was known for raiding other lawyers' clients, having made his name in a grandstanding ambulance chase when a munitions ship had exploded in Galveston Harbor and he had filed a class action suit.

"Your name will appear on the case," Garrison added, indicating that Deutsch would pay all future expenses, including the trip to Washington. It was clear to Organ that more than five thousand dollars was involved.

"Don, you know my situation," Jim added. Organ did know. Jim lived from hand to mouth.

"Jim, go ahead," Organ said. "But I won't be on a case with Eberhard Deutsch." Garrison was clearly relieved.

In Washington, Gremillion reminded the justices that federal judges had been "criticized vociferously in my state," a reference to Judge Skelly Wright, who had been much abused in Louisiana for ordering desegregation of the New Orleans schools. Jim Garrison sat in the audience with Robert Haik. "You lost," Haik told Garrison, but Garrison was confident. "How many former district attorneys were up there?" he said. "Three. I had three going in. . . ." Pershing appeared at the hotel with his collar open, his belly hanging over his pants. "Isn't this a wonderful day to fuck a little boy in the ass!" Pershing said.

For *Garrison v. Louisiana*, Justice William Brennan wrote the majority opinion, rejecting Louisiana's defamation statute as antiquated. Now the Supreme Court enlarged the right to criticize public officials, an important expansion of *New York Times v. Sullivan*. Even "erroneous statement," inevitable in free debate, was to be protected.

On upholding the Bill of Rights, Jim Garrison never wavered. He refused to charge the manager of a Doubleday bookstore for selling James Baldwin's novel *Another Country*, no matter that the head of the vice squad, Frederick A. Soule, called it "filthy and pornographic." When the powerful (White) Citizens' Council attacked Garrison, he welcomed the challenge. "The Bill of Rights lives in a kind of oxygen tent," Jim Garrison said. "And a 24-hour watch is needed because someone is always turning off the oxygen—always in the interest of justice—of course."

Malcolm O'Hara's 1965 campaign to unseat Jim Garrison was so well financed that Garrison wondered whether the money came from right-wing Louisiana senator Allen Ellender, and behind him Lyndon Johnson. At once O'Hara made Pershing Gervais a major issue. Implicated in the theft of illegal football cards from a safe at Clarence's Bar, Pershing was forced to resign from the district attorney's office. Jim Garrison bid the single most vicious nemesis of his life an official, if not yet an actual, farewell.

Pershing set up shop at the Fontainebleau Motor Hotel where he extorted money from the families of defendants, pretending to have influence sufficient to prevent charges from being filed by the district attorney's office. He would, Pershing promised, return the money if he failed. At least half the time, he would collect, even as he had nothing to do with the decision of whether or not to prosecute. So Pershing "played results." He grew even more virulent, summoning lawyer Lou Trent one day and threatening, "You're on the verge of going to the bottom of the Mississippi River!"

O'Hara played another card: he produced Jim Garrison's military records, and claimed that Garrison, given a "medical discharge" by the Army for "neurosis" and an "anxiety reaction," was unfit for public office. In 1951, given a choice between remaining with the FBI or going back into service in Korea, Garrison had chosen to serve. Then, on his first day at Fort Sill, he found that he "just couldn't make it."

"I know this sounds crazy, but this is how I feel," he said. The Korean conflict was ending as Garrison was admitted to Brooke Army Hospital at Fort Sam Houston in Texas.

Garrison remembered his wartime service in Europe, flying toward the enemy as closely as possible until he was shot at. He was apparently suffering now from what has been termed "post-traumatic stress syndrome." Just before he had entered law school, suffering from an inexplicable exhaustion following a trip to Mexico, a Dr. Matthews at LSU had said "his trouble was a deep-seated, chronic, severe psychoneurosis."

The Army concurred. Jim Garrison was a garden variety neurotic, with "no signs of pathologic personality." He was an "introverted" man, who could be "anti-social," even as he had never suffered fools gladly. He was prone to allergies that were psychogenic in origin, but only a "moderate" degree of "neurasthenia or a hypochondriasis." The cause was his "over-solicitous mother," who "made every effort to monopolize his affections."

Anyone who knew Jim Garrison was aware of this "marked mother dependency." Jane Garrison had remarried, and was now "Mrs. Lyon Gardiner of Laurel, Mississippi." When she wrote to her son at the hospital, he did not reply. Yet he would always admire his mother for how during the Depression she had managed to find jobs so that she could take care of him and his sister, even as many men remained unemployed. Watching one of the women's films of the 1940s with his son, Lyon (Snapper), years later, Garrison remarked that the strong heroine reminded him of his mother.

Out of an essentially innocuous Army medical report, O'Hara fashioned a nasty personal attack. There is an "ugly force" that "drives him to destroy everyone who fails to bow to his will," O'Hara said, a "Napoleonic complex," an amusing vulgarism given Garrison's great height.

"Possessing another man's army record carries a federal penalty of up to ten years in prison," Garrison pointed out, "just about the length of time remaining in O'Hara's term [as judge]." He demanded to know the source of the report. A "close friend" of yours, O'Hara lied.

The source of the report was Raymond Huff, a regional commissioner for the U.S. Customs Office in New Orleans, and a former commander of the Louisiana National Guard. Huff was another Kohn informant, and a close friend of right-wing anti-Communist and former FBI Special Agent in Charge in Chicago, Guy Banister, now running a detective agency at 531 Lafayette Street in New Orleans. Jim Garrison's strong stand against a series of Klan-inspired nighttime fire bombings following a CORE march for voting rights had angered Huff. Huff had visited segregationist leader Leander Perez, who had been a Garrison supporter dating from the time of Garrison's successful prosecution of a reckless driver who had killed Perez's daughter-in-law. "I consider him very dangerous," Huff said of Jim Garrison. "Something ought to be done about it."

Yet another campaign issue was Garrison's sexual infidelities. At thirty-seven, his mother had pressured him to marry for the sake of his political future. He chose a file clerk at the Deutsch law firm named Leah Ziegler, nicknamed "Liz." His friends were astonished. In his signature white dinner jacket, Jim Garrison had long been a Quarter habitué; Tuesday afternoons he and Denis Barry had participated in orgies in a rented apartment, once a slave quarters, where strippers stripped and women were shared. Settling down seemed anathema.

His marriage also seemed a mismatch, since Liz lacked his education and his intellect. He had been dating others, among them cement company heiress, Evelyn Jahncke.

Nor was Garrison certain of his feelings. He had run into Peggie Baker one day and told her he was thinking of getting married, but was not sure. "How do you know if you're in love?" he asked. When Liz told him she was pregnant, he married her, he confided to Denis Barry, to Robert Haik and soon to his new girlfriend Phyllis Weinert. On the honeymoon at Jane Gardiner's house in Mississippi, Liz announced that she had a miscarriage, and she had spoken so matter-of-factly that Jim and Jane both had to wonder.

On the day of the run-off for district attorney, Jim Garrison was with an airline attendant named Judy Chambers, dubbed "scrambled eggs" by Haik because she had appeared at breakfast. But at the moment of his victory, yet another rival had appeared, pushing Liz aside as Jim made his way to the podium. "I belong up there," Jane Gardiner said, "I'm responsible for him being here today. You've been only a hindrance. Get out of my way!"

It was with "scrambled eggs," and not his wife, that Garrison traveled to Washington, D.C., with Denis Barry for the purpose of meeting President John F. Kennedy. The trip had been arranged by Chep Morrison, now Kennedy's representative to the Organization of American States. After a raucous night, Garrison overslept. The next day he had to face an irritated attorney general, the president's brother.

"How did it go?" Haik asked on his return.

"Well, I met Bobby," Garrison said. "Bob, you can always meet a president. But you can't always get a piece of ass like that!"

"Sex has nothing to do with morality," Garrison told John Volz.

Liz was "sweet"; she was like a little pixie, beautiful, blonde, effervescent. But he saw no reason to mend his ways, even as their family grew. He adored his children and gave them affectionate nicknames. "We're going to have a Snapper," Jim reassured Liz during her difficult fourth pregnancy. He was referring to Edward H. ("Snapper") Garrison, a late-nineteenth-century jockey famous for lagging behind only to sprint to victory for a "Garrison finish." Ever after Lyon Garrison would be known as "Snapper."

Garrison soundly defeated Malcolm O'Hara in the first primary, 82,460 to 47,324. Then he took up his pen and wrote an essay about evil entitled "A Heritage of Stone" as the introduction to his former assistant Ralph Slovenko's book, *Crime, Law and Corrections.* "In the looking-glass world produced by the Nazi culture," Garrison writes, "truth was an enemy, compassion a stranger, only the innocent were punished, only the guilty were rewarded and the meek inherited the earth." He closed with the image of a passer-by picking up a human skull, and peering "through the goggled sockets at the dusty hollow where a handful of grey tissue once took the measure of the universe." The illustration was that photograph snapped by Garrison at Dachau. He submitted "A Heritage of Stone" to *Commentary* magazine, but they turned it down.

Through the spring, the summer, and the autumn of 1966, Jim Garrison studied the Warren Commission volumes. After he finally received his three copies, it seemed as if reading about the Kennedy assassination was "all that he did." "Most of the people they called had nothing to do with it," he concluded. He read Harold Weisberg's *Whitewash*, Mark Lane's *Rush to Judgment* and Edward J. Epstein's *Inquest.*

A *Life* magazine stringer, who had authored a favorable article about him published in the *Saturday Evening Post* under the byline of "James Phelan," encouraged him. "You're in a unique position to get to the bottom of this," David Chandler said, "because you can subpoena people. A lot of the principal people involved hung around New Orleans. You can ask questions. You can do something." Soon Chandler reported to Aaron Kohn that Jim Garrison was working on the Kennedy assassination.

Garrison had long opposed his office's intervention in pardons, yet that year he supported the pardon of the sexiest stripper in the Quarter, a diminutive beauty named Linda Brigette, known as "the cupid doll." Linda did her "Dance of a Lover's Dream" at Frank Caracci's 500 Club; she liked Frank, who had warned her against

Pershing Gervais. "Don't mess with him because he ain't no good," Caracci said. The law was that a stripper could not put her hand into any part of her vagina. One night police officers Robert Buras and Norman Knaps saw Linda touch herself and arrested her for lewd dancing. It was her second arrest.

Before long, Linda faced the prospect of serving two fifteen-day sentences. Her lawyer Louis Trent requested that Jim Garrison "use your influence" in having a pardon signed by Governor McKeithen. Garrison sent his assistant James Alcock to the pardon board hearing and when Brigette's name came up, he was to advocate the pardon. (The New Orleans rumor was that there had been a private party, where Jim Garrison, intoxicated and playing a ukelele, sang, "I can yodel in the canyon if I want to," a sexual preference he recounted frankly to male friends.)

On the day Linda was to go to jail, a taxi sped from Baton Rouge with Governor McKeithen's pardon. It was this pardon that provided fuel for the first attacks on Garrison's fledgling investigation into the murder of John F. Kennedy. At first Garrison took the criticism with his usual sardonic disdain. "Mr. Garrison, I cannot believe that you helped that stripper get a pardon!" a woman told him one day. "Well, Madam, obviously I was paid $50,000," Garrison said.

Aaron Kohn now opened a full attack, insisting to anyone in the press who would listen that the pardon of Brigette, who was married to a Garrison friend named Larry Lamarca, proved that Jim Garrison had Mafia connections. Kohn sent a telegram to Governor McKeithen asserting "the economic importance of Linda Brigette to organized crime," since "Carlos Marcello is behind Lamarca." Even public relations man and CIA asset, and another Kohn informant, Jesse Core, had to tell Kohn it was silly "to think that a dancer could be important to organized crime." Kohn's real target was Jim Garrison.

At first Garrison did not take Kohn seriously. Connecting him to the mob through Brigette was "the silliest thing to come along since the Flat Earth Society's latest press release," he quipped. When Kohn persisted, Garrison called the Metropolitan Crime Commission a "Big Brother operation right out of George Orwell's *1984* . . . a kind of super Soviet-type NKVD."

Undeterred, Kohn continued to construct his dossier against Jim Garrison, one based on innuendo, lies, and half truths. On his list was that Garrison had invited Lamarca and Brigette to sit at his table at a press club dinner. Included as well was that Garrison had bought a new house on Owens Boulevard from a Mafia-connected builder named Frank Occhipinti, no matter that the $52,000 mortgage was so onerous it would take Garrison virtually the rest of his life to pay it off. Garrison had gotten Brigette a divorce, Kohn charged, although in fact, it had been Garrison's law partner, Denis Barry. Garrison had been involved in a mortgage loan to a dubious person named Mike Roach, another false accusation, as Barry explained to Kohn: Garrison had merely witnessed the signatures, and had received no financial benefit from the transaction.

A vendetta against Garrison had begun, one in which the U.S. Attorney Louis LaCour joined to insist that Carlos Marcello had "interests" in New Orleans, as well as in Jefferson Parish, and hence should have been brought to justice by the Orleans Parish district attorney. When Garrison called him to testify before a grand jury, Lacour pleaded executive privilege. Garrison subpoenaed Kohn as well, even as he scoffed at Kohn's charges: "We will undoubtedly learn that I have been seen on a street car at the same time as Bugsy Schwartz, the famous burglar, or that I was in New York City at the same time as Machine-Gun Brady."

"Put up or shut up!" Garrison demanded of Kohn on the front page of the *Times-Picayune.*

Kohn testified before the Orleans Parish grand jury for three hours, but could produce only the innuendo that there was a relationship between Carlos Marcello and a municipal court judge named Andrew Bucaro. Furious, Garrison ordered that his staff mark all mail from the Metropolitan Crime Commission MCC "return to sender."

Garrison was in fact perplexed. In 1962 Kohn had praised his office, which had moved so "vigorously against criminal elements." Only a year earlier, in 1965, Kohn had again praised Garrison's efforts, allowing himself to be quoted in a supplement to the Sunday *Times-Picayune* about the achievements of Garrison's office. He had no way of knowing that Kohn's current attacks were connected to the investigation he had barely begun.

Only a week after President Kennedy's death, the MCC had published a pamphlet rich in biographical facts, with a photograph of Lee Harvey Oswald holding a "Mannlicher Carcano rifle" on its cover. It asserted that Oswald had "acted alone"—this before the Warren Commission had even convened. In the late 1970s, New Orleans homicide officer L. J. Delsa and now a former New Orleans police intelligence officer Robert Buras, working for the House Select Committee on Assassinations (HSCA), would question Kohn on how he had obtained the photograph of Oswald and all that information so quickly. "This is evidence," Delsa said.

"We got avenues," Kohn said.

By the late autumn of 1966, the CIA and the FBI, working in tandem, had already begun to subvert Jim Garrison's investigation. The strategy, as manifested by Kohn's attack, was to undermine Jim Garrison's credibility by accusing him of Mafia connections. HSCA Miami investigator Gaeton Fonzi discovered from his informant Rolando Otero what Jim Garrison could not yet begin to surmise: "The Mafia angle was first injected at the time of Garrison's investigation when the Agency decided it was a way of short-circuiting his efforts."

Plants were placed in Garrison's office, among them Pershing's replacement, Raymond L. Beck, a former FBI agent disgraced in a shoplifting incident. Pershing Gervais is "advising Garrison on his investigation," Beck told Special Agent Regis Kennedy. To FBI night clerk William Walter, Beck confided: he had been asked by the FBI to spy on Jim Garrison. Garrison intends "to expose errors in the Warren Report," Beck told them.

As Garrison read, he concluded that the man who during the summer of 1963 had distributed leaflets in New Orleans urging "Fair Play for Cuba" was no left-winger at all. Only one of his Marine Corps acquaintances, Kerry Thornley, had thought Oswald was a Marxist, despite his subscription to *Pravda*.

Oswald, rather, must have been a low-level operative of the Central Intelligence Agency, "sheep-dipped" or disguised as pro-Castro. Garrison had no evidence that Oswald, who had defected to the Soviet Union in 1959, had been participating in CIA Counter Intelligence chief James Angleton's false defector program. He did pause when he discovered that a file marked "Oswald and the U-2" had been marked "classified." Oswald's radar training with U-2s, the fact that his return from the Soviet Union had been funded with State Department money, while he was accompanied by a wife with family connections to the Soviet secret police, did not add up to his being a leftist. Then, within a few months, Oswald had repaid his entire debt, despite straitened circumstances. Oswald's tax records were "classified," Garrison was soon told. Refused the 1,200 CIA files among the Warren Commission findings, he kept on.

Garrison focused on a passage in the Commission volumes on Oswald's "Military and Civilian Occupational Specialities and Education," and the fact that Oswald had "cross-trained" at Keesler Air Force Base in Mississippi. Only special people had "cross-training," Garrison knew. On February 25, 1959, Oswald had three more answers right than wrong on a Russian examination, overall two more right than wrong. "That's like saying my dog is really stupid," Garrison would say. "When we play chess, I can beat him three games out of five."

Garrison searched New Orleans for traces of Oswald's five-month residence, but the FBI had swept everything clean. On the day after the assassination they had appeared at the New Orleans Public Library and confiscated Oswald's book-borrowing records. As late as the 1990s, the Bureau was destroying evidence, as agents marched into the Tulane Library special collections and confiscated from the Hale Boggs papers all of Boggs' notes and Warren Commission evidence. These included telephone records of Jack Ruby, who had called a New Orleans friend of Ruth Paine, with whom Marina Oswald was living at the time of the assassination.

Garrison compared the moral indifference of those who accepted the Warren Report unquestioningly with the residents of Dachau passing the concentration camp and pretending "they didn't know what that smoke was that was pouring out of the crematorium."

In the homicide business themselves, Garrison's staff were dubious that Oswald, with a bolt-action rifle, its telescopic sight loose, and a tree obstructing his vision, could have done the crime alone. It was a conspiracy, they concurred, and Oswald was "in on it."

Jim Garrison marked the moment when he officially began his investigation with an October 1966 lunch at Broussard's French Quarter restaurant with that same Cajun jive-talking lawyer Dean Andrews to whom Eugene Davis had sent William Livesay, instructing him to say that "Mr. Bertrand" had sent him. Blinking behind dark glasses, Andrews sat, clearly uncomfortable. In addition to representing small-time criminals, he was also a mob lawyer, "a little like Pershing," Herman Kohlman, now a Garrison assistant, thought. Andrews had applied to the FBI for employment only to be turned down as "unstable" and a "big talker." Disdainful, Andrews called FBI agents "feebees," the same term used by the Secret Service, according to Lee Harvey Oswald's brother, Robert.

Another of those requiring legal assistance from Andrews had been Lee Oswald, who had turned up at Andrews' office in the company of some "gay Mexicanos," Andrews had told the Secret Service. Fearing his citizenship was in jeopardy, Oswald had come to challenge his "undesirable" discharge from the Marines. The men who accompanied Oswald "possibly frequent the Gaslight Bar in the French Quarter," Andrews told the Warren Commission, referring to that gay redoubt where William Livesay met Hardy Davis to set him up, the same bar where Livesay had killed Perry Tettenburn. Hardy Davis thought Oswald was a member of a "homosexual clique." Davis, married but in the closet himself, might well have known something about Oswald's sexual proclivities.

Now Garrison wished to question Andrews about that call he had described to the FBI, the Secret Service and the Warren Commission, and which he received on the day after the assassination. It was a call from the same "Clay Bertrand" Eugene Davis had instructed the young men he sent to Andrews to invoke. Ill with pneumonia, Andrews had informed "Bertrand," and all his clients, that should they need to speak to him, he could be reached at the Hotel Dieu Hospital. When Bertrand called asking that he go to Dallas to represent Lee Oswald, Andrews was delighted. "We'll go to Dallas and become famous!" Andrews told his investigator Prentiss Davis. As soon as his secretary Eva Springer arrived, he asked her, "Do we have a file on Lee Oswald?"

On Sunday morning, realizing he was too sick to go anywhere, Andrews had called his friend and fellow attorney Monk Zelden to go to Dallas in his place. During a second call to Zelden, the point became moot. "Don't worry about it," Zelden said, "Your client just got shot."

"We just lost a client," Andrews told Davis when he visited a while later. That Sunday afternoon, Andrews phoned a television station, and the Secret Service, to report he had seen Oswald on three occasions. Dean Andrews would be interviewed six times by the FBI, and three by the Secret Service. He told FBI agent Donald L. Hughes that "Clay Bertrand" had accompanied Oswald to his office, and Regis Kennedy that Clay Bertrand was "a French Quarter queer."

By Wednesday, alarmed at this attention, Andrews had telephoned Jim Garrison's office, where he reached Raymond Comstock. Trying to figure out what Comstock knew, Andrews pretended he was trying to identify "Clay Bertrand." Comstock picked up the telephone and called Regis Kennedy at the FBI field office ("Big Regis," as Andrews called him). Kennedy, it turned out, had already enlisted Comstock to search New Orleans for "Bertrand."

By now, having been enlisted in a cover-up of the Kennedy assassination, the Bureau had developed the strategy that Andrews had dreamed up the call from Clay Bertrand. "Big Regis was pushing me pretty hard," Andrews later remembered, and so he had succumbed. He had been under sedation, he said, the call from Bertrand "a figment of my imagination." An FBI report reveals that Andrews did not receive any sedation until eight at night that Saturday, hours after Bertrand's call.

"Write what you want, that I am nuts, I don't care," Andrews pleaded. Kennedy did just that. The whole story, Big Regis wrote, was "a figment of his imagination," no matter that Kennedy had between thirty and forty men combing New Orleans in search of that "figment," Bertrand. Later, under oath, before Garrison assistant James Alcock, Regis Kennedy would admit the FBI had been searching for "Bertrand" even before Dean Andrews had come forward.

By the time he testified before the Warren Commission, Andrews was terrified. The Commission did not bother to interview Prentiss Davis, Eva Springer or Monk Zelden to corroborate his story. He began to alter his description of Bertrand. The man who was one or two inches over six feet, as Andrews had told the Bureau, was now five foot eight. Bertrand hung out at Cosimo's, in the Quarter, Andrews said slyly—as good liars always plant a truth among their obfuscations. He had run into Oswald giving out his leaflets, Andrews told Wesley Liebeler, and reminded Oswald that he owed the office twenty-five dollars. "It's a job," Oswald had said, "I'm being paid." So Oswald had signaled to Andrews, as he would to others, that he was no Castro supporter.

"Your friends down the street are trying to find you," Liebeler told Andrews, referring to the FBI.

"De Brueys?" Andrews asked, alarmed. Big Regis was one thing, but Warren de Brueys, the FBI's most intelligent, shrewd and trusted agent in New Orleans, although he was not Special Agent in Charge, was quite another. It was de Brueys who had flown to Dallas on November 23rd to write the FBI's report that would become the voluminous Commission Document 75, dated December 2nd.

At their historic lunch, Jim Garrison thrust a copy of *Whitewash* under Andrews' nose. What he wanted, what Andrews would not yield, was the real identity of "Clay Bertrand." You're worse than the feebees, Andrews told Garrison. But Garrison persisted, threatening to summon Andrews to the grand jury and charge him with perjury. Andrews begged to speak "off the record." Garrison refused. According to Garrison, Andrews then grew frantic.

It would mean "a bullet in my head," he pleaded. Garrison wondered whether Oswald had ever been told that Dean Andrews would be representing him, whether he had reacted to this possibility in one of those unrecorded telephone calls he made from the Dallas jail. It was never intended that Andrews actually represent Oswald, Garrison thought.

Oswald, famously, had requested that Communist party lawyer John Abt represent him, an obvious signal to his intelligence handlers that his Marxist cover remained intact, that he was loyal still, and they could count on his silence, even as something had gone terribly wrong. Whatever Oswald had been told, it could not have been that he would be standing before the press in a Dallas jail accused of having murdered the president of the United States. This crime he categorically denied having committed.

Garrison speculated: in requesting Abt, "Oswald is still playing out his assignment as an undercover intelligence agent for the government," continuing the "false front scenario created by the covert action dramatists."

Garrison had enlisted his youngest assistant, a former boxer named Andrew (Moo Moo) Sciambra, in the Kennedy investigation because "Moo Moo doesn't yet know what can't be done," and so might be aggressive. Now Garrison sent Moo Moo to Cosimo's bar in search of the identity of the elusive "Bertrand."

CLAY SHAW
COSIGNS A LOAN 3

The key to the whole case is through the looking glass. Black is white: white is black. . . .
—Jim Garrison

A MONTH LATER, IN NOVEMBER of 1966, Jim Garrison flew to New York to attend a petroleum conference in the company of oil tycoon Joseph Rault and Louisiana senator Russell Long. His investigation well under way, all week he talked of nothing but the Kennedy assassination as he sought to gain the support of these powerful friends. "He chewed my ear off about the Kennedy assassination," Long told his daughter as soon as he got off the plane. He had "always thought" a second person was involved, Long immediately told the press, proposing a new investigation to supersede the Warren Commission.

Garrison had fired disloyal Raymond Beck by getting him a job with his friend Willard Robertson, who ran the Volkswagen franchise, replacing Beck with Lou Ivon. Chief assistant Charlie Ward now handled the routine duties of the district attorney's office as Garrison devoted himself single-mindedly to unraveling the conspiracy that resulted in the assassination. "Nothing else matters but bringing out the truth about what they did to John Kennedy," he would say, "and not only that, bringing out the truth about what's happened to this country before it's too late." As tragic as the murder was, the consequences for the Republic, in terms of the survival of democratic institutions, were even more catastrophic.

Garrison dubbed the staff working on the Kennedy case "The Smith Group," after Winston Smith, the beleaguered hero of George Orwell's *1984*. In his first set of code names, John F. Kennedy was

"Jack Smith." Jack Ruby was "Red." Oswald was "Patsy." David Ferrie was "Lindbergh." Fidel Castro was "Lefty Beard." The Cuban Revolutionary Council, which met at Guy Banister's office, was the "Land Recovery Company," the word "company" reflecting its patron, the CIA. Texas oil man H. L. Hunt was "Harry Blue."

No suspect was eliminated, from anti-Castro Cubans to Cuban Communists. Nor, *Life* magazine editor Richard Billings would write in the notes he took while observing Jim Garrison's investigation, "did Garrison ignore the possible implication of right-wing militants, segregationists, or the mob." Frank Klein was assigned to investigate whether Jack Ruby had ever made contact with the Marcello organization, since he had hired a stripper, "Jada," wife of one of the Conforto brothers. Garrison put the question to Pershing. "Nothing to it," Pershing said.

It was David Ferrie, "Lindbergh," whose Civil Air Patrol attachment Lee Oswald had joined, who was, as he had been in 1963, once more Garrison's chief suspect. A natural as an aviator, Ferrie, a native of Cleveland, had sacrificed a vocation in the priesthood, dismissed from a seminary for "emotional instability." Shortly thereafter, he was fired from a high school teaching job for "over-attachment" to his young male students.

In New Orleans, having become an Eastern Airlines pilot, Ferrie gathered boys around him, showing them pornographic movies and taking nude photographs. He held forth to a crowd of mostly fatherless young men, for whom he was called "Dad," on subjects from Jesus to rockets, sometimes hypnotizing them. Ferrie himself boasted of only a bachelor's degree from a fifth-rate college called Baldwin-Wallace in Bera, Ohio, and a bogus Ph.D. from "Phoenix University" in Bari, Italy.

One of the boys, Eric Michael Crouchet, upset by Ferrie's sexual advances, filed a complaint against him with the police. When Ferrie, in the company of a tough Cuban, tried to persuade Crouchet to drop the charge, he was arrested for extortion. A fifteen-year-old named Al Landry ran away from home and took refuge with Ferrie. His mother sought help from the police. "The reason she raised all this hell was because I wouldn't screw her," Ferrie said.

His person was distinctive because he didn't have a single hair on his body, the result of an onset in 1932 of "alopecia areata"; he was first treated at a clinic in Cleveland. Depressed, lamenting his ugliness, he glued a piece of reddish brown fur onto his head, and, as Aaron Kohn described him, "little swatches of carpet pasted on for eyebrows." On his wall Ferrie hung the saying, "People are no damn good." Machine guns sat on the landing of his apartment, which housed a library including *Summa Theologica* in Latin, *War and Peace*, and *Firearms Investigation, Identification and Evidence*. There were a priest's vestments and crucifixes; heavy dumbbells joined a microscope and cages of white mice, along with a fragment of a cancer treatise. Ferrie's ambitions included ordination as a bishop in the Apostolic Orthodox Old Catholic Church of North America. Some aspect of cancer research was another of his interests, although he had no formal training in science. Ignorantly, he talked to his boys about how parasites could enter the sole of the foot and eat away at the brain.

Ferrie had managed to accumulate friends in high places. He had served as a police informant for an officer of dubious ethics named Sanford Krasnoff. According to Ferrie's closest young friend, Alvin Beaubouef, it was through Dave's connections that Krasnoff's friend, Edward Sapir, fresh out of law school, became a very young judge.

Dave had flown Carlos Marcello back to New Orleans after Robert Kennedy had him deported. Prior to that, Ferrie had traveled to Guatemala to arrange a false passport for Marcello; returning to New Orleans, Ferrie had taped this passport to his chest. When Eastern Airlines fired Ferrie because of his police record, redolent of crimes against nature, his attorney had been a Carlos Marcello lawyer, G. Wray Gill. Dave was paying Gill back by working on the Marcello case, which was heard on November 22, 1963.

It was Ferrie's political affiliations that interested Jim Garrison. Ferrie had flown for the CIA as a contract pilot, taking off from Tampa, the Keys and Venice, Florida, in sabotage missions: he burned sugarcane fields, dropped propaganda leaflets, and infiltrated and exfiltrated anti-Castro activists. His handler was Eladio del Valle, a mob-connected Cuban exile, who was also involved in setting up training camps to wage war against Castro. Del Valle paid Ferrie between $1,000 and $1,500 a mission, missions tracked by Cuban intelligence. Ferrie also flew for South Central Air Lines, a CIA proprietary. Ferrie's CIA employment has been confirmed by ex-CIA employee Victor Marchetti. By 1959, U.S. Customs had put David Ferrie under twenty-four-hour surveillance.

On occasion, Ferrie flew with another CIA contract pilot named E. Carl McNabb, who would later join Jim Garrison's investigation in an attempt to redeem a murderous past. One day they arrived at the School of the Americas in the Panama Canal Zone, a joint project of Robert Kennedy and the CIA for training of the Latin American military. McNabb met with some resistance. Dave walked in as if he owned the place.

"I didn't know your security clearance was so high," McNabb laughed, a light glittering in his ice-blue eyes.

"I didn't know yours was so low!" Ferrie rejoined.

"Kennedy is no good, Kennedy is a nigger lover," Ferrie told the boys under his spell. CIA and Kennedy together screwed up the Bay of Pigs, he ranted. On his blackboard before an audience of rapt boys he had drawn plans for the invasion of Cuba, then accused Kennedy of making a deal to support the invasion only to back out. He spoke of his CIA connections openly.

Among the CIA's schemes to kill Castro under OPERATION MONGOOSE was a plan concocted by Desmond Fitzgerald, chief of the Cuban Task Force, who was encouraged by Robert Kennedy to effect the assassination of Fidel Castro, already a CIA project. It involved the placement of a seashell rigged with explosives where Castro was known to enjoy diving. A midget submarine was needed to put the shell in place; on November 22, 1963, one such submarine sat in David Ferrie's apartment, "the kind designed for skin divers," Carlos Quiroga, an anti-Castro Cuban who worked for the Cuban Revolutionary Council, says. Quiroga watched Ferrie try to install its motor, as Ferrie talked of how he could build a mini-submarine armed with a bomb to propel into Havana harbor.

Jim Garrison's next move was to invite Jack Martin to Tulane and Broad. Martin, who had awakened New Orleans to the Oswald-Ferrie connection, was a small man, five foot nine, in his forties, with a small mustache. He dressed perpetually in a gray suit and a black porkpie hat, his tie pulled down. Jack bore the pallor of an alcoholic and looked out at you through weak blue eyes ("a skinny, messy little guy," Garrison's secretary Sharon Herkes thought).

Jack Martin had a scar on his chin, chain-smoked and subsisted on bad coffee. He seemed a broken-down, harmless individual, a hanger-on. A would-be journalist, he had worked for the *Westbank Herald*, a right-wing paper owned by a Major Stewart, who bore intelligence ties to Latin America. In 1958 Guy Banister had been publisher. Jack also worked for Banister as a sometime private eye, describing himself as "a con man who has stayed just within the law." He had mysterious access to police records, information he peddled. Like David Ferrie, he was a religious zealot, belonging to the same "church." Martin was, Robert Buras says, "a type of Ferrie," both men "highly intelligent."

Jack Martin also bore a checkered criminal history. He had been caught in a crime against nature with a homosexual named "Mona Lisa," and had a police record ranging from disturbing the peace, vagrancy and drunkenness to a 1952 murder charge in Houston, Texas, which had miraculously vanished. Despite all this, Martin was on a first-name basis with Senator Russell Long and enjoyed access to the office of Attorney General Jack P. F. Gremillion. Jack could get you a letter certifying you were an honorary attorney general of the state of Louisiana. Yet on the instructions of Plaquemines Parish czar Leander Perez, Martin had filed a petition to disqualify Gremillion as a candidate for reelection.

In November of 1963, Jack Martin's business card read, "Martin, Newbrough & Dalzell, Private Investigations." The telephone number rang through at Guy Banister's detective agency, even as Banister's own intelligence connections ranged from the expected FBI to the Office of Naval Intelligence (ONI) and CIA. William Dalzell was a CIA operative, as was Joseph Newbrough, a steady asset of the Domestic Contact Service, which in New Orleans also supervised the clandestine services. Newbrough was close to another CIA figure shortly to enter this story, Fred Lee Crisman. Dalzell's criminal charges had disappeared in a manner similar to Martin's. He had joined the Agency in the early fifties, a cryptologist with a "top secret" clearance, and was acquainted with David Ferrie. In New Orleans, CIA and FBI shared information about Dalzell.

Almost from the start Jim Garrison had come to believe that Lee Harvey Oswald was not observed with anyone who was *not* connected with the Central Intelligence Agency. Garrison's own witnesses, no less than his suspects, were equally Agency-involved. His instincts were correct, although he never learned that Jack Martin, his first real witness, not only served with military intelligence, but was himself a former CIA employee. Jack's real name was John J. Martin, and he worked for the Agency throughout the 1950s. His close intelligence ties he kept hidden. At one point in Garrison's investigation, Martin became hysterical at the thought that a television reporter had his photograph. "There are no photographs of me!" Jack insisted.

John J. Martin was a low-ranking intelligence assistant. He joined the Agency in November of 1950 and left supposedly in June of 1958 on a "disability retirement." He had been a GS-7 in the Transportation Branch, Services Division. Like David Ferrie, his rival and nemesis in matters ecclesiastical, Martin had been born in Cleveland, in 1913. Ferrie was born in 1918.

What emerges from the record is that John J. Martin, Jack

Martin, never left the Agency. In New Orleans, Martin was assigned to a young man named Thomas Edward Beckham, in a manner similar to Ferrie's relationship with Lee Oswald. Beckham was to notice that Martin had in his possession a variety of police credentials, and often posed as a police officer.

In Louisville, Martin had worked for "Echo Blue," a publication of the Fraternal Order of Police, where he also came to know Archbishop Carl Stanley. In New Orleans, Martin still carried "numerous police commissions," making it his business to spy on other policemen. The "S" in the New Orleans name of Jack S. Martin stood for "Suggs," Stanley told the FBI. But it was the same man he knew as John J. Martin.

Stanley created churches. He raised funds and mixed in politics, and John J. Martin had requested that Stanley consecrate him as a bishop to go to Cuba. He admitted to Stanley that he worked for the CIA and saw to it that Stanley did not promote David Ferrie in his quest to become a bishop.

CIA documents describe John Martin as suffering from "telephonitis," as Jack Martin was known not to be able to stay off the telephone; often he called the Agency itself. "Judging from his rambling talk during his phone calls," CIA wrote for the record, "and the ridiculous reason given for these calls, it would appear that the Subject is of unsound mind." CIA's John J. Martin, Louisville's John J. Martin, another rambling talker, was also identical in appearance to the New Orleans Jack S. Martin: five foot nine, one hundred fifty pounds with a small mustache. Like John J., Jack called himself a "newspaperman." "Bishop" John J. was a con man, like Jack. Jack's wife told the FBI right after the assassination that he would take off "alone for several months every year," his true identity obviously a mystery even to her.

Jim Garrison knew enough to listen to Jack Martin, then verify his facts. Almost always, unless he intended it otherwise, what Jack Martin told you checked out. One day Martin had invited Joe Newbrough to meet him at nine A.M. at a coffee shop. While Newbrough, "the fat man," ate his hearty breakfast, and Jack sipped his bad coffee, a limousine pulled up. Suddenly Newbrough saw Carlos Marcello being hustled off. It was the day Marcello was deported, and Jack had foreknowledge of the kidnapping of the Mafia don engineered by Robert Kennedy.

In 1971, when Jim Garrison was arrested for allegedly accepting bribes from pinball gambling interests and was driven to the Wild Life and Fisheries building for booking, at the front of a crowd of spectators stood that man who always knew what was happening in New Orleans.

"They had to frame a case on the DA!" Jack Martin called out loudly. "How about that!" Then Martin led the crowd in applause. "Let's hear it for the DA!" Martin shouted.

States-Item reporter Hoke May, himself a CIA asset, and for whom Jack Martin was an entirely reliable source, concluded that Jack Martin had been badly discredited by the FBI on purpose, made to seem an alcoholic, a mental case and a person not to be taken seriously, when in fact he was entirely credible.

In December of 1966, Jack Martin told Pershing Gervais, who had reappeared at Tulane and Broad in a semi-official capacity, that David Ferrie had blackmailed G. Wray Gill and Carlos Marcello to pay for the service station he opened in 1964. Ferrie had told his friend and fellow CIA asset Herb Wagner, who ran a finance company, not to bother with charges because the "government" was paying for his gas. For Jack Martin and David Ferrie, there was no contradiction here.

The day after his interview with Pershing, Jack Martin told Jim Garrison that Oswald had "offices" in the Newman building, Guy Banister's building. The janitor kept Oswald's belongings after he was gone. He had spotted Ferrie "once or twice maybe" with Oswald at Banister's. Once Ferrie walked in wearing "an army type fatigue suit and sunglasses," accompanied by three or four young men, one of whom was named "Lee." "He used to be with me in the CAP when he was a little kid," Ferrie said of Oswald. "Oswald is a friend of mine." There's a photograph of Oswald with Ferrie at a cook-out, Jack said.

Then came another bombshell. David Ferrie made a trip to Dallas during the time Oswald was there and lied about it, Jack revealed. He was in Dallas or Fort Worth two days before the assassination. His assignment was to fly three people from Texas to Laredo, or to Matamoros, in Mexico. Jim Garrison was unable to verify Ferrie's trip to Dallas. Yet it was so.

Having been turned over to the Secret Service on November 25, 1963, Ferrie told John Rice, the Special Agent in Charge, that he had not been in Dallas "for the last eight to ten years." Soon the Secret Service yielded to the FBI's insistence that it take over all investigating. "In the last fifteen years, I have been in Dallas, Texas, very infrequently," Ferrie told the FBI, typing his own statement for Regis Kennedy. Ferrie lied, too, when he said he did not know Lee Oswald. Ferrie's friends knew otherwise.

Benton Wilson knew David Ferrie from having served at Keesler

Air Force Base where Ferrie took his CAP recruits on occasion. Wilson worked at National Car Rental with another Ferrie friend, Jim Lewallen, who was a tenant at one of the French Quarter properties renovated by Clay Shaw, the managing director of the International Trade Mart. Ferrie and the Wilsons met often at the Old Loyalty Bar on North Rampart Street, where Ben Wilson and his brother John lived.

Jim Lewallen confided to the Wilsons that he was the lover of both Clay Shaw and David Ferrie, and that of course Shaw knew Ferrie. Lewallen and Ben Wilson bore so remarkable a resemblance that, later, when Jim Garrison's staff were interviewing Lewallen, Garrison walked in and said, "Congratulations, you finally got Wilson!"

The Wilsons admired David Ferrie for his passion, for his genius as an aviator, for his erudition, and for his superior vocabulary. More, they knew Ferrie as someone who would help people out, like an old merchant seaman named Joe Karl, who, in a case of mistaken identity, had been threatened by some mob characters. Once Ferrie became involved, the problem vanished.

One day during the third week of November 1963, Dave arrived at the Old Loyalty Bar wearing a hunting costume, full camouflage, complete with vest and cap.

"Why are you dressed like that?" Ben Wilson wanted to know.

"We're going on a hunting trip to Dallas," Ferrie said.

"What are you hunting for?" John asked. He was twenty-two years old.

"Big game! Big game!" Dave said cryptically. On the day President Kennedy was killed, Ben Wilson was certain. "They did it! They killed Kennedy!" he said, shaking his brother out of a deep sleep and referring to David Ferrie. A right-winger, like Dave, Ben shed no tears for a president he despised.

A few days after the assassination, John Wilson ran into Ferrie again. Dave was still in his hunting clothes, that same outfit Jack Martin had described Ferrie wearing during the summer when he appeared at Guy Banister's office with Oswald.

"Did you get any big game?" John joked.

"Damn right. You know it," Dave laughed.

At the law offices of G. Wray Gill, the week of the assassination, Gill instructed David Ferrie to rent an airplane since his own plane needed repair. Dave approached Herb Wagner, from whom he had borrowed money in the past—like the $5,000 Dave needed to bribe

Jefferson Parish assistant district attorney A. J. Graffagnino in the Crouchet case (Graffagnino later went to jail on another matter). Dave had also invited Wagner, who, like Dave, held rank in the Civil Air Patrol, to join OPERATION MONGOOSE, the CIA's project to assassinate Fidel Castro. Wagner was a short, stocky man, with thinning hair and glasses, resembling no one so much as the director, Mr. Hoover, himself. "It's called Operation Mosquito," Dave laughed; OPERATION MONGOOSE had not yet officially begun, but Dave knew about it. "The government knows what we're doing. As a matter of fact, they're backing us!"

Wagner declined, but he did help the CIA with its training camps of anti-Castro Cubans north of Lake Pontchartrain. It was apparently Wagner who was the pilot on an occasion sponsored by Ferrie when two soldiers-of-fortune, Gerald Patrick Hemming and Howard K. Davis, went to Louisiana in search of training camp sites. Herb also flew reconnaissance planes for the CIA into Cuba. His own flights, Dave told Wagner, were "the most patriotic thing I've ever done."

Now Dave wanted $400 to rent a plane to fly to Dallas, a trip Wagner later concluded was to take care of prearrangements for the assassination. He would be coming right back—the same day. That Dave flew to Dallas that week is also confirmed by Allen Campbell, a young Banister operative, who was Ferrie's next-door neighbor at the airport. Campbell knew Ferrie with his "red brillo pad" glued to his head and his "circus," the tough young kids with whom he surrounded himself. Yes, Campbell says, Dave flew to Dallas that week.

Wagner wanted collateral for the loan, and so Dave offered his dubious 1948 blue Stinson Voyager. "Does this plane have an Air Worthiness Certificate?" Herb asked, with the German exactitude that led Ferrie to nickname him "Von Wagner." They went up in the Stinson; Wagner was not impressed. When he later told Jim Garrison that Ferrie's plane was airworthy, Wagner lied. Even Ferrie had to admit to the FBI after the assassination that "the plane has not been airworthy since the license expired in the spring of 1962." The only planes he would have access to would be "rental planes," a fact the FBI verified.

When Wagner insisted that Dave find someone to cosign the four hundred dollar loan, Dave produced Clay Shaw himself, the man Jim Garrison was to place on trial for conspiracy in the murder of President Kennedy. Vehemently, yet calmly, Shaw would always deny he had ever met David Ferrie. Yet he did cosign that loan. In 1967, Wagner wondered whether he should show the loan document to Jim Garrison. He consulted his friend Roger E. Johnston Jr., then a deputy marshal for the Kenner Police Department.

"I have a document that would really be beneficial to Jim Garrison's probe," Wagner confided. He opened a drawer at the bottom of one of his filing cabinets, and pulled out a tan manila folder. It was a loan contract.

"Here in front of my eyes," Johnston says, "was the proof." The borrower's signature read: "David Ferrie." The cosigner was "Clay Shaw." The document proved not only that Ferrie and Shaw knew each other, but that they participated together in preparations for the assassination, reflecting their mutual foreknowledge of the crime.

In the 1980s, a retired Louisiana state trooper named Norbert A. Gurtner told the FBI that, shortly before the assassination, he was copilot with David Ferrie on a Beech D-18 flight from New Orleans Lakefront Airport to New Orleans Moisant and on to Love Field, Dallas. None of the passengers carried baggage. Nor did Ferrie introduce Gurtner to any of them. Gurtner identified Lee Harvey Oswald and Clay Shaw, and a young man named Perry Russo as passengers, and while this configuration demands pause, Gurtner's revelation, apparently without an ulterior motive, should be noted. Gurtner said he was willing to take a polygraph if the FBI had any interest. It hadn't.

Although Jim Garrison never learned about that loan granted to David Ferrie and cosigned by Clay Shaw, there was further evidence that persuaded him that Ferrie was connected to the assassination. Jack Martin, during the weekend of the assassination, had said that when Oswald was arrested, he had Ferrie's library card with him, information he could not have gleaned from New Orleans television. When the FBI questioned Ferrie, he denied emphatically that he had loaned the card to Oswald. "The card has never been out of my possession," Ferrie said. Then he wandered around town inquiring whether anyone knew about Oswald's possessing his library card. He asked Oswald's neighbor, Mrs. Doris Eames, if she knew "whose library card Oswald had." He questioned Oswald's landlady, Mrs. Lena Garner: "They found my library card on Oswald," Ferrie said.

Jim Garrison concluded that if there were no evidence linking a library card found on Oswald to Ferrie, the FBI would never have put the issue in its report. If "Oswald had a library card on him bearing the name 'George Washington,'" it would not be reasonable to state in an investigative report that David Ferrie denied lending his library card to Oswald." Later Garrison learned from a source that Ferrie's library card had indeed been found on Oswald, "but has since been destroyed."

Despite Ferrie's denials, his CAP cadets reported that Oswald had been among them. Ferrie, expecting protection from higher authority, was so bold as to name Jerry Paradis as willing to confirm that Oswald had not served under his command. But in 1978, an attorney now, Paradis clearly remembered for the House Select Committee that Oswald and Ferrie were "in the unit together" at ten or fifteen meetings. "I'm not saying that they may have been there together. I'm saying it was a certainty."

Ferrie told Jim Lewallen that there might be a photograph of himself and Oswald together—just as Jack Martin had revealed to Jim Garrison. There they are together, Ferrie and Oswald, indeed at a cook-out, as Jack Martin had said, in an unearthed photo album belonging to a cadet named John Ciravolo, who was in the CAP in 1955 and 1956. Ciravolo remembers Oswald as "a boy with a nose too big for his face."

The evidence that David Ferrie knew Lee Oswald well goes far beyond the testimony of the CAP cadets. John Wilson one day had spotted Oswald distributing pro-Castro leaflets on Canal Street. "A commie nut," Wilson thought. Then he had seen the very same fellow at Dave Ferrie's apartment. "What was he doing at Dave's!" Wilson thought. Another young man in New Orleans, Thomas Lewis Clark, told Garrison that "at one time Dave told me he had taught Oswald."

There remain yet other witnesses to Oswald's close connection to David Ferrie. It was mid-September of 1959 when Oswald traveled from Fort Worth to the city of his birth where he contacted Clay Shaw's travel agent, Lewis E. Hopkins, at the International Trade Mart. Oswald's destination was a mystery, although his cousin Marilyn Murret, who worked for the CIA, knew it, and would so inform Lee's half brother John Pic, even before Lee reached the Soviet Union. "Do you ever hear from Lee?" John asked Marilyn when he ran into her in Japan.

"Oh, he's in Russia," Marilyn Murret said. At that point no one but the CIA knew where Oswald was headed.

Lee had time to kill during that steamy New Orleans September. But you could relax at the Old Pontchartrain Beach amusement park, ride the ferris wheel, have a mechanical gypsy tell your fortune, or knock lead milk bottles off their stool with a ball.

Van Burns, a recent high school graduate, was in charge of the parakeet stand while he awaited Marine Corps boot camp. You threw a nickel onto a plate and earned a free parakeet. On the night in question, Van's friend Bob Boylston wandered by in the company of two men. Six months earlier, Bob had been inducted into the Army. Now, surprisingly, he was out. He mumbled something about the Civil Air Patrol. Van would wonder later whether the man accompanying Bob Boylston that night had liberated him from the Army for some purpose. The Civil Air Patrol interested Van Burns. The fad among the cadets, he had learned, had switched from learning German to studying Russian.

Bob introduced Van to his companions. One was an older man with odd hair. His name was David Ferrie. The other was named "Lee."

"Lee, Lee Oswald," he said. He threw a few nickels at the plates, but missed. He did not win a parakeet, a creature he had once bought for his mother out of the first money he ever earned. He was in the Marine Corps, Lee told Van. "In recon."

"What do you do in recon?" Van said, genuinely interested. Lee scowled.

"We take pictures," Lee said finally, moving away toward the greyhound booth where Bob Boylston stood. So among Oswald's possessions after his death would be a Minox camera used for microdot work, an artifact of espionage. "Possession of same in Eastern Europe is in itself sufficient to deny egress across borders," one of Garrison's anonymous leads states.

Boylston returned. "He's a great pilot," he said, referring to Ferrie, who had wandered off. "I know what you're thinking," Boylston said quickly to Burns. "Maybe he is and maybe he isn't. But he's never approached me." Ferrie in fact reserved his sexual advances for a select few of his acolytes.

Boylston confided that Lee traveled with him and Ferrie on flights to Cuba where Lee took pictures. The three appeared to be so intimate as to seem to form a special clique, Van Burns thought. When he learned of Jim Garrison's investigation, he did not come forward with the information that he had seen Oswald and Ferrie together.

Bob Boylston did provide some information to Jim Garrison's investigators. He was close enough to Ferrie for Ferrie to have paid his Loyola University tuition, he said. Ferrie had talked in 1961 of "secret orders" having to do with Cuba, of having been wounded and shot down on one of his flights. Bob was in charge of CAP records, which were sent to Washington, but when Jim Garrison attempted to subpoena these records, he was told they did not exist.

Boylston also had told Van Burns of having gone to Dallas several times with Dave, and how Dave spoke of a "super-special army always ready to fight." Once he had driven Dave to the airport as Dave was headed for one of his trips to Cuba. He must never talk about the training going on over the Lake, no matter what happens, Dave told Boylston. "Even if 'it' didn't go. They were "taking care of something," something very serious.

From the mid-fifties, Ferrie kept in touch with Oswald. In Russia as a false defector, Oswald wrote on a form that, should his first child be a boy, he was to be named "David Lee Oswald." The only "David" in his life was Ferrie.

Among Jim Garrison's most important contributions to understanding the assassination of President Kennedy, among his earliest insights and efforts, was his exploration of Oswald's connections to the U.S. government. Marguerite Oswald had told the Warren Commission that her son was "an agent of the government," working for the CIA. Garrison came to believe her, suspecting that the Marine Reserve "recruiting officer," who had come personally to her home to help an underage sixteen-year-old Lee join the Marines, was Ferrie himself. Lee went to the Marine Corps "because of the Civil Air Patrol," Mrs. Oswald had testified. Her son was "already preparing himself . . . to become an agent."

Garrison wrote to Mrs. Oswald that Ferrie was "probably" the person who helped Lee "get selected for intelligence work after he went into the Marines." Ferrie was behind Oswald's movement into "the covert operations division of the Office of Naval Intelligence," as so many of Ferrie's CAP cadets wound up in the military. Garrison wrote to Oswald's mother: he had not believed at first that "your son was working for the C.I.A." Now he did.

In his interview with Jim Garrison, Jack Martin had also dropped the name "Thomas Edward Beckham." Another Garrison witness, a runner for Guy Banister named David Lewis, who also called himself a "leg man" for Jack Martin, told Garrison that Beckham knew Oswald and had even distributed leaflets with him. This was partially true. Beckham did not, however, hand out any leaflets. Yet they were casually acquainted, and Oswald had occasionally visited a mission where Tommy had been placed by Jack Martin and where money was collected for the anti-Castro cause.

Leaving Jim Garrison, Martin at once telephoned Regis Kennedy at the Bureau. He had nothing to do "with the Garrison investigation of the Kennedy assassination," Martin insisted. Garrison "is trying to hatch an egg and you know what happens when an egg does not hatch. There is a big smell." Martin now again implicated that young man whom he had known since his teens, Thomas Edward Beckham. Beckham "was associated with Oswald and assisted Oswald in passing out leaflets," Jack told Big Regis.

Yet Jack Martin had done Garrison a service. He had confirmed not only that Ferrie, his suspect, was connected to Oswald, but that both Ferrie and Oswald were involved with Guy Banister. He also revealed that Oswald had indeed been "sheep-dipped" and was no Marxist. "Ferrie was anti-Communist, but he and Oswald were tight. *See?*" Martin told Garrison. With the assignment to distribute "Fair Play for Cuba" leaflets, Oswald was being set up as part of a plan to blame Castro for the assassination. In placing Oswald at Guy Banister's office, Jack Martin banished any doubts Garrison might have had that Oswald was the patsy and not the assassin of the president.

Garrison studied his 1963 interviews with Ferrie, Alvin Beaubouef and Melvin Coffey, his traveling companions on an automobile trip to Galveston and Houston on the weekend of the assassination. In presenting the trip as spur of the moment, Coffey had lied. Beaubouef told Garrison the truth: the trip had been planned "at least a week in advance," as John Wilson knew as well.

Who was David Ferrie? Garrison wondered, as he perused the documents taken from Ferrie's apartment on the evening of November 24th. Ferrie was a CIA contract employee. He had organized crime relationships at the highest level. Not knowing of the joint efforts of the CIA and the Mafia in OPERATION MONGOOSE, Garrison was perplexed. "Why does an apparently minor homosexual have a connection with Wasserman [Jack Wasserman was Carlos Marcello's Washington lawyer] and, by implication, Marcello?" The Warren Commission had concluded there was no "real Mafia motive" in the assassination. But Jack Ruby's background, Garrison considered, was "redolent of organized crime and labor racketeering." He had not given up the possibility that there had been significant Mafia involvement in the assassination.

The day after Garrison talked to Jack Martin, David Ferrie appeared for questioning at Tulane and Broad. The interviewer was John Volz, who had done his homework. In April of 1963, Volz wrote in his memo, Kennedy had "come out publicly against anti-Castro raids on Cuba by refugees based in Miami." That policy had come home to Louisiana on July 31st, 1963, when, on Kennedy's instructions, the FBI had raided a major anti-Castro training camp northwest of Lake Pontchartrain.

The Warren Commission, pointedly, had not called David Ferrie. But three months into his investigation, Jim Garrison had a suspect who had actually participated in the planning and implementation of the murder of the president. Facing tough prosecutor Volz sat David Ferrie himself.

Ferrie lied, evaded and obfuscated. He denied he was "acquainted" with Oswald. He admitted to being in Dallas only "in March or April of this year," which was 1966. Asked why he had invited arch-enemy Jack Martin to help him contact witnesses in his case against Eastern Airlines, Ferrie replied with a question, "How do you explain a psychopath?" as he enlisted the FBI's strategy of discrediting Jack Martin. As for why he went to Houston and Galveston on the weekend of the assassination, Ferrie professed, as "a Yankee," to be fond of ice skating. He didn't bother to repeat his original 1963 lie that he had talked to the owner "at length" about how to operate an ice-skating rink, suspecting that by now Chuck Rolland had revealed that no such conversation had taken place. Ferrie added a new explanation: the purpose of the trip was now an errand for Gill, a meeting with a man named Marion James Johnson.

In 1963 Ferrie had also claimed on that car trip to have gone goose hunting, only to have admitted to Frank Klein there were no guns in the car. He had lied about the guns, he confessed to his adopted "godson," Morris Brownlee, because he didn't want to give the district attorney anything. Alvin Beauboeuf confirms that Ferrie told him to lie and tell the police there were no guns, because he didn't want his guns confiscated.

Now Ferrie admits to Volz that there *were* guns in the car. He confides that Brownlee has been "in a lot of trouble during the last ten or twelve years," neglecting to mention that Brownlee had broken with him after Ferrie had forged his name on a good character affidavit presented at the Eastern Airlines hearing.

Where is Pershing? Ferrie asks. Pershing, he is certain, could explain to him why he is being questioned by the district attorney's office.

OSWALD
AND CUSTOMS 4

Is this Juan's apartment?
    —Lee Harvey Oswald

J IM GARRISON WAS ALMOST from the start certain of Oswald's connections to both the FBI and CIA. Even more startling are government documents, released since Garrison's investigation, that suggest that Oswald shared, like Miami customs agent Cesario Diosdado, an affiliation with not only the FBI and the CIA, but also with U.S. Customs. A New Orleans patrolman remembered arresting Ferrie and Oswald together at the lake front and taking them to Levee Board headquarters where Oswald's Customs connections soon emerged.

At Customs, Oswald's handler was a man named David Smith. Oswald's employment with Customs was so sensitive that the HSCA interview with bar owner and FBI informant Orestes Peña was sealed for twenty-five years. As an FBI informant, Peña reported to Warren de Brueys beginning in 1959 or 1960. Peña placed Oswald with Customs officials on a regular basis. So explosive were Peña's revelations about Oswald's relationships with Customs officers that Peña's files were systematically destroyed by the FBI in a multicity effort that stretched across Europe. A document survives, a teletype directed to J. Edgar Hoover, dated January 14, 1976: "Rome file regarding 'Orestes Peña: IS—Cuba' Destroyed."

Peña was uniquely placed to observe the interconnections between the FBI, the CIA, Customs, and the Immigration and Naturalization Service (INS). Cubans arriving illegally in the United States at the Port of New Orleans were brought to Peña through a "Mr. Johnson" of the INS. Peña's role was to offer room and board and help find them jobs.

In the mornings, Peña revealed, Oswald frequented a Greek restaurant on Decatur and Iberville with "other federal agents from the Customs House Building," which housed FBI, ONI, CIA and Immigration. At least ten or twelve times, Peña testified, he observed Oswald sharing breakfast with his Customs handlers. He had witnessed his own handler Warren de Brueys at that same Greek restaurant when Oswald was there with federal agents. "I believe they knew each other very, very well," Peña said of Oswald and de Brueys. Peña talked at length to Jim Garrison, although no memos survive.

Peña had also observed Oswald, de Brueys, David Smith and Wendall Roache of the Immigration Service leave the restaurant together and head for the Customs House building. In 1976, staff members of the Church Committee knew that Smith "was involved in CIA operations in the New Orleans area in the early 1960s." In his testimony, Warren de Brueys acknowledged his acquaintance with "Border Patrol" Agent Smith. And Roache also admitted his acquaintance with Warren de Brueys. "I knew him," Roache said curtly. An investigator for the INS in New Orleans, Theophanis E. Pappelis, swore under oath before the Church Committee that de Brueys "had a working relationship with the New Orleans INS office."

As senior patrol inspector in 1961, Roache, according to an FBI document, was investigating David Ferrie who "had been trying to purchase a C-47 airplane for $30,000 and supposedly had a cache of arms in the New Orleans area." From this vantage, it appears that Oswald was investigating Ferrie, rather than the other way around. Hunter Leake, of the New Orleans field office of CIA, later told Roache, "Garrison had something. I read his reports in the newspaper and they were correct. He received good intelligence information, whether he was using it for politics or not."

After the assassination, David Smith was transferred to Uruguay. Wendall Roache was moved to Puerto Rico. When Roache was finally contacted by the Church Committee in 1975, he said, "I've been waiting twelve years to talk to someone about this." His testimony remains classified to this day.

Only fragments of what Roache knew have emerged. Roache mentions the name of "Ron L. Smith," a Border Patrol inspector with the New Orleans Station of the INS, who received a call from the New Orleans police about Oswald being arrested. Oswald claimed to be Russian, insisting he spoke only "Russian." He was released when he admitted he was American. The story Smith finally told the Church Committee was that Oswald claimed to be a

Cuban alien. (On August 9th, when Oswald was arrested in New Orleans, he also told the arresting police officers that he was Cuban-born.) Smith had interviewed Oswald on April 10, 1963, having gone down to see Oswald in jail "to verify or disprove this status." In 1963, both INS inspectors testified, INS had responsibility for surveilling certain Cuban groups in New Orleans, an assignment from the Department of Justice.

"Smith had an office in. . . ." Roache began. Then the interviewer suddenly cuts him off. The interview of "James Smith" of U.S. Customs remains classified. Roache, too, observed Oswald "going into the offices of Ferrie's group," and said "Oswald was known to be one of the men in the group."

Roache swore under oath that David Ferrie took movies at a Cuban exile training camp north of Lake Pontchartrain. A piece of that film was viewed by the deputy legal counsel of HSCA, Robert K. Tanenbaum. It included Oswald, Ferrie and CIA Western Hemisphere chief David Atlee Phillips, as well as Alpha 66 operative Antonio Veciana, the CIA's AMSHALE, with whom Guy Banister's people worked closely. Roache also states that there were no organized crime tie-ins involving the Louisiana aspects of the assassination, a point Aaron Kohn himself would confirm in his testimony before the House Select Committee.

Yet other witnesses of Oswald's involvement with Customs were Russell Bruce and Edward L. Cupp, who ran the INS District Office, people Jim Garrison never reached. Garrison did cast a long look at one Sergio Arcacha Smith, a Cuban in exile who worked for all three agencies too, FBI, CIA and Customs, as a CIA document of May of 1967 reveals: Arcacha "maintained extensive relations" with Immigration and the FBI. His FBI case officer was . . . Warren de Brueys. CIA admitted at the start of Jim Garrison's investigation that it was coordinating its activities with the FBI, Immigration and Naturalization Service and with Customs, disseminating to them all "pertinent intelligence information." Neither of the two INS inspectors in New Orleans were interviewed by the FBI for the ostensible investigation mandated by the Warren Commission.

Lee Harvey Oswald's other demonstrable link to Customs was his close relationship with a Cuban customs house broker, as he defined himself, named Juan Valdes. Valdes was a short, plump, meticulous fellow with fair skin, but extremely hairy; hair covered his back, his chest and arms, although his hairline receded from his forehead, so that he seemed "horseshoe bald." In conversation, he often used the term "BC," meaning "before Castro."

Sometimes Juan called himself a "coffee broker," but the pastime he pursued assiduously was growing orchids, particularly prize-winning phalaenopsis. Orchids of every color of the rainbow crowded the surfaces of his apartment. He also raised macaws. A nasty red chow was always by his side. A year before Oswald came to New Orleans, Juan lived at the Wohl Apartments on St. Charles.

Juan was gay. Soon he had made sexual advances to the boyfriend of his neighbor, Gretchen Bomboy. So persistent was he that Bomboy and her boyfriend went to the police, and a restraining order was issued. Juan Valdes, now in his mid thirties, moved to the Patios Apartments at 3101 St. Charles, a redoubt of Uptown bohemians.

Among the tenants at the Patios was a well-respected orthopedic surgeon and oncologist named Mary Sherman, an attractive woman in her early fifties with masses of dark braided hair. When she entered medicine in the 1940s, Sherman had been one of only three women orthopedists in the country. A widow, she came to New Orleans in 1952 from the University of Chicago where she joined the staff of the hospital created by Dr. Alton Ochsner, a longtime CIA asset.

During the summer of 1963, Mr. and Mrs. Owen Hawes were Valdes' next-door neighbors at the Patios. Hawes worked for NASA, so that at times his whereabouts were unknown even to his wife, Victoria. She came to know Juan, who looked "like a little Jewish accountant." Juan told her he was born in Miami. He spoke almost without an accent.

Soon Juan was asking Mrs. Hawes to accept packages for him when he wasn't home, mostly orchids and plants that he imported from Latin American countries. Some, she speculates, might well have included drugs. One day Juan knocked at her door and asked if he might use her telephone. He had his own telephone, he explained, but to make his long distance calls, he wished to use hers. He promised to pay her back at the end of each month. Many of the calls, she noticed, were to Cuba. Others were to Miami.

Shortly after Juan made his request, Mrs. Hawes opened her door to another caller. A man stood there. "Is this Juan's apartment?" the young man asked. He was very polite, a nondescript young man. Yet Victoria Hawes recognized him at once. They had attended Beauregard Junior High School on Canal Street together, she and this wispy, sad young man, who in school had been so shy that he had gravitated toward anyone who would pay him some attention. He was a "sidelines" fellow, she had thought, and people tended to ignore him, while he seemed not to want to be seen. He was never invited to the King Cake parties the class enjoyed, nor did "Harvey" host any King Cake parties.

At home with small children, Victoria now saw Lee Oswald frequently visiting Juan Valdes. She thought it odd because Juan was so much older. Together Lee and Juan came to her apartment to make the telephone calls to Miami and to Cuba. The walls were so thin that when they were in Juan's apartment, she could hear them talking in the bathroom, then flushing the toilet over and over, maybe twenty times in a row, and she thought they must be destroying paper. She was curious about them both, not least Juan who often returned from mysterious walks at four o'clock in the morning.

Victoria Hawes noticed as well that Oswald and Valdes were both friendly with Dr. Mary Sherman, to whom Juan spoke in Spanish, an odd association, she thought, between a respectable orthopedist and pathologist and a gay Latino orchid grower whose name even seemed dubious. It now seems apparent that Oswald the Customs agent and Valdes who worked at the Customs House, and at various import-export companies, obvious CIA proprietaries, had much in common. Oswald as a PSI, or Potential Security Informant, would report violations of the Neutrality Act, which forbade self-styled raids into Cuba. The information he conveyed might well have come, in part, from Valdes, now working for a company called "All Transport, Inc.," located at Clay Shaw's International Trade Mart.

In 1964, relations between Mary Sherman and Juan Valdes deteriorated. They fought over the garbage. In anger, Valdes threw a bunch of flowers onto Sherman's private patio area. She told her maid that Juan was obnoxious, a "pest," and ordered that he no longer be admitted to her apartment. But Sherman's maid was to remember Dr. Sherman having dinner with Juan at an earlier time.

Although he lived at the other end of the semi-circular floor, when smoke issued from Mary Sherman's apartment in the early morning hours of July 21st, it was Juan Valdes who telephoned, not the fire department, but, oddly, the police. Mary Sherman's body was found with unspeakable wounds: on the right side of her body, flesh and bone had evaporated, so that her right rib cage and all of her right arm had disintegrated, leaving a stub, with the lung and other organs exposed to view. The massive conflagration necessary to cause her bones to evaporate would have converted the entire apartment complex to ashes had her injuries been inflicted at the Patios. Yet the curtains hadn't even caught on fire. The immediate cause of death was a knife wound to the heart. After Mary Sherman's death, her genitals had been mutilated carelessly through her clothes to make it seem that the crime was somehow sex related. There was no forced entry. Her wallet remained, untouched.

Juan had been heard to come in at dawn by his downstairs neighbor, Helen Wattley.

"If I had to say now who did it, it would be Juan," homicide detective Frank Hayward said. No record remains of a search warrant of Valdes' apartment or of his being interviewed at the scene, although Hayward later revealed he had seen orchids everywhere, proving he had been inside Juan's apartment. Interviewed at police headquarters, Valdes was permitted to type his own statement. Then, although Hayward wanted to question him further, Lieutenant James Kruebbe ushered Valdes quickly out the door. Later, as a polygraph operator, Kruebbe would be instrumental in challenging the credibility of important Garrison witnesses.

Hayward and his partner Robert Townsend continued to demand that Valdes submit to a polygraph, and Valdes agreed, making an appointment. He did not keep it. His lawyer had advised him to decline, Valdes explained.

The police wondered if Mary Sherman might have found out something about Valdes, implicating him in her death. One secret that has been kept until now is, of course, Valdes' acquaintance with Lee Harvey Oswald the previous summer. After a month, the police were ordered by higher authority to cease investigating the Mary Sherman murder entirely. Four months later, Townsend concluded: "they didn't want this thing solved."

Mary Sherman was known to do nighttime work, perhaps with a linear particle accelerator, one of which was known to have been in use in New Orleans at the time, and that could account for her bone injuries, injuries even a crematorium would not approximate. Only that her work was top secret explains why, if she had been injured in an accident, an ambulance was not immediately summoned. The heavy wiring capability at the soon-vacated U.S. Public Health Hospital at the end of Magazine Street, nicknamed, "the Lab," was close to where Oswald had resided with Marina. Circumstantial evidence suggests that this hospital was Sherman's extracurricular destination and the scene of her bizarre injuries. At "the Lab," secret research—black ops—proceeded in the dead of night. Sherman worked frequently until midnight, and Juan Valdes was given to those nighttime walks.

"The Lab" was later quarantined and guarded by armed police, suggesting too that secret government research proceeded there. In 1999, Robert Buras discovered that the facility, now empty, was still guarded by armed police. The remains of heavy wiring suggest equipment of great force, like a nuclear particle accelerator through which cancer cells might be transferred from one animal to another, or toxic biological weapons developed, likely projects for secret research. Less likely was that Sherman was merely working on an anticancer vaccine. That CIA secret research was proceeding in New Orleans matches Dr. Alton Ochsner's status as a CIA asset.

A blank vaccination card signed by "Dr. A. J. Hideel" was found in the possession of Oswald when he was arrested in Dallas; the card had been issued by this same hospital. The fact that Oswald hung around the U. S. Public Health Service Hospital places his summertime companion Ferrie there as well, even as Oswald's connection to Juan Valdes connects him to Mary Sherman.

Reporter David Chandler confirmed to New Orleans author Don Lee Keith that Mary Sherman was doing "research with cancer cases." A former FBI agent named Edgar Saux (Sachs), administrative director of the Ochsner Clinic, where Mary worked at her day job, said Sherman had special connections to obtain valuable drugs and was writing a book on bone cancer. Could she have had some relationship to David Ferrie? her colleague Gordon McFarland was asked. "Absolutely," he said. Jim Garrison first thought that a fragmentary treatise on cancer research found at David Ferrie's apartment might have been authored by Mary Sherman, and the white mice at Ferrie's apartment might once have belonged to her. Mary Sherman was also a good friend of Ferrie's doctor, Martin Palmer.

Don Lee Keith, attempting to track down Juan Valdes in the late 1970s, interviewed a Mr. Gilley at Emery Ocean Freight, one place where Juan had worked. "You don't want anything to do with him!" Gilley said. Then, abruptly, he hung up. At All Transport, Inc., a Mr. Quartler remembered Valdes well. "I'll never forget him!" Quartler said. "Anything I could tell you about him, I wouldn't tell you over the phone." Quartler was told the reporter had something belonging to Valdes and wanted to give it to him in person. "Throw it away!" Quartler advised.

All references to Dr. Ochsner or his clinic were expunged from the police report of Mary Sherman's death, although he was her employer. Mr. and Mrs. Hawes were left with a sixty dollar unpaid telephone bill. Then an anonymous telephone call came, the voice sounding like Juan's: "You better move," the man said. They did. When Owen Hawes brought the telephone bill to the FBI during

Jim Garrison's investigation, another call came: "Stop sticking your nose in business that doesn't concern you!" So they moved again.

On May 24, 1967, Jim Garrison subpoenaed Juan Valdes before the Orleans Parish grand jury. The *Times-Picayune* described him as a "Latin playwright." Valdes was interviewed not by the grand jury, but by a once-and-future CIA operative who had joined Garrison's staff, William Martin. Two months later, on July 28th, Martin finally produced a memo of this interview.

Of photographs he was shown, Valdes identified Clay Shaw, whom he had "seen in and around the International Trade Mart for many years." He had "never associated with or been a member of any of the Cuban Revolutionary anti-Castro groups," he said. The subject of Oswald and the subject of Mary Sherman did not arise, according to this report. Martin writes that Valdes was "fat," a "soft and mild-mannered person and would not appear to be the stocky powerful Cuban we are looking for." Garrison had instructed all his investigators to search for a thick-necked, pockmarked Cuban who had appeared on a WDSU television film of Oswald.

Later, appalled by Martin's disloyalty, Garrison would tell his staff when he received questionable information, "sign the memo 'Jones Harris' [another of his less-than-reliable volunteers] or 'William Martin' because if the files are ever grabbed by the U.S. government, this one will not be appreciated." Martin was certainly an FBI informant as well. The day after Martin interviewed Valdes, the FBI's Division Five (Intelligence) did a name check on Valdes for "All References (Subversive & Nonsubversive)." A laundry list of documents involving Valdes emerged from the Bureau files. One, a 105 file, belonging to "Lee Harvey Oswald," and dated November 1963, was marked "destroyed."

By 1969, Juan Valdes had disappeared from the New Orleans City Directory.

Years later, Edward Butler, head of INCA, the Information Council of the Americas, a right-wing anti-Communist propaganda group, met with Dr. Ochsner, who financed INCA. Butler revealed he knew Juan Valdes, even as Mary Sherman had been a financial contributor to INCA. And long after his official investigation had come to a halt, Garrison learned Mary Sherman had donated money to one of the anti-Castro training camps, a fact known to *Life* magazine. She had taken care of the trainees there.

CIA reporter Hoke May told Don Lee Keith that Mary Sherman had indeed been a close friend of David Ferrie, a fact Jim Garrison was never able to prove. May thought that Ferrie worked with Mary Sherman on a cure for cancer. Ferrie, an expert at medical documentation, worked on medical briefs for G. Wray Gill. Ferrie's brother Parmely had said that Ferrie had once flirted with the idea of becoming a doctor.

David Ferrie's association with Mary Sherman is not as far-fetched as it first appears. There had been thousands of mice in the U.S. Public Health Service building. Ferrie had possessed cages of white mice that some speculate had come to him from Mary Sherman. These mice he at one time stored at the apartment of one of his young boy-acolytes, Michael Otty Clyde Wakeling, at 209 Vinet Street, where a "sickening odor" pervaded. Wakeling testified for Jim Garrison that Ferrie was using these mice "to develop a cure for cancer." But, rather than searching for a cure, Ferrie was more likely to be injecting mice with viruses to learn how to transfer cancer from one organism to another, in keeping with his history of schemes to assassinate Fidel Castro. His experiments with mice seemed to match his fantasy of sending a bomb-laden mini-submarine into Havana harbor.

Hoke May's source was Jack Martin, who knew that Ferrie and Mary Sherman had a close personal connection. Sherman had been initiated into involvement in clandestine Cuban activities by David Ferrie, Martin told May. Having heard rumors that David Ferrie either had killed Mary Sherman, or at least been partially responsible for her death, Garrison told *Playboy* he wondered whether Sherman's death was connected to her association with David Ferrie. Without more evidence, he could go no further.

Forty years later, detective Frank Hayward remained too uneasy to discuss what he knew about the unsolved Mary Sherman case, even with a fellow retired police officer. Sherman's connections to Valdes, Valdes' connections to Oswald, Oswald's connections to Ferrie, Ferrie's connections to Clay Shaw, and Shaw's close connection to his fellow CIA operative, Dr. Alton Ochsner—all link the mystery of Mary Sherman's tragic death to the Kennedy assassination. It is true that there is no direct line of evidence between the murder of Mary Sherman—or Mary Sherman's nighttime research—and the assassination of John F. Kennedy. Yet a close colleague of Lee Harvey Oswald, the man blamed for Kennedy's death, a man as Oswald's cohort hitherto unknown to students of the assassination, was the chief suspect in Sherman's murder.

Historians have remained unable to connect Mary Sherman to Oswald's mentor, David Ferrie, despite Jim Garrison's speculation that there was a connection. Yet Garrison's source, Jack Martin, whose bona fides have over and over been established, whose CIA background emerges in this history for the first time, told Hoke May that Ferrie and Sherman were connected and well-known to each other. It was, of course, Jack Martin who opened the Louisiana case by revealing on November 22, 1963, the connection between Ferrie and Oswald, which, despite Ferrie's disclaimers, turns out to have been more true than historians have even realized. Moreover, the government cover-up of Mary Sherman's death rivals that of the Kennedy assassination itself.

Although he never quite connected Oswald with Juan Valdes, Garrison worked hard to develop leads placing Oswald with anti-Castro Cubans. "The Cuban threat runs so clearly through this that the theory on which we started no longer is a theory to us," Garrison said. Cubans were "in the picture continually." Jack Martin had told him that Oswald knew Sergio Arcacha Smith, who was close to Bobby Kennedy and his special group training to assassinate Fidel Castro, a group that was watching Oswald, so that he seemed almost to have been admitted into its ranks.

In New Orleans, Oswald had visited the clothing store Casa Roca, managed by the New Orleans representative of a CIA-funded militant anti-Castro group called Directorio Revolucionario Estudantil (DRE). The Miami DRE in the summer of 1963 was handled by a seasoned CIA operative, George Joannides, who specialized in psychological warfare and propaganda.

In New Orleans, Oswald enacted a well-orchestrated scenario designed to establish his public identity as a pro-Castro Marxist. Having approached the DRE representative, Carlos Bringuier, with an offer to join his group, Oswald then engaged in a street scuffle on Canal Street with Bringuier and two followers.

In a letter dated August 1st and postmarked August 4th, five days before he jostled with Bringuier, Oswald wrote to V. T. Lee of the Fair Play for Cuba Committee, describing a confrontation with anti-Castro Cubans while he was demonstrating that had not yet taken place. "Through the efforts of some cuban-exile 'gusanos,'" Oswald writes, "a street demonstration was attacked and we were officialy [sic] cautioned by police."

In this public display of Oswald as a Marxist, the DRE played a major role, even as those many telephone calls to Miami from the apartment of Victoria Hawes, recorded on her telephone bills, and having vanished into the maws of the FBI, allowed Oswald to have been directed in his confrontations with the DRE by Joannides, their CIA handler and a skilled propagandist. Joannides' chief DRE contact in Miami, Luis Fernandez-Rocha, quickly discerned that Joannides was the handler not only of the DRE, but of others as well.

The DRE also helped Oswald make his nonexistent Marxism public in New Orleans through the assistance of CIA media asset Bill Stuckey, who moderated a radio debate between Oswald and Bringuier that summer. It would appear that Joannides' intelligence clearances became more profound from December 1962 on, when he was approved for access to "Special Intelligence." Nearly fifteen years after Jim Garrison's death, the CIA, which had released the personnel files of many dead agents, concealed Joannides' records, refusing to release them, and willing to subject themselves to a bitter FOIA (Freedom of Information Act) lawsuit.

Oswald had located Bringuier through his fellow FBI informant, Arnesto Rodriguez (1213-S). Rodriguez's father was a CIA asset (AMJUTE-1), the cryptonym standing for the CIA's on-island surveillance network. But Arnesto's brother, Emilio, was an even more significant Agency employee, receiving posthumously the CIA Medal of Merit, its second highest award.

Emilio's address book was a veritable *Who's Who* of CIA notables. It included the telephone number of David Atlee Phillips and the means of contacting CIA officials from Desmond Fitzgerald to Richard Helms himself. In pursuing the Rodriguez family, Jim Garrison would be cutting across CIA sources, methods and operations, past and present. Emilio, who had remained behind in Cuba after the Bay of Pigs, continued to work for the CIA under Desmond Fitzgerald and was with the CIA during the Garrison investigation.

Oswald surprised Rodriguez by already knowing that there was a training camp north of Lake Pontchartrain; he wanted to help the Cubans kill Castro, Oswald said.

"I can infiltrate your organization and find out what you're doing here any time," Warren de Brueys had told Bringuier, only for Oswald suddenly to materialize. Meanwhile Bringuier himself was an FBI and CIA informant; de Brueys remembers him as a "source." While Bringuier called himself the DRE's public relations officer in New Orleans, his file resided in the DRE files in its *military section.*

Bringuier treated Oswald on Canal Street, distributing his leaflets as if he were actually a Marxist. But young leftists in New Orleans saw through Oswald at once. What leftist would ignore all left-wing organizations, from the Southern Conference Education Fund

(SCEF) to CORE (Congress of Racial Equality) to the pale Council on Peaceful Alternatives? None in history, young Bob Heller and Tulane student Hugh Murray both thought. Heller's roommate, Oliver St. Pe, took a look at the Fair Play for Cuba leaflet, considered replying to the post office box of "Hidell," stamped on it, then changed his mind. It must be a trap, he decided.

Guy Banister had hired a young man named Daniel Campbell to spy on leftist groups, but he was never asked to consider Oswald, whose leaflet bore the address 544 Camp Street, the side entrance of Banister's own building. The day before Oswald scuffled with Bringuier, August 8th, the FBI already had in its possession a copy of the pamphlet he distributed that day, "The Crime Against Cuba," written by Corliss Lamont. The FBI's regular informants, who had been watching for the establishment of a branch of Fair Play for Cuba, did not report on Oswald's activity.

That the CIA itself had infiltrated Fair Play for Cuba is well documented. CIA strategy was for its "appropriate cut-outs" to infiltrate Fair Play, then plant "deceptive information which might embarrass the Fair Play for Cuba Committee in areas where it does have some support abroad." The FBI was enlisted to help by stealing Fair Play stationery and mailing lists so that it could forge "large quantities of propaganda in the name of the Committee." As CIA's Joseph Burkholder Smith admitted, "The Counter Intelligence staff was very interested in the Fair Play for Cuba Committee and getting a penetration into it would have been a high priority effort."

In charge of all these manipulations was CIA disinformation specialist David Atlee Phillips, George Joannides' immediate superior. "The DRE. Dave Phillips ran that for us," CIA operative E. Howard Hunt told the HSCA; this was the same Hunt who, as part of the CIA's vendetta against the president, had invented State Department cables, forgeries that implicated John F. Kennedy in the November 2nd CIA-sponsored assassination of South Vietnamese president Ngo Dinh Diem. Later, Alpha 66 activist Antonio Veciana said that he had spotted his own handler, "Maurice Bishop," certainly Phillips, with Lee Harvey Oswald in Dallas.

The Canal Street incident bears the stamp of a chain of command that went from Joannides in Miami to David Phillips and upward to Richard Helms, DDP (Deputy Director, Plans), in charge of the CIA's clandestine services. According to documents released by the CIA through his attorney Jim Lesar to author Jefferson Morley, Joannides traveled from Miami to New Orleans around April 1st,

1964, prior to Carlos Bringuier's interview with the Warren Commission. Concluding his tour at the Miami CIA station, JMWAVE, on May 15, Joannides returned to Washington. Five days later, on May 20th, he traveled from CIA headquarters back to New Orleans, purpose unexplained.

Those who believed that the CIA orchestrated the Canal Street incident range from former DRE leader Isidro Borja, who knew that "the CIA had Oswald under surveillance for a long time," to CIA assets in New Orleans, such as William Gaudet. "Why would someone come to tell Bringuier that Oswald was in the street handing out pro-Castro leaflets?" Borja speculates. "And who was that person?" Gaudet, editor of *Latin American Reports*, a CIA proprietary journal funded by Dr. Alton Ochsner, and issuing from Gaudet's office at the International Trade Mart, also concluded that the incident had been staged: "a sort of PR operation . . . put on, I think, mostly by Junior Butler [head of INCA]. I think Carlos went there on purpose," Gaudet said.

Jim Garrison later received an eye-witness account of the brouhaha. A tourist named Matt O. Wilson told him he had seen Bringuier and two colleagues emerge out of nowhere, as if "they must have been standing right there in front of one of the buildings." Then, suddenly, they grabbed Oswald's literature, tore it up, and shoved him to the ground. A "funny look" came onto Oswald's face, a "sneery look," as if "he didn't care what happened." Harry Dean, infiltrating Fair Play on behalf of the CIA in Chicago, told both Jim Garrison and Marguerite Oswald that Oswald was "doing the same job as I was."

Orestes Peña, whose Habana Bar at 117 Decatur Street placed him next door to Bringuier's store, swore under oath that during Bringuier's tussle with Oswald, he saw the FBI taking photographs, which meant that they had advance notice of the event. Peña knew as well that Gaudet was a "CIA-FBI agent." The incident, in its clever use of propaganda, closely resembles Phillips' masterminding of the overthrow of President Arbenz in Guatemala. In Oswald's case, the ultimate goal of making public future "assassin" Oswald's pro-Castro sympathies was to blame Castro for the assassination, precipitating a ground war in Cuba.

Oswald and Bringuier were both arrested, even as the police officers at the scene had to wonder: Oswald seemed as if he were "being used by these people." The police report states that Oswald was "very uninformed and knows very little about this organization that he belongs to and its ultimate purpose or goal." Oswald and Bringuier wound up at the First District police station. Soon Bringuier was seeking legal advice from Kent Courtney, a right-wing professional anti-Communist and segregationist supporter of Senator Joseph McCarthy. Courtney edited a sheet called the *Independent American*, a publication at which no Marxist would have applied for a job. Yet Oswald did.

Oswald, the supposed Marxist, was seen that summer in Kent Courtney's company at political gatherings in Baton Rouge. Courtney introduced Oswald as "Leon," a man who did construction work for him. "Leon" agreed with Courtney. American foreign policy was "soft on Communism," he said. On one such trip they were accompanied by two silent Latinos. Marguerite Oswald knew of her son's association with Kent Courtney because she telephoned him on October 27, 1964, demanding to know if he "had ever had any personal contact with my son, Lee." Writing to J. Edgar Hoover the next day, Courtney denied ever having known Oswald.

Bringuier would be so hostile to Jim Garrison's investigation that he was admonished by DRE leader Juan Manuel Salvat. "The entire matter of the assassination is very serious," Salvat says he told Bringuier. "You should refrain from making any statements or expressing personal speculations." Salvat himself had "no quarrel with Jim Garrison or his investigation."

Following his arrest, Oswald was questioned by Lieutenant Francis Martello, formerly of New Orleans police intelligence. Just as at the American Embassy in the Soviet Union in 1959, Oswald had handed the senior consular official a handwritten note, requesting that his citizenship be revoked, so now he handed Martello a note on a piece of paper torn from his notebook. Its reverse side included the Moscow telephone numbers of United Press International and the Associated Press.

Oswald pointed to a number scribbled at the top of the note. "Just call the FBI," Oswald told Martello. "Tell them you have Lee Oswald in custody. When they arrive, hand them this note." Oswald added that he wished to be visited by a particular agent: Warren de Brueys.

In the predawn hours of that Saturday morning a young FBI clerk named William Walter took Martello's call. There was only one agent present at the field office, John Quigley. With the number Martello relayed in hand, Quigley ordered Walter to search the office indices for records of a "Lee Oswald." Walter found 105 files, which related to espionage and Cuba, not surprising given Oswald's Customs affiliation, and 134 (Informant) files.

There was also a security file in the locked filing cabinet of SAC Harry Maynor. Two names appeared on the file jacket: "Lee Oswald" and "Warren de Brueys." Oswald's file resided with those connected to ongoing surveillance and paid informants, and were locked up "for some security purpose." Later Walter told Jim Garrison that, during the summer of 1963, the FBI had two distinct sets of files on Oswald and were communicating with him on a regular basis.

Quigley telephoned Warren de Brueys, whose excuse for not visiting Oswald in jail was that he had to attend a barbecue. Quigley himself was to interview Oswald, an interview lasting more than an hour and a half. Later Quigley said he burned his notes. Martello kept Oswald's original note, transcribed part of it for the FBI, and kept the original with its fuller detail. This he secreted among his personal possessions for the next thirty years. The original is a hodgepodge of English and Russian, filled with cryptic abbreviations: MAPURIS. HA PUS. None of the numbers correspond exactly to the numbers on files at the New Orleans FBI office.

Jim Garrison perused Francis Martello's testimony before the Warren Commission, and, without knowing anything of his conversation with Oswald, shook his head. "Martello is a man of no mentality at all," he said impatiently. Martello had concocted a story of how the note had suddenly appeared with Oswald's passport photograph. He had concealed how Oswald had handed him the note and told him to call the FBI.

Martello lied, too, when he testified that he had turned the original of this note over to the Secret Service. He told neither the Warren Commission nor the Secret Service about how Oswald had ordered him to call the FBI. Nor then did Garrison know that Francis Martello had long been Guy Banister's police department contact. Martello was among those who used the transposition "Harvey Lee Oswald." So Martello joined U.S. Army Intelligence, the 112th Intelligence Group, and two Office of Naval Intelligence teletypes of November 27, 1963. By August 9th, Martello possessed more information about Lee Harvey Oswald than he would ever admit. Two others to use that same transposition were Clay Shaw and a CIA courier named Donald P. Norton, who was to be interviewed by Jim Garrison.

When years later the HSCA requested Francis Martello's file from the FBI, the Bureau sent instead the file of a "Frank Martello" from California. The error was never corrected.

Leaving John Volz, David Ferrie rushed over to Carlos Bringuier's store. Where is Sergio Arcacha Smith? he demanded, revealing that he knew of Arcacha's connections—to Oswald, to Bobby Kennedy, and to the agency he hoped would protect him. Jim Garrison is trying to frame me, Ferrie said.

"This is a free country," Bringuier told Ferrie, whose sexual preferences were not to his liking. "Nobody can be framed without evidence." That afternoon, Ferrie called Lou Ivon. The next day, he sought the protection of the FBI. He began to carry a loaded rifle in his 1954 Chevrolet.

Jim Garrison now requested the FBI's 1963 reports on David Ferrie. The Bureau refused, continuing to conceal information from him, including details of Ruby's FBI file; the New York field office had reported a "mention or overhear" of Ruby on August 6, 1962, suggesting that Jack Ruby was of interest and concern to the Bureau more than a year before the assassination. Garrison was to receive none of these records.

The FBI instead installed a wiretap in Garrison's office through T. Chandler Josey, a Garrison acquaintance. The local police ceased to cooperate with his investigation. The FBI and CIA's media assets agreed to help discredit the "allegations of various authors" who either denied that Oswald was the lone assassin or that Ruby and Oswald were connected and knew each other. Hugh Aynesworth of the *Dallas Morning News* requested only that the Bureau not disclose his identity "outside the Bureau."

When eager volunteers turned up at Tulane and Broad, trusting Jim Garrison did no background checks. An Englishman with "bright blue eyes" named Tom Bethell gained favor because he had graduated from Oxford University. "The real Oxford?" Jim Garrison asked, impressed. Bethell claimed to have arrived in New Orleans in 1966, although during the summer of 1963 he had befriended the roommate of Oswald's Marine Corps antagonist Kerry Thornley, and had been seen in Thornley's dubious company.

William Gurvich, a local detective specializing in security for government-subsidized shipping in the Port of New Orleans, turned up. His father, Samuel C. "Gurevich," had been an FBI agent whom Hoover had denounced as "an unscrupulous rascal," having "violated all manner of Bureau rules and regulations." Dean Andrews, whose sympathies were not with Jim Garrison, had to remark that in New Orleans the "Gurvich family are known as character-assassins and black-mailers—ask any lawyer."

Impressed that Gurvich was willing to work as a "dollar a year investigator," that Gurvich could come up at a moment's notice with a bunch of Dallas phone numbers, and that he brought as a gift a color television set for the office, Garrison took him on. "Like a Greek bearing gifts," Garrison would say later. He permitted Gurvich to use his private office. When Gurvich requested the office master file, so he could go through the files at night to be up on the case, Garrison agreed.

"I don't trust Gurvich," Lou Ivon said, refusing to give Gurvich the files. "You can't distrust everybody," Garrison said. Ivon gave Gurvich only the least-sensitive material. Garrison also ignored other warnings. Former Banister partner Joe Oster said, "You're making a big mistake in having Bill Gurvich around here. I think he's a plant." Soon letters from potential witnesses addressed to Jim Garrison were finding their way into the files of the New Orleans FBI field office.

Jim Garrison enjoyed the company of intelligent people, and welcomed *Life* magazine editor Richard N. Billings. Billings flew to New Orleans in December of 1966, suspecting that Garrison was "onto something." A tall, angular man in his late thirties, Billings was smart and worldly, and, like Garrison, no stranger to irony. When Garrison compared lawyer G. Wray Gill's incarceration at Angola for murdering a girlfriend to Theodore Dreiser's *An American Tragedy,* Billings knew what he was talking about.

From behind his desk, Garrison flipped a photograph to Billings. Billings saw: "a guy in a wig."

"He may not be the assassin, but he'll do," Garrison said, with a straight face. Ferrie was "a helluva pilot, also a hypnotist, a defrocked priest, and a fag," Garrison pointed out, and Billings felt as if he were entering a strange land. Garrison later wrote to Billings: "If he [Ferrie] turns out to be our man, you must agree there has never been a more interesting suspect." Yet acknowledging the possibility of "coincidence," he was not ready to move against Ferrie. Soon they were exchanging information, as Billings learned of a CAP cadet who revealed that "Ferrie had flown Oswald to Cuba in 1959 in a Stinson."

Garrison also revealed that he had extracted from Gill his office phone bills for the telephone David Ferrie had used in 1962 and 1963. There were long distance calls to Houston, Dallas, and Irving, Texas. The bill for November 1963 was missing.

As he searched for telephone matches between Oswald, Ruby and Ferrie, Garrison was attracted to a call on September 24, 1963, the day before Oswald departed from New Orleans. Ferrie had called an apartment house called "Delaware Towers" in Chicago where a close cohort of Jack Ruby's named Lawrence V. Meyers met his mistress Jean Aase (West). Was it this call that resulted in Meyers and Aase meeting with Ruby in Dallas at the Cabana Motel on November 21, 1963? Was Meyers Jack Ruby's handler? On November 23rd, Ruby had telephoned Meyers three times, once at Galveston, where Ferrie had gone to "ice-skate" and "hunt geese." Meanwhile in Houston on November 23rd, Ferrie converged with Jack Ruby's friend Breck Wall. Ruby phoned Wall just before midnight that same evening. Why did Breck Wall, an entertainer, rush to Galveston when Kennedy was shot?

Garrison now had David Ferrie under twenty-four-hour surveillance. Oswald's Fair Play for Cuba leaflets were "probably a cover," he suspected, correctly. But was there any significance in Oswald consorting with so many homosexuals, not the least of whom was Ferrie? Garrison did not yet know of even stronger homosexual connections of Lee Harvey Oswald. As Garrison had begun to investigate, Tulane psychiatrist Harold Lief was treating a homosexual patient.

He had seen Lee Harvey Oswald at one of the parties of Clay Shaw, his patient told Lief. After the assassination, he had recognized him at once on television. "Oswald was there!" he said, as he described Clay Shaw's house in minute detail, including the wooden beams upstairs in the master bedroom, to which pulleys had been attached. Lief knew he was telling the truth because at one point Lief himself had rented Clay Shaw's house.

"You should come forward and tell Jim Garrison what you know," Lief said. "Oh, no, oh God, no!" the man cried. His parents thought his problem was depression and knew nothing of his sexual orientation. "Oswald was there," he repeated.

Garrison constructed a "biography" of Lee Harvey Oswald, terming Oswald "a rebel looking for a cause." The Cubans crossing his path were "self-designated revolutionaries from the lunatic fringe of the Cuba movement." He learned that at the age of fifteen, Oswald had tried to join the New Orleans Astronomy Club, although he had no particular interest in astronomy.

Oswald had wanted "to play the infiltrator" out of a "distorted need to belong to something," William Wulf, the president of the Astronomy Club, told Garrison. That the FBI was well aware of Oswald's entire history in New Orleans is reflected in yet another fact: on Sunday morning November 24th, only minutes after Jack Ruby shot Oswald, the Bureau was on the telephone to William Wulf.

Oswald's penchant for "infiltrating" was based on his admiration for FBI spy Herbert Philbrick, hero of *"I Led Three Lives,"* who had infiltrated the Communist Party. Philbrick had lived on Magazine Street in Cambridge as Oswald took up residence on New Orleans' Magazine Street. Oswald's teenaged letters to social organizations, his assignment of infiltrating the Soviet Union as a false defector and his approach to the DRE—each had been a moment toward his fulfilling a lifelong dream, one based on a real-life, anti-Communist model.

THE BANISTER MENAGERIE 5

What number Camp?
            —Jim Garrison

"**W**HERE IS CLAY BERTRAND? And why did he disappear after Smith's death?" Garrison sat brainstorming with his reporter friend David Chandler. Bertrand spoke Spanish. Bertrand was rich. Bertrand sent gay men to Dean Andrews as clients. Bertrand's first name was "Clay." There was no "Clay Bertrand" in the New Orleans telephone book, although Justice Department records would later reveal that among the four people to whom one phone number was registered was a "C. Bertrand."

"Only one person meets all these conditions!" Chandler said excitedly. "That's Clay Shaw!" Chandler was "a bit of an agent provocateur," the New Orleans entrepreneur and self-styled electronics expert soon to enter Garrison's investigation, Gordon Novel, thought. But Chandler was right. When Moo Moo's uncle called the bartender at Cosimo's on Moo Moo's behalf, this time the bartender told the truth: "Everyone down here knows who Clay Bertrand is. It's Clay Shaw."

Just before Christmas 1966, Jim Garrison had police investigator Lester Otillio pick up for questioning both Shaw and Layton Martens, a Ferrie lover who had been staying in his apartment on November 22, 1963. Martens, "a white-haired little punk," Novel calls him, was also a frequent Shaw guest, "for drinks and a chess game."

Shaw appeared at Tulane and Broad, six feet four inches tall and distinguished, with kinky gray hair, sharply chiseled features and a dark complexion. His eyes were silver blue, his poise that of a self-invented, self-educated man. Moo Moo faced a former member of military intelligence and an experienced CIA operative.

I never met Oswald, Shaw lies, as he invents a story of how his assistant, J. B. Dauenhauer, had told him a young man asked for permission to distribute leaflets outside, only for Shaw to object. He had gone downstairs, but the man had vanished, Shaw says. It is unfortunate that I did not meet him, "since then I might possibly have had a tiny footnote in history."

"Are you Clay Bertrand?" Moo Moo says suddenly. He has never met anyone named Clay Bertrand, Shaw says. He denies that he knows David Ferrie. He denies that he knows Dean Andrews. "What does Mr. Andrews do for a living?" Shaw says. Then he wishes Jim Garrison and Moo Moo Sciambra a Merry Christmas.

Later Shaw will write with dark laughter in a typewritten *Diary*: "Clay Bertrand? Who he?" At parties that Christmas season, he jokes about being a Garrison suspect. He is so confident that he doesn't bother to brief his close friend and fellow homosexual, Dauenhauer, with whom he had served in the military, so that when Garrison assistants Sciambra and Alcock interview Dauenhauer on February 10th, he reveals that Shaw had lied. Dauenhauer had not been visited by Oswald before he distributed the leaflets; he had never asked Shaw for permission for Oswald to do so.

Jim Garrison considered what he termed "propinquities." Didn't Ferrie's friend James Lewallen live next door to Shaw? Didn't a young man named Dante Marochini, who in 1963 worked for Oswald's employer, William Reily, also know Ferrie? Lewallen had admitted he introduced Marochini to Shaw, even as Marochini denied to Jim Garrison that he knew Shaw. "First Garrison got all the fruits, now he wants the cherry," Marochini had joked.

In search of Cuban help to locate the dark Cuban photographed with Oswald, Jim Garrison enlisted New Orleans' Director of International Relations Alberto Fowler, dubbing him "a legitimate Cuban." Alberto had joined the 26th of July movement only for Fidel Castro to demand that he demonstrate his loyalty by murdering a Batista functionary, the mayor of a small town near the Fowler family sugar mill. Alberto complied, only to become disillusioned with the man who gave a speech entitled *"Elecciónes, para qué?"*

Perceiving there was no room for him in "the New Society," Alberto moved to Miami, and then back to the city of his birth, New Orleans. "The revolution wasn't a mistake," he said. "The man was." Now a veteran of the Bay of Pigs and of Castro's prisons, Alberto was uniquely placed to help Jim Garrison, even as he remained of independent mind. He refused to join Butler's fanatic INCA, which Alberto immediately perceived was "something other than it appears to be." The CIA had wanted to appoint not Sergio Arcacha Smith, but Alberto Fowler to head the New Orleans branch of the Cuban Revolutionary Council. Alberto turned them down.

"Jim, I didn't kill him . . . but I wish I had," Alberto joked when Garrison called to invite him to participate in his investigation. Learning that Fowler, who was "hardly pro-Castro," was working with Jim Garrison, Clay Shaw blanched.

Alberto Fowler at once began to help "Big Jim." He revealed that he had run into William Gaudet in Guatemala, and Gaudet "had been either an FBI or CIA agent." He knew that Arcacha and his friend David Ferrie frequented a restaurant named Pedro's, also a redoubt of Customs agents.

"I think Guy Banister's office is near there," Garrison said during a discussion recorded on tape. "We might take a look all the way up Lafayette Street, all the way up Camp, all around there." Then he stopped. "What number Camp?" Garrison said. It was at that moment that Jim Garrison realized that Oswald had used as his headquarters the building that housed Guy Banister's detective agency. "It's one of my great discoveries," Garrison said a decade later, "and I'm sure the CIA is eternally grateful."

"A legitimate group wouldn't fool with Oswald," Garrison said, noting the close proximity to Banister's office of the Old Post Office Building where CIA employees, Oswald, Kerry Thornley, Jack Martin and Thomas Edward Beckham among them, kept post office boxes. Garrison dubbed them "keys to the Club." Half a block away was the Crescent City garage run by Adrian Alba, also a CIA contact; here Oswald sat reading gun advertisements. A few doors down was Oswald's employer, the Reily coffee company, whose owner, William Reily, was the subject of two CIA files in the Office of Security, a "B" file and a "C" file, indicating that he was both a covert and an overt CIA asset.

Oswald's "not with anybody who's not with the CIA," Garrison concluded even without possessing Oswald's Marine Unit diary. This traced his movements from Keesler Air Force Base, a training for which only five of his cohorts were selected, to Henderson Hall in Arlington, Virginia, through which the files of intelligence operatives passed. Oswald stayed at the Marine barracks at Hardwick Hall, arriving already qualified as an electronics operator with training in counterintelligence.

Other CIA assets Oswald encountered in New Orleans included

Ed Butler, who debated him on the radio. "Mr. Butler is a very cooperative contact and has always welcomed an opportunity to assist the CIA," Butler's Domestic Contact Service Source Information Sheet reads. Yet the CIA asked Butler to leave its "Free Voice of Latin America" because he was too right wing. Other Butler CIA documents emanate from the Office of Security.

In an extraordinary slip, Butler revealed in a 1967 interview that he knew Oswald was a scapegoat, not guilty of killing President Kennedy. He compared Oswald with Marinus Van der Lubbe, a twenty-four-year old Communist, as Oswald was twenty-four when President Kennedy was killed. Van der Lubbe, entirely innocent, was "caught walking out of the burning Reichstag and the Nazis used him for the showcase trial in 1933 to wipe out the Communist plot." Both were pawns, Butler says, the two cases "almost identical."

Even Joseph Rault, who was helping to fund Jim Garrison's investigation, was a CIA asset, having been cleared to assist JMWAVE as president of a CIA proprietary with the cryptonym YCOUGH. Rault used his own petroleum business, Rault Petroleum Corporation, as a funding mechanism for YCOUGH. Other oil companies in which Rault had an interest were used as "back-stopping cover of JMWAVE operational vessels," bound for sabotage in Cuba. Rault was also enlisted in a CIA project with the cryptonym ECHO, and recommended other New Orleans businessmen to participate in CIA activities. JMWAVE contacted him several times a month.

What was true for Oswald was equally so for the hatchet-faced Guy Banister, another impeccably dressed, gray-haired man in this story. Banister added a fresh flower to his lapel every day. Virtually everyone connected with Banister worked for one intelligence agency or another, so that Garrison finally said, "It's almost semantics to discuss whether Banister was ONI or CIA. What difference does it make?"

Under the cover of a moribund "detective agency," Banister collected and stored weapons for anti-Castro operatives. On behalf of the CIA, he paid off its operatives, and functioned as a conduit for Company money at the training camps north of Lake Pontchartrain. Money flowed through his office in 1963. Sometimes he sent his runner, Thomas Edward Beckham, to make deliveries to the camps. Sometimes he sent Joe Newbrough, a fellow CIA asset, to demonstrate training techniques. "Why not get rid of Jack Martin?" Allen Campbell asked Banister one day. He needed Jack for surveillance jobs, Banister said vaguely.

Banister was close to the CIA field office chief William P. Burke, having been approved on November 10, 1960, "for contact use as a routine source of foreign positive intelligence," all the CIA would admit on paper. CIA's J. C. King considered Banister's operation a vital component of the CIA's Western Hemisphere Division. Banister also reported to the New Orleans head of naval intelligence, Guy Johnson. With Guy Johnson and another CIA asset, Maurice B. Gatlin, Banister had been involved in shipping jeeps to Cuba.

When Banister hired young men to infiltrate left organizations, later selling this information, he cleared them first with Guy Johnson. It was "intelligence for sale," Daniel Campbell says. Johnson, who had brought Sergio Arcacha Smith to New Orleans, showed Jack Martin a document, more evidence that Robert Kennedy had put out a "personal contract" on Fidel Castro.

During the summer after the Bay of Pigs, when the Schlumberger ammunition dump at Houma seemed ripe for the picking, Banister, together with CIA's David Atlee Phillips, organized a burglary. The thieves included David Ferrie and Layton Martens. By 1967 Phillips was keeping an eye on Jim Garrison, fearing that he would discover that the CIA were "the actual operators" of the Belle Chasse training camp, which was "entirely Agency controlled and the training was conducted by Agency personnel." Phillips was worried that Alberto Fowler would help Garrison locate the camp.

Banister chatted on a regular basis with J. Edgar Hoover; Regis Kennedy was a frequent visitor to Banister's office. Banister was also very close to G. Wray Gill, who had ordered Ferrie to go to Dallas the week of the assassination.

Other visitors to Banister's office included Nazi George Lincoln Rockwell, in town to protest the screening of Leon Uris' *Exodus,* and who was introduced to Banister by Jack Martin; General Edwin Walker; the ubiquitous Ed Butler; and Klan stalwarts Alvin Cobb and A. Roswell Thompson, who drove up in a big black Cadillac. Yet another Banister cohort was Jim Garrison's enemy, Raymond Huff of Customs, who, with Banister and the CIA, was another of those who had participated in the overthrow of President Arbenz of Guatemala.

Banister did little detective work, and rarely paid his occasional employee Lawrence Guchereau. Instead, he ran a spying operation, keeping files on everyone of note in New Orleans. Banister had files on Hale Boggs; on young FBI clerk William F. Walter; on Tulane psychiatrist Harold Lief. The most important files were numbered "1013," the "10" standing for Communism, the "13" for New Orleans.

When David Ferrie showed Banister some photographs he had taken of Shaw in full female drag, Banister put them in his Shaw file, although Banister and Shaw were friendly, meeting frequently at the Old Absinthe House. Banister enjoyed an equally close friendship with Dr. Alton Ochsner. Banister kept his Lee Harvey Oswald file isolated from the others.

That Lee Harvey Oswald set up shop at intelligence operative Guy Banister's establishment, there is no doubt. Both Allen and Daniel Campbell had known Oswald as a boy at the Bethlehem Orphans' home. Allen remembers Oswald as a withdrawn child, trying to console the little girls who were abused by one of the people in charge. "Allen, don't worry, someday we'll find somebody who will love us," Campbell says he recalls Oswald remarking.

"Can I use the phone?" Oswald asked Dan Campbell, who remembered him instantly. On another occasion, Campbell saw Oswald just sitting on the second floor, his eyes closed. Others who spotted Oswald with Banister include William Gaudet, who saw the two "deep in conversation right by the post office box. They were leaning over and talking and it was an earnest conversation." By now Gaudet was certain the Agency knew Oswald. Orestes Peña also saw Oswald enter the building at 531 Lafayette Street.

Banister's secretary, Delphine Roberts, remembered Oswald walking in and asking for an application to be an operative. To her surprise, he was invited into Banister's office. The door closed behind him. Soon Oswald was using a room upstairs, depositing his leaflets there. When Delphine observed him giving out his leaflets, she went to Banister: why hadn't he checked this man out?

Banister was angry, famously, only when Oswald stamped "544 Camp Street" on one of his pamphlets. "He's with us," Banister finally told Delphine. Soon she suspected Oswald had a relationship with the FBI. Soon she learned that Oswald and Ferrie had traveled together across Lake Pontchartrain to a training camp. A local farmer named George Wilcox, out fishing near Bedico Creek, saw them as well: Ferrie, Oswald and some Cubans in military camouflage, carrying rifles and conducting a "military training maneuver." Ferrie and Oswald were the only two "white men" among fifteen to twenty Hispanics. It was that camp to which Wendall Roache had referred and of which Robert Tanenbaum had viewed a fragment of film.

After a while, Banister no longer bothered to keep a secret of his acquaintance with Oswald. Together, according to then–history student Michael Kurtz, they appeared at LSU where Banister discussed the evils of integration and attacked John F. Kennedy's politics. Banister called for a full-scale military invasion of Cuba, while Oswald kept silent. On the next occasion, Oswald himself denounced Kennedy for his civil rights policies. Later, Kurtz says, he spied the two eating together at Mancuso's restaurant.

During Garrison's investigation, neither of the Campbells; nor Gaudet; nor Delphine Roberts; nor Kurtz; nor Banister's wife Mary, who saw the "Fair Play for Cuba" leaflets in Banister's possession; nor Banister's brother Ross, who met Oswald and called him "rather stupid"—none of these potential witnesses came forward. Even Garrison's chess partner, lawyer Thomas Baumler, only later admitted that "Oswald worked for Banister." Banister cohort Vernon Gerdes informed only Clay Shaw's defense team that he had seen Banister, Ferrie and Oswald together. Late in 1968 a Garrison volunteer found one of Banister's student infiltrators, George Higginbotham, who penetrated left-wing groups under the code name "Dale." Higginbotham revealed how he had kidded Banister one day about sharing a building with people distributing pro-Castro leafets.

"Cool it!" Banister had said. "One of them is mine." Higginbotham promised more information, but would speak only to Jim Garrison personally. When Garrison met with Higginbotham, he was "close-mouthed." Garrison was forced to write: "Contributed nothing." No more cooperative was Banister's landlord, Sam Newman.

"You must have seen Oswald up there," Garrison said.

"I didn't see nothing," Newman said. Only for the HSCA would Banister secretary Mary Helen Brengel admit that both Banister and Delphine Roberts had "some prior knowledge of the assassination."

Jim Garrison did know that Banister had pistol-whipped Jack Martin on the evening of the assassination. Jack had called police intelligence officer Major Presley J. Trosclair Jr. on that occasion, in itself unusual. Trosclair would be someone you would call if the issue were Oswald and the Kennedy assassination, not for a simple assault. No ordinary citizen could have gotten to Trosclair, Robert Buras says. But, with his intelligence connections, Jack could. The police report written up by Francis Martello, who interviewed Martin, says only that Martin and Banister had been discussing "personal and political subjects." Martin did not press charges against Banister, his fellow operative.

It was a "god damned lie" that he had stolen any of Banister's files, Martin lied to Jim Garrison.

On November 22nd, in the company of Joe Newbrough, Banister

had stopped at a print shop and so learned about the assassination. "Now all we have to do is kill Earl Warren and the country will clear up!" Banister said. Later, refreshing himself at the Katz 'n' Jammer bar at 540 Camp Street, he speculated, "I wonder why Bobby wasn't included. ("I'm glad," Delphine had said when she heard the news of John F. Kennedy's death.)

That Banister had a role in the assassination even Regis Kennedy believed. "Guy Banister is a key to everything that happened in New Orleans," Big Regis told Moo Moo Sciambra, "and was in on everything from the very beginning to the very end." Big Regis believed Jack had stolen some of Banister's CIA files, and this had led to the pistol-whipping.

Jim Garrison never interviewed Banister, who died on June 6, 1964, of "natural causes."

"If I'm dead in a week, no matter what the circumstances look like," Banister had told Guy Johnson a week earlier, "it won't be from natural causes." Allen Campbell says a single round shot came in through the window, and that Delphine Roberts was present; she called Allen, who, in possession of Banister's keys, headed for 531 Lafayette to remove files involved in the "ongoing internal security of the United States."

Mary Banister called her friend Ruth Lichtblau in terror. "Guy's been shot!" she said. There was blood on the walls. Soon Mary left New Orleans for good. "Don't try to get in touch with me," she told Lichtblau. Delphine later told Robert Buras she believed both Banister and Ferrie were murdered; she had kept silent in fear. Kent Courtney also believed Banister was murdered.

The *Times-Picayune* reported that Banister died alone. Allen Campbell says he knows who shot Guy Banister. Lou Ivon went to the morgue to look at Banister's body: there was no head wound of any kind.

Jim Garrison uncovered more than one Oswald-Banister connection. William Dalzell had conceived of a front for Arcacha's Cuban Revolutionary Council, to be called "Friends of Democratic Cuba," and Banister had helped draw up the charter. On January 20, 1961, two men, claiming to represent "Friends of Democratic Cuba," had visited the New Orleans Bolton Ford dealership to purchase trucks for shipment to Cuba. They called themselves "Joseph Moore" and "Oswald," even as the real Oswald was in the Soviet Union at the time. Later, shown a photograph of Oswald by the FBI, Bolton assistant manager Oscar Deslatte said this was not the man who had called himself "Oswald." When the vice-president of Bolton called the FBI, the agent, who arrived at once, grabbed the bid form, which was never to be seen again, certainly not by the Warren Commission.

This "Oswald," Deslatte later told Jim Garrison, was an aggressive, unpleasant man. When the bid was made out in Moore's name, "Oswald" had objected: "I'm the man handling the money! You should have my name too." His companion was a heavyset Cuban with a scar over his left eye, a description confirmed by Bolton truck manager Fred Sewell. The one called "Oswald" was small and thin, about five feet seven inches tall. To confuse the issue, William Dalzell's landlady and girlfriend, Betty Parent, nicknamed "Betty Parrott," a Regis Kennedy informant, insisted to Sciambra that Moore was five feet eight, with blonde hair and blue eyes, not Cuban at all.

A month after it was created, Friends of Democratic Cuba dissolved, as if it had existed only for the purpose of the Bolton Ford truck-bidding incident. According to its president, Martin L. McAuliffe, a "Mr. Call" of the FBI had ordered them to dissolve because they were "in violation of the law to work with a foreign power," even as no such "Mr. Call" existed at the FBI. Insisting he never heard of Joseph Moore or the incident, McAuliffe did not fear lying to Jim Garrison. He, too, was a CIA asset, having visited the New Orleans field office three times by June 1961.

An informant told Garrison that a Joseph Moore had once liberated William Dalzell from jail, had "worked in intelligence in the Marines," and was now CIA. Garrison also uncovered an FBI interview with a car salesman named James A. Spencer at Dumas and Milnes Chevrolet.

Some time between February and August of 1961, when, again, Oswald was still in the Soviet Union, a man who identified himself as "Lee Oswald," with a Magazine Street address, had come into this Chevrolet dealership to purchase an automobile. This "Lee Oswald" had spoken *favorably* of Fidel Castro. Spencer remembered him because he came in twice, although he did not purchase an automobile. The only New Orleans people who knew Oswald's name at that time were Oswald's Marine acquaintance Kerry Thornley—and David Ferrie.

Warren Commission historian Mary Ferrell discovered that the descriptions of Oswald when he was out of the United States listed him as five feet eleven inches tall, while at home he was always five feet nine. Some forms said his eyes were gray, others that they were blue, as if he were deliberately obscuring his identity, the simpler to "infiltrate," the more easily to be impersonated.

Only now has Jack Martin's protégé, Thomas Edward Beckham, revealed what inspired Banister to a rage so virulent that on the evening of the Kennedy assassination it sent Martin bloody and reeling to Baptist Hospital in a police patrol car.

It is a sultry November day in 1963. Jack Martin and Thomas Edward Beckham, on whom, as his charge, Jack keeps an ever-watchful eye, are at Guy Banister's office. As Jack closets himself with Banister, Tommy, as he is known, chats with Delphine Roberts.

"Do you have many girlfriends?" Delphine asks flirtatiously.

Tommy is twenty-one years old, cute in a Pat Boone sort of way. He is small and boyish, only five feet seven inches tall, and maybe 157 pounds. Charming and pliant, he exudes dimples and an ingratiating smile. When his hair turns gray suddenly, he dyes it black. Tommy dropped out of school in the third grade and can neither read nor write, but he has begun to learn by reading the labels on liquor bottles. His mother is Jewish, his father not.

Tommy has a strong, clear voice, and he can entertain you by playing the guitar and singing, even yodeling. Under the name "Mark C. Evans," he is a rock/folk singer of some ability, performing at high school hops. He says that he even appeared on "Louisiana Hayride," the country music radio program of live concerts out of Shreveport, a virtual "cradle of the stars" that launched Hank Williams, Elvis Presley and Johnny Cash.

Sometimes Tommy makes as much as two or three hundred dollars a week. He earns money as a barker in the Quarter. For a time, with his deep, crystal-clear voice, he is a radio announcer. He has also worked for the Greyhound company calling out bus departures: "Welcome aboard Greyhound, now boarding at Gate Three!"

Tommy's father originally brought him together with Jack Martin, giving Jack some money in the hope that Jack would help Tommy in his singing career. Through Jack, Tommy finds himself often in the company of a group of older men who gather at Thompson's cafeteria. At Holsum's, another hangout, Jack introduces Tommy to A. Roswell Thompson, who is active in the Klan. In his white robes, once a year, in broad daylight, "Rozzy" lays a wreath at the foot of the statue of Robert E. Lee at Lee Circle. Tommy hears that he was involved in desecrating a Jewish cemetery. Rozzy's belt buckle, a gift, reads: "To A. Roswell Thompson, From Huey P. Long. Share The Wealth. Every Man A King."

Thompson takes an interest in Tommy. Another of the men in this group is Clay Shaw, who offers Tommy the opportunity to have sex with a man.

"I don't go for that," Tommy says.

"Everybody to his own way," Shaw says. One day he introduces Tommy to a Cuban girl named Gloria Borja. "You be careful, kid," Shaw tells Tommy, only Shaw calls him "Thomas."

When Jack and Guy Banister go out to Moisant Airport to welcome former Cuban dictator Fulgencio Batista, Tommy begs to go along. Batista is part-owner of a Jefferson Parish gambling casino called "The Beverly Club," his partner, Carlos Marcello.

At Walgreen's on Canal, near South Rampart and near the International Trade Mart, Tommy finds Jack engaged in conversation with the Nazi George Lincoln Rockwell. When Rockwell is later arrested, it is Hardy Davis who will bail him out.

Jack seems annoyed to see Tommy today. "What the hell are you doing here?" Jack growls. "Do you know who this is?"

"I'm a Jew," Tommy says.

"I was a decorated Army man," Rockwell says. "If I quit, would you hire me? There's people who want me to fight their battles." Later Rockwell is spotted with Clay Shaw at a gay establishment called Dixie's Bar of Music. Encountering at Banister's office young Daniel Campbell, who has been assigned to attend meetings of the New American Nazi party and take down names, Rockwell invites him to a gay bar. Campbell declines.

Rockwell's presence at Guy Banister's office, and in the company of Clay Shaw, helps to define the politics of those with whom Oswald consorted in New Orleans. Fulgencio Batista the brutal dictator and George Lincoln Rockwell the Nazi—these were typical Banister acquaintances.

At Jack Martin's apartment, Tommy spots a woman and a baby, a glimpse into mysterious Jack's private life, since he never speaks of anything personal, seeming always unanchored and without connections, without a past. One day Tommy observes at Jack's five men in Roman collars, one in a big clerical hat, another with a huge crucifix swinging diagonally across his chest. On another visit, Tommy notices filing cabinets with locks. Jack speaks of "safe houses." Tommy asks Jack if he has intelligence connections, to which years later Jack will admit, evasively: "only for short periods and never officially."

On yet another day, Tommy walks into Walgreen's, and there is Jack speaking Spanish with Sergio Arcacha Smith and Luis Rabel.

One of them calls John F. Kennedy a "Communist." The Bay of Pigs has come and gone.

Jack has Tommy ordained in his church, the Old Orthodox Church of North America, and a phony degree arrives from Earl Anglin James in Toronto. Jack has sent James a gold key to the city of New Orleans that he wears on his watch chain. David Ferrie's 1962 and 1963 telephone records include seven calls to the unlisted number of Earl Anglin James. The only call he got from New Orleans was from Jack Martin, James will lie.

Tommy has no particular interest in being a priest, but he does what Jack tells him to do. He is soon in charge of a "Mission" at 352 North Rampart Street called "United Catholic Mission Fathers," which, he says, really meant "United Cuban Revolutionary Forces." Tommy is given a card that reads: "Priest in charge of the Holy Chapel for Peace." Printed as well is his name: "Father Evans." The purpose of the Mission is collecting money for the struggle against Castro, for which they use containers supplied by the Continental Can Company. Among those who visit the Mission are David Ferrie and mercenaries Loran Hall and Lawrence Howard, trained by the CIA at No Name Key in Florida for sabotage against Cuba. Howard's CIA affiliation is masked by his role as an informant for the Alcohol, Tobacco, Tax Unit of the Internal Revenue Service, with the CIA reimbursing his salary.

Lawrence Howard is a large, burly man, at least 235 pounds. He is Mexican, with a luxuriant head of black hair and a flowing mustache, your image of Pancho Villa. He, too, has been heard to complain about Kennedy's withdrawing air support at Playa Giron. The leader at No Name Key, Gerald Patrick Hemming, says that Howard was sent to spy on him by a CIA handler.

Tommy and Gloria Borja have sex at the Mission. When she becomes pregnant, Jack Martin finds a New Orleans character named W. T. Grant to pose as a judge and "marry" them. But Tommy suggests they run away and marry legitimately in Las Vegas. When their financial circumstances force Tommy back to New Orleans, Jack is right there waiting for him.

Tommy now becomes a courier, transporting the money they raise at the Mission to Miami. One day he is arrested at the airport and driven to the First District police station. The money disappears; there are no charges.

After Jack introduces Tommy to Guy Banister, Banister asks Tommy to spy on Jack for him. "Sometimes I like to see how my people are doing," Banister says. Loyal, Tommy reports the conversation to Jack. Jack now begins to give Tommy puzzling advice. Jack tells him to throw himself down the stairs at Thompson's cafeteria, and "act like you're knocked out. Then go to a doctor."

One day Tommy is arrested at the Mission for impersonating a priest, and he suspects that Jack is somehow behind this arrest. Jack advises him to commit himself to the Charity Hospital's "third floor," the psychiatric ward. A while later Jack tells him to commit himself voluntarily to the mental hospital at Mandeville. "It's to protect you," Jack says. This time Tommy obeys. Accompanied by his mother and one of his brothers, he goes to the Mandeville hospital. He wears his priest collar and the people think it surely must be his brother being committed, not the priest. A psychiatric record is being built against him, and he cannot imagine why.

In the spring of 1963, upstairs at Walgreen's, Tommy meets a young man about his own age named Lee Oswald. When Tommy first sees him, Oswald is doing a flexing exercise, pushing his hands together.

"What do you do, work out?" Tommy says.

"If you do this, it will help your arms and enlarge your chest," Oswald says, eager to be friendly. He learned the exercise in the Marines.

They run into each other often. He has just returned from Mexico City, Oswald says one day. He tells Tommy that he has lived in the Soviet Union.

"Why?" Tommy says.

"We can't pick the place where we are born, but we can choose where we want to live," Oswald says. He compares himself to Hemingway, who lived in Paris. From the start it is apparent that Lee is acquainted with the other members of the group.

The subject of homosexuality arises. "Shaw is homosexual," Tommy says.

"I know," Lee says.

Oswald mentions his "undesirable" Navy discharge, which brings him to anger. He blames John Connally, former Secretary of the Navy, and now the governor of Texas, for his troubles. He says he has written to Connally. "I have and always had the full sanction of the U.S. Embassy, Moscow, USSR, and hence the U.S. government," Oswald had written, demanding that Connally "take the necessary steps to repair the damage done to me and my family." It was to change his discharge that he consulted lawyer Dean Andrews.

Lee and Tommy grow friendlier. Lee has money and is always ready to pick up a check. He buys Tommy lunch. "Don't you want a piece of pie?" Lee asks Jack Martin, "Don't you want something to eat?" It's almost as if he's trying to buy friends, Tommy thinks. But Jack sticks to his diet of bad coffee and cigarettes. Tommy cannot understand why Jack seems to dislike Lee so much, especially since he's always trying to pick up Jack's check.

Sometimes Tommy sees Lee at Thompson's restaurant. He runs into Lee at Guy Banister's office where he hears Lee call Banister "the chief." He hears Lee attacking Governor Connally. "I hate that son of a bitch," Oswald says. "Connally was a target," Gerald Patrick Hemming believes, as did CIA operative Richard Case Nagell. Nagell, in New Orleans that summer, heard talk of the assassination not only of President Kennedy, but of "other highly placed government officials."

Lee visits the Mission. Together Tommy and Lee visit Orestes Peña's Habana Bar. One day when Oswald is distributing his leaflets outside the International Trade Mart, Tommy goes along. A cameraman appears, and it's clear the press has been invited in advance. On his heels is Jack Martin, furious.

"Get away from there!" Jack shoos Tommy from the area. "What are you trying to do, get yourself in trouble?"

A photograph survives of Thomas Edward Beckham, dressed all in black, in front of the International Trade Mart as Oswald enters the building. Beckham confirms that it is, indeed, he.

It is August 16, 1963, another suffocating summer day in New Orleans. Standing just inside the doors of the Trade Mart is Warren de Brueys, Oswald's handler, his shadow. Oswald enters the Press Club where he asks for a glass of ice water. Seated at the bar is *States-Item* reporter on the police beat, Jack Dempsey, a big, bluff, generous Irishman in his characteristic long-sleeved white shirt, and bow tie, his straw hat beside him. Still holding one of Oswald's "Fair Play for Cuba" leaflets, Dempsey offers Oswald a beer.

"No, thank you, sir," Oswald says. "Water would do me better than a beer or a coke."

"Have you read the leaflet?" Oswald says.

MORE EVIDENCE DENIED TO JIM GARRISON

6

I knew I was dancing with the CIA. I wasn't guessing.
—Jim Garrison

TOMMY ATTENDS MEETINGS at Algiers, on the West Bank of the Mississippi River, but still part of Orleans Parish, and at the Town and Country Motel in Jefferson Parish. The subject is always the same: what is to be done about John F. Kennedy? The group assesses the news that Kennedy has assigned his school friend William Attwood to meet with Fidel Castro, seeking rapprochement. This effort, not yet reported in the press, is known to everyone here.

Sometimes Clay Shaw is present, but everyone here calls him "Clay Bertrand." He looks like movie actor Jeff Chandler, Tommy thinks. At every meeting there is also someone with a criminal background, like Tony Marullo, who is related to the Marcellos by blood. Guy Banister himself never attends, but sends a woman named Anna Burglass to represent him. G. Wray Gill sometimes makes an appearance.

"Are you serious about killing John F. Kennedy?" Tommy asks Jack Martin one day.

"You don't kill a president. You assassinate him," Jack says.

Lee attends some of these meetings, as does Jack Ruby, owner of the Carousel Club in Dallas. Tommy has already been introduced to Ruby. One day, Tommy and Clay Shaw are together in the lobby of the Monteleone Hotel on Royal Street, when they run into Jack Ruby, who is a regular at this hotbed of international intrigue. Jack Ruby is well known to the Monteleone doorman, Kelley, a homosexual, who, on at least one occasion, has been thrown out of Dixie's Bar of Music for unwelcome advances to some young man. Kelley's acquaintance with Ruby, the subject of an FBI report, adds credence to Beckham's memory of having met Ruby at Kelley's place of employment.

"Where are you hanging your hat these days?" Shaw asks Ruby. Ruby motions—upstairs. There is talk of Tommy entertaining at Ruby's club. Ruby has deep roots in Louisiana, and one of his cousins owns The Court of Two Sisters restaurant. A year before the assassination, Ruby was treated for rectal cancer at the Ochsner clinic.

At Holsum's, Tommy runs into Jack Martin's partner, Joe Newbrough, who is sitting with a man named Fred Lee Crisman. Joe is asking for advice from Crisman about federal fraud charges looming against him.

"Didn't it scare you when you read, *United States of America v. Joseph Newbrough*?" Crisman says. "How did that hit you?" Crisman then turns to Tommy and introduces himself. Soon they are meeting alone. Crisman says he's a teacher, and can teach Tommy to read and write. He can help Tommy speak correctly so that he doesn't say "worser" and "you knowed."

"If it kills me, I'm going to teach you English," Fred says. They begin to meet often. It is some time later that Tommy will summon his nerve. "Fred, I know you're a government agent, an operative," Tommy will venture. Crisman will only laugh.

When Jack Martin is finally finished talking with Guy Banister this hot November day in 1963, he and Tommy walk over to the Old Post Office. Jack reads his mail, then puts it back into his box. He is lingering, peering outside. Half an hour passes. Tommy becomes impatient.

"It's a lot cooler in here than it is out there," Jack says. "I'm waiting for someone. If you want to go, go." Finally Jack has seen what he needs to see. "I've got to go back over there," Jack says. "I left my damn package in Guy's office. I've got to go get it. I want you to talk to Delphine."

They walk back to 531 Lafayette. "Tell Guy I'm out here and I want my package," Jack tells Delphine. "Tell Guy to hand me that package."

"What package?" Delphine says.

He never had a package, Tommy thinks.

"He's gone," Delphine says.

"Well, hon, I'm gonna grab it and get out of your hair," Jack says. He rushes into Banister's office as Delphine continues to flirt with Tommy. Jack emerges with a brown envelope. He has a file folder tucked under his arm so that Delphine can't see it.

"Come on!" Jack says as he walks out very fast.

Later Guy Banister telephones Tommy at his parents' house. They must meet. His secretary told him Jack took an envelope, Banister says. Did he also take a file? "Yes, he did," Tommy says.

"Do you know where he went with it afterwards?"

"He went to the Roosevelt Hotel," Tommy says. The color seems to drain from Banister's face. "There are documents that concern me. They could get me in a lot of trouble," Banister says. Later Tommy would conclude that the file had been connected to the murder of John F. Kennedy. The pistol-whipping followed.

Before the assassination, Tommy is given one last assignment. He is sent to the law offices of G. Wray Gill in the Pere Marquette building at 150 Baronne Street. Clay Shaw is there, accompanied by a young man who, Tommy thinks, couldn't weigh more than ninety pounds soaking wet, and "queerer than a three dollar bill." It's Layton Martens. Ubiquitous, Jack Martin is present, as is David Ferrie.

"Do you want to make two hundred dollars?" Dave says.

Laid out on a desk are drawings of buildings, sketched in detail, with an automobile on the street below. The view is from a high angle looking down, as if the car were in a gully. There are also 8x10 photographs in black and white, mounted on heavy paper: charts, diagrams, maps, photographs. Someone scoops them up and places them in a large envelope. Tommy is to carry this package to Dallas and hand-deliver it to a man he knows from the Mission, Ferrie explains. Gill gives him money, and more directions. Ferrie, Tommy has noticed, never has any cash.

"No jewelry!" Gill says, looking at Tommy's cheap watch and rings glittering with fake stones. "Get that jewelry off!" Jack says harshly.

They drive Thomas Edward Beckham to the airport, where he is handed a magazine in which to secrete the envelope. "Tommy, I know how talkative you are," Gill says. "I don't want to hurt your feelings, but this is important." Tommy is not to speak to anyone on the airplane. He is given a room number at the Executive Inn where he must deliver the package.

Arriving in Dallas, Tommy takes a taxi. But he doesn't even have to enter the Executive Inn because waiting for him outside in an old

Chevrolet is Lawrence Howard, he of the Pancho Villa mustache. Howard is mean-looking, Tommy thinks, as he hands him the package. As Howard ruffles through the envelope, his face darkens.

"Are you sure this is all of it?" Howard says. He seems to suspect that Tommy has stolen some money out of the package.

"I didn't take nothing out," Tommy says. "If you want to call them, go call them. I didn't mess with nothing in that envelope." He was not able to read what was inside.

President Kennedy was murdered so soon after Tommy delivered the package that he was certain it had contained plans for the assassination. One of the maps he took would in fact be found in Lee Harvey Oswald's room.

"Lee did it!" Tommy tells Rozzy on November 22nd.

"No, he didn't," Thompson says. "Two of our guys did."

When Jack Ruby killed Lee Harvey Oswald on Sunday, Tommy was outraged. "How could Jack kill Lee?" he said, well aware of their acquaintance.

When he asked how Jack had gained entry to the police station where Lee was held, he was told, "one of our friends, a CIA man, had walked him in, saying 'he's with me.'" David Ferrie would tell his friend, Raymond Broshears, that the Dallas police were informed by their superiors that Jack "was going to kill the bastard and that they would be patriotic to turn the other way." Broshears already knew: Ferrie and Oswald were connected to the CIA, and Jack Martin, keeping a close rein on Beckham, had introduced Beckham to David Ferrie.

The Louisiana mob, always present at those meetings in Algiers, not to mention at Carlos Marcello's Town and Country, apparently lent a hand in arranging for Ruby to kill Oswald, just as the CIA had enlisted the Mafia in its attempts to murder Fidel Castro. Marcello's man Joe Civello, of St. Landry Parish, whose responsibilities were in Dallas, had dealt with the Dallas police, being close to Sergeant Patrick T. Dean, who was in charge of basement security at the Dallas police station. Civello was also close to Egyptian Lounge owner Joe Campisi, whose family hailed as well from St. Landry Parish, and who was designated to be Jack Ruby's first jailhouse visitor. A Louisiana politician visiting Dallas had listened to Campisi brag at length about his role in helping Ruby murder Oswald.

Terrified, Tommy decided to leave town. He knew too much. They might kill him, too.

"There's $8,000 in your post office box," Jack Martin told Tommy. With the assistance of Fred Lee Crisman, Tommy embarked on the wandering life of a con man. Jim Garrison did not discover that Thomas Edward Beckham had delivered that package until years after his investigation had ground to a halt, although he would locate traces of the charts, maps and diagrams.

For years Tommy kept silent. But David Ferrie began to carry around a manila file, which he nicknamed "the Bomb." It would "blow this city apart if he ever released it," Ferrie said. A Ferrie acolyte named Jimmy Johnson, who worked undercover for Jim Garrison, went through Ferrie's papers one day and found a notebook marked "Files, 1963," which included a "loose-leaf paper with a diagram on it." Johnson would later describe what he had seen:

> [A] diagram of a figure of a man with . . . what could be called a bullet hole in the back of his head and right shoulder. Also, a diagram of a man side-facing with arrows pointing starting from the back coming to the front of his throat. At the top of the page there is a triangular line going up with markings 60 feet high with a line coming down 2,500 feet long. At the bottom is a diagram of an airplane.

Jimmy Johnson would later elaborate: "They had a building ten stories high, a drawing. It implied that it was 109 stories high and so many feet, and there was a convertible. It had a drawing of the street, there was a convertible, a few people in it, and it had an airplane . . . the line was the airplane, coming down over the building and over the convertible and in, going up at a high angle of attack."

In 1969, Jim Garrison learned more about these maps and diagrams from a friend of conservative congressman F. Edward Hebert, no supporter of his. Her name was Clara (Bootsie) Gay, and she was an antiques dealer. On the Tuesday after the assassination, November 26th, Gay saw a batch of those same diagrams as David Ferrie's desk was being cleaned out at the offices of G. Wray Gill. Gay was there because Gill was her lawyer.

Bootsie Gay had met Ferrie at Gill's offices, and at first had sympathized with him as he described the injustice of his having been fired by Eastern Airlines. At the very persuasive Ferrie's request, Gay had sought Congressman Hebert's help on Ferrie's behalf. "Officials of airlines like to keep members of Congress happy," Ferrie had said. He's a "Saint on Earth," although a "little fanatic," Gay said of Ferrie, her explanation for why "he has been so tormented." A feisty widow, Gay herself had been broke and Ferrie had made flying trips for her business at no charge. At Gill's offices, "he seemed always to be saying his rosary."

Hebert turned her down. When she told Ferrie, he became furious, and never spoke to her again. "Talking religion is one thing, but living it is another," Gay wrote in a note to Ferrie. A Gill stenographer later told her Ferrie "went into a fit" when he read it.

Learning that Ferrie had been questioned by the district attorney in connection with the Kennedy assassination, Gay telephoned Gill's office to find the secretaries "in a turmoil." One told her, "Mr. Gill knew nothing about Ferrie—it was all new to him." Bootsie knew otherwise. She went to Gill's office only to find Gill employee Regina Franchevich packing up Ferrie's papers. If Ferrie walked into the office, we would all walk out, someone said.

Bootsie sat watching as Regina took a chart, it looked like a diagram, of an automobile from a high angle looking down, surrounded by buildings at what was clearly Dealey Plaza. When Franchevich tossed it into a wastebasket, Bootsie fished it out.

"This should be turned over to the FBI or the Secret Service," Bootsie said.

Franchevich angrily snatched the diagram back. "It's nothing," she said. She threw it back into the trash. Again Bootsie plucked it out. "I'll give it to the FBI," she said. Franchevich grabbed the paper, this time for good, if not before Bootsie Gay spotted on that diagram the words "Elm Street."

Bootsie Gay later reconstructed the diagram for Jim Garrison. She drew a square, denoting a building. Inside a second square, she wrote "VIP," explaining that this square represented a vehicle. She had come forward, she explained, because she considered herself "a good citizen and a damn good and loyal American." David Ferrie, she now believed, "must have done something pretty evil."

As Bootsie Gay had left Gill's office that late November day, one of the secretaries imparted a word of advice. "Mrs. Gay, if I were you I wouldn't call Mr. Gill's house for a while. I'm sure his phones are tapped."

Still determined to locate the Cubans pictured with Oswald, Garrison extended his investigation to Dallas and to Miami. In Dallas in late September of 1963, three men had visited a Cuban exile named Sylvia Odio. Two of the men, calling themselves "Angelo" and "Leopoldo," were Latins, with one, Odio thought, speaking not with a Cuban, but with a Mexican accent. The third was an American whom the others called "Leon Oswald." They had just come from New Orleans, and were, they claimed, collecting for Odio's father's organization, JURE.

A day or two later, "Leopoldo" called Odio and confided that "Leon" had raved about wanting President Kennedy dead. He was an ex-Marine, and wanted to help in the Cuban underground, exactly what Lee Harvey Oswald in New Orleans had told Arnesto Rodriguez and Carlos Bringuier.

"Leon" had accused the Cubans of lacking "guts." He insisted that "President Kennedy should have been assassinated after the Bay of Pigs and some Cubans should have done that, because he was the one that was holding the freedom of Cuba. . . ."

During the weekend of the assassination, both Sylvia and her younger sister Annie at once recognized Lee Harvey Oswald as "Leon." The visit demonstrated at once foreknowledge of the assassination as being committed by somebody named "Oswald," in an obvious conspiracy. Odio would not identify the other two, although she did describe the unusual configuration of "Leopoldo's" forehead.

J. Edgar Hoover then adopted for Sylvia Odio the same policy he had enlisted for all inconvenient witnesses. Regis Kennedy had called Jack Martin a "nut." Oswald's Marine friend Nelson Delgado, who testified that Oswald was a poor shot, was not only a liar and overweight, but "immature and below average in intelligence." Sylvia Odio, Big Regis now said, "was suffering from a mental condition described as 'grand hysteria.'" She was "unstable," and suffered from a "crying need for recognition." Warren de Brueys says to this day that Garrison was a "nut."

Alberto Fowler, on Jim Garrison's behalf, flew to San Juan, Puerto Rico, in an attempt to interview Sylvia Odio, with no success. Having accused the FBI of persecuting her, she remained too disillusioned by her treatment by the Warren Commission and the FBI to cooperate with Jim Garrison's investigation. Garrison did locate Odio's uncle, Augustin Guitart, a physics professor at Xavier University in New Orleans. "The FBI asked me many questions about Sylvia's possible insanity," Guitart told Frank Klein. "I do not feel that she is insane and [I believe] that she is telling the truth about what happened in Dallas."

"There is no question about her honesty," Garrison concluded. Sylvia Odio's story remained, as researcher Sylvia Meagher put it, "proof of the plot," proof that there had been a conspiracy. Spies in his office were everywhere, and Joe Oster, Banister's former partner, reported to Regis Kennedy that the "testimony of Sylvia O . . . was of considerable interest" to Garrison.

By now Garrison was so immersed in the investigation that he instructed his secretary to interrupt him only for calls from Willard Robertson or Governor McKeithen. One day Garrison told her he would not take any calls, "not even if it's Jesus Christ." A few moments later, a call came in from the governor's mansion.

"Governor McKeithen, if he's not going to take a call from Jesus Christ," Sharon Herkes said, "I know he's not going to take a call from you."

At home, Jim Garrison was permissive, a district attorney who did not believe in punishment, his daughter Elizabeth says. "What purpose did that serve?" he might ask an errant child, and you walked out of the room feeling terrible because you had let down your dad. Jim Garrison was not a conventional father and did not attend Little League games. He did recite "The Cat and the Fiddle," which he knew by heart, and taught those of his children old enough about Graham Greene and Shakespeare. Liz encouraged the children to appreciate their father and their love for him grew stronger as the investigation took its toll.

For help in Miami, Alberto Fowler enlisted fellow Bay of Pigs veteran Bernardo Gonzalez de Torres Aguilar, a rangy thirty-three-year-old with thinning black hair, large dark eyes and olive skin, now set up in a Miami detective agency. Unknown to both Fowler and Jim Garrison, de Torres had been working for the CIA since December of 1962. When a CIA/FBI liaison offered the FBI information about members of Brigade 2506 (Bay of Pigs) which "CIA had some knowledge of or indirect contact with," that document was placed in de Torres' FBI file. A CIA document, informing the FBI of those CIA supported as part of the Cuban Revolutionary Council, also contains the name "Bernardo R. Gonzalez de Torres Aguilar." De Torres informed against fellow members of Brigade 2506 to the Bureau.

Among de Torres' efforts was an alliance with Luis Somoza, former Nicaraguan dictator, to use a B-26 bomber to hit Fidel Castro. The FBI, alarmed, reported these plans to the CIA, which yawned. That report had come from de Torres' own father, who, by August of 1966, was still informing against his son. The word in Miami was that de Torres worked with Charles Siragusa, head of the Federal Bureau of Narcotics, and Gene Marshall, both of whom also worked for the CIA. Under CIA protection, Bernardo de Torres told the FBI that he "cannot and will not cease his efforts to fight Communism in Cuba."

Jim Garrison sent Sergeant Thomas Duffy to Miami to recruit Bernardo de Torres, who was all too eager to work only for expenses. De Torres contributed nothing true to Jim Garrison's effort. Visiting Jim Garrison in New Orleans, he insisted that Sylvia Odio had inquired whether the men who visited her had been sent by a man named "Leonardo." He insisted that Leopoldo's real name was "Antonio." As will later be revealed in this story he had reason to know otherwise.

De Torres imposed another name: Jorge Rodriguez Alvarado, the person the Warren Commission suggested might have sent Odio her visitors. Soldier of Fortune Gerald Patrick Hemming, who knew de Torres well, suggests that the visit to Odio's was arranged by a CIA agent, working simultaneously for U.S. Customs, named Steve Czukas, who was also the supervisor of Bernardo de Torres in his real assignment. This was the surveillance of Lee Harvey Oswald.

Jim Garrison welcomed de Torres, FBI informant and CIA operative, as he speculated that the men who visited Mrs. Odio, plus Oswald, plus "the people who organized it here," comprised the "assassination plotters," which was not quite the truth. De Torres repeatedly fed him disinformation: that Oswald was in Tampa when President Kennedy was there, four days before Oswald went to Dallas; that a person involved in the assassination named "Lolita Matamoros" was a "Communist"; that a man named Rafael Mola had flown to Cuba "a few days after the Smith event," information that came to de Torres, he claimed, through "an agent of the 26th of July." None of this went anywhere.

Jim Garrison was dubious. One thing he did know was that Oswald was no Communist. He became suspicious when de Torres said he had classified information about an Oswald visit to Miami, and told a tale about the "Miami planning in the summer of 1963," what seemed like an attempt to draw Jim Garrison's attention away from New Orleans, although it was in fact true: Oswald had been in Miami. By January 7th, Garrison had ordered his staff "under no circumstances" to offer any information to de Torres. On January 11, 1967, Garrison wrote at the top of one of de Torres' memos: "His reliability is not established."

Pershing had begun to inform to the FBI on Jim Garrison's investigation, insisting he himself had told Garrison to "forget the matter"; he "would not assist Garrison in the investigation." Now Gervais and Gurvich were joined by de Torres, who told his handlers at JMWAVE everything he knew about the Garrison investigation. "Everybody is looking for me," de Torres said. CIA passed the news on to the FBI. Hoover paused. Bernardo de Torres had been a useful informant up to this point; now they must hold him at arm's length. "Be certain . . . don't use Torres as an informant now in any capacity," Hoover scrawled. Soon the FBI was insisting that Bernardo de Torres had never been one of their informants.

De Torres gave Alberto Fowler the name of Ferrie's contact, "Eladio del Valle," to keep Garrison interested. The expenses de Torres claimed to have generated were hefty—by mid-February $1,500—catastrophic for the investigation. One bill was for $598, the single largest expenditure for the Garrison investigation to date. For the three months he "worked" for Jim Garrison, de Torres accounted for half the total expenditures up to that time.

Near the end of February, de Torres told Fowler he had "new information." With the help of del Valle, he had identified the stocky Latin in the photograph with Oswald as a Lebanese businessman and pilot named Roberto Verdaguer. Major Verdaguer had in fact been Castro's air force chief, who, with his brother Guillermo, had brought in a Cuban air freighter, requesting political asylum in the United States. He was hardly the Lebanese businessman de Torres claimed him to be.

Garrison now cut de Torres loose. On the morning of March 2, 1967, de Torres gave the CIA his final report on Jim Garrison. On paper, the Agency says it told de Torres to take this information to the FBI. Meanwhile they informed their own Soviet section, as well as the FBI.

For the HSCA, Gaeton Fonzi discovered that de Torres' CIA handler had been Paul Bethel. One of Fonzi's Miami sources, "Juan Adames," revealed that de Torres had admitted to him that he knew Oswald and "knows some of the people who were involved in it." He and de Torres had forged documents for hit teams, meeting in Cuban hangouts all over Florida, Adames told Fonzi. De Torres had "direct access to Santos Trafficante, who did in fact exhibit foreknowledge of the Kennedy assassination. Kennedy "is going to be hit," Trafficante told José Aleman a year before the event." And de Torres had been "pretty edgy" about this new HSCA investigation.

Further evidence of the complicity of de Torres in the events that he was ostensibly helping Jim Garrison to investigate includes a Justice Department document of March 14, 1967. A Cuban-American had gone to the FBI with information received from Arceli Mastrapa, a secretary at the Cuban embassy in Mexico City: "Cuban exile Bernardo Torres at Miami had developed evidence that it was a Cuban refugee group which had carried out the assassination of President Kennedy."

"One day, sooner or later, they're gonna come and talk to me," de Torres said.

"Well, did anybody [you know] have anything to do with it?" Adames said.

"They will never find out what happened," Bernardo said. Did he believe Oswald killed Kennedy?

"I don't believe it because I know some of the people who were involved in it," de Torres said, as he admitted he worked with the CIA. When Adames denied he himself had any connection to the Agency, de Torres said, "Well, we all say that."

Fonzi discovered from an FBI report that a man named Arturo Cobos identified de Torres as "the man to call with contacts on a high level with the CIA in Washington." A 1969 document identifies de Torres as working for "Pentagon intelligence."

A person who knew de Torres well was a "terrorist" named Rolando Otero, already a Fonzi source.

Both Bernardo de Torres and E. Howard Hunt had been involved in the Kennedy assassination, Otero, who had already talked to the FBI, told Fonzi, echoing Adames. "Oswald was a CIA agent." A decade after Jim Garrison's investigation, his suspicions that the CIA had plotted the murder were being confirmed. Otero had demonstrated his credibility. He knew what few did, for example, that Robert Kennedy had sent a representative from the criminal division of the Justice Department to Dallas on the day President Kennedy was killed. That man was Walter Sheridan. De Torres had "worked with Oswald," even as de Torres had posed "as a photographer at Dealey Plaza."

Adames confirmed that de Torres had in his possession photographs taken during the assassination.

When de Torres was subpoenaed by the HSCA, Fonzi wrote out a long list of questions: Had his penetration of Garrison's office been "motivated by his relationship with any United States intelligence agency or any person?" Had he reported on Jim Garrison's investigation to any Agency or person? Had he supplied false information to Garrison? With what agencies was he associated at that time and what functions did he perform "on their behalf?" Fonzi already knew of de Torres' telephone calls to CIA about his appearance before the committee, calls registered to "Mclean, Virginia," as calls to the CIA always were.

In Washington, Fonzi's researcher Edwin Lopez requested that

A FAREWELL TO JUSTICE

the CIA give the House Committee its files on Bernardo de Torres. Five or six sanitized documents appeared. Lopez complained to chief counsel G. Robert Blakey, only for thirteen more documents to arrive. But at the bottom of one page, someone had forgotten to erase a number. Lopez then requested of the CIA all documents relating to that number, purposely not mentioning the name "Bernardo Gonzalez de Torres Aguilar." Suddenly a cartload of documents arrived.

As he had placed the HSCA under the control of the CIA from the day he replaced Richard A. Sprague, Blakey and his deputy, Gary Cornwell, accepted Bernardo de Torres' request for immunity. Then, as if this weren't questionable enough, Blakey permitted a visit from the CIA right before de Torres was interviewed. The CIA demanded that the committee not ask de Torres anything about the time frame when de Torres was its operative, a period that included the Kennedy assassination. Accusing de Torres of being a double agent, working as well for Castro, which seems a preposterous claim, the CIA departed with Blakey's assurances. Virtually moments later, an FBI emissary appeared. The Bureau proposed its own time period about which de Torres must not be questioned. Blakey acquiesced in everything the CIA and the FBI requested.

Fonzi watched as de Torres finally entered the room, with "an air of dapper and casual confidence." Here, Fonzi thought, was a true professional. Government lawyer William Triplett told de Torres he was no longer bound by "any prior secrecy oath to the CIA," as if the committee were not itself bound by secret agreements with the Agency.

Asked how he came to work for Jim Garrison, de Torres evaded. "I don't know how I was chosen by him," he lied. He never met Frank Sturgis or Howard Hunt, de Torres claimed. All he knew about David Ferrie he had learned from Garrison. "I never worked for the CIA," de Torres lied. "I never talked to anybody associated with the CIA." He possessed no photographs of the assassination, and did not know the pockmarked, stocky Cuban Garrison sought. He had never met Oswald. "I have never been contacted by a CIA member, to my knowledge," de Torres repeated. Representative Christopher Dodd was not quite ready to let him go. "Have you ever been an agent of the Central Intelligence Agency?" Dodd demanded in the face of de Torres' denials.

"No, sir," de Torres said.

Fonzi sat, spellbound. This guy has so much faith in the protective shell the Agency provided that he doesn't need to exhibit an iota of arrogance, Fonzi thought. If an uninformed outsider were sitting in the room, he would have wondered why, of all the hundreds of thousands of Cubans in Miami, we picked this guy to call to Washington.

Jim Garrison now focused on two "wildcat Cubans," Miguel Torres and Emilio Santana. Partners in crime in New Orleans, they dined, rumor had it, with an Oswald friend named "Chico" at an apartment in the 1300 block of Dauphine Street, where Clay Shaw lived. (In December of 1962, five months before his arrival in New Orleans, a "tall man, about 6-foot tall and dark complected, a man with a slight mustache," who signed a Christmas card "Chico," had visited Oswald in Texas.)

Garrison was aware, as Gaeton Fonzi was to put it, that "in almost every incident of a known Cuban association with Oswald, that individual has a direct tie with other Cubans or a Cuban organization headquartered in Miami." For help in locating his Miami suspects, Jim Garrison turned to the Miami/Dade States Attorney, tough, one-eyed, free-wheeling Richard Gerstein, the only district attorney in the country willing to help him.

"Don't waste your time," Gerstein's administrative assistant, Seymour Gelber, told Gerstein.

"He's a fellow district attorney," Gerstein said.

Gerstein placed his own chief investigator, Martin F. Dardis, at the disposal of Garrison's investigators Lester Otillio and Douglas Ward, as they sought the short, stocky Cuban photographed with Oswald. If he could find this Cuban, Garrison believed, "we will have the other murderer of President Kennedy." Garrison nicknamed his Cuban suspects: El Guapo; El Gravo; El Toro. As "El Indio," CIA asset David Sanchez Morales had been involved with David Atlee Phillips in the CIA's overthrow of President Arbenz.

Dardis, his soft blue eyes and strawberry-blond hair notwithstanding, was a hard-boiled cynic who had earned a silver star at the Battle of the Bulge. Already he knew that the CIA's Cuban cadre was receiving checks from Eastern Airlines and Sears, among other companies, and the checks were drawn on the First National Bank of Miami. CIA's JMWAVE enjoyed free rein from the local FBI, Border Patrol, INS, Customs, the Coast Guard, the FCC, the Navy and, of course, the local police.

There was no paper trail Dardis could not follow, as in later years he demonstrated by being perhaps the single most important figure in helping Woodward and Bernstein unravel the money trail in the Watergate case, the brouhaha over Mark Felt notwithstanding. Garrison told Dardis that the name of the Cuban in question was "Manuel García Gonzalez," a name he had pried out of Dean Andrews. He hangs around Cuban bars. He carries a red toolbox and fixes boats, Garrison said.

"I should be able to find him," Dardis said, finding the request absurd. "I knew you could," Garrison said, missing Dardis' irony. Garrison had nicknamed this Cuban "Bugs Bunny."

At the airport to meet Garrison's investigators, Dardis held up a sign echoing the nickname Ward enjoyed at Tulane and Broad: "Mr. Wonderful." "I'm not getting you any women," Dardis said, aware of Pershing's role. Like Lou Ivon, Dardis had utter contempt for Gervais.

Dardis by himself telephoned every marina in Miami until he found the Cuban with the red toolbox. It was the wrong man. Garrison assistant James Alcock arrived, but Miami police intelligence offered little help. Alphonso L. Tarabochia, in charge of monitoring Cuban refugees and the Cuban underworld in Miami, honored Dardis' request and put Alcock in touch with José Antonio Lanuza of the DRE. He had seen "El Toro," before, Lanuza said, evasively, but could not identify him.

Alcock met Laureano Batista, who ran a training camp north of Lake Pontchartrain, and learned of how right-wing National States Rights Party member Joseph Milteer had predicted the triangulated gunfire of the assassination "from an office building with a high-powered rifle" in a February 9, 1963, tape made by a Miami police intelligence informant named Willie Somersett. Milteer knew that there would be a scapegoat. "Oh, somebody is going to have to go to jail," he had speculated. "Just like Bruno Hauptmann in the Lindbergh case." The Miami police had altered President Kennedy's November 18th itinerary, canceling the motorcade.

Somersett later told Jim Garrison that Milteer had telephoned him from Dallas at 10:30 A.M. on November 22nd. Kennedy would probably never return to Miami," Milteer had said. "Don't worry about your friend, Jack. We're going to take care of him today." Even Bernardo de Torres would insist that the Secret Service had been warned that Kennedy was in danger, although they denied it.

Alberto Fowler continued to work for Jim Garrison, whom he found *simpático*. He remained loyal, so that when David Chandler's wife Patricia asked him for photographs of the Cubans whom Garrison was investigating, Alberto sent her to Laureano Batista in Miami, giving her nothing.

"Poor Jim is swimming upstream," Alberto told his son. Alberto agreed with Jim Garrison that Kennedy "was taken out by the military industrial complex," and that CIA employees had been involved in the plot. They were making a ton of money in Texas after Kennedy died, he noted. Fowler also believed that Carlos Bringuier was aware of Oswald's affiliation with the CIA, and that the two of them had "staged their confrontation on Canal Street."

One day Alberto, his wife Paulette, and their two children were at dinner at their home in the Garden district. Suddenly a brick came crashing through the window, landing in the middle of the table. Dishes broke. Glass shattered. A note was attached to the brick: "We know you're working for the Garrison investigation."

"Get the shotgun!" Alberto yelled very loudly. There was no gun in the house. Alberto hated guns.

"I should think twice about working on the Garrison investigation," an anonymous caller soon whispered. "We can have someone look at your taxes."

"My taxes are fine," Alberto said.

"I don't think you understand," the caller said. "There will be a mistake on your taxes."

Now Alberto did go out and buy a gun.

TIGER BY THE TAIL 7

[The district attorney] knows he's got a tiger by the tail.
—David Ferrie

O N VALENTINE'S DAY, 1967, Emilio Santana, who had worked for the CIA from the first night he arrived in the United States, was interviewed at Tulane and Broad. Short-staffed, Garrison permitted Carlos Bringuier to interview Santana. In a matter of days, Bringuier was warning J. Edgar Hoover: Garrison was putting the blame for the assassination not only on the CIA, but "on you!" something Garrison never did.

Knowing that Garrison hoped that Santana would place Sergio Arcacha Smith in New Orleans during the summer of 1963, corroborating David Lewis' testimony, Bringuier attempted to steer Santana into stating that the person he met representing Alpha 66 was not Arcacha, but one Luis Bretos. Thomas Edward Beckham could have corroborated that Arcacha had visited New Orleans that summer, but he was to be among the most elusive of Garrison witnesses.

For Santana's polygraph the next day, the translator was Alberto Fowler. Had he met Miguel Torres at a 1963 dinner in the 1300 block of Dauphine Street hosted by Arcacha? Santana said no, and the machine registered deception. Santana was asked about a piano player named "Jean Vales." When he said he didn't know "Jean Vales," the machine signaled its alarm. Was the similarity between the names "Jean Vales" and "Juan Valdes" the reason? Garrison wondered.

Meanwhile, interviewed at Parish Prison, Miguel Torres said Santana had definitely been at that dinner where the subject was "revolutionary actions with regard to Cuba." During his polygraph, when Torres denied that he knew Clay Shaw, the machine revealed that he, too, was lying.

Garrison pondered more propinquities. Oswald had used as a job reference a man who lived at 2705 Magazine Street, while Torres said he met Santana often at the 2700 block of Magazine. A witness who could have helped Garrison with respect to Santana was a contractor named Woodrow H. Hardy, but Hardy confided only in his lawyer, Samuel Exnicios. Hardy worked for Clay Shaw, supervising the renovations of his many French Quarter properties. By the summer of 1963, Woodrow Hardy had worked for Shaw for years and had his own key to the patio door of Shaw's house at 1313 Dauphine Street. Hardy was accustomed to letting himself in when he had work to do.

It was twelve noon, an hour when Hardy did not expect to find Shaw at home. He let himself in through the patio door only to discover in the big downstairs room, deep in conversation, Clay Shaw, David Ferrie and Lee Harvey Oswald. Usually Shaw made time to talk to Hardy about construction matters. Now, Shaw rose quickly to his feet. Firmly, he ushered Hardy out the door.

"I'm engaged in a conference right now," Shaw said.

After the assassination, having recognized Oswald, having read of witnesses in the case dying, Hardy feared for his life. Hardy told his lawyer that he had seen Shaw, Ferrie and Oswald together only because Sam's brother, Hugh Exnicios, had been in some trouble over the Garrison investigation.

Jim Garrison did receive an anonymous letter naming Hardy. Hardy had told the author of the letter that he had seen many Cubans visiting Shaw. Among them was "Emilio Santana." The letter, which Garrison could not follow up, was signed, "a citizen who believes in your case."

Orestes Peña knew Santana as "Juan Elerio Cabellero," a member of the CIA's clandestine services.

Carlos Bringuier laughed to himself when he passed Garrison's polygraph. He had denied being contacted by the CIA, and the machine did not demur. It wasn't a lie because it was at *his own request* that he had at least four interviews with the CIA by then. Even New Orleans CIA agent Hunter Leake registered discomfort at this.

As Garrison sought still the stocky, swarthy Cuban with the pockmarked complexion, Billings dubbed him "Oswald's Latin shepherd." Could he have been "Angelo," the heavier man at Sylvia Odio's? Dallas deputy sheriff Roger Craig spoke of the driver of a station wagon who was "very dark complected," with "real dark short hair."

Dallas district attorney Henry Wade identified a "dark complected Latin with long black hair, and a stocky build," a man with "numerous bumps on his face" sitting with Oswald at Ruby's Carousel Club. The issue of Ruby's acquaintance with Oswald was, from the earliest days, part of Garrison's focus. Thomas Edward Beckham confirms that Oswald and Ruby knew each other. Even without Beckham's testimony, Garrison knew this was true. The owner of Bruning's Seafood Restaurant told Tommy Baumler, then working for Banister, that he had seen Oswald and Ruby together. Baumler was informed about a telephone operator who overheard a conversation between Ruby and Oswald with Ruby in New Orleans and Oswald already back in Texas. When the operator came forward, the FBI ignored her. Sam (Monk) Zelden, was the attorney for a trucking firm to which Oswald applied for employment. Among Oswald's three job references was Jack Ruby.

The Dallas evidence, too, is rich in examples of people testifying to having seen Oswald at the Carousel Club. Among them is ventriloquist-magician Bill DeMar, who performed the week before the assassination when he spotted Oswald in the audience. Interviewed by the Warren Commission, DeMar was perplexed when, for purposes of identification, he was given a photograph of a young man on the stage with a stripper who didn't even work at Ruby's club. Oswald had been sitting at a table, DeMar remembers. He had never been on the stage.

Jim Garrison sent John Volz to Dallas in search of the pockmarked Cuban, nicknamed "Bugs Bunny." Volz came up empty only for Jim Garrison to be incredulous. "You know, you have the imagination of an FBI man!" Garrison said. Before long, Volz was promoted to chief of narcotics. Later, as U. S. Attorney, Volz would prosecute Governor Edwin Edwards and Carlos Marcello. Marcello he convicted, but Edwards eluded him. One day Edwards had turned up alone at Volz's office without an appointment.

"What would I have to do to make this go away?" Edwards said.

"Nothing," Volz said. (Edwards' conviction had to await another day.)

Of all Banister's associates, people whom he suspected of being acquainted with Lee Harvey Oswald, Garrison wanted to talk to Sergio Arcacha Smith, who had been present at the robbery of the Schlumberger ammunition dump, and was paid by David Ferrie. He concentrated on Arcacha and Shaw, hoping to link them to Oswald and Ferrie. Both Arcacha and Ferrie had worked for U.S. Customs, Garrison knew, even as he did not know Oswald had done so as well. Arcacha had maintained his connections with the CIA, the FBI and Customs, and in fact was well-acquainted with Oswald. He had moved to Dallas where he was warned by both Bringuier and his own assistant, Carlos Quiroga, that Garrison's men were coming.

Gurvich and Alcock arrived with a warrant for Arcacha's arrest for participating in the Schlumberger burglary, which had been planned in Orleans Parish. "I had expected them earlier," Arcacha said, suave as ever. He invoked "Mr. Bobby Kennedy," whom he had called whenever he needed advice, and who "knew what we were doing all the time." This, of course, turns out to be true.

Governor Connally invited Arcacha to Austin, embraced him and reassured him that he would not extradite him back to Louisiana. Shortly before his death, Arcacha admitted he had traveled back and forth to New Orleans frequently during the summer of 1963 and was even gleeful that he had evaded Jim Garrison. To the end of his life, Arcacha denied he knew Oswald, which was *not* true. He had told his public relations man and supporter Ronny Caire that "Oswald was nutty as a fruitcake. He didn't know which side he was working for." But higher authority shielded Arcacha to the end, so that Garrison was forced to conclude that his connection to the crime was "remote" and his own efforts "a waste of time."

Garrison developed a list of "standard questions." Had a witness seen Oswald either in Banister's building or in Mancuso's restaurant? (Allen Campbell reveals that you could enter Mancuso's from 531 Lafayette without even going into the street.) Had the witness seen Ruby at 531 Lafayette? Did the witness recognize Banister, Arcacha, Ferrie or Bringuier? Had the witness seen Oswald with Banister, Ferrie or Ruby? Garrison wondered whether Banister had the same CIA handler, a man named "Logan Stewart," as Arcacha did. An informant told him that Banister had joined the New Orleans police as a "single step phase" of "sterilizing" him from his intelligence connections.

No answers were forthcoming from Banister associates such as Joe Newbrough, who claimed he did not know what was stored in the boxes of war materiel at Banister's office. Newbrough was willing to say that "David Ferrie is capable of almost anything," and to report that Ferrie had asked him to sign a statement based on a lie, that one of the boys whom Ferrie had been charged with molesting, Eric Crouchet, was "habituating homosexual hangouts." It was for Regis

Kennedy, and not for Jim Garrison or Lou Ivon, that Joe Oster, Big Regis' informant #1309-C, produced a photograph taken by Newbrough of jeeps and trucks being shipped to Cuba in 1960 from a New Orleans dock.

A Banister client reported that "he had heard Banister remark on several occasions that someone should do away with Kennedy." I. E. Nitschke, a former FBI agent close to Banister, reported that Banister was bidding on the security contract for NASA's Michoud's assembly facility where so many employees of Reily Coffee went to work after the assassination, and where Oswald said he hoped to land a job. Nitschke remembered a "short, stocky" Cuban "with obviously large arms and neck," whom Banister had confided was "exceptionally adept in guerrilla warfare and guerrilla type tactics."

Was his name Manuel Gonzalez? Garrison said.

Gonzalez, yes, Nitschke said. He was in fact looking at a photograph of longtime CIA operative David Sanchez Morales. Exasperated, Garrison dubbed the group of Cubans he was seeking "Winkin', Blinkin' and "Nod" after the nursery rhyme.

Nitschke did urge Delphine Roberts to turn everything she had over to the district attorney's office. Roberts refused. She volunteered only that Banister "belonged to a worldwide intelligence network to receive information from all areas." Mary Banister concealed that she had sold some of her husband's files to Kent Courtney.

David Lewis had told Jim Garrison that Carlos Quiroga, Arcacha's assistant, had introduced him to "Lee Harvey." Quiroga had driven the Schlumberger arms to Miami in a U-Haul truck. During the summer of 1963, at the suggestion of Bringuier, Quiroga had gone to Oswald's house, requesting an application form for Fair Play for Cuba. Oswald had told him, Quiroga said, that he was studying Russian at Tulane. When Quiroga heard (but how?) that Oswald was distributing leaflets outside the International Trade Mart, he had telephoned New Orleans police intelligence, then rushed over himself. Quiroga says his plan was to "physically attack" Oswald, but he arrived too late. The incident seems a potential carbon copy of Bringuier's Canal Street fracas.

Quiroga was to be a most unpromising Garrison witness. He was given to reporting the names of students at "pro-Castro" meetings to Warren de Brueys, his informant file (134) having been opened with de Brueys on November 30, 1966. Ultimately the FBI rejected Quiroga as a permanent informant because of his "apparent detective complex."

At Tulane and Broad, Quiroga faced tough Frank Klein. On

Klein's desk was a statement from Bringuier to the Secret Service that Quiroga had visited Oswald *on several occasions*, not just the once to which he admitted.

Ferrie is a "Communist" who has been arrested "for Communist activities," Quiroga says, obvious disinformation that Klein ignores. "Ferrie is plenty scared," he adds.

Klein asks Quiroga about Banister's role in the front. "You mean about the arms?" Quiroga says.

"I didn't say anything about arms," Klein says.

"Well, he didn't have anything to do with arms," Quiroga says. Then he smiles. Klein thinks: He smiles involuntarily or smirks when he is not telling the truth. Klein asks about training camps, and Quiroga replies with a question: "The one here or the one across the lake?"

Klein concluded "This man knows a lot more than he is telling me." Garrison scribbled on Klein's statement: "Quiroga seems impelled to reinforce Oswald's cover."

Garrison subpoenaed Quiroga for another round of questions. He had been seen at Mancuso's and had introduced David Lewis to "Lee Harvey," Garrison said. It was a point on which Lewis had passed his polygraph, reflecting the same response as he did when asked his own name. Richard Billings read the transcript and also wondered about Quiroga: "He's evasive about Mancuso cafe." Asked if he knew a "Clay Bertrand," Quiroga admitted he had heard the name.

"One of the things we have learned is that Oswald was not a Communist at all. Would it surprise you if I told you that Oswald was anti-Castro?" Garrison said.

"He had to be a Communist," Quiroga insisted. "He told me he would kill American soldiers if they land in Cuba." Showing Quiroga a photograph of Oswald with anti-Castro Cubans, Garrison persisted. He would reveal "confidential information" to Quiroga, proof that Oswald's plan had been to enter Cuba as a Communist, and then, as he had been ordered, to kill Fidel Castro. Branding him a Communist was part of a scenario that would blame Castro for the assassination of President Kennedy.

Quiroga immediately reported to Aaron Kohn, accusing Garrison of being "un-American." Then he denounced Garrison as being "un-American" to the House Un-American Activities Committee. Even Kohn was astonished. Quiroga then called de Brueys at home, complaining that Jack Martin had threatened to kill him for going to the district attorney's office.

On April 15th, Quiroga took a polygraph at Tulane and Broad.

On whether he had seen Oswald only once, on the day he visited him on Magazine Street, Quiroga failed. On that he was aware that Fair Play for Cuba was a cover, he failed. On whether Arcacha and Banister knew Oswald, the box all but blew up. Had Arcacha visited New Orleans on any occasion in 1963? Quiroga said no, and failed. Even on whether he had seen any of the guns used in the assassination, he failed. And while this was unlikely, suggesting that Quiroga was so nervous as not to be a suitable polygraph subject, Quiroga did pass other questions with no difficulty.

Quiroga testified before the Orleans Parish grand jury, only to be asked to return. He begged the FBI to help him, pleading the Fifth Amendment. His father was in prison in Cuba. He would not testify because he had been threatened with a perjury charge, he said.

"We only charge people with perjury when they lie under oath," Jim Garrison said. He referred Quiroga to that pro-Castro Oswald pamphlet with "544 Camp Street" stamped on it. Quiroga remained silent.

By the third week of February 1967, Jim Garrison was convinced: David Ferrie was the "transportation manager" of the assassination, in charge of shepherding people in and out of Dallas. He was also an Oswald babysitter. But Garrison wanted more evidence. Believing Ferrie was close to confessing, Lou Ivon disagreed. Ivon urged that they take Ferrie into custody immediately.

New evidence against Ferrie did continue to arrive. At White Rock Airport in Dallas, a mechanic named Fred Lenz identified Ferrie as having been there in "October or November of 1963," piloting a plane in and out of Dallas. Ferrie had worn a "checkered, brown and light gray or white sport jacket," similar to a coat Ferrie was wearing in the photograph William Gurvich now showed Lenz. Lenz remembered being shown "Ferrie's credentials." The owner of Ted Hill Aviation corroborated Lenz's identification. A student pilot also identified Ferrie from photographs.

David Ferrie was indeed "plenty scared." In panic, he telephoned Pershing. "I've got some interesting ideas," Dave said. "There may have been a second assassin." Would Pershing please arrange an interview with Jim Garrison? "Playing for results," as always, Gervais called not Jim Garrison, but Regis Kennedy. Now Ferrie hired an attorney, one of his flying students, Gerald Aurillo, who had once been a Garrison assistant.

After hiring Max Gonzales undercover to tell Ferrie he wanted to buy a plane, Garrison drew into his investigation that young blond

Ferrie friend, Jimmy Johnson, who would report on some of the contents of "the Bomb." Unlike the majority of the Ferrie boys, he was married. A parole violator on a weapons charge, Johnson helped Garrison, he said later, "to keep myself out of trouble." Lou Ivon named him "Undercover Agent #1." A measure of Ivon's professionalism is that for nearly forty years neither Alvin Beaubouef nor Morris Brownlee knew that Jimmy Johnson was working for Jim Garrison.

On January 18, 1967, Johnson reported that he retrieved for Ferrie an 8 x 10 envelope under the seat of a white Chevrolet with no license plates. "I'm going to buy a new car, because I've just got hold of some cash," Ferrie told him. Police investigator Lynn Loisel learned that Ferrie now had between thirty-five and forty-five thousand dollars and was planning to buy a DC-3 airplane to run guns to Cuba. Ferrie's only visible means of support was from teaching students to fly, although his license was no longer valid. One night he delivered a truckload of hand grenades to a friend's house for safe keeping.

Ferrie wrote obscene letters. One, beginning, "Dear Bastard," described a sex movie: "some dude fucking this broad . . . he got his nuts jerking under her knee, she blew him, he fucked her in the ass twice, and in the pussy twice . . . I could have raped an exhaust pipe they made me so hot." He asked Johnson to line up women to pose while they were having intercourse with Johnson for fifteen dollars an hour. They would split the profits. He asked Johnson to burglarize a man's house because he knew the man always kept a thousand dollars in cash at home.

One night a patrolling police car light hit Ferrie's porch. "The police suspect me," Dave said. Yet he laughed at Jim Garrison. "They won't be able to get anything on me. I'm so much smarter than those people." Later Johnson remembered they discussed the assassination maybe "a hundred times." Ferrie obviously knew a lot about Oswald. Johnson concluded that Ferrie had been involved in a plot to assassinate President Kennedy with Cubans at Houston, Texas, and that Ferrie was to have flown the airplane helping the assassin get away. That Ferrie knew Oswald there was no question.

Despite his bravado, Ferrie began to deteriorate. He rarely bathed. The rifle in his car was now always loaded. He talked of killing himself. He telephoned the Reverend Raymond Broshears and said he feared that he was going to be killed. Depressed, he confided to Jimmy Johnson that Garrison had picked up his friend Mike (Crouchet), and had questioned him about Ferrie.

Ferrie quarreled with Jimmy Johnson, but Ivon told Johnson

to patch it up. "That's no problem," Johnson said, "David Ferrie is in love with me." Evenings, Ferrie reclined on the couch, talking on the telephone. Between eleven thirty and midnight, he removed his false eyebrows, put down two pillows and a blanket and went to sleep on the floor.

Now Ferrie began to telephone Lou Ivon. His persistent themes were that he feared for his life and that he was sick and would die soon anyway.

"What's happening with the Cubans?" Ferrie asked in one of these calls.

"Dave, the best thing is for you to come talk to us," Ivon said. Ferrie refused. Yet, Jim Garrison concluded later, "in his need to talk to Ivon, he was showing signs of conscience."

Judge Thomas Brahney tipped off reporter Jack Dempsey. "Gervais and all those big investigators have been going to Dallas and Miami," he said. "What do you think they're going there for?" On another day, Brahney told Dempsey that Jimmy Alcock, the assistant assigned to his section, had been replaced. "I hear Alcock has been going to Dallas," he said. Dempsey had City Hall reporter Dave Snyder examine the air ticket vouchers put through the accounting office from the district attorney's office fines and fees account: There were twelve trips to Miami alone. Dempsey soon noticed two names on the grand jury agenda: Joseph Newbrough and David William Ferrie.

That Jim Garrison was investigating the Kennedy assassination was by now an open secret in New Orleans. Reporter Sam Depino was babbling, as was Pershing, as was Carlos Bringuier. On February 17th, the *States-Item* broke the story: "DA Here Launches Full JFK Death 'Plot' Probe." David Ferrie, not mentioned by name, was described as a man who had been arrested in New Orleans and booked as a fugitive from Texas, November 26, 1963. It could be no one else.

Ferrie showed the article to Allen Campbell, his hangar neighbor at the airport.

"I'm a dead man!" Ferrie said.

Ferrie was particularly agitated by a quotation attributed to Jim Garrison, saying "none of the people mentioned in the press so far are very important in the investigation." That was "a big joke." If he wasn't important, why was the DA harassing him? He reached Pershing. "Get your licks in first," Pershing advised, and so Ferrie called the FBI and reporter Snyder and gave him an interview.

Discovering that a law enforcement officer, the first, was investigating the murder of President Kennedy, the world press converged on New Orleans. Arrests are certainly "months away," Jim Garrison told them in an attempt to deflect attention from his real plan, which was soon to arrest David Ferrie. "Jim Garrison has some information the Warren Commission didn't have," Senator Russell Long announced, making public his support of Jim Garrison. Garrison had requested that Long not "tell the FBI what he was doing and I didn't."

WDSU was the New Orleans NBC affiliate owned by Edgar and Edith Stern that had helped the CIA establish Oswald's cover as a Marxist in that August 1963 radio debate. They at once opposed Jim Garrison's investigation. He should turn his information over to the federal authorities, WDSU insisted. Garrison replied in a press release. These authorities, he said, have "been able to develop very little after three long years." As for who had jurisdiction, he pointed out, murdering the president was not a federal crime on November 22, 1963: "The Federal Government has about as much jurisdiction over a murder in New Orleans as the S.P.C.A. [Society for the Prevention of Cruelty to Animals]"

It was now that Jim Lewallen told Ferrie's friends to stay away from Ferrie's apartment. "Dave is hot, very hot," Lewallen told the Wilson brothers. "A lot of shit is coming down, so just stay away." Soon Lewallen would reveal that Ferrie had for a time lived at one of Clay Shaw's French Quarter properties.

On Saturday, February 18th, the day after the story that Jim Garrison was investigating the Kennedy assassination broke, Ivon and Sciambra drove over to 3330 Louisiana Avenue Parkway where Ferrie rented an apartment from Eddie Sapir and his father. Their purpose was to gauge Ferrie's reaction to the news. "I'm glad you finally decided to come and talk with me," Ferrie said. "I've been trying to get in touch with Garrison or Ivon for days."

He is sick, Ferrie says, and has been unable to keep anything in his stomach. In the living room, Ferrie lies down on the sofa. As a result of rumors of my arrest, I've been asked to leave the airport, he says, not mentioning that he was banished because he had no license to give flying lessons.

"Garrison is using Miguel Torres to frame me," Ferrie complains. He curses Jack Martin, who "started all this." He wants to speak to Garrison to see if he is serious. He brings up the trip to Houston and Galveston the weekend of the assassination. "It was the worst trip of my life," Ferrie says, leaving it at that.

"Who do you think killed the president?" Sciambra says. Ferrie launches into a lecture on ballistic trajectories, and even produces some sketches of the assassination scene, leftovers from that package Tommy Beckham delivered to Lawrence Howard on instructions from Ferrie and G. Wray Gill, vestiges of "the Bomb."

Sciambra knows that Ferrie did not arrive at his alibi location, Thomas Compton's Southeastern Louisiana College dorm room, until five in the morning on the Sunday night he returned from Houston and Galveston, although he had left New Orleans at nine or ten and Hammond was only an hour and a half away. Sciambra asks Ferrie to explain his whereabouts during those missing hours.

"Go to hell," Ferrie says.

"Did you stay with Clay Shaw?" Sciambra persists.

"Who's Clay Shaw?" Ferrie says.

"If that doesn't ring a bell, how about Clay Bertrand?" Sciambra says.

"Who's Clay Bertrand?" Ferrie says.

"Clay Bertrand and Clay Shaw are the same person," Sciambra says.

"Who said that?" Ferrie blurts out, a question he would not have asked if he had not associated the two names with each other, if he did not know that Shaw was Bertrand. It was the Oswald library card follies all over again.

"Dean Andrews told us," Sciambra fibs.

"Dean Andrews might tell you guys anything," Ferrie says, ignoring that he has already denied that he knew Andrews. Ferrie now changes the subject and starts talking about Arlen Specter's magic bullet theory.

"Save it for another day," Louie says.

The following afternoon, just as Ivon was sitting down to Sunday dinner, his telephone rang. "My life is being threatened," Ferrie said. "They're going to kill me!" He pleaded for protection.

"David, hold still," Ivon said. "I'll be right over." Ivon drove first to Jim Garrison's house.

"Check him in at the Fontainebleau," Garrison said. By four o'clock, Ferrie was checked in under a false name. Now he sat down and talked to Lou Ivon. He admitted that he had worked for the CIA.

"How do you think I got the man out of Guatemala?" he said, referring to his rescue of Carlos Marcello. "Ain't no ordinary person could do that."

Both he and Clay Shaw, whom he had known for a long time,

had been involved with the CIA. Of course Shaw was Bertrand. Shaw hated John F. Kennedy, Ferrie said.

Yes, Oswald had often been at Guy Banister's office. Oswald had also visited the training camps across the lake. Ferrie talked freely about his own part in the burglary of the CIA-affiliated Schlumberger ammunition dump in Houma. His sponsor, Ferrie said, was Robert Kennedy, who had given him and Layton Martens "letters of marque." He had received checks from the White House through a CIA account.

"You're on the right track," Ferrie told Ivon. "But you won't get anywhere because of the government." Then he added, "You guys don't know what you're dealing with. You all can't handle this."

In his report, Ivon wrote that Ferrie had been the babysitter for Lee Harvey Oswald, a role assigned to him by the CIA. Clay Shaw had served as the conduit of information from Washington.

At four A.M. Louie finally went home, leaving Lynn Loisel to keep an eye on Dave. When Loisel went out for cigarettes, Ferrie fled. So that there would be no leak, Ivon decided not to have his report typed by an office secretary but to give Jim Garrison his handwritten notes directly.

The next morning, Orestes Peña spotted Ferrie walking on Decatur Street. He must find Sergio Arcacha Smith and Wilfredo Mas, Ferrie told Peña. Mas was with both FBI and CIA; his brother in Miami belonged to the DRE. Peña suggested that Ferrie ask DRE member Bringuier. Then Peña telephoned Garrison's office and told investigator Frank Meloche that he had just seen Ferrie.

"Garrison is trying to frame me because he wants the publicity to run for higher office," Ferrie tells Bringuier. Assuming that Bringuier would know, Ferrie asks him for the date when the conspiracy started. He needs help in finding Arcacha. "All judges should be hanged," Ferrie remarks. Bringuier's back goes up. In Cuba, his father had been a judge.

"You should go to a psychiatrist," Ferrie finally tells Bringuier, "because anyone who believes in a Communist conspiracy to kill Kennedy needs to go to a psychiatrist." David Ferrie has renewed his acquaintance with the truth.

The next day, Tuesday, Ferrie sits at the New Orleans Public Library perusing the Warren Commission volumes. He sells his airplane. He is being harassed because he helped Carlos Marcello, he says. He has figured out that Jimmy Johnson has been spying on him but does nothing about it. He meets up with his old friend, now former policeman Sandy Krasnoff, who knows he is close to Shaw. "I'm going to kill myself," Ferrie says. "I'm fed up with life." He plans to use poison.

In the early morning hours of Wednesday, February 22nd, Ferrie was interviewed at his apartment by George Lardner of the *Washington Post.* To this particular reporter, according to Lardner's published story, he lied, as if by rote. He said he did not remember having met Lee Harvey Oswald since they were "in different units" of the CAP. He was "hunting geese" the weekend of the assassination. The district attorney knows "he's got a tiger by the tail," Ferrie says. Lardner departed at 4 A.M.

At 11:45 A.M. on that Wednesday, Jimmy Johnson arrived to pack up Ferrie's papers. The door was locked, so Johnson let himself in through a window. Ferrie lay dead, naked in his bed. His false eyebrows were still glued on, which was unlike him. On a coffee table sat two sealed envelopes. One was addressed to his brother Parmely, the other to Gerald Aurillo. Jimmy Johnson saw these two letters. Twenty-five minutes later he noticed that they had disappeared.

There were two typewritten suicide notes in the room. In "Suicide Note A," which was sitting in the typewriter, Ferrie talked of life as "loathsome," and leaving it a "sweet prospect." A "somewhat Messianic district attorney" was "unfit for office," Ferrie writes, as were two judges, J. Bernard Cocke and Federal Judge Herbert Christenberry, who denied "defendants due process of law."

"Suicide Note B," unsigned, was addressed to Alvin Beaubouef. "I offered you love," Dave pleaded to his heir. He was dying, "alone and unloved," for which he blamed Al's girlfriend and future wife, Carol. Under Dave's microscope was a smear, cells being checked for venereal disease. Krasnoff arrived at the scene, while his wife rushed to have someone remove the Eddie Sapir campaign sign from the front lawn. Beaubouef would keep some of Dave's possessions but throw most of his library into the city dump. In one of Ferrie's law books a particular section was highlighted: "the conditions under which the District Attorney of New Orleans could be removed from office."

Coroner Nicholas Chetta knelt down and sniffed the corpse. "Poison! Poison!" he said. But Chetta ruled finally that Ferrie had died of natural causes, a ruptured blood vessel at the base of the brain, a "beury aneurysm." Chetta's verdict did not match Ferrie's recent symptoms, his difficulty in walking, his lethargy. The autopsy was "slipshod," Ferrie's doctor Martin Palmer contends. It was only partial and they did not even open the brain case, casting the beury aneurysm verdict into doubt. Chetta at once reported to the highly interested FBI that "Suicide Note A" was "not a suicide note."

Empty bottles of the thyroid medication Proloid were at the scene and could have been traceable through the high iodine content in the blood had the coroner run that test. Drugs, too, might cause an aneurysm, but samples of Ferrie's blood were not kept. Leonard Gurvich, William's brother, who had also attached himself to the Garrison investigation, noted that the inside of Ferrie's mouth was "all burned up as a result of taking some type of acid drug." Dr. Frank Minyard, later coroner of Orleans Parish, also has noted in the report reference to a contusion, perhaps caused by "something traumatically inserted into Ferrie's mouth."

Other ambiguities persist. "I can't get hit in the head," Ferrie had told Daniel Campbell, referring to his "eggshell cranium." Morris Brownlee had told Garrison's investigators that Ferrie "knew he was going to die from the weakened arterie [sic] in his head."

In 1969, Dr. Dimitri L. Contoslavlos, a Pennsylvania medical examiner, tried to reach Jim Garrison. He wanted to point out that a blow to the side of the head just below the ear could cause an aneurysm to burst, and there need be no external tissue damage. A karate blow, or even a punch to the side of the neck, could do someone in.

Dr. Chetta ruled that the time of death was before midnight, only for reporter Lardner to contend that he had been with Ferrie until just before four in the morning. Chetta then dutifully altered the time of death: "I can't rule out the possibility he may have died as late as 4 A.M.," Chetta said. It was a "major inconsistency," Garrison noted, "one of the mysteries we don't understand."

That night, Robert Kennedy reportedly telephoned Dr. Chetta, inquiring as to the cause of David Ferrie's death as he kept an ever-watchful eye on Jim Garrison's investigation. Garrison issued a press release cautiously referring to the "apparent suicide" of David Ferrie. He had planned to arrest Ferrie early the following week. "Apparently we waited too long," it read. One of his assistants added a phrase, terming David Ferrie "one of history's most important individuals." These were not Jim Garrison's words. Garrison did suggest an appropriate epitaph for Ferrie from the last words of Serb partisan Draja Mihailovic, shot by Tito for collaboration: "I was swept up in the gales of history." Regarding the cause of death, Garrison would not "rule out anything." Ferrie was "a man of lights and shadows, mountains and valleys," Garrison summed up.

Young John Wilson thought, "Dave just wouldn't kill himself. He was looking forward to the coming bullshit. He would love all the publicity, and he believed that he was much more intelligent than Jim Garrison. It would be a fun time for Dave." Most of the people who knew Ferrie believed he did not die of natural causes, as Dr. Chetta ruled. Wendall Roache, who had worked with Oswald in Customs, testified before the Church Committee to his belief that Ferrie was murdered.

Jack Martin noted that Nicholas Chetta was famous for selling "natural causes" verdicts, "just like a prostitute." So Chetta had ruled in other suspicious deaths, from the wife of sheriff Johnny Grosch to the demise of Corrine Morrison, wife of mayor Chep Morrison. Only that past December, Martin, referring to the death of Ferrie's mother, had remarked to Jim Garrison that there "are a lot of ways of killing a guy without showing in an autopsy." Ferrie is "the key to everything," Martin believed.

Benton Wilson was certain the CIA had murdered Dave, and because Wilson knew so much about Ferrie's connection to the assassination, he began to fear the Agency might come after him as well. He began to carry a knife. When Jim Garrison sought him for questioning, Ben Wilson fled the state of Louisiana, not to return for decades. He settled in a remote part of the country, in a town so small that any strangers would be noticed. In the ensuing years, he would not talk to his sons about the assassination or about Ferrie for fear that they might become vulnerable, and he carried a 9 mm automatic in his belt. In his house, following David Ferrie's example, he placed a machine gun on the upstairs landing. When he saw the movie, *JFK*, all Ben Wilson said was, "It wasn't like that."

Twenty-four hours after Ferrie died, his CIA Miami contact Eladio del Valle was found shot through the heart. Del Valle's skull had been cut open from ear to ear with a machete, his body discovered not far from the apartment of Bernardo de Torres. Kennedy "must be killed to solve the Cuban problem," del Valle had said. Del Valle had identified the Cuban Manuel García Gonzales from a photograph, and had promised to help Alberto Fowler.

CIA General Counsel Lawrence Houston suspected that in late 1966 Del Valle had alerted President Duvalier about a plot led by Rolando Masferrer, with covert CIA encouragement, to invade Haiti. That may well have been the motive for his murder, the CIA wrote for the record, ignoring the extraordinary coincidence of Ferrie and Del Valle dying within twenty-four hours of each other.

In the 1990s, General Fabian Escalante, former head of Cuba's intelligence services, confided in author Dick Russell. Tony Cuesta, a Cuban about to leave Havana after a hospital stay and grateful for the care, named in a written declaration two people as having been involved in the plotting of the Kennedy assassination. One was Eladio del Valle, the other Herminio Díaz García, a "dark-skinned" Cuban who may have been the man Jim Garrison had identified as having been seen with Oswald, and often with Ferrie.

Jim Garrison held a staff meeting right after Ferrie's death. Everyone, not least Charlie Ward, who had political ambitions of his own, recommended that he drop the investigation, turn what he had over to the federal government and resume his political career. By now Garrison thoroughly hated politics. "What am I supposed to do? Go out and cut ribbons?" he argued. He would continue. If anyone wished to leave the investigation, they were free to do so.

John Volz and Jimmy Alcock tried one last time to persuade Garrison to cease and desist. Together they entered his private office where no one went casually.

Your main witness is dead, they pleaded. You can't go any further. Jim Garrison was so brilliant, Volz thought. You could explain a legal problem, or a public relations problem, to him in two sentences and he would come up with an instant answer, and a good one. On the subject of the Kennedy assassination, however, he was unmovable.

"Jim, we don't have the wherewithal," Volz said. "How many people do we have? It's time to take this ball and roll it down the hill. It's over."

"You must be crazy," Garrison said. "We're just beginning to crack this case!"

Coda: There is a CIA document dated February 8, 1973, six years after David Ferrie's death. It is a Memorandum For File, signed by Bruce L. Solie, Deputy Chief of the Special Research Section. The subject is Ferrie, David W., #523949, and Ferrie is described as being "of continuing interest . . . relative to the case of Kenneth Ralph Tolliver, #538049." Solie writes that "no action of any kind should be taken on Subject case without consulting the TOLLIVER file," as if action on the dead Ferrie were still pending.

Lest anyone doubt Ferrie's CIA connections, or Louis Ivon's account of his last conversation with Ferrie, Kenneth R. Tolliver became a member of the Association of Former Intelligence Officers, whose presidency was filled for a time by David Atlee Phillips. He is the author of *A Defector in Place*, a roman à clef about "Raya," the Soviet Embassy code clerk in Mexico City who became a defector in place. An early Tolliver work was *5Gtc: An Authorization Code*. Espionage is his subject. Agent Tolliver was connected to Ferrie in another aspect: he is a pilot of "fixed wing aircraft," a subscriber to *Sport Aviation*.

Tolliver's name surfaces in the Warren Commission questioning of Birchite Revilo Pendleton Oliver, a professor of classical philology at the University of Illinois. Oliver Exhibit No. 8 is a photostatic reprint of an article headlined, "A lot to remember, McComb Army officer big part in Kennedy funeral," by Kenneth Tolliver. Tolliver writes about one Captain Richard C. Cloy who helped conduct the Kennedy funeral, including a quote from his wife on how the funeral was "one of the most moving experiences of her life." The story appeared in the Jackson, Mississippi, *Clarion-Ledger* on February 21, 1964, and is of interest in its reflecting a certain interest on the part of Tolliver in the assassination of President Kennedy.

As to what the CIA contemplated on Ferrie's case, action they were forbidden to undertake without consulting "the TOLLIVER file," is unknown to the author at this time.

A WITNESS COMES FORWARD AND INTRIGUE AT THE VIP ROOM

8

He was hardly Joe Smith, American.
—Jim Garrison

T HE DEATH OF DAVID FERRIE frightened potential witnesses. Garrison tried to combat this fear by telling reporters that his office had "solved" the case "two weeks ago." On February 25th, he announced that he knew "the key individuals, the cities involved and how it was done." Arrests were forthcoming. Senator Russell Long proposed that the federal government offer a "substantial reward" to "loosen the lips of some people." Operating on a shoestring, Garrison borrowed $2,500 from Volkswagen dealer Willard Robertson, who would donate almost $30,000 dollars to the investigation.

Joseph Rault, along with a chemical engineer named Cecil Shilstone and Robertson, then formed a committee called "Truth and Consequences." Fifty businessmen pledged one hundred dollars a month for a minimum of three months. That Robertson and Shilstone were simultaneously also on the board of INCA they did not view as a contradiction. Helping uncover the murderers of President Kennedy was their patriotic duty, a "civic effort," Rault said. The public deserved "something better than the snow job the Warren Commission gave," Robertson added. Contributors ranged from private citizens like David Ferrie's insurance agent, Avery Spear, to Governor John McKeithen. A flippant reporter asked Garrison whether he expected a contribution to "Truth and Consequences" from the CIA. Garrison laughed.

"No, but I am expecting some from the FBI," he said.

Reporters attempted to extract from Shilstone the names of contributors. "Even if I did know, I would not tell you gentlemen," he said. There were reprisals against those who dared help Jim Garrison. In May of 1968, Shilstone reported to the FBI a rumor that he had been involved in the murder of Martin Luther King Jr. FBI's Joseph Sylvester checked on Rault and discovered that he was a longtime Bureau informant.

One attack on the group focused on the presumed illegality of the district attorney's accepting private funds. Louise Korns checked and found that such private contributions were entirely legal. Garrison was a "parochial officer, and does not operate a state agency," she wrote. Korns established that the existing law did not apply to Truth and Consequences' contributions. Pressure on the group to reveal its records persisted.

By June 1967, Garrison had spent a paltry $9,032. That summer he admitted that Truth and Consequences had "disappeared completely. . . all of a sudden one day came and they didn't meet anymore."

A Dallas cab driver named Raymond Cummings, having read that David Ferrie had denied being in Dallas in 1963, came forward. Between January and May 1963, Cummings said, he had picked up Lee Harvey Oswald at the Irving Continental Bus Station. A week later, he had picked up Oswald, David Ferrie and another man and driven them to Jack Ruby's club. William Gurvich handled Cummings' polygraph, with a cohort named Roy Jacob, who pronounced Cummings a liar. Cummings was sent back to Dallas. A decade later, Garrison knew Jacob could not be trusted and regretted that he had not accepted Cummings as a witness. Cummings had provided a "possibly good lead," he wrote, "but temporarily torpedoed by 'lie detector' test arranged by Gurvich." A Ruby employee named Clyde Limbough by then had revealed that he had seen Oswald in Ruby's office on three occasions, as the evidence that Oswald and Ruby were well acquainted accumulated.

Ferrie's death also brought to Jim Garrison E. Carl McNabb, who had flown those missions with Ferrie. McNabb thought he had better warn Garrison that in dealing with Ferrie, he was also dealing with the CIA. McNabb wished to convey from his own experience how closely the various intelligence agencies worked together: "One organization would loan me out to the other."

So lean that he seemed to be without a shadow and able to evaporate at will, pale, bone-thin, and chain-smoking, thriving on danger, McNabb, like Garrison, like Oswald, was another person in this story who never knew his father. Like Ferrie, he had flown under the Soviet radar, setting down on Cuban beaches by the dark of the moon, infiltrating and exfiltrating. Now McNabb joined Jim Garrison's efforts. He was nicknamed by volunteer and former FBI agent, William Turner "Jim" for Garrison and "Rose" for the Rose Bowl.

Reading of Ferrie's death, a young insurance salesman in Baton Rouge named Perry Raymond Russo wrote to Jim Garrison. The letter never reached him. Frightened that he might himself be arrested, Russo then contacted the Baton Rouge sheriff's office. Call a newspaper, he was told. "We will get him and it won't be long," Russo quoted Ferrie to the *Baton Rouge State-Times.* The February 24, 1967, headline read: "Local Man Says He Recalls Remark By David Ferrie About Getting JFK." The story of Russo's acquaintance with Ferrie appeared on a Friday. On Saturday, Moo Moo Sciambra drove up to Baton Rouge.

There is no doubt that Ferrie knew Russo. In Ferrie's self-serving statement defending himself against charges he had shielded the runaway Alexander Landry Jr., he refers to "one Perry Russo" as a "hard" character, who hangs out at a bar frequented by "known homosexuals, sex perverts and dope addicts," typical Ferrie charges against the young men whom he feared might do him harm.

On that Saturday, Russo told Moo Moo Sciambra about a gathering he had attended at the apartment of David Ferrie. The guests included an older man named "Clem Bertrand" and a figure named "Leon," who seemed to be Ferrie's roommate, so close did they appear. This man Russo identified as Lee Harvey Oswald. That Oswald had visited David Ferrie's apartment is corroborated by John Wilson, who also saw Oswald at Ferrie's apartment. That Oswald was sometimes called "Leon" is corroborated by Sylvia Odio's testimony, and by those to whom Oswald was introduced by Kent Courtney as "Leon."

That night the group sat discussing the ways and means of assassinating President Kennedy, Russo said. Both "Bertrand" and Ferrie discussed what their alibis would be for the day when Kennedy was shot. "Bertrand" would be in California, Ferrie at Southeastern Louisiana College at Hammond. All these men shared a hatred of Kennedy, including Russo, who had taunted one of his liberal Loyola professors when Kennedy died: "Your boy's been shot!" Russo gloated.

Now on Saturday afternoon, Moo Moo removed from his briefcase a sheaf of photographs. "Tell me anybody you know," he instructed Russo. Russo identified Ferrie at once. He knew Miguel Torres, Emilio Santana and a Cuban named Julian Busnedo. Oswald's picture appeared. "Yeah, I know him," Russo said. "That's David Ferrie's roommate, but he was a little dirtier. He was "unshaven" and had a "bushy beard." As soon as he had climbed the stairs to Ferrie's apartment that night, Ferrie had introduced him to "Leon Oswald."

"I knew the guy," Russo told Loyola classmates after the assassination.

The last photograph was of a gray-haired man.

"That's Bertrand." Russo said. "Clem Bertrand."

"*Clem* Bertrand?" Sciambra said. "It wasn't Clay?"

No, he was called "Clem," Russo insisted. When Sciambra asked whether Russo had seen this man with Ferrie on other occasions, Russo recounted how he had observed "Clem Bertrand" at Ferrie's gas station on Veteran's Highway in, he thought, 1965. Bertrand had been driving a 1959 Thunderbird convertible, an automobile Clay Shaw did own until 1964. He had also spotted Bertrand at the Nashville Avenue wharf when John F. Kennedy came to New Orleans to give a speech.

Sciambra invited Russo to New Orleans to talk to Jim Garrison. When Russo balked, Sciambra appealed to his "civic duty." By 9:30 Monday morning, February 27, 1967, Russo was at Tulane and Broad. Police artists worked to create a portrait of "Leon Oswald." Once stubble was sketched onto the face, Russo identified the figure as Lee Harvey Oswald.

But that was not the more important of the police composites sketched. Robert Buras, a police officer of unimpeachable integrity, worked as the artist. Buras' great talent at school had been in art, his favorite subject. Now, as Russo provided the description, Buras drew the person Russo called "Clem Bertrand." Finally Russo was satisfied.

What Buras had produced turned out to be an exact likeness of . . . Clay Shaw.

Through Perry Russo, Jim Garrison could establish that Clay Shaw had lied when he said he did not know David Ferrie; that Shaw knew Oswald; that Shaw was indeed the "Clay Bertrand" who had telephoned Dean Andrews; and that Shaw had been discussing the implementation of the assassination three months before the murder. Garrison wanted more details of that extraordinary gathering at 3330 Louisiana Avenue Parkway. That afternoon, at 3:28 P.M., in a session supervised by Dr. Nicholas Chetta, Russo was placed under sodium pentothal. The purpose, as Lou Ivon puts it, was "to add to what we already had." Sciambra did the questioning, mentioning the name "Bertrand," which he would not have done had Russo himself not already on Saturday mentioned that a person of that name had been present during the discussion of the assassination at Ferrie's apartment. He used the name "Clay," only for Russo to correct him. Russo insisted he had met not Clay Shaw, but "Clem Bertrand." He knew "a Bertrand and he is a queer."

Russo described "Clem Bertrand" as "a tall man with white kinky hair, sort of slender." At the Nashville Avenue wharf, he had stood out because he was the only person not looking at President Kennedy. Shaw was "hawking some kid who was not too far away from him," Russo said. At the gathering, Ferrie had said, "We are going to kill John F. Kennedy" and "It won't be long."

Dr. Chetta was persuaded: "There's not a chance at all that what this kid said is not true. It had to have happened." Another session and hypnosis would follow, but Russo never wavered in his story.

Yet Jim Garrison still was not satisfied. The next day Moo Moo drove Russo to 1313 Dauphine Street. Russo knocked at the door, and there he was, "Bertrand," with his big hands, chiseled face, and chiseled hair. By the end of the day, February 28th, 1967, Garrison requested two subpoenas. One was for Clay Shaw. The other was for James Lewallen, whom Russo had told him had been in bed together with Ferrie and Shaw. During a lie detector test, Lewallen had failed on the question of whether he had sex with either Ferrie or Shaw.

For Richard Billings, who continued his own investigation, Russo's friends Ken Carter, Niles Peterson, and Ted and Jerry Kirschenstein corroborated that Oswald had been the bearded "roommate" at Ferrie's. Garrison also had identifications of Shaw as Bertrand not only from the Cosimo's bartender but from Joe Oster, who said that Shaw, not David Ferrie, had been the man the levee board policeman had spotted with Oswald. Shaw was Bertrand, Oster said. In his interview with the Garrison office, Dauenhauer had revealed that Shaw lied. Shaw was also lying when he denied he knew Andrews. Gordon Novel told Jim Garrison that he and Dean

Andrews had met with Shaw about Novel's opening a food concession at the International Trade Mart. Novel knew as well that Andrews and Shaw had met in the steam room of the New Orleans Athletic Club.

There was further corroboration later that Shaw had been lying from a former Shaw secretary, Mrs. Jeff Hug, who said Andrews had visited Shaw's office one day and picked up an envelope of money. Shaw had also lied about his alibi. He had not been "en route" to San Francisco when the assassination occurred, but in bed at the St. Francis Hotel with a man named James Dondson. That Shaw was in San Francisco confirmed the essence of Russo's testimony.

Jim Garrison discovered that on November 11, 1963, Shaw had solicited a speaking engagement from the director of the San Francisco World Trade Center, Monroe Sullivan. That Shaw flew to San Francisco was very unusual, since, frightened of flying, he generally took the train. On the Monday after the assassination, Shaw appeared in Portland, Oregon, where he was scheduled to speak at an import-export conference, a "lone, grim, meditative figure." Only one other person turned up for the conference, canceled in the wake of the president's death. The evidence of Shaw's involvement in a conspiracy that led to the arrest of Lee Harvey Oswald was already considerable.

Garrison had lost David Ferrie. Now he wanted Clay Shaw arrested at once. This arrest, he hoped, would "detonate a chain reaction" and other witnesses would come forward. He waited at his refuge from the office's many leaks, the New Orleans Athletic Club, where he was interviewed by French journalist Bernard Giquel. "Through the famous Looking Glass, the black objects can appear to be white and the white objects can appear to be black," Garrison said. He did not volunteer much else.

On March 1st, David Ferrie was buried. His sole living relative, his brother Parmely, did not attend. On that same day, J. Edgar Hoover designated Jim Garrison "as a person not to be contacted without prior Bureau approval." Russo's story was already known to the Bureau. Division 5 ordered a review of files relating to "who knew where and with whom Oswald was living during this last month in New Orleans."

In the late morning, the sheriff handed Clay Shaw a subpoena. Lester Otillio again drove Shaw to Tulane and Broad "for questioning." The plan was that Shaw be given a lie detector test. "If he passes the box, we'll see what happens," Garrison said. While Shaw waited in a room with a one-way mirror, so that he could be observed without knowing it, Sciambra brought Russo in to make one final identification. Once more Russo identified Shaw as "Clem Bertrand." *Life* photographer Lynn Pelham photographed Shaw to determine his mood. Shaw seemed "very nervous." Then Sciambra questioned him, producing photographs of Dante Marochini and Lewallen.

"What would you say if we told you we had three witnesses proving you knew David Ferrie?" Sciambra said.

"I've never seen Ferrie in my life," Shaw said. He again insisted that he never met Oswald. Sciambra produced photographs of various Cubans, all of whom Shaw denied knowing. Then Sciambra requested that Shaw take a lie detector test, implying that he would be arrested if he declined. It was, John Volz says, a not uncommon practice to offer a suspect the option of taking a polygraph; if he was telling the truth, he might not be arrested. Later Shaw would claim he refused because he did not want his private life exposed, although his homosexuality was an open secret in New Orleans.

Shaw had assembled a legal team well before his March 1st arrest. With Edward F. Wegmann out of town, Salvatore Panzeca, whom Shaw describes in his diary as a "dark-haired Italian boy" with a "bantam cock attitude," arrived. *"Está maricón?"* Panzeca said, interviewing his client in the men's room. *"Sí,"* Shaw replied. Panzeca then told Jim Garrison he would not permit a lie detector test unless he could "review all the questions that would be asked." He preferred to wait until the next day, he said.

"You must be kidding," Garrison said. He planned to arrest Clay Shaw "for conspiracy to kill the president of the United States." In panic, Panzeca looked over at his Tulane classmate, Garrison assistant Al Oser. Oser looked grim.

Lou Ivon read Clay Shaw his rights at 5:30 on the afternoon of March 1st, arresting him for conspiracy, a "felony" committed "from April 24, 1963, the date of Lee Harvey Oswald's arrival in New Orleans, to November 22, 1963." William Gurvich, pleading it was his birthday, insisted on making the announcement to the press as Garrison staff members exchanged glances.

An hour later, Ivon had a search warrant ready. It listed the certainty of Shaw's being "Clay Bertrand," probable cause being the meeting recounted to Sciambra by Russo in Baton Rouge. At that event, Shaw had discussed the killing of President Kennedy as well as "the means and manner of carrying out this agreement." Ivon also swore under oath that the information offered by Russo under sodium pentothal only "verified, corroborated and reaffirmed his earlier statements."

At 8 P.M., Clay Shaw, handcuffed and with Edward Wegmann by his side, was brought to Central Lock-Up where he was finger-printed. The booking officer, Aloysius Habighorst, knew nothing about Jim Garrison's case and had never heard the name "Bertrand." While, as was customary, Wegmann waited in the door-way, Habighorst questioned Shaw as he typed the booking card. He was born in New Orleans, Shaw said, although in fact his birth-place was Kentwood. Shaw's CIA personnel file reveals the same error, as he maintained the consistency of his self-invention.

"What names other than Clay L. Shaw do you use?" Habighorst said. It was a routine question.

"Clay Bertrand," Shaw said. Habighorst typed "Clay Bertrand" onto the Bureau of Identification fingerprint card. The booking sheet also carried the "Clay Bertrand" alias. Habighorst sat openly in view and could not unobserved have copied the alias from the field arrest report written by Ivon. No one, including Clay Shaw's attorney, saw him refer to any other documents as he typed the booking card.

The search of Clay Shaw's house produced a chess set on a lac-quered board and a calorie counter, revealing that Shaw's interests in more than literary matters coincided with Jim Garrison's. Down-stairs, the walls were covered with pale green silk, the floors with Oriental carpets. Upstairs, it was as if an entirely different man lived here. Attached to the beams in the ceiling over the bed in the master bedroom, just as Dr. Lief's patient had described them, were huge hooks with chains fitted with wrist straps hanging free, hooks large enough to hang a human body.

On the ceiling were bloody palm prints. Many hands had been suspended there, William Alford thought, and he wondered whether anyone had died or been seriously injured in this room. A black gown bore "whip marks," William Gurvich noticed. Five whips bore traces of blood. A cat-o'-nine-tails sat in the closet.

"Let's dust and lift those prints," Alford said. Ivon refused. The boss didn't want to make Shaw's sexuality an issue.

At 11:15, Garrison's investigators emerged from 1313 Dauphine Street with five cardboard boxes containing ropes, whips, chains, marble phalluses, the black cape, a black hood and black lacquer Asian-type sandals with white satin linings that had never touched pavement, belying the later contention that these were Mardi Gras costumes. Shaw's notebooks contained the names of European aristocrats.

Jim Garrison sent the phalluses, whips and chains to Robert Heath, the head of psychiatry at Tulane. Heath concluded that Shaw's motive for becoming involved in a conspiracy to murder President Kennedy "could very possibly have been rooted in his "sadistic, homosexual abnormality," a thesis Jim Garrison rejected.

"I don't want that factor to enter this case," Garrison reiterated, even as, privately, he called Shaw a "Phi Beta Kappa sadist." Nor would he investigate whether violent sex crimes had emanated from behind those red doors at 1313 Dauphine Street. He did not pursue complaints against Shaw stemming from sexual evenings when violent practices were rumored to have gotten out of hand.

Alford's suspicions about those bloody handprints had been well founded. Shaw's maid, Virginia Johnson, would reveal that there had been a "mysterious death or killing of somebody in the house," and although the coroner had come to pick up the body, there had been no police investigation. Al Oser discovered that only two weeks before Shaw's arrest, the police were called "because Clay Shaw, a white male, and two colored males were on the patio naked and using wine bottles on each other."

Among the first people Shaw notified after his arrest was Fred Lee Crisman, Tommy Beckham's mentor. He was in trouble, Shaw told fellow CIA operative Crisman. In addition to their political affiliations, Shaw and Crisman had sexual proclivities in common. Crisman would describe himself as "being sadistic in sexual practice preferences."

Clay Shaw's friends at once insisted that Jim Garrison had arrested him only to further his own career. Garrison denied this charge vehemently: "I'd have to be a terribly cynical and corrupt man to place another human being on trial for conspiracy to murder the president of the United States just to gratify my political ambition," he said. He told CBS reporter Joe Wershba, "I have nothing personal against this man. I have more in common with Clay Shaw than with many members of my staff. He loves music, he writes plays. . . ."

Yet even Garrison's own friends wondered at the arrest of the respectable director of the International Trade Mart, a socialite who escorted rich women, like funeral home heiress Muriel Bultman, nicknamed "the fruit fly," to opera and theater; Shaw the playwright; Shaw who flew businessmen to Latin America to help make their fortunes; Shaw the war hero. Could this man have been involved in the murder of the president?

"Is this another Wilmer?" Jack Bremermann wrote jokingly to Garrison, referring to Wilmer Thomas whom Garrison had put up for Tulane student body president. He received no reply. G. Wray Gill, according to David Ferrie's godson Morris Brownlee, seemed troubled, exhibiting "personal fear."

Damage control began at once. David Chandler invented a story that Donald V. Organ, who had represented Garrison in the defamation suit brought by the judges, had telephoned Shaw and offered to represent him for free. Organ says he never spoke to Shaw in his life.

Then a more persistent rumor took wing. Two weeks before Shaw's arrest, Garrison and his wife, Liz, had been at dinner at Brennan's with Charlie Ward and his wife, Lenore. They were seated in the middle of the room, as Garrison preferred.

He had no great admiration for Frank Sinatra, Garrison said. Sammy Davis Jr. was the most talented member of the "rat pack."

"Say what you may," Lenore Ward began, attempting to enliven the evening with the worst thing she could think of saying. "Sammy is a good entertainer, but he can't carry a tune. He's nothing but a one-eyed nigger Jew!"

Jim Garrison, she knew, was sometimes naive and always took people at face value.

"You're the most bigoted person I've ever met!" Garrison told Mrs. Ward.

"I don't think that's quite fair," Liz Garrison said, and Garrison threw his glass of water in her face. Retaliating, Liz threw her water back at him. He threw wine; she threw wine.

Seated just beyond Lenore Ward was a table of men. A *Look* magazine writer was dining with Jack Sawyer, who directed the news for the ABC affiliate, WVUE. At this table as well was Clay Shaw.

"He threw a glass of wine," Shaw said. He got up and went over to the Garrison table. "I know you're the district attorney, but you're no gentleman," Shaw said.

Jim Garrison looked at him, unperturbed.

Liz departed, ordering Lenore, "You go back and sit down and say, 'you don't scare me, you bastard.'"

Back home, Garrison showed the Wards the photographs he had taken at the Dachau concentration camp. It was his way of explaining why he could not tolerate any form of racism or bigotry.

But the story hit the streets. Shaw had "humiliated" Garrison, it was said, and this was the reason why Shaw had been arrested, a story Shaw would repeat four years later: "On one occasion, I saw him throw a glass of wine in his wife's face and it's very difficult to forgive anybody who has seen you at your most undignified." Reporter Rosemary James, who numbered Pershing Gervais among her important sources, placed Ella Brennan at Shaw's table, where Brennan says she had never been. Wilmer Thomas, that same Tulane student candidate, says Liz had thrown red wine only for Jim to duck, so that the wine landed on Shaw's white linen suit. In another embellishment, Jim Garrison, drunk, had threatened to "get" Shaw, a threat Mrs. Ward says did not happen.

In Jack Sawyer's memory, Shaw never got up from his seat.

Shaw was indubitably "Clay Bertrand." The FBI knew it if only because informant Lawrence Schiller reported that three homosexual sources in New Orleans and two in San Francisco had confirmed that Shaw was "Clay Bertrand." Between fifteen and twenty "independent and unrelated homosexual sources in New Orleans" had mentioned the name "Clay Bertrand." The FBI told Schiller it had developed handwriting comparisons between Clay Bertrand and Shaw. Before long, the CIA would create a document including both names, "Shaw, Clay" and "Bertrand, Clay."

Jim Garrison was not so fortunate as the FBI in garnering witnesses willing to testify on the record that they knew Clay Shaw as "Clay Bertrand." Pat O'Brien's chanteuse Barbara Bennett had turned on the television and seen Shaw being arrested: "There's Clay Bertrand!" she shouted out. Shaw was a frequent visitor to Pat O'Brien's, and Bennett his sometime party guest. She did not come forward. Nor did her friend, Quarter businesswoman Rickey Planche, who owned a dress shop at the corner of Pirates Alley and Royal. Only when she saw "Clay Bertrand" on television, Planche says, did she, too, learn that his real name was Clay Shaw. Neither Barbara Bennett nor Rickey Planche contacted Jim Garrison. "We were intelligent women," Planche explains. Telling what they knew could only put their lives in jeopardy, they believed.

Fred Leemans Jr., owner of a Canal Street Turkish bath, saw "Clay Bertrand" with a fellow named "Lee" who was "always popping off about something." Leemans wanted money for his testimony. Shaw's maid Virginia Johnson told acquaintances but would not admit to Garrison investigators that she saw a letter addressed to "Clay Bertrand."

Yet potential witnesses kept surfacing. One Valentine Ashworth insisted he had seen Oswald with "Clay Bertrand" and was able to identify a photograph of Shaw. Near Baker, Garrison's driver, police officer Steve Bordelon, found a witness who said Shaw had been asking about jobs for people using the name "Clay Bertrand." In

Abita Springs, a homosexual named Greg Donnelly knew Shaw, sometimes as Bertrand, sometimes as "Le Verne" or "Lavergne," Shaw's middle name. In California, William Turner said he discovered a man named Thomas Breitner who claimed that on the day after the assassination Shaw was introduced to him as "Bertrand."

In the process of corroborating the identification of Shaw as Bertrand, and of connecting Shaw with Oswald and Ferrie, Garrison inevitably uncovered details of Clay Shaw's sexual life. Many in New Orleans knew Shaw as the head of a "disciplinary crew of queers," as businessman Charles Franks, who traveled with Shaw to Latin America, put it. If a homosexual called attention to the group by being arrested, Shaw, dressed as a French executioner, held a tribunal with punishment dispensed in a sadomasochistic ritual. The culprit was chained and lashed with the cat-o'-nine-tails. There was a sign in Murphy's Barber Shop on Iberville: "Hair cuts—xxx. Shave—xx. Whippings—See Clay Shaw for prices on request."

Years later Joseph Newbrough would talk about how when David Ferrie was arrested on one of his "crimes against nature" charges, bail bondsman Hardy Davis had been paid by the "Clement Bertrand Society." The name derived from Pope Clement V (hence "Clem" Bertrand), whose surname was "Bertrand D'Agout or De Got." In the fourteenth-century church, this pope had sheltered homosexuals. Clay Shaw was Pope Clement V's spiritual descendant, offering legal help to homosexuals. The FBI soon uncovered the "Clement Bertrand Society" with Bertrand "the name adopted by Clay Shaw and Doug Jones and other Uptown homosexuals."

Under the name "Clay Bertrand," the Clement Bertrand Society rented an apartment on Chartres Street. It was a mail drop for pornographic literature and photographs, and for those transactions for gay men caught in the web of an intolerant legal system. Cash by courier was the means of payment to help these young men. An envelope bearing the name "Clay Bertrand" and this Chartres address was spotted by a Bureau informant. The postal carrier reported the delivery of a letter to "Clay Bertrand" to Garrison's former girlfriend, Evelyn Jahncke.

Lee Harvey Oswald and David Ferrie figured prominently in Shaw's sexual pursuits. The Reverend Raymond Broshears of the Universal Life Church told Jim Garrison that one day Ferrie introduced Shaw to him as "Clara" at Dixie's Bar of Music. Ferrie had confided that Oswald did not kill President Kennedy. His own assignment had been to fly two of the assassins from "south of

Houston on down through Central and South America." Shaw was close to Kent Courtney, Ferrie had told him, corroborating other witnesses. Shaw knew arms dealer, Richard Lauchli. Ferrie had also introduced Broshears to Kerry Thornley, with whom Broshears had sex. "I had sex with Thornley and I know his slender hips," Broshears bragged. Back in California, Broshears sent back praise for the professionalism of Louis Ivon: "Mr. Ivon is one of the best cops I've ever met," Broshears wrote, "in the South, that is."

Evidence accumulated and continued to accumulate that, despite Shaw's denials, he certainly was close to David Ferrie. One day Guy Banister asked Joe Newbrough to get Clay Shaw on the telephone. Then he handed the receiver to Ferrie, a scene Newbrough did not convey to Jim Garrison. A Shaw secretary named Aura Lee told a group of doctors at Ochsner that "she had seen Ferrie go into Shaw's office on a number of occasions," that Ferrie had privileged access. Herb Wagner never came forward to tell Jim Garrison that Shaw had cosigned a loan for Ferrie, although he did identify Shaw as possibly the "big fellow who walked with a very slight limp . . . who used to go around Dave's service station."

There were others, such as businessman L. P. Davis, who called Charlie Ward to report that Ferrie had made a reservation for Shaw to go fishing on Free Mason Island. At the fishing camp the owners identified Ferrie and Shaw, remembering them because the trip had occurred so close to the time of Hurricane Betsy in 1965. In Hammond, the owner of a funeral home, Carroll S. Thomas, a friend of Clay Shaw's, told the FBI he met Ferrie through Shaw; he wondered how Shaw, so conservative, could have been involved with someone so "left wing" as Oswald. Even Layton Martens admitted to Jim Garrison that Oswald "apparently knew someone by the name of Clay."

Some of Shaw's sexual partners drew a highly graphic picture of his proclivities. A Northwestern University professor named Henry Lesnick persuaded a young friend named David Logan to contact Jim Garrison about his having been Clay Shaw's lover. Logan had seen Shaw and Ferrie together at a party and at Dixie's Bar of Music, where Barbara Bennett also ran into Shaw. Bennett had spotted Oswald there as well. Oswald seemed to "want to associate with gay guys."

After dinner, Shaw took Logan up to the bedroom where the hooks extended from the ceiling beams. He asked Logan to beat him with a whip, then "to shit in his mouth and pee in his mouth and all over him." Logan's testimony is in part corroborated by his knowledge that Shaw had only one nipple. Another witness described

Shaw defecating over him on glass, and also said Shaw had one nipple.

Yet another witness, a Texas inmate, imprisoned on a crime-against-nature charge, had been introduced to "Clay Bertrand" by Eugene Davis for "sexual purposes." Bertrand "wasn't the butchest thing in the world," Willie Morris reported. He also identified a short, fat man he had seen with Bertrand as Jack Ruby. On whether he knew Morris, Eugene Davis was evasive: "I wouldn't say yes and I wouldn't say no," he said while his lawyer, G. Wray Gill, looked on. But Morris' testimony was confirmed by the doorman of The Court of Two Sisters, Leander D'Avy. He had seen Oswald, he had seen Ferrie with Eugene Davis, and Oswald had asked to see "Clay Bertrand."

In December 1968, still refusing to admit he had met Oswald, Eugene Davis did reveal that he knew Shaw and had seen him in a "long black car," perhaps a Cadillac or a Chrysler. FBI informant Betty Parrott knew Davis had been fired as night manager at The Court of Two Sisters for bringing Oswald upstairs. Only in the late 1970s would D'Avy tell the whole story. Oswald had come up and asked "if there was a Clay Bertrand working there." D'Avy didn't know. Then Eugene Davis had ambled by.

"Send this young man in. I'll talk to him," Davis said. A few moments later, Davis told a waitress. "He's just come from behind the Iron Curtain!" D'Avy had seen Shaw talking with Eugene Davis and Oswald and Ferrie, all together in the upstairs apartment.

Jim Garrison was to use none of these witnesses. "Throughout our trial," he would say, "in every thing I have ever written and in every public statement I have ever made—I never once made any reference to Clay Shaw's alleged homosexuality." It had only been in his attempt to identify Shaw as Bertrand that details of Clay Shaw's sexual life had been exposed. In the public proceedings of the district attorney's office regarding Shaw, his homosexuality was never mentioned.

At a playful moment in December 1966, Clay Shaw signed the guest book at the VIP lounge at the Eastern Airlines terminal at Moisant International Airport: "Clay Bertrand." There was a witness, Ronald R. Raymond, a sergeant on the Kenner police force, who confirmed that Shaw was there on that day. Then he told Jim Garrison that he "did not want to be involved."

Exhibiting greater courage was the hostess of the VIP room, Mrs. Jessie Parker. Among Parker's assignments was to request that people who entered the VIP room sign the registration book.

Mrs. Parker identified Clay Shaw as the man who on December 14th had signed "Clay Bertrand." Numa Bertel checked her out since she was the seamstress for a family he knew and worked for an established funeral home. When Mrs. Parker's statement for Jim Garrison leaked out, she began to receive telephone calls threatening, among other things, that she would lose custody of her little boy. Numa reassured her in his avuncular way. Mrs. Parker passed her polygraph, as Jim Garrison, with photographs of the guest book in hand, began to search for corroborating witnesses.

On the same page as Clay Bertrand's appeared the signature of a businessman named Alfred J. Moran, a member of the board of the International Trade Mart. Well-acquainted with Clay Shaw, Moran was also a CIA operative, part of the clandestine services under the "Deputy Director for Plans," Richard Helms. Like Shaw, Moran wore the hat of two CIA components and was an asset of the Domestic Contact Service. Moran served the Miami CIA station, JMWAVE, too. Only nine days before Jim Garrison reached him, he had performed a task to the satisfaction of his Miami CIA handlers. In New Orleans, Moran was so close to the CIA field office that he was the "personal surety" on Hunter Leake's notarial bond, testifying to the solvency of the field office.

Jim Garrison sent James Alcock to interview Moran. A handwriting expert has confirmed that the signature "Clem Bertrand" was written by Shaw, Alcock said, Perry Russo's testimony obviously in mind. The signature reads "Clay."

He knew Shaw "fairly well," Moran admitted, but he was positive Shaw was *not* at the airport on that day. He would have recalled his presence since he disliked him so much. He approved of Jim Garrison's investigation 100 percent, Moran told Alcock heartily. The only true statement Alfred Moran made to Alcock that day was that, offended by Shaw's homosexuality and objecting to the CIA's enlistment of homosexuals, he disliked Shaw intensely.

The next day, November 14, 1967, Moran hosted a cocktail party. Among his guests was the CIA's Hunter Leake. He had been contacted by a member of Jim Garrison's staff, Moran confided. They had the names of people who had been at the VIP room on the day Shaw signed the guest book as "Clay Bertrand." I saw Clay Shaw that day, Moran admitted to Leake. He despised Shaw, he added. He had "objected strenuously" when Shaw was appointed Managing Director of the Trade Mart because "of his alleged homosexual tendencies and consequent susceptibility to blackmail."

"Jim Garrison has an ironclad case," Moran said.

All Leake registered, as he reported to his superior, Lloyd Ray, were the words "ironclad case." He forgot that Moran had, dutifully, despite his personal abhorrence of Shaw, not told Alcock the truth. Ray wrote to CIA headquarters for instructions. At once CIA ran a check on Moran and examined his complex history with the Agency.

The CIA now turned to protecting its operative Shaw, who had revealed so carelessly that he was the Bertrand who had telephoned Dean Andrews for Oswald. First, it had to be determined whether Moran "knows Jim Garrison personally? Is he favorably disposed toward him, his staff or his investigation?" So sensitive was the matter of Moran and Shaw that it was handled by the CIA's General Counsel, Lawrence Houston himself.

Deciding to cleanse the record, Houston chose the strategy of neutralizing Lloyd Ray's memo of November 15th in which he had put into writing Moran's having told Leake that Garrison had "an ironclad case" against Shaw. The files had now to be sanitized, altered so as to contradict and deny the veracity of Ray's original memo.

Houston was not overly worried. Moran would certainly do whatever the CIA asked since he had "always been most helpful and cooperative with the Agency." Houston would cleanse the files and erase the Lloyd Ray memorandum by having Moran explicitly deny that he had seen Shaw in the VIP room. Further, Moran was to declare his certainty that Shaw and Bertrand "were two different people." The entire enterprise reveals of course that Houston knew perfectly well that Shaw was Clay Bertrand.

A duck hunt in which both Moran and Leake were already scheduled to take part would be the venue for Leake's extracting Moran's denial that he had seen Shaw at the VIP room. Then a slipped disk sent Moran to bed, canceling his attendance at the duck hunt. Under the pretext that Leake required Moran's signature on the annual affidavit of solvency for the CIA field office, a bedside visit was planned. Houston wanted this visit to be "as soon as propitious." Leake was to "obtain casually the additional information desired."

On December 11th, Leake appeared in Moran's bedroom. He poured forth a tale of Jim Garrison's absurdities, fortified by press reports. Garrison has "flipped his lid," Leake said, referring to Garrison's having considered whether a shooter at Dealey Plaza had been concealed in a sewer manhole.

Two days later, Lloyd Ray reported to Lawrence Houston that the mission had been accomplished. The file had been cleansed. Moran was on the record as having denied that he ever "independently" said he saw Shaw at the VIP room that day. He had, rather, only repeated Alcock's assertion that a handwriting expert had made a positive identification. Moran asserted that he had no independent knowledge of Shaw's having been at the VIP room. Having told the truth to Leake at the cocktail party, now he lied.

Ray infused his final memorandum to Houston on the subject with a defense of Clay Shaw. It is "inconceivable to us," he wrote for the record, that Clay Shaw would use an alias at the VIP room since he was so well known to the Eastern Airlines officials. Ray was, however, worried. Should Moran and Arthur Q. Davis, an architect, whose name appears directly above Shaw's in the registration book, identify their signatures, and should a handwriting expert also identify "Clay Bertrand" as Clay Shaw, "then Clay Shaw is in serious trouble."

Had Clay Shaw's use of the alias Clay Bertrand not implicated Shaw in the Kennedy assassination, Houston would not have felt the need to sanitize CIA files with lies. Nor would the CIA have enlisted such highly placed personnel as Houston in an effort to sabotage Jim Garrison's investigation.

AN OPERATIVE
IN ACTION

9

It is fair to conclude that "Centro Mondiale" is not your basic civic organization.

—Jim Garrison

O N THE MORNING OF March 2, 1967, the day after Jim Garrison arrested Clay Shaw, attorney-general designate Ramsey Clark, about to replace Nicholas Katzenbach, who succeeded Bobby Kennedy, phoned Cartha DeLoach at the FBI. Did the FBI know anything about Clay Shaw?

Shaw's name came up in our investigation in December 1963, "Deke" told Clark. Few documents survive of this early FBI interest in Shaw, but for a suggestive fragment signed by Hoover from the "Latent Fingerprint Section" (Identification Division). Addressed to the SAC in San Francisco and dated December 5, 1963, it requests an examination of "five train tickets" from Southern Pacific. That this document was connected to an investigation of Clay Shaw is reflected in the fact that a copy went not only to Dallas, but also to New Orleans.

A reporter that afternoon asked Clark whether Shaw had been "checked and found clear, more or less."

"That's right. That's true," Clark said. Information Officer Cliff Sessions added that the Justice Department knew "that Mr. Bertrand and Mr. Shaw were the same man."

For this leak, Deke chastised Sessions mercilessly. "This is the danger of telling Clark anything," Hoover raged. "He can't refrain from talking to the press." Clark says now he would never have made that statement about Shaw "without prior knowledge," had DeLoach not briefed him that morning. "Manipulated" by the FBI, as he puts it, Clark was kept in the dark as well by CIA's Richard Helms who, he has said, "lied to me about Oswald." In June, the Justice Department issued a statement denying that Shaw had ever been investigated by the FBI in connection with the assassination.

"I never used any alias in my life," Shaw said in a press conference on March 2nd. "I did not know Harvey Lee Oswald." He had never met "Mr. Dave Ferrie." Nor did he "know Dean Andrews."

He was "wound up as tight as a dimestore toy," one reporter noted. Alberto Fowler thought Shaw was "quite calm and assured." It had to be "because he feels that high-ranking government officials are involved and will see that no harm comes to him." Alberto had now concluded that "federal employees acting on their own were involved in the plot."

Clay Shaw claimed that he was a liberal, a "great admirer" of John F. Kennedy. But Shaw was no liberal, as a young professor at the Tulane School of Law and future Garrison assistant Ralph Slovenko had discovered in April 1957. Slovenko was giving his first public talk, his subject, the nationalization of the Suez Canal. With no treaty in force, Slovenko argued, Egyptian president Gamal Nasser had been justified in seizing the canal and using the profits from its operation to finance the Aswan Dam, which would "benefit the entire population."

The assigned commentator then rose to his feet, his steel blue eyes flat. Stone-faced, supercilious, he treated Slovenko with contempt.

"Nasser had no business" nationalizing the Suez Canal, Clay Shaw said. Slovenko's argument was "a lot of tripe."

Shaw's political friends were extreme conservatives, like L. P. Davis of the Citizens' Council. He was seen with anti-Castro Cubans, and aided a contract pilot named Leslie Norman Bradley. Shaw was "helping us," Bradley said. CIA files term Bradley an "unscrupulous adventurer." Another of Shaw's acquaintances was "Bob Sands," who raised money for the sabotage of Cuba.

Shaw did maintain a liberal facade. His conversation ranged from French Quarter architectural renovations to the theater and he numbered among his acquaintances playwright Tennessee Williams and novelist Gore Vidal. One night Vidal got into an argument with one of Shaw's professor friends named Don Scheuler, who had invoked the "Platonic verities," an idea Vidal greeted with scorn. In mock exasperation, Shaw threw up his hands.

"I believe in beauty and ecstasy," Shaw said.

Although he consorted with some socialites, Clay Shaw was not someone of whom Uptown society approved. Alberto Fowler's niece says that because of his lower-middle-class origins, her family would never have seen Shaw socially. His racial origins, too, seemed questionable. "They say I'm an octoroon," Shaw readily admitted. Asked if Shaw could ever have been Rex at Mardi Gras, Jim Garrison quipped, "He would have a better chance of becoming the King of England."

When the Duke and Duchess of Windsor visited New Orleans, Clay Shaw handled the protocol. All the ex-Rexes wanted to meet the Windsors. Should they bow? Yet they were kings no less than he, perhaps more so. Perhaps he should bow to *them*. It was Clay Shaw's favorite New Orleans story.

Clay Lavergne Shaw was born on March 17, 1913, in the hamlet of Kentwood in "bloody" Tangipahoa Parish where the Mob disposed of inconvenient corpses. His grandfather, named Clay Shaw, was a six foot six inch sheriff, wounded twice in action. Grandfather Clay Shaw killed several people as he rose to the rank of federal marshal. "I want you to know I don't have any of those tendencies. I wouldn't hurt a fly," grandson joked to Dr. Harold Lief, then his tenant. "If there were no guns," Shaw told Jesse Core, who urged that he be armed after a house he was renting was vandalized, "the world would be a better place." But when the district attorney's investigators searched Shaw's house, they did discover a gun. Shaw's father was a lumberman and a federal revenue agent.

When he was five, Shaw's mother took him to live in New Orleans. Shaw's play "Memorial," written under the pen name of "Allen White," for his two maternal grandmothers, enjoys autobiographical resonances. He reveals himself to have been the victim of an emotionally suffocating mother, who tries to bind her son to her "so strongly that he could never get free." He grew up an overweight schoolboy, the butt of bullies, big, yet timid and helpless.

In the eleventh grade, Clay Shaw dropped out of Warren Easton High School, an institution attended later by Lee Harvey Oswald. Shaw escaped to New York where he worked for Western Union and for a lecture bureau. In November 1942, he enlisted in the Army, which placed him in the medical corps. "I didn't even know what a fracture was," he said later. Two days before graduating from Officer Candidate School, he slipped trying to swing on a rope across a ditch. Rather than risk losing his rank as a second lieutenant, he didn't consult a doctor, and would limp for the rest of his life.

Military intelligence discovered him. Never having seen a day of combat, Shaw rose to the rank of major as aide-de-camp to General Charles O. Thrasher, who was in charge of transferring German prisoners of war to the French. Thrasher was a man of such cruel disposition that he horrified the French liaison officer. Appalled by Thrasher's callous treatment of the German prisoners in his charge, Major William H. Haight swore out a deposition against him for the inhumane means by which he handled and transferred the Germans, who were being starved to death and were in a condition "worse than the former German concentration camps."

Shaw himself moved with ease through an Army Counterintelligence group called the "Special Operations Section." Still without having stepped onto a battlefield to face enemy fire, he was to receive a Croix de Guerre, and a Legion of Merit from France, and a similar decoration from Belgium.

Returning to New Orleans, he joined a CIA proprietary, the Mississippi Shipping Company, run by a fellow homosexual, Theodore Brent. When the Agency sponsored the first of its international trade centers in New Orleans (there would be another in Rome), its "principal backer and developer" was a lawyer named Lloyd J. Cobb, who had received his Covert Security Clearance from the CIA in October 1953. Among the consulates located at the International Trade Mart was that of Belgium, later to figure in this story.

The International Trade Mart was run by CIA operatives, its public relations handled by David G. Baldwin, who later would acknowledge his own "CIA connections." Baldwin's successor, Jesse Core, was also with the CIA. It was a matter of saving the Agency "shoe leather," Core would say. The Trade Mart donated money to CIA asset Ed Butler's INCA. Every consulate within its bowels was bugged.

Arriving for work his first day dressed in his major's uniform, Shaw became a spokesman for trade, decrying tariffs and urging Soviet bloc countries to seek economic independence, although he had no formal training in economics whatsoever. He hired fellow single men and could be spotted driving in his Thunderbird convertible filled with boys, their blond hair blowing in the wind. When Theodore Brent died, he left Shaw a legacy, a legal defense fund for gay men that Shaw dispensed as "Clay Bertrand."

Shaw had begun to work for the CIA at Mississippi Shipping, paid one hundred dollars a month, according to Guy Banister's brother, Ross. Eventually he bought an apartment house in Madrid. His official Domestic Contact Record breaks off in 1956, even as it was standard procedure to deny an agent or asset's employment for *at least* the preceding five years. When a reporter told William Gaudet that the CIA had given the end date of his service as 1955, as one document suggests, Gaudet laughed and corrected him: it was 1969, he said on that occasion.

As managing director of the International Trade Mart, Shaw moved on to CIA operations, pursuing initiatives outlined by the Agency. Far from being a mere informant providing information, he was enlisted for specific assignments. The use of the present tense in a 1967 document suggests he continued to be an operative with the Domestic Operations Division of Clandestine Services, his new number 402897-A, into the 1960s. Richard Helms' assistant, Thomas Karamessines, told the CIA's Victor Marchetti that Shaw was a top CIA operative in New Orleans.

In 1976, with the HSCA investigation looming, J. Walton Moore wrote to the head of the Domestic Collection Division, formerly Domestic Contact, for help in handling "the exposure of Shaw's connections with CIA." It was no simple matter because CIA had papered the file, insisting that Shaw's contact "was limited to Domestic Contact activities." Moore knew that this was not the truth. "We cannot determine the nature of DCD's relationship with Shaw from our files," he pleaded.

As the years passed, Shaw's CIA jackets changed. File #33412 was destroyed, and Shaw became #12274. His security clearance number also changed as he enjoyed the highest of six CIA categories. To unravel Shaw's Agency relationships, following his "five agency" clearance on March 23, 1949, Domestic Contact applied to the Security Branch. In 1952, Shaw had been cleared for project QKENCHANT, along with E. Howard Hunt and Monroe Sullivan, his San Francisco host during the weekend of the assassination. QKENCHANT authorized trusted CIA personnel for clearance to recruit or enlist "civilians," people not officially with the Agency, to discuss "projects, activities and possible relationships." It supported "an array of CIA activities." An author named Hugh Chisholm McDonald was cleared under QKENCHANT to be "used for intelligence procurement."

QKENCHANT clearance meant you were a safe contact, and could be utilized as a "cut out," with the CIA giving you only a certain amount of information. You might be told to contact someone you didn't know. You might not know the planner of an operation, or its ultimate sponsors. You might know something about who is running an operation, but not everything. But QKENCHANT, in CIA's own words, was an "operational project."

AN OPERATIVE IN ACTION

Shaw, then, could recruit other agents, granting them security approvals. His QKENCHANT records resided not with Domestic Contact, but in the Agency's "operational files." Shaw used his QKENCHANT clearance "to plan or coordinate CIA activities, as well as to "initiate relationships with . . . non-Agency persons or institutions." Shaw was part of the Agency's clandestine services with Covert Security Approval, working under cover.

One day Garrison assistant Richard Burnes placed a telephone call to Clay Shaw's house, and asked to speak to "John Shaw."

"This is Clay Shaw speaking," Shaw said.

"Does a John Shaw live at this address?" Burnes persisted.

"Who are you from? Who sent you?" Shaw demanded. Burnes, a tough and savvy lawyer, concluded that Shaw was in the habit "of receiving calls from persons whom he did not know, and who had been sent to him." It was a peculiar form of salutation at the least, Richard Billings had to agree.

Among those whom Shaw recruited under his QKENCHANT clearance was Guy Banister. The date was August 1960. A recently uncovered "Secret" CIA document reveals that Guy Banister Associates, Inc., was of interest to the Agency "for QKENCHANT purposes." The QKENCHANT recruiter in New Orleans was, of course, Clay Shaw, no matter that Shaw steered clear of Banister and his operation publicly. The Agency went on to do a thorough investigation of Banister, including his having been fired by the New Orleans Police Department. A complex credit check was part of the vetting of Banister. The Banister investigation was completed in September out of Los Angeles, where "Central Cover Staff" (CCS) material was routinely processed, including the investigation of potential front companies and people, like Banister, that CIA thought it might utilize.

Shaw also assisted in helping the CIA maintain the fabrication that it was involved only in the gathering of intelligence abroad. In that capacity, he hosted the appearance in New Orleans of General Charles Cabell. "The Central Intelligence Agency is not a policy-making agency. We merely serve the policy makers," Cabell told his audience. As moderator of that event, Shaw permitted no questions from the floor.

Shaw's first assignments for the Agency involved reporting on with whom Trade Mart tenants were doing business. By 1955, he had traveled to a Czechoslovak engineering exhibition at Erno, assigned as "a CIA observer," a trip for which he was paid separately. Czech intelligence activities in the United States were his specialty, as he located space for an obvious front, a New Orleans "Czecho-slovakian Industrial Fair." That year William P. Burke, then chief of the New Orleans field office, wrote to the Contact Division that he would be compromising a "Y" number ("YY" meant radio communications) should he refer them to "the reports supported by Clay Shaw."

Shaw did corporate spying for the agency, inquiring whether the Hall Mack Refining Company was an active client of the John A. Marshall Company in chemical manufacturing. Shaw found out. In 1956, he spied for the CIA on mercury producers in Spain and Italy, "to ascertain for us the extent of the Spanish and Italian mercury stocks on hand." CIA furnished him with names and addresses to make his inquiries. Another assignment led Shaw to attempt to thwart the use of West German money to help East Germany and Czechoslovakia increase their exports to the West, thereby earning them dollars. So, General Cabell's assertions notwithstanding, he helped the CIA in its policy making.

In Latin America, Shaw sought intelligence on revolutionary movements. One assignment was to ascertain whether the local military was loyal to the CIA. In Peru, he explored the nature of the opposition to the Odria regime, then urged the CIA to oppose a Lt. Colonel named Alfonso Llosa, Minister of Public Works, who was a possible successor to Odria. In Chile, Shaw was assigned to search for "indications of serious unrest, particularly in the armed forces."

In Nicaragua, his job was to assess the strength of General Somoza. In Argentina, the CIA asked him to gauge the political influence of Peron supporter Juan Pistarini, whose relations with the army and with labor were of concern to the Agency. Shaw reported that Peron and his wife Evita "are jealous of each other's power and . . . maintain two separate and independent political organizations." He cautioned the Agency: that Pistarini was Peron's "most influential and valuable supporter would seem to be a bit exaggerated." Always Shaw was briefed in advance and given areas to investigate in each country to which he traveled under the cover of fostering trade.

Jim Garrison could discover no documents clarifying his suspicion of Shaw's Agency relationships. Empirically, from observing him with Oswald and Ferrie, both also intelligence assets, and from Perry Russo's testimony, Garrison concluded that Shaw had been on assignment for the Agency in the implementation of the plot to kill President Kennedy. Shaw's functions for CIA, Garrison decided, even without reviewing Shaw's CIA files, were various and included covert action, spying, and supervising CIA proprietaries at the Trade Mart.

Garrison did uncover a Louisiana-based CIA operation in which Shaw had been involved. Shaw had flown to Cuba in 1959 as part of a CIA project to refine Cuban nickel at a Louisiana refinery in Plaquemines Parish through a firm called Freeport Sulphur. The pilot was David Ferrie. On board was a Freeport director named Charles A. Wright. When the embargo against Fidel Castro took effect and Castro prevented Freeport from owning land in Cuba, CIA reversed the plan, creating a triangular trade. The raw nickel would journey from Cuba to Canada, and then to Louisiana. In late 1961 or early 1962, Ferrie flew Shaw again for Freeport Sulphur, this time to Canada. Shaw sat at the back of the plane. Beside him was a stocky Cuban with a dark complexion.

Garrison's source was one Jules Ricco Kimble, both a Klan member and an FBI informant on the Klan. Kimble was also a CIA informant and a CIA operative, recruited for special assignments. He knew Ferrie, Kimble told Garrison. In fact, Jack M. Helm, the Imperial Dragon himself, had asked Kimble to drive him to Ferrie's house the day after Ferrie's death. Helm had emerged with a briefcase.

That A. Roswell Thompson, another Klan eminence in this story, was close to Ferrie, to Beckham, and to the entire Louisiana assassination contingent, adds credibility to Kimble's testimony. It didn't matter to Jim Garrison that the Clay Shaw trial had come and gone by the time Kimble came forward. Investigating the assassination was his lifelong cause.

He had met David Ferrie at the Golden Lantern bar, Kimble claimed. Ferrie had introduced him to Shaw, and it was then that Ferrie invited him to join them on that flight to Canada. The Cuban with Shaw was "kind of heavy set, dark complexion, balding in front," the feature Sylvia Odio had noticed about "Leopoldo." Back at Lakefront Airport, Ferrie, Shaw and the Cuban had gone off together.

A former newscaster told Garrison that Shaw and two others had negotiated for the purchase of a closed-down nickel ore plant in Brathwaite, Louisiana. Moo Moo Sciambra interviewed Freeport vice-president Dick Wight, who confirmed that Shaw had flown to Cuba with Ferrie; Wight had been on board. When the U.S. government financed the Braithwaite nickel plant, the deal had been checked out by Ferrie and Jack Martin, on assignment from Guy Banister.

Further confirmation came from a James J. Plaine of Houston, who was enlisted by Dick Wight in an attempt on the life of Fidel Castro. Plaine had been in New Orleans during the summer of 1963 and had in his possession a "Fair Play for Cuba" leaflet, signed "I will be up to see you soon, Lee." In 1969, Paul A. Fabry, president of International House, sister organization of the International Trade Mart, showed a Japanese trade group a film about Freeport Sulphur. During the HSCA investigation, Gaeton Fonzi learned that David Atlee Phillips, too, had been in contact with the Freeport Sulphur people. That Freeport Sulphur was a CIA proprietary, and that Clay Shaw as a CIA operative assisted in its efforts is well documented.

After Shaw's arrest, Jim Garrison received from Ralph Schoenman, philosopher Bertrand Russell's secretary in London, copies of a series of articles published in an Italian newspaper of the independent left called *Paese Sera*. The articles had been assigned six months earlier to expose the CIA's pernicious attempt to influence European electoral politics and to thwart the democratic process in more than one country. They focused on "Centro Mondiale Commerciale," the world trade center in Rome, as a CIA front, one modeled, according to a 1958 State Department document, on the original CIA-created International Trade Mart in New Orleans. *Paese Sera*, of course, did not possess this document. Its evidence came first hand.

Centro Mondiale Commerciale was, by the U.S. government's own admission, a CIA front, channeling money not only into legal political parties, but also into right-wing movements. Among them was the virulent paramilitary OAS *(Organisation Armée Secrète)* in France, which employed terrorism to oppose the independence of Algeria, and was among the "most notorious fascist organizations in French history." In New Orleans, Guy Banister and L. P. Davis had been OAS supporters.

The most notorious OAS-sponsored effort was the attempted assassination of Charles de Gaulle in 1962. Banister operative Tommy Baumler remarked that "those who killed John F. Kennedy were those who wanted to kill de Gaulle." He was referring to the CIA, Clay Shaw, Banister, and Centro's parent organization, PERMINDEX (Permanent Industrial Exhibition), based in Switzerland.

Having been accused of "shady speculation" by the Swiss, PERMINDEX had created the Centro Mondiale Commerciale in Rome, ostensibly to develop industry and trade in Italy. The Centro, however, was a trade association that rarely if ever organized an exhibit; it facilitated no commercial transactions.

CIA had, in fact, founded PERMINDEX to organize its political policymaking. In Italy, this had meant opposition to a coalition of socialists and communists that would have resulted in a majority government. The CIA preferred the Christian Democratic Party and so

CIA Counter Intelligence chief James Angleton filtered ten million dollars of CIA money to the Christian Democrats. In *Les Echos* newspaper, de Gaulle named PERMINDEX as having been involved in the attempt on his life. The French, no less than the Italians, considered PERMINDEX a "subsidiary of the CIA." *Paese Sera* would call PERMINDEX "a creature of the CIA . . . set up as a cover for the transfer of CIA funds in Italy for illegal political espionage activities."

In the ranks of PERMINDEX were actual Nazis and neo-Nazis, terrorists and Mafia operatives. Typical was Prince Guterez di Spadafora, a former Mussolini undersecretary, whose son had married the daughter of Hitler's finance minister, Hjalmar Schact, tried for war crimes at Nuremberg. The leadership of PERMINDEX included a long-time asset of CIA Deputy Director for Plans, Frank Wisner. His name was Ferenc Nagy, and he was the president of PERMINDEX. Nagy had been chairman of the Hungarian's "People's Party" or "Independent Party of Small Holders." Briefly, in 1945, he had been prime minister of Hungary. But it was Nagy's CIA history that catapulted him to the leadership of PERMINDEX. Its general secretary, Bela Kovacs, was also a CIA asset. Kovacs had been arrested by the Soviet security police and charged with spying for "a Western intelligence service."

Nagy had been on Frank Wisner's list of the individuals with whom his office would "have dealings in connection with our authorized activities" since September 22, 1948. Wisner then had been Assistant Director of CIA as well as "Assistant Director for Policy Coordination." Nagy had been a "cleared contact of the International Organizations Division of the Agency," among Wisner's most trusted Eastern European contacts.

Nagy's history with the CIA dates from its beginnings and links PERMINDEX with the Agency's clandestine services. Confirming de Gaulle's thesis that PERMINDEX funded the OAS is that Nagy was a "munificent contributor" to Jacques Soustelle, former professor at the *École pratique des hautes études* and former Algerian governor general. Soustelle became an OAS supporter, and his organization, *Conseil national de la resistance,* was all but identical to OAS. In 1960, Soustelle met in Washington, D.C., with Richard Bissell, then heading the CIA's clandestine services. A year later, Soustelle went into exile to avoid being arrested by de Gaulle's police. Two years after that he would be accused of colluding with OAS in the attempted assassination of de Gaulle. Soustelle had openly "advocated overthrowing de Gaulle," while condoning OAS violence.

In New Orleans, Delphine Roberts identified Nagy from his photograph as someone she had seen at Guy Banister's office.

Nagy's partner in the leadership of PERMINDEX was Giorgio Mantello, a.k.a. Georges Mandel, who during World War II had traded in Jewish refugees, profiting handsomely from their misery from his perch at the consulate of El Salvador in Bern. It was Mandel who had been the official founder of PERMINDEX. CIA kept silent, but the State Department learned that, as "Georges Mandel," Mantello had been engaged in the "wartime Jewish refugee racket" until he was expelled from Switzerland.

Although Centro Mondiale Commerciale refused to reveal the origins of its vast income, the paper trail leads to a Miami bank, Astalde Vaduz, and to the CIA front "Double-Chek." CMC was connected as well to L. M. Bloomfield in Montreal, and to the Seligman banking family in Basel; Seligman banking in turn was allied with Sullivan and Cromwell, the law firm of CIA Director of Central Intelligence, Allen Dulles. "My parents are very interested in PERMINDEX," Peter Seligman-Schurch wrote to Clay Shaw.

In Switzerland, PERMINDEX soon aroused "widespread public suspicion." Nagy and Seligman stonewalled the concerned American consulate in Bern after the Swiss complained they had "insufficient confidence in the business integrity" of PERMINDEX.

In the spring of 1958, Enrico Mantello, the vice president of PERMINDEX and brother of Giorgio, visited New Orleans. Touring the Trade Mart, he invited Clay Shaw to join the board of directors as a means of defusing the criticism of PERMINDEX; its critics by now included the State Department itself. Nagy appeared at the American Embassy in Rome to announce that he intended "to strengthen U.S. control in PERMINDEX by adding to its Board of Directors a Mr. Shaw, who is in charge of the New Orleans, Louisiana permanent exhibit."

Nagy claimed that Shaw "had from the outset great interest in the PERMINDEX project," and Shaw did use the term "delighted" in his cable of acceptance. He made plans to visit Italy, then canceled, despite Mantello's urgings. When he added his PERMINDEX directorship to *"Who's Who in the South and the Southeast,"* the Department of Commerce warned Shaw about "this shadowy organization." But, as in all his CIA assignments, grateful for the career CIA made for him, Clay Shaw honored his obligation.

Internal evidence that PERMINDEX was a CIA front emerges in the fact that the CIA included PERMINDEX materials in its asset Clay Shaw's files, three years before as well as after the Kennedy assassination. One of these documents, dated March 16, 1967, reveals that at the time of his arrest Clay Shaw was working with the

Domestic Operations Division of the CIA's clandestine services. This was only a seeming contradiction since the CIA's operational component in New Orleans had resided under the umbrella of the Domestic Contact Division, at least since November 19, 1964, according to a CIA document on "Garrison and the Kennedy Assassination," MEMORANDUM No. 8.

"Most of us consider the CIA with abhorrence," Shaw wrote in his *Diary* for the record, with his customary dark laughter.

In 1962, Centro Mondiale Commerciale was expelled from Italy, ostensibly for financial malfeasance, and specious real estate dealings, but actually for subversion and illegal intelligence activity. "Who was giving money to the CMC and what was it being used for?" *Paese Sera* demanded. PERMINDEX relocated to a more compatible political venue, apartheid South Africa. Clay Shaw remained on its board, providing space at the Trade Mart for a permanent PERMINDEX display.

The editors of *Paese Sera* were astonished when their March 1967 publication date for the series on PERMINDEX coincided with the arrest of Clay Shaw. They had been working on the series for months, former editor Giorgio Fanti says. Now they headlined Clay Shaw's involvement in PERMINDEX, with a subhead revealing that he had been arrested by Jim Garrison in New Orleans. *Paese Sera* noted that Shaw's name had first appeared in connection with the CMC on February 14, 1962, in a *Paese Sera* article on the financial machinations of the organization. He had gone to Rome "during the time preceding the disbanding of the CMC," Shaw admitted to a *Paese Sera* interviewer. *Paese Sera* wondered, too, about Shaw's leaving the United States two days after the assassination, remaining abroad for two years with only intermittent visits to America.

Shaw affected his customary disdain. He had agreed to be on the PERMINDEX board, he claimed, because "a young Italian came to see me in New Orleans and told me about a world trade center that was being planned in Rome." He also told the *Paese Sera* interviewer that he "accepted the position in exchange for two New Orleans–Rome air tickets." Even his closest friends were appalled. "There must have been blackmail involved—they're very famous for that, the CIA," Patricia Chandler says.

Jim Garrison had charged that the CIA had plotted the assassination of John F. Kennedy, for which they were aided and abetted in New Orleans by their operative, Clay Shaw. Thirty-five years later, a series of attacks on *Paese Sera* began to appear, accompanied by an excoriation of Jim Garrison. Among the publications sanctioning these attacks was the CIA's own Web site, "Studies In Intelligence." Journalist Max Holland repeated in a series of magazine articles the erroneous thesis that the only reason that *Paese Sera* believed that the CIA was behind PERMINDEX was that the newspaper was the victim of KGB disinformation. Jim Garrison, therefore, had connected the CIA to the Kennedy assassination and to Shaw only owing to a KGB lie.

Rather, Garrison's attribution of the planning of the assassination to the CIA was based on his discovery of the CIA connections of Lee Harvey Oswald, and not those of Clay Shaw, an inconvenient detail Holland omits. The truth is that Garrison had focused on the CIA in December 1966 and January 1967, well before the March publication of the *Paese Sera* articles.

Holland was regurgitating a scenario laid down by Richard Helms. In 1961, Helms was doing damage control for the Agency by attacking European newspapers that were exposing the role of the CIA in influencing the elections in Italy, and in funding such dubious movements as the coup in Algeria designed to maintain French colonial control.

The CIA had made *Paese Sera* a target two years before the Kennedy assassination. Then assistant Deputy Director for Plans Helms, later to be convicted in federal court of perjury, charged, falsely, before the Senate Internal Security Subcommittee that *Paese Sera* was an outlet for Soviet Communist propaganda for daring to suggest that the attempted putsch against Charles de Gaulle by four Algerian-based generals enjoyed the support of the CIA. The fact was that *Paese Sera* was printing the truth. Later the Agency would accuse its old nemesis, *Paese Sera,* of being a Soviet conduit for disinformation fed to Jim Garrison.

Despite those denials by Helms, the *New York Times* itself reported that "CIA agents have recently been in touch with the anti-Gaullist generals." The CIA had even hosted a luncheon in Washington for Jacques Soustelle. Reports had arrived from Paris that the CIA was "in touch with the insurrectionists who tried to overthrow the de Gaulle government of France." Although Helms blamed *Paese Sera,* the original story had run first in France, in *L'-Express.* No matter, Helms accused *Paese Sera* of being an "outlet for disguised Soviet propaganda," planted in Italy. Helms was obviously attempting to discredit the newspapers that dared expose CIA interference in European electoral politics.

Max Holland's Helms-echoing attacks on *Paese Sera,* and his accusation that Jim Garrison was a dupe of Soviet anti-CIA propaganda, have met with outrage by the surviving *Paese Sera* editors. They despised the KGB and the CIA equally, they say. The Italian Communist party never made more than a token financial contribution to *Paese Sera*. It is "totally absurd that either the Italian or the Soviet Communist Party had any influence whatsoever in editorial policy or the political direction of the paper," says Edo Parpalione, a staff writer at the time. Calling *Paese Sera* a conduit for KGB disinformation is "a conscious lie." Giorgio Fanti agrees. *Paese Sera,* he says with pride, was a paper of the independent left, like *La Repubblica* today.

Jean-Franco Corsini, who wrote for *Paese Sera* between 1964 and 1974, is also appalled by Holland's charges. Corsini calls the false connection being made between *Paese Sera* and the KGB "the usual manipulation of the CIA." As for supposed "proof" from the newly opened KGB archives, Corsini raises an eyebrow. He says he sees "no reason to trust new CIA documents any more than old KGB documents," and hopes for the simultaneous demise of both the CIA and the KGB. "Their time will come," he predicts, if not in his lifetime, then "in that of my children and grandchildren." As for the Kennedy assassination itself, the writers at *Paese Sera,* like many Europeans, General de Gaulle not least, saw it as "an internal plot inside the United States government."

Max Holland's strategy of connecting Jim Garrision's focus on CIA involvement in the assassination with KGB propaganda originates not only in Richard Helms' false 1961 testimony. Holland is consulting another blueprint as well, a CIA document dated April 4, 1967. Titled "Countering Criticism of the Warren Report," it is addressed to "Chief, Certain Stations and Bases" and outlines how the CIA's media assets should respond to critics.

This document appears in fact to be aimed at one particular challenger to the Warren Commission, the one receiving national attention in New Orleans in 1967. CIA should "employ propaganda assets to answer and refute the attacks of the critic" through "book reviews and feature articles," CIA advises. Jim Garrison, a war hero, could not be credibly accused of "Communist sympathies," an outworn strategy by the millennium in any case. But he might— and this is what Max Holland has done in a barrage of articles—be attacked as part of "a planned Soviet propaganda operation."

Holland combined his CIA-authored charge that Jim Garrison was a dupe of the KGB through *Paese Sera* with a defense of Clay Shaw. Shaw was only one of 150,000 Americans who "volunteered information to the CIA that he *routinely* gathered during his frequent trips abroad," he writes. None of Shaw's assignments was "routine," of course; each was initiated by the Agency.

Yet, as if they had been briefed collectively, Holland and a group of fellow writers repeat verbatim, using the same language, this falsification of the CIA career of Clay Shaw. Patricia Lambert, in a book-length attack on Jim Garrison published in 1998, writes that "Clay Shaw at one time did provide *routine* information to the CIA's Domestic Contact Service," while, she adds, QKENCHANT was "a program for *routine debriefing* of individuals involved in international trade," which, of course, was not the case at all. (Emphasis added.)

Before Lambert, came a CIA and FBI media asset, James Phelan, who wrote that Shaw had "merely been one of the many that had been *routinely debriefed. . . .*" Holland refers to a "devastating expose of Garrison's sources and methods" by James Phelan. This same distortion is repeated by Helms in his autobiography, *A Look Over My Shoulder,* where he invokes positively both Lambert and Holland's article on the CIA Web site.

This verbatim disinformation recalls the climax of Costa Gavras' brilliant 1967 film *Z,* in which the fascist Greek colonels and the hired killers who assassinated Dr. Grigorios Lambrakis in Salonika, six months before John F. Kennedy died, are exposed in their conspiracy: on separate occasions, they utilize the identical phrase, "lithe and fierce like a tiger."

When Jim Garrison shared the *Paese Sera* articles with Richard Billings, Billings discovered that "Centro Mondiale Commerciale specialized in the financing of political groups considered to be intransigent anti-communists." Billings' research revealed that *Paese Sera* was "rarely proven to be basically wrong." When *Paese* Sera telephoned Garrison from Rome, he could tell them only that he had discovered that the International Trade Mart has "turned over varying sums of money to the associations of so-called Cubans in exile." Then both he and Billings put aside the *Paese Sera* articles. Garrison lacked the resources to investigate in Rome. By the time he published his memoir, *On the Trail of the Assassins,* in the late 1980s, he had entirely forgotten when he even read the *Paese Sera* articles. Misremembering, he wrote that they had come to his attention only after the trial of Clay Shaw.

Garrison's uncovering of Shaw's CIA service alarmed the Agency. Lloyd Ray sought guidance again from Lawrence Houston. What should he do if "called upon by Mr. Garrison or any of his investigators?" Ray was authorized to refuse any requests for information, and to state that he was "under an oath of secrecy and could not discuss any official business of the Central Intelligence Agency." Nor was the CIA pleased when on April 5th, only a few weeks after the *Paese Sera* articles appeared, the FBI reported to the CIA that Jim Garrison "has information that Clay Shaw has some connection with CIA."

The Agency now collected the manifold Shaw records from its Office of Security. Lloyd Ray put it on the record that *his* office had no conversations with Clay Shaw since May 1956. CIA then lied to the FBI, insisting that Shaw had only been "of interest" to DCS (Domestic Contact Service) from December 1948 to May 1956. As for actual records on Shaw, all they could locate was that Shaw had introduced General Charles Cabell to the Foreign Policy Association in New Orleans.

Establishing Shaw's operational efforts for the CIA was virtually impossible for Jim Garrison, to whom access to the CIA's files was denied. Testifying in 1978 for the HSCA was John Whitten, a long-time officer in the clandestine services, in charge of reviewing counter intelligence operations. Known in CIA circles as "John Scelso," Whitten lifted part of the curtain of CIA opacity.

The distinction between CIA "employee" and "agent," Whitten explained, was hypothetical. There are "certain types of high-level agents who are staff agents, who have staff status, but they are not employees." Personnel files were routinely purged, Whitten revealed. Even if the record stated that someone had retired or contacts with them had ceased, there could be "a buried operational file somewhere indicating that the person was still working for the Agency." He might have been describing Clay Shaw.

Far from being a mere asset for the Domestic Contact Service, Clay Shaw was a CIA operative. His records resided with Counter Intelligence. Arthur Dooley of the Counter Intelligence Research and Analysis Staff headed by Raymond Rocca, nicknamed "The Rock" by chief James Angleton, one day telephoned John P. Dempsey, the Director of Research. Dooley revealed how well aware he was of Clay Lavergne Shaw. He did not bother with the fantasy of attaching an ending date to Clay Shaw's Counter Intelligence service.

A SKITTISH WITNESS 10

I think the only possible maxim to apply in this case is "Let Justice Be Done Though The Heavens Fall."
—Jim Garrison

"WRACKED BY EXHAUSTION," Jim Garrison flew to Las Vegas three days after the arrest of Clay Shaw. A man recognized him at the airport: "You're Jim Garrison!" "Who?" Garrison said. "Never heard of the guy." He checked into the Sands Hotel under the name of his maternal grandfather, "Robinson." He was not a gambling man, preferring to sit in the dry desert sun by the pool, talking on the telephone.

On his heels came reporter James Phelan, who clung to him like a ferret. At first Garrison welcomed Phelan, who, in June of 1963, had arranged for the *Saturday Evening Post's* publication of David Chandler's story, newly titled as "The Vice Man Cometh." The article had called Garrison "the best DA's office New Orleans ever had." The trusting Garrison handed over to Phelan Sciambra's two memos of his interviews with Perry Russo. Ivon and Alcock were appalled.

Phelan rushed to a photocopier. Then he paid a call on Robert Maheu, longtime CIA asset and former FBI agent, and Guy Banister associate. Notorious as the liaison between mobster Johnny Rosselli and the CIA in OPERATION MONGOOSE, that plan to assassinate Fidel Castro, Maheu enjoyed covert security approval for "use in the United States" in "extremely sensitive cases." His company was a public relations cover for Agency employees.

Having made contact with Maheu, Phelan flew to Washington, where he informed the FBI's H. P. Leinbaugh, who reported directly to Deke DeLoach, of everything he knew about Garrison's investigation. He handed over Sciambra's memos, which soon reached The Director himself. Phelan asked only that Leinbaugh hold the Garrison documents "closely," so that his role as an FBI informant remain secret. The CIA was also using Phelan as an informant "of interest in connection with," in Agency jargon, "a sensitive SPS [Special Projects Staff] activity."

James Phelan had begun his concerted effort, as he admitted to photographer Matt Herron, to discredit Jim Garrison and derail his investigation. Phelan had already warned Mark Lane: "If you associate with Jim Garrison, your credibility will be gone. He's going to undo all the good work you've done." Lane at once made plans to fly to New Orleans to assist Garrison. "It would be a good idea to write an article attacking the Garrison investigation," Phelan then urged Professor Richard Popkin, who had written a book called *The Second Oswald*.

With Maheu in Las Vegas was his CIA handler, James O'Connell, and his lawyer, Edward Morgan, but also Johnny Rosselli, the mobster to whom Maheu had offered $150,000 to kill Fidel Castro. The coinciding of Jim Garrison's visit to Las Vegas with Rosselli's appearance there became an opportunity for the CIA to smear Garrison by accusing him of mob connections. In the May 23, 1967, CIA Inspector General's Report there is a sudden nonsequitur: Jim Garrison met with Johnny Rosselli in Las Vegas. The Inspector General adds, "The Rosselli-Garrison contact in Las Vegas in March is particularly disturbing." The Report offers no date, place or occasion for the meeting. It states only that Rosselli's talking to Garrison "lends substance to reports that Castro had something to do with the Kennedy assassination in retaliation for U.S. attempts on Castro's life."

By now, the Agency had reason to fear Jim Garrison. It believed that, as the Inspector General's report states, when he revealed his full case, "we should expect to find CIA prominently displayed." CIA had admitted to plots against Castro in part "because it is already out and may boil up afresh from the Garrison case."

By Garrison's having penetrated its plots to kill Castro ("Unhappily, it now appears that Garrison may also know this"), and his discovering that Rosselli might be involved, the district attorney might well develop evidence of the CIA's role in the assassination, CIA feared. The "unhappily" refers to CIA displeasure that Garrison might expose the CIA's own murder plots. This was what was "disturbing," not that Garrison's mob connections might emerge, since he had none. The lie that Garrison had met Rosselli would be perpetuated into the 1990s by former *Frontline* corre-spondent Scott Malone, who named Richard Billings as his source. Billings denies he said any such thing.

Testifying before the Church Committee, Richard Helms all but revealed that the false Garrison-Rosselli connection originated as CIA disinformation. "It might have been the lawyer Ed Morgan, it might be Rosselli, it might be Maheu, or Garrison, who was out in Las Vegas with Maheu and some of the others," Helms said vaguely. Garrison, of course, was in Vegas, but he was not "with Maheu and some of the others," ever. His companion was *Life* photographer Lynn Pelham. He was joined by William Gurvich. Had Garrison met with Rosselli, or even Maheu, either Phelan or Gurvich would cer-tainly have exposed the fact. Maheu told the Church Committee he had no recollection "of seeing Garrison in person." With no reason to lie, Rosselli stated that he had never met Jim Garrison.

For the rest of his life, Garrison would be shadowed by the CIA lie that he had met with Rosselli. "I suppose it is an honor to have the CIA sufficiently concerned about you to have to discredit you," Garrison said, incredulous at the idea of his having talked to Johnny Rosselli. "You remember the guy that was killed with a bul-let in his stomach and his legs cut off—and put in a barrel and dropped in the bay off Florida?"

In Vegas, Garrison did meet James Dondson, who had been in bed with Clay Shaw at the time of the assassination. Dondson was escorted to Las Vegas by FBI informant Lawrence Schiller. Garrison's hope that Dondson might corroborate that Shaw was "Bertrand" turned out to be futile.

Back in New Orleans, Garrison readied himself for a Prelimi-nary Hearing. Under then-Louisiana law, he was not obliged to re-veal to the Shaw defense the names of his witnesses. Yet "because of the enormity of this accusation," Garrison decided to "lean over backward and give the defendant every chance." He would expose to the public his confidential informant Perry Russo. Garrison had also in mind that Louisiana law permitted testimony given at a pre-liminary hearing to be heard at the trial if a witness was no longer available, a significant issue since so many witnesses to the Kennedy assassination had died.

Garrison had faith in Russo. A reporter had discovered in Russo's apartment, among the law books he was apparently study-ing, some of Oswald's "Fair Play for Cuba" leaflets. Russo's crucial placing of Shaw with Oswald and Ferrie during a discussion of the assassination was the overt act Garrison needed under the Louisiana conspiracy law to convict Clay Shaw: "a visit by one of the parties to his co-conspirator for the common purpose of discussing details." This overt act need not have necessarily aided in the direct commission of the crime. It need not even have in itself been wrong, only that the "combination" led to the crime. The very use of the name "Oswald" placed Shaw in collusion with the president's accused assassin, even as John Wilson's having seen Oswald at Ferrie's apartment suggests for history that the man Russo identified was indeed Oswald.

Russo agreed to take a lie detector test. But faced with Gurvich's Roy Jacob, he became so nervous that Jacob couldn't obtain a reading. Police polygrapher Edward O'Donnell, who would claim, with no tape or even a written record, that Russo had told him verbally that he was lying about having seen Clay Shaw at Ferrie's, had no better luck. Russo's "general nervous tension" made him an unsuitable subject for the test.

O'Donnell, the man said to have the coldest eyes in New Orleans, was a bitter enemy of Jim Garrison and close to the Gurviches. Garrison had brought up police brutality charges against him and his partner, Tony Polito. Although no indictments had resulted, some of the police were infuriated that black victims were afforded the dignity of coming forward to state their case by Garrison's office. Garrison investigator Frank Meloche was to remember of Polito and O'Donnell: "They were brutal, but they cleared some cases." O'Donnell was also named by Wendall C. Roache as working for the INS, among those who had "detailed knowledge of Cuban exile activities in New Orleans." Not least was the fact that O'Donnell informed to the FBI on Russo's polygraph.

For corroboration, Garrison had also attempted to extradite Sandra Moffett, Russo's date at the Ferrie gathering. Now married to a part-time preacher and living in Nebraska, Moffett refused. Her husband told Garrison's staff rudely, "Don't bug me!" Finally, aided by lawyers she could not possibly have afforded on her own, she was spirited across the state line to Iowa, where fugitives were safe. Moffett would be only the first of potential Garrison witnesses whom governors would refuse to extradite back to Louisiana.

Russo remained so nervous that Dr. Chetta had to give him a tranquilizer before he could take the stand. Under oath, Russo again described the conversation about the assassination at David Ferrie's apartment. "Diversionary tactics" would be employed, and "a triangulation of cross fire," the same term used by Joseph Milteer in Miami, Russo explained. There would be a "scapegoat" who had to be "sacrificed" and an escape flight to Mexico, Brazil or Cuba, although "Bertrand" had cautioned that they could never make it out of Cuba.

Ferrie had also suggested on that evening that they should all be "in the public eye on the day of the assassination, making sure they were making a speech or there were enough people around to witness that Dave Ferrie was at such-and-such a place and at such-and-such a time." "Mr. Bertrand" planned to travel on business "to the West Coast." "Leon" had complained to Ferrie about his wife being angry with him, and Ferrie had promised to "handle it."

When Garrison asked Russo to come down from the stand and make his identification, Russo positioned himself behind Shaw's chair. While Shaw sat motionless, a burning cigarette in his hand, Russo placed his open palm a few inches over Shaw's head.

"You weren't part of it?" F. Irvin Dymond, now Shaw's lead counsel, demanded of Russo under cross-examination. The clock had begun ticking on the two years the Shaw defense would have to undermine Perry Russo. "Do you believe in God, Russo?" Dymond demanded.

Perry Russo emerged as a strong witness. "I was there and Dave Ferrie was there, and Leon Oswald," Russo repeated. "Clay Shaw was there, but his name was not Clay, it was Clem." That Russo had undergone both sodium pentothal and hypnosis did not emerge as significant. A Tulane Medical School professor testified how difficult it would be even for a pathological liar to lie under hypnosis.

Garrison's other major witness was a black narcotics addict named Vernon Bundy, whose criminal record was minor: five years' probation for burglary of a cigarette machine. During his morning polygraph, Bundy was asked only two questions: Was he acting on someone's instructions and was the information he was giving true?" In charge of the polygraph, James Kruebbe had to admit, "No one put him up to it." Then Kruebbe, the man who was to help Juan Valdes evade his polygraph, insisted that Bundy had failed.

Bundy had identified Oswald's leaflets as being yellow. Lou Ivon had then telephoned Carlos Quiroga to confirm the color, a call Quiroga misinterpreted to mean that Lou Ivon himself didn't know. So the amateur detective revealed his inexperience. Ivon would never have asked the question had he *not* known the color of the leaflets.

From photographs, Bundy had identified Shaw and Oswald, who looked "dirty," Bundy said, corroborating Russo. He identified the composite of Oswald "with the beard stubble," which had not been made public.

On the day Bundy was to testify, John Volz took him to a window where he might observe Shaw entering the courthouse using the sheriff's entrance. "That's him!" Bundy said. He repeated the identification in the courthouse foyer, identifying Shaw by his limp. At that point, not even the district attorney's staff had known that Shaw limped. "I've talked to a lot of liars," Volz says. "I can tell when someone is shucking me." Bundy was telling the truth.

On the stand, Bundy recounted a hot summer day in 1963 between nine and ten in the morning. He had been walking "towards the colored section of Lake Pontchartrain," preparing to inject himself with heroin. A four-door black sedan appeared, an automobile Bundy had described in his prison interview as a "black limousine." Fearing the vice had caught up with him, he closed up his "outfit," the two caps of heroin, the cooker, and the bottles. If he's a cop, Bundy decided, he would throw everything into the lake.

"It's a hot day," the man said cordially, passing behind Bundy.

"He was a tall, settled man," Bundy said, describing Clay Shaw, over six feet tall, with gray hair. "White man." Five minutes later, a younger man appeared, looking like "a junkie or beatnik type of guy," wearing white jeans and a T-shirt, and in need of a shave.

"What am I going to tell her?" he had said loudly, again echoing Russo's testimony. "Don't worry about it. I told you I'm going to take care of it," the tall gray-haired man said. He handed the younger man a roll of money. Without counting it, the younger man put it in his pocket, from which some leaflets were protruding. They left. As Bundy was looking for paper to wrap his "works," he spotted something that had fallen from the young man's pocket. It was a yellow piece of paper, "something about free Cuba." Asked if he saw either of the men in the courtroom, Bundy walked down and stood behind the gray-haired man he had seen at the lakefront. He put his hand over Clay Shaw's head.

By the close of the hearing, Dymond was reduced to requesting that the Warren Report be placed into evidence. The Report had insisted there had been no conspiracy, and so his client could not be guilty.

"You're not serious, are you?" Judge Bagert said, dismissing the Warren Report as "fraught with hearsay and contradictions." After thirty minutes of deliberation, the three judges ruled that "sufficient evidence" had been presented and ordered that Shaw be held for trial. It was, Jim Garrison noted with pride, the first judicial decision challenging the Warren Report.

Garrison then brought Russo before the Grand Jury. Its foreman was Albert LaBiche, a close friend of Garrison's archenemy Raymond Huff, who termed LaBiche "totally honest, courageous and incorruptible." Both LaBiche and grand jury member Larry Centola were in turn close to Cartha DeLoach, Deke himself. Neither had any sympathy for Jim Garrison.

Clay Shaw was charged with conspiracy with David W. Ferrie, with Lee Harvey Oswald and with "others, not herein named" to murder John F. Kennedy. He pled "not guilty." Meeting the press on April 4th, Shaw, a martini in his hand, described his politics as "of the Wilson-Franklin Roosevelt persuasion."

With the Sciambra memos in hand, James Phelan now set about the task of subverting Perry Russo as a witness. Phelan would argue that until he was under sodium pentothal, Russo had not told Sciambra about the gathering at which he had seen "Leon" Oswald, Clem Bertrand and David Ferrie. The scene where the assassination was discussed was a concoction suggested to Russo, who was being used so that Jim Garrison could frame Clay Shaw.

Phelan believed he could get away with this sleight of hand because of some confusion in Sciambra's memos: Moo Moo had written the memo of the sodium penothal session of Monday, February 27th first, before he had penned his account of his Saturday afternoon interview with Russo in Baton Rouge. It was this memo written first, but about a subsequent event, that contained the description of the gathering at Ferrie's apartment where the assassination was discussed.

Days later, Sciambra wrote up the Saturday February 25th meeting with Russo. This memo of their first interview did not contain a discussion of the meeting at Ferrie's house because Sciambra felt he had already covered the subject in the previous memo. The memo of that Saturday does describe Russo identifying a photograph of Clay Shaw as "Clem Bertrand," which could not have occurred unless Russo had also discussed the gathering on that first day.

The memo of the February 27th session is more comprehensive. Russo refers to "two other occasions" when he saw Shaw, suggesting that he had mentioned the more important occasion, the gathering at Ferrie's, during his first meeting with Sciambra. Sciambra's questions at the sodium pentothal session also assume Russo had already told him about Bertrand, even as Ivon's search warrant for

Shaw's house reflects knowledge of the party; it was sworn out before either of the memos were written. Yet it was sloppy of Sciambra not to have included all the details of the most crucial evidence, that of the gathering at Ferrie's, in the memo devoted to the Saturday afternoon when Russo first brought it up.

Phelan attempted to dissuade other Garrison witnesses from cooperating. Not everyone was susceptible to his crude maneuvers. "Go to hell!" the Reverend Broshears told Phelan.

Soon Phelan was demanding Sciambra's original notes. Indignant, Sciambra told him he had burned them. Phelan tried to hire Pershing in his effort to destroy Jim Garrison's investigation, but Pershing saw right through him. "You can't afford to pay what I would charge," Pershing said, "and even after I completed the investigation, if you call me six days later and told me you wanted a different conclusion, I would conduct an investigation leading to almost any conclusion or viewpoint."

When Phelan requested interviews with Perry Russo, Jim Garrison approved, then had Russo wired. "I want to know what these people are thinking," Garrison said.

"I understand that you did have emotional problems," Phelan began. Russo remained unshaken.

"As far as I'm concerned," Russo said, "Bertrand and Shaw are the same." He insisted that he had told Sciambra about the gathering at Ferrie's apartment at their first meeting in Baton Rouge. When Phelan suggested that Russo had seen Guy Banister, not Shaw, Russo remained adamant. He had encountered Clay Shaw.

When all else failed, Phelan began to threaten Russo. "You could be the patsy," Phelan warned. Russo would find himself in jail. What if the Shaw people could demonstrate that Shaw had been out of the country on the day of that gathering? (Of course, they could not.) Immediately Phelan sent copies of his interviews with Russo to the FBI in Washington. Phelan's behavior, Lou Ivon reflects, was "a casebook in the obstruction of justice."

Assisting Phelan was Hugh Aynesworth, who warned Richard Billings: "You're getting too close to Garrison." The extant record reveals that Aynesworth had attempted to join the CIA in 1963. He also reported to the FBI, which kept copious files on Aynesworth, including a 1964 report that Aynesworth was caught in bed with the wife of an ex-convict, the irate husband then stabbing him in the neck. The FBI placed this document in a Lee Harvey Oswald file.

By late February, Aynesworth boasted of having informants in place in Garrison's office. Gurvich stole files and handed them over to Aynesworth, who then passed them on to the CIA. According to reporter Lonnie Hudkins, Aynesworth, like himself, was working for the CIA. Through Aynesworth, the CIA learned of Jim Garrison's interest in the firm of Brown & Root.

Aynesworth reported as well to the Houston field office of the FBI, anxious to furnish "facts of alleged intimidation, bribery, coercion of persons whom New Orleans district attorney Garrison is attempting to have testify." Like Quiroga, he denounced Garrison to the House Un-American Activities Committee.

With cover now as a *Newsweek* reporter, Aynesworth devoted himself to undermining Jim Garrison's case. He met with Clay Shaw's defense team at his Texas home. He provided photographs of Mark Lane "during a sex orgy" to the Shaw defense, which distributed them to interested parties. He slipped the Shaw defense copies of Garrison's press releases, while Edward Wegmann shared copies of his motions and private correspondence. Aynesworth even interviewed witnesses for the Shaw defense.

Aynesworth adopted the FBI's strategy for his attacks on Jim Garrison. Garrison is "losing his sanity," Aynesworth insisted. People who had changed their minds about testifying for Garrison were now "in danger of being harmed and possibly killed." In yet another fabrication, he said Garrison had called Oswald a "Mafia hood." He repeated Phelan's lie about how Sciambra's memos had discredited Perry Russo. "Bertrand didn't exist," Aynesworth wrote in *Newsweek.* When Aynesworth sent Jim Garrison a scurrilous telegram, Garrison scrawled at the bottom, "No answer needed." Then he consigned the document to his "Nut file."

Connecting Clay Shaw with Lee Harvey Oswald and David Ferrie and all of them to the CIA was not enough. Garrison had to connect the CIA to the assassination. He believed he found a witness who could help him in a CIA operative named Richard Case Nagell. Garrison came to believe that Nagell was "the closest thing to the key [to the assassination mystery] that there is in one man, if he wanted to be." CIA had assigned to Nagell the surveillance of Oswald in New Orleans in the summer of 1963, only for Nagell to uncover the plot to murder President Kennedy. "If you find out what I had to do with Oswald and he had to do with me, you will know what this is all about," Nagell wrote to Richard Popkin.

That Oswald was under surveillance by the intelligence community at least a year before the assassination has been well established. The most recent evidence places Oswald under CIA surveillance through the files of the 112th Military Intelligence Group, which requested Oswald files from the 502nd Military Intelligence Battalion in Seoul, Korea, in September of 1962. Shortly thereafter, a request came for information on Nagell, complete with his CIA code name, "Laredo."

"Well, they're watching Oswald like a hawk," career military man Jim Southwood told Dick Russell, Nagell's biographer, "and this guy Nagell is the guy doing it." For Southwood, this meant, at the least, "that Oswald had been an intelligence operative." It was another vindication of Jim Garrison's work, more than a decade after his death.

Serving as a military intelligence officer with the Counter Intelligence Corps of the Army, having been recruited to the CIA in 1955, Nagell had first met Oswald in Japan. There he observed Oswald attempting to recruit KGB assets, such as Fujisawa Chikao, a Tokyo University professor. Back home in California, Nagell worked for the CIA's red squad, spying on dissident organizations. "I investigated an associate of the now deceased right-wing extremist David W. Ferrie," he wrote, referring to Sergio Arcacha Smith. When Nagell ran into Fujisawa in the United States, the CIA told him to turn his information over to the FBI.

For the CIA, Nagell went to Louisiana as "Oswald's manager." Before long, he connected Arcacha with Eladio del Valle, and "Angel" (Angelo) with exile leader Manuel Artime, and the notorious Rolando Masferrer. Under the code name "Laredo," Nagell infiltrated Oswald's circle, the "Ferrie-Banister Group," as he put it. He knew about the training camps north of Lake Pontchartrain and discovered that Oswald had become the pawn of those acquaintances of David Ferrie, "Angel" and "Leopoldo." Oswald had been told, falsely, that "Angel" and "Leopoldo" (the names of Sylvia Odio's visitors) were agents of the Cuban G-2 (Dirección General de Inteligencia), Fidel Castro's intelligence service. Defining themselves as "special emissaries from Fidel," and insisting they had been "personally sent to kill JFK," Angel and Leopoldo promised to furnish Oswald "safe conduct to Cuba when it was over."

Nagell would also contend that he met Oswald in Jackson Square where the two were photographed together by a street vendor. Oswald told him that he was to pick up five hundred dollars in his post office box and meet his contact, "Oaxaca," in Mexico City. Nagell warned him that "Angel" and "Leopoldo" were, in fact, CIA-financed anti-Castro Cubans, part of a "violence-prone faction of a CIA financed group." But, protecting his cover, Oswald continued to call himself a "friend of the Cuban revolution." Knowing how much Oswald hated Governor Connally, Nagell made certain never to mention that name.

Nagell believed Oswald was being utilized to ruin Kennedy's rapprochement with Cuba, which was being implemented by William Attwood. This disruption would be followed by a military invasion of Cuba. Nagell tried to warn Oswald. But, "upset and visibly shaken," Oswald was unable to extricate himself in time. Too late, Oswald discovered that he had "become involved in a domestic-inspired, domestic-formulated and domestic-sponsored plot to assassinate President Kennedy." All this confirmed Jim Garrison's suspicions.

One day Nagell looked up and his CIA handler had vanished. It was September 17, 1963. He wrote to J. Edgar Hoover, warning that Kennedy was about to be assassinated, naming two of Oswald's aliases to establish his own bona fides. Then he wrote to Desmond Fitzgerald at JMWAVE, returning the five hundred dollars he was supposed to have supplied to Oswald.

Now fearing the CIA and knowing there were alternate patsies in the wings to be blamed for the assassination should Oswald bolt, on September 20, 1963, Nagell walked into an El Paso, Texas, bank and fired off a weapon. "I'm glad you caught me," he told an El Paso police officer, "I really don't want to be in Dallas." In his possession was Lee Harvey Oswald's Uniformed Services Identification and Privileges Card and a social security card with Oswald's name and number. Arrested, Nagell behaved as if he were Oswald, a Marxist. "Now I won't have to go to Cuba," he said, attacking "our capitalistic system." Instead of the short stay in federal prison he expected, Nagell was sentenced to ten years. By now Nagell was thirty-seven years old with a long scar running down the paralyzed left side of his face, the result of a plane crash. He had a mouth full of gold teeth and was battle-weary.

To signal his continuing loyalty to the CIA, Nagell claimed that the Soviet Union had ordered him to kill Oswald to prevent him from murdering President Kennedy, a preposterous idea. To Robert Kennedy, he wrote part of the truth: "Any conspiracy of which I had cognizance was neither Communist inspired nor instigated by any foreign government." Later Nagell would admit that his actions were the result of his having had foreknowledge of the assassination. By March 1969, he had repudiated his original statement that he was working for the Soviets. Rather, he had worked "with Lee Harvey Oswald in an assignment with a U.S. Intelligence Agency."

The FBI rolled out that tactic it enlisted with a wide variety of witnesses who knew "too much" about the assassination. It accused Nagell of taking bribes from organized crime and pronounced him crazy so that he was shipped off to the federal psychiatric facility at Springfield, Missouri.

Jim Garrison heard about Nagell from a bona fide member of "Fair Play for Cuba" in Los Angeles, Vaughn Snipes, who wrote to Garrison under the name "Don Morgan." Soon Nagell's half-sister had told Garrison of a tape of Oswald and Nagell, which also included the voices of "Angel" and "Leopoldo."

Garrison abided by Nagell's conditions. He signed a form promising not to charge Nagell as an accessory or hold him as the material witness he obviously was. He would not prosecute him for withholding evidence or issue a search warrant for the "recording tape" containing Oswald's voice. Then Garrison assigned to interview Nagell the same William Martin who would go on to sabotage his investigation of Juan Valdes. Martin's CIA history included his father's having worked for the United Fruit Company and Martin's own position as chief investigator for Maurice Gatlin's Anti-Communist Committee of the Americas.

Jim Garrison had "his hands full with amateur sleuths who were coming out of the woodwork," Nagell remarked, allowing Martin to know he was aware of what was going on at Tulane and Broad. He paraphrased Garrison: "Let justice be done though the heavens crumble," close enough.

The same group of people had created three separate plots to kill President Kennedy, Nagell told William Martin, in Miami, Los Angeles and Dallas. Garrison had been correct to focus on anti-Castro Cubans. Neither Alpha 66, JURE or the "Cuban Revolutionary Democratic Front" had killed the president. Rather, the perpetrators were Cubans as individuals, aided by "a few United States citizens." The assassination was made to seem as if it had been ordered by Fidel Castro.

Nagell saw through William Martin at once. He asked whether Garrison had received any cooperation from the CIA or FBI; Martin does not record his own response in his memo. When, in his first memo, Martin wrote that Nagell had infiltrated the assassination plot for the Soviets, Nagell was furious. He then denied vehemently that he had ever acted on behalf of the Soviets. When Martin identified one of the voices on Nagell's tape (which he had not heard) as Arcacha's, Nagell dismissed Martin's memos as "distorted." Later Lou Ivon would pronounce Martin's work for Jim Garrison "of no help."

Martin had admitted to Nagell that he was a "former CIA officer assigned to Latin American operations," and knew Desmond Fitzgerald and Tracey Barnes. To Nagell, this meant that Martin was a "former member of the CIA's Dirty Tricks Division [clandestine services], who, by his own admission, is still in the reserves." Martin's purpose, Nagell concluded, was to learn what Nagell thought about his CIA superiors and the assassination and then report back to the Agency. He vowed never to permit Martin to retrieve the tape of himself, Oswald, Angel and Leopoldo. By the end of June 1967, the FBI had in its possession all the private correspondence between William Martin and Richard Case Nagell.

Richard Popkin concluded that Martin was a "professional spy," noting that he had an office inside the Cordell Hull Foundation, a CIA conduit to fund Latin American dictators. Martin had money in several currencies and three passports from three countries in three different names, Popkin discovered. When Martin finally departed from Garrison's office in December 1967, he resumed open contact with the CIA, expressing officially his willingness to cooperate with them.

Nagell's letters, written in semi-code to Arthur Greenstein, a friend living in Mexico, reveal his close acquaintance with the New Orleans conspiracy. He terms Oswald "the ghoul," and Ferrie "Hairy de Fairy," giving Ferrie's correct address on Louisiana Avenue Parkway. He names "Dirty Dick" (Helms, who ran CIA's "dirty tricks" division) as the person who gave the order for John F. Kennedy's murder, a view shared by Colonel William Bishop, a Nagell CIA associate. Bishop told author Gary Shaw, "Richard Helms gave the order for the assassination." Gerry Patrick Hemming concurs with too many others not to be credible here: "Helms is behind the entire operation to kill JFK."

"Clay Shaw will probably be convicted, as he is guilty," Nagell writes. "Clay will be slurred as fruit." Nagell knew that there were others "much more deserving of conviction than Shaw," although Shaw was "of more importance than Ferrie." Nagell noted that Oswald "did not visit Ferry's [sic] training camp at the same time Shaw was purportedly there, at least not while I was Oswald's manager." As for the motive for the assassination: CIA, and Counter Intelligence in particular, "hated" John F. Kennedy "for planning to curb activities of spook outfits, especially CIA." CIA was further incensed that Kennedy was "thinking of effecting rapprochement with Fidel and establishing better relation with USSR. Fidel not adverse."

"Bang bang," Nagell concludes. "JFK dead. CIA et al. expand powers. CIA most powerful."

Nagell's assertion that he met with Lee Harvey Oswald in Mexico City in July 1963 is corroborated by Thomas Edward Beckham. Beckham remembers that at one point that summer in New Orleans Oswald remarked that he had just returned from Mexico. By 1969, Nagell had also revealed that at the time he was meeting with William Martin, he was visited by CIA agents who "cautioned him to keep his mouth shut about his ties with Oswald."

In yet another attempt to deflect Garrison's investigation, a character named Ronald Lee Augustinovich popped up, mimicking Nagell's story. He had been assigned to Oswald as part of a CIA team "trying to find the source of an intelligence leak," "Augustinovich" claimed. He told Garrison just enough to seem credible, that Oswald worked for the CIA, and that "a pilot in New Orleans was silenced by the CIA and they made it look like suicide," this pilot, David Ferrie, being one of Augustinovich's own informants.

One of Garrison's inexperienced volunteers fell for the story, insisting that Augustinovich was "the only person that might give us an Oswald-CIA link in sworn testimony." Jimmy Alcock flew to Miami where he heard Augustinovich's story of Oswald in New York infiltrating an assassination plot, only for the plotters to use Oswald as a patsy. On behalf of the CIA, Augustinovich said, he had attempted to infiltrate the group. It was all patent disinformation, designed to move Garrison away from blaming the CIA for the crime. Later CIA-FBI liaison files were to reveal that Augustinovich was indeed a CIA agent, but not one inclined to offer Jim Garrison any valuable assistance.

A more intriguing source with information connecting Oswald and Shaw appeared in the person of a self-proclaimed former CIA employee named Donold P. Norton, recorded in Garrison's files as "Donald." On a British Columbia radio station, Norton described delivering a package of money to "Harvey Lee Oswald" in Monterrey, Mexico. He had gone with his information first to the *Vancouver Sun*, only for CIA temporarily to kill the article "because there was no truth in it." Charlie Ward, a skeptic in all matters conspiratorial, went to Vancouver to interview Norton, since he was from Ward's home town of Columbus, Georgia.

Ward found himself in the presence of a very nervous, nondescript-looking man in glasses, whom he believed sufficiently to invite to Tulane and Broad. He had been recruited in 1957 by the CIA at Fort Benning, Georgia, Norton said, speaking very rapidly. A professional organist and pianist, with a master's degree in music, Norton had been playing in the Main Officers' Open Mess. His CIA handler, he says, had requested that he pretend to be homosexual, the better to spy on possible homosexuals. He went on to uncover a general who spent an evening with him in drag.

Before long, Norton said, he was working under James Angleton at Counter Intelligence, his assignments issuing from "The Captain," E. B. Worrell, who had been an acting postmaster under President Eisenhower. Oswald had gone to the Soviet Union under Angleton, Norton said. When Norton became a courier, the CIA paid him, he says, first one thousand, then two thousand dollars a week.

Residing in Minneapolis in September 1962, Norton was approached by a man he knew as "Mr. Bertrand," who handed him an attaché case. His assignment was to deliver this case to a "Harvey Lee" at the Hotel Yamajel in Monterrey, Mexico. It contained $50,000 and was destined for the anti-Castro movement.

Norton says he had previously met Bertrand at the Double Gate Country Club in Albany, Georgia, where he had been performing. He had also heard that Bertrand had been flown to Georgia by a man named "Hugh Pharris," who had appeared at the club in sunglasses.

At the Yamajel, "Harvey Lee" told Norton he was from "New Orleans." A southerner himself, Norton verified that Oswald's accent was both correct and unlikely to be faked. "Harvey Lee" was a man of slight build with thinning hair and extremely reticent. There was no question in Norton's mind but that he was an Agency employee. (That Oswald was living in Fort Worth, working at Leslie Welding, did not preclude his having met Norton in Monterrey.)

In return for the attaché case, Oswald handed him a portfolio of documents, which Norton said he delivered to a CIA operative in Calgary, Alberta. He had recognized Oswald right after the assassination, although he had not known him as "Oswald." Later another Norton CIA contact, Edgar A. Horhorouny (Eddie Horouny), whose cover was as a still photographer at WDAK-TV, channel 28, in Columbus, told Norton that the real name of "Bertrand" was Clay Shaw.

In New Orleans Donold P. Norton identified Oswald's photograph, and also Clay Shaw's as the man he had known as "Mr. Bertrand." He looked at a photograph of David Ferrie. The "repulsive photograph" was not "Hugh Pharris," Norton said.

He hadn't come forward because he feared for his life, Norton explained. He didn't believe Oswald shot President Kennedy because he was with the CIA, "and if he did it, then you'd better believe the whole CIA was involved." He was willing to testify against Clay Shaw in court.

Checking out Norton's background, Garrison discovered he had been arrested once, but never convicted of anything. He thought Norton might be a former CIA employee who "had encountered a corner of the operation." Yet there was a "question mark and we don't need him."

No information in Garrison's office was safe from the CIA, which soon did a check on Norton, on "Hugh Pharris" and on Norton's "bodyguard," a plainclothes Royal Canadian Mounted Police officer and Norton friend named Lou Reisig. CIA then issued its standard boilerplate denial: "We can find no record of any of the names involved and have never had any association with them." For someone of whom they had never heard, the CIA made a concerted effort, scouring the Cuban Operations Group at JMWAVE and Counter Intelligence for traces of "Donald P. Norton."

In New Orleans, Irvin Dymond requested that Lloyd Ray, an old friend, put him in touch with someone "in authority in CIA" about the *Vancouver Sun's* Norton article. The request went up to Lawrence Houston himself, who responded favorably: "We have means of getting this information to Dymond for use in preparing Shaw case without involving Hunter [Leake] or Agency." The Shaw lawyers had a particular request: they wanted Lloyd Ray publicly to deny that Norton "had ever worked for the Agency."

CIA complied. Donovan V. Pratt even had a ready explanation for this extraordinary interference in a state prosecution: It is suggested that "the only reason given for our interest is that Norton has made false allegations that CIA employed him."

In September 1967, Reisig was assaulted by three men in white shirts and ties in a Vancouver parking lot. "Keep your nose out of anything that concerns the United States," he was told. In a written statement, Reisig said he believed "that these were CIA men who would have reason to beat [me] because of my association with Norton." Asked if he believed the CIA was behind Kennedy's death, Reisig said, "I don't think. I know they were."

Learning of the incident, Jim Garrison requested a copy of the police report from the Royal Canadian Mounted Police. Instead, the Vancouver police sent the Reisig file to J. E. Milnes, SAC at the FBI's Seattle field office, refusing Garrison on the ground that they could furnish information only to "police agencies." Vancouver offered Milnes the opportunity to decide "what portion if any of the information" should be made available to the district attorney's office in New Orleans.

Milnes stonewalled, then insisted he was not "in a position in this case to advise you concerning the disposition of material from your files." He would not authorize the Vancouver police to release any files to New Orleans. The reaches of the FBI to protect the CIA and to thwart Jim Garrison extended well north of the border.

The Warren Commission did not summon Richard Case Nagell, who was available, and even wrote to J. Lee Rankin offering to testify. Nor did they call Norton, who was not. The Warren Commission volumes quote Nagell only in an FBI report in which Nagell claims that "his association with Oswald was purely social." There is no mention of New Orleans, or, Jim Garrison noted, why Nagell was even questioned.

JOHN F. KENNEDY, JIM GARRISON AND THE CIA

11

I've got to do something about those CIA bastards.
—John Fitzgerald Kennedy

THE HISTORICAL RECORD CORROBORATES Richard Case Nagell's view that the CIA hated Kennedy most "for planning to curb activities of spook outfits, especially CIA." Reading an April 1966 *New York Times* article, "C.I.A.: Maker of Policy, or Tool?" Jim Garrison also registered Kennedy's profound warfare with the Agency. He circled the paragraph where Kennedy was quoted by an insider as threatening to "splinter the C.I.A. in a thousand pieces and scatter it to the wind." He also marked a sentence where Kennedy countermanded President Eisenhower, who had exempted the CIA from control by American ambassadors abroad. Kennedy reversed that, putting the ambassadors in control.

By the end of 1966, Garrison was persuaded that Kennedy was murdered as a result of his struggle with the CIA, and, behind it, the Pentagon's "war machine," which was determined to have its ground war, if not in Cuba, then elsewhere. A month after Kennedy's death, former president Harry Truman expressed on the front page of the *Washington Post* his dismay that the CIA he created had been running a shadow government, becoming "operational." Truman declared that the CIA was "in urgent need of correction." (Brazenly, Allen Dulles had even told a reporter to think of the CIA as "the State Department for unfriendly countries").

New York Times columnist Arthur Krock had warned of CIA malfeasance two months earlier. The CIA, Krock wrote, was a "malignancy" on the body politic. With startling prescience, in October of 1963, Krock in his outrage all but predicted the Kennedy assassination. If the United States ever experiences an attempted coup, Krock wrote, "It will come from the C.I.A. and not the Pentagon." Between Kennedy and the CIA there was now raging "an intra-administration war," with the CIA serving the needs of the military and those corporations that stood most to gain from a ground war.

Liberal journalist Walter Lippmann could not help but note that the CIA was bursting the bounds of its mandate. Forty years later, historian Arthur Schlesinger Jr., a Kennedy adviser, would remark quietly to Jim Garrison's old classmate Wilmer Thomas that they had been at war with "the National Security people." That the CIA exacted its revenge on Kennedy has been an open secret since 1963.

After the CIA in 1954 had overthrown President Arbenz in Guatemala, its first "solo flight" as a policy-maker, President Eisenhower recognized that the Agency was dangerously out of control. He established a "President's Board of Consultants on Foreign Intelligence Activities." Its conclusion was that the CIA's clandestine services were "operating for the most part on an autonomous and free-wheeling basis in highly critical areas," in direct conflict with State Department policy; its recommendation was that Eisenhower fire Allen Dulles, or at the very least force him to accept an administrative deputy. Eisenhower's reward was that the clandestine services, then run by Richard Bissell, former assistant of Frank Wisner, sabotaged the May 1, 1960 foray of the U-2 flown by Francis Gary Powers. The U-2 fleet had been dubbed "RBAF," which stood for "Richard Bissell's Air Force," one more indication of CIA arrogance. The Agency lied directly to Eisenhower, insisting that should the plane be shot down, neither the aircraft nor the pilot would survive. So Bissell would lie to John F. Kennedy and insist that "failure was almost impossible" at the Bay of Pigs.

Despite Eisenhower's reluctance, the CIA insisted upon a flight close to the time of Eisenhower's scheduled May 16th summit with Khrushchev, de Gaulle and Macmillan, arguing, with no discernible evidence, that this last flight was urgent. Years later, the CIA would admit in hearings before the Senate that this flight wasn't particularly necessary at all. The issue of CIA malfeasance in the failure of Powers' mission was not even raised.

Eisenhower, reluctantly, had declared that the cut-off date for U-2 flights was May 1st, assuming that meant the CIA would organize the flight during the last two weeks of April. But it was on May 1 that Francis Gary Powers was sent aloft. In insisting on that one additional overflight, Bissell succeeded in making policy, which meant destroying detente and with it Eisenhower's desire to cut the country's defense budget. Rapprochement with the Soviet Union meant for Eisenhower a subsequent redirecting of the country's resources to its domestic needs. This was not to be.

Powers' mission seems to have been doomed. Both the circumstantial and the direct evidence that Powers' flight was interfered with by those in charge are overwhelming. "Powers came down because his aircraft was fixed to fail," stated retired Air Force Colonel L. Fletcher Prouty, who was in charge of providing military support for the clandestine services, and whose data should not be disregarded because of his speculations about a "secret team." Powers' flight was made to fail by a shortage of the proper fuel, Prouty concluded. Prouty was also alarmed that the flight violated standard procedure. Powers was laden with identification, not least a Department of Defense identification card. The U-2 itself bore identifying marks, violating a National Security Council edict. Whereas Powers should have been bearing no identity, he was possessed of enough for the Soviets promptly to announce that he was a "spy" from the United States. "That is why Powers survived and why they landed in good shape," Prouty reasoned. "'They' equals Powers and the U-2."

Other evidence suggests that the CIA deliberately routed Powers into the path of nests of Soviet missiles it knew could shoot him down if he was flying too low. That Powers' top secret camera had been removed suggested that someone knew this plane was not coming home. It was a catastrophe timed to thwart the May 16th summit with Premier Khrushchev that Eisenhower hoped would cap his presidency.

Seizing the high road, Khrushchev immediately demanded that Eisenhower admit he had no knowledge of the flight and fire Dulles and Bissell. The CIA had forced Eisenhower's hand, realizing that he "could not honestly say that he didn't know what was going on," Prouty writes in The Secret Team. "At the same time he had to announce to the world that he had known about the flight." "The White House and the other agencies did not so much approve the flights as hold a veto power over them," David Wise and Thomas B. Ross write in their very cautious little book, The U-2 Affair. When Eisenhower in his much-quoted farewell address warned of the dangers of the military-industrial complex, Prouty speculates, he had in mind his own political sabotage at the hands of the CIA in the U-2 fiasco. During the summit that failed, a trigger-happy Pentagon man even put the U.S. military on alert for ten hours, fanning the flames of Cold War belligerence Eisenhower had intended the summit to defuse.

Powers himself could not help but note that he had been given a "dog" of a plane, which had never flown right and was possessed of a fuel tank "which wouldn't feed all its fuel." There had been almost no overflights from early 1958 until April 1960, Powers notes. The purpose of his own flight he did not know. Even before he reached the Soviet border, Powers writes in his memoir, "I had the feeling they knew I was coming." Powers concludes: "No man, even in the privacy of his innermost thoughts, likes to admit he has been used."

Powers writes that he was disgusted when his defense counsel argued that it should have been Allen Dulles and the CIA in that Moscow dock. It was in fact so. Questioned by the Senate Foreign Relations Committee on where he had received the authority for Powers' flight, Dulles replied, "Well, we had a group." Bissell was conspicuously absent that day.

If U-2 flights were suspended routinely at politically sensitive moments, they certainly were not suspended this time. No credible explanation for this was provided at the inquiry. The proceedings were edited by Chip Bohlen and Richard Helms, who had replaced Bissell has deputy director for plans. Helms moves to the heart of the U-2 story, just as he will to the assassination of President Kennedy. Under the practiced hand of Helms, a censored version of the hearing was produced. Nothing from Dulles' five-and-a-half hour testimony was quoted. Some records were burned.

A few years later, Powers resigned from the CIA. When the Agency awarded its "intelligence star" to pilots who had participated in the U-2 program, Powers was not among them.

Powers adds that a CIA officer was given a leave of absence so that he might help prepare material on the U-2 incident for President Eisenhower's memoirs, so nervous was the Agency with regard to its role in the U-2 incident. Powers goes so far as to admit that there are "clues" that the CIA "betrayed" his final U-2 flight, only, suddenly, in an abrupt reversal, to term that betrayal, which he has already documented, a "wild fantasy."

When, years later, a writer as careful as Michael Beschloss suggested the fragility and instability of the U-2, no less a high level CIA figure than Lawrence R. Houston accused Beschloss of getting his facts wrong in the pages of *Periscope*, the journal of the Association of Former Intelligence Officers. That the U-2 was not shot down and obliterated in itself suggests that the Soviets were very well informed of its capabilities and peculiar, indeed, "fragility." Confusing the issue was that radar expert Lee Harvey Oswald had already been dispatched into the Soviet Union, and would even appear at Francis Gary Powers' trial. In fact, the Soviets were well aware that there were U-2's at Atsugi.

A startling new FBI document of April 21, 1966, reveals that the Soviets knew not only that U-2's were being dispatched, but how to disable them. The information provided to the Soviets did not come from Lee Harvey Oswald. Rather, the source was a former United States Army sergeant named Jack Edward Dunlap, assigned to the National Security Agency. Committing treason, Dunlap had given the Soviets "important information regarding the U-2 flights over the USSR." It was Dunlap's information that "provided the Soviet Union with the capability of shooting down the Powers U-2 aircraft."

As late as March 18, 1971, a "top secret" document notification was placed in the files of both Jack Edward Dunlap and "Gary Francis Powers" [sic] with "direct reference" to the "TS document" revealing that Dunlap had admitted to his wife "that he furnished information to the Soviets for money."

An "extremely sensitive source who has furnished reliable information in the past" told the FBI as well that "as a result of Dunlap's information the Soviets were well aware of when the U-2 planes crossed over the Soviet Union. The Soviets always had their anti-aircraft guns trained on these planes." It was in part as a result of his being pressed by China that Khrushchev shot down Powers' U-2 aircraft. Khrushchev had planned to use Dunlap's information at the United Nations, but was dissuaded because it might compromise Soviet agent Dunlap. Dunlap also "gave the Soviets lists of sources of information the Americans had in the Soviet Union and a lot of reports on Central Intelligence Agency matters." That the CIA knew about Dunlap's reporting to the Soviets on the U-2 seems apparent.

On the night of July 22–23, 1963, Jack Edward Dunlap committed suicide.

Within a month of Kennedy's inauguration, the CIA had also defied *him*, meeting on February 16, 1961, without his knowledge, with assassins planning the murder of President Trujillo in the Dominican Republic. Kennedy's policy was that the United States should not initiate the overthrow of Trujillo, at least not before we knew what government would succeed him. Concealing its actions from the president and defying his expressed wishes, the CIA went ahead anyway. It had attempted the assassination of Patrice

Lumumba in the Congo without clearing the idea with Eisenhower, and saw no reason to relinquish its power to the new young president. A CIA cable on the Trujillo assassination reads: "This matter is not to be discussed with State Department."

In violation of its charter, CIA had long been operating domestically, creating a Domestic Operations Division to "handle all of this domestic activity." Led by C. Tracey Barnes, CIA opened offices from New York to Los Angeles. In 1975 James Angleton admitted, "Going back to OSS days, we've had operations that were domestic." The FBI's intelligence service was increasingly nervous. As D. J. Brennan put it, echoing Eisenhower's President's Board of Consultants on Foreign Intelligence Activities, "CIA is too prone to freewheeling."

The CIA put John Kennedy on notice from the moment he took office. Allen Dulles, the Director of Central Intelligence, and Richard Bissell invited a dozen White House aides to the all-male Alibi Club. Already Bissell was superintending the CIA's attempts to murder Fidel Castro using biological contamination. "Liquid bacteria might be best," Bissell advised, "in his coffee, tea or bouillon."

After dinner, Bissell addressed his guests. "I'm your man-eating shark," he declared. Listening, CIA man Robert Amory approved. Bissell was getting "a head start on State," warning the Kennedy team that "the CIA was a secret state of its own." Nor had this CIA shadow government bothered to inform President-elect Kennedy that the CIA had enlisted the Mafia in its attempts to murder Castro. Running this government within the government was a group at the highest level of the CIA: Dulles, Bissell, Helms, Frank Wisner and Kim Roosevelt, as well as the ubiquitous Lawrence Houston. James Angleton, chief of Counter Intelligence, was on board. On the agenda were assassinations that "did not appear on paper."

"Never will," Helms later told the Church Committee defiantly, as he would take his secrets to the grave.

Four months into his presidency, John Kennedy, whom onetime CIA asset Gerald Patrick Hemming calls "the last President to believe he could take power," refused to submit to CIA blackmail and commit land troops to Brigade 2506 about to land at the Bay of Pigs. He cut short the expected air cover.

What the U-2 incident was to Eisenhower's presidency, the Bay of Pigs was to Kennedy's. Both Eisenhower and Kennedy were wary of military buildup, wary of a bankrupting deficit that a burgeoning defense budget and military forays engendered. Both were opposed by a CIA pursuing a policy of fierce militarism. "Any person who doesn't clearly understand that national security and national solvency are mutually dependent and that permanent maintenance of a crushing weight of military power would eventually produce dictatorship should not be entrusted with any kind of responsibility in our country," Eisenhower had said passionately. Kennedy would have agreed.

The old soldier in Eisenhower could not disavow the CIA, let alone fire its leader, even though Eisenhower's son John thought his father did John Kennedy "a disservice by not firing Dulles." Kennedy felt no such constraint. After Brigade 2506's inevitable defeat and Kennedy's refusal to be blackmailed into invading Cuba, he fired Allen Dulles, which also meant the departure of his subordinate, General Charles Cabell, whose brother, Jim Garrison would often note, was mayor of Dallas at the moment Kennedy was murdered. Soon Bissell was banished from the clandestine services. Helms confessed years later that after Kennedy had defied the Agency, Helms had vowed he would "fall in front of the onrushing train instead of letting that happen again."

Kennedy replaced Dulles with John McCone, whom William Harvey, in charge of CIA assassinations, chose not to debrief, as the CIA's attempts to murder Fidel Castro proceeded. Harvey, as his CIA colleague John Whitten described him, was "a really hard-boiled, unsubtle, ruthless guy . . . a very dangerous man." Harvey had already obtained the approval of Richard Helms not to brief the Director of Central Intelligence (DCI) on Johnny Rosselli's involvement in the attempt to murder Fidel Castro, and didn't do so. Nor did Helms, when he took over the clandestine services, involve McCone, granting him "plausible deniability." It was "not necessary or advisable," Helms decided. McCone, a devout Catholic, might have been disturbed, Helms said. Lawrence Houston agreed.

John F. Kennedy set himself on a course of eviscerating the power of the CIA. He began to cut away at its operational jurisdiction. He reevaluated the CIA budget and the Agency's financial autonomy. As Norman Polmar points out in *Spyplane,* "under a law passed on June 20, 1949, the Director of Central Intelligence was designated the only U.S. government employee who could obligate federal funds without the use of vouchers."

Kennedy dared to challenge this prerogative.

In May of 1961, only a month after the Bay of Pigs, Kennedy formed his own "Special Group," meeting as the president's Foreign Intelligence Advisory Board. Its express purpose was to bring the CIA under the control of the president. "Covert action programs of the

CIA may not have been worth the risk nor worth the great expenditure of manpower and money," Kennedy told the group on May 15th. CIA should continue its "intelligence gathering." He, however, was undertaking a "total reassessment of U.S. covert action policies and programs," with the help of General Maxwell Taylor, whom he appointed special assistant for intelligence "on top of covert operations." Kennedy told the press he was resisting the pressure of the "intelligence community" to assassinate Castro, although in fact both he and his brother were to be directly involved in plots to murder the Cuban leader.

Soon overflights bound for Cuba would be in the hands of the Strategic Air Command, not the CIA. The Navy would participate. Kennedy created a Defense Intelligence Agency, responsible to him. He commissioned a list of directives defining precisely what the CIA could and could not do. By the close of 1961, the "Special Group" had seventeen recommendations for the "reorganization and redirection of CIA." Kennedy also signed a National Security Action Memorandum limiting CIA operations that required "greater firepower than that generated by handguns." It effectively prevented CIA covert operations except for small skirmishes.

The CIA retaliated by withholding intelligence from the president. By June 7, 1961, Kennedy was complaining that he was "receiving inadequate information concerning developments in a number of countries." As his ally General James H. Doolittle had put it, the "covert operations dog is wagging the intelligence tail." In one of his final acts, General Cabell delayed the distribution of the Inspector General's Report on the Bay of Pigs from being distributed to Kennedy's Foreign Intelligence Advisory Board.

"I've got to do something about those CIA bastards," Kennedy said. It was the persistent refrain of his presidency. By the turn of the New Year 1962, he demanded not only a reorganization of the Agency, but a redefinition of the role of the Director of Central Intelligence.

It was the independence and power of the CIA that John Kennedy fought, its undermining of his authority, and its secret alliance with the military. With one particular virulent policy, the assassination of Fidel Castro, he did not disagree, as the record amply reveals. Robert Kennedy, representing his brother before the Foreign Intelligence Advisory Board, began openly to encourage the assassination of Fidel Castro, with, Helms would testify, "no limitations" on how that was to be accomplished.

William Harvey would testify under oath before the Church Committee that on at least two occasions there was White House approval and "initiative" of the "specific Rosselli operation" to murder Castro. Sabotage against Cuba was a given, accepted by both sides. In June 1963, President Kennedy approved "a broad economic sabotage program directed against refineries, shipping facilities and other areas of the Cuban economy." Robert Kennedy sent a message from the president that "more priority should be given to mount sabotage operations."

Bobby instructed his "hero," General Edward Lansdale, to send a memo to CIA's William Harvey to come up with "assassination contingency plans" and to plan "concrete action against Cuba." When Ramsey Clark became attorney general, among items remaining from Bobby's tenure, left there during the Katzenbach period, he discovered copies of Lansdale's memos to Bobby outlining how Castro could be murdered. Calling Castro "primary target," Bobby urged Lansdale to be ever "new and imaginative" in getting rid of the Castro regime.

Unknowingly Bobby was enlisting the CIA's murder apparatus ("executive action" capability), the very apparatus soon to be turned against his brother. So Bobby Kennedy fell into a CIA trap that would render him silent about the murder of his brother for the rest of his life. Facilitating that macabre double-cross, not yet aware that it had already been accomplished, the White House itself had requested that the CIA "create an Executive Action (assassination) capability."

Furious at the ascendancy of Lansdale, the CIA decided not to attempt to "unseat him," but to deny him direct access to their Task Force W, "the CIA contribution to the Inter-Agency Mongoose effort" run by the Special Group Augmented. Bobby was its chair, reporting to the Foreign Intelligence Advisory Board. Even as their policies coincided, even as they agreed on the murder of Castro, the CIA was angry. It was the first time an Attorney General "was actively engaged in giving instruction and directions to the CIA."

The CIA now concealed its own ongoing efforts to assassinate Castro, although it was required to disclose them. "The question was never asked," Bissell told Frank Church. Bobby's group had hoped to "keep its hand tightly" on the CIA. It was not to be. Bobby requested that the CIA at least inform him if they were to continue to use Mafia elements in the assassination attempts on Castro. The CIA ignored him and went ahead anyway. Feeling no loyalty toward Bobby, Lansdale informed the FBI and the National Security Agency that both John and Robert Kennedy were deeply involved in the schemes to kill Castro.

The CIA Miami station, JMWAVE, enjoyed an "operational relationship" with several editors and reporters on the *Miami Herald*. These were designated by the cryptonym AMCARBON, the "carbon" connoting that they were media assets. Among them, as AMCARBON-1, was Al Burt, the *Herald's* Latin American editor, easily identified on a ten-page CIA report dated four months after the assassination that contains Burt's journalistic biography, beginning with his work at City Desk. The *Miami Herald* is spelled out, unredacted, as "Iden[tity] 3."

Burt, JMWAVE acknowledge, was "by no means an expert on Latin America." What he provided for the agency was domestic intelligence. Like other AMCARBONs, Burt was willing, CIA notes in this document, "to bring potentially significant operational leads to JMWAVE's attention" and to "carry out certain operational support tasks." This, of course, was exactly what its New Orleans asset Clay Shaw also accomplished for the agency.

Among Burt's "contacts and sources," from whose efforts he had provided CIA with information, was Edmund Leahy of the Washington News Bureau. Leahy was "particularly interesting," Burt told JMWAVE; his daughter was "a secretary in the office of Attorney General Robert Kennedy." What this explosive CIA document, issuing from its Miami station, offers is concrete evidence that Bobby was being spied on "from within," to use the phrase he used in his book on the Mafia.

Bobby had the wrong enemy, however. Someone on his staff, whom, like Edward Lansdale, he believed he could trust, was betraying him to the enemy from whom he and his brother had the most to fear, and which, in their youthful inexperience, they underestimated. This was the Central Intelligence Agency, which had been charting the Kennedy brothers' every move.

John Kennedy continued to attempt to curtail CIA operations. "We become prisoners of our agents," his aide Richard Goodwin would reflect. Kennedy sent Goodwin down to No Name Key to meet with that free lance soldier of fortune Gerald Patrick Hemming and his fellow mercenaries. Would they be interested in taking over the CIA radio station on Swan Island where the CIA monitored its illegal flights into Cuba?

Hemming preferred to remain on good terms with the CIA. Shrewdly, he perceived that its power exceeded that of John F. Kennedy. His loyalty was to James Angleton anyway, on whose behalf he had infiltrated Castro's 26th of July movement, even participating in Castro's "execution squads" until the Cuban leader threw him out. He would not be co-opted by a mere president. "We want to be involved in combat operations. We don't want to be office pinkies," Hemming said, sending Goodwin home. The Swan Island operation remained under the control of CIA's David Atlee Phillips, who was before long to be spotted with Lee Harvey Oswald in Dallas and Louisiana.

As the CIA continued to keep John F. Kennedy in the dark, Kennedy instructed his friend Bill Baggs, editor of the *Miami News,* to report to him on the actions of JMWAVE. He told Baggs he doubted the CIA was giving him a true picture of "Cuban matters." Bewildered, Kennedy blamed John McCone.

On July 1, 1962, Baggs convened a group of characters, including a Kennedy backer named Theodore Racoosin. Racoosin invited his friend, soldier of fortune Howard K. Davis, who invited Hemming along. Present as well were the CIA-sponsored Cubans, Eduardo "Bayo" Perez ("Eddie Bayo"), who had served in the 26th of July movement under Raoul Castro, and Tony Cuesta. Lawrence Laborde, who would become a Jim Garrison suspect, was also on hand. The meeting, a measure of Kennedy's helplessness, degenerated into a farce as the Cubans complained about CIA failures to keep promises regarding money and materiel for their anti-Castro operations.

Kennedy wanted to know about opposition to Castro within Cuba. Richard Helms, in charge of such information, would tell him nothing. Defiant, the CIA now sponsored an "OPERATION FORTY" in Miami, training Cubans in methods of torture and letting its own low-level operatives run free, to Kennedy's chagrin.

When it came to manipulating the press, David Atlee Phillips was second to none. In October of 1962, as Kennedy was negotiating with Khrushchev over the missiles the Soviet Union had placed in Cuba, Phillips timed raids into Cuba by the terrorist group Alpha 66. At a Washington press conference, Phillips' asset Antonio Veciana announced that Alpha 66 had just attacked a Russian ship in a Cuban harbor, and had engaged in a firefight with Russian troops. It was Eisenhower and the U-2 all over again. Kennedy fought back, and the CIA failed once more in its ongoing effort to provoke a ground war in Cuba.

Throughout the missile crisis, the CIA withheld information from President Kennedy. Instead, it briefed Senator Kenneth Keating of New York, whose wife, Mary, had been "Dickie" Bissell's secretary. Keating rose to the floor of the Senate on October 9, 1962, announcing "at least a half-dozen launching sites for intermediate range tactical missiles in Cuba," facts not yet in Kennedy's possession. Keating attacked Kennedy for "a tremendous error and serious concession to the Soviets." He had been supplied with films of Cuba by CIA asset, and future Garrison suspect, Loran Hall.

"Who's giving Keating this stuff?" Kennedy demanded, even now not quite fully aware of the intensity of the CIA opposition to him. When he finally figured it out, he became apoplectic. "Those CIA bastards. I'm going to get those bastards if it's the last thing I ever do," he vowed again. It was Bobby, brother of the dead president, who got even by running against Keating for his New York Senate seat, and beating him.

The warfare between Kennedy and the CIA had grown so intense that McCone threatened to resign. During the summer of 1963, Kennedy shut down those CIA-sponsored anti-Castro training camps in Florida and Louisiana. In the autumn, he authorized a rapprochement with Castro through his old schoolmate William Attwood as "a gesture to try to establish communication." Meanwhile Bobby, Lansdale and McCone were still working on a "Guideline for a Post-Castro Program." Even McCone was amazed at how openly President Kennedy "suggested the possibility of pursuing both courses at the same time."

In the intra-government warfare that exploded in the murder of John F. Kennedy, the president represented not a white knight for peace and brotherhood, but a different economic perspective. In Vietnam, he wanted not the ground war that would lead to a catastrophic death toll and an insupportable deficit, but the use of Special Forces, aided by an indigenous military. Castro he wanted dead not by the military invasion the CIA pressed for throughout his presidency, but by "clandestine means." A Georgetown dinner party found Kennedy inquiring of former British intelligence agent Ian Fleming what his fictional creation James Bond would have done to get rid of Fidel Castro.

At a meeting of the Special Group Augmented, Robert Kennedy did not object when someone said—and Richard Goodwin remembers that it might well have been Bobby himself—that "the only real solution would be to assassinate Castro." Asked whether Kennedy was involved in those assassination plots, Goodwin would reply only with an analogy: It was like Henry II's asking, "Who will rid me of this turbulent priest?" referring to the king's veiled order for the assassination of his adversary, Thomas à Becket.

At times, the Kennedy brothers' efforts to murder Castro were quite open. At their request, New Orleans' own Guy Johnson, a former naval commander and ONI operative, brought to the White House Lieutenant Commander Richard Gordon. In the presence of both John and Robert Kennedy and Secretary of State Dean Rusk, Gordon was enlisted to train a marksman to kill Castro. The sniper set forth, only for Castro, forewarned, to meet him at the airport. Gordon was punished with residence at Bellevue Hospital in New York City, where, as a favor to Guy Johnson, F. Lee Bailey represented him against the Navy and won his release.

That pragmatism governed the Kennedy family has been well documented. Kennedy intimate Charles Bartlett would conclude that Kennedy confounded the national interest with his own reelection. From Louisiana comes one painful example. According to former congressman John R. Rarick, who had seen the Angola records, now gone, Kennedy's sister Rosemary Kennedy, who was declared retarded, her level of psychological disarray unclear, and later subjected to a lobotomy, who became an icon to "mental health awareness," was actually a thief. She had been incarcerated at Angola for writing bad checks.

A "doctor's appointment" was arranged in Baton Rouge, and Rosemary was seen no more in the state of Louisiana. It was her criminal activity that apparently prompted the family decision to label this woman as hopelessly damaged, Rarick suggests.

"They're going to throw our asses out of there at almost any point," Kennedy had feared, referring to Vietnam, as he signed National Security Memorandum (263) mandating the withdrawal of one thousand soldiers from Vietnam. But long before he decided against a ground war in Vietnam, Kennedy's fate had been sealed.

At the November 22, 1963, meeting of the Foreign Intelligence Advisory Board," McCone demanded that President Kennedy "try to correct the CIA's public image." McCone wanted the president himself to refute Arthur Krock's charge that the CIA functioned as a "third government in South Vietnam." The clandestine services, however, which had managed the murder of President Diem and plotted against Lumumba, had its own idea of how to deal with John F. Kennedy.

After the death of his brother, Robert Kennedy, viewing the CIA as his chief suspect, immediately confronted John McCone. "Did the CIA kill my brother?" he demanded. Then he called Enrique ("Harry") Williams, among the favorite Cubans in his "special project."

"One of your guys did it!" Bobby declared. He asked his aide, Frank Mankiewicz, whether "any of our people were involved," and Mankiewicz thought, did you think there might be? On the chance that the Mafia might have planned the assassination, Bobby sent Justice Department lawyer and his personal operative, Walter Sheridan, to Dallas to inquire whether the Mafia had anything to do with the murder of his brother. The answer came back in the negative.

Then Bobby called Chicago lawyer Julius Draznin and charged him "to find out what the word in Chicago was on the hit." In two to four days, as Draznin remembers, he had his answer: the assassination had *not* been a Mafia-organized operation. Draznin, an FBI liaison with organized crime, based in the field office of the NLRB, spent that week in close communication with Sheridan and Bobby. When Sheridan in 1975 told the Church Committee that the "mob" had been behind the assassination, he knew better. Bobby Kennedy reportedly even asked Daniel Patrick Moynihan to investigate whether Jimmy Hoffa could have blackmailed the Secret Service. The answer again came back to him: There was no evidence that organized crime had masterminded the murder of his brother. Complicit in those plots to kill Castro, Lee Harvey Oswald in the company of his own people, along with other, more important participants in the assassination of his brother, Bobby now had no alternative but to protect the Agency.

Oswald, Jim Garrison concluded, had been "an employee of the CIA which skillfully nurtured him and convinced him that he was performing undercover intelligence assignments for the government." Oswald was "bright and deeply experienced, if low level, and had he not been eliminated, he'd still be talking," Garrison said. The Agency, Garrison was firmly convinced, was behind the assassination. "The CIA is a major menace to the democracy I thought we lived in," he told the press.

"Jim," William Alford said on a day when he was exhausted, "If the CIA killed the President, there's nothing a chicken shit assistant district attorney from New Orleans is going to be able to do about it." Knowing how deeply Garrison believed in his case, Alford figured he would be fired on the spot. Instead, Garrison burst out laughing.

"There's probably nothing a chicken shit District Attorney is going to be able to do about it either," he said.

Worried, the CIA watched. On February 6th, 1967, Lloyd Ray wrote to the Director of the Domestic Contact Service that there was "some truth in the allegation of the Garrison investigation." He feared "Garrison will expose some CIA operations in Louisiana." From the moment of its 1948 agreement with the CIA, the FBI had acquiesced in the CIA's operating at home as well as abroad. Now the Agency relied on the FBI to help subvert Garrison's work.

"Due to Garrison's irresponsible actions," Hoover raged, "no contact is being made with him or any member of his staff." Should any agents be asked for information, they were to say, "No comment." Robert Rightmyer, now the Special Agent in Charge in New Orleans, was warned: "Give Garrison nothing!" All personnel in New Orleans were to "keep their mouths shut." The FBI hated Garrison with an "intense passion," Gordon Novel was to discover from his own contacts with the Bureau. The only investigation they were making was of Garrison himself, even as the FBI claimed its interest was in continuing to investigate the murder of the president.

All leads reported to the FBI were suppressed. John Alice, working at an import-export firm at the International Trade Mart, came forward to the FBI and identified several figures in the photographs of Oswald handing out his leaflets. Jim Garrison was not informed. There was a call from a woman named Cecilia Pizzo, a friend of Delphine Roberts, who knew that "Clay Shaw and Clay Bertrand were one and the same person." This, too, was suppressed. When Joe Oster reported that Oswald had frequented Thomas Edward Beckham's mission, the FBI did not tell Jim Garrison. Examples of the FBI concealing valuable leads from Jim Garrison are manifold. Many Louisiana citizens believed that in presenting evidence to the FBI, they were simultaneously helping Garrison. It was not so.

The FBI papered its files with disinformation. "The Bureau's extensive investigation of Ferrie failed to develop any evidence that he was known to Lee Harvey Oswald," insists a statement issued in April 1967 by the intelligence component, Division 5.

Whether or not Hoover received a written warning from CIA operative Richard Case Nagell that the assassination of the president was being planned in New Orleans, there are on the record other suggestions of FBI foreknowledge. Dallas FBI agent James Hosty, in charge of Oswald, was ordered not to attend the luncheon for President Kennedy on November 22nd to which he had been invited. "If I knew what was good for me, I'd better stay away from there," Hosty reported to the Church Committee that he was told.

Garrison perused a letter Oswald had written to the Soviet embassy in Mexico City on November 12, 1963, revealing that Oswald knew that an official at the Cuban embassy named Eusebio Azque was being recalled on November 18th, an extraordinary fact. In every interview Garrison gave he talked about Oswald's intelligence connections. Langley contacted Lloyd Ray, while James Angleton briefed

J. Edgar Hoover about the *Paese Sera* articles, with the CIA insisting, falsely, that the CIA "has not been in contact with Clay Shaw since May 1956." The Agency was further dismayed when "Oswald was allegedly linked with CIA in some early newspaper stories." In the *States-Item,* Hoke May was writing that Clay Shaw was and still is a CIA agent.

Lawrence Houston instructed Lloyd Ray to notify Washington at once should anyone in the New Orleans FBI or CIA be subpoenaed. John McCone repeated the boilerplate denial he had offered the Warren Commission on Angleton's instructions: "Lee Harvey Oswald was never associated or connected directly or indirectly, in any way whatsoever with the Agency."

Together, FBI and CIA had to figure out how to "allay the story of CIA's possible sponsorship of Oswald's activity." Helms knew how to be emphatic. There was no record of Oswald contact with CIA, even "in the mind of any individuals," was how Helms put it. Allen Dulles insisted he had no knowledge of Oswald. The Rock's office put out the statement that there was "no record or indication that any other US government agency had used him as a source or had considered him for recruitment," which was patently false.

It was Angleton who had run the false defector program. It was Angleton who moved people between the CIA and Customs, from Charles Siragusa, his World War II friend, to Oswald. If the CIA opened Oswald's "201" file a year after he "defected," at the end of 1960, his Counter Intelligence "SIG" file had long been in place. In 1976 the Church Committee would conclude that counter-intelligence was the "focal point" of Oswald's employment with the CIA, as documentation denied to Jim Garrison began to emerge.

Garrison did learn of a memo reflecting that Oswald "less than six weeks before the assassination . . . was under surveillance by both the FBI and the CIA." It came in a notarized affidavit from State Department Officer James D. Crowley: "The first time I remember learning of Oswald's existence was when I received copies of a telegraphic message, dated October 10, 1963, from the Central Intelligence Agency, which contained information pertaining to his current activities."

Most of the documentation of Oswald's CIA connections emerged after Jim Garrison's investigation. This includes a document in which Thomas Casasin, a CIA employee in the "Soviet Realities" section, reveals that he wished to debrief Oswald after his return from the Soviet Union only to be thwarted by Counter Intelligence. In a

November 25, 1963, document, Casasin recounts that the Soviet Realities branch had an "operational intelligence interest in the Harvey story," and had approached Oswald to use him as an outside contact. "It makes little difference now," Casasin writes to Walter P. Haltigan after Oswald's death, "but REDWOOD had at one time an OI interest in Oswald." It was the summer of 1960. They had backed off because "this individual looks odd."

Casasin then discovered that Counter Intelligence had possessed all the information he required, but was refusing to share it with him and the "6 branch." Casasin had assumed that if Oswald had been debriefed, he would have been informed, yet he was not. Counter Intelligence Special Investigation Group (CI/SIG) knew Oswald well and were concealing what they knew from other Agency components, as one branch of the CIA reveals that Oswald worked for another, but had been kept in the dark about it.

Another example of counterintelligence protecting its pre-assassination relationship with Oswald was CIA's concealing FBI reports on Oswald's Canal Street fracas from its own Mexico City chief of station, Win Scott. This detail further corroborates that the CIA had orchestrated that Canal Street brouhaha with the DRE, whether through David Atlee Phillips or his deputy George Joannides.

Yet another trace of Oswald's CIA connection appeared a decade after Garrison had officially concluded his investigation in a CIA telegram, a document marked #304-113. In the Soviet Union, the CIA had "interviewed a former Marine who worked at the Minsk radio plant." Dated December 4, 1963, the telegram read: "Source reported Sov Con Gen told him 30 Nov that Oswald sent to USSR and married Svt girl under CIA instructions." Yet another document has surfaced, placed in Oswald's file in Mexico City. Its subject is a CIA proprietary called "Transcontinental SA," an import-export company which, among other activities, bought up bankrupt factories and rebuilt them.

Transcontinental purchased helicopters in Los Angeles destined for Cuba. A third party served as intermediary in a mirror image of the Freeport Sulphur operation. The date is October 12, 1961, when Oswald was serving counter-intelligence in the Soviet Union, the same time that Oswald's name was placed on that truck order at Bolton Ford in New Orleans. That Oswald's name is on the Transcontinental document suggests his assignment with U.S. Customs.

Further evidence of the intelligence agencies' awareness of Oswald emerges in fragments of the Church Committee files that reveal that, on November 22, 1963, Oswald's name popped up on a National Security Agency "Rhyming Dictionary," a list of names on other agency lists ("rhyming" was jargon for "comparison"). Both the CIA and the FBI contributed names to the NSA for its watch list, people who represented a "threat to the internal security of the country," some because of "their training, violent tendencies and prominence in subversive activity." Within NSA, the watch list was supervised by a CIA employee named Mabel Hoover. FBI, CIA and NSA have all publicly denied that Oswald was on their lists. The NSA material sent to the Warren Commission remains classified.

A CIA accountant with "top secret" clearance named James Wilcott, who had been with Oswald at Atsugi, had retired in 1966, having become disenchanted with the Agency. Wilcott, who never became a Garrison witness, revealed that Oswald had indeed been debriefed—at Atsugi—after he returned from the Soviet Union. On November 24th, Agency employees in Japan buzzed about "Oswald's connection with the CIA," and concluded that the assassination had been an "outright project of Headquarters with the approval of McCone, or under the direction of Dulles and Bissell." The murder of President Kennedy was at the level of the DDP (Helms), Wilcott said, with Oswald having been "recruited from the military for the express purpose of becoming a 'double agent.'"

Wilcott was certain: Oswald, who, he was told, had drawn an advance on his salary "some time in the past from you," was "an employee of the agency and was an agent." Oswald received "a full-time salary for operational work." There were at least six or seven people who "either know or believed Oswald to be an agent of the CIA," Wilcott said.

Wilcott concluded that "Ruby was paid by CIA to do away with Oswald," the plan being to "kill Kennedy, link Oswald to Castro and use this pretext to invade Cuba." Marina had been a "sleeper agent," recruited before Oswald's false defection; CIA had made a deal to get her out of the USSR with Oswald. "The phony link to the Cuban government could not be established firmly enough to serve as an excuse to attack Cuba," Wilcott concluded, hence the need to brand Oswald as the lone assassin.

As an insider, Wilcott was dangerous. In the waning days of the CIA-dominated HSCA, Robert Blakey chose Harold Leap to discredit Wilcott. Having come to HSCA from longtime service at the Drug Enforcement Agency, Harold Leap was the Agency's man; whenever there was a CIA agent or asset to be interviewed, Blakey's deputy, Gary Cornwell, sent Leap to New Orleans. Leap accompanied Robert Buras on his interview with William Gaudet.

Now Leap seized on Wilcott's vagueness about naming the specific case officers who had initially informed him of Oswald's CIA relationship. That Wilcott could not remember Oswald's cryptonym also was useful to Leap in his effort to undermine Wilcott's story. Questioning CIA people who had been at the Tokyo station, Leap fulfilled his mission: "None of the individuals had seen any documents or heard any information indicating that Lee Harvey Oswald was a CIA agent."

Leap had trouble discrediting Wilcott, who in 1965 had passed his CIA polygraph. There was only one unfavorable comment: "Subject considered a very naive man." Then Leap thought he hit pay dirt. "Jerry," Jerome E. Fox, an intelligence analyst whom Wilcott had named as having talked to him about the Oswald-CIA connection, had returned to the United States in 1962! A relieved HSCA could now continue to protect the CIA unimpeded. Meanwhile Gaeton Fonzi, HSCA's Miami investigator, learned from his own CIA source, Rolando Otero, that "Oswald was sent to Russia as a CIA agent and that the decision to kill Kennedy was made before his return to the United States."

Antonio Veciana was an asset both for the CIA under the cryptonym AMSHALE, and for 902nd Military Intelligence, one of the military intelligence groups, William Pepper reveals in *Orders to Kill,* instrumental in the assassination of Martin Luther King Jr. The 902nd was under the command of Major General William P. Yarborough, the army's assistant chief of staff for intelligence, notorious for having founded the Green Berets at Fort Bragg. The 902nd, Pepper writes, "carried out some of the most sensitive assignments" and was "a highly secretive operation." At CIA, Yarborough met directly with Richard Helms. So CIA and military intelligence worked hand in glove.

Veciana had told Gaeton Fonzi that he had seen his CIA handler David Atlee Phillips with Oswald in August of 1963. In an outline for a novel to be called *"The AMLASH Legacy,"* a *roman à clef* about the assassination, David Atlee Phillips has his hero, Harold Harrison, based on himself, acknowledge: "I was one of the two case officers who handled Lee Harvey Oswald. After working to establish his Marxist bona fides, we gave him the mission of killing Fidel Castro in Cuba."

Phillips has his Oswald character develop the Dealey Plaza plan, shooting with a sniper's rifle from an upper floor window of a building on the route where Castro often drove in an open jeep. Unknowingly he is manipulated into assassinating John F. Kennedy instead of Castro. Slyly, Phillips places "Harrison" (himself) on the high seas at the moment when Veciana claimed he had seen his handler, Maurice Bishop, with Oswald.

Phillips blames the Soviet Union for masterminding the assassination, mingling truth with fiction. Warren Commission critics, as Helms had outlined, were dupes of the KGB, as Max Holland's thesis about Jim Garrison once more can be traced, not only to Helms, but also to the most skillful of CIA propagandists, David Atlee Phillips. In an amusing side note, CIA's Win Scott steals Harrison's journal, even as, in real life, it was James Angleton who broke into *Scott's* files after his death and stole his novel manuscript.

Yet another trace of David Atlee Phillips' connections to the events of November 22nd, which included both the assassination of President Kennedy and the arming of Rolando Cubela with the means to assassinate Fidel Castro, emerges in a CIA cable. Miami is informing its Mexico City station that one "Henry J. Sloman," an alias for longtime CIA asset Anthony (Tony) Sforza, would be arriving in Mexico on November 22nd. Because the CIA was fond of providing Mafia cover for some of its assets, many people mistakenly concluded that the Mafia had been behind the assassination of President Kennedy. CIA's Sloman, himself, as Seymour M. Hersh points out, "was considered a professional gambler and a high-risk smuggler directly linked to the Mafia."

In Mexico City, Sloman/Sforza was to meet the wife of an agent designated as AMHALF-2, and retrieve a message regarding the "Martime Exfil of headquarters asset" who was to arrive in Mexico "on 22 November," and may have been Fidel Castro's sister, Juanita. Sloman was ordered to contact Phillips, mentioned here under his longtime alias "[Michael] Choaden," on the next day and pick up the information that had arrived from "[02] Exit-3." AMHALF would be a link person, part of the communication circuit providing intercepts for island assets. Between 1960 and 1963, there were something like 350,000 such intercepts either by land lines or on island assets, all directed to CIA.

Sloman was the case officer for, among others, Emilio Rodriguez, the oldest son of Arnesto Rodriguez and brother of Arnesto, Junior, whom Oswald had visited in New Orleans in an attempt to learn how he might involve himself in training camps for sabotage against Castro.

The header of this November 22nd, 1963, CIA cable includes the cryptonym PBRUMEN, which referred to Cuba. By its timing it suggests the Cubela assassination attempt of November 22nd. It also seems to suggest that Oswald believed that he was involved in the attempts on Castro's life and did not know he would be linked to the shooting in Dealey Plaza.

This extraordinary document, if fragmentary, is interesting, too, because it provides an alibi for David Atlee Phillips under the alias he used in Cuba, "Michael Choaden." If Phillips was down in Mexico, as he would be expected to be, waiting to be contacted by Sloman, he was not in Texas; this cable would confirm for any record that David Atlee Phillips was somewhere other than at Dealey Plaza on November 22, 1963.

David Atlee Phillips' nephew Shawn recounts a conversation in which Phillips, dying of lung cancer, admitted to his estranged brother James Atlee Phillips that he was indeed in Dealey Plaza on November 22nd. "Were you in Dallas that day?" James Atlee Phillips, Shawn's father, asked. From everything James Atlee Phillips knew, he suspected strongly that his brother was at the scene of the shooting of President Kennedy. David said "Yes," Shawn told author Dick Russell. Then he broke down crying. After this they hung up the phone, as if all that needed to be said had finally been said. This moment of understanding created a peace that had eluded the brothers for some years.

Yet another witness who died before Jim Garrison could reach him was a former military affairs editor at *Life* named J. Garrett Underhill, a CIA informant. "A small clique in the CIA" killed President Kennedy, Underhill told his friends. He knew the people involved and they knew what he knew. As he prepared "to blow the whistle on the CIA," Underhill was found in bed with a bullet wound behind his left ear. The date was May 8, 1964.

Jim Garrison forged ahead. He subpoenaed CIA asset Lawrence J. Laborde, a terrorist, who, piloting his *Tejana III*, had blown up a ship "running machinery to Cuba." Even Hemming calls him "plug-ugly" and "cold-blooded," a "trained CIA assassin" who had bungled two jobs in Mexico, attempting to murder Mexican politicians under the orders of Win Scott. The CIA granted Laborde "Provisional Covert Security Approval." Should he leave the country?

Laborde asked Lloyd Ray as Jim Garrison closed in on him. The Rock, pulling Laborde's CIA files, was pleased to note that he had never been paid directly by the Agency. Ray was ordered never to meet with Laborde again.

Jim Garrison was interested in Laborde because he now believed that Laborde—who was notorious in this regard—had enlisted for the assassination the same assets CIA had utilized for sabotage against Cuba. Based in New Orleans, Laborde was under Garrison's jurisdiction. Garrison wondered whether he had been involved.

A deadly chess game ensued between Jim Garrison and the CIA. The CIA compiled a Garrison dossier, including a list of its New Orleans assets and employees, conveniently omitting, for one, Carl Trettin, Deputy Chief of the Counter Intelligence Branch of the Cuban Operations Group, who knew Carlos Bringuier. CIA asset Edward Butler's page is blank, with "RI trace in progress." David Ferrie's page reads "no identifiable traces." Memoranda, labeled "CASE 49364"—"The Garrison Case"—flowed from the Agency. One memorandum was titled: "CIA Involvement with Cubans and Cuban Groups Now or Potentially Involved in The Garrison Investigation."

The CIA maintained a "target file" of people the agency considered to be hostile. According to Chester Vigurie, who worked as a file clerk for the CIA field office in New Orleans in the late 1960s, and later as a probation officer in Jefferson Parish, "Jim Garrison and everyone connected to his probe of the JFK case were in the CIA's target file."

In search of negative information about Jim Garrison, Richard Helms breakfasted with Louisiana congressman F. Edward Hebert, chairman of the House Armed Services Committee, who was "friendly and well-disposed toward the Agency." Garrison in turn subpoenaed Helms, demanding that the CIA produce a photograph of Oswald and a Cuban companion in Mexico City. He worried about how his staff would cope with the smooth Helms. "The guy's going to come in a thousand dollar suit, and my guys will be awed," he told Mark Lane.

Garrison needn't have worried. Lawrence Houston wrote to Judge Bagert on Helms' behalf: New Orleans had no jurisdiction. Helms would make no personal appearances in New Orleans. Undeterred, Garrison subpoenaed Allen Dulles. The subpoena was returned undelivered, only for Dulles to declare on television that he had no objection to going to New Orleans, only he hadn't been served with a subpoena.

Garrison also subpoenaed Regis Kennedy and Warren de Brueys, who had already been transferred to Washington, D.C., out of harm's way. Thwarted by the intelligence agencies, Garrison turned increasingly to the press, accusing "our investigative federal agencies" of being deeply involved in the "concealment of essential information relating to the assassination of President Kennedy."

He charged that the CIA was paying lawyers representing his suspects, and that made the papers on May 11, 1967: William Martin had told him Stephen B. Lemann, as a special counsel, was handling the CIA's clandestine New Orleans payroll. Martin's informant had been Clay Shaw's friend, David Baldwin. Garrison also charged that "federal agents involved are taking the fifth amendment." There were so many articles about Garrison that Lloyd Ray, ordered to send five copies of every article to "interested Agency components," dubbed his office "Ray's Clip Joint."

De Brueys was gone, but Regis Kennedy remained in New Orleans. In Washington, Regis Kennedy's reports were at once sealed. Judge Bagert ruled that the Executive Branch did not enjoy "unlimited authority." Big Regis must appear before the Orleans Parish grand jury. Ramsey Clark ordered Kennedy to reveal no information acquired in the performance of his official duties. Then, just before Kennedy entered the grand jury room, two of U.S. Attorney Louis Lacour's assistants, fearing that a blanket invocation of privilege might lead to judicial review, told him he should use "his own judgment" about when to invoke privilege.

On the stand, when he invoked privilege, as opposed to a simple denial, it seemed as if the tall, lean, red-haired Kennedy was making admissions. He invoked privilege in reply to whether he knew the connection between Oswald and any Cubans; he did not say that he did not know. He invoked privilege on whether he knew Jack Ruby's New Orleans contacts. He admitted he knew of federal agents in New Orleans who had known Oswald. He admitted he knew the answer to whether the Justice Department had determined that Shaw and Bertrand were the same man. He invoked privilege on the question of whether the Justice Department had investigated Clay Shaw, and whether there was an FBI file on Shaw.

For his honesty, Kennedy was attacked by Assistant Attorney General Fred Vinson and by Ramsey Clark, while Lacour's assistants, a veritable Rosencrantz and Guildenstern, denied they had told him to use his own judgment. Watching from Langley, Lawrence Houston decided that CIA people should claim "executive privilege" were they to be subpoenaed. Special Agent in Charge Rightmyer, in Regis Kennedy's defense, reminded Hoover of how helpful the New Orleans field office had been in providing the CIA with information.

Jack N. Rogers, New Orleans CIA asset and counsel to the Louisiana Un-American Activities Committee, solicited liaisons with anti-Castro guerrillas in the Escambray Mountains. Like Oswald, Rogers worked with Customs, helping to head off the entrance into the United States of Communist propaganda from Cuba. Like Guy Banister, Rogers dispatched spies to watch Cuban students at LSU, then reported to both FBI and CIA. Calling on Jim Garrison at Tulane and Broad, Rogers came away believing that Garrison could prove "a close association between Oswald and Jack Ruby and a conspiracy involving Clay Shaw."

The war between Garrison and the CIA continued to rage, as Garrison spoke of "two Americas," one in which the government, serving a "warfare complex," thought it had the right to lie to the people. On WWL-TV, Garrison called Oswald "an anti-Communist doing work for the CIA," with the CIA "paying lawyers" to block his investigation. He charged that the CIA had more power than "the Gestapo and NKVD of Russia." Could the CIA halt his investigation? he was asked.

"It can slow it up," Garrison granted. The "principal responsible people" were "former employees of the CIA." He blamed "the Bay of Pigs sector—that's where the rabid people are." This was a veiled reference to Phillips. Garrison insisted he might not be a perfect person, "but I don't happen to be a liar."

Watching Garrison on ABC-TV's "Issues and Answers," CIA asset Eustis Reily told Aaron Kohn that anyone listening to Garrison "would also be convinced he is on solid ground." Jack Anderson arrived in New Orleans with a "hostile viewpoint" toward Garrison. By the end of a six-hour conversation, Anderson admitted he "began to believe Garrison's story," and so reported to Deke. There was "authenticity in Garrison's claim that Shaw had been approved by the CIA "to engineer a plot that would result in the assassination of Fidel Castro only for the assignment to change," Anderson said. Furious, Deke wrote a memo calling Anderson a "sitting duck" for Garrison's "wild accusations."

It wasn't a good day for Deke. Only the night before, he had had an unwelcome telephone call from Johnson aide Marvin Watson. President Johnson was persuaded that there had been a conspiracy and "that CIA had something to do with this plot." Could the FBI give them "any further information?" Deke was livid.

Jack Anderson also talked to Lyndon Johnson's press secretary, George Christian, who was "convinced that there must be some truth to Garrison's allegations." Another reporter persuaded by Jim Garrison "against my will and my judgment" was Fred Powledge of

The New Republic, who put the lie to the Agency's formula for describing Jim Garrison as "politically ambitious" and longing to be "governor of Louisiana" while his case was "jerry-built" and "flimsy." To Powledge, Garrison seemed neither crazy nor connected to organized crime.

Back at Langley, The Rock raged. Garrison had outstripped even "the foreign Communist press" in attacking the CIA, "vehemently, viciously, and mendaciously." In fact, Garrison had taken the very position that had cost John F. Kennedy his life: that the "CIA should be drastically curtailed or destroyed." Garrison also had concluded that there had been internecine warfare within the CIA itself, which the Inspector General's report, a document he was never to read, reveals amply.

The murder of John F. Kennedy, Jim Garrison believed, was ratified by the entire Agency "as an Agency policy" because "the Agency did not want it known that Agency elements were involved." Fully aware of the forces in the media unleashed to discredit him, Garrison commented that "he who controls the past controls the future."

"WHITE PAPER" 12

They didn't want to just discredit Jim Garrison. They wanted him destroyed.

—William Alford

ENLISTED IN THE FRONT LINE of the media attack to discredit Jim Garrison and ruin his case was Justice Department lawyer Walter Sheridan. In 1963 it was Sheridan who had determined, at Bobby Kennedy's request, that the Mafia had not planned his brother's assassination. Whether he had been sent directly to New Orleans by Bobby, or on Bobby's behalf by Herbert J. Miller Jr., who had been rushed to Dallas to forestall any investigation of the assassination by the state of Texas, Sheridan appeared in New Orleans virtually as soon as Garrison considered the CIA a suspect and began to examine the involvement of anti-Castro Cubans. By February 20th, Sheridan had enlisted that young entrepreneur and FBI informant Gordon Novel to penetrate Garrison's office. On February 26th, four days before Clay Shaw's arrest, Sheridan knocked on his door at 1313 Dauphine Street.

Sheridan's background included service to vast areas of the intelligence community: to the FBI; to the CIA, which had cleared him as an investigator in 1955 and 1956; and to the National Security Agency, which granted him "security approval for liaison."

At the Justice Department, Sheridan had made himself indispensable to Bobby Kennedy in his relentless pursuit of Teamster president Jimmy Hoffa. With the help of a vicious Louisiana criminal named Edward Grady Partin, and using blackmail, threats of violence and wiretapping, Sheridan had succeeded in engineering Hoffa's conviction. Like Sheridan, Partin also reported directly to Herbert J. Miller Jr. For a time, future Garrison lawyer Lou Merhige had represented Partin. When they severed their relationship, Partin owed Merhige ten thousand dollars. "You won't sue me and I won't have you killed," Partin said. When Hoffa was finally behind bars, Bobby Kennedy rewarded Partin with his heart's desire: a "Lotus Ford" racing car.

Sheridan next demanded that Ramsey Clark ensure that Clark's father, Justice Tom Clark, not vote to reverse the Hoffa conviction. Despite Earl Warren's dissent, the Supreme Court complied.

Put in contact with the Shaw defense team by Walter Sheridan, Miller went on to serve as the liaison between Shaw's lawyers and Richard Lansdale, a lawyer in Lawrence Houston's. On a regular basis, Edward Wegmann sent his briefs to Miller, who then forwarded them to the CIA. Houston had been ordered to cooperate with the Shaw defense by Richard Helms. Throughout the Garrison investigation, the CIA's highest legal officer, Houston, worked to help Shaw evade justice. The sanitizing of Alfred Moran's file had been but one example.

By the time he was assigned to the Garrison investigation, Sheridan, according to author Jim Hougan, "disposed over the personnel and currency of whole units of the Central Intelligence Agency." Simultaneously, he worked for Bobby Kennedy as his personal intelligence agency, head of his wiretapping unit. Sheridan was a short, stocky man with a beaky nose and slitlike eyes. "His almost angelic appearance hides a core of toughness," wrote Bobby Kennedy, ever given to hero-worship of brutal men.

Sheridan now began a four-year effort to discredit Jim Garrison and, enlisting his Internal Revenue capabilities, to try to put him in jail. Not the first federal agent to pose as a journalist, he traveled to New Orleans ostensibly as a producer of NBC documentaries, a cover he had established in Detroit. In *Newsweek*, Hugh Aynesworth called Sheridan a "reporter" or "journalist" four times in a one-page article. Sheridan was nothing of the sort.

Jim Garrison was astonished by Sheridan's single-minded effort to destroy his investigation, given that it so obviously emanated from Bobby Kennedy. Bobby's opposition perplexed him. "If my brother were killed," Garrison said quietly, "I would be interested in getting the individuals involved, no matter who they were." Unaware that Bobby had reasons to behave otherwise, Garrison told Joe Wershba on the CBS program, "Mike Wallace at Large," "I cannot go into his mind."

All Garrison knew for sure was that, although he admired "Jack" Kennedy, and openly said so, inexplicably, Bobby was attempting to "torpedo" his case. That Bobby "never really wanted any investigation" had long been clear to his staff. Whether it was Herbert J. Miller Jr. personally who sent Sheridan to New Orleans, as Edwin Guthman says, or Bobby directly, or the two in tandem, certainly Bobby allowed Walter Sheridan to tell people that it was Bobby himself who dispatched him to New Orleans.

Claiming to be investigating not Garrison, but the Kennedy assassination, Sheridan met Garrison, courtesy of Dick Billings. When Sheridan mentioned he had been with the Office of Naval Intelligence, Garrison raised an eyebrow. Later he would liken Sheridan's arrival to "artillery" being moved into the area. ONI liaison Guy Johnson was well aware of Sheridan's assignment: Sheridan "was clearly sent here by the Kennedys to spike Garrison." He had gone to "bury" Garrison, Sheridan told Herbert J. Miller Jr. at one point, suggesting that it was, indeed, Bobby Kennedy who had sent him. Immediately Sheridan began reporting to Miller, and through Miller to the CIA on everything he learned about Garrison. Miller then turned the information over to Richard H. Lansdale for Lawrence Houston.

Sheridan would have preferred to report directly to the CIA on "Garrison's schemes and instructions." Miller tried to obtain that privilege for him, pleading his case before the Agency. Sheridan is "completely trustworthy and will live up to whatever arrangements are made," Miller said. Sheridan would accept "any terms we propose," he told Lansdale.

The CIA, obviously uncomfortable with a representative of Bobby Kennedy, preferred to keep Sheridan at one remove and deal with the intermediary, Miller. Miller would protect Sheridan and his nefarious role in the Garrison investigation from later government inquiries into the 1990s. Not only did Miller refuse to reply to the ARRB's questions about Sheridan and the Garrison investigation, but he went on to facilitate the removal of Sheridan's papers from the Kennedy Library when the government petitioned that they be moved to the National Archives and be made available to scholars, so obviously were they assassination records, and thus by law the property of the U.S. government. Sheridan's papers were consigned to the oblivion of his family—with Miller representing the Sheridan family interests.

Shortly after Sheridan's arrival in New Orleans, the CIA had Emilio Santana's police file. At Counter Intelligence, Raymond Rocca, "The Rock," decreed that Sheridan not be authorized to use Santana on his projected NBC "White Paper" because then the

Jim Garrison's maternal grandfather, William Oliver Robinson, seven foot three inches tall, as Uncle Sam, in Knoxville, Iowa *(photograph courtesy of Lyon Garrison).*

Jim Garrison at the age of three, with his sister, Judy Denison, Iowa. c. 1924 *(photograph courtesy of Richard N. Billings).*

Garrison, right, at age sixteen or seventeen, on the Baker family boat. At left is Warren Malhiot, who married Peggie's sister, Wilma *(photograph courtesy of Wilma Malhiot).*

Garrison, age nineteen, drops out of college and enlists in the army. He is shown here with his mother, Jane Garrison, in 1940 *(photograph courtesy of Garrison's personal collection).*

Garrison at Dachau concentration camp. "What I saw there has haunted me ever since," Garrison said years later *(photograph courtesy of Garrison's personal collection).*

Garrison at his desk. "The longer you sat in his office, the better your chances that the prosecutor would recommend no jail time at all."

District Attorney Garrison: "Just another day at Tulane and Broad." *(photograph courtesy of Judge Louis P. Trent)*.

Garrison with Liz Garrison and Benny Goodman *(photograph courtesy of Lyon Garrison).*

President Lyndon B. Johnson, six foot three and three-quarter inches tall, steps forward quickly so as not to appear smaller than Garrison *(photograph courtesy of Lyon Garrison).*

Pershing Gervais: "The Devil Incarnate." 1962
(photograph by Terry Friedman, copyright The
Times-Picayune).

Garrison in court with
Donald V. Organ: Judges
like "the sacred cows of
India," 1963 (photograph
by P.A Hughes, courtesy of
Donald V. Organ).

Garrison shared with John F. Kennedy an affinity for the media, and
television in particular.

Garrison 1965
reelection
advertisement:
"Possessing another
man's army record
carries a federal
penalty of up
to ten years
in prison."

WHAT MOTIVATES A DISTRICT ATTORNEY?

"The same thing that motivates you, really. Your children
and mine are the future. What else really matters?

"Let's keep making this a better city -- for them."

Jim Garrison

Paid for by Jim

Linda Brigette: The Cupid Doll *(photograph courtesy of the late Linda Brigette)*.

Aaron Kohn: "the economic importance of Linda Brigette to organized crime" *(photograph courtesy of AARC)*.

Garrison in 1967: "The Bill of Rights lives in an oxygen tent." *(photograph by Lynn Pelham).*

David Ferrie, left. Ferrie took movies at a Cuban exile training camp north of Lake Pontchartrain.

Ferrie: "People are no damn good."

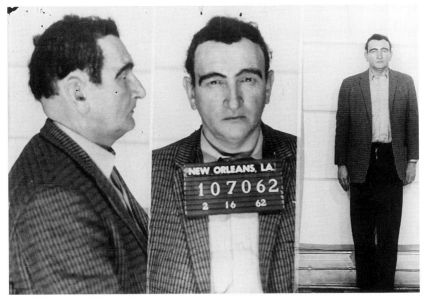

Ferrie: "We're going on a hunting trip to Dallas."

A Civil Air Patrol (CAP) cook-out: Lee Harvey Oswald, in white T-shirt, smiles, at right. John Ciravolo is to Oswald's right. David Ferrie, in helmet, is second from left *(photograph courtesy of John B. Ciravolo, Jr.).*

Oswald distributing leaflets urging "Fair Play for Cuba" outside the International Trade Mart in New Orleans: "Through the efforts of some Cuban-exile 'gusanos,' a street demonstration was attacked."

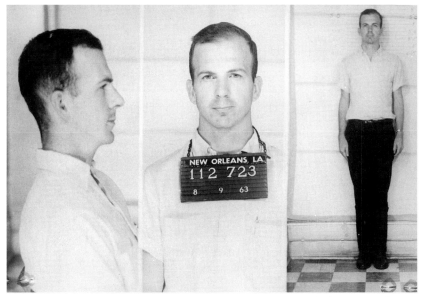

Oswald arrested in New Orleans, August 1963: "Just call the FBI. Tell them you have Lee Oswald in custody."

Official FBI photograph of William Walter, 1963 (photograph courtesy of William Walter).

Juan Valdes wins the best flower award from the New Orleans orchid society, April 1962: "they must be destroying paper."

Mary Sherman: "a close friend of David Ferrie."

William Gurvich with Jim Garrison in Las Vegas, March 1967. "Like a Greek bearing gifts." *(photograph by Lynn Pelham)*.

New Orleans Police Sergeant, Intelligence Division, Subversive Section, Robert Buras, protecting the civil rights of Ku Klux Klan stalwart A. Roswell Thompson. Thompson is about to lay his annual wreath at the foot of the statue of Robert E. Lee *(photograph courtesy of Robert Buras)*.

Guy Banister: "Now all we have to do is kill Earl Warren and the country will clear up" *(photograph courtesy of the J. Gary Shaw Collection).*

Thomas Edward Beckham, in black, photographed outside the International Trade Mart, as Oswald walks inside: "What are you trying to do? Get yourself in trouble?" Beckham confirms that this is indeed he.

Director of International
Affairs for the City of New
Orleans, Alberto Fowler,
with his wife, Paulette: "Jim,
I didn't kill him. . . ."
*(photograph courtesy of
Alberto A. Fowler).*

Garrison during his
investigation, 1965-1969:
"I knew I was dancing with
the CIA" *(photograph by
Lynn Pelham).*

Martin F. Dardis, center, Richard Gerstein, right: "I should be able to find him" *(photograph courtesy of Martin F. Dardis)*.

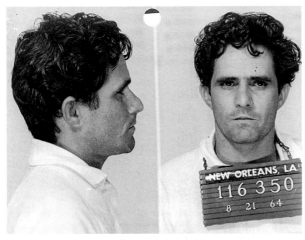

Emilio Santana: "Wildcat Cubans."

Bernardo de Torres is at the right: "They will never find out what happened" *(photograph courtesy of Christopher Sharrett).*

Clay Shaw's signature as "Clay Bertrand" at the Eastern Airlines VIP room: "I saw Clay Shaw that day."

CIA's "relationship with Santana will come out." Clearly the NBC "White Paper" on Jim Garrison was controlled by the CIA.

Sheridan sent his deputy, Frank Grimsley, to the New Orleans Athletic Club to dig up dirt on Jim Garrison.

To assist him in the destruction of Garrison, Sheridan hired Richard Townley of the New Orleans NBC affiliate, WDSU, that longtime CIA media asset. "I can make a lot of statements he can't," Townley admitted, referring to Sheridan. When Townley arrived armed at the home of Ferrie's godson, Morris Brownlee, Brownlee, who had been wired by Jim Garrison, looked at him askance. "A squad of federal marshals" will protect you if you agree to talk to NBC, Townley promised.

Townley remarked to the FBI that his instructions from Sheridan regarding Garrison were to "shoot him down." Gene S. Palmisano, an assistant United States attorney, rushed to the FBI with news it already had: Sheridan's "White Paper" "would destroy the credibility of Garrison's investigation." Loose-tongued Townley told Aaron Kohn that the "White Paper" was being coordinated with "a reporter named Ainsworth [sic] of *Newsweek*."

Kohn soon joined the team, providing Sheridan with a list of "sixteen offenses" committed by Jim Garrison, dating back to the Marc Antony grand jury's refusal to indict Chep Morrison and Provost Dayries, which had not been Jim Garrison's decision. Included was Garrison's "admiration for Huey Long!" Sheridan urged Kohn to go before the NBC cameras and state that Garrison's Las Vegas expenses, including his $5,000 line of credit, had been picked up by Carlos Marcello. "No such credit had been established for Carlos Marcello," Kohn had to tell Sheridan. Kohn did supply Sheridan with Garrison's medical records from his military file. Then he told Sheridan to locate Pershing Gervais.

The middleman between Sheridan and Gervais would be Zachary "Red" Strate, who had been convicted with Jimmy Hoffa of the illegal use of Teamster funds in the building of the New Orleans Fontainebleau Motor Hotel. If Strate would deliver Gervais, Sheridan promised, Strate's Chicago conviction would be overturned. At their meeting at the Bourbon-Orleans Hotel, arranged by lawyer Edward Baldwin, Strate brought Malcolm O'Hara with him. Baldwin had lured O'Hara to this conference by explaining the purpose of Sheridan's documentary: it "was to end the problem, destroy Garrison or get him to resign."

"I am here in New Orleans representing Robert Kennedy,"

Sheridan said, "and I have been sent down here to stop the probe, no matter what it takes." He needed Gervais to make Perry Russo change his story, a story the Shaw defense obviously believed. When Strate informed Gervais of Sheridan's attempt to bribe him, Pershing suggested they "go see Garrison right away and tell him."

In Chicago, Strate took the stand and testified to Sheridan's attempt to bribe him. Represented by Herbert J. Miller Jr., Sheridan lied, denying that he had ever attempted to bribe Strate. Once more he escaped censure.

Jim Garrison had become aware that the FBI knew too much about his investigation. That his telephones were tapped was a continuing irritation. "Joe, I'd be glad to talk to you," he told CBS correspondent Joe Wershba, "if only we could get the number one faggot in Washington off my line." One day the FBI received a call from someone trying to reach Jim Garrison. "Mr. Garrison informed us that if we could not reach him at home," the man said, "he could be reached through the sound room of the FBI." Russell Long told Cartha DeLoach that Garrison did not mind so much the FBI tapping *his* wires. But they had also tapped the wires of his girlfriend!

"That's a damned lie!" Deke sputtered. The FBI now had between ten and fifteen agents following Jim Garrison's investigators, and Hoover was supposedly sending a daily report on the Garrison investigation to Lyndon Johnson, a fact Warren de Brueys believes entirely possible.

Sheridan assigned Gordon Novel as an operative inside Garrison's office. Novel garnered the assignment to "debug" the offices at Tulane and Broad with the help of Truth and Consequences backer, Willard Robertson. When Garrison complained that the FBI was tapping his phones, Robertson, who had known Novel since he was a wild Metairie teenager, proposed that the problem by solved by this young "electronics expert."

Novel was already an FBI informant when he signed on with Sheridan, informing the Bureau of the details of the robbery at the Schlumberger ammunition dump. He did not mention to the FBI his later contention that Guy Banister had provided him with a key to the bunker, even as Novel's former wife, Marlene Mancuso, who was present, reports that the bunker locks had been removed with bolt cutters; no key was needed.

"Bob thinks this is a fraud," Sheridan told Novel when he enlisted him. Novel's first question to Sheridan had been, "Who do you represent, Mr. Kennedy or NBC?" Novel was to claim that Sheridan hired him as his "chief of security," a role he later pretended Garrison had also given him. He would be a triple agent, Novel smiled to himself, working for the FBI, for Sheridan, and for Garrison.

Novel reported to the FBI the day he entered Garrison's office. "In five days" Garrison planned to arrest David Ferrie, Novel said. The next day, February 22nd, the day of Ferrie's death, Novel told the FBI that Garrison was persuaded that Clay Shaw was Clay Bertrand. He informed to the FBI on the 23rd as well. With the help of Novel, the FBI was now monitoring every Garrison lead. "Find the loop holes so we can plug them!" Hoover ordered. "Compared to the FBI, the Mafia look like altar boys," Novel concluded.

A man named "Luis Angel Castillo" was arrested on March 2nd in the Philippines in connection with an assassination plot against President Ferdinand Marcos. Castillo testified he had been "programmed" to kill a man riding in an open car in Dallas on November 22, 1963. Already fully informed about Garrison's case, the FBI ordered that, under hypnosis, Castillo be asked about a list of names, all from the Garrison case: David Ferrie, Layton Martens, Alvin Beaubouef, Lillie Mae McMaines [Sandra Moffett], Perry Russo and Clay Shaw.

"David Ferrie" drew an extreme physical reaction; Castillo seemed to know "Lillie McMaines" as a party girl. The CIA located Castillo's 201 file in its Far East Division. What is to be noted is not whether Castillo had great value as a Kennedy assassination suspect, but that the FBI took seriously the names of Garrison's witnesses, that they were in the Bureau's early possession, and that they were being used in FBI interrogations as valid leads.

Ever talkative, in the short time before Garrison banished Novel, Garrison mentioned in his presence that he was exploring whether Carlos Marcello was connected with Jack Ruby. He planned to bring Marcello before the Orleans Parish grand jury, Garrison confided to Novel. Novel then reported to the FBI that Garrison planned to *indict* Marcello.

Novel stole Garrison's office memos, including copies of lie detector tests administered to witnesses, and handed them over to Walter Sheridan. He gave Sheridan tape recordings of meetings he attended with Garrison and his staff, his expertise in taping second to none.

Novel gave Sheridan tapes of conversations between Garrison and Willard Robertson. He supplied Sheridan with the list of Garrison's Truth and Consequences supporters. The FBI then sent letters to the members of Truth and Consequences, accusing Garrison of being a schizophrenic and a homosexual. Aaron Kohn requested that Dr. Lief declare that Garrison was a "paranoid schizophrenic . . . obsessed with fear of his own active or latent homosexuality, coupled with the use of his prosecutive power in an attempt to destroy homosexuals."

Jim Garrison had obtained a photograph of a laundry truck that he thought might resemble the one used at Houma, and was perhaps utilized in Dallas. He showed it to Novel, who sold it to Sheridan for five hundred dollars. That night, Sheridan not only told William Gurvich that Novel had sold him this photograph, but also that he had been meeting with Novel on a regular basis. Gurvich, ever anxious to secure his position with Garrison, reported to his boss and the "chief of security" was seen no more at Tulane and Broad.

"You're going to be investigated," a friend of one of Shaw's lawyers told Marlene Mancuso. She would look "bad" unless she talked to Sheridan. Richard Townley found Mancuso on May 18, 1967, working as a cashier in the French Quarter at Lucky Pierre's. "If you do a taped interview with us, we'll show you in a good light," Townley said. "We're going to destroy Jim Garrison. Everybody is going down." Mancuso was to state for the "White Paper" that Garrison had coerced her into giving testimony on the Schlumberger ammunition dump raid.

"You're the one who's trying to coerce me," Mancuso said. A friend of Novel named Gerry Munday then called Mancuso. He didn't want to see her hurt "or face federal perjury charges," Munday said. Finally, Walter Sheridan appeared in person at Lucky Pierre's.

"You might as well talk to us now," Sheridan began. If Mancuso would denounce Garrison, he would get her a job on "The Tonight Show." Mancuso was a former Miss New Orleans, dark-haired, sultry and very beautiful. The offer was not far-fetched.

"He's going down the drain and you're going with him," the pint-sized Ness said in Mafia-speak. He demanded to know why she had hired G. Wray Gill. Didn't she realize he was Carlos Marcello's lawyer? Garrison violated people's civil rights, Sheridan said, although the truth was that Garrison had violated no one's rights. It was Walter Sheridan who trampled persistently on the Bill of Rights.

At 6 A.M. Mancuso set off for home, with Sheridan dogging her footsteps. They arrived at the St. Louis Cathedral on Jackson Square. "I want to go inside and say a little prayer," Sheridan said. His hypocrisy, Mancuso thought, was "stifling."

Another day, Sheridan and Townley showed up at Mancuso's

home. They were looking for Gordon Novel, they said. "I have rights too," Mancuso said to Bobby's man. "If you don't get out, you could get killed," Townley told Mancuso on the telephone the next day.

"I can't take the harassment anymore," Mancuso finally told Jim Garrison. "They're trying to destroy you and I'm not going to be part of anything like that."

"Would you mind signing a statement?" Garrison said.

"That's why I'm here," Mancuso said. She swore out an affidavit accusing Sheridan of attempting to bribe her to change her testimony and to coerce her into appearing on his program. In contrast, she says, Garrison and Lou Ivon behaved "like gentlemen."

Sheridan worked on other Garrison witnesses. He paid Jules Ricco Kimble five hundred dollars for information about the papers and tapes Jack Helms had taken from Ferrie's apartment. Kimble should stop talking to Garrison and hide out in Canada where he would be "safe," Sheridan advised. Sheridan enlisted an FBI agent named Clement Hood to tell Kimble that if Garrison subpoenaed him, Hood would help him in exchange for Kimble's full cooperation with Sheridan now.

Sheridan tried to enlist police officer Fred Williams, who had been a Garrison investigator. He handed Williams a PT-109 tie clasp. This was nice, Williams thought, but he didn't trust Sheridan. If Jim had nothing, why were these strong efforts being made against him? (In later years, disgusted with the false promises of the Kennedy's, Sergio Arcacha Smith would give away his P-T 109 souvenir to author Gus Russo.)

Nina Sulzer, whose husband Jefferson was a close friend of Clay Shaw, was a social worker at Orleans Parish Prison. "You're on the wrong team," she told Vernon Bundy on Sheridan's behalf. "What are they doing for you?" she said, referring to Garrison's office.

"There's nobody doing nothing for me," Bundy said. Then he turned his back on Sulzer.

Jack Martin also refused to have anything to do with Sheridan, accusing him of "extortion."

"If you say it was a hoax that's all we need from you," Townley coaxed. "I hear you're gonna blast Marcello," Martin replied, fishing. Then Townley, on tape, told Jack Martin what Sheridan had admitted: the Marcellos had nothing to do with the assassination.

"I'm not the guy you think I am," Martin said, as of course he was not.

"Walter's still working for the CIA," Martin told Townley, "and you're being paid by them whether you know it or not." Martin had a last word for Aaron Kohn as well: "Why don't you quit working for the CIA?"

Sheridan's primary target was Perry Russo. James Phelan, an "excellent pipeline," Townley thought, had begged Russo to agree to a private meeting with Clay Shaw, without letting Russo know that Walter Sheridan would also attend. Russo had turned him down. Phelan continued to work on Russo for Sheridan while Richard Townley paid Russo three separate visits, putting on what Russo was to term "a tremendous amount of pressure."

"Shaw is innocent," Townley told Russo. Then he threatened that the Shaw lawyers would prove Russo was a drug addict and he would be "ruined for life." If Russo would only admit that his testimony had been "doctored," Irvin Dymond would not slander his character.

"I want you to understand something right off the bat," Sheridan said when he met Perry Russo. "I think you're making up some of this, that you're lying. I think you dreamed up some of it and I think the D.A. shoved some stuff in your head."

"Well, you're entitled to your opinion," Russo said.

"When did you first mention the party?" Sheridan demanded, moving into Phelan's strategy involving the Sciambra memos.

"To Sciambra. In Baton Rouge . . . that was the basic reason Sciambra wanted me to come to New Orleans that Monday. There was no other reason for me to come down. Just because I knew Ferrie was not enough reason. . . ." Russo said.

"We're going to take Garrison out of this," Sheridan said, unfazed. "We can't allow this to go any further. Garrison is going to jail and you're going to jail."

When Russo grew weary, Sheridan laid out his plan. Russo was to go to Biloxi, Mississippi, out of Garrison's jurisdiction. Shaw would be at a motel where they would talk. Then, with the cameras rolling, Russo would go outside and state that he had never before met Clay Shaw, or anybody named Oswald. He had never heard anything about the shooting of the president back in the summer of 1963. He had very little contact with Ferrie, who was "crazy."

"You might be able to save yourself. We're getting Garrison. He's done with. We'll finish him off," Sheridan said onto Russo's tape.

When Sheridan asked Russo where he would most like to live, Russo named Los Angeles. Sheridan then promised him a monthly check for five years, and a fake job. He need not fear extradition. Part of Sheridan's assignment was to see to it that no state governor extradited a witness for Garrison. When Richard Helms asked his assistant, Thomas Karamessines, "Are we giving that guy down there all the help he needs?" he was referring, in part, to Sheridan's efforts on behalf of Clay Shaw, who told friends like Jefferson Sulzer how much the CIA was helping his defense team.

On June 21st, Russo signed an affidavit against Phelan, Townley and Sheridan. All three had offered him attorneys if only he would say that he had lied, while a "high official of NBC" would get him a job in California. In this document, Russo reiterates his testimony that he had heard Ferrie, "Clem Bertrand" and "Leon" Oswald discussing the assassination of President Kennedy.

Sheridan made good on one threat: In October 1968, *Time* magazine printed that Russo was a "known drug addict." Russo sued and won; *Time* paid him $15,000. In two more attempts to slander Russo, the FBI was told he was a "known homosexual," who frequented the 100 block of Royal setting up "chickens"; a homosexual named Elmer Renfroe, working with the Shaw defense, claimed to have attended "the wedding of David Ferrie and Perry Russo."

In 1990, Jim Garrison was offered one last corroboration of Russo's testimony. A former Shaw lover called to say that Garrison had been "absolutely correct" in charting Shaw and Ferrie's involvement in President Kennedy's assassination. He had heard them both "saying things no American should ever say." He had valued his relationship with Shaw and so remained silent. This source also believed that Ferrie had been murdered because he had talked too much.

Sheridan's "White Paper" was aired on June 19, 1967. Years later, disturbed by this and so many press attacks, Garrison's children would ask how he could bear it. "What do you expect from a pig but a grunt?" Garrison told his eldest son, Jasper.

Gordon Novel could not appear since, when Jim Garrison filed a material witness warrant against him, he fled the jurisdiction, alighting in McLean, Virginia, "lair of the CIA," as Garrison put it. There Novel took a lie detector test in the presence of Walter Sheridan, administered by a former Army intelligence officer and CIA contact, Lloyd B. Furr. Knowing the questions in advance, Novel passed. Then Novel flew to Columbus, Ohio. The FBI could always reach him through Walter Sheridan, he told them. "I was doing everything in my power to destroy Jim Garrison," Novel admits.

In Ohio, Novel entertained members of the Shaw defense team, whom he told that Garrison's staff had written Ferrie's "suicide notes." Among Novel's scams was the forgery of a letter to a "Mr.

Weiss," supposedly proof that Novel was with the CIA. Weiss, Novel claims, was "a high security official, in charge of the State Department Intelligence and Security Division." "That was cute," Novel says. The *States-Item* reported that he was a CIA operative.

Other of Novel's mischievous actions included filing a damage suit against Jim Garrison and Truth and Consequences because Garrison had "ruined his reputation as a man of honesty, honor and probity." Judge James A. Comiskey ruled that Novel had to return to New Orleans to pursue the lawsuit. Later Novel filed a libel suit against Garrison and *Playboy*, based on Garrison's mentioning him in his *Playboy* interview, a suit Novel claimed was financed by the White House. At CIA Counter Intelligence, The Rock stated for the record: it was NBC and Sheridan who were "supporting and financing Novel."

When Jim Garrison tried to extradite Novel, Walter Sheridan telephoned Ohio governor Rhodes and invoked national security. It was Deke himself who had decided that Novel not be extradited. "It would be deplorable if the Department of Justice and the FBI had to be of assistance to Garrison," DeLoach said. Hoover scribbled onto Deke's memo to Clyde Tolson, "I certainly agree."

Some of Sheridan's "White Paper" is devoted to challenging Perry Russo's contention that the real Lee Harvey Oswald was present at Ferrie's gathering. On camera, Layton Martens claims that "Leon" was really James Lewallen, no matter that Lewallen was well over six feet tall. When Russo's friend, Lefty Peterson, says he doesn't remember the name of Ferrie's roommate, Sheridan prompts him: "Could it have been Jim?" Martens adds his persistent lie that Ferrie admired President Kennedy.

Martens under oath had denied having been present at the Schlumberger robbery, or that he had ever met Novel, or Juan Valdes. On April 5th, Martens had been indicted for perjury; Garrison termed it "arrogant perjury." Martens was to admit for Sheridan another of his lies to Jack Martin: there had been no "letters of marque" from Robert Kennedy to David Ferrie and himself, only an ordinary letter. On the "White Paper," Sheridan, of course, does not mention that Martens had been indicted.

Dean Andrews appears, pale and sweating profusely. He could have invented the names "Manuel García Gonzalez" and "Richard Davis," he says, although off camera he had admitted to Sheridan that they were real people. On the air, Sheridan keeps only Andrews' line, "If it is the Manuel García Gonzalez that I told him, he has got the right ta-ta, but the wrong ho-ho." On the unedited tape, Sheridan asks, "You made them up?" and Andrews replies, "Fags use aliases as females use make-up."

Jim Garrison had persisted in attempting to extract the real identity of "Clay Bertrand" from Andrews. Protesting, Andrews insisted they had a deal: if only Andrews would just reply, "I don't know if he is, and I don't know if he isn't," Garrison would back off. He wouldn't.

Andrews sought help from the FBI. In panic, he lied to Townley and to the Shaw defense, enlisting that lie that Clay Bertrand was "married and the father of four children," as he settled on the strategy of implicating Eugene Davis, to Davis' extreme indignation. Andrews told Garrison that Bertrand's voice was "deep," while telling *Life*'s Marc St. Gill that Bertrand had a "soft voice."

Among Andrews' perjuries before the grand jury was his denial that Ferrie had ever called him on behalf of a client. The grand jury only that morning had heard Thomas Lewis Clark testify to the reverse. Andrews swore he never told his investigator Prentiss Davis the name "Clay Bertrand." Davis testified that he had.

Andrews knew how important it was for Garrison to identify Shaw as Bertrand: "If Giant gets past that, he is home clear," Andrews admitted. He wanted "to live," he told a radio interviewer. "I love to breathe," he told Harold Weisberg, admitting that Shaw was Bertrand. He had confided to Mark Lane, "They told me if I said anything I would have a hole blown in my head."

Jim Garrison indicted Dean Andrews for perjury on April 12th. In the hallway, Andrews paraphrased Humphrey Bogart in *Casablanca*, referring to Oswald: "Of all the offices, he has to walk into mine."

On the "White Paper," after Andrews denies on camera that Shaw is Bertrand, host Frank McGee stares earnestly into the camera and confides that they have learned the real name of Clay Bertrand, which they have sent to the Justice Department. No name is mentioned.

Other "White Paper" witnesses include two convicts, Miguel Torres and John Cancler ("John the Baptist"). Both insist Vernon Bundy admitted that he made up his story of seeing Shaw and Oswald at the sea wall. Cancler adds that Ivon and Loisel had asked him to plant "something" in Clay Shaw's house, and that Garrison had promised he would be paroled out of his nine-year prison sentence if he lied and said Shaw, using the name "Bertrand," had approached him sexually. In August, Torres would demand of Nina Sulzer that in exchange for his having lied for Sheridan,

Judge Frederick Heebe should suspend his three-year federal prison sentence.

James Phelan repeats his Sciambra-memo story, adding another lie, that Russo's lie detector test had indicated deception. Sheridan did not dare put polygrapher Roy Jacob on camera. Sandra Moffett appears, insisting that Jim Garrison had offered her money to appear before his grand jury, a lie that NBC found it worth traveling to Iowa to tape.

Fred Leemans, taped in Aaron Kohn's office, lies by denying he saw Shaw with Oswald at his Turkish bath, a denial he would repudiate. Leemans later swore that Sheridan's people had threatened that unless he said he was bribed by Jim Garrison's office, he and his family "would be in physical danger." He had been visited "by a man with a badge," claiming to be a "government agent," and checking Slidell bar owners for "possible income tax violations." It had to have been Sheridan, wearing his familiar Internal Revenue Service hat.

On camera, Alvin Beaubouef looks grim. On March 9th, Ivon and Loisel had visited Beaubouef at home. The next day, Beaubouef accused Loisel of trying to bribe him with three thousand dollars to lie about Ferrie. Ivon says he went along precisely to witness the events and be certain nothing untoward occurred. Witness or criminal or suspect, virtually everyone in this story agrees that Ivon was always, as even Gordon Novel puts it, entirely "honorable."

Loisel did offer Beaubouef money, and a job, but the offer was predicated on Beaubouef's telling the truth and taking a lie detector test to prove it. Lies were of no interest to Garrison, who was determined to prove who killed President Kennedy for history. "We would never suborn perjury," he said.

The next day, at the office of Beauboeuf's lawyer, Hugh Exnicios, Loisel repeated his offer. Exnicios secretly taped him, as a sleazy scenario began to unfold. Even as the tape was doctored, Exnicios attempted to sell it. He first approached Jefferson Parish district attorney Frank Langridge, who wasn't interested. Then Exnicios peddled the tape to the Shaw defense, which was. Irvin Dymond wound up with the tape.

At Tulane and Broad, Beaubouef admitted in the presence of Alcock and Ivon that he had been told they wanted only the truth. Beaubouef even signed an affidavit that there had been "no bribe." Soon Beaubouef was accusing Ivon of putting a gun down his throat, and of having signed the affidavit under duress. Aynesworth reported to the FBI that Beaubouef had been "offered bribe and later intimidated."

Richard Townley sent Beaubouef and his lawyer, Dymond intimate Burton Klein, to Washington, a trip Klein says was entirely "wasted." Even Walter Sheridan's designated polygrapher would not ask Beaubouef whether Lou Ivon had put a gun down his throat.

Herbert J. Miller Jr. wanted the CIA's lawyers to talk to Beaubouef, but Richard Lansdale backed away. "This matter is not within our authority," Lansdale wrote for the record, "notwithstanding that we obviously are involved." Beaubouef would report he was "jockeyed all around Washington, not knowing who he was seeing or what he was saying to whom." The trajectory of information went from Hoover to CIA Counter Intelligence and James Angleton.

Eventually the New Orleans police, led by Major Presley Trosclair, investigated Beaubouef's charges against Loisel and Ivon. Trosclair quickly unearthed that Beaubouef had helped Garrison, contacting a witness named James Louviere—after Loisel and Ivon's visit, and after the Loisel taping. Burton Klein was unable to offer specifics. "Read *Newsweek*," Klein had told Trosclair, defiantly. Klein insisted that Beaubouef had called to hire him, although that was not so: it was Shaw's lawyer, Irvin Dymond, Klein's close friend, who had arranged for him to represent Beaubouef.

Exnicios would not permit the police to copy the tape, even in his presence, and Beaubouef's wife would not corroborate his accusation that Loisel had threatened him with "lead being sent in the direction of his posterior." What statement of Loisel's gave you the impression that he wanted you to fabricate a story?" Trosclair asked. "The whole conversation," was all Beaubouef would say. The police discovered that the tape had been altered, and the exoneration of Loisel and Ivon made the front pages.

For Sheridan's "White Paper," the WDSU director had to tell Beaubouef, as they taped, "Don't drop your eyes so quickly." Beaubouef, clearly nervous, insists he and "others" were intimidated, but names no names. The NBC correspondent holds a binder purporting to be the "full" transcript of Loisel's "bribery offer," but it is never opened. Sheridan does not mention that Ivon and Loisel had been cleared. Nor does Sheridan reveal that Exnicios had offered to sell him the Loisel tape for five thousand dollars.

Appalled by Aaron Kohn's public endorsement of the "White Paper," Jim Garrison summoned him to Tulane and Broad. Kohn was questioned by the fiercest of Garrison's assistants, Richard Burnes. Honest, ethical and relentless, Burnes had a master's degree and was skilled in the cornering of a suspect. Liars wilted when they faced Richard Burnes.

Burton Klein had requested of Garrison's office that he, Klein, instead of his client Beaubouef, who was "uneducated," be permitted to appear before the grand jury. "If I am wrong, tell me to leave," Klein told the wrong man.

"You are wrong," Burnes said.

Like the FBI, Kohn withheld evidence from Garrison. Jimmy Hoffa's private investigator, Bernard Spindel, possessed tapes and evidence about the Kennedy assassination that he wished to make public. Spindel asked Kohn what he should do. "The Bureau won't touch it," Spindel said. "The CIA won't touch it because their people are involved. The DIA won't touch it because they won't interfere. NSA won't touch it." Jim Garrison never received these materials.

Timed with the "White Paper" was the defection of William Gurvich, who, having called Perry Russo "a most convincing witness" and his evidence "sound," now, in a scenario directed by Sheridan, publicly denounced Jim Garrison. Gurvich flew to New York, where he was "hiding out," he told Joe and Shirley Wershba.

Sheridan phoned Gurvich at the Wershba apartment. For his compliance, Sheridan then rewarded him with a private meeting with Bobby Kennedy, both at his office and in a car as Kennedy was driven to the airport. When Bobby learned that an article on Gurvich's visit would appear in Bill Moyers' *Newsday*, he asked Moyers not to run it. Moyers laughed and ran it anyway. "Bobby was 'extremely grateful' to learn Jim Garrison had nothing," Gurvich says in *Newsday*. He had promoted himself to being Garrison's "chief assistant," and is so described. He had never read the Warren Report, and Bobby had confided that he had never read it either, Gurvich adds.

Back in New Orleans, Gurvich handed the Shaw defense all that he hadn't yet given them of Garrison's "Master File." He accused Garrison of ordering the "arrest and physical beating of two newsmen, Townley and Sheridan," and easily "passed" a Roy Jacob polygraph not only on this question, but also on his assertion that Jim Garrison planned to raid the FBI field office "with red pepper guns"—reflecting an Ivon office joke: "If we catch anybody, we'll shoot them with red pepper guns." Gurvich was sheltered by Sheridan's lawyer, Edward Baldwin, whose CIA-employed brother worked for Clay Shaw.

Before the Orleans Parish grand jury, Richard Burnes demanded that Gurvich name any members of Garrison's staff who had done anything illegal. Gurvich could not under oath offer a single name.

Then, in the company of Baldwin, he visited the publisher of the *Times-Picayune*, George Healy, himself a frequent FBI informant; like Phelan, Healy requested only that the Bureau protect his identity. When Gurvich complained about the pro-Garrison reporting of Hoke May and Ross Yockey, both were at once removed from covering the Garrison case.

On July 27th, Garrison charged Sheridan and Townley with four counts of public bribery as well as intimidation of a witness, including "violence, force and threats upon Marlene Mancuso, with intent to influence her conduct in relation to her duties as a witness." Sheridan was also charged with conspiracy to commit burglary over the photograph of the truck stolen for him by Gordon Novel. Sheridan fled to Detroit. He would emerge unscathed from Jim Garrison's indictment. In 1970, the U.S. Supreme Court disposed of the charges against Sheridan and Townley.

On Sheridan's behalf, Bobby Kennedy went public: "It is not possible that Mr. Sheridan would do anything that would in the slightest degree compromise the truth in regard to the investigation in New Orleans," Bobby said. As for Sheridan the man, "I have the utmost confidence in his integrity, both personal and professional." Robert F. Kennedy now had less than a year to live; it was not his finest hour.

Bobby apparently felt he had no choice but to do everything in his power to destroy Jim Garrison's investigation. As will be shown later, in the months preceding the assassination Oswald had become well-known to Bobby and his closest colleagues in the anti-Castro movement, among them Angelo Murgado, Manuel Artime, and Manolo Reboso. Were even his awareness of Oswald to emerge, Bobby might seem in the public perception to have been complicit in the death of his brother, and no better than his CIA adversaries.

Gerald Patrick Hemming tells a tale that might serve as a metaphor to explain Bobby's conundrum. Without corroboration, offering none, Hemming spins a story of Bobby choppering from Palm Beach to a training facility near Homestead Air Force base. There, Hemming imagines, Bobby met with Cubans, many of them Bay of Pigs veterans, who were part of his Special Group. According to Hemming, among the Cubans that day stood one Lee Harvey Oswald, even as independent corroboration does indeed place Oswald in Miami that summer of 1963. The story recalls the scene in the Oval Office witnessed by attorney F. Lee Bailey.

Hemming postulates that Bobby greeted these Cuban men who considered themselves patriots so that they would know that this time, unlike the Bay of Pigs, the highest authority was backing them. Bobby wanted to know the names and view the faces of those involved. Along with Oswald, Hemming places in that company Bernardo de Torres, whose role was to tail Oswald; this was indeed a de Torres' assignment.

The scene may or may not have taken place as Hemming colors it. That Robert Kennedy did everything possible to stop Jim Garrison from investigating the murder of the President is certainly true. That Bobby repeatedly insisted that he would investigate what had happened once he became president, is also true, although it makes little sense—who could guarantee such an electoral outcome? Rumor has it as well that at a Kennedy family meeting Bobby told those assembled that he would have to gain the presidency to deal with the facts of his brother's death. Only his own complicity in Castro's planned assassination, however, his acquaintance with the people who turned against his brother, explains Bobby's active effort to sabotage Jim Garrison's investigation, and, in that cause, to assist the CIA in its cover-up.

John Cancler was not so fortunate as Walter Sheridan. Before the Orleans Parish grand jury on July 12th, he was asked by Richard Burnes whether he had made statements for an NBC newscaster. Cancler invoked the Fifth Amendment, and Alcock at once cited him for contempt. In September, Cancler called his FBI handler, Delbert Hahn, and offered him supposedly compromising photographs of Jim Garrison and an "unidentified Negro female."

Burnes disposed with equal proficiency of Miguel Torres, who was represented by Burton Klein. "Have we ever asked you to tell us anything but the truth?" Burnes demanded. "No," Torres had to admit.

Burnes also reexamined Dean Andrews, as on July 18th new perjury charges were filed. Just the statement that Shaw positively was not Bertrand made the case against Andrews, Burnes thought. If Andrews really didn't know who Bertrand was, how could he be so certain it was not Shaw? Alcock had sought testimony from Wesley Liebeler, who had interviewed Andrews for the Warren Commission. Liebeler refused.

"We could subpoena you," Alcock said, and did. A Vermont judge made the New Orleans summons evaporate.

It had done Andrews no good to name Eugene Davis as Bertrand. Andrews was convicted and sentenced to eighteen months in jail.

Ross Scaccia, now an assistant U.S. attorney, wanted to know for sure whether Andrews was lying. They met in the parking lot of a filling station. Andrews was morose. Was Clay Shaw Clay Bertrand? Scaccia asked. Andrews did not deny it. He seemed terrified.

In 1970, Scaccia became Eugene Davis' lawyer, taking care of his homosexual friends, as once Dean Andrews had done. "Gene, you and I are very close," Scaccia said. "Is Clay Bertrand Clay Shaw?"

"Yep," Davis admitted. "He is."

Jim Garrison had filed a six-page complaint with the FCC, demanding equal time and arguing that Walter Sheridan had interfered "with the prosecution of an open case." NBC offered half an hour, in a panel format, an offer Garrison rejected. He would have to spend half his time educating the panelists, he feared, because they wouldn't have read the Warren Report. The Shaw defense attempted to enjoin Garrison from appearing at all, but Judge Haggerty ruled that Jim Garrison, too, enjoyed "a citizen's right to free speech."

Garrison chose "a low key fireside chat," in contrast with what even Tom Bethell called Sheridan's "shrill" program. He had compiled a list of the people Sheridan had attempted to bribe in the Hoffa case, and a retired police officer named Herman Frazier had agreed to send a confirming affidavit. Garrison did not use it.

Dressed in a light-colored suit, pipe in hand, Garrison perches on the edge of a desk and speaks directly to the viewing audience. He raises the question of whether Oswald acted alone, and whether there had been a conspiracy to murder President Kennedy. This country was not built on the idea that a "handful of nobles" should determine what the people are allowed to know, he says.

He lays the conspiracy to murder President Kennedy at the door of men "once connected with the Central Intelligence Agency." Oswald himself was "in the employ of U.S. intelligence agencies," he says. He ridicules Arlen Specter's single bullet theory, without which Oswald could not have been condemned as having acted alone. One bullet somersaulting through both Kennedy and Connally was like "an elephant hanging from a cliff with his tail tied to a daisy; it may be mathematically possible, but it is not likely."

Garrison also defended his office against the charge that they had used "improper methods." I have always defended the rights of individuals, he says. He mentions that Beaubouef's charges had been repudiated by the police, and that Cancler and Torres had not stood by their stories when faced by a grand jury.

"If we still live in the same country in which we were born," Garrison says, "the attempt to conceal the truth will be a failure." The people will decide, not a handful of men in Washington and New York. "As long as I am alive," Jim Garrison promises in a passionate closing, "no one is going to stop me from seeing that you obtain the full truth and nothing less than the full truth and no fairy tales."

Garrison was being optimistic. As amateurish, as unbalanced as Sheridan's "White Paper" appears today, despite its NBC imprimatur, it had its effect. In September, three months after the "White Paper" aired, Lyndon Johnson sat perusing a Harris poll. He was pleased that, whereas in March 1967, 45 percent of respondents thought Jim Garrison would "shed light on JFK death," by September the figure had dropped to 32 percent. Now 60 percent of those polled had lost faith that much would come of Jim Garrison's investigation.

SMOKING GUNS IN A RURAL PARISH 13

Why was his name erased?
        —Francis Fruge

WHILE WALTER SHERIDAN was spending six months traveling back and forth to New Orleans attempting to destroy Jim Garrison's case, evidence entirely unknown to him was emerging in two rural Louisiana hamlets north of Baton Rouge. The Garrison investigators were Francis Fruge—a lean, shrewd Cajun state police officer specializing in narcotics, an intense man with piercing black eyes—and Anne Dischler—an undercover investigator for sheriffs' offices and for the State Sovereignty Commission whose role was to thwart the desegregation of Louisiana's public institutions. In her thirties, Dischler was a strong, determined woman, strikingly attractive with hazel eyes that took on the color purple. She was the mother of seven children.

Through the painstaking work of Dischler and Fruge, Jim Garrison was able to chart how Lee Harvey Oswald had been set up as the "patsy" who would be blamed for the murder of President Kennedy. Three months before the assassination, Garrison would be able to demonstrate, the cover-up had begun, making it apparent that the same people who had planned the crime were behind the cover-up.

Late in February 1967, a St. Francisville businessman named A. H. Magruder telephoned Garrison about a hunting trip he had taken with a friend, Dr. Victor J. Weiss. Weiss was a clinician at the East Louisiana State Hospital at Jackson, the mental hospital, nicknamed "East" by local residents. On November 22, 1963, at "East," Weiss had encountered a female patient who spoke of being "involved with a group of men in the assassination of Kennedy."

Rose Cheramie was a twenty-eight-year-old prostitute and drug addict with a long police record and time served at Angola. She had worked for a Basile whorehouse called the Silver Slipper Lounge once owned by Jack Ruby. In 1963, Rose, like others of her trade, plied that strip of Highway 190 extending from Opelousas, birthplace of Jim Bowie, to the Texas border where a gas station more than likely doubled as a brothel. One night in November 1963, Rose had been beaten and tossed from an automobile on this highway. A state trooper booked her as a suspected narcotics addict.

Because Francis Fruge was from Basile and already knew Rose, as he did most of the women frequenting that route, the doctor at the hospital where Rose was taken called him. When Fruge heard what Rose had to say, he called fellow trooper Donald White, who also had encountered Cheramie. "I've got your lady friend here in jail," Fruge said. "She's got something to share with us."

Three men were traveling from Florida to Texas to kill John F. Kennedy, Rose recounted. "These Cubans are crazy. They're going to Dallas to kill Kennedy in a few days." When Rose cut her ankle with a razor blade, Dr. F. J. Derouin signed commitment papers and Fruge was ordered to drive her to East. Rose was no stranger to the East Louisiana State Hospital at Jackson. Under the name Melba Christine Youngblood Marcades, she had previously been incarcerated there.

On Friday, November 22nd, at twenty minutes before noon, Rose was watching television in the hospital recreation area. Scenes in Dallas flashed on the screen. President Kennedy was on his way.

"Somebody's got to do something!" Rose shouted. "They're going to kill the president!" No one paid any attention. The motorcade pulled into view. "Watch!" Rose cried out. "This is when it's going to happen! They're going to get him! They're going to get him at the underpass!"

"POW!" Rose yelled as the shots rang out.

All that weekend Rose talked. Dr. Weiss heard her say she knew Jack Ruby. She believed Kennedy was assassinated because of narcotics traffic on the Mexican border. She herself was connected to a drug syndicate. She was not only a stripper for Jack Ruby, Rose confided. She was one of his drug runners. She had seen Lee Harvey Oswald sitting at a table at Ruby's Carousel Club.

That weekend Francis Fruge thought he and Donald White should come forward and "tell what we know." White urged silence, but Fruge telephoned the FBI in Lafayette. "This lady warned us about the assassination," Fruge said.

"They've already got their man," the agent said. "Case closed." Fruge also informed his State Police superior, Captain Ben Morgan, and Colonel Thomas Burbank himself.

"This is significant," Fruge said.

"Francis, get her the hell out of Louisiana," Burbank said. "I don't want her here." The doctor who released Rose Cheramie from East was Malcolm Pierson, a temporary employee with a checkered past. Having been caught with drugs and punished with a suspended license, Pierson was attempting to work his way back into medicine with service at East, a dumping ground for medical men under a cloud.

On November 28, 1963, a tense Rose Cheramie, in the custody of Fruge and trooper Wayne Morein, flew in a state police plane to Houston. Rose continued to talk. She had been a stripper at another Ruby-owned club, The Pink Door. Oswald and Ruby were "them two queer son-of-a-bitches." They've "been shacking up for years," Rose said. Ruby's nickname was "Pinky." Unsuccessful in penetrating the drug ring Rose described, Fruge returned to Louisiana.

"Find Rose!" Jim Garrison told his investigator Frank Meloche, who had taken Magruder's call.

"You're working for Jim Garrison now," Colonel Burbank told Fruge. "You're assigned to him on the Kennedy assassination on twenty-four-hour call."

"Find her, I want her!" Garrison told Fruge. On March 6, 1967, in search of Rose Cheramie, Fruge flew to Houston with Meloche and Anne Dischler. Rose's mother and sister denied they knew a "Rose Cheramie." Back in New Orleans, Garrison uncovered Rose's twenty aliases and her crimes. Her name appeared in many places, but not in any of the Warren Commission indices of names. The state police had not taken her photograph or prints. Finally Fruge came up with an old mug shot and a rap sheet.

Fruge discovered that in 1965 Rose had been again thrown from a car and this time had been run over. Her suitcases had been placed in the middle of a deserted country road near Big Sandy, an unlikely place to be hitchhiking. Although a motorist had hit Rose, she was alive. Once more she talked, this time to a Texas Highway Patrol officer named J. A. Andrews: She was a stripper for Ruby. Ruby and Oswald were bed partners.

Rose Cheramie's death certificate reads "bullet hole in head," although hospital records mention no bullet hole. Her death was ruled "accidental." Fruge could uncover no record of the driver who killed Rose at the address he had provided. Jim Garrison requested that Rose Cheramie's body be exhumed, but Texas authorities refused to comply.

In Basile, convinced that Rose Cheramie had direct knowledge of the assassination plot, Fruge showed photographs of Cubans provided by Garrison to Hadley Manuel, the manager of the Silver Slipper. Of the two men he had seen with Rose, Manuel identified Sergio Arcacha Smith (a "dapper, mustachioed, ex-fink for the CIA," Richard Case Nagell called him), and a man he called "Osanto," the CIA's own Emilio Santana. Will Fritz, the Dallas police captain, told Fruge of diagrams of the Dealey Plaza sewer system that had been found in Arcacha's Dallas apartment.

The FBI never informed Garrison about its November 28, 1963 interview with a Margaret Kay Kauffman in Pennsylvania, who had contacted the state police about a Silver Slipper flier she had found. On the back, in pencil, was the name "Lee Oswald." To the right was "Rubenstein, Jack Ruby" and at the bottom "Dallas Texas." A Cuban doctor named "Julio Fernandez" had lived next door, Kauffman said.

Dischler and Fruge began to investigate reports that Lee Harvey Oswald had been spotted in towns radiating out of Baton Rouge. Because people were frightened to talk to them, Dischler sometimes identified herself as a reporter for the Lafayette *Daily Advertiser*. Cal Kelly was positive he had seen Oswald in June 1963 at a restaurant in Walker, Louisiana, having doughnuts and coffee. The waitress had remarked to him that he looked like a stranger.

"Probably I am," Oswald said. "I just came from Cuba. I caught a freight truck out of Florida. I'm on my way to Dallas, as soon as the driver gets some sleep." In the parking lot was a truck with a man asleep at the wheel. When Kelly and his twelve-year-old grandson watched the assassination events on television, they were both positive the man had been Lee Harvey Oswald.

In April, Dischler and Fruge followed up a lead involving a brawl at the Lafayette Holiday Inn lounge. The source had been Robert J. Angers, whose column, "Anecdotes and Antidotes," appeared in the *Daily Advertiser*. This was one incident that Angers did not share with his readers.

Angers was a longtime CIA asset, who wrote for William Gaudet's *Latin American Reports*. Having run into Angers in Guatemala, Alberto Fowler pegged him as a "right-wing extremist," who worked undercover for the FBI. In May 1963, Angers had been honored by Arcacha's Cuban Revolutionary Council for an editorial in his paper, the Franklin *Banner Tribune,* which read, in part, "America can no more afford the risk of a Communist Cuba than she can a Communist Louisiana."

Angers was "tight-lipped" and obviously holding back when Fruge and Dischler asked what he knew about the ruckus "Oswald" had created at the Holiday Inn. They turned to witnesses at the scene. A belligerent troublemaker, introducing himself as "Lee Harvey Oswald," had created a disturbance as he criticized the Kennedy family. A barmaid named Lou Domingue was so upset she began to cry. In the ensuing skirmish "over another queer at the lounge," a knife flashed, then fell to the ground. The lounge manager, Harold Guidry, picked it up.

"Lee Harvey Oswald" had signed his bar slip "Hidell," then fled without paying. Fruge and Dischler had no photographs to show the lounge manager. They did discover that there was no "Hidell" registered at the hotel, although Jessie Romero, working behind the desk, remembered the man named "Oswald." Romero thought he had returned after the assassination, claiming to be a cosmetics salesman, a "cousin" of Lee Harvey Oswald. He was a "good size" man with hazel eyes and blonde hair, although when Romero saw a photograph of the actual Oswald, she said *he* "greatly resembled the man in the incident." Another witness, Ernie Broussard, was also certain the man had been there in September, "a few months before the assassination," only to return a few weeks later. Dischler and Fruge were unable to discover whether charges had been filed against "Hidell" for running out on his bill.

Frank Meloche told Dischler and Fruge that Jim Garrison was "very interested in Oswald being in Lafayette. If you need anything, holler." Garrison in New Orleans, and Fruge and Dischler in the field, began to discover that there were quite a few men that summer and autumn who went around calling themselves "Oswald." An artist, Cedric Rolleston, said a man in the lobby of the Bentley Hotel in Alexandria on October 11th or 12th said his name was "Lee Harvey Oswald." He had predicted that "a lot of Catholic rulers are going to be killed in a few months." After the assassination, Rolleston called the FBI, which dismissed his information as "unreliable."

Dischler and Fruge concluded that the man at the Holiday Inn had been a decoy who had foreknowledge of the assassination, as reflected in his enlisting the real Oswald's alias, "Hidell." The State Police had tracked him from Morgan City, up to Lafayette, then to Beaumont, Texas, Houston and Dallas. A "foreign lady" had been with him in an old car. It was late September or early October.

In New Orleans, a witness named Corinne Verges Villard, who worked at the New Port Motel in Morgan City, whose part-owner was Carlos Marcello, told Garrison of having seen Oswald. Jack Ruby was a frequent customer. Villard said Ruby returned in mid-November in search of her boss, Pete Guarisco. Accompanying Ruby on this visit was a young man who "appeared very nervous." He wore a T-shirt and faded blue jeans. Villard then identified a photograph of Lee Harvey Oswald as the man with Ruby that day.

When the FBI arrived, Villard spoke of Ruby, but did not volunteer that Oswald had been there, or that in late September or early October a woman with a foreign accent asking for a room had been accompanied by the same man who had been with Ruby. The woman's hair, she remembered, was a "golden reddish color," not Marina's brown.

Some time later, Governor McKeithen's aide, Aubrey Young, found a woman named Barbara Messina, who had dinner with Ruby several times in 1963; each time she was picked up by a gray-haired man in a Cadillac. On these occasions, there was a nice-looking young man with Ruby, one whose picture she "saw on television after the assassination." Then Messina disappeared, too frightened to meet Moo Moo and Steve Bordelon.

Yet another decoy surfaced: a man by the name of Lee Harvey Oswald had replied to an ad for a garage apartment in Baton Rouge, on October 25, 1963. Fruge's supervisor revealed that they had reports of a "traveling Oswald" causing disturbances all along the route to Texas, all recorded by the state police.

On April 28th, Fruge and Dischler met with Garrison's staff at Tulane and Broad. "Frank Jeanette," Rose Cheramie's pimp, had been seen at "Jim's Lounge" with a Ruby stripper, they learned. They wanted to proceed to Shreveport, following the trajectory of the Holiday Inn lead. Two sets of Oswald tracks, one heading for Texas by way of Clinton and Shreveport, the other by way of Morgan City and Lake Charles, with a man calling himself "Oswald" and attacking the Kennedys, suggested that a cover-up was in place well before the assassination. Later Ned Touchstone, editor of *The Councilor* newspaper, who had also been investigating the Louisiana roots of the assassination, would apologize to his readers for not pursuing the divergent tracks of Oswald, who "could have had a double."

Jim Garrison put aside this set of leads in favor of an incident he believed was more promising. Fruge and Dischler had discovered that people in East Feliciana Parish had observed Oswald in the company of both David Ferrie and Clay Shaw. Information of the trio traveling together in the area had begun to circulate early in 1964.

John R. Rarick, district judge for the Feliciana parishes, East and West, was having his thick black hair cut at the Jackson barber shop of his supporter, Lea McGehee. The quintessential gossiping barber, McGehee had been a Navy cryptographer in Korea handling "top secret" matters and working with surveillance aircraft. The barber was nothing if not observant. The judge, in turn, was a good listener.

"Oswald was here," McGehee told Rarick. It had been late summer of 1963, an afternoon so quiet that you could have shot a cannon down the street and not hit anyone. But that day was less sultry than usual. Not bothering to turn on his air conditioner, McGehee opened the door. A young man who didn't need a haircut entered. McGehee had seen a battered green automobile with a woman and a bassinet in back. Idly, he wondered whether the man had arrived in that car.

"A barbershop is a good place for a haircut and information," Oswald said.

McGehee eyed him with suspicion. He knew "all or most everybody in town." This must be one of those CORE workers. By 1960 only ten Negroes were exercising their franchise, and CORE had targeted East Feliciana Parish for a major voter registration drive. Hanging on McGehee's wall was a poster given him by Judge Rarick of Martin Luther King Jr. at the "Communist" Highlander School in Monteagle, Tennessee, "proof" of how the civil rights movement was Communist-controlled. Hoping for a juicy argument, McGehee turned Oswald's chair so that he stared directly into the face of Martin Luther King. But Oswald did not react. Oswald said nothing at all about the poster. Instead he remarked that he had come from New Orleans in search of work.

"Don't you have any friends in New Orleans who can help you?" McGehee asks. Oswald has come a long way.

"I have no friends," Oswald says. Then he volunteers that he is looking for a job at the East Louisiana State Hospital.

"Do you know this is a mental hospital?" McGehee says.

"Oh!" Oswald says. He is surprised. Then he asks whether they "have all sorts of jobs, like electrician." The largest employer in the area, East had a sheet metal shop, a power plant, a dairy. . . .

"You have to know somebody to get a job there," McGehee says. "If you know somebody you have a better chance." The sanction of the right politician was crucial.

"That's a nice haircut," Oswald says, standing up. Pleased by the compliment, McGehee directs him to the home of state representative Reeves Morgan, who controls patronage in East Feliciana Parish. He even draws Oswald a map.

"Do you have change for a five?" Oswald asks. As he departs, McGehee, washing his hands, looks out the window. The green car is nowhere in sight. Suddenly a large black car with a big wraparound bumper pulls up from Church Street, adjacent to the Washateria next door. (In Jackson, the churches are on Bank Street and the banks are on Church Street.) Oswald is seated in back, his arms splayed across the back of the front seat. There are two people in front, and they are all laughing as the car, pulling onto State Road 10, passes in front of the barbershop on its way to Clinton.

At the home of Reeves Morgan, Oswald introduces himself as "Oswald." Morgan's teenaged daughter Mary, anxious for a better look at this young man, parades through the living room on her way to the freezer out on the porch. Outside, seated up in a tree, Morgan's young son Van is playing "Tarzan." He eyes the black Cadillac in the yard and the man with white hair behind the wheel.

Morgan explains that you must register to vote to get a job at East. If none of his constituents wants a job right now, Oswald might have one, Morgan says.

"What do you mean by 'constituent?'" Oswald says. He is indignant. "You mean you have to see a politician to get a job!" Soon he is again cordial, offering his full name, "Lee Oswald." But he is too late. Morgan has made up his mind. "A smart aleck white boy who evidently was a nigger lover appeared in a black Cadillac," Morgan said later. When Morgan went outside to see Oswald off, the Cadillac sped off so quickly that he was almost run over in his own driveway.

After the assassination, Reeves Morgan, in Jackson for a haircut, talked with McGehee about the man both of them recognized from television as their visitor.

"Mr. Reeves, we need to call the FBI," McGehee said.

"I already have," Morgan said. "They told me they knew Oswald was in the area." A few days later, the FBI had called and asked what Oswald had been wearing.

It had been a summer of strangers in East Feliciana Parish. A big, olive-complected "Cuban," a tough "soldier-of-fortune type" with wavy black hair and a heavy beard, had come in three or four times for a haircut. McGehee had chatted about Honduras. He thought the man worked at lawyer Lloyd Cobb's Marydale Farms—the same Cobb who was Clay Shaw's superior at the International Trade Mart. In April 1978, during HSCA depositions, McGehee would reach for the photo identification book and select "Lawrence Howard" as his 1963 customer. Alarmed, lawyer Jonathan Blackmer quickly changed the subject to McGehee's stint as a Navy cryptographer.

Reeves Morgan identified that same photograph as Lawrence Howard. "This one here looks similar to a fellow I saw on the streets of Jackson!" he said. When Blackmer quickly pulled out a Xerox of another picture of Howard, and Morgan did not connect it immediately to Howard's photograph, Blackmer cried out in triumph: "Let the record reflect that the Xerox photograph was a newspaper photograph of Lawrence Howard taken in 1967 and is not familiar to the witness!"

In his sharp country way, Morgan, unruffled by Blackmer's attempt to manipulate the interview, then strengthened his identification. "This picture in here looks more like when I saw him around here. I just knew that somebody said he was one of them Mexicans over there," he said, referring to Marydale Farms. Howard was indeed of Mexican origin. "He didn't have no looseness, in none of his pants or nothing. He walked like a wrestler."

Henry Earl Palmer, the registrar of voters in 1963, also identified Lawrence Howard. "I have seen a man similar to that," he said. Howard might have worked for Mr. Louie, Louis Roussel, the oil billionaire who owned a farm next door to Lloyd Cobb's. The HSCA never investigated Marydale Farms.

Judge Rarick did not doubt Lea McGehee's story of Oswald and his haircut because he had observed the black Cadillac himself. He had been standing with District Attorney Richard Kilbourne, observing the CORE registration drive. Kilbourne was a tall man with a short mustache who, when upset, would roll his eyes back as far as they would go, then abruptly raise his head. He was no friend of Rarick's. Kilbourne headed the local Citizens' Council, which he used as his personal campaign organization. He watched approvingly as the only police officer in Clinton, Town Marshal John Manchester, a ruddy six-footer, approached a black Cadillac.

Manchester, from a dirt-poor family, was proud of being a police officer; his other job was reading gas meters. He favored a ten-gallon hat, and on the orders of Special Counsel Richard Van Buskirk, questioned all strangers who appeared in East Feliciana Parish. He was especially proud of having arrested CORE volunteer Michael Lesser, who had been sitting on the stairs leading up to the Registrar's office. Manchester charged Lesser with "criminal anarchy," a capital crime in Louisiana, tantamount to treason. Having learned that efforts would be made to integrate the courtroom on the day of Lesser's hearing, Kilbourne filed a motion for a continuance—and got it.

That summer a black activist named Mama Jo Holmes, who sheltered CORE volunteers, noticed her gas bill was unusually high. Then her house was robbed and the papers of the CORE people stolen. Crosses were burned on State Road 10, and you knew where a Klan member lived because he had planted a white camellia tree in his front yard. Lloyd Cobb's brother Alvin, that friend of Guy Banister, headed a "White Camellia Organization," a unit of the Klan.

Now Kilbourne and Rarick notice that Manchester has two men spread-eagled on the black Cadillac.

"We've been occupied by the Fed," Kilbourne drawls, "and now the Feds are fixing it so the Negroes can take over." When Manchester spots Kilbourne watching, he joins him and Rarick. "We pulled that guy over!" Manchester says. He had asked to see their drivers' licenses. "They claimed they didn't have anything to do with this. It was two dudes out of New Orleans." They were lost, coming up from Baton Rouge on Plank Road, Manchester says, referring to the area of Reeves Morgan's house. They were circling around, looking for Jackson.

Returning home from his haircut a year later, Judge Rarick telephoned his friend Ned Touchstone. Then he called Jack Rogers, who, from the day of the assassination, had a private detective named J. D. Vinson developing information on Oswald, whom he presumed was a Communist.

"Why don't you tell Jim Garrison about this?" Rarick told Rogers. According to McGehee, Rarick then wrote a little story on the appearance of Oswald in Jackson and Clinton for the *Councilor.* Soon Jack Rogers and Ned Touchstone paid their own visit to McGehee's barbershop, taking notes as McGehee talked. Rogers informed State

Sovereignty Commission official Fred Dent Jr. about the appearance of Oswald, Ferrie and Shaw in East Feliciana Parish. By the time Dent told Dischler and Fruge, they knew that and more.

Rogers scrawled his later notes on a 1965 calendar. A man named David Broman reported to Rogers that the FBI had interviewed Rose Cheramie. He learned Rose had laughed when she read in the papers that there was no connection between Ruby and Oswald. One of his "operators," as Rogers termed his informants, said he found a woman in Laredo, Texas, who had a photograph of Oswald and Ruby taken in February 1963, "Laredo," recalling Richard Case Nagell's code name.

Rogers also believed he had made a major discovery: Rose Cheramie had a sister in Jackson named Gladys Palmer. Although Palmer's maiden name was Ragland and two of her sisters were alive to inform Rogers that Rose was not their sister, Rogers had nonetheless stumbled onto an important lead. After "Rose Cheramie" his source did write the words "maiden name Ragland." Gladys Palmer worked as a stripper at the Carousel Club for Jack Ruby; she and Rose Cheramie were "sisters" in the trade. During the summer of 1963, Gladys had driven back to Louisiana in a steel blue Mercury registered to Jack Ruby. During that summer, Gladys Palmer had been seen often with Lee Harvey Oswald.

Everywhere in Clinton, Fruge and Dischler met witnesses who spoke of Gladys Palmer, a skinny, dark-haired woman always impeccably made up. Gladys was outspoken, and cutting. If her sisters asked her to do something, she would reply, "Why don't you do it yourself!" Wild, a terrific dancer, promiscuous, noisy and boozy, Gladys took drugs, again rendering her a double for Rose Cheramie.

Sometimes deputy sheriff Carl Bunch had to lock Gladys up. Her husband was Matt Junior Palmer, whose aunt, Peggy Palmer, ran the "Bayou Sara Lounge" near the St. Francisville ferry landing, and Gladys, even in her forties a "hot number," could often be found there. It was after one of her big blowouts with Matt Junior that she fled to Texas to work for Jack Ruby.

Jim Garrison confirmed some parts of this lead. On March 17th, a Thomas Williams reported that Matt Junior Palmer's ex-wife had been employed by Jack Ruby. She had returned to Jackson driving a "black Lincoln Continental" and been placed at East for drug treatment. Williams also reported that a pilot named Billy Kemp, whose wife, Maxine, worked at East, had been approached three or four weeks before the assassination to fly a group of people out of the country for $25,000.

By 1967, Gladys was shunned in East Feliciana Parish. "Don't give her any money for the funeral because she'll use it for drugs," Josephine Palmer, Henry Earl's sister, said when Matt Junior died. "Once she put him in the ground she walked off." Henry Earl Palmer, Matt Junior's cousin, thought Oswald wanted a job at East to be near Gladys.

Fruge and Dischler learned that Gladys had been spotted with Lee Harvey Oswald at two bars east of Baton Rouge: the Audubon and the Hawaiian Lounge. Sometimes they were accompanied by Gladys' eighteen-year-old cousin, Gloria Wilson, an emaciated girl. Gladys drove Gloria to Acadia Parish to meet Gloria's lover—in a black Cadillac. This lover, terrified after the assassination because he had seen Gloria with Lee Harvey Oswald, confided to Anne Dischler that both he and Gloria knew Oswald. He had seen Oswald at the drugstore, he told Anne Dischler later. He had been frightened for Gloria when he saw her in that Cadillac. Gloria worked at Cochran's Drug Store in Jackson; some said she was "dating" Oswald. "Got in car," Dischler's notebook reads.

Fruge and Dischler discovered that deputy Alvin Doucet and special sheriff's deputy Hardy Travis had confirmed that the steel blue Mercury that took Gladys home was registered in the name "Jack Ruby." D. J. Blanchard, an engineer at East, saw Gladys drive with Oswald in this blue car to the Audubon. The FBI had interviewed Gladys, Henry Earl Palmer reported to Fruge and Dischler. As Rose Cheramie's name does not appear, so neither is there a reference to "Gladys Palmer" in any of the indices of names attached to the Warren Commission findings. By the time Jim Garrison's investigation found Gladys Palmer, she had married a man named Earl Wilson and moved to Baton Rouge.

Jim Garrison directed Fruge and Dischler to focus on the appearance of Oswald, Ferrie and Shaw in Clinton where Oswald had attempted to register to vote. Oswald in the presence of Shaw would corroborate Perry Russo, and render Clay Shaw, who had denied ever having met Oswald and Ferrie, a perjurer, at the very least.

On May 23, 1967, Fruge and Dischler appeared at Henry Earl Palmer's office. On this first visit, they intended only to make contact; Dischler had not even brought along her notebook. She did have her tape recorder, which resembled a briefcase. It lay flat on the floor and ran throughout the interview.

Palmer was a tall, rangy man, unrelenting in his opposition to black people voting. On his wall was one of the Martin Luther King Jr.

posters; a doll hung from a noose on his door. "Daddy was in the Klan," his daughter says. Palmer in fact was an "Exalted Cyclops." Robert Buras points out that if you were white in that era and lived north of Baton Rouge, you were more than likely to join the Klan, or at the very least, the Citizens' Council. Palmer and John Manchester were even suspicious of John Rarick because, having been born in Indiana, he was a northerner. The notion that Palmer's testimony was not credible simply because of his Klan affiliation is fatuous.

Women were also treated as of no account. When Henry Earl Palmer spoke, he ignored Dischler, addressing himself entirely to Francis Fruge.

"Oswald registered to vote up here," Palmer remarked. He took out his big registration book, opened it, and pointed to a place on one of the pages. "Look," he said, "this is where Oswald registered."

The name had been erased and written over, but you could still see the big "O" and the space where "Lee H." had been signed. Over the erasure, another name had been written, but you could make out the pentimento, the shadow of "Oswald," the truth beneath the surface.

"Why was his name erased?" Fruge said.

Henry Earl offered no explanation. Instead, he explained how you had to be acquainted with two registered parish voters in order to register. Oswald had mentioned two doctors at East: one was "Dr. Frank Silva," the medical director of the hospital that summer. He was "living with Dr. Frank Silva," Oswald had claimed. The other was Dr. Malcolm Pierson, who was at East because Dr. Silva, who was married to the daughter of the hospital administrator, Warren Price, had tried to assist in his rehabilitation by recommending him.

Oswald had produced separation papers from the Navy, Palmer said. On the strength of his having mentioned Dr. Silva, Palmer had permitted him to register. Palmer then described Oswald's companions: a man fitting Clay Shaw's description had driven to Jackson in a black Cadillac. He had been accompanied by a shorter man, "sloppily dressed with dark bushy eyebrows." Palmer thought he saw another well-dressed man, placing four men in the car. John Manchester, too, would later tell John Rarick three men had remained in the car after Oswald had gotten on line to register to vote.

"We'd like to come back tomorrow," Fruge said, planning to have the registration book copied. Palmer agreed, adding that at first he and Manchester had decided not to say anything about Oswald being up there. This was later corroborated by a garage owner named

Joe Phelps to whom Palmer and Manchester had both denied they had seen a black Cadillac. Then they changed their minds.

When Fruge and Dischler appeared at Palmer's office the next day, the big registration book had disappeared. Palmer expressed surprise. He offered no explanation. He did not deny that he had said that Oswald had registered. "Nobody can erase that from my memory," Dischler says today.

In the months to come, Fruge and Dischler met with Palmer several more times. Never again did he mention that Oswald had registered successfully. Soon Palmer began to talk as if Oswald had *failed* to register. "Why eased off on statement in comparison to tape?" Dischler writes in her notebook. Nor did Palmer ever mention again that Oswald had invoked "Dr. Frank Silva." He mentioned only Dr. Pierson, and only to say that Dr. Pierson himself was not a registered voter in East Feliciana Parish. This, Henry Earl said, was why he refused to permit Oswald to register.

Dischler and Fruge concluded that Oswald had attempted to register twice: he failed the first time, the second not. Oswald had been in Jackson already in May, when he was spotted with Gladys Palmer and Gloria Wilson.

It would be the same with Oswald's job application at East. All evidence of his presence there had disappeared, too. Palmer also told Dischler and Fruge, inaccurately, that John Manchester had asked the radio operator to run a 1028 identification on the Cadillac, only to find it registered to the International Trade Mart, an event that did not occur. It would have been unlikely in those days to make the long-distance call in the hope of reaching the Bureau of Identification to request a license check. But Palmer was seeking to regularize what had happened on that day.

"John Manchester can identify the men in the car," Palmer said. But Manchester wanted to tell his story only to Jim Garrison. "I'm not talking to some damn state trooper!" Manchester said.

John Rarick was serving as intermediary between Garrison and John Manchester.

"I can't drive all the way up there," Garrison told Rarick. Rarick turned out to be invaluable. His law partner was married to one of Henry Earl's sisters, and Henry Earl's first wife, "Pinkie," a medical doctor, was now married to Jack Rogers. "Jim was always a finer man than some of history has recorded," Rarick says with a sardonic tone that matches that of his Tulane classmate.

Eventually Manchester talked to Francis Fruge in John Rarick's office, while Anne Dischler took notes. Manchester seemed to know, she thought, that Oswald had registered to vote. "What do you think of Oswald's having registered?" Fruge said, and Manchester knew exactly what he meant.

Manchester had examined the driver's license of the white-haired man behind the wheel. It read: "Clay Shaw." Shaw had then volunteered that he worked for the International Trade Mart. When Henry Earl a few moments later asked what they were doing in Clinton, Manchester had quipped, "Selling bananas, I guess." The CORE people had not nicknamed him "Barney" from the Andy Griffith Show for nothing.

As Dischler and Fruge continued to interview the residents of Clinton and Jackson, a narrative emerged: Oswald, Clay Shaw and David Ferrie had driven into Clinton at 9 A.M. Oswald got out of the car, and joined the already long line of black people waiting to attempt to register to vote. It was a Thursday, one of the three days a week Henry Earl deigned to open his doors: the other days were Friday and Saturday. It appears to have been September 19th.

A witness named Henry Brown said he thought he saw a hospital employee named Estes Morgan sitting briefly in the back of the car with Oswald. Estes was related to Reeves Morgan. People said they saw two white men in line together, and this was apparently Estes Morgan and Oswald.

"It's useless to try to register because the only people who can register in Clinton are black people," Morgan remarked to Oswald as they stood together in line.

"You're right," Oswald said. "The black people will eventually take over."

For black people, passing the test was, in fact, all but hopeless. That summer, William Dunn, a driver on a sugar cane farm, attempted to register nine or ten times. Furious, he joined CORE. One black woman failed to register because she had not placed the dot directly over the "i" in the word "parish." One woman, succeeding, thanked Jesus Christ.

"Don't come thanking Jesus in here," Henry Earl said. "It's just the goodness of me passing you."

That day the white man Estes Morgan also failed to register.

Following his own failure, Oswald headed for East, entering the old Parker Building, since the majestic Greek revival "Center Building" was being remodeled. He approached receptionist Bobbie Dedon and asked for directions to the personnel department. The hospital application, issued by the Civil Service, inquired whether you had ever been arrested. Question fifteen asked whether you were a registered voter in the state of Louisiana. As he went off to take his pre-employment physical, Oswald was told: if you're not a registered voter, you won't be able to work here.

Wearing a T-shirt, obstreperous and calling attention to himself, Oswald falls into conversation with some hospital attendants. His subject is Cuba and what it will take to bring Fidel Castro down. His voice is loud.

The director of medical services passes by and hears him. It is Dr. Frank Silva. One of the attendants, who is from Texas, calls Dr. Silva over.

"Dr. Silva is from Cuba," the attendant tells Oswald. Oswald behaves as if he is already aware of that fact. Now Dr. Silva, an elegant man with a profound sense of propriety, takes a long, penetrating look at the uncouth young man purporting to be looking for a job. The young man is bragging about how proficient he is with guns, how he served in the Marines, how he will go to Cuba.

"I'm involved with getting rid of Fidel Castro," Oswald says. "I'm using my skills as a Marine." This man is as belligerent as the one who signed his Holiday Inn bar bill "Hidell" and ran off without paying, as rude as the man who, applying for a job at the *States-Item* in August, twice visited the news room. There he posed as a "rabid *supporter* of Fidel Castro," according to an article in the *States-Item* the day after the assassination; he was so annoyed by the complicated application process that he threw his uncompleted form into a trash can.

It was Oswald the infiltrator, playing his hero Herbert Philbrick, leading his own multiple lives. At the East Louisiana State Hospital, he was not the pro-Castroite, but the man described in David Atlee Phillips' *The Amlash Legacy,* in which his hero recounts, "I was one of those officers who handled Lee Harvey Oswald. We gave him the mission of killing Fidel Castro in Cuba. . . ."

In 1955, having graduated from the University of Havana Medical School, Dr. Francisco Silva Clarens had left Cuba to continue his studies at Tulane University. He has no love for Fidel Castro. He is a man more interested in art, literature and history than in politics, an intellectual, and the psychiatrist who would come to be known as the "father of psychiatry in Baton Rouge." Jim Garrison would have viewed him, like Alberto Fowler, as a "legitimate Cuban." Dr. Frank Silva was spiritually light years from his second cousin, Francisco Bartes Clarens, a CIA asset and mercenary who flew murderous missions for the Agency in the Congo. Dr. Silva has met this cousin,

Frank Bartes, only once. "I don't get involved with people for whom I have no respect," he says. He is certain that Frank Bartes, who appeared on the scene immediately after Oswald's court appearance over the Canal Street fracas with Carlos Bringuier, has no idea that he is working in Clinton.

Now Dr. Silva concludes that this disrespectful, impolite man ranting about killing Fidel Castro has no idea what he's talking about. He is a troubled man making a spectacle of himself while applying for a job at a mental hospital.

"I've come to get a job at the suggestion of Dr. Malcolm Pierson," Oswald says. It flashes through Dr. Silva's mind that they might know each other because both are homosexual. So Pierson has imported one of his New Orleans boyfriends up here, Dr. Silva thinks.

I would never give a job to this person, Dr. Silva decides as he walks off. Armed with the name "Dr. Frank Silva," Oswald then returned to Henry Earl's office. Dr. Silva had registered to vote in Clinton in 1962; Henry Earl then permitted Oswald to register.

Assigned by Jim Garrison to help Fruge and Dischler, Moo Moo Sciambra interviewed Dr. Frank Silva. His memo of that meeting claims that Dr. Silva "had never seen or heard of Lee Harvey Oswald." This is not what Dr. Silva told him, however. Dr. Silva says that Moo Moo had been so vague that he had concluded that all Sciambra had come to discuss was Rose Cheramie's story.

Dr. Silva had begun to tell Moo Moo about the man at the hospital talking about Cuba. Then, feeling ill, he pleaded he had the flu. He had more to say. Could Sciambra come back at a later time? Moo Moo never returned to interview this witness who had encountered Lee Harvey Oswald, one whose integrity and credibility could never have been challenged.

AN UNSUNG
HERO AND THE
DO-NOT-FILE FILE

14

By the time I get there, he better be back in jail.
—Corrie Collins

A T THE EAST LOUISIANA STATE Hospital at Jackson, Fruge and Dischler interviewed Merryl Hudson, secretary at the personnel office headed by Guy Broyles. They examined Dr. Pierson's file. Jack Darsey, the hospital executive assistant, said that Dr. Pierson was "about to crack up, worrying about something." Pierson himself gave Fruge and Dischler the name of a nurse, Charlie Wilbans, who had talked to Rose Cheramie.

Maxine Kemp, who also worked in personnel, confirmed that Oswald had applied for a job. She would show them the form. Kemp searched all personnel files, "active" and dormant. "It's missing," she told Fruge. She, too, remembered the black Cadillac, which had stopped at her father's Texaco station outside Clinton.

Dischler and Fruge interviewed another employee, Aline Woodside, who also said she had seen Oswald's application. Receptionist Bobbie Dedon identified Oswald from his photograph. She had seen no likeness of Oswald until Fruge showed her his. Independently, a "former Army intelligence officer" told Ned Touchstone that a man who looked like Oswald and used his name had applied for work at East. He had arrived in a big automobile "believed to belong to a wealthy New Orleans man."

Sciambra did his own set of interviews. Reeves Morgan confirmed that Aline Woodside had said she saw an application with Oswald's name on it. Henry Earl Palmer told Moo Moo that there were two white people on the "long line of colored people," and identified Estes Morgan as the second man. Palmer gave his description of the two white males sitting in front of the black Cadillac as it waited for Oswald. He identified David Ferrie in a photograph from his "heavy eyebrows." He thought the gray-haired man might have worn a hat. Palmer marked with an "X" the photographs of Ferrie and Shaw as "likely identifications." There was no doubt in his mind when he saw Oswald's picture: "That's him!" he said. Henry Earl had, after all, run into Oswald twice.

Palmer was vague only when Moo Moo asked him the name of the doctor with whom Oswald said he was living. He now claimed he urged Oswald either to obtain a letter from someone who had lived in Jackson for six months, or to register in New Orleans. He had told Oswald he did not need to be a registered voter to get a job at the hospital—which was technically true. "That's the last time I saw Oswald," Palmer lied to Sciambra. Warren Price and Dr. Silva were too prominent to be drawn into this mess, and Palmer was now circumspect.

According to Henry Earl Palmer, Gloria Wilson, emerging from Cochran's, had taunted him: "Your civil rights workers are riding better than you now. That boy in line with the niggers got in the black Cadillac and left with it." Palmer was "sure" that Gloria and her boss Mrs. Cochran had "talked to the people in the car."

Moo Moo tracked down CORE activist Verla Bell in Indiana. She had seen the black Cadillac, and a man in it with a big straw hat. She saw "Barney" (Manchester) talking to the men in the car, and Palmer talking to Manchester, and a man named Andrew Dunn sitting on a bench in front of Wright's barbershop. Bell said she could not positively identify the men in the car.

John Manchester was now willing to sign an affidavit that the gray-haired man said he "was from the International Trade Mart." He had not run a "1028," but had examined "Clay Shaw's" driver's license.

Jim Garrison tried to locate the owner of the black Cadillac. Moo Moo learned that G. Wray Gill made his automobile available to David Ferrie "in the scope of his employment." Shaw's friend Jeff Biddison owned a similar automobile, which Shaw borrowed on occasion. Banister's cohort A. Roswell Thompson also drove a black Cadillac. When John Volz scrutinized Shaw's appointment books for the summer of 1963, nothing demonstrated that he could not have been in Clinton.

By now, Francis Fruge had a small snapshot of the black Cadillac that had been taken by a local resident. It pictured four figures, their faces indistinct. The "well-dressed" fourth man seen in the

Cadillac by Henry Earl remained unidentified. Joseph Cooper, a Baton Rouge police officer working undercover for the FBI infiltrating the Klan, told Moo Moo that Guy Banister had attended events in Baton Rouge at the Jack Tar Capitol House Hotel in the company of local attorney Richard Van Buskirk. One such occasion was a speech given by right-wing General Edwin Walker in 1963, the same General Walker at whom Oswald purportedly took some shots. The other was a 1964 speech by Dr. Carl McIntire, whose assistant Edgar Eugene Bradley would figure in the Garrison case. Cooper said that Van Buskirk, McIntire, General Walker and Guy Banister all knew each other.

Cooper also confirmed that Billy Kemp had indeed been offered $25,000 to fly two passengers to South America on November 22, 1963. Kemp had refused.

Cooper was ready to testify before the Orleans Parish grand jury when he was seriously injured in an automobile accident. While he was in the hospital, members of the Louisiana State Police and representatives from the governor's office both attempted to take possession of his files, which were in the custody of the Slidell police. Cooper was persuaded that Oswald was a naval intelligence agent. Cooper also told Sciambra that Banister had a file on Lee Harvey Oswald, which of course was true.

The possibility that Banister had been in Clinton led Moo Moo once more to Henry Earl Palmer. It was not Guy Banister in the black Cadillac, Henry Earl insisted. He had run into Banister in 1944 when he was in the Army, stationed in Orlando. He would certainly have recognized Banister, he claimed.

Andrew Dunn, who had been sitting in front of the barbershop, as Verla Bell said, told Fruge and Dischler, and Moo Moo as well, that he had seen four men in the car. It was a Thursday. Dunn, unemployed and the town drunk, had time on his hands. Townspeople told Fruge and Dischler that Dunn's memory was good despite his affliction. He was not an unstable man.

He saw a tall man with black hair, Dunn said. The driver was tall, well dressed and gray at the temples, with darkish hair. He wore a blue suit. All of the men got out of the car. From photographs, Dunn immediately identified Ferrie, Oswald and Shaw. He could not find a photograph in the group depicting the fourth man. He would know him if he saw him, Dunn insisted. Dunn had also seen Oswald with Estes Morgan. He knew Morgan well and had seen him go upstairs to the registrar's office, but not anywhere near the car. He was definitely not the fourth man.

Anne Dischler's notes reflect Dunn's testimony: "There were four men in the car. There was a tall, well-dressed man driving the car. The other three men in the car were not as tall and not as well dressed. I have identified three pictures of the men in the car. He did not have a picture of the fourth man." Three men had returned to the car, while the fourth got into the registration line. Dunn's was the best interview Dischler and Fruge had conducted that July.

Four days later, Dunn confirmed that he was "absolutely sure" there were four people in the car. Moo Moo pulled out his set of photographs and now Dunn found the fourth man. It was Guy Banister. He was driving, Dunn said. Then he examined the photograph of Clay Shaw again and corrected himself. No, it was Shaw who was driving. Banister had been in the backseat. Gloria Wilson also told her best friend Veda Freeman that "four men were in the car."

After Dunn had identified Banister for Sciambra, Dischler again studied the 3 x 5 photograph of the black Cadillac. It was Ferrie at the wheel, she decided, with Oswald beside him. In back, were Shaw and another older man, more bulky: two middle-aged, gray-haired men were seated side by side in the backseat. Dischler was persuaded that it was Guy Banister. Back in New Orleans, Garrison's staff blew up the photograph, but the larger it became, the more distorted were the faces.

Fear of talking cut across race and class lines. "We're working for Mr. Garrison's office," Dischler and Fruge would say. "We're trying to find out what happened to our president." Few found it in their interest to come forward. Black people had no sympathy for Shaw or Oswald, but they had heard of witnesses dying, and held back. The white people were cautious. Barber Wright would say only, "Possibly I did see the Cadillac."

Lawyer William ("Billy") Kline, whose office was right across the street from Palmer's, told someone he had "talked to men in car." It took a call from Jack Rogers before he would even meet Fruge and Dischler. "I didn't see anything," Kline would say ever after. "Try Richard Van Buskirk." Van Buskirk was that Clinton town attorney who filed the motions against CORE seeking injunctions to thwart its voter registration drive, and he was close to the Klan. Van Buskirk, friend of General Walker, friend of Guy Banister, was the least likely person in East Feliciana Parish to help Dischler and Fruge. Kline was sending a not-so-veiled message. John Rarick speculates about Kline's refusal to come forward: "Just don't want to get involved. Fear of being regarded as controversial."

By the end of August, the Sovereignty Commission, whose interests in forestalling integration did not mesh with Jim Garrison's effort to uncover the murderers of John F. Kennedy, told Anne Dischler she was being terminated. The excuse was that her expenses were too high, even as these were paid by the Orleans Parish district attorney's office. A seasoned politician, Garrison thanked Henry Sibley for "the cooperation of the Sovereignty Commission with regard to our case." "Do not resign," Moo Moo told Dischler. "Go back to work on Monday." Garrison would intervene.

"Are you interested in witnesses who could identify Shaw as a homosexual?" Dischler asked Garrison when they met in New Orleans that August. He was not.

Fruge and Sciambra interviewed the mother of Layton Martens, now incarcerated at East. In September 1963, Marguerite Martens had claimed in a letter to a Father Toups that at their home she had overheard her son Layton, Ferrie, Banister and Shaw talking about killing Kennedy. Her son, she added, was just an innocent bystander. With Guy Banister's assistance, Martens had her committed to the mental ward at Charity Hospital. Martens told a friend, Beverly Farley, that he had his mother committed because "she complained that the FBI was questioning her." On November 30, 1966, just as Jim Garrison was beginning his investigation, Ferrie and Martens had her committed in Mandeville. Now she resided at the mental hospital at Jackson.

Marguerite Martens' psychiatrist was present during her interview with Fruge and Sciambra. "Why didn't you contact the authorities?" Fruge asked.

"Who's going to believe a nut?" Mrs. Martens said.

In August, Fruge and Dischler continued to uncover evidence linking Gladys Palmer to Ruby and Oswald. Alba Claudine Ross, a telephone operator at East and "close to Gladys" until Gladys seduced Alba's husband, Troy, might be a witness. Gladys had stayed at one point with Hilda Perpera, Ross said. Dischler confirmed not only that Gladys had returned from Texas in that steel blue Mercury, but that she had been in the company of a "blondish" man with blue eyes and fair skin, five foot eight or nine inches tall, a man who fit the description of the person at the Holiday Inn lounge who had signed his bar bill "Hidell." In helping the decoy become "Oswald," it appeared that Gladys herself, three months in advance, had foreknowledge of the assassination.

Gladys was known to have borrowed an old model Ford and driven to Jackson. If Lea McGehee did see Oswald emerge from an old car near the Washateria, a car with a woman in it, that woman could well have been Gladys. McGehee remains certain Oswald departed in a black Cadillac. Both Fruge and Dischler saw Gladys as a key witness.

On August 22nd, Fruge and Sciambra found Gladys at her home on Evangeline Street. She had already been interviewed by Jack Rogers and Ned Touchstone, she said testily. She did not know anything "that would lend any assistance." She had never seen or heard of Lee Harvey Oswald "in her life" before the assassination. She had never heard of Jack Ruby until he shot Oswald. She had never been in Dallas. As for that new light blue Mercury, she bought it herself and it was registered in her own name. It had since been repossessed. She could identify no photographs. Estes Morgan did look familiar, she said as she ushered Sciambra and Fruge out the door.

Yet witnesses continued to contradict Gladys Palmer. Cal Kelly's daughter, Elizabeth Kelly Graham, told Sciambra she heard Oswald had been at the hospital seeking employment—in the company of Gladys Palmer. She had talked to people who had seen Oswald and Gladys together, although she was not ready to provide their names. Neither Graham nor Gladys Palmer was subpoenaed to appear before the Orleans Parish grand jury.

So far, Jim Garrison had only white witnesses to testify to the presence of Oswald, Ferrie and Shaw in Clinton, and he didn't even have all that many of those. Jack Rogers' investigator, Ronald Johnston, saw Shaw and Oswald together at the Clinton courthouse "looking for something"—information Rogers did not share with Jim Garrison.

Moo Moo Sciambra presided over a town meeting at Mount Hope Missionary Baptist Church on State Road 10. He showed slides to an audience of about sixty black people and four or five whites. Images of Ferrie, Shaw and Oswald flashed on a screen.

"Does anybody recognize any of these pictures?" Moo Moo said.

Silence rang out. The meeting produced "no positive result," Dischler wrote in her notebook. Sciambra told Jim Garrison that "we must win their confidence more in order for them to talk freely . . . they seem to be very suspicious of white people."

The audience was in fact filled with people who could identify those slides. One woman recognized Ferrie at once. "It looked like he had on a false face," she said later. "False eyelashes, reddish looking, like it was plastered on." Experience cautioned silence. "We don't know where our enemy is," she said. A friend echoed her: "It's too dangerous to fool with." Community leader Charlotte Greenup also would not testify. "If you don't have to die, you don't want to die," Greenup said.

On September 12th, Dischler and Fruge produced their final witness, Henry Burnell Clark, a twenty-nine-year-old clerk at the Stewart & Carroll General Merchandise Store. Shortly before noon, Clark said, he saw approaching him "a tall man in a dark business suit, who was wearing a shirt and tie." He entered a black automobile, backed the car onto Main Street, and drove past the bank. Clark signed the photograph identifying Clay Shaw. "He reminded me of a movie actor I remembered seeing on the screen, and because he was unusually tall, standing well over six feet," Clark said.

"Jeff Chandler?" Garrison wrote onto Clark's statement. The other man had "unusual" hair, "bushy" hair. He had walked up to the pay telephone. Clark also identified the photograph of David Ferrie. The notary who signed Clark's statement, and witnessed Clark's signature on the Ferrie and Shaw photographs, was— William F. Kline Jr.

"One who might help you is Corrie Collins of Baton Rouge," a CORE member named Christine Wright told Fruge and Dischler. "Corrie C. Collins—female. May be in E. Baton Rouge Ph [Parish]," Dischler wrote.

Tall and broad-faced, with quiet courage, Corrie Collins, a man, was the East Feliciana chairman of CORE. At eighteen, he had been drafted into the Army; at twenty-one, a Vietnam veteran, he had attempted to register in Clinton. Henry Earl Palmer failed Collins because he answered all six questions correctly. To pass, you needed only four right answers. "You didn't follow instructions!" Palmer said nastily.

Ten days later, the waiting time required by law, Collins returned and registered to vote. By now, he had joined CORE. When the town of Clinton issued an injunction against demonstrations, arguing that "Communist-front" operators had infiltrated CORE, Collins went to court to have the injunction lifted. Lined up against him were Van Buskirk, Kilbourne, "Billy" Kline, and a lawyer named William E. Woodward.

It seemed that every week Collins found himself in Judge Rarick's court. Rarick admits today that the only violence resulting from the CORE voter registration drive came when the rapscallion son of deputy sheriff Carl Bunch threw a brick and broke the window of a black Baptist church. At the time, Rarick more than once jailed CORE leaders, and Collins in particular, for "criminal conspiracy." Once he ordered a deputy sheriff to force "a Negro wearing a CORE T-shirt" in court to put on a coat.

Corrie Collins could not be intimidated. A fellow CORE worker later explained that Collins would go down before he would give in "unless the lives of his family were threatened." His mother had died when he was three years old. This brought him a certain stoicism. The worst had already happened, he says. Now he had nothing to fear. When a CORE worker, arrested for demonstrating, was dragged from jail by a lynch mob, Collins sent a message that the man be brought back to jail. "By the time I get there, he better be back in jail," Collins said. He was.

If Collins discovered that a Klan meeting was in the works— the Klan met regularly at a TV repair shop—if he saw the cars lined up outside, he walked in, just to let the Klan members know he knew they were there. The Klan burned crosses in the yards of CORE members like James Bell, who would not testify for Jim Garrison. They stayed away from the Collins house. "They knew better," Collins says. It was Collins who had nicknamed Manchester "Barney."

His enemies were formidable. Collins was fired from his job at the Villa Feliciana Geriatric Hospital because he missed work when he was jailed for participating in the voter education project. The days of work he missed did not equal the leave days he had kept in reserve. Still, he was fired. Protesting before the Louisiana Civil Service Commission, he was reinstated. It was just another day in East Feliciana Parish.

Two weeks after Collins registered, Oswald had appeared. Collins was standing beside Verla Bell outside Palmer's office dressed in blue overalls, the signature outfit of the civil rights worker, when the black Cadillac rolled up with four men in it. When, later, Collins said there were three, he was referring to the time after the fourth white man had gotten in line to register to vote. It was between nine and ten in the morning.

"It may be an FBI car," Collins said. The driver was a tall man with white hair. A shorter man was sloppy, with bushy eyebrows. One of the men in the back wore white pants, definitely not hospital whites, but casual pants. The white pants recall Vernon Bundy's testimony that Oswald had been in "white jeans" at the lakefront. The fourth man was the same age as Oswald, Collins says, ruling out speculation that this was not Oswald, but a male nurse in his late forties named Winslow Foster. Foster would not have been registering in East Feliciana Parish, where he did not reside.

Collins decided the men had been sent to disrupt the registration drive. The two young men got out of the car and joined the line to register. Later in the day, Collins strolled upstairs to the Registrar's office. In the hallway he observed Lee Harvey Oswald deep in conversation with a man Collins identified easily from his wig, David Ferrie. Nor did Collins have trouble identifying Clay Shaw, who had gotten out of the car and was walking around.

On his second try, Francis Fruge found Corrie Collins at his home in Baton Rouge.

"Why me?" Collins said.

"They told me, anything that happened in Clinton during that time, you would know," Fruge said.

Collins examined the photograph of the black Cadillac, but the faces weren't clear. He easily identified photographs of Shaw, Ferrie and Oswald. When Moo Moo came to interview him, Collins told him how he had seen Ferrie and Oswald upstairs. Sciambra did not write this down, creating yet another potential Russo-memo problem.

Late in January, Moo Moo returned with Jimmy Alcock. If he wore blue overalls, it had to be a Wednesday or a Thursday, his days off, Corrie Collins said. He had heard Manchester joke that the Federal people looked like they were trading with the enemy, a line Verla Bell also remembered. "Scrubbs" Dunn had been sitting on a bench and had identified Oswald later as getting out of the car.

The driver had on a light hat, Collins said, echoing Henry Earl Palmer and Verla Bell. Years later, he had forgotten the hat, but his testimony remains unimpeached. On January 31, 1968, Corrie Collins signed the back of the photographs of Oswald, Shaw and Ferrie. A measure of how strained Garrison's office had become is that on the back of the Shaw photograph, someone wrote: "Chg: conspiracy to commit murder of Pres. Johnson." Corrie Collins would prove to be among Jim Garrison's staunchest Clinton witnesses.

Fruge and Dischler persisted until the end of September 1967. Both Bobbie Dedon and her husband, Joe, repeated that they had seen Oswald in Jackson with Gladys Palmer. "Oswald may have been at the Audubon Bar with Gladys," Joe said. Dischler passed a note to Fruge: "Recorder is on floor." D. J. ("Cotton") Blanchard reiterated that he had seen Gladys in Opelousas in a Cadillac, as the tape recorder whirred, undetected. "Too many men," Emily Bailey, who had worked at the Audubon, said of Gladys. Mrs. Cochran said she saw Gladys getting into the black Cadillac. Dischler and Fruge corroborated that the registration, revealing that the Mercury was owned by Jack Ruby, had been rechecked by Sheriff Archie Doughty and his deputy, Alvin Doucet.

On October 9th, Anne Dischler wrote the last page in her third notebook. The Winslow Foster lead had gone nowhere. "We don't want to stop," Dischler pleaded with Moo Moo. She and Fruge had not yet even interviewed Dr. Frank Silva. Her list included tracking down "old churches," at Garrison's suggestion, and talking to Dr. Silva, Gladys Palmer and Cal Kelly again. Did Ned Touchstone have any photographs they needed? she writes. Fruge had his own list of tasks as yet unaccomplished:

1. Shaw's credit cards for Aug–Oct. 1963.
2. Any civil rights organizations in Trade Mart?
3. Dunn affidavit: is it complete?
4. Have we spoken to Estes Morgan's relatives?
5. Justice dept (FBI) who were around during registration may well have spoken to Oswald.
6. Should we check with Doris Shaw Yarbough?
7. Old dark beat up car at Barber Shop (may well be same as one sold by Oswald at Junk Yard).
8. Have we talked to Morgan's daughter?
9. Person Morain [sic] heard of at hospital who said Pres. to be shot was probably the Ruby stripper. . . .

"Mr. Garrison said stop," Moo Moo repeated. The state police had now formally removed Fruge from the investigation with the excuse that "we're short of people." A state legislator had called for the return of the expenses paid to "a state police detective and a woman state employee who worked together on a mysterious investigation."

Working alone, Sciambra was inundated with disinformation. A hospital attendant named Pete Reech identified a photograph of Sergio Arcacha Smith and insisted that Frank Silva had introduced them, although he knew Dr. Silva only as someone to whom he delivered the newspaper. Once, Dr. Silva had invited Reech in for scrambled eggs. Dr. Silva states that he never met Sergio Arcacha Smith. Henry Earl Palmer reported Manchester's false contention that a boy who fit Oswald's description had emerged from a CORE meeting, and that Manchester followed him in the direction of Jackson. Corrie Collins is adamant that no such white person at that time attended a CORE meeting.

Some witnesses retracted their testimony. Cal Kelly denied he was sitting on that bench with Andrew Dunn. Dunn again identified Guy Banister, but now placed Jack Ruby as the driver of the black Cadillac. Later Dunn admitted he changed his testimony because he thought "Dischler and Fruge were FBI agents." The only new witness was CORE activist William Dunn.

Still, by June 1968, thirteen East Feliciana Parish witnesses had agreed to testify at the trial of Clay Shaw.

Jim Garrison would continue to pursue East Feliciana leads even after the Shaw trial. Sciambra found Ed Dwyer, willing to discuss his neighbor Lloyd Cobb's Marydale Farms. "Clay Shaw visited that farm," Dwyer said, "for sure." He believed Shaw supplied funds to the Klan in the area, and that Edward Grady Partin's man, with the surname Sylvester, might know whom Shaw knew in Clinton and St. Francisville. At the end of April 1969, Moo Moo found Jerry Sylvester, who turned out to be a good friend of John Manchester. Sylvester agreed to help, only two months later to die in a small plane that crashed on take-off.

In the late 1970s, Garrison turned over to the HSCA some of these leads, including the statement of Corinne Villard. He noted that Patterson, where Villard had seen Oswald and the "foreign lady," was on the same route David Ferrie had taken on his trip to Houston and Galveston on the weekend of the assassination. The HSCA chose not to follow up.

The FBI would forever deny that they had received a telephone call from Reeves Morgan, informing them that Oswald had been in Clinton and Jackson. On January 22, 1968, Moo Moo wrote to Elmer B. Litchfield, the FBI's resident agent in charge at Baton Rouge. He had learned that Mr. Reeves Morgan "called your office to inform you of Oswald's presence in the area," Sciambra wrote. He would like to meet with Litchfield. Given official FBI policy, Litchfield couldn't have met with Sciambra even if he wanted to.

Alerted, J. Edgar Hoover sent a message to all Louisiana agents: they were not to acknowledge Sciambra's letter "because we are not becoming involved in any way in Garrison's investigation." Division 5's William Branigan ordered that agent Joseph Sylvester have Sciambra's letter hand-delivered to the U.S. attorney, who had to be alerted in the event that Litchfield was subpoenaed. Litchfield composed a formal denial that the FBI in Baton Rouge had received Morgan's call and sent it to Robert E. Rightmyer, the SAC in New Orleans. He "did not receive any telephone calls from Mr. Reeves

Morgan, or from anyone else that Oswald was there," Litchfield wrote. Two of his underlings, Earl R. Petersen and Michael Baron, wrote identical denials.

Hoover now ordered Ramsey Clark to state that a review of his files "fails to reveal any contact with Mr. Reeves Morgan in connection with the assassination investigation." Hoover added, malignantly, that Morgan's name did appear in his files; Morgan had fired a Negro trucker "because the Negro had participated in voter registration activities."

Moo Moo and Jimmy Alcock drove up to the Baton Rouge FBI office and asked to speak to Litchfield. They were told he was not available, and, no, they could not wait. Litchfield at once informed Rightmyer, who reassured Hoover that no "effort would be made to contact Sciambra and Alcock." Litchfield comments today, "Everything went through the Seat of Government."

On February 1, 1968, a nervous William Branigan again telephoned Joseph Sylvester at the New Orleans field office. Should Litchfield be contacted at home or away from the office by Alcock or Sciambra, he should be "brief," offer "no comment," and declare that "any information he might have acquired as a Special Agent of the FBI cannot be divulged." Assistant U.S. Attorney Gene S. Palmisano on February 14th wrote Sciambra that Reeves Morgan's only contact with the FBI was "on a totally unrelated matter," while "the FBI has no record of any such contact by Mr. Morgan." The term "no record" calls to mind the FBI's "do-not-file file."

Five days later, Moo Moo wrote to Hoover: "Our office has information indicating that Lee Harvey Oswald was in the Jackson and Clinton, Louisiana area some time in the late summer of 1963. Would you please send any information you have relative to Oswald's presence in the area at that time?" He hoped to force Hoover into an outright lie. "If you have no information relative to Oswald's presence . . . we would also appreciate a reply from you, indicating this." Hoover replied—with silence. Sciambra then repeated the request to Palmisano. He may not have been clear. "Irrespective of Mr. Reeves' telephone contact with the Bureau's Baton Rouge office," he asks, did the FBI have any information?

On April 18th, Branigan again telephoned Rightmyer, requesting that the New Orleans field office review its files to see if they had any information about Oswald "being in the Jackson-Clinton area during the summer or 'late' fall of 1963." It was so urgent that Rightmyer was to reply the same day. Rightmyer dutifully reported that the review "failed to uncover any information that Oswald was in the Jackson and Clinton areas." Now Hoover told the U.S. attorney's office that they should "refer Mr. Sciambra to the material published by the Warren Commission in its Report and the twenty-six volumes of testimony and exhibits." This Hoover memo was distributed to all assistant U.S. attorneys, to Division 5, and to Hoover's own special team, starting with Clyde Tolson and Deke.

Research has revealed that the FBI, from Hoover on down, was lying. The Bureau was fully aware of Oswald's presence in Clinton and at the East Louisiana State Hospital at Jackson. On November 26th or 27th—the witness, Merryl Hudson, is not certain which—the Tuesday or Wednesday after the assassination, an FBI agent appeared at East. He headed for the office of the personnel director, Guy Broyles. Had Oswald appeared at the hospital? he asked disingenuously, producing a small, glossy 3 x 5 photograph of Lee Harvey Oswald.

He showed this photograph to Broyles and to his secretary, Hudson. Had they ever seen this man?

"He is supposed to have turned in an application," the agent said. Hudson at once denied seeing Oswald or the application, but Maxine Kemp has "some thoughts" about Oswald's missing application: "I believe the personnel officer, Guy Broyles, had his secretary take it out of there."

Forty years later, just as Merryl Hudson reveals that the FBI knew perfectly well about Oswald's visit to East Feliciana Parish and the hospital, so Elmer Litchfield admits that the FBI knew that Oswald had been in Clinton and Jackson that summer of 1963. Litchfield remembers driving with a fellow agent by the Clinton courthouse shortly after the assassination.

"That must be where that guy thought he saw Oswald," his subordinate remarked to Litchfield.

Evidence reveals, too, that the FBI followed the "Oswald" of the Lafayette Holiday Inn fracas. Right after the assassination, the resident FBI agent out of Lafayette had gone to the Holiday Inn lounge and seized as "evidence" both Oswald's knife and that bar slip signed "Hidell." Lou Ivon says that too few resources and too little time made it impossible for the Garrison office to follow up properly on the Holiday Inn incident.

(Research reveals as well that the FBI also destroyed other Kennedy assassination records. During the 1970s House Select Committee investigation, Chief Counsel G. Robert Blakey requested of the Bureau that his personal notes made from "certain FBI files" be retained at FBI headquarters yet not be considered "agency records" and so subject to Freedom of Information Act requests from historians. Rather, they were to be "congressional documents," safeguarded by the FBI, which would exercise no control over them. That prerogative would remain with Blakey himself.

The FBI counsel would have granted this request, but the assistant director of the Records Management Division, showing scant respect for Blakey, overrode his decision. "Not necessary to correspond with Blakey," he wrote onto the recommendation. "Notes were taken from informant files *and will be destroyed after HSCA completes inv.*" (Emphasis added.)

When leaks brought the Clinton evidence their way, the Shaw defense team borrowed from tactics honed by Walter Sheridan. Believing it would be easy to intimidate the "country folk," they dispatched Hugh Aynsworth and James Phelan up to Clinton either to bribe or to frighten the Clinton and Jackson witnesses from testifying that they had seen Shaw and Oswald together. Many of the people were already terrified.

Aynesworth chose to focus on John Manchester because he was the most potentially damaging witness. Manchester was a law enforcement officer, and it was to him that the driver of that black Cadillac had shown a driver's license in the name of "Clay Shaw." It was to Manchester that the driver had admitted that he worked for the International Trade Mart. Aynesworth produced a copy of Manchester's statement stolen from the locked filing cabinet in Lou Ivon's office.

"You could have a job as a CIA handler in Mexico for $38,000 dollars a year," Aynesworth said. All Manchester had to do was leave the state of Louisiana and not return to testify at the trial of Clay Shaw.

It turned out that Manchester was not "Barney" after all. Manchester was livid.

"I advise you to leave the area," Manchester told Aynesworth. "Otherwise, I'll cut you a new asshole!"

When Manchester reported the incident to Jim Garrison, Aynesworth denied that it had happened. Manchester submitted to both a polygraph and an interview under sodium pentothal. He had been telling the truth. Garrison then subpoenaed Aynesworth before the Orleans Parish grand jury. "It has been determined that the CIA is his true employer," Garrison concluded about Aynesworth. The charge reads: "Hugh Aynesworth tried in February of 1968 to bribe a Louisiana police officer, Clinton City Marshal John Manchester, to keep Mr. Manchester from testifying about the covert activities of Lee Harvey Oswald, Jack Ruby, and Clay Shaw at a civil rights function there in 1963." Even when he was offered immunity, Aynesworth would not appear to answer the charges.

In March 1968, Clay Shaw decided to commission a book about the case, to be written from his point of view. It would attack Jim Garrison as a homophobe and assert that he was being victimized because he was homosexual. Shaw called a friend named Stuart Timmons, who declined. He called his friend James Leo Herlihy, author of *Midnight Cowboy,* who also turned him down. But Herlihy recommended James Kirkwood, later to coauthor *A Chorus Line.* Kirkwood would pretend to be "objective." Kirkwood's editor at Simon & Schuster, Richard Kluger, says he would never have signed up *American Grotesque* had he known of Kirkwood's special relationship with Clay Shaw.

In the company of Aynesworth and Gurvich, Kirkwood drove up to Clinton where Gurvich commandeered Deputy Carl Bunch, for whom the summer of 1963 meant, "We shall overcome and being busy with them niggers." According to Kirkwood, they "barged" into the Collins home, odd language since the door was always left unlocked. Kirkwood writes that he encountered Corrie Collins' father Emmett "Snowball" Collins, "with fear in his eyes." He insists he found a "white-haired man of seventy." In 1968, as in the year 2001, Emmett Collins had jet black hair, despite his nickname of "Snowball."

Nor could it have been a case of mistaken identity: there was no white-haired grandfather on the scene. Corrie Collins doubts that the event could have occurred for another reason. He had put the local police on notice not to bother his father. "Bother me, not him," Collins said. By then no one had any doubt that he meant it.

There is no documentary explanation of why Clay Shaw was instructed by the CIA to bring Oswald to East Feliciana Parish where he was to be employed at East. Garrison and his staff speculated from the evidence. Employment at the huge East Louisiana State Hospital would provide Oswald with a cover and a legitimate job, removing suspicion that he had been a wandering intelligence agent with an FBI informant's number, Numa Bertel thinks. But why at East?

Jim Garrison wondered whether Oswald's job at a notorious "insane asylum" might have led to fabricated evidence that he was a patient, and not an employee. Perhaps unsuccessful shock treatments would have been offered as the cause of his having become the "deranged" assassin. The "crazed" part of Oswald's profile would be accomplished at Jackson.

Before Dr. Frank Silva, Oswald had behaved erratically, attracting attention and not behaving as a person actually seeking a job would. Oswald had not known, Garrison concluded, that "he would be the turkey on Thanksgiving day." But he might well have believed that he was participating in a scheme to murder Fidel Castro, as the comments overheard by Dr. Silva indicated.

What if, Garrison wondered, with Oswald on the payroll, corrupted doctors, at a place where many doctors were temporary and recovering from misdemeanors, had said they tested him and found him insane, suffering from aggression "beyond control?" He might escape to "unknown parts." The hospital would have papers to prove that, "acting funny" one day, Oswald had been locked down, only to emerge as the "lone nut" at Dealey Plaza.

The entire escapade of Shaw and Ferrie bringing Oswald north of Baton Rouge provides strong evidence that the cover-up began before the assassination. Oswald was being converted to a "patsy," an innocent man being readied to be held responsible for the heinous crime. The Warren Report, lacking any motive for Oswald as the perpetrator, challenges his sanity, defining him as a classic sociopath: "He does not appear to have been able to establish meaningful relationships with other people"; he is "a man whose view of the world has been twisted"; he is a "troubled American citizen"; he is an "unstable character, whose actions are highly unpredictable." Oswald's appearance at a mental hospital may be easily connected to the scenario of the coming cover-up. A decade after the Warren Report, the FBI was still calling Oswald "a rather disoriented individual with bizarre ideas."

The two Clinton eye-witnesses who identified Guy Banister as having been in Clinton did not survive. In 1964, Gloria Wilson suddenly fell ill. Her legs swelled up so that it seemed as if her flesh would burst. So rapidly did her body shut down that people speculated that she had been poisoned. She was nineteen years old. The family had a history of heart trouble, Deputy Carl Bunch says. Gloria's lover, who lived west of Opelousas, was terrified that she had been murdered because she knew too much. Anne Dischler discovered that Gloria had left a diary locked in her private drawer at Cochran's. When her sister Flo went to collect Gloria's possessions, the diary was gone.

On July 6, 1968, Andrew Dunn, being held in the Clinton jail on a charge of public intoxication, was found hanged in his cell—while lying flat on his bunk.

Into the millennium, Shaw lawyer Salvatore Panzeca would claim that his client had never appeared in East Feliciana Parish with Lee Harvey Oswald. "It never happened," Panzeca insists. Patricia Lambert had introduced the fantasy that Winslow Foster, not Oswald, was the second white man in Clinton, even after she read Anne Dischler's 1967 notebooks, which demonstrated otherwise.

In July of 2000, Dischler formally repudiated Lambert's book. Her statement accuses Lambert of having "twisted my report to fit her own 'Clinton scenario,' leaving out important facts that would have shed a different light on the actual truth of the Clinton, Lousiana story!" Dischler wrote Lambert that she was "appalled at, and ashamed" that her work was mentioned as any part of what Lambert had written.

The evidence that Oswald, Shaw and Ferrie appeared together in Clinton is massive and even includes G. Wray Gill's telephone records. Two calls had gone out from David Ferrie's phone at Gill's office, distinguishable by an "04" on the bills. One was to Clinton, to the phone booth at the corner of Henry Earl Palmer's office, on May 18th, 1963. The other was to Jackson on November 16th.

Other people attempting to deny that Shaw had been seen with Oswald have included Ferrie's friend Alvin Beaubouef, who said the Clinton witnesses had been "bribed." Rosemary James would echo Panzeca: Shaw "just wasn't there," she insists. It was Guy Banister, "who looked so much like Clay, it was unbelievable."

A TALE OF TWO KINGS AND SOME SOLDIERS OF FORTUNE

15

The Warren Report in many respects unfortunately is in the position of Humpty Dumpty. It can never be put back together again.
—Jim Garrison

A N ANONYMOUS LETTER IN MAY 1967 directed Jim Garrison to Omaha, where he might find Thomas Edward Beckham. An "army" of men had been collecting money for a new invasion of Cuba, among them Arcacha, Fred L. Crisman, Martin Grassi and "Lucian" Rabel. The mistaking of "Lucian" or "Lucius" for "Luis" places Beckham himself as the source of the information. A second anonymous letter, from the same source, dated January 9, 1968, informs "Mr. G." that Fred L. Crisman, "a Washington man," had been advising "Mark Evans" (Beckham), an Omaha man, to hide out in Iowa. Beckham had delivered $200,000 of Cuban money. "Is it not odd that Crisman is a friend of Clay's as well as Beckham?" the letter says. "Is it not strange that he knew Tippit?" His source knew David Ferrie and Lee Harvey Oswald personally. The writer was Beckham's sometime manager Bob Lavender, a former Treasury agent.

"Keep digging, Jim," Lavender adds. Thomas Edward Beckham reports that everything in Lavender's letters is true. Crisman flew to New Orleans eleven times in 1964, seventeen in 1965 and twenty-four in 1967. Crisman was indeed the first person Clay Shaw telephoned when he was in trouble. Beckham himself called Crisman right after the assassination. Garrison now renewed his efforts to locate Thomas Edward Beckham.

Jim Garrison would never work unimpeded by intelligence plants in his office. William C. Wood, a former CIA staff agent and instructor, became one of his investigators in April 1967. Garrison thought Wood might supply "general information as to the operations of the agency." He hired him, even after Wood failed a polygraph. Wood's explanation was that he failed because he was upset about James Wilcott's revelations that Oswald had been a CIA employee.

A second polygraph suggested that Wood had been sent to penetrate Garrison's office. Yet Garrison ignored the suspicions of his staff. Eyebrows were raised as Wood disappeared for weeks at a time. All along, Wood, whom Garrison renamed "Bill Boxley," maintained contact with the Agency, passing on "information which had come to his attention." As recently as February 1967 he had applied for re-employment to the CIA. He had contacted the Agency in March as well.

A thin-lipped, hatchet-faced man with hair "the color of thunderstorm clouds," Boxley looked like "a slightly seedy insurance adjuster." His work bore a twisted logic: "Sea-land company" became "Land-Sea." Boxley seized every opportunity to deflect Jim Garrison from examining the role of the CIA in planning the assassination. Over and over, he would place the blame on the FBI or other agencies. In Dallas, Boxley informed Police Chief Jesse Curry that "there were more intelligence agencies than the CIA and FBI on hand in Dealey Plaza that day."

Banister, Boxley insisted to Garrison, revealed "much more closely an FBI affiliation than a CIA affiliation," or one with naval intelligence, which "runs operations totally independent of CIA operations." He analyzed a Banister memo to Guy Johnson about TACA airlines, a CIA proprietary: "It appears that we may have cut across a CIA operation here and great care must be taken not to expose it." For Boxley, this exonerated Banister of CIA connections.

Boxley urged Garrison to see Lee Harvey Oswald as "an FBI penetration into Russia instead of a CIA project." It was the FBI that used Oswald to infiltrate pro-Communist organizations within this country, Boxley claimed, incorrectly, ignoring that the Fair Play for Cuba Committee was a CIA project supervised by David Atlee Phillips. Boxley read Nelson Delgado's Warren Commission testimony about a man in civilian dress coming to the gate of El Toro when Oswald was on guard duty. "Now this tableau is much more indicative of general FBI procedures than CIA," Boxley claimed.

Gerald Patrick Hemming, a would-be CIA counter intelligence operative, claims to be that man at the gate, and his loyalty was to
James Angleton, never to the FBI, whether or not Angleton returned
the favor.

As a primary source, Boxley hooked up with oil man H. L. Hunt's
security chief, Paul Rothermel, a former FBI agent and CIA asset. "I
can tell you positively that Jack Ruby was a paid FBI informant,"
Rothermel told Boxley. Boxley then reassured Rothermel that "Mr.
Garrison knows Mr. Hunt is not involved," and would never "embarrass Mr. Hunt." Denying that he remained a CIA agent, Boxley spoke
at the September 1968 conference of Garrison investigators, declaring that he had "solid evidence" that the "ONI and the FBI were involved in this thing from the minute Oswald returned to Fort Worth"
and "heavily after he arrived in New Orleans." Boxley insisted that
FBI agents Regis Kennedy and Warren de Brueys were "closely cooperating with the Office of Naval Intelligence."

Boxley attempted to ingratiate himself into all subsequent leads,
including one from a Canadian insurance salesman named Richard
Giesbrecht. In February 1964, Giesbrecht had heard a man at the
Winnipeg airport he later identified as David Ferrie talking about Oswald and the assassination. Oswald had been hanging around with
"Isaacs," Giesbrecht heard, a lead Boxley mangled by accusing the
wrong "Charles Isaacs," whose name appeared in Jack Ruby's notebook. Boxley so confused the story that Garrison suspected that the
Giesbrecht scenario had been a "planted lead."

Yet despite the Isaacs fiasco, Garrison assigned Boxley to interview Bob Lavender in Seattle in his continuing effort to track down
Thomas Edward Beckham. At once, Boxley discredited Lavender: "I
got the distinct feeling that Lavender was on stage reiterating a
story which he had been encouraged to tell us," Boxley wrote. He
insisted Lavender's story "bears a distinct Jack Martin flavor," and
recommended that the facts Lavender offered "be taken with a generous portion of salt." The basis of his criticism was that he knew
no one in the CIA who would entrust a large sum of money to people like Beckham, "or permit such funds to be flown around the
country in a suitcase." Yet Lavender had pointed Jim Garrison to
people—Beckham and Crisman—who had direct knowledge of the
planning of the assassination.

At Tulane and Broad, during the period their tenure overlapped,
two CIA plants—those doppelgangers, twin disruptors of Jim Garrison's investigation—William Martin and William Wood ("Boxley")—
squabbled. Their animosity was exacerbated by the fact that Martin

had been placed in charge of Boxley's burgeoning expense account. Boxley bragged he had a sketch of Ruby and Oswald drawn by an informant. When Martin asked to see it, Boxley declined. Boxley attempted to undermine Martin by pointing to Martin's CIA connections. Didn't these render his loyalty dubious? Hadn't he been chief investigator for the Banister group, the Anti-Communist League of the Caribbean, which had sent $100,000 to the Organization of the Secret Army, which had attempted to assassinate Charles de Gaulle?

Ivon disliked both of them. He called Martin a version of cult TV Detective Maxwell Smart, Agent 86. Boxley, Ivon noted, was always less than forthcoming.

Yet another attack on Jim Garrison issued from his perpetual adversary, Raymond Huff, that close cohort of Guy Banister and Aaron Kohn. Huff now collaborated with the FBI to end Jim Garrison's service with the Louisiana National Guard, with the assistance of National Guard Adjutant General Erbon W. Wise. To secure his own promotion, Wise had made a sizable contribution to John McKeithen's campaign. He now saw Garrison, who was so close to Governor McKeithen, as an obstacle. With the help of Wise, Huff found the grounds for an attack: Garrison had not been properly subordinate, appearing in the company of the governor and flying off in his private plane when he was scheduled for duty.

Dissatisfied with Wise's progress in the campaign against Garrison, Huff confided to Kohn that Wise was "very weak and naive." Taking matters into his own hands, Huff saw to it that not only was Jim Garrison not promoted to brigadier general, but he was removed from the National Guard entirely. Garrison was a "dangerous man," Huff told Kohn. He himself loved America and hated "anyone who damages it," he said, making it clear that if in 1965 it had been Garrison's liberal politics that annoyed him, it was Garrison's Kennedy probe that now inspired Huff's attempts to destroy his reputation. Huff wanted to thwart Jim Garrison's mobilization in the Army reserves as well, and contacted the FBI for help. The Bureau consulted the Department of the Army. At the Justice Department two Garrison adversaries, Fred Vinson and J. Walter Yeagley, were contacted.

Huff attempted to discredit Garrison's investigation by accusing him of granting comfort to the Cold War enemy: Garrison's "denouncing statements of federal authority," Huff declared, "are being wisely used in propaganda by the Communist countries and by the anti-American nations around the world." The Army backed away, claiming that Jim Garrison as a civilian did not come within its investigative jurisdiction. Fearing criticism for intervening in Garrison's investigation, the FBI recommended "no further action be taken." "OK," Hoover affixed his double horseshoe signature to a memorandum to Division 5's William Sullivan. Jim Garrison would now be in the Army Reserves, "kicked upstairs," as a disappointed Huff put it.

Neither Walter Sheridan nor Aaron Kohn nor Raymond Huff nor the eponymous Boxley could prevent new witnesses from coming forward. The Reverend Clyde Johnson was a blue-eyed, curly-haired cherubic ex-inmate from the Mississippi State Penitentiary sporting a skull and crossbones on his left forearm. His first incarceration came when he was eighteen. Now an evangelical Christian, Johnson had made a desultory run against John McKeithen in the 1964 gubernatorial campaign. He hailed from Kentwood, Clay Shaw's hometown.

On September 2, 1963, Johnson said, he met with Clay Shaw, Jack Ruby and Lee Harvey Oswald in the Jack Tar Capitol House Hotel in Baton Rouge. Introducing himself as "Alton Bernard," Shaw had contributed five thousand dollars in one hundred dollar bills to Johnson's campaign. He liked the Reverend Johnson's anti-Kennedy speeches, Shaw said.

At the Capitol House, "Bernard" introduced Johnson to "Leon," a young man about five feet nine inches tall, he thought, with a stubble. Jack Ruby joined them, while a "tall, big Mexican-looking fellow," a dead-ringer for Lawrence Howard, stood at the door. "Bernard" doled out money in brown envelopes to Jack, to "Leon," and to Clyde Johnson. Now Johnson had come forward "in the cause of justice," but also because he feared for his life. Corroboration arrived from the man who had run for lieutenant governor with Clyde Johnson, Ed McMillan. On election night of the run-off, he had been in Johnson's room at the Monteleone Hotel when "Alton Bernard," whom he now identified as Shaw, had been present.

There was further corroboration from a Jacksonville, Florida, inmate named Edward Whalen, who stated that Clay Shaw and David Ferrie had tried to recruit him to kill Jim Garrison. Garrison was skeptical, only for Whalen to describe how Ferrie had talked about the same meeting in Baton Rouge between Shaw, Ruby and Oswald. "Oswald was an agent of the CIA," Ferrie had told him. Whalen knew how proud Ferrie was of his aviation skills; Ferrie offered to fly him out of the country, an offer Ferrie frequently made to men. Whalen said Ferrie referred to Shaw as "Clay Bertrand," and if Whalen was mistaken about the configuration of Ferrie's apartment, he was able to identify Ferrie friends who had not been in the news, like Dante Marochini.

Clyde Johnson never wavered from his original statement. "Any time you step on a pig's tail, you can hear it squeal, and there's lots of pigs squealing," he remarked. As for the Warren Report, he added, "As the Bible says, 'No man is as blind as the man that don't want to see.'"

Gurvich stole a copy of Johnson's statement, and soon Clay Shaw's lawyers requested that the CIA and the Justice Department find out where Ruby and Oswald were between September 1st and 5th. Gurvich had to admit that Jim Garrison had not bribed Clyde Johnson; he gave him only ten or twenty dollars for his transportation. Clyde Johnson's information was damaging enough for Edward and William Wegmann and Dymond to fly to Dallas to trace Jack Ruby's early September movements. William Alexander at the Dallas district attorney's office provided details of a Ruby traffic violation. Aynesworth lent his customary assistance. Yet Clyde Johnson's story stood, unimpeached.

On WVUE-TV, FBI media asset Sam Depino stated that Clyde Johnson needed psychiatric help.

Even after Gurvich was gone, files continued to disappear from Garrison's office.

One day Boxley opened a letter from a "Duncan Miller." "The same oil man who bought the Oswald guns," Miller wrote, was "the subject of a collusive use of a post-office box in Dallas." On the very day Oswald received his guns, a Denver oil man and gun collector, John J. King, had been implicated in a fraudulent land scheme for oil leases in Alaska. This same King had sued the government for the release of Oswald's weapons on behalf of Marina, and lost. John J. King told Penn Jones of *The Midlothian Mirror* that he wanted to contribute to Jim Garrison's investigation. Boxley brought him to Tulane and Broad where he sat twirling his Annapolis class ring.

When Jim Garrison attempted to show King assassination photographs and documents, he manifested no interest.

"What would it take to stop you from this thing you're on?" King said. "Suppose you were offered a federal judgeship? Would you continue to be involved?" When Garrison asked what it would take for him to be appointed to the federal bench, King said, "Stop the investigation."

"There's nothing they could offer me," Garrison said. The "propinquity" of King's post office box to Oswald's led Garrison to conclude that King, called "Miller" in *On the Trail of the Assassins,* was a government plant.

By appealing to the audience, satirist Mort Sahl had goaded Johnny Carson into inviting Jim Garrison to be a guest on "The Tonight Show." In his relentless campaign to destroy Jim Garrison's investigation, Bobby Kennedy telephoned Carson and requested that he not put Garrison on, but he was too late. Walter Sheridan and his sidekick, Frank Grimsley, had to fly to Los Angeles to brief Carson.

On the air, Garrison was reasonable and engaging. Carson, however, had metamorphosed from the affable imaginary golfer to a rigid prosecutor as he read from Sheridan-authored index cards. Hadn't Garrison alternately blamed Cubans, Nazis, oil-rich millionaires and "high officials in the United States government?" for the assassination? Carson demanded.

His knowledge had evolved, Garrison explained patiently. "There have been refinements." He offered a conceit: An elephant has a tail, is gray, but also has four legs. Descriptions would change based on one's perspective. On his main point, he had never wavered: "We have found that the Central Intelligence Agency, without any question, had individuals who were connected with it involved." Did Garrison have "absolute facts and proof of that?" Carson sputtered.

"I wouldn't say so otherwise," Garrison said.

"It's not going too well," Garrison remarked to Carson during one of the breaks. "Would you like me to do a tap dance?" This was not an idle suggestion. Phyllis had taught him the soft shoe, which he performed ably with a cane.

"Not on my fucking show you won't," Carson said.

When Carson provided a list of Warren Report supporters from Dean Rusk and Robert S. McNamara to J. Edgar Hoover and Robert F. Kennedy, Garrison said, "What difference does it make, Johnny, how many honorable men are involved when the critical evidence is continually being concealed from the American people?"

Garrison challenged NBC to show the Zapruder film. Then concealed from the American public, this 8mm movie reveals how Kennedy's skull was shattered by a shot from a gunman positioned at the front of the motorcade. Garrison told the audience that the

Warren Commission files had been locked away until the year 2039, so that his eight-year-old son Jasper would be seventy years old before he could read "the CIA file on Lee Harvey Oswald."

Afterward, Garrison and Carson exchanged harsh words, and Carson stalked out. So many people wrote to NBC complaining of Carson's rudeness to Jim Garrison on the air that the station disseminated a form letter: "I can assure you that Mr. Garrison was not in the least discomfited by Mr. Carson's questions, and he left the studio in an atmosphere of cordiality." Garrison's version was different. "I didn't like Carson and he didn't like me so there was virtually no colloquy," he said. Later Garrison added, "Carson is no Noel Coward as far as conversation is concerned."

Investigation funds dwindled. In Miami, Garrison met a financier and horse-racing aficionado named Louis Wolfson, whose horse, Affirmed, would win the Triple Crown in 1978. Wolfson shared his interest in the ponies with a local broadcaster named Larry King, to whom Wolfson periodically lent money, none of which was ever repaid. Eventually Wolfson swore out complaints against King. States Attorney Richard Gerstein liked both the ponies and King and refused to accept charges on King's bad checks or Wolfson's complaints.

In March 1968, Jim Garrison appeared on Larry King's Miami television program where he blamed a "reactionary clique" at the CIA for the assassination. The network vice-president at once reported to Richard Helms that Garrison had attacked "the integrity of the Central Intelligence Agency."

Gerstein suggested to Larry King that he enlist Wolfson to make a contribution to Jim Garrison's investigation. At the top floor of the Miami Beach Doral Hotel, Garrison met with Wolfson, King, Gerstein and Wolfson's right-hand man, Arvin Rothschild. He talked. Wolfson grew dejected as he heard Garrison blame the CIA for the assassination.

"I hope you fall flat on your face," Wolfson told Garrison. Wolfson hoped that Garrison was wrong, that an agency of the government had not murdered the president; but he believed as well that the American people had the right to know the truth.

When Wolfson asked how much was needed to complete his investigation, Garrison said $25,000. This sum Wolfson at once pledged, in $5,000 installments, to be conveyed by Gerstein. Wolfson decided to send Garrison the money through an intermediary because of his troubles over a Nixon-concocted securities violation.

He did not want at that moment publicly to expose his support for Jim Garrison.

He was going to New Orleans, Larry King piped up. He would be happy to deliver the money.

Larry King never delivered any money to Tulane and Broad. Challenged, he insisted he had given all the money to Gerstein. When the second installment was sent to King, he claimed he gave Gerstein that money, too. Soon Wolfson discovered that Garrison had received only a portion of his contribution. Before it was over, King and Gerstein had stolen about half of the money.

Wolfson swore out a complaint against Larry King. "Larry King was the lowest person I've ever run into," Wolfson says. This time King was arrested, charged with grand larceny and booked on December 17, 1971. Gerstein recused himself. The special prosecutor would be Alfonso Sepe, who had already investigated an assassination incident at the "Parrott Jungle," where a Cuban spoke of his sharp-shooter friend "Lee," who could speak Russian. Sepe, who himself would later serve jail time, ruled that King should go free since the statute of limitations had run out.

Later Gerstein claimed that the missing money had been residing all along in his office safe. He had been so "forgetful" that he had never gotten around to giving Garrison the money. At a press conference Gerstein made a show of producing notes he had made of the original serial numbers on the Wolfson money. Then he opened the safe and declared that the money inside bore the same serial numbers.

Martin F. Dardis, Gerstein's own chief investigator, who himself had arrested King twice, once for bad checks, laughed. Dardis noticed that the bills Gerstein was holding up were printed after the incident occurred and could not possibly have been Wolfson's money earmarked for Jim Garrison. Having Larry King deliver money to Garrison, Dardis says, was like "having the fox guard the hen house." No money had been put in any safe. Wolfson never spoke to Gerstein again; King never apologized to Wolfson.

Gerstein now had to be certain that Garrison would not reveal the truth to ace *Miami Herald* reporter James Savage. When Savage called Tulane and Broad, Garrison, ever loyal, telephoned Gerstein. Talk only to Gene Miller, Gerstein said, referring to a friendlier reporter.

When Miller called, Garrison lied to protect Gerstein. He had "accidentally misled Wolfson in February 1970 by failing to report that Gerstein had been trying to give him $5,000 he was holding," Garrison said. It was an "oversight," due to his own "absentmindedness." He had promised to go to Miami, and then never went. Gerstein had even called and said, "I have another $5,000," only for Garrison to be hospitalized with a slipped disk. Garrison's creative chronology reveals how conscientiously he sought to protect Gerstein: he was at Hotel Dieu Hospital in December 1969; Wolfson dispensed the money in 1968.

In his memoir, *Larry King by Larry King,* King refers to the incident, claiming the amount of money he stole was $5,000, which in fact was not the actual amount, but the figure decided on by the court for prosecution purposes. "Garrison was something of an eccentric who would disappear for weeks at a time and not let anyone know where he was, so Dick hung on to the money," King writes.

Indifferent to money, Garrison never noticed that only $9,500 of Wolfson's $25,000 ever reached him.

"There's been a delay in sending the rest of the money," Garrison was told one day in 1970 when the jig was up for Gerstein and King.

"What money?" Jim Garrison said.

A steady steam of people bent on sidetracking Garrison's investigation beat an unholy path to Tulane and Broad. An intellectual, more interested in ideas than practicalities, Garrison was a gullible man. "I regret to say, I trust everyone and am easily fooled," he would acknowledge. That soldier of fortune who had scorned John F. Kennedy's offer that he take over the CIA's Radio Swan, arrived unannounced on July 7, 1967. Gerald Patrick Hemming wore green camouflage fatigues and jungle boots with treads, as if he had just interrupted guerrilla maneuvers.

From serving as a CIA courier, like Beckham, like Donald P. Norton, Hemming in Cuba had participated in those assassination squads of Batista functionaries. CIA media asset William Stuckey had written in the New Orleans *States-Item* that Hemming could handle "two heavy machine guns from the hip at the same time." The CIA liked that Hemming "appears to be little influenced by deep beliefs in democratic principles."

On orders from Robert Kennedy to pursue the untimely death of Fidel Castro exclusive of the efforts of the CIA's clandestine services, General Edward Lansdale had solicited the help of Gerald Patrick Hemming. Lansdale had requested of the CIA its Hemming file, only to be told CIA had "a dosier [sic] about an inch thick." CIA had offered its sanction: "As far as they are concerned he is OK," a Colonel

Patchell writes Lansdale in a handwritten memo. "They consider him helpful to their cause." Hemming believed that it was "one or more of Bobby's boys gone bad" who had killed his brother, as Bobby shared operatives with CIA executioner William Harvey, tool of the DDP, Richard Helms. If Jim Garrison was perplexed by Bobby's efforts to "torpedo" his investigation, Hemming understood them well.

Hemming had heard Garrison had been looking at "his men." "We're going to be indicted by Jim Garrison for the JFK thing," Hemming told his cohort, Roy Hargraves. Hargraves would later admit he was in Dallas on November 22nd, armed with fake Secret Service credentials. His later FBI COINTELPRO service would include the planting of bombs against the Black Panthers. Lawrence Howard, "fat Larry," another Hemming No Name Key associate, had also been in Dallas on that day. Hemming had good reason to fear that Garrison might consider as suspects the men training with him for sabotage against Cuba. An anonymous letter mailed from Miami stated that the "person that shot at President Kennedy was Hector Aguero (Indio Mikoyan), who was prepared in Miami by two Americans to kill Fidel Castro, those Americans are named Chery and Davis."

Examining that note, William Martin had told Garrison that "Chery" was the way a Latin-American would pronounce "Jerry". "Davis" must be the Howard Davis who flew with Hemming over Covington in search of training camp sites. El Indio ("Mikoyan") would be exposed by Gaeton Fonzi as David Sanchez Morales, a CIA officer involved in the overthrow of President Arbenz in Guatemala.

"Investigate in Miami," the writer advises Garrison.

On June 28th, one Wiley Yates had written to Garrison suggesting that Loran Hall, another Hemming cohort, should be a suspect. Yates' source was a Dallas businessman named Wally Welch, who had been together with Hemming and Hall in Cuba. Concluding that Hemming had been involved in "assassination training," Garrison had been showing witnesses those photographs of Hall, Howard and William Seymour, whom he had nicknamed "Winkin', Blinkin' and Nod."

Accompanying Hemming now was Roy Hargraves. Hemming made him wait downstairs. The CIA, aware of the presence of Hemming at Tulane and Broad, watched.

He was writing an article for *Life* magazine, Hemming told Garrison. (Richard Billings smiles and denies that this was so.) "You're heading back to No Name Key and you're leading back to me," Hemming said. "Either I'm stupid or someone is trying to frame my ass, and you're taking the bait." Hemming's alibi is that he was in Miami on November 22nd, at the office of the *Miami News*. There, he ran into CIA media asset Hal Hendrix, who was about to write a story linking him to Oswald until Angleton's people stopped him, Hemming claims.

Hemming fears that he is being recorded. He fears that his foreknowledge of the Kennedy assassination is tantamount to treason. He worries that Garrison's attention will cause him to lose a possible appointment to the CIA's Agency for International Development (AID) in Vietnam. His strategy, like Boxley's, is to divert Garrison's attention away from the CIA.

"There were numerous teams of adventurers with paramilitary inclinations trying to get Kennedy," Hemming says. There were two hundred conspiracies. "Maybe Oswald got there ahead of them." He is gifted at double-talk, as he extrapolates about teams blackmailing their sponsors, pretending to have killed Kennedy and demanding money for their silence. Then the sponsors hired the Mafia to silence them. Later Hemming will claim that Guy Banister was one of these sponsors, offering Hemming a suitcase full of cash to shoot Kennedy. Howard K. Davis, present on that occasion, suggests that Hemming could not have resisted telling him about such an offer had it been made.

"Just to have this queer pilot isn't enough," Hemming says, as if the dead David Ferrie and not Clay Shaw was now Garrison's chief suspect. "You need to begin all over again." Hemming floats a laundry list of suspects: Dennis Harber; a Minuteman from California named "Colonel Gale"; a Jim Keith; an Edward Claude, a former intelligence officer for the Dade County sheriff; G. Clinton Wheat, an ex-Klansman; oil man H. L. Hunt.

He is willing to give up Loran Hall, who, Hemming confides, was in Dallas and could "very well have assassinated the president." Hall was fooling around with Communists, Hemming suggests, an unlikely scenario that Garrison saw through at once. Hall had gotten Sylvia Odio's name from a Ford motor salesman named Nico Crespi. Howard and Seymour, however, Hemming claims, had nothing to do with the assassination. Hemming does not tell Garrison, as he later will tell others, that it was "his people" who were with Oswald when he visited Sylvia Odio and who were "working Oswald on the assassination of Castro operation."

"I don't know who you work for," Lou Ivon tells Hemming. Ivon is not easy to fool, the reason why of all the people Hemming meets this day, it is Ivon he respects. "There were more snitches in there than cops," Hemming would remember.

"If you knew to a T, it wouldn't do any good," Hemming tells Garrison harshly. "You can't cause me any trouble." Only when Garrison appears not to know the name "Angleton" does Hemming breathe a secret sigh of relief. He offers to "join forces" with Garrison, and asks to read Garrison's files, so that for a month Hemming believes he is actually working for Jim Garrison. He telephones Tom Bethell that he has been unable to find "Nico Crespi," and is irritated that Garrison has not sent him the twenty-six Warren Commission volumes. His phone bill is high, Hemming complains, attempting to pull a Bernardo de Torres. No one at Tulane and Broad falls for it.

Upon departing from New Orleans, Hemming telephoned Angleton's office. "Do you think Garrison has heard of U.S. Customs?" Angleton asked, well knowing the role of Customs in Oswald's activities. "Would he go after them?" Hemming says that Garrison had not placed Customs in the case. Yet, Hemming knew, "that's where all the family jewels were." Other information Hemming withheld from Jim Garrison was how Angleton, hating Kennedy, termed him a "KGB mole running the country," and how Allen Dulles, no longer DCI, had ordered the FBI to have Hall recant on the Sylvia Odio story, and say he was not, after all, at Sylvia Odio's.

Hemming knew that Bernardo de Torres was working for the CIA during the Garrison investigation. He knew that not only Clay Shaw, but also Oswald had "Q" clearance from the CIA. He calls Lawrence Howard "one of the best shots in the world," and places him at Dealey Plaza as a shooter. At times he lies, as when he told a Garrison volunteer that he knew Thomas Edward Beckham, who was "five foot eleven inches tall," off by four inches. He lies convincingly, with so much passion, that it seems inconceivable that he doesn't believe what he is saying. Digression is his tactic, doubt a stranger.

"There is reason to believe he is still working for the CIA," Garrison remarked when Hemming was gone. He drew this conclusion without knowing that only four months earlier, Hemming had turned up at CIA officer Justin P. Gleichauf's house to report on Rolando Masferrer's projected Haitian invasion. CIA concluded that Hemming was targeting his own assets. Hemming "was an informer for the CIA," while claiming to be with Naval Intelligence. When Hemming had applied for regular employment with the Agency in January 1962, he had been turned down, even as Lawrence Houston pondered more than forty reports to his CIA handler filed by Hemming in the fall of 1960 upon his return from Cuba.

Hemming did not get the job with AID. His visit to Jim Garrison's office led to CIA's checking again on Hemming and his Interpen

(Intercontinental Penetration Forces), Hemming's group of soldiers of fortune training at No Name Key in Florida for sabotage against Cuba. CIA was troubled that Hemming's visit might lead Garrison to focus on Robert K. Brown and on the JMWAVE station's activities. The Agency had to admit to the FBI that Hemming was a source. Soon the ONI was inquiring of Hoover what information he had on Hemming. Then the Defense Investigative Program Office asked Naval Intelligence for its Hemming files.

Five days after Hemming's visit, Lawrence Laborde's son, Michael, appeared at Tulane and Broad. His goal was to divert Jim Garrison's attention from his father and to implicate Hemming and Hargraves. Hargraves had called David Ferrie shortly before the assassination, Michael claimed. Then he told the Bureau: "You have to stop Garrison before he harms the country."

At the end of July another CIA asset, Frank Bartes, that cousin of Dr. Frank Silva, whose name appears in Oswald's notebook as "Bardes," arrived with a message from Hemming. He wants to be a friend to this office; he wants "to do whatever he can to help you," Bartes says.

A decade later, Hemming admitted to HSCA investigator Gaeton Fonzi that he had lied to Jim Garrison. "I created smoke myself," he confessed. He had passed on to Garrison useless "smoked" names through "cut-outs." Garrison's West Coast volunteers had begun to focus on the specious Hemming names, California-based right-wingers who had nothing to do with the assassination. Garrison perceived, correctly, that Hemming's "mission was to add to the confusion."

That CIA contract pilot, Jim Rose, who had flown with David Ferrie, had begun to work for Garrison, even as he continued his missions for the clandestine services. Did he think the Agency was so big it could be out of control? Garrison asked Rose. The first time Rose walked into Tulane and Broad, Ivon frisked him, only to ignore a ballpoint pen.

"It's napalm," Rose said. "If I shot you, your face would go up in flames." Garrison dubbed him "Winston Smith," then "Winnie the Pooh," then "Rosalie." Rose worked on Shaw's telephone records and found the number of Sergio Arcacha Smith's lawyer. He identified one more CIA courier, William Cuthbert Brady. He knew Loran Hall and Lawrence Howard personally as "proficient riflemen and top-level guerrilla fighters."

In 1966, Rose had joined former Batista executioner Rolando

Masferrer's invasion of Haiti to depose the dictator Duvalier. In his attempt to escape, he shot a man square in the face. McNabb, "Rose," was a stone-cold killer. He knew that among those working for Masferrer was William Seymour of No Name Key notoriety. Terming Masferrer "the most dangerous man in the United States," Rose suggested that if any anti-Castro leader were involved in the assassination, "his first choice" would be one of the Masferrer brothers.

Rose proposed a Miami-based scheme to Jim Garrison. To locate those Cubans photographed with Oswald outside the International Trade Mart, he would pretend to recruit mercenaries for a CIA project in Biafra. A concealed Garrison investigator would photograph the applicants. Should Rose be exposed, Richard Gerstein would have him arrested and "put on the next flight to New Orleans."

In this effort, Rose contacted several CIA-linked reporters, among them, Donald Bohning, CIA's AMCARBON-3. "AM" stood for Cuba; "Carbon" was that CIA cryptonym for its writer assets. Bohning, who became the Latin American editor for *Miami Herald,* an Al Burt doppelganger, lunched weekly with CIA's Jake Esterline, one of the reluctant engineers of the Bay of Pigs operation. Bohning had received his Provisional Covert Security Approval as a CIA confidential informant on August 21, 1967, then Covert Security Approval itself on November 14th. On July 31st, the DDP himself approved the use of Bohning in the CIA's Cuban operations.

Bohning informed Esterline of Rose's visit on March 28, 1968. A "Winston Smith," working for Jim Garrison, was looking into the activities of Rolando Masferrer in 1963, before the assassination. Rose was attempting to identify certain Cubans who had appeared in photographs. He was leaving for Biafra to fight as a mercenary next month.

Bohning declined to help Jim Rose. Later he found other journalists of his acquaintance had also been contacted, but with Rose using the name "Carl McNab"[sic]. "I use many different names for different purposes," Rose explained to Bohning when next they met. "I used to have still a different war name with the Company." That was "Carl Davis."

During that sojourn in Miami, while JMWAVE watched his every move, Rose met with Lawrence Howard. He didn't believe Masferrer was involved in the assassination, Howard said smoothly. "He's too smart for that." But others "in the ring around him could well have been." Masferrer had been sentenced to twenty-four years in prison for the abortive Haitian escapade, but Rose managed to meet with him. He could help Masferrer leave the country, Rose promised.

Lawrence Houston watched, concerned that Garrison might indeed locate the "seven" Cubans for whom he was searching among the Masferrer group.

The scheme progressed. Masferrer told Rose he had ten aides ready to go to Biafra. Rose proposed an Austin, Texas, mail drop. But he was nervous: It was a violation of federal law to recruit personnel for foreign service. He asked Masferrer to submit photographs of the volunteers. When Masferrer hesitated, the Garrison volunteer who was to take the photographs, Gary Sanders, urged Rose to ask other groups for pilots and troop instructors to give Masferrer some competition.

"My next assignment is to fly arms into a little revolution in Biafra," Rose lied to his old friend Martin Xavier Casey, a veteran of the Haitian expedition. Casey, too, believed that the "CIA was probably involved" in the assassination. All the while, Rose feared that Masferrer might talk to Lawrence Howard and learn Rose's real identity.

Interviews with the CIA-sponsored Cubans willing to sign on for Biafra were set up at the Howard Johnson's in Coral Gables where Rose was registered as "Winston Smith" of Los Angeles. Sanders would take the photographs and ship them to Garrison at a mail drop on Chef Menteur Highway. A "short, skinny guy" named Ralph Schlafter ("Skinny Ralph") arrived. Skinny Ralph was the #2 man of the tramps arrested at Dealey Plaza, CIA photographer Tom Dunkin told Rose. He was also one of Hemming's men at No Name Key. Some thought they had spotted him in November 22nd footage.

Rose and Sanders remained in Miami for six days, March 28th to April 2nd, 1968, interviewing Cubans. According to Rose, Masferrer himself identified the Cuban with the scar who had been Ferrie's and Oswald's companion as one of his own lieutenants. This heavyset man, with a "bull neck," was now in New York. Rose was ready to fly to New York in pursuit, but nothing came of it, or of Rose's escapade involving the imaginary expedition to Biafra.

After Rose left Miami, still in search of the "heavy-set thick-necked Latin with a scar over one eyebrow and pock-marks on his face," Garrison wrote to Gerstein, requesting any records of the "Masferrer group," especially of his "lieutenants." This is "extremely important," Garrison wrote, requesting that Gerstein "assign this to someone who follows through."

WITNESSES AND ROUSTABOUTS 16

Apparently I am not very highly regarded by the Mafia if they won't even pick up my phone bill.
—Jim Garrison

W ITH WALTER SHERIDAN TEMPORARILY at bay, J. Edgar Hoover devised a new scheme to discredit Jim Garrison. His instrument would be a reporter named Sandy Smith, writing for *Life* magazine. "The Director likes to do things for Sandy," Richard Billings was told when he heard about *Life's* projected series on organized crime. Despite its seeming national scope—the Mafia rampant in America—the raison d'être of the two *Life* articles, running on September 1 and 8, 1967, was to impute Mafia connections to Jim Garrison.

Garrison readily agreed to an interview with Sandy Smith, who arrived in the company of Billings. Smith bided his time as Garrison outlined the achievements of his office. Then Smith came to the point: "Let's talk about Marcello for a moment." Garrison admitted that the Sands had picked up his tab during his March 1967 Las Vegas vacation, while he had paid his personal expenses and phone bill. "If I was a friend of the mob, as you seem to insinuate, and I knew the mob controlled the hotel," Garrison told Smith, "I would have told them to take the bill and shove it."

When Billings tossed off the name "Frank Timphony" as one of "the top racketeers down here," Garrison said he had "never heard of him." Garrison writes in his unpublished manuscript, *Coup d'État:* "I shook my head and answered that I had never heard of him. The editor shrugged, as if to say, 'See what I mean?' He held out his hands. 'There you are,' he said. 'You should have had a dossier on him by now.'"

In the presence of Smith and Billings, Garrison telephoned Pershing. In *Life's* description of that call, Pershing Gervais replied that Timphony was "one of the biggest bookies in New Orleans." Garrison's version was that Gervais had registered no positive response, no recognition of the name.

The local research for the articles was done by David Chandler, with the assistance of Aaron Kohn. Chandler rushed to inform the FBI of the details of Billings' and Smith's interview with Garrison. Despite Chandler's supposed skills as an investigative reporter, the articles do not mention Felix Bonoura, the "chicken man" of Magnolia Broilers. Yet Bonoura was the crime boss who paid Victor Schiro $10,000 in a "campaign contribution" so that he would appoint Joseph I. Giarrusso as superintendent of police, all Bonoura needed to continue unimpeded. Bonoura and Giarrusso were partners in a security company, as the line between police and organized crime blurred. None of this had any connection to Jim Garrison.

Carlos Marcello funded political adversaries, as would later become common practice with American corporations. When John R. Rarick ran against John McKeithen in 1968, a Marcello emissary met with Rarick's campaign manager, $100,000 in hand. "Big John's already got his," Marcello's man said. Rarick turned him down. None of this had anything to do with Jim Garrison, either.

Chandler wrote only that Garrison was "very friendly" with Sammy Marcello and Joseph Marcello, and that Garrison's Las Vegas expenses were paid for by a Mario Marino, once a Marcello floor boss at the Flamingo Club. The $5,000 credit that was extended to Jim Garrison was investigated by James Phelan, who had to tell Chandler, as he had informed Walter Sheridan, that "no such credit had been established for Carlos Marcello." Billings admits there was never any proof Garrison either used the credit or came away with any of the $5,000.

Garrison was "friendly with some Marcello henchmen," the September 8 *Life* article says vaguely. There were "frequent meetings" with Marcello, although *Life* does not even claim Garrison was present at any of them. Timphony is said to have done business in New Orleans in a betting establishment. That was all they needed "for me to become *Life's* version of 'The Man Who Broke the Bank at Monte Carlo,'" Garrison said later.

Sandy Smith had described telephone calls from Carlos Marcello to McKeithen aide Aubrey Young, who had indeed worked as a bartender at a Marcello-owned establishment. Suspicious of how Smith could have obtained those records, Billings requested that he reveal his source. Smith refused. Billings then dialed FBI head-quarters in Washington and asked to speak to Sandy Smith.

"He's not in today," the woman said. Like Sheridan, mas-querading as a journalist, Smith was a full-fledged employee of the FBI whose assignment was to discredit Jim Garrison by charging him with mob complicity. Smith was particularly close to Deke, who called Smith "a good friend of the Chicago office."

WDSU television reported that "an associate of Cosa Nostra kingpin Carlos Marcello signed the tab for Jim Garrison," some-thing the *Life* articles never dared claim. Jim Garrison attempted to defend himself: "I've never used a dollar of gambling credit any-where in the world in my life because I don't gamble," he said, of-fering to resign.

McKeithen was asked why he thought *Life* had focused its sto-ries on Louisiana. "I still think it has something to do with Sheri-dan being indicted down here," he said. Bob Hamm, on KATC-TV in Lafayette, quoting an FBI report titled "Garrison and the Mafia," stated that Garrison had placed organized crime along with anti-Castroites as participating in the assassination. Hamm referred to "FNU (first name unknown) Santanna [sic]" as having been in Dealey Plaza.

At a meeting with *Life* editors in New York, McKeithen blinked and admitted there was evidence of organized crime in Louisiana. When he appointed Chandler to be a "Special Investigator," Garri-son was furious. "He's got a wonderful face," he said of McKeithen. "He's got the face of a wagon train leader traversing the continent, but when he got back to New Orleans, this BLOB stepped off the plane." Garrison demanded that Chandler present what evidence he had before a grand jury.

Chandler, like Sheridan, evaded the grand jury by seeking relief in the federal courts. He told the LSU student newspaper that Garri-son was "helping the Mafia," and alluded to bribery, so that even Tom Bethell had to demur: "No one said anything about bribery, only gambling." Chandler then threatened McKeithen that unless he stopped supporting Garrison, they would do to him what they had done to Garrison. "I can't support you openly now," McKeithen told Garrison.

"We had Huey Long and we called him 'the Kingfish.' We're going to call you 'the Crawfish,'" Garrison replied. Garrison was so angry that when McKeithen came to testify before the Orleans Parish grand jury, Garrison let him wait for an hour in the hall. "Aren't you going to ask him to come inside?" Sharon Herkes asked.

"Let him sit out there like everyone else," Garrison said.

Pershing testified before the grand jury. "If there were any [organized crime] here, I think I would know about it," Pershing said. Gordon Novel joined this latest campaign to discredit Jim Garrison by informing to the FBI of an old May 1963 charge: that Marcello had supposedly offered Pershing $3,000 a week so that Garrison would not appeal a slot machine case Marcello had already lost. In June 1962, as Garrison was taking office, the Louisiana Supreme Court ruled that electronic devices constituted slot machines; Jim Garrison had no say in the matter either way. The whole "bribe" story had been another "Gervais," a public relations ploy. Pershing admitted he had lied. "I said it was good public relations to always tell the truth," an irritated Garrison told him.

On the day before Christmas 1967, Garrison wrote a memo for his archives, "Organized Crime Aspects of the Assassination." There had been indications of organized crime in Ruby's involvement, he wrote, but "they had never quite flowered into any kind of evidence." (Later he would call Ruby "a member of the Mafia branch of the Agency.") Given that the mob had "a special interest in Cuba," there was "some involvement of individuals who seem to have organized crime connections."

He had considered that Ferrie worked for Marcello's lawyer. But it was "beyond the bounds of reason" to suppose that the mob could "accomplish the long-range preliminary nurturing of a scapegoat, thereafter break through the defense net protecting the president, and then follow this up by having the government help cover it up for you." It did not make sense that the FBI would help conceal "assassination participation by representatives of the Genovese, Gambino, Bonanno, Columbo and Luchese families." His own involvements, he was to say, were "the same connections with organized crime as Mother Theresa and Pope Paul."

In April 1968, Garrison considered suing *Life*, which stood ready with G. Robert Blakey—like Novel, ubiquitous in his efforts to undermine Jim Garrison—on its legal team. He contacted Donald V. Organ, who had represented him against the judges, producing his Las Vegas records. "Apparently I am not very highly regarded by the Mafia if they won't even pick up my phone bill," Garrison wrote Organ. He supported *Life's* First Amendment rights, but these stories represented "a form of reality for millions of people." Did he have a case for malice, a "specific exception" to *New York Times v. Sullivan?* Garrison wanted to know. Organ discouraged him. He would be a public figure suing a news establishment with no way really to prove malice, Organ thought.

"I made it up," Chandler revealed later of his charge that Garrison was connected to organized crime. "It was like throwing a pebble into a pool. . . ."

Discouraged by his experience with *Life,* Garrison met with editors of *Look* magazine, whose managing editor, William Attwood, had been Kennedy's emissary with Castro. Garrison outlined his investigation through lunch, dinner and into the night. According to Associate Editor Chandler Broussard, Attwood was so impressed that he telephoned Bobby Kennedy at one in the morning. Bobby's reply was, reportedly, "We know a good deal of this." Press Secretary Pierre Salinger, according to Richard Billings, attributes to Bobby a similar statement: "We know who the bastards are and we're going to get them." Simultaneous contradictory policies were, of course, the modus operandi of the Kennedys. The fact remains that Bobby Kennedy did everything he could to stop Jim Garrison as he waited for the presidency that would never come.

At four that morning, Attwood suffered a heart attack. Broussard was soon fired. No positive story was forthcoming in *Look.*

Yet another witness made his way to Tulane and Broad. Dago Garner's file jacket reads "Jack Armstrong," reflecting Jim Garrison's sardonic irony. Darrell Wayne Garner was a pimp and an alcoholic, a car thief and gun runner, with thirty arrests to his credit between 1957 and 1964. In Dallas, Garner was a Ruby hanger-on. He decided to come forward when his girlfriend, Ruby dancer Nancy Mooney, in jail for disturbing the peace, died by hanging herself with her toreador pants.

Fearing for his life and seeing accidents befall people he knew, including members of his own car-jacking gang, Garner went to his lawyer, who sent him to Hugh Aynesworth. In New Orleans, Aynesworth attempted to prevent Garner from talking to Jim Garrison. "You better get out of New Orleans because Jim Garrison will hang you by your balls," he said. Ignoring Aynesworth, Garner found a lawyer named Jim McPherson. Irvin Dymond's office was right down the hall. McPherson sent Garner to Jim Garrison instead.

On July 18, 1967, Garner told Garrison he had known Officer Tippit, as a part-time gun runner. He knew Warren Reynolds, a witness to the Tippit murder, who was killed two days after talking to the FBI. Shown a photograph of Clay Shaw, Garner was cautious. He had seen a man resembling Shaw with Jack Ruby. Shown a photograph of Emilio Santana, he had no doubt that this was the man who shot Warren Reynolds. "This guy was with Jack Ruby a lot," Garner said. He had heard Reynolds say the name "Shaw" many times. Garner also identified Santana's friend Miguel Torres. He knew, too, that instead of driving toward the assassination scene when John F. Kennedy was shot, Tippit had driven away from it. Hugh Aynesworth had told him, Garner added, that he was representing Clay Shaw.

A witness Jim Garrison never was able to question was Ruby's factotum, the twenty-two-year-old drifter Curtis (Larry) Crafard. Ruby had introduced Crafard to his friends as "Oswald," so that Crafard took a good hard look when one day Oswald walked into the Carousel Club. Garrison wondered whether Crafard had shot Tippit, whom Crafard now admits to knowing. Crafard says he saw Rose Cheramie dance at the Carousel. He admits to knowing Lawrence V. Meyers, who met with Ruby the night before the assassination. This was the same Meyers who contributed to the Dallas State Fair where Crafard worked with a check made out to Jack Ruby.

"I think he's a professional killer," Jim Garrison concluded, even as, years later, Crafard would tell researcher Peter Whitmey that he had been a "hit man" in the 1960s. "We get good leads," Garrison said, lamenting that he lacked the resources to trace Crafard's associations, and to determine whether they led to the Mob or to the Agency. He pondered Crafard's "special Army discharge." Crafard's not having surfaced in New Orleans led Garrison to postpone that lead. But he remained intrigued about the man who set up "light housekeeping at the Carousel Lounge —nobody has ever lived there before or since—and he's gone the day after the assassination." Crafard's brother Edward says that Curtis was "heavily involved in the assassination." Curtis "was involved in helping Ruby that weekend," and knew that Ruby was acquainted with Oswald before the assassination. Curtis, his brother adds, did not leave Dallas until after Jack Ruby shot Lee Harvey Oswald, in contrast to Crafard's Warren Commission testimony that he had departed on November 23rd.

Hugh Aynesworth reported to the Shaw defense that Dago Garner had seen Ruby, Tippit, Oswald and a white-haired man at the Carousel Club. They speculated that Jim Garrison must be giving Garner money. But, as in the case of the Reverend Clyde Johnson, it was not true. "Money don't mean that much to me," Garner says on tape, speaking to Lou Ivon. "I don't care if I don't get a penny. I can go to work."

"We don't want you to lie to us," Ivon says.

Garner was more forthcoming on November 12, 1967. He had known Jack Ruby since the fifties, he now told Jim Garrison. At the Carousel Club, in Ruby's presence, Clay Shaw had talked about "bounty hunting," killing President Kennedy, the same term John Wilson had heard David Ferrie use. Garner had seen Oswald at the Carousel several times. Clay Shaw had paid Garner's bus fare to New Orleans. They were to meet at Wanda's Bar, owned by Eugene Davis, the man who advised young men in trouble to visit Dean Andrews and say "Bertrand" sent them.

Garner had engaged in a skirmish at the Carousel Club with Lawrence Howard and identified his photograph easily. In a December interview with Mark Lane, Garner further demonstrated his bona fides not only in identifying Emilio Santana as a Ruby associate, but also in his knowledge that Jack Ruby had owned the Silver Slipper in Eunice. Like Rose Cheramie, Garner knew that Ruby's nickname was "Pinky." He knew Oswald did not know how to drive an automobile. He knew Shaw's sexual practices, adding, he "liked to be whipped with ping pong paddles."

Other Garrison witnesses, Richard and June Rolfe, public relations people who had worked for Sergio Arcacha Smith, testified to Garner's credibility. Rolfe had seen Jack Ruby put his arm around Garner and the two walk out of the office together. Garner was a "totally honest person," Rolfe thought.

In New York, Jimmy Alcock interviewed a New Orleans native and certified public accountant named Charles I. Spiesel, who had met David Ferrie at Lafitte's Blacksmith Shop. Ferrie had invited him to a party where Clay Shaw appeared, and a man Spiesel identified from the composite of Oswald "with the beard drawn on it." As at the gathering at Ferrie's apartment described by Perry Russo, the group discussed "means and methods to be used in killing the president." They had agreed that "a high powered rifle with a telescopic sight" would do the job. Shaw had asked Ferrie whether the man doing the shooting could be flown to safety, a subject that had also come up at the gathering Russo had attended. When Spiesel asked for help in getting accountancy work, Ferrie told him to call Clay Shaw.

Alcock knew that Spiesel was far from an ideal witness. He had a habit of subpoenaing public officials to court (once he had subpoenaed Aaron Kohn). He believed every human being has a "double," so that he took photographs of members of his family, including his mother. When he saw them later, he would check the person against the photograph. He even fingerprinted his daughter every six months to be sure he was not talking to her double.

Skeptical, Alcock wondered if this was "a very obvious nut." CBS reporter Bob Richter had telephoned Tulane and Broad to say he had heard Spiesel's story and was dubious about the man. Yet Spiesel had revealed so much that was concrete and verifiable that his testimony could not be dismissed.

Garrison had more confidence in a Dealey Plaza witness named Julia Ann Mercer, who appeared in New Orleans with her husband Kern Stinson, an Illinois state legislator. Handing Garrison a copy of her original affidavit to the Dallas sheriff on November 22nd, Mercer said, "They have me saying just the opposite of what I really told them."

Mercer had witnessed a green Ford pickup truck parked on Elm Street at 10:50 A.M., just beyond the triple underpass in front of the Stemmons Freeway. She identified the driver as Jack Ruby. A man had gotten out of the truck and carried a package wrapped in brown paper up the grassy knoll. Her statement to the sheriff's office bore a notary stamp, although no notary had been present. That there was certainly such a truck is born out by Dallas police records: a dispatcher reported that a wrecker was needed to tow one away.

Interviewed again the next day, November 23rd, Mercer had identified a picture of the man she was certain had driven the truck. Idly turning it over, she had read a name written on the back: "Jack Ruby." By Monday, the sheriff's office had inserted the words "Air Conditioning" onto the side of the truck, even as Mercer insisted that no identifying words were written on the vehicle she had seen. Soon the FBI would claim that no air conditioning companies in Dallas had a green pickup. After four interviews, the FBI wrote that Mercer "could not" identify any of the photographs of the man behind the wheel, which was patently untrue.

After her fifth interview, the FBI insisted again that Mercer was not certain the driver was Ruby. She was. Ruby's alibi, a Swiss cheese of obfuscations, would turn out to be consistent with the possibility that he could have been at Dealey Plaza at 10:50 A.M. He himself told the Warren Commission he "believ[ed]" he had arrived at the Dallas *Morning News* where he was placing an ad for his club at 10:30 or 11:00. He insisted that he talked to two employees who were together, although it emerged that they were not together at the time. One of them, Gladys Craddock, who had once worked at the Carousel as a "hostess," destroyed her credibility by placing herself as working on Ruby's ads at a time prior to when Ruby claimed to have been composing them. Later she changed this part of her story.

Watching television on Sunday morning, November 24th, Mercer told Jim Garrison, she had again recognized Jack Ruby as "the man I saw in the truck. I looked right in his face and he looked at me twice." The FBI report had reversed everything, stating she "could not identify" Ruby, but could identify the man who removed the gun case from the truck. The reverse was true.

Garrison wondered whether the man with the gun case had been Curtis Crafard, but he did not have a photograph of Crafard for her to identify. Nor had the FBI shown Julia Mercer a photograph of Crafard, although, living at Ruby's club, he seemed a logical suspect. They did show her Oswald's photo. He was not the man who had gotten out of the truck, Mercer said.

Dallas Secret Service agent Forest Sorrell, the first person to interview Ruby, told the Warren Commission that although "this lady said she saw somebody that looked like they had a gun case," he did not pursue it. Julia Ann Mercer had placed Ruby at the assassination scene, connected to the crime before he shot Oswald. Yet the Warren Commission did not invite her to testify.

For Garrison now, Mercer wrote out a statement denying that the signature on the November 22nd affidavit was hers. Mercer was terrified, and, in exchange, Garrison promised not to subpoena her in the Shaw case, "assuming we can ever get the defendant on trial." He wanted, rather, "a record as to where the truth is as against the organized effort to portray me as a liar and an insane person as well."

Neither Crafard, whom Garrison came to suspect as Officer Tippit's murderer, not least because the man at the site had fled into an "Odd Church" in a light-colored windbreaker like one Crafard wears in an FBI photograph, nor Mercer was interviewed by the HSCA. Gaeton Fonzi searched for Crafard's military discharge papers, which had been seized by the Warren Commission when he testified. They were nowhere to be found in the exhibits.

"No other witness so completely illuminated the extent of the cover-up," Garrison wrote of Mercer. He had offered to provide the HSCA with her married name and address, if they would make "a serious effort to protect her." He received no reply. The HSCA final report claims they "had been unable to locate her."

At the close of 1967, Garrison's investigation took so unfortunate a turn that Garrison could not bring himself to mention it in *On the Trail of the Assassins*. Neither Ivon nor Alcock would have been capable of the incompetence volunteers William Turner and "Bill Boxley" now exhibited. One day Turner was leafing through Garrison's "crank file" when he found a letter from a man named Thomas Thornhill.

Believing there was something dubious about this lead, which incriminated a man named Edgar Eugene Bradley in the assassination, Assistant District Attorney Mike Karamazin had tucked it away deep in Garrison's filing cabinet. There Turner unearthed it. Although it addressed neither Clay Shaw's, David Ferrie's, nor Oswald's intelligence connections, Turner pronounced this lead viable. The California volunteers had begun to steer Jim Garrison to those false names "smoked" by Gerald Patrick Hemming, disobeying Garrison's order: "I don't care about who the shooters were. I care about who the planners were." No greater disservice was done to Jim Garrison's work than Turner's and Boxley's targetting of Edgar Eugene Bradley.

Bradley was the California representative, at a salary of about $500 a month, of a right-wing preacher, the Reverend Carl McIntire. Admired by Jack Rogers, friend of Guy Banister and Richard Van Buskirk, McIntire had been approved for CIA contact use in 1954. Garrison had been right in connecting right-wing churches and the CIA. McIntire had even met with Guy Banister on another occasion, in 1963 at the Capitol House Hotel in Baton Rouge at a meeting of the National States Rights Party.

But this was a far cry from McIntire's assistant Edgar Eugene Bradley's being involved in the assassination. Thornhill claimed Bradley had tried to hire people to assassinate President Kennedy during a California campaign trip. The fee was to be $50,000. Bradley supposedly produced a layout of the storm drain system where Kennedy was to speak. Thornhill claimed Bradley had tried to persuade one Carol Aydelotte to get her husband to kill President Kennedy.

In December 1967, as the Bradley scenario was being developed by Turner and Boxley, Jim Garrison headed west to California for speaking engagements. There, a brouhaha arose over a radio personality reportedly having discovered that there was a San Francisco Mafia contract on Garrison's life. Hoover yawned. "Right," he wrote. "It is another diversionary tactic by Garrison." In the middle of all the distractions that followed was Boxley.

In Albuquerque, where Garrison was traveling under the name "John Armstrong," Boxley appeared without prior notification, armed with his .45. Garrison was livid. "I don't appreciate your dumping this paranoid garbage on me," he said. He had instructed his staff not to pass on death threats. But against Garrison's instructions, Boxley called the Albuquerque sheriff's office, and, impersonating an FBI agent, said the Mafia had "decided that Garrison should be killed." The "syndicate contract" turned out to be a hoax.

Sending Boxley home, Garrison went to Los Angeles, where he tells of an incident in the airport men's room. Despite a long line of empty stalls, someone had taken a stall right next to his. He heard "low whispering voices." Fearing he might be set up with a "sex misdemeanor charge," Garrison suddenly thought of a telephone call from a client he had once represented on a federal case.

Garrison writes of the incident in *On the Trail of the Assassins*. He remembered the man as "a grimy, furtive and disheveled homosexual who sold pornographic photographs for a living." Only three weeks before the airport incident the man had called. "He was thinking of visiting New Orleans during the next Mardi Gras," and hoped they might get together. Now Garrison wondered if this bizarre incident was somehow connected to the call from a person he had not heard of for years, yet who had managed to find his unlisted home telephone number.

Believing his investigation was in jeopardy, that a public scandal would be catastrophic for the case, he fled. He had to brush past two airport policemen blocking the bathroom exit door. A ring of policemen stood outside.

In Los Angeles, Boxley awaited him. Registered as "Clyde Ballou," Garrison was surprised when a bellhop delivered a manila envelope addressed to "Jim Garrison." Inside was a hard object.

"It's an explosive!" Boxley shouted. He threw the envelope in the bathtub and turned on cold water. The object was Lawrence Schiller's new book.

Boxley said he was in California to pursue the Bradley lead. Together, Turner and Boxley interviewed Thornhill and Aydelotte, who claimed that Bradley had CIA connections. They put Turner and Boxley in touch with Denis Mower, a "self-avowed Minuteman," and with a Reverend Wesley Brice of the Hollywood Bible Presbyterian Church.

Manifesting increasingly dubious judgment, Turner and Boxley then met Mower in a motel room where Mower insisted that in 1960 Bradley had attempted to recruit him to assassinate President Kennedy from the storm drain system of Sears, promising to pay him with "government money." He had told all this to the FBI, Mower said. Brice's story was that Bradley had admitted to him that he was in Dallas on the day of the assassination, staying a block from Dealey Plaza. This fact was confirmed by Bradley's wife, who had purportedly said, "Guess where Gene is! He's in Dallas!" Because he was a man of the cloth, Brice was to be the one person in this ugly charade whom Bradley would never forgive.

Boxley announced that Bradley was "a former intelligence operative, a covert FBI employee and a current FBI undercover employee," guilty of involvement in the assassination. It fit his persistent scenario of focusing involvement for the crime on the FBI and away from the CIA. Neither he nor Turner managed to uncover that Thornhill and Aydelotte had been in litigation with Bradley over a quarrel within the right-wing church movement. Aydelotte blamed Bradley for her expulsion from the John Birch Society.

"That's Gene Bradley!" Aydelotte told Boxley, pointing to a Fort Worth *Star Telegram* photograph of two men standing in front of the Dallas School Book Depository. Other less-than-helpful volunteers suggested that Bradley was one of the "tramps" arrested at Dealey Plaza.

Garrison sent Moo Moo out to Lakefront Airport in search of anyone who might have seen Bradley with David Ferrie. The only person they had seen in 1963 was that CIA contract pilot *Leslie* Bradley, "dressed in a Castro fatigue outfit, complete with hat and beard," and "sleeping on the second floor." Bradley was soon to be rescued by Clay Shaw.

On the reassurances of Turner and Boxley, Jim Garrison decided to charge Edgar Eugene Bradley. Dubious, troubled, retaining his integrity, Jimmy Alcock refused to sign the Bill of Information. Sciambra agreed with him. Richard Burnes wanted no part of it. Whatever Bradley did was not in New Orleans, Burnes pointed out. With no connection to Shaw, it would mean they would now have two conspiracies emanating from New Orleans. Charlie Ward examined the tramp photographs and was certain Bradley was not one of them.

By telephone, Garrison threatened to fire them all were they not to obey his instructions. Only with the deepest reluctance did Garrison's assistants charge Edgar Eugene Bradley with participation in a conspiracy to murder John F. Kennedy. When Bradley's lawyer vowed to "fight extradition every inch of the way," Ivon and Alcock breathed a sigh of relief.

In retrospect, this unfortunate event seems part of a general sabotage from within of the Garrison investigation. Turner had attempted to draw the Minutemen into the case. Bradley stated that Colonel Gale, the leader of the California Rangers allied to the Minutemen, whose name Hemming had also brought into Garrison's office, was nothing more than a "nut" and "an extremist." For Boxley, Turner and Rose, Bradley's perspective was inconvenient.

If Bradley's politics were to the right, that hardly implicated him in the assassination. A former CIA agent named Chris Gugas in Omaha, where the CIA had a strong presence at the Offutt Air Force Base, did Bradley's polygraph, but Bradley pleads that it was Gugas who had contacted him. That Bradley had supported J. Edgar Hoover for president, that he was an informant to the FBI's Los Angeles field office, did not implicate him, either.

Jim Garrison allowed himself to believe that he had found evidence against Bradley from Dallas deputy sheriff Roger Craig, who insisted he was "positive" that Bradley was a man, "standing among some Dallas policemen," to whom he spoke on the steps of the school book depository. Craig said he had shared information with Bradley about a young man entering a waiting light-colored Nash station wagon with a Latin-seeming driver. Garrison had welcomed Roger Craig when he had revealed that the Dallas police had been told specifically "to take NO part whatsoever in the security of that motorcade." Then he went on to trust Craig far too much.

The evidence Garrison sent to California for Bradley's extradition hearing included an affidavit from Max Gonzales. Gonzales swears he met David Ferrie in the company of Edgar Eugene Bradley between June and August 1963. "I don't believe it," Numa Bertel says. The FBI's Division 5 agreed, suggesting that Garrison may have "manufactured" a witness. All Garrison supplied for the extradition hearing was this Gonzales statement, his own affidavit and Roger Craig's.

The Bradley problem was further exacerbated when another California volunteer, a UCLA film student, Stephen Jaffe, calling himself a "photographic expert," insisted in a memo to Lou Ivon that Bradley was one of the tramps "beyond any shadow of doubt, and absolutely beyond any possibility of fabrication." Another "expert," Richard E. Sprague, insisted Bradley did not resemble the tall tramp enough because Bradley "had an operation performed since November 22nd, which altered his appearance"! Eventually Bradley would go on television holding the tramp photograph, and proving that it was not he.

Another California volunteer "helping" Garrison was a KHJ-TV reporter named Art Kevin, an FBI informant. Alberto Fowler was at once suspicious and broke their appointment, "for some unknown reason," Kevin thought. Kevin dispatched a reporter to the Van Nuys Airport with a photograph of Bradley where he spoke to a flight instructor with American Flight Service, a CIA proprietary. William Burchette said Bradley would supposedly be back about one; he wasn't. Before long, Burchette had quit. No evidence materialized. Bill Turner then sent Jim Rose to the same airport, where Rose reported a pilot he knew had said he had taken Bradley on "government missions."

Not yet done, Kevin found a pseudonymous witness named "Margaret McLeigh," who insisted she could identify from photographs that Clay Shaw was the tall, broad-shouldered, white-haired man, who had visited Bradley "quite often." None of what she said could be verified. Meanwhile Turner and Rose suggested that Jim Braden (Eugene Hale Brading), questioned in the Dal Tex building on November 22nd, was in fact Edgar Eugene Bradley. The only testimony that rings true was from a Tulsa woman named Betty Helm, who would not confirm Bradley's statement that he was in Tulsa with her on November 22nd. Bradley had asked her to sign an affidavit to that effect, she said, but she had refused.

When Bill Turner flew to New Orleans and addressed Jim Garrison's investigators, barely had he uttered a word when Charlie Ward and Jimmy Alcock bombarded him with questions: Why had Bradley been accused of conspiracy? Where was the evidence? Turner was vague. When it was over, Alcock vowed that he would never prosecute Edgar Eugene Bradley.

More of Hemming's names began to be heard at Tulane and Broad: Colonel Gale, Clint Wheat. Carol Aydelotte now claimed that Stanley Drennan "wrote prescriptions for Lauren [sic] Hall," that Hall had met Bradley at Clint Wheat's house, and that Bradley knew Kent Courtney.

As the months passed, Bradley became increasingly alarmed. He contacted the CIA, offering to assist them, as he had the FBI. Fearing that the charge might stick, he asserted that he had "the greatest respect for the former CIA people whom he knew and for the Agency itself."

On June 5, 1968, California held Bradley's extradition hearing. Jim Garrison sent no one from New Orleans to examine witnesses. Bradley's lawyer was assisted by Hugh Aynesworth, who had supplied the Bill of Particulars filed for Sergio Arcacha Smith in his successful effort to avoid extradition from Texas. It wasn't until October 1st that California denied Louisiana's extradition request in the matter of Edgar Eugene Bradley.

A coda: After the Shaw trial, Jim Garrison wrote to Bradley. Bradley replied graciously. He had come to the conclusion that Garrison had been "set up" for failure, for being discredited, Bradley wrote back, "to discourage any future attempts by anyone to solve the mystery surrounding the assassination of John F. Kennedy." When Roger Craig approached Bradley attempting to extort money, Bradley pleaded with Jim Garrison to come to Los Angeles. "Please, Mr. Garrison, try to make arrangements to see me as soon as possible," he wrote. By now Roger Craig was offered no quarter at Tulane and Broad.

On March 30, 1974, Jim Garrison wrote a formal exoneration of Edgar Eugene Bradley. "To Whom It May Concern," Garrison begins: "This is to state that several years ago, I dismissed the charges which had been lodged in this jurisdiction." One witness had volunteered information and "subsequently failed to testify truthfully in the trial on another matter." Another was "a representative of a domestic intelligence operation of the federal government which was seeking to complicate and interfere with our inquiry into the New Orleans part of that operation which ended with the assassination of President Kennedy." A third had died. They had "initiated an injustice," Garrison admitted.

"Mr. Bradley was the victim of the above-described individuals and consequently I consider him innocent of any real connection with the president's assassination."

"I would like to meet you as much as you would like to meet me," Garrison, as he neared the end of his life, told Bradley. Jim Garrison and Edgar Eugene Bradley finally met in 1991 in New Orleans. At lunch at the New Orleans Athletic Club, Bradley saw at once: Jim Garrison seemed pale, not well.

He had been set up, Garrison told Bradley. Bradley explained that Thornhill and Aydelotte had been lovers; they had demanded that property of Aydelotte's mother be put in Thornhill's name. Bradley had served as an auxiliary police officer, and had already picked up some of their friends on a gun-running charge. "Margaret McLeigh" had been a disgruntled neighbor.

They discussed Max Gonzales, and Roger Craig, who would say "anything I wanted him to say if I would give him money," Bradley said. They joked about the mistaken identification of Leslie Norman Bradley. Having been charged in the murder of the president, his name splashed across the nation's newspapers in banner head-lines, Bradley had suffered lasting consequences. He had lost his job. He spent years supporting lawyers.

"Bradley, we were both set up," Garrison said. His sympathy, Bradley concluded, was genuine. "I think I know who set me up. I don't know who set you up," Garrison added. "The government sent me false information."

Edgar Eugene Bradley liked Jim Garrison, whom he viewed as a "fine country gentleman." At their lunch, Garrison presented him with a copy of *On the Trail of the Assassins*. It was inscribed: "April 1991. For Gene Bradley, with warmest regards, and my appreciation of a fine American. Jim Garrison."

JACKALS FOR THE CIA 17

In Washington, the failure to tell the whole truth is not considered to be an offense.
—Jim Garrison

WHEN JIM GARRISON READ the Warren Commission testimony of Oswald's Marine acquaintance Kerry Thornley, he branded it as so "heavy-handed that this goes back to before the Barrymores." A "total fabrication," it exposed Thornley as a "pathological liar in the service of some clandestine operation connected to the assassination." Only Kerry Thornley had testified that Oswald was a Marxist, preparing for Fidel Castro to be blamed for the assassination. Thornley's portrait of Oswald, Garrison thought, was "synthetic and representative of the fictional nature of the entire fraudulent 'investigation.'"

In Oswald's Marine Corps unit, Thornley and Oswald, along with John Moretti and Major A. F. Boland, were all working for the CIA. Other than Thornley, not a single Marine who knew Oswald said he was a Communist, a Marxist or even a Socialist. Peter Francis Conor said Oswald called his namesake Robert E. Lee "the greatest man in history." Mack Osborne said that Oswald laughed when, caught studying Russian, he was accused of being a spy. Henry J. Roussel Jr. said Oswald called people "comrade" in jest. "Nothing socialist, mind you," Nelson Delgado said.

Thornley had told the Warren Commission not only that Oswald was a Communist, but also that he was "crazy," with a "definite tendency toward irrationality at times, an emotional instability." Why, Garrison asked, did Thornley decide to write a book about Oswald if he was such a "nebbish?" Thornley's decision to write about Oswald was made even before Oswald "defected," Garrison believed, and made sense only if Thornley knew that Oswald would be accused of killing the president.

The most blatant of Thornley's lies concerned Oswald's height. He made Oswald five foot five, four inches shorter than he was. (Thornley had told Warren commission counsel Albert Jenner he was five foot ten; Oswald was said to be five foot eleven on most documents, five foot nine on others.) It would be, Garrison said later, as if he himself called Gerald Patrick Hemming, at six foot seven, and an inch taller than himself, "a rather short fellow." It seemed as if Thornley was suggesting that he and Oswald were so different in appearance that one could never be taken for the other. Both were pale, slender, brown-haired men with receding hairlines, a year apart in age.

Seeing them together at the Bourbon House, Quarter habituée Barbara Reid called Oswald and Thornley "the Gold Dust twins." Both had resided at the Hotel McBeath; both frequented the Ryder Coffee House, whose guest book bore Oswald's signature. Other CIA types hung out there, too, like CIA courier William Cuthbert Brady.

To the Warren Commission, under oath, Thornley denied he had seen Oswald since 1959. He claimed he heard Oswald speaking Russian with another Marine. Over lunch, Albert Jenner suggested it must have been John René Heindel, nicknamed "Hidell" by Marine buddies. Soon Thornley created an affidavit recounting how *he* came to identify Heindel as the man who spoke Russian with Oswald. The rapport between Thornley and Jenner, Garrison was to say scornfully, was "more suggestive of Rudolph Nureyev and Margot Fonteyn performing Swan Lake together than it is of an inquiry of a witness who was in close association with the alleged murderer of the President of the United States shortly before the assassination."

When Garrison subpoenaed Louisiana resident Heindel to the grand jury, Heindel swore that he spoke no foreign languages. He had known Oswald slightly, at Atsugi (where Thornley was not present), but not in California where Thornley supposedly heard him talking Russian with Oswald.

"If he speaks Russian, he fooled me," Jimmy Alcock said after Heindel had been dismissed.

Garrison discovered that Thornley had been elated at the news of the assassination. "I'm glad," he proclaimed. "Have you heard the good news?" Thornley had asked Bernard Goldsmith, a member of the discussion group at Ivon's. Oswald was "not a Communist," Thornley had confided to Goldsmith. "When it is all over . . . I may yet go piss on JFK's grave," Thornley wrote to his friend Philip Boatwright in 1964. Garrison learned that Thornley had left New

Orleans right after the assassination, leaving a room filled with confetti, torn up paper soaked in water, so that no writing was legible. Thornley then moved to Arlington, Virginia, where his rent cost more than his salary as a doorman.

In January 1968, Garrison pondered Thornley's August 1963 trip to Mexico City, unaware that Oswald, too, had made a midsummer trip to Mexico. "All info re LHO in Mexico City is clouded with a mist as if it were something that happened about the time of the Druids," Garrison said. "This place is the thing wherein we'll catch the conscience of the Queen Bee."

He assigned Max Gonzales to fly to Cuba with photographs of Thornley, Novel and Beckham, those "slim young men-on-the-make," if only to learn who really talked to Sylvia Duran at the Cuban embassy in Mexico City. "Pearl" Gonzales might learn the truth. "At the very least we can enjoy the novelty of encountering the truth from a government official for a change," Garrison said. The trip never happened. One day, flying in his little plane over Lake Pontchartrain, Gonzales disappeared, never to be heard from again.

J. Edgar Hoover had told J. Lee Rankin, Warren Commission chief counsel, that Oswald had ordered and picked up his pro-Castro leaflets at the Jones Printing Company. But owner Douglas Jones told the FBI on December 3, 1963, that he "did not believe the person ordering the printing of the handbills was Oswald." Jones' assistant, Myra Silver, concurred.

On December 13, 1967, Harold Weisberg, on behalf of Jim Garrison and armed with dozens of photographs, including four of Kerry Thornley, interviewed Jones. One photo had been retouched and showed Thornley with a bushy beard, in case, Weisberg reasoned, he had worn a beard during the summer of 1963. Jones identified all four photographs as being of the man who had picked up the leaflets: all were of Thornley. "He called himself 'Lee Osborne,'" Jones said.

When Boxley, who had insisted on tagging along, denied back at Tulane and Broad that Jones had made the identification of Thornley, Weisberg played the tape for Lou Ivon. Soon the tape vanished. Weisberg returned to reinterview Jones and Silver, this time separately, and without Boxley. Each again selected only photographs of Thornley as the man who had picked up the leaflets.

On January 8, 1968, Richard Burnes sent a material witness warrant to Tampa, requesting Thornley's attendance before the Orleans Parish grand jury. There would be no immunity. Garrison's press release focused on Thornley's denial that he had seen Oswald in September 1963 when, in fact, they were "frequent companion[s]." Heindel is "a CIA agent," Thornley sputtered as he fought the subpoena, demanding to be "formally extradited."

Garrison had a plethora of witnesses who had seen Oswald and Thornley together during that summer of 1963. Among them was Barbara Reid, who provided a sworn statement that she had seen the two together at the Bourbon House. She had also seen Oswald on WDSU being interviewed by Bill Stuckey. "I am positive that the person sitting at the table with Kerry Thornley was Lee Harvey Oswald," Reid said.

Peter Deageano was at Reid's table, and saw Oswald walk in and join Thornley. Deageano had observed the two together on another occasion, "in either August or September." Oswald was eating a hamburger while chatting with Thornley and his girlfriend, Jeanne Hack. Deageano had also seen Oswald distributing his leaflets on Canal Street, and identified him as "being identical" to the person he saw at the Bourbon House.

Another witness was L. P. Davis, who had also seen Oswald and Thornley at the Bourbon House, the two wearing black slacks and white shirts, so that they might have been twins. A newsman named Cliff Hall told Richard Burnes that Thornley had admitted to him right after the assassination that he had seen Oswald during the summer of 1963. Jeanne Hack said Thornley knew about Oswald's "Fair Play for Cuba" activity. On the day of the assassination, he told her, "Oswald did not do it alone but had help."

After the assassination, Thornley had visited Reid's house. Pointing to a photograph of Oswald, she had said, "This is the fellow that you introduced me to."

"Did I?" Thornley said.

Before the Orleans Parish grand jury, Kerry Thornley repeated his denial that he had seen Oswald in New Orleans during the summer of 1963. He professed not to know that Oswald had even been in New Orleans. Terming Oswald "accident prone," he insisted that Oswald had called communism "the best system" and that "Heidel" spoke Russian with him.

Thornley admitted to having met Clay Shaw ("a big tan guy with silver hair") and talking to him twice. The name "Guy Banister" rang a bell. No, he had never been at Jones Printing. He had never met Marina Oswald.

Marina was the next witness, passing Thornley in the hall without reacting. Had she ever seen this man before? Moo Moo Sciambra asked.

She had never heard the name Kerry Thornley, Marina said. Asked about George Bouhe, whom she and Lee knew well, a man who gave her English lessons and who lived next door to Jack Ruby, she become nervous. "It was coincidence," Marina finally said. Oswald was never gone "late in the evenings," but home every night. Garrison mentioned an Alabama priest who had said Lee was away from home often, but Marina held firm, apparently knowing she must undermine the evidence that Oswald had been in Clinton and Jackson.

She had cut herself off from Ruth Paine. Paine "was sympathizing with the CIA," Marina said. Garrison did not raise Marina's having attended the English Language Institute at the University of Michigan, a hotbed of Soviet defectors and CIA assets, although he was aware that she had. He did not ask her if she knew former KGB officer Alexander Orlov, resident there, placed by the CIA to be debriefed on what he knew about Soviet espionage.

Later Marina Oswald Porter would describe Jim Garrison as a "gentleman" with an "idealistic spirit," which was "a comfort" to her. There was "nobility" in his effort. Only in the 1990s would she say that Oswald, innocent, had worked for some part of the American government. By then she had long since sacrificed her credibility.

Ruth Paine followed Marina, her testimony a carbon copy of Thornley's. Oswald was "a Marxist," Paine stated. She herself did not work for the CIA. A chilling moment came when Paine struggled to explain why she had failed to honor Oswald's request that she call lawyer John Abt on his behalf.

Back in Irving, Texas, Paine wrote a schoolgirlish letter to Jim Garrison, signing it "Ruth," as if they were friends. Praising the "sheer force of your personality," another Gerald Patrick Hemming, she offered Jim Garrison her "help." Soon she would be testifying for Clay Shaw.

Kerry Thornley was charged with perjury on February 21st, 1968. At once Garrison was vindicated as the news brought new witnesses forward. LSU professor Martin McAuliffe remembered that Thornley had mentioned Oswald to him at the Bourbon House that summer. Jeanne Hack, now Napoli, had been surprised that Thornley, like Oswald, had a post office box at the Lafayette Square station, far from his customary venues. Thornley had once taken her to a meeting at the back of Carlos Bringuier's store. John Schwegmann Jr. told Garrison he had seen Thornley at the Oswald residence on Magazine Street.

Myrtle and Tony LaSavia were both "positive" they had seen Thornley walking past their house at 919 Upperline with Marina on the way to the Winn-Dixie supermarket on Prytania Street. Tony LaSavia was certain: It was not Oswald, but "another man," accompanying Marina to the market. When he saw Thornley on television, as well as in the newspaper, he immediately recognized him "as being the person who used to walk with Marina to the Winn-Dixie food store."

Mrs. Doris Dowell, assistant manager of Shilington House where Thornley was the doorman, said Thornley had told her he "met Oswald again in New Orleans at a place in the French Quarter." And Allen Campbell says now that Oswald and Thornley were in constant contact.

Was it Thornley at the Levee Board ranting about fascism? Garrison wondered. Both were intelligence agents, he believed.

For the HSCA, Thornley concocted yet another affidavit. Clint Bolton, a *Vieux Carre Courier* columnist, Thornley writes, knew Shaw and Banister; Banister had ordered Bolton to coach him in "rewritting" [sic] his book about Oswald. Bolton had "fed" him the view that Oswald was a Marxist; Bolton had told him Oswald was a government agent who was slated to kill Castro, but "somehow flipped out and killed Kennedy instead." Thornley had, nonetheless, dedicated his 1965 book *Oswald* to Clint Bolton.

In New Orleans, Thornley had known only "the second Oswald or Leon Oswald." Admitting he had discussed his book with Guy Banister, Thornley insisted that meant that the CIA "knew I was writing a book on Lee Oswald." David Chandler, he added, "knew more about the assassination than he was telling."

Reading this fifty-page affidavit, Gaeton Fonzi concluded that Thornley was making "a rather strained effort to portray an instability of character," mimicking his false picture of Oswald and hoping to avoid further scrutiny of his own role. A "confidential" Los Angeles Sheriff's Department interview with a friend of Thornley's father on November 26, 1963, reveals that Oswald and Thornley had been corresponding regularly. Kerry, his father Ken had revealed, had "numerous letters from Oswald, some of which are of recent date."

From the Department of Defense files comes a document placing Thornley as a CIA employee who attended Chemical and Biological Warfare School. Receiving "technical instruction" in Washington, D.C., Thornley moved up from "confidential" to "secret" clearance. His course in "Atomic, Biological and Chemical Warfare" ran from June to August 1960, and had begun at Atsugi, Japan.

On December 29th, Garrison had subpoenaed Loran Hall, Lawrence Howard and Thomas Edward Beckham. Los Angeles Police intelligence forwarded Hall's files to New Orleans. But Howard was too well protected. They had nothing on Howard, they said. The subpoena to Howard cited him for association with David Ferrie in 1963 in New Orleans. These witnesses were relevant, Garrison told the press, unlike the "preposterous irrelevancies" called by the Warren Commission: "Theodore Roosevelt, Franklin D. Roosevelt, Rudy Vallee and Xavier Cugat."

CIA at once announced it had "no connection" with Howard. Hall was a domestic contact, but only in 1959, cross-referenced with Hemming. When a reporter asked Howard whether his training of guerrilla forces "had any connection with the U.S. Central Intelligence Agency," Howard did not bother to deny it. "No comment," Howard said.

To Art Kevin, Howard denied he had ever met Ferrie, Ruby, Oswald, or Shaw. "He can prove he was working in Los Angeles at the time of the assassination," Kevin wrote to Garrison, which was not so. For Garrison volunteer Steven Burton, Howard produced falsified "employment records." When Burton showed him a photograph of Oswald, Howard exclaimed "That's Leon Oswald!" as if he were confirming that he had visited Sylvia Odio.

Having been relieved by friendly California courts of Garrison's subpoenas, Howard and Hall went to New Orleans voluntarily, in exchange for immunity. They would talk, not at the grand jury, but in Jim Garrison's office. Howard demanded that Garrison make his cooperation "public." Then he began to lie: He insisted he was unable to identify his companion Loran Hall from photographs. He looked at beautiful Sylvia Odio's picture and said, "I've never seen her, but I'd like to." He gave himself away in referring to Odio as someone Gerry Patrick "had gone out with," reflecting a story Hemming still spins of a liaison with Odio in Cuba.

"Do you think he could be CIA?" Garrison asked Howard about Hemming. "There's no question he could have told us a lot more than he did."

Howard kept a straight face. Asked if any of the Cubans "have any connection with the Central Intelligence Agency," Howard evaded the question. Garrison knew that when in October 1963 Oswald was registered at the Dallas YMCA, Howard was there too. Now Howard insisted someone else had signed his name to the register.

Then Howard began to insert false names into the discussion:

Nico Crespi ("he's a Cuban"); Clint Wheat, an ex-Klan member who held meetings at his house where they discussed the assassination, and who disappeared after Garrison attempted to have him subpoenaed; William Gale. Howard opened his address book and gave Garrison the useless number of Colonel William Gale. When Garrison mentioned Thomas Edward Beckham, the man who had delivered maps and diagrams to Howard in Dallas the week of the assassination, Howard remained calm.

"I've heard the name Tom Beckham," Howard said coolly. "I know you subpoenaed him."

"That's the only way you know him?" Garrison said.

"Yeah," Howard said. He added that Hemming "could have been" CIA because "he had the connections," as he revealed his knowledge that Gerald Patrick Hemming had two uncles, Robert and Art Simpson, who had been shipbuilding partners with John McCone during World War II and who stayed close to the intelligence community so that as a young man, Hemming claims, he was introduced to Frank Wisner and James Angleton.

Howard revealed one startling truth. Jerry Cohen of the *Los Angeles Times* and Lawrence Schiller had promised him representation from Clay Shaw's lawyer. He didn't have to talk to Garrison at all. Disarmed, Garrison told Howard, "It's perfectly obvious that you're completely honest." In a press release of February 28th, Garrison called Howard "extremely cooperative," his appearance "very helpful."

Off balance, he was exonerating a man involved in the implementation of the murder of the president. Lawrence Howard "was not personally connected in any way with the assassination of President Kennedy," Garrison said. Lou Ivon thought otherwise: Howard should have been followed up more thoroughly, Ivon says. A year before the Shaw trial, Garrison's staff was exhausted, and Howard slipped through their fingers.

Cohen and Schiller also attempted to prevent Loran Hall from going to New Orleans. Garrison would hold him in "contempt of court" and put him in jail for five years, Schiller told Hall. Billings' *Life* colleague Mike Acoca also worked on Loran Hall. Garrison is out to hang you, Acoca told Hall.

To Harold Weisberg, echoing Hemming, Hall insisted that Jim Garrison "will never solve the thing . . . somebody a lot higher than you or I masterminded the whole thing . . . there is people up in Washington, DC." Approximately two weeks after the assassination, Harry Dean of the Chicago Fair Play for Cuba Committee met with an FBI agent named Rapp, of the Pomona, California, office, who told him not to talk to anyone else. Dean told Rapp that he had heard Loran Hall state that a Communist would be framed for the murder of President Kennedy.

Hall's interviews were laced with disinformation. He had a "source" who saw Clay Shaw enter the home of Edgar Eugene Bradley, he said. Schiller and Cohen both believed Bradley was involved, Hall said.

Hall knew that Hemming was telling people that he was in Dallas on November 22nd, armed with Hemming's Johnson .06 rifle, complete with telescopic sight. Garrison was told by an informant named Jack Huston that Hall knew Oswald in Dallas. He knew from Wiley Yates that Hall had spent time in New Orleans.

The meeting between Hall and Oswald is confirmed in an Army Intelligence, 11th MI Group (III), document authored by Charles N. Phillips, and dated June 19, 1970. The "source" mentioned is Roy Hargraves, who reveals that both Lawrence Howard and Loran Hall met with Lee Harvey Oswald in Texas in October while en route to Florida before the assassination. It states that both Howard and Hall were connected with the CIA. This document also has Hemming explaining to Hargraves that "the assassination was a Central Intelligence Agency plot to do away with Kennedy." Hall and Howard, both CIA-sponsored, were involved, according to this Army intelligence document. Hargraves reveals that he confronted Lawrence Howard with the question of his involvement, only for Howard to have "clammed up" and become very nervous.

Hall's intelligence connections were manifold: arrested in Dallas that October for having dexadrine in his glove compartment, a parade of agents—CIA, FBI, military intelligence—visited him in jail. Later he would call himself a "jackal for the CIA." Just before he boarded the plane for New Orleans, Hall contacted first the FBI and then the CIA to ask if they had any objections to his going. Was there anything they wanted him to tell Jim Garrison?

It was May 6, 1968, by the time Hall reached Tulane and Broad. "You can make a great contribution to this country if you so choose," Garrison had pleaded. But Hall only repeated the scenario of his fellow Cuba infiltrator Hemming that there had been many plots to kill John F. Kennedy. He had been part of a conspiracy of Mafia demons (Giancana, Rosselli and Trafficante) to kill Castro, but not of "*the* conspiracy." There was no "one person" assigned to kill President Kennedy, Hall said. Then he regurgitated the Hemming litany of names: Clint Wheat and Colonel Gale; the National States Rights Party and Nico Crespi; Dr. Drennan. He threw in the name of

Dr. Crocket, whom Hemming insisted was holding his Johnson .06, only for Crocket to deny it.

Hall claimed he had never spent time in New Orleans.

Did Hall know Thomas Edward Beckham?

"No, I seen pictures of Beckham," Hall said. Yes, he could identify Garrison's thick-necked Cuban: it was "José Duarte, who, in fact, was a long-time and current asset of JMWAVE." Two months later Hall would send a photograph of "Duarte" to Lou Ivon, with greetings for "the big man."

As he had for Howard, Jim Garrison issued a public statement exonerating Hall. Then Steve Bordelon took Hall for a drink at the Habana Bar.

"Welcome back, Lorenzo!" the bartender said, calling Hall by his real name, which was Lorenzo Pascillio. Loran Hall was, of course, no stranger to the Crescent City.

A month later Manolo Aguilar, a Naval Intelligence operative, with cover as head of the FRAC (Frente Revolucionaria Anti-Communista), told the Miami police, but not Jim Garrison, that Lawrence Howard had "said that the FBI was giving him a very bad time because of his part in the assassination." Hall had told the FBI that "Howard has been involved." Hemming himself had informed on Howard, Hall and Seymour to the CIA.

Hall was to tell the HSCA that a woman named Mrs. Mildred Hyatt could provide an alibi for him for November 22nd, but Hyatt did not back him up. He had never heard the name Oswald before the assassination, Hall claimed, although Nico Crespi was with Oswald in Dallas in May, June or July. Both Hall and Howard denied they had been in New Orleans, except, Hall said, once in January 1963 to "gas up." Lawyer William Triplett concluded that Hall seemed to have been "not only rehearsed but almost programmed."

"I was not a CIA agent . . . a card-bearing certified CIA agent," Howard told the HSCA. "Perhaps indirectly I was working for them." Howard was not questioned about the package delivered by Thomas Edward Beckham, although the HSCA staff knew about it. Nor did Blakey's lawyers question Howard about his having been identified at Marydale Farms in East Feliciana Parish during the summer of 1963. That he was a very dangerous man Howard himself confirmed to Louisiana investigator L. J. Delsa. "If the president would call me and ask me to go over to Cuba and kill Castro," Howard told L. J., "I promise I would get to the tip of Florida and if I had to swim, I promise you he would be dead."

A few days before the assassination, still in Los Angeles, Hall had made an admission to a private detective named Leroy Payne. Payne worked for Richard Hathcock, to whom Hall had pawned and redeemed the Johnson rifle. I have no time to talk, Hall said. I'm taking a plane to Dallas.

"You better have a good alibi for November 22nd," Payne, who had told the FBI about the Johnson rifle, remarked to Hall some time later. Hall professed not to be worried. He had fifty witnesses who could testify that he was in the lobby of a Dallas hotel at the time the president was shot, Hall declared. None of those witnesses were to check out. Shortly after the assassination, Hall, who had been chronically unemployed, and had been begging for "quarters and canned goods," suddenly opened a tavern and motel in Kern County, California.

Forever after, Lawrence Howard would insist he was not in Dallas on November 22nd, but in California. It was not so. Shortly before the assassination, Howard did return to Los Angeles, bitter that Fidel Castro remained alive. To a friend named Richard Magison, he hinted that "they were going to do something so monumental, bad, heinous, terrible, shocking, important, that the United States would definitely invade Cuba."

"Was the CIA involved?" Magison said.

In reply, Howard removed a piece of paper with a name and a telephone number from his billfold: "E. Howard Hunt."

On the day of the assassination, Magison drove to the Air Fan Manufacturing Company where Howard worked, anxious to discuss the president's death with Howard and his friend, "Tex," whose real name was William Seymour. He had not seen Howard for several days, his boss said, nor did he know where Howard was. Howard was to lie both to Jim Garrison, insisting "work was disrupted" on that day in Los Angeles, and to the HSCA, whom he also told he was "working, I was right on the job. I was right on the job." Magison remembered something else. Howard had just bought a light blue or green Nash Rambler, even as Garrison witness Edward Girnus was to mention a light-colored station wagon parked "on the railroad track to the rear of the School Book Depository near Dealey Plaza."

In 1968, when newspapers reported that Garrison had subpoenaed Lawrence Howard, Magison drove over to his house. The burly Howard faced him from behind the barrel of a gun. He was "heavily armed and fearful for his life," Magison was to remember. Magison made a hasty departure.

Harry Dean, that CIA Fair Play for Cuba infiltrator, also knew that Howard was in Dallas on November 22, 1963. "I think Howard took a shot [at Kennedy]," Dean said, and "he was in Dallas and all those other crumbs . . . I don't believe Oswald did."

Perry Russo had told New Orleans CIA asset, lawyer Jack Rogers, that Lawrence Howard was a personal friend of David Ferrie, and he had met Howard with Ferrie. Both Howard and Seymour, Russo believed, were "at the scene of the assassination in Dallas," where Howard met both Ruby and Oswald.

Clay Shaw's lawyer, Edward Wegmann, was also persuaded that "Lawrence Howard was in association with David Ferrie in New Orleans in 1963," and had appeared at Beckham's Mission. In Dallas, Wegmann had learned, Howard "was in contact with Jack Ruby" and was also "in association with Lee Harvey Oswald in Dallas."

After the assassination, Thomas Edward Beckham had taken to the road. Penniless, terrified, but always a survivor, with an infinite capacity to reinvent himself, he lived on the streets, moving from town to town. As "Mark Evans," he sang on weekends at clubs. Small and agile, game for anything, at "All American Shows," a carnival out of Florida, which toured the biggest state fairs in the country, he rode a stripped-down motor bike inside a drum with centrifugal force holding him up. Running was better than thinking what might happen to you.

Fred Lee Crisman seemed able always to find him. Together with Bob Lavender (until a counterfeiting scheme alienated the two), Fred promoted Tommy's singing career. In Olympia, Washington, a fake license on Crisman's office read: "Crisman and Beckham Psychological Services." Nobody came. Later Crisman signed the name over to Beckham: "International Association of Pastoral Psychologists."

"Use that as back-up," Crisman said. Among the businesses incorporated by Fred and Tommy in Olympia were: marketing of a tear gas pistol; a school to train police officers; and the "Northwest Relief Society," which existed solely to solicit funds, like the New Orleans Mission on North Rampart. By 1968 Crisman would be investigated for narcotics activity in connection with a group called "Servants of Awareness."

Sometimes Tommy drives Fred out to an Army base in Tacoma, where he is known. At Boeing aircraft, where Crisman had been employed, Fred takes him into the top security area. There is also church activity, like the World Wide Church, run out of Springfield, Missouri, by a CIA asset named Herman Keck.

Keck called himself a "bishop" in the Anglican church and said he was part of an international clergymen's association. He was a master engraver, and he delivered documents to the CIA through Crisman. He traveled far and wide on a diplomatic passport. "I'm the paper man for the Company," Keck told Beckham. And Crisman confirmed it. "Look kid," Keck said. "If they need KGB identification, I'll provide it." Later, Keck would be one of those to set up a safe house for Tommy and to advise him to stay away from Jim Garrison. "They'll just write him up as another nut," Keck said of Garrison. He called Tommy "cowboy" and said he had been "lucky" to get through it safely. By "it" he meant the assassination.

It is now, finally, that Beckham draws his conclusion.

"Fred, I know you're a government agent," Tommy says one day.

"Yeah," Fred says, and Tommy realizes, as Jim Garrison had, that "the CIA can do a lot under cover of religion."

Tommy practices medicine without a license. He poses as a police officer. He gets into trouble over a bad check and languishes in jail until Fred arrives, handcuffs Tommy and then explains to the police, "I'm an FBI man." They walk out.

To get away from Fred, Tommy ships out with the Merchant Marine.

Nebraska finds Tommy as it once did potential Garrison witness Sandra Moffett. Two weeks later, Fred Lee Crisman is on his doorstep.

"What do you take me for?" Fred says.

"I just felt like moving on," Tommy says.

"Kid, you're not in a position to move on," Fred says. He takes Tommy to Offutt Air Force base in Omaha, home of the Strategic Air Command's Operation Looking Glass, which kept nuclear bombs in the air at all times, and was a base for reconnaissance flights bound for China and Cuba. Crisman shows identification and walks right in, Tommy by his side. "This is Agent Beckham," Crisman says as they pass through security where top secret clearance is required.

Soon Fred has introduced Tommy to Lieutenant Colonel Lawrence Lowry, director of the Operators' Office of the Planning Division of the Strategic Air Command with, indeed, top secret clearance. Lowry, in charge of "Plans" at Offutt, is deeply connected to the CIA. As "OI/SD Lt. Col. Lowrie," his name appears in the CIA's JMWAVE files of Customs/CIA officer Cesario Diosdado. A trace reference remains: In September 1966, "Col. was consulted" by the Agency regarding the acquisition of some explosives. The cable originated from the DCI, the Director of Central Intelligence himself.

"I want you to look after my boy," Crisman tells Lowry. Thomas Edward Beckham and Colonel Lowry grow close. Lowry can telephone and talk to a plane in midair, Tommy notices. Lowry places Tommy at a second-hand junk shop, which they name the B & L Enterprises Thrift Shoppe, with his wife in charge. Lowry's unlikely story is that he met Tommy after cutting out an advertisement in a local newspaper in which one "Mark Evans" was looking for investors in a recording studio.

Lowry says he answered the ad, and planned for Tommy to cut some records. They opened up a used furniture and book store. He loves music, Lowry says, which was why he befriended Beckham, and hoped to split the profit from the records. "Gentleman Jim [Reeves]" is his favorite Beckham song. Lowry is not ready to admit any relationship with Fred Lee Crisman, whose CIA connection entitled him to ask favors of highly placed military people.

It was one more baby-sitting operation, a waste of time until they needed him for something, Tommy knew. During his days with Lowry, Tommy asks Jack P. F. Gremillion to send Lowry a certificate designating him as an "honorary attorney general" of the state of Louisiana. On May 17, 1967, the certificate arrived.

Mrs. Lowry sits with Tommy in the store. They never sell anything. Tommy writes to the Reverend Raymond Broshears, whom he knows through David Ferrie, about setting up a branch of the Universal Life Church using the Thrift Shoppe storefront as its headquarters. He begins to dress as a church man in a black vest and white collar.

When Jim Garrison subpoenaed Beckham in January 1968, the Inspector General of the Strategic Air Command looked into Lieutenant Colonel Lowry's relationship with Beckham, and began to investigate Lowry himself. Lowry had been in the Air Force for more than nineteen years. They didn't pull his clearance, but Lowry was at once removed from involvement in anything classified.

The Inspector General also looked into the B & L Enterprises Thrift Shoppe and found it had operated only for a month, May to June 1967, with Mrs. Lowry writing the first month's rent check. The stock, from old refrigerators and washing machines to used books, was worth only between two and three hundred dollars. According to Colonel Lowry, Tommy paid him back five thousand dollars that he invested. Never to meet Beckham again, Lowry calls him "a fine gentleman." Anyone seeing the two together would have assumed they were, indeed, good friends.

One day in Omaha, Tommy received a telephone call from Jack Martin, whom he had not seen since the assassination. He remembered Jack's CIA and FBI identification cards, his four passports from four countries and his New Orleans police identification. Jack had always said the government used him when they needed him.

Tommy still fears Jack. Now Jack orders him to go to a safe house in Council Bluffs, Iowa, just across the bridge, Iowa being a state where Beckham, like Sandra Moffett, can avoid extradition to Louisiana. To avoid Jim Garrison's subpoena, Beckham moves back and forth between Nebraska and Iowa.

The one person who helps him is a man named Joe Martin, a disc jockey at KOWH-AM radio in Omaha. This Martin is a mild, unassuming man, a right-wing Republican who began in radio in the 1940s with Johnny Carson at Omaha's WOW. Although Joe Martin seems to be unconnected, a nobody, he was selected to compose the theme song for the 1964 Republican National Convention. It made station manager Mike Starr wonder: Joe Martin from lowly Omaha?

Many employees at station KOWH have Air Force backgrounds. The majority owner is William F. Buckley Jr., whose brother Ross lives in New Orleans on the 1200 block of Dauphine Street, not far from Clay Shaw. Ross also participated in the Friday night discussion groups at the Ryder Coffee House with Kerry Thornley and William Cuthbert Brady. Together with Brady, in 1962 Ross Buckley organized a "Fair Cuba Committee." William Buckley never comes to Omaha, and Joe Martin denies that he knows him. Both are CIA assets.

From his employees, Starr hears of secret phone calls to Joe Martin, whispered conversations. Martin would disappear with no explanation for hours at a time. He is in fact involved in shielding and protecting Garrison witnesses and helping them avoid his subpoenas.

After he hears from Thomas Edward Beckham, whom he is now ordered to shield, Joe Martin confides in Mike Starr. He is running a CIA safe house, he reveals. Starr, a young graduate of the Georgetown School of Law, who serves as a judge advocate at Offutt Air Force base, raises an eyebrow. At the safe house, Martin says, he has been recording the stories of those he is shielding on tapes he plans to play on KOWH. Starr fears he will lose his FCC license or be prosecuted and says, "absolutely not!" Somehow New Orleans authorities have learned that Joe Martin is helping Beckham, and the Omaha police interview him about aiding and abetting a fugitive.

The only people who know that Tommy is in Council Bluffs are friends from Offutt Air Force base like Colonel Lowry, Jack Martin and Joe Martin. Jack Martin calls and tells Tommy to return to

Omaha. Almost as soon as he arrives back in Omaha, Thomas Edward Beckham is served with a subpoena. Tommy's own brothers had pointed Garrison to Nebraska, ending the long search for Beckham begun by Garrison in February 1967. The Omaha Better Business Bureau terms him a "con artist."

One night, six weeks after Joe Martin asked for airtime to play his assassination tapes, there is a loud banging at the door of radio station KOWH. Everyone but Mike Starr and Joe Martin has left for the evening. The porch light is on, and through the circular plate glass window, Mike Starr sees two men in trench coats. He opens the door a crack, and tries to prevent them from entering. Flashing badges with photo ID cards, they brush past Starr. "CIA!" one of them says.

"CIA?" Starr says. "In Omaha?" Meanwhile Joe Martin has bolted from Studio A and raced down to the basement fallout shelter. In pursuit, the government agents grab him. One clutches his right arm, the other his left, and they drag Joe off into the night.

"Where are you taking him? When will he be back?" Starr says.

"We don't know," one of the men says. They disappear. When Starr telephones, the CIA denies it has any men in Omaha.

Beckham believes that one of the men must have been Fred Lee Crisman because, suddenly, there he was.

"I might as well return to New Orleans," Beckham says. "I can lie, or say nothing."

"You might say something you shouldn't say," Fred laughs. "Smart as I am, even I make mistakes."

Beckham returned to New Orleans to testify before the Orleans Parish grand jury. Through Bob Lavender, Crisman sent him one more message: "If I am subpoenaed as a result of anything he says to that grand jury, I'll kill him!"

Three days after Joe Martin disappeared, Mike Starr received a telephone call from the psychiatric unit at St. Mary's Hospital. Did he want to pick up Joe Martin?

When Starr arrived, Martin was cowering in a corner of the room, unshaven and disheveled. Martin tried to talk, but could not remember anything about the last three days. He would be unable ever to go on the air again. All he would say, when finally he could speak, was that he had been working with somebody who had tried to get away from him.

UPHEAVAL 18

This is going to be a test of whether we really have justice in America.

—Jim Garrison

ARRIVING IN NEW ORLEANS, Tommy assures the press that the only time he was ever in Dallas was "late last year" with Dr. F. Lee Crisman, with whom he works as a psychologist and who manages his entertainment career. Should he testify before a grand jury, his mother's life would be in danger, he had been warned. He is an ordained priest in the Orthodox Catholic Church of North America. When he runs into David Lewis, Tommy says that he and his brother Jim "are CIA agents." Uppermost in his mind is Fred's threat that death awaits him should Fred be subpoenaed as a result of what he tells Jim Garrison. He seems to have exhausted himself in several lifetimes, and yet he is only twenty-seven years old.

Thomas Edward Beckham is not permitted to roam unsupervised in New Orleans. A. Roswell Thompson assumes the role of handler. "Don't worry," Rozzy reassures him. "We've got it covered." "They" have someone working for them inside Garrison's office, Tommy is told. He is terrified of Rozzy and his Society for the Preservation of Southern Tradition, vigilantes who bury black people alive upside down. He fears Rozzy more than he fears Jack Martin—or Jim Garrison, who has granted him only limited immunity—for actions that occurred prior to the assassination. Garrison, he believes, could put him in jail for criminal conspiracy.

As A. Roswell Thompson sits outside in the hallway waiting, Thomas Edward Beckham appears before the Orleans Parish grand jury. It is February 15, 1968. As he is about to enter the jury room, he runs into Jack Dempsey, ever on the police beat. "Stick around," Tommy says. "After this is over, I'm going to give you something that will blow the district attorney out of office."

Inside, Jimmy Alcock explains his constitutional rights.

"I have none," Tommy says. Then, he begins to lie. He lies about his education, claiming he has been to college and is a psychologist, although by the afternoon he will admit to having dropped out of school in the seventh grade. Even this isn't true: he made it only to the third grade. He cannot recall, he says, whether he was in New Orleans in 1963. He met F. Lee Crisman in Washington State—after the assassination. He met Crisman through an ad, he says, using Colonel Lowry's cover story for how Lowry met Beckham.

Did Crisman advise him to go to Iowa when he was subpoenaed? No, he says, another lie. He met David Ferrie only once, at the office of G. Wray Gill, a partial truth since Ferrie was there that day Gill sent him to Dallas with the maps and diagrams for Lawrence Howard. His Mission was to feed the poor, he lies, "nothing to do with Cuba." He has never carried money for anyone. He lies so energetically that he cannot remember the name of the church in which he was supposedly ordained. He denies knowing the Reverend Raymond Broshears, then takes the fifth amendment on whether he ever discussed the CIA with Guy Banister.

A dark-faced Richard Burnes listens, furious.

Jim Garrison remains calm. Was he an employee directly or indirectly of the Central Intelligence Agency?

"I worked for Mr. Banister," Tommy says, "and if Mr. Banister worked for the Central Intelligence Agency, then indirectly I worked for them." "Indirectly" is that same term Lawrence Howard had used for Jim Garrison and will later enlist for the HSCA. Beckham is shown photographs of Thornley, Howard and Hall, all of whom he knows. He says he cannot identify them. Jim Garrison asks whether he ever visited the Old Post Office Building in connection with the CIA. "I have been to that building, but not for no CIA," Tommy says. He admits he had a post office box at the Old Post Office Building, but only to receive business cards.

Asked if he is aware that Mr. Fred Lee Crisman is with the CIA, Tommy hedges. "I knew he was formerly an intelligence officer, or combat officer or something," he says. He professes not to know that the first person Clay Shaw telephoned after his arrest was "Dr. Crisman."

Good liars lace their fabrications with filaments of the truth. Tommy admits he brought Guy Banister information on Jack Martin, which is true. He mentions a narcotics-laden "German ship" arriving at the Port of New Orleans in 1962, details of which Jack Martin knew. Martin apparently informed the FBI and an item had appeared in the *Times-Picayune* about a German ship en route to Cuba being tied up. I'm sure it was Jack, he says.

He denies that he ever met Lee Harvey Oswald.

"You are lying," Jim Garrison says, finally. "I don't care what your connection with the federal government is, and what Mr. Crisman told you."

"I don't have no connection," Tommy says. "Mr. Garrison, why are you trying to make me out to be a CIA agent?"

"You are lying," Garrison repeats, insisting that after lunch there be "no more lies . . . because the name of that is perjury." But in the afternoon there are more lies, as Tommy denies meeting Clay Shaw, Jack Ruby and Lawrence Howard. A few times he says too much, as when he remarks that Shaw was run out of Italy "for being a front for the CIA," and when he admits to knowing a "Joe Martin," although Garrison has no idea this is an Omaha CIA asset.

A decade later Thomas Edward Beckham will change his answer to every one of these questions.

"Why don't you tell the jury what the information is that's going to knock District Attorney Garrison out of office," Burnes finally demands. Beckham then talks about a French Quarter affidavit exposing Garrison's "intimate affairs" with "a male prostitute." He invents a name, "David Richards," whose real name is "Marcello." He calls "this guy Bertrand" another Garrison sexual partner. His source is Eugene Davis, he claims. He had gone to Wanda's Bar to ask Davis why Garrison had called him. Only that Beckham knew him as an intermediary for Clay Shaw accounts for his invoking Eugene Davis.

Richard Burnes had reached his limit. Burnes had been so skeptical of the charging of Edgar Eugene Bradley that he had inquired about malpractice insurance for public officials. When Numa Bertel rejected an offer from Camille Gravel's law firm in Alexandria, Burnes accepted, with no regrets about leaving the Kennedy case behind.

Garrison was prevented from focusing effectively on Beckham's handler, Fred Lee Crisman, by inept investigative work. Richard E. Sprague insisted that Crisman, like Bradley, was one of the tramps arrested at Dealey Plaza. Bill Turner confused Crisman's stepfather with a sinister contact. Armed with ten $100 bills from Jim Garrison, Jim Rose had blundered into Crisman's Tacoma "advertising agency," obviously enjoying the breaking-in, but accomplishing nothing.

Crisman remained an enigma, a short man with a boxer's nose and scars, a ruddy complexion and a crew-cut. He *was* notorious—for having been on the scene of the 1947 "Maury Island incident" in Washington State involving the supposed sighting of UFOs. Some thought the entire brouhaha was a scam to cover up a Boeing aircraft accident involving radioactive material. Boeing refused to supply Garrison with Crisman's employment records.

Crisman, who, like David Ferrie, had been fired from a high school teaching job, was another right-wing extremist, carrying an ID card from Interpol and two letters from Governor McKeithen praising his work on behalf of the state of Louisiana. His Ph.D. was from "Brantridge Forest School" in England, a degree as phony as David Ferrie's.

Garrison issued a subpoena for Fred Lee Crisman on October 31, 1968. His press release accuses Crisman of having been "engaged in undercover activity for a part of the industrial warfare complex for years." Crisman told reporters that he had been summoned to New Orleans solely because he knew Beckham, whom he denounced as the "banker" for the "free Cubans." There was a conspiracy all right in the assassination, Crisman said, but he had "nothing whatsoever to do with it."

Jim Garrison didn't even attend Crisman's appearance at the grand jury on November 21, 1968. There, Crisman repeated Beckham's lies about their meeting in Washington State, insisting that his first visit to New Orleans was in 1966. He did not know Clay Shaw. He was a writer, an English teacher. No, he did not work for the CIA. Alcock's questioning was halfhearted.

Garrison sought to clarify how the CIA utilized a "bizarre cluster of 'Old Church' evangelical sects" in implementing the assassination. They were "the most natural of safe houses," he thought. You could raise money there without serious inquiry. The Reverend Broshears, Jack Martin, Joe Newbrough, David Ferrie, Beckham, Crisman, and even Ruby's factotum, Curtis Crafard, had been connected to these churches. Jack Martin persuaded an Archbishop Walter M. Propheta of the American Orthodox Catholic Church to write to Jim Garrison, praising Garrison's "real courage," but Garrison was not diverted. He wanted to investigate the Abundant Life Temple near the scene of Officer Tippit's murder.

Some church figures tried to help, like Reverend Thomas A. Fairbanks, who told Garrison that Ferrie and Jack Martin were so close that Martin used Ferrie's credit card. Fairbanks suggested not only that Ferrie had set Oswald up "as a patsy," but that Ferrie had "ordained" William Seymour as an Oswald double.

Crisman, Beckham's "mentor and sponsor," was "an operative at a deep cover level in a long-range clandestine intelligence mission . . . an operative at a supervisory level, a Fagin to the Artful Dodger," Garrison believed. Crisman had been "cut out" for the operation at Banister's. The "Old Church" covers used by Beckham and Crisman, Martin and Ferrie, were designed to divert attention. Such churches had been utilized by the O.S.S. during World War II, Garrison discovered.

In March 1968, Garrison hosted the National Convention of District Attorneys. No one from Dallas attended. The recipient of the distinguished service award that year, Bill Cahn of Nassau County, New York, later went to jail on gambling violations. J. Edgar Hoover was to be awarded honorary membership in the National District Attorneys' Association.

At a Wednesday breakfast meeting, Garrison discussed how the federal government had protected David Chandler. *Life* magazine was "performing a vital function for the present administration . . . by withholding the Zapruder film, which showed that President Kennedy was shot from the front." State government, Garrison suggested, was "the last defense in this country against totalitarianism."

The week would culminate in a Saturday night awards banquet with Vice-President Hubert Humphrey as the dinner speaker. But as soon as Humphrey heard that Garrison had criticized Lyndon Johnson for withholding the Zapruder film, he canceled his appearance. Jim Garrison, instead, would address the group. Hoover refused to allow his representative to be in the same room with Jim Garrison so that his award had to be presented on Friday afternoon when Garrison would not be present.

The organizing committee faced a dilemma: What would Garrison say in his speech? They consulted Charlie Ward, who was chairman of the convention committee.

"The last thing I'm going to do is tell Jim Garrison what he can say," Ward said. "I would be wasting my time." Garrison did agree to meet with the committee at two in the afternoon on the day of the banquet. There Bill Raggio, DA of Reno, Nevada, told him he was not to attack either the president or federal judges, and he must not discuss the Kennedy assassination at all.

"Gentlemen, if that's all that's on your minds," Garrison said, "I can put you at ease. I'm not only going to speak about it, but I'm going to speak about it at length. What would you think the delegates would like to hear me talk about—the French and Spanish influence on contemporary New Orleans architecture?" He admitted he planned to "go into the activities of Lyndon Johnson in concealing vital evidence concerning the murder of John F. Kennedy."

When Raggio requested an advance written copy of Garrison's remarks, Garrison laughed. When Raggio said, "there will be no speech by you tonight," Garrison told him not to worry because he was not going to talk at the banquet. . . . Garrison paused. "Because there will be no banquet."

Instead there would be a dance. Garrison shipped the banquet food to local orphanages: St. Elizabeth's, St. Vincent's, and the Protestant Children's Home. He commandeered the banquet room, and no other hotel would cross the Orleans Parish district attorney by providing another. Among those that night in New Orleans who went to bed "without their supper," as one newspaper put it, was G. Robert Blakey, now an adviser to the President's Commission on Law Enforcement.

Jim Garrison offered a parting word to his colleagues, each of whom had paid eight dollars for the dinner.

"If you want the money for your tickets back," Garrison said, "you can sue me in federal court!"

Later, on television, Garrison said that Mr. Raggio should consider the lost $3,000 his fee for the lesson in free speech. Only one district attorney attended the dance, Charlie Marlin Moylan, who dubbed the incident the "last supper." As a swing band played "You're the Cream in My Coffee," Jim Garrison took the microphone and sang. Departing, he confiscated the official flag of the district attorneys.

"Jim, you can't do that," Liz protested.

"I just did," he said.

As the investigation wound down, the Shaw defense sought refuge in the friendly federal courts. "How many witnesses have you intimidated?" William Wegmann dared to ask Moo Moo Sciambra on the stand.

Tom Bethell had been assigned to compile a list of potential prosecution witnesses for the Shaw trial. It began with Perry Russo and Vernon Bundy, and included Charles Spiesel and Francis Martello. Bethell asked a volunteer named Jim Brown to write up everything that went on in the office.

On June 6th, 1968, Tom Bethell ran into Shaw lawyer Salvatore

Panzeca in the hallway of the federal courthouse. Bethell confided to Panzeca that he had just written a memorandum of the list of trial witnesses, a list the prosecution was then under no legal obligation to share with the defense. Driving off in Panzeca's car, Bethell blurted out the names of the prosecution witnesses while Panzeca spoke them back aloud, memorizing. By the end of the day, Panzeca had a copy of Bethell's memo in his clutches. Meeting with Bethell two days later at the Cafe du Monde, Panzeca remarked that the Shaw defense would now investigate each of the witnesses named in the memo.

It wasn't until January 1969 that Garrison's staff surmised that someone in the office had provided the Shaw defense team with a list of their witnesses. Bethell feared Garrison's staff might suspect him and subject him to a polygraph. He asked Panzeca's advice.

You should express your indignation and refuse, Panzeca said. And, by the way, was the prosecution planning to use Fred Leemans? By now Leemans had admitted that he had lied for Walter Sheridan.

On January 13th, a weeping Tom Bethell confessed to Lou Ivon. Immune to the tears, Ivon inquired where Bethell got the extra copy of the trial memo. When Panzeca had driven him back to the courthouse, he had made the copy, Bethell admitted.

Five days later, David Chandler invited Bethell to a party, his official welcome to the Shaw team. Was Perry Russo going to be the main witness for the state? Chandler wanted to know.

With fewer leads materializing, in the hope of obtaining more evidence, Jim Garrison was not averse to making contact with foreign intelligence agencies. William Turner sent Jim Rose to the Soviet embassy in Mexico City to ask for information about the Kennedy assassination. Rose was told that a "package would arrive with everything we know." During that trip, ever flirtatious, Rose picked up two women. He told them that in the current *Newsweek* they could read the name of the person who financed the assassination: the article was about Texas millionaire Gordon McClendon.

A month later, in March of 1968, Jim Garrison had in his possession a manuscript called *The Plot,* which he renamed *Farewell America.* It came from the NKVD, Boxley declared. *Farewell America* was a ragtag jumble of disinformation designed for no purpose other than to distract Jim Garrison from naming the CIA as his chief suspect. "The upper sphere of the CIA were certainly not informed of the preparations for the assassination," pseudonymous author "James Hepburn" writes. Accepting that there had been a conspiracy, *Farewell America* invokes a kitchen sink of sponsors, including even "agency rogue elements," which "might" have had a hand.

But the real sponsor was South Texas oil interests and the Hunt family. The Hemming litany of false sponsors appears: Drennan, Wheat and Gale, Minutemen and Birchites. *Farewell America* damns John F. Kennedy as a "socialist," and blames his aide Kenny O'Donnell for not taking precautions to protect him. Jackie is indicted for snobbery and unseemly curtsying to the Duke of Edinburgh on the day of her husband's funeral, while the Duke eyes her with disdain. Like Clay Shaw, "Hepburn" affects admiration for Woodrow Wilson.

Farewell America, which contained no footnotes, was so shoddy that no American publisher would touch it. Although Garrison requested "Hepburn's" source notes, no documentation would ever be forthcoming. The next volume would name the murderer, "Frontiers Publishing" promised. Garrison sent the greenest of his California volunteers to Geneva in pursuit of the notes, but Stephen Jaffe returned empty-handed. The author, Herve Lamarre, turned out to be not a KGB operative, but a scion of French intelligence doing the CIA a favor.

Lamarre offered Jaffe a share of the profits should he find an American publisher for *Farewell America*, which would have made Jaffe a Garrison volunteer accomplishing the Agency's disinformational work. For a film version, a Robert Kennedy acolyte named Richard Lubic put a copy of the Zapruder film into Lamarre's hands. Bobby had so compromised himself that he was once again directly helping the CIA cover up the death of his brother. Jaffe's youth was met by Harold Weisberg's aging foolishness: Weisberg now showed H. L. Hunt's man Paul Rothermel documents Garrison had entrusted to him. Rothermel then sent them off at once to J. Gordon Shanklin, SAC in Dallas, and to Congressman Earle Cabell. Carbons went to the CIA.

Jim Garrison, at this late stage of his investigation, wanted to believe that *Farewell America* was genuine, that an intelligence agency of a foreign country had been "extremely cooperative," and, having "penetrated the assassination operation," had provided valuable information. In fact, *Farewell* America was a fraud. When the film version portrayed Edgar Eugene Bradley as one of the tramps, something Garrison now doubted, he at last stepped back and repudiated it. The film echoes Boxley in blaming J. Edgar Hoover for the assassination. As one of the more sober California volunteers realized, the film of *Farewell America* was nothing more than "a sophisticated piece of anti-Garrison propaganda."

Boxley's final attempt to derail Jim Garrison's investigation was his identifying the man who fired the fatal shot on the grassy knoll as Robert Lee Perrin, a Ruby gun runner whose wife, Nancy, had been a bartender at the Carousel Club. Nancy Perrin Rich had told the Warren Commission that she and her husband had been involved in exfiltrating Cubans and infiltrating Enfield rifles to Cuba; the group's paymaster was Jack Ruby. Officer Tippit had been the first person she contacted when she moved to Dallas in 1961. Boxley then claimed that Tippit had been killed because he knew that Perrin was one of the assassins. He had "solved the case," Boxley said.

The trouble was that Perrin had died in New Orleans on August 28, 1962. Boxley had an answer for that. Perrin had not died at all, he claimed; the body found belonged to an itinerant Venezuelan sailor. Helping Boxley with this scenario, which would have destroyed Garrison's investigation, was a *Confidential* magazine writer named Joel Palmer.

Boxley termed Edgar Eugene Bradley "the most important CIA executioner." He declared that he had located a family who lived in Perrin's building and connected Bradley to Perrin. Boxley also named a "Bertram Norwood Youngblood" as a witness who had met Perrin, using the pseudonym Jack Starr, a month after Perrin's purported death, not realizing that the name "Youngblood" belonged to a Dealey Plaza witness, no less than to Rose Cheramie. The Perrins had first planned to assassinate Kennedy at the Nashville wharf, Boxley and Palmer insisted.

Lou Ivon had lost his patience. Ivon demanded that Boxley must go. When Garrison persisted in defending him, and permitted him to remain with the office, Ivon "quit." In Oliver Stone's *JFK*, Ivon makes the first move and returns to Tulane and Broad. In real life, Jim Garrison admitted his mistake, and knowing that he could not continue without Ivon, *he* telephoned. "Come back," he said. Louie rested for a few days, and then returned.

Together with Moo Moo Sciambra, Lou Ivon reinvestigated the Perrin lead, only to discover that Perrin's landlord Kruschevski denied everything Boxley had claimed: he had not said Perrin was fifty years old, as Boxley claimed, a necessary distortion because there was a fourteen-year difference between Perrin and the "Jack Starr" he supposedly became. He had not seen a man wearing a reddish brown wig, as Boxley had attempted to throw David Ferrie into the mix. A neighbor named Mason Kittess told Sciambra and Ivon that it was Boxley who had identified Bradley, and told him that Bradley had been involved: Kittess had never identified a photograph of Bradley. Boxley had shown him the tramp photograph, himself insisting that it pictured Edgar Eugene Bradley.

Moo Moo and Louie saved Jim Garrison from issuing an arrest warrant for the dead Perrin. Palmer then retaliated by claiming that Garrison planned further charges against Bradley, which was not true. Now Ivon compiled his evidence against Boxley: Boxley had falsely accused Barbara Reid of being an "agent." He was inexplicably secretive, so that once, riding with Ivon, he hid his face as a car passed theirs. Boxley's role in the charging of Bradley had been unconscionable. There was a common denominator to Boxley's work: his fervent effort to exonerate the CIA.

The entire California contingent with which Boxley had worked now left the investigation. Steve Burton mailed back his credentials, admitting that "certain of the actions of my colleagues" had "dramatized what inexperience can do to embarrass the investigation." He was referring to Jaffe. "Who was Clay Shaw?" Jim Rose would say years later, as if that name were entirely irrelevant to what he was doing for Jim Garrison. On November 25th, Bill Turner sent in his final memo. Invoking the name of H. L. Hunt, he had come up with a new witness, "Elmer Robert Hyde." He had a new fact, too: there were two hundred French agents at Dealey Plaza.

"Flak!" Garrison wrote onto Turner's memo. "We're close to Berlin. Not worth follow-up!" On December 9, with the encouragement of his friend, Philadelphia lawyer Vincent Salandria, Garrison finally fired Boxley, accusing him of being "an operative of the Central Intelligence Agency." Jimmy Alcock had become tight-lipped "with an edge of bitterness"; both he and Ivon believed it would have been better not to go public about Boxley.

On the advice of William Turner, Boxley fled New Orleans. On December 27th, Boxley telephoned Dr. Stephen Aldrich at the CIA, offering information, and on the next day he called again. The CIA, noting that Boxley had reapplied for employment not only in February, but also in March of 1967, enlisted the FBI to visit Boxley and "request elucidation," adding they were "prepared to listen." CIA had been "keeping an eye on him."

Boxley drove to Texas and requested a job with the Hunt organization and Paul Rothermel. Rothermel was to call Jim Garrison "a most vindictive left-winger," and claim that with Boxley's help he had all along been attempting to "guide" Jim Garrison's investigation. Boxley now told Rothermel *Jim Garrison* believed Edgar Eugene Bradley lived across the street from Robert Perrin! It was Garrison who believed that Perrin was involved in a conspiracy with Clay

Shaw! Boxley offered to distribute the specious *Farewell America*. William Turner took on that role, even arranging for a 2002 reissue of the fraudulent book.

In the midst of all this intrigue, Jim Garrison was accused of being connected with a bankrupt, shady finance organization called Louisiana Loan and Thrift. When they first incorporated, he had considered borrowing money to buy stock. Two days later he had changed his mind. Even the auditors had to admit, despite Aaron Kohn's rumors: Jim Garrison "was not a stockholder."

Agents of the Intelligence Division of the IRS had appeared in New Orleans, threatening Garrison with "criminal prosecution." They visited Security Homestead, which held the mortgage on his house. "I only owe $50,000," Garrison said with his customary sardonic irony. Refusing the IRS permission to go through his papers ("I'm not going to cooperate with the federal government," he said), he told the press that this IRS effort was connected with his investigation. "It never occurred to them," Garrison added, "that a state would investigate the assassination."

In preparation for the Shaw trial, Garrison went into federal court in Washington, DC and requested forty-five photographs and twenty-four X-rays taken before and during John F. Kennedy's autopsy. The government stalled. Judge Charles Halleck ruled that Garrison had first to produce evidence that the president was fired upon from two directions. "When is that circus in New Orleans going to end so that the real carnival [Mardi Gras] can begin?" Halleck was to say of the Shaw trial. The effort to obtain the medical evidence dragged on after the Shaw trial had begun.

"You will see," Garrison wrote Halleck on February 3, 1969, responding to the government's request for a copy of his opening statement, with irony dripping from his pen, "that a substantial part of our case rests upon the actual shooting of President Kennedy in Dealey Plaza." It would not matter: the photographs that revealed a gaping exit wound in the rear of Kennedy's skull, to the dismay of the photographers who took those pictures, had long since disappeared from the medical "evidence."

The first half of *State of Louisiana v. Clay* Shaw would be devoted to proving that a conspiracy had in fact occurred at Dealey Plaza. Then Clay Shaw's involvement had to be demonstrated. At the heart of Garrison's dilemma was that he was connecting Clay Shaw to Oswald, not because Oswald had been the shooter of

President Kennedy, but because he had been set up to be. Nor would Garrison be able to prove that Shaw had originated the plan to manipulate Oswald into assuming the blame for the murder. Yet Shaw was guilty, nonetheless, of the federal crime of treason. "Misprision of treason" includes harboring knowledge of an act of treason or a treasonable plot.

The choice of witnesses reflected the inadequacy of Garrison's tiny, overburdened staff. In early January of 1969, a Garrison assistant telephoned Dr. Robert N. McClelland, a surgeon who had attended John F. Kennedy at Parkland Hospital. "We want you to testify," he said, adding, "If you won't, we'll subpoena you." Dr. McClelland, who believed that his loyalty was to history and not to power, was taken aback. He was entirely willing to testify. "I wonder why you didn't call me much earlier," he said.

The assistant wanted to know first if Dr. McClelland would confirm the handwritten note he had written, stating that there was "a gunshot wound of the left temple." They planned, Dr. McClelland surmised, to suggest that there had been a gunman in the storm sewer on the left side of the motorcade. "No, I would not testify to that," McClelland said, "I made a mistake." He had only written that line about the wound to the left temple because Dr. Jenkins had told him so. So drenched with blood had the head been that no one could have observed such a bullet wound.

The voice of Garrison's assistant rose three octaves. "What!" he sputtered. Abruptly, he concluded the conversation. Had he talked with Dr. McClelland a moment longer, he would have learned that from his examination of the head, McClelland believed that the fatal shot had come from behind the picket fence at the grassy knoll, in front of the motorcade and not from the Texas School Book Depository.

Dr. McClelland, positioned behind the head as he assisted in the tracheotomy, holding the retractor and leaning over the president's head, had observed that the back of the president's head had been blown out, and he had been willing to so testify. Viewing the Zapruder film later confirmed Dr. McClelland in his conviction. Someone had hit the president from behind first, so that he was leaning slightly forward before his head exploded and he was thrown violently back against the seat of the car.

In 1988, at the National Archives, Dr. McClelland saw an X-ray with the right orbit injured, although, as he remembered, President Kennedy's eyes and face had not been injured. It was either a fake or mixed up with someone else's X-ray. He also discovered a faked photograph: you could see the thumb and forefinger of a gloved hand—it belonged to Dr. J. Thornton Boswell—pulling the flap of the scalp over the wound together and forward, and making it seem as if the back of the head was intact. He had seen no flap of scalp as, for ten or twelve minutes, Dr. McClelland had stood at the head of the gurney, looking down, deep into the head wound.

So the prosecution lost its best medical witness.

Richard Case Nagell could have identified both Oswald and Clay Shaw as CIA agents. But Nagell refused to name the government organization he had worked for in 1963. He would not name the CIA in court. Garrison concluded that this reticence would have led the defense to eviscerate him as a witness. Nagell was "the most important witness there is," Garrison believed, "absolutely genuine." Finally, Nagell was of no use to him.

Nagell's recalcitrance, his fear that the CIA might try to "eliminate him," prevented the prosecution from connecting Shaw to the CIA. "Whoever's taking care of him can't be too unhappy with him," Garrison later told Dick Russell. He acknowledged that nothing Nagell said "turned out to be untrue."

There was a plethora of witnesses who would not come forward: Alfred Moran, who had seen Shaw sign his name as "Bertrand," was one. Another was Herbert Wagner, who had witnessed Clay Shaw co-signing that loan for David Ferrie. Woodrow Hardy had seen Shaw, Ferrie, and Oswald deep in conversation at Shaw's house, but he lived in fear. Banister cohort Vernon Gerdes, who had seen Oswald and Shaw together, worked for the Shaw defense. Fred Leemans had contradicted himself. Juan Valdes had melted into the night.

William Turner had not included Thomas Breitner's claim that Shaw had been introduced to him as "Bertrand" in California in his first report of their interview. Garrison was dubious about using Breitner, as he was about "Donald P. Norton," who was willing to testify. There was no hope of involving Thomas Edward Beckham, Fred Lee Crisman, Lawrence Howard, Loran Hall, Jack Martin or A. Roswell Thompson. Fear that their homosexuality might become public prevented David Logan and Dr. Lief's patient from coming forward. Even Eugene Davis would not risk public exposure.

Garrison then further limited himself by deciding not to call any witness who had been in trouble with the law. This ruled out Jules Ricco Kimble, who might have testified that he flew with Shaw and Ferrie to Montreal; it ruled out Edward Whalen, who said "Bertrand" (Shaw) had tried to hire him to murder Jim Garrison. Serving time for bank robbery, Edward J. Girnus had said he saw Ferrie and

Shaw together and produced a flight plan for April 8, 1963, in which the pilot, named Ferrie, was accompanied by "Hidell" and "Lambert," a Shaw look-alike. He, too, was ruled out. The Reverend Broshears had been consigned by federal courts to an institution.

Jim Hicks, a surveyor and Navy veteran, had told the Orleans Parish grand jury that he could place shots as originating from the grassy knoll. He described consistently how he had seen Kennedy's head explode. Since his trip to New Orleans, things had not gone well for Hicks. He had been incarcerated at Western State Mental Hospital at Fort Supply, Oklahoma. He was residing now at the Garfield County jail for passing bad checks.

Hicks bragged that he would be Garrison's first or second witness; after all, he had seen a man by the name of Clay Bertrand, who looked just like Clay Shaw, at Dealey Plaza. Hicks asked Jim Garrison to liberate him from jail so he could come testify at the Shaw trial. He would not be needed, Garrison replied.

Dago Garner, who had met Shaw through Jack Ruby, had embroidered so much, Garrison thought, that it was "like flying at night with no lights." Mark Lane lobbied hard that Charles Spiesel, who believed everyone had a "double," was too eccentric, too great a risk. Forget Spiesel, use Dago Garner, Lane advised. Garner, at least, knew Shaw had one nipple.

"With my luck, Shaw will drop his pants and he'll have three testicles," Garrison joked.

Garrison considered calling Julia Ann Mercer, and later thought he "probably made a mistake not calling her." He made her appearance voluntary. "Frozen with fear," as Garrison put it, Mrs. Stinson did not rise to the challenge of citizenship. Another witness who could testify to a conspiracy was William Walter, but the FBI sealed his lips. Moo Moo's inefficiency cost Garrison two Clinton-Jackson witnesses, Gladys Palmer and Dr. Frank Silva.

Violence erased some of Garrison's potential witnesses. Andrew Dunn had died in a Clinton jail. Dallas policeman Buddy Walthers, who had agreed to testify for Jim Garrison, was murdered before he could describe the fourth bullet he found that ruled out Oswald as the lone shooter.

The Reverend Clyde Johnson, who could place Shaw, Oswald and Ruby together at the Capitol House Hotel, termed himself "the ace-in-the-hole" in Jim Garrison's case. To protect Johnson, Garrison put him up at a women's dormitory at Southeastern Louisiana College at Hammond. On the day before he was scheduled to testify, Clyde Johnson was beaten up so badly he had to be hospitalized. A few months later, he was shot to death.

Governor John Connally, who had always insisted that one bullet did not strike both him and President Kennedy, again ruling out Oswald as the sole shooter, traveled to New Orleans with his wife.

"The CIA must have gotten to him. He wouldn't have come unless the CIA had gotten to him," Garrison said. Mortified, William Alford drove out to the airport to inform Connally that he would not be needed after all. But even Hugh Aynesworth believed Connally's animosity toward Jim Garrison disqualified him as a state witness.

Despite their possessing the prosecution witness list, the Shaw defense was worried. Those they feared the most were Raymond Cummings, the Dallas cab driver who had driven Oswald and Ferrie to the Carousel Club; Dago Garner; the ubiquitous Emilio Santana; and former O.S.S. officer, now a Montreal banker, Major L. M. Bloomfield, who could talk about Shaw's relationship to the Centro Mondiale Commerciale, with whom he shared board membership. By January 30th, through Aynesworth, the Shaw team was aware that Jim Garrison knew about Charles Spiesel's peculiarities.

Shaw's lawyers wanted to call Richard N. Billings. He had been "unable to make a final determination of Russo's credibility," Billings said. He considered Perry Russo "a fairly respectable witness," and believed "elements of his story."

The best direct evidence Garrison had that Shaw knew he was participating in the murder of President Kennedy was in Perry Russo's testimony. Although his behavior did not have to be criminal, according to Louisiana conspiracy law, Shaw had to have performed an overt act to further the criminal agreement. One of his coconspirators had to be involved, while the state also had to demonstrate that Clay Shaw knew the general scope and aims of the conspiracy. The jury would have to believe Perry Russo's account of the gathering at Ferrie's apartment, where "Leon Oswald" had been present, and the assassination discussed.

"I wasn't ready," Garrison would reflect later. "But I had to go." He had believed that the government would never "let it go to trial." They'll kill me first, he told Bill Alford. Now the trial was upon him.

STATE OF LOUISIANA
V. CLAY SHAW

19

I will not be able to produce any bank presidents. I will not be able to present any presidents of Chambers of Commerce. I will not be able to produce any newspaper publishers as witnesses. Because there were no people like that around any of the meetings that were taking place.

—Jim Garrison

T HE OBSTACLES THRUST INTO Jim Garrison's path as he attempted to expose the conspiracy to assassinate President Kennedy had been murderous, sinister and unrelenting. They ranged from the untimely death of David Ferrie and the illegal efforts of Walter Sheridan to the lies published by the CIA's media assets who had attached themselves to the Shaw defense team. They included the ambush of a key witness, Clyde Johnson, and the discrediting of another key witness, Perry Russo.

Garrison was also concerned that, to a jury, talking about Shaw's work for the CIA would be like "talking about UFOs." Later, Garrison would compare himself to Santiago, the aged fisherman in Ernest Hemingway's *The Old Man and the Sea.* Garrison, too, had caught a "monster fish." But by the time he reached shore, went to trial, that prize specimen had "long since been picked apart by sharks." It was among his most apt conceits.

Sensitive to accusations that he had been in search of personal publicity all along, Garrison chose not to prosecute the Shaw case himself, entrusting Jimmy Alcock and Al Oser with that task. Hong Kong flu had given way to viral encephalitis, and Garrison was not well. His back was so painful that he could stand for only a few hours a day. Mort Sahl and Mark Lane appeared in his bedroom one morning only for Garrison to haul himself out of bed and crawl across the room on his hands and knees. "Gentlemen," Garrison said, as he passed them on his way to the bathroom, "you are looking at one of the most powerful men in the state of Louisiana!"

Garrison made the opening statement, defining the Louisiana conspiracy statute. He outlined a series of overt acts, of which he needed only one to convict Clay Shaw. "Oswald" shooting at the president was an overt act, but Garrison did not state that Lee Harvey Oswald fired a rifle at Dealey Plaza. He had long been convinced from the paraffin test and other evidence that Oswald was not a shooter.

Nor did he insist that the "Leon Oswald" at Ferrie's was Oswald himself. That "Leon" was a "slightly erroneous game card," he was to say. Yet the mention of any "Oswald" at all demonstrated foreknowledge and participation in the conspiracy, since history had connected an "Oswald" to the assassination, whether he was the patsy Oswald himself said he was, or a killer. Anyone associated with someone named "Oswald" was a coconspirator.

In his opening statement, F. Irvin Dymond declared that Clay Shaw never knew David Ferrie or Lee Harvey Oswald. It was so blatant a falsehood that it seemed from the start as if Shaw had suborned perjury from his own lawyer. James Phelan had laid the groundwork for Dymond's case with his false contention that Perry Russo had not mentioned Shaw at his first meeting with Moo Moo Sciambra. To defend Shaw, Dymond required the falsehood that Shaw's presence at Ferrie's gathering was a lie suggested to Perry Russo under sodium pentothal.

The Clinton witnesses, black and white, were put on first. None could be shaken in their certainty that they had witnessed Shaw, Ferrie and Oswald together. John Manchester "put it all together," James Kirkwood was to write, but it was ludicrous that Corrie Collins would have participated in a Manchester-engineered plot. Nor did either Garrison or Alcock prepare these witnesses in advance, as the Shaw lawyers charged. To the dismay of barber Lea McGehee, they had not been prepared at all.

Unable to shake a feisty Manchester, Dymond resorted to civil rights baiting: Hadn't Manchester tried "everything within your power" to keep blacks from "getting registered?" Discrepancies between the earlier interviews with the Clinton witnesses and their trial testimony were negligible: Oswald's pants were never hospital whites. Shaw may or may not have put on a hat.

With the African-American witnesses, Dymond played to what he assumed would be the lower-middle-class jury's racism, the two black jurors notwithstanding.

"This is your testimony under oath?" Dymond demanded belligerently of Corrie Collins, as he would of no white witness.

"Beg your pardon?" Collins said. Boos and hisses issued from the audience at Dymond's palpable display of disrespect. Even Judge Haggerty was offended.

"You don't have to repeat that, Mr. Dymond. It is obvious he took the oath," Haggerty said.

"I am trying to make sure he realizes it, Judge," Dymond replied brazenly. "I am trying to find out whether he had forgotten it."

"No, I haven't forgotten it," Corrie Collins said.

A note from his employer, the U.S. Postal Service, demanded that Collins report for work early on Saturday morning, even as they knew he had been testifying in New Orleans. Corrie Collins never bothered to inform Jim Garrison that he had been fired for testifying at the Shaw trial. Lea McGehee returned home to Jackson to discover a man trespassing on his property. Arrested by deputies Hardy Travis and Alvin Doucet, the man telephoned the International Trade Mart in New Orleans.

"Our main case was the perjury case," Garrison said later, acknowledging that the prosecution's inability to connect Shaw's trip to Clinton and Jackson in the company of Oswald and Ferrie with the assassination rendered that evidence only partially effective. Richard Popkin, more sanguine, considered Shaw's appearance in Clinton and Jackson "the one real piece of linkage" with the assassination. The other was the identification of Shaw as Clay Bertrand.

That Shaw was less than open with his lawyers is reflected in an advertisement Wegmann and Dymond placed that week: "Will the person who signed the name 'Clay Bertrand' in the guest register of the Eastern Airlines Lounge, Moisant Airport, please call! . . ." Or perhaps the advertisement was a desperate New Orleans lawyer's publicity stunt.

On the stand, Vernon Bundy, despite his understandable unwillingness to acknowledge that he had been convicted of stealing from a cigarette machine, repeated how he had observed Oswald and Shaw at the sea wall. Bundy requested that Shaw walk to the rear of the courtroom. Then Bundy sat down in Shaw's chair and asked Shaw to approach him.

"I watched his foot the way it twisted," Bundy said. "That is the foot that was twisted that day." He denied he had made any admissions in Parish Prison to Miguel Torres or "John the Baptist." Dymond's attempt to impugn Bundy as a narcotics fiend went nowhere.

On the matter of Charles Spiesel's eccentricities—fingerprinting his daughter and his theory that everyone had a double—the prosecution played Russian roulette, not fully registering the harm Tom Bethell's theft of the witness list had done. On direct examination, Spiesel did well, as he described a conversation in June 1963 between Shaw and Ferrie regarding whether the assassin could be flown away from the assassination safely. Spiesel revealed that Shaw, moving as if he believed he was graced with impunity, spoke openly about the murder of President Kennedy.

At a party at 906 Esplanade, a house that had been owned by Clay Shaw only the previous month, next door to an identical house, 908 Esplanade, still owned by Shaw, Spiesel heard talk of a "high-powered rifle with a telescopic sight." Shaw and his friend Arthur J. Bidderson had apartments at 906. If Spiesel did not identify the exact building, he was close.

The Shaw defense had hired Walter R. Holloway, a former FBI agent, to investigate Spiesel. "They've even contacted our boy in New York, Charles Spiesel," Alcock had told Bethell when the jig was up. On January 30th, Aynesworth wrote to Wegmann: "Garrison knows that you know about Spiesel and that we have tried to contact him."

The CIA had already provided the Shaw defense with information about Spiesel's furrier father, Boris, and had produced a letter from Spiesel to John McCone, dated October 4, 1962, complaining about how he had been "hypnotized continuously" and "harassed" by police officers. Aaron Kohn provided a 1965 letter from Spiesel, and stated Spiesel was "emotionally disturbed." Fearing that Spiesel might be the "Russo of the trial," the Shaw defense had sought ammunition to undermine this witness—and found it. Panzeca would later claim that the Shaw defense learned the truth about Spiesel only "four minutes" before cross-examination, but the evidence is otherwise. "The Jack O'Diamonds was prepared for him," Jack Dempsey says.

Under cross-examination, Dymond elicited Spiesel's history of lawsuits charging his enemies with using disguises. He exposed how Spiesel viewed the New York police as enemies who hypnotized him and harassed him. And he forced Spiesel to admit that when his daughter returned home from LSU at the end of a semester, he fingerprinted her to be certain this was the same girl he had sent off to college.

At that moment, coming on February 8, 1969, he saw his case flying out the window, "like a Tom turkey," and reasonable doubt flying in, Jim Garrison said later. William Alford concluded that Spiesel had been "one of those plants" placed to destroy Garrison's case, even as Spiesel's knowledge of Shaw's real estate had been established to lure Garrison into accepting him as a witness. Richard Popkin viewed Spiesel as a "set-up." Spiesel was, Garrison would conclude, "a pleasant-mannered bomb unloaded on us for the trial by the Company." For the government, "destroying an old-fashioned state jury trial was like shooting a fish in a barrel with a shotgun."

As Perry Russo prepared to take the stand two days later, the Shaw defense visited his father to ask whether Perry was receiving psychiatric treatment.

"Bunk!" Frank Russo said. Nor had he ever known his son to lie. The Shaw team subpoenaed Russo senior, then chose not to call him.

On the stand, Russo quoted the talk at Ferrie's gathering of "three-sided triangulation," of two shooters escaping and one being "captured as a scapegoat or a patsy for the other two." He told how Shaw and Ferrie had outlined their alibis, and swore that during Sciambra's first visit, he had identified not only photographs of Shaw, but of Ferrie, Oswald, Arcacha and Santana. Sciambra's memo of his Saturday meeting with Russo had omitted other items, such as their discussion of who would replace Fidel Castro, Che Guevara or Raoul Castro? He had seen "Clem Bertrand" wearing a hat, Russo added.

In an exhausting cross-examination that runs to hundreds of pages, Dymond focused on undermining the identification of "Leon Oswald" as the "real Oswald," even as the name itself indicts Shaw. Russo understood that it didn't matter whether "Leon" was "the Oswald that showed up in Dallas," or was someone posing as Lee Harvey Oswald who "wanted to be remembered in that place at a certain time."

Having gotten nowhere in shaking Russo, on the second day of his cross-examination, Dymond tried to threaten the witness by suggesting that if he was present during the talk of killing John F. Kennedy, and yet had not stated his disagreement with the plan, he himself was implicated in the murder of the president. Alcock objected.

"This is the first time I have ever been accused of badgering a witness," Dymond said.

"You used the word," Alcock said.

Sciambra testified that he had burned his notes of his first meeting with Russo because of the "tremendous problems" the office had with leaks; he cited the example of "a person who works for a national news magazine," referring to Hugh Aynesworth. He had reported what Russo had told him on February 25th "to the best of my ability," Sciambra said. "That would make me a sloppy memorandum writer, but it doesn't make me a prostitute."

The news reporting of the trial was distorted. Martin Waldron at the *New York Times* added the word "torture" to Spiesel's description of how his enemies had harassed him. Waldron wrote that Bundy had "yawned" on the stand; he had not. Waldron altered Russo's term "bull session" to "it was a bull session and not serious," the last three words entirely Waldron's invention.

Midway through the trial, to prove that there had been more than one shooter, and hence a conspiracy, the state showed Abraham Zapruder's home movie of the assassination. It was the first time the film had been screened in a public forum. Zapruder himself testified how he had witnessed Kennedy being shot in the head from the front, his brains splashing backward out of his head. Then the jury watched, spellbound. Smoking in the darkness, Shaw rose from his seat clutching his cigarette, and stared. The film was screened six times in two days, while Garrison had one hundred copies made and distributed to universities.

"They can run it a hundred times if they want to," Judge Haggerty replied to Dymond's objection. James Phelan attempted to spin away the reality everyone in the courtroom had observed. Kennedy had experienced a "gas expulsion backwards," Phelan said. But bona fide members of the press were stunned. The state's Dealey Plaza witnesses, like Mrs. E. C. Walton, who heard not only four shots, but shots coming from the "front right," were persuasive.

Alcock hoped to connect Clay Shaw to the events in Dallas not only through Russo and Spiesel, but also to his identity as "Clay Bertrand," the man who had telephoned Dean Andrews the day after the assassination on Oswald's behalf. He wanted Big Regis to testify to the FBI's search for Clay Bertrand even before Dean Andrews called them. Now serving the Shaw defense, Harry Connick, an assistant U.S. attorney, advised Big Regis. The jury was excused.

Had he been seeking Clay Bertrand in connection with his investigation of the assassination before he talked to Dean Andrews? Alcock asked.

"I was," Big Regis admitted. This meant that the FBI knew that Clay Shaw was connected to the assassination independently of Bertrand's call to Andrews. Obviously honoring a prearranged agreement, Alcock stopped there. He did not ask why or under what circumstances the FBI had learned about Shaw's involvement. Irvin

Dymond stood silent. Out of the hearing of the jury, the state was vindicated in its prosecution of Clay Shaw, in its contention that Clay Shaw had been involved in the planning of the assassination.

Pittsburgh forensic pathologist Cyril Wecht had testified in Washington for Garrison in his unsuccessful attempt to dislodge the X-rays and autopsy photographs from the government—and the uncooperative Kennedy family. Wecht declined to appear at the Shaw trial. Wecht was uneasy about speaking only with the Zapruder film as evidence. Dr. John Nichols of Kansas City did agree, and became at once the subject of a full-scale CIA counter intelligence investigation. Nichols had, in fact, been one of the CIA's own; in 1957 he had been approved by the Domestic Contact Service, to whom he had reported as recently as 1964. CIA noted now that he had "flunked out" of West Virginia University.

If Garrison's case was lost when Charles Spiesel confided that he fingerprinted his daughter, it was now lost a second time. For a year the CIA had worried about that booking card filled out by officer Aloysius Habighorst in which Shaw admitted to the alias "Clay Bertrand." From the CIA field office, Hunter Leake had solicited suggestions from Washington on what to do about Shaw's admission. The trace memo does not reveal what those suggestions were.

Many CIA records pertaining to Oswald and Shaw have disappeared. According to a Louisiana history professor, Michael Kurtz, Hunter Leake admitted to him that after the assassination he had destroyed many of the field office's files on Lee Harvey Oswald. The remaining Oswald documents Leake loaded "to the brim" onto a truck. Then he personally drove the Oswald files to CIA headquarters in Langley, Virginia. These files contained many references to PERMINDEX, once more linking Oswald to Shaw, and both to the CIA.

That the New Orleans field office of the CIA kept Oswald files there is no doubt. Chester Vigurie, that CIA file clerk who reported that the CIA had "target files," told the HSCA in 1977 as well that he had had occasion to check the CIA file of Oswald in the late sixties, only to discover that it had been retyped some time after 1968; he knew this because "some time in 1968 the CIA began using a particular kind of 'type' to print up their file reports." Oswald's file was printed with this new type. Vigurie's suggestion was that the HSCA determine "what happened to the earlier files pertaining to Oswald."

Now came what Garrison would call "the Haggerty bomb," which "tore as big a hole in our case—modest enough a venture to begin with—as did Charles Spiesel, our dreamy accountant." With the jury again excused, Lou Ivon swore that he had arrested Clay Shaw and read him his Miranda rights in the presence of his lawyer. Habighorst appeared in dark glasses, shaky from a hit-and-run accident the day before. Inexplicably removed from Mardi Gras duty early, he had been rammed by a truck on his way home.

As Habighorst typed out the booking card, Edward Wegmann had stood at the door at Central Lockup, in keeping with New Orleans police policy. Habighorst had never heard the name "Clay Bertrand" before Shaw's arrest on March 1st. There was "no way for Habighorst to come up with that name on his own," Lou Ivon says.

Desperate, the Shaw defense produced a police sergeant named Jonas Butzman, but Butzman had to admit he had not heard Habighorst's questions and Shaw's answers, and he had not even been present "during the whole time" that Shaw was processed. Captain Curole admitted that Wegmann had never requested permission to enter the Bureau of Identification room, which he would have done had he believed that the law guaranteeing Shaw's Miranda rights necessitated his presence as the booking card was being filled out.

The Shaw defense had developed its strategy on the advice of Edward O'Donnell, ever anxious to sabotage the Garrison case, who said technicians in Central Lockup sometimes completed the fingerprint cards by using information on the arrest register, rather than asking the person arrested himself. Out of this vague generality, the Shaw lawyers now claimed, with no evidence whatsoever, that this was what Habighorst had done.

Habighorst had taken the alias off the field arrest report, Dymond now asserted, although he was unable to produce a single witness who saw Habighorst doing it. Wegmann had to admit that Shaw had been handed the blue copy of the Arrest Register, and it did not include the alias. Shaw himself then took the stand. Had he been asked whether he had an alias?

"I certainly was not," Shaw lied. Did Habighorst consult any other documents while he was typing? Shaw fudged.

"He may well have, I don't know," Shaw said. He referred to his height—six feet four inches tall—although he had to admit that papers piled up on the counter had not obstructed his view of Habighorst at any point.

Alcock went on to argue that Shaw's Miranda rights had not been violated because, as far as Habighorst was concerned, the alias bore no relation to the crime. Yet Judge Haggerty ruled that the booking card could not be admitted because Shaw's Miranda rights had been violated. He should have been warned of his right to remain silent.

"Even if Officer Habighorst is telling the truth. . . ." Haggerty said.

"Your honor!" Alcock said, his face red.

"I do not believe Officer Habighorst. I don't believe Habighorst!" Haggerty sputtered, ruling the booking card inadmissible because Wegmann had not been permitted to be with Shaw during the booking, so violating *Escobedo v. Illinois* as well. The ruling was so capricious that some wondered whether Haggerty was affected by dislike of Habighorst's brother Norbert, a bad cop, who had held back information and was now serving ten years for killing the brother of police superintendent Joseph Scheuering.

Alcock moved for a mistrial, and didn't get it. He filed a writ, only to be denied by the Louisiana Supreme Court. He asked Haggerty to let the jury decide, but Haggerty insisted that Shaw should have been told that the question was detrimental and that he didn't have to answer it.

Years later, when Jim Garrison was a judge himself, he asked his former assistant, Ralph Whalen, to research Haggerty's decision. It was wrong in 1969 and it was wrong in the late 1980s, Whalen said. A later decision, *Rhode Island v. Innis* (1980) did not consider the booking process "interrogation" if what was involved were "words normally attendant to arrest and custody," just as Alcock had argued. It had not been universally known that Shaw was the Bertrand who had telephoned on behalf of Oswald; the incriminating response had to be related directly to the offense for which the person was being booked.

The Bertrand alias was "the product of the imagination of investigating officers," Dymond declared.

"The State rests," Alcock said.

The defense was desultory. Marina Oswald testified she had never heard the name Shaw or "Bertrand," but that Lee was not a Communist. She insisted that on the night he had seen General Walker, he didn't have his rifle with him. Lloyd Cobb admitted that Clay Shaw's job as managing director at the International Trade Mart was an honorary one, even as Gordon Novel points out that Shaw could never have had that position at the International Trade Mart "without having a relationship with the CIA." Shaw had been absent from New Orleans only one day that summer, September 25th. On that day he had to obtain "leases," Cobb said, although the truth was that Cobb had hired a man named James Lawrence, who spent ten weeks between July and October 1963 specifically for the purpose of handling the leases for the new trade mart. Shaw was "a liberal," Cobb insisted.

Dr. Pierre Finck, the only doctor at President Kennedy's autopsy who was a competent forensic pathologist, came to testify for Clay Shaw. Harry Connick briefed him. On the stand, Dr. Finck insisted that the fatal head wound struck the back of Kennedy's head. He attempted to undermine the evidentiary importance of the Zapruder film by insisting that a film was "not the material of choice to determine the direction of the shots." Yet Al Oser forced Finck to admit to so many autopsy irregularities as to render the government's medical evidence of scant value.

Dr. Finck admitted that before they began the autopsy, the doctors were told that Kennedy had been shot from behind, with the clear suggestion that their finding should confirm that fact. They were ordered not to dissect the neck wound, or the track of the back wound. On Robert Kennedy's orders, Dr. Finck had not been allowed to see the X-rays and photographs when he prepared his Warren Commission testimony.

Finck recounted that when Dr. Humes had asked, "Who's in charge here?" the reply came back: an Army General. (Could it have been Air Force General Curtis LeMay? Cyril Wecht wonders.) The autopsy room had been filled with FBI agents, federal military personnel, Secret Service, two Admirals, Galloway and Kinney, and a Brigadier General of the Air Force. The ringmaster was a four star general. "An officer who outranked me," Finck admitted, prevented him from examining Kennedy's back wound, or even looking at the clothing he wore.

Alarm bells rang in Washington. Could Pierre Finck be trusted? Dr. J. Thornton Boswell was put on a plane to New Orleans by the Justice Department "to refute Finck's testimony, if necessary." Boswell, a government man, had convened a medical panel officially chaired by Ramsey Clark to undermine the Garrison case a year before.

An admiral had told him only three shots had been fired, Finck continued. He could not explain the discrepancy between the location of the hole on Kennedy's shirt and the apparent entry wound on the neck. To the question of how one bullet—the so-called magic bullet—could have inflicted all the wounds they said it did, Finck replied, "I don't know." Admiral Galloway had ordered them to put the word "presumably" in the statement "the second wound presumably of entry." Part of the autopsy report was based on a false news account that said Kennedy fell face forward. Then Finck volunteered that the doctors had not removed the organs of the neck, or traced the track of the neck wound because "the [Kennedy] family wanted an examination of the head and chest . . . only."

Oser bore in. "I am asking you why you didn't do this as a pathologist." Finck repeated: "I was told not to, but I don't remember by whom."

"You didn't burn your notes also, did you?" Oser demanded, referring to Dr. Humes' admitting to having burned his. Oser got Dr. Finck to agree that the wound in the back of the neck, purportedly an entry wound, was larger than the "exit wound," the wound in the throat, which defied scientific fact, and alone rendered the official autopsy findings preposterous. Dr. Finck admitted the drawing they used was "incorrect." He admitted that the left side of the brain had not been examined. By the time Oser was done, the entire autopsy had been called into question. Jim Garrison was to consider Al Oser's cross-examination of Dr. Finck among the strongest moments of the state's case.

Returning to Washington, Colonel Finck composed a memo for the record stating that he had gone to New Orleans without a court order or Army orders. He had refused any expert witness fee. In later years, the quintessential Swiss gentleman, Dr. Finck retired to his native land, returning only to testify before the HSCA. Morose, he would not discuss the Kennedy autopsy, except to say he was "very, very unhappy, very frustrated."

"I wish I could talk about it," he told Cyril Wecht.

In the waning days of the Shaw trial, Dean Andrews perjured himself yet again by testifying that Clay Shaw was not "Clay Bertrand." On the grounds of "self-incrimination," he refused to answer every one of Alcock's questions about his Warren Commission testimony. He added the lie that Eugene Davis was Clay Bertrand. In a nuisance suit, he then went on to sue Jim Garrison for perjury.

CIA clandestine services operative Lloyd Cobb located Charles Andrew Appel, his fellow CIA asset and founder of the FBI laboratory, to dispute Shaw's Eastern Airlines lounge signature. Appel was notorious for having "proved" that Bruno Richard Hauptmann had written the Lindbergh kidnapping ransom note.

"The defendant Clay Shaw did not write the entry in the book," Appel said.

Alcock exposed the lie perpetrated by James Phelan. Why, if Russo had mentioned "Clem Bertrand" only in New Orleans, under sodium pentothal, didn't Phelan include that fact in his six-thousand-word *Saturday Evening Post* article, "Rush to Judgment in New Orleans"? He had kept this fact "in reserve" for Sheridan's "White Paper," Phelan admitted, revealing that his effort to discredit Jim Garrison for the government meant more to him than his journalistic integrity.

With his word against Russo's, Edward O'Donnell testified that Russo had denied in his presence that Shaw was at Ferrie's gathering. Alcock did not attempt to penetrate O'Donnell's animosity toward Jim Garrison.

Then only one defense witness remained—the defendant himself. Handed their photographs, Clay Shaw once more denied that he had ever met Oswald or Ferrie or Russo. He had never in his life worn a hat. He had never been in Clinton. He was not "Clay Bertrand" or "Clem Bertrand." He was on the West Coast at the time of the assassination, Shaw lied, because he had an invitation to speak in Oregon; he did not mention that he had solicited that invitation to speak in San Francisco from fellow CIA asset, Monroe Sullivan.

Was he a supporter of President Kennedy?

"I was," Shaw said, smiling slightly.

The state had blinked before the effort to connect Shaw with the CIA and the CIA with the assassination. When Irvin Dymond asked, "Have you ever worked for the Central Intelligence Agency?" it was the first time the Agency had been mentioned at the trial.

"No, I have not," Shaw lied.

Salvatore Panzeca insists that Shaw told his lawyers "everything," implying that they all participated together in suborned perjury. The record suggests that Shaw told his lawyers very little. Edward Wegmann had speculated that Jim Garrison had "not even concocted evidence, that Shaw was connected with the CIA." In September 1967, Dymond and Wegmann requested that the Justice Department obtain information for them of the possible CIA connections of a long list of individuals; Clay Shaw was among them.

"Justice got very clear impression Shaw had not told them [his lawyers] of his previous contacts with CIA," an astonished Lawrence Houston wrote. He searched, but could not locate a record of Shaw's having signed a secrecy agreement: he perjured himself on his own initiative.

At the trial, CIA officers were "in attendance throughout," even as Langley told the New Orleans field office: "Case is of interest to several Agency components, covering aspects which relate to Agency." The Justice Department sent William S. Block as "an undercover agent for the government observing the trial."

Garrison and his staff had been faced with the decision of whether and how to show Shaw's intelligence activity and his connection to the CIA. They had no access to the CIA's complex Shaw files, and were unable even to invoke the *Paese Sera* articles because newspaper articles are, finally, only hearsay. Nor did the *Paese Sera* articles prove conclusively that Centro Mondiale Commerciale was a CIA front distributing laundered money to influence Italian politics. The documentary evidence that Ferenc Nagy, at the helm of the CMC, was a longtime CIA asset emerged only in the 1990s. Lacking the resources to investigate in Italy, unable to appreciate the "fullness" of Shaw's involvement in CMC, Jim Garrison had read the *Paese Sera* series only in a cursory manner.

"We did not have any evidence that Shaw worked for the CIA," Garrison summed up. He knew it in his bones, he said later, "once we learned that it was he who had called Andrews," and that Shaw was "a pal of Ferrie's." Moreover, Garrison believed that the jury was not ready for the concept of "domestic espionage," even as he knew he was "taking the risk of leaving out motive."

It was only in 1973, Garrison was to say, "thanks to Victor Marchetti," that he knew for certain "that Shaw and Ferrie were both CIA employees, which means that we were not wrong with regard to the trial of Shaw." In addition to his recounting how Helms had revealed he was helping Clay Shaw, Marchetti would explain that Shaw's Project QKENCHANT files resided under CIA "Operations," rather than with "Domestic Contact."

In February 1969, all Alcock could do was to expose Shaw's lies, among them Shaw's outright fabrication that he did not solicit that invitation to San Francisco. Alcock did uncover yet another Shaw lie: Shaw's denial that he had been at the Lake Front Airport in 1963. State witnesses Nicholas Tadin and his wife Mathilde identified Shaw as having been present when they were observing their son's flying lessons with David Ferrie. Salvatore Panzeca considers the Tadins to have been the most damaging state witnesses. Frank Meloche, who knew the Tadins, was certain: "They would never have lied."

Dymond asked for a directed verdict on the strength that he had proven that the name "Clay Bertrand" "had a completely fictitious origin."

Alcock's closing was passionate and reflected his belief that Clay Shaw was guilty. He said he had proven Shaw a liar "within four hours" through the Clinton witnesses. The premise that Shaw did not know Ferrie or Oswald "lay shattered, broken, and forever irretrievable in the dust of Clinton, Louisiana." If Shaw had lied on any material issue, he told the jury, they were free to "disregard his entire testimony." He did not apologize for Spiesel, who had remembered Clay Shaw because he had telephoned Shaw later at Ferrie's suggestion about work in New Orleans. Whatever his eccentricities, Spiesel was a functioning businessman who had been to college and served in the military.

Alcock asked the jury to consider how Russo could have known what Shaw's alibi would be. "Leon" had said he was going to look for work in Houston, a fact confirmed by Ruth Paine. Clay Shaw, Alcock concluded, was "unworthy of your belief."

Al Oser had the easier job of proving a conspiracy in the assassination at Dealey Plaza. He repeated Dr. Nichols' testimony that if President Kennedy had been hit in the back of the head, he would have been driven forward from the blow, the bullet traveling at 2,175 feet per second, with a wallop of 1,676 pounds. "That's a wallop! That's a wallop!" Oser said. He pointed to a blow-up of the crime scene with people running toward the grassy knoll. "Where is everybody running to in the photograph, gentlemen?" he asked the jury.

A defiant Dymond had written his closing statement the night before, he bragged to his friend Burton Klein, while in the act of being ministered to by a woman of the night. If the State meant to charge the government with "dishonest, unscrupulous conduct," they should have done so, he said. "As a loyal American citizen," he believed in the Warren Commission. Critics of the Warren Report," Dymond said, pandering to a Southern ethos where dissent meant integration and communism, were "a group of vultures, no better than supporters of the Soviet Union."

Anticommunism and racism were then aligned to class snobbery as Dymond asked the jury to compare the credibility of the Clinton witnesses with that of so distinguished a figure as Lloyd Cobb. "There is no way in the world that this defendant could have been in Clinton, Louisiana when the State claims he was there," Dymond said. "Bertrand" was an invention of Andrews, he insisted. "Only a lunatic" would have signed that guest book 'Clay Bertrand,'" Dymond said.

In rebuttal, Oser expressed his indignation at being called "un-American." He explained why, although the state had subpoenaed

FBI ballistics expert Robert Frazier, Frazier became a defense witness instead, going on to testify that the windshield of Kennedy's limousine had been broken—from the inside.

Frazier had arrived in New Orleans only to demand that Harry Connick accompany him at all times. Connick then told William Alford that he could not talk to the witness unless he revealed his questions to Connick in advance.

"Harry, I'm not going to tell you that," Alford said in his cordial way. "It's none of your business."

"Well, I think it is," Connick said. When Alford insisted that the purpose of the statute was to protect the witness, not for Connick to demand that Alford divulge his case, Connick held firm. "If you don't tell me, you're not talking to him." Disgusted, Alford threw both Connick and Frazier out of his office.

Alcock concluded by referring to the defendant as "a veritable Dr. Jekyll and Mr. Hyde." Where Clay Shaw spent his time was a mystery to Lloyd Cobb and to his own secretary. He was glad, Alcock said, that the case had reached "a jury like yourselves despite the efforts of the Jim Phelans, the Walter Sheridans and the [Fred] Frieds of NBC."

There were tears in Jimmy Alcock's eyes. He knew he was going to lose, he had told Frank Meloche. He had given his all.

Jim Garrison delivered the final closing statement. He loved his country, he said. But justice "did not happen automatically. Men have to make it occur." He called the Warren Report "the greatest fraud in the history of our country," one only the jury could correct. The trial might be over, he added, but he intended still "to fight for the truth." Contemptuous of poor Pierre Finck, who had obeyed a general not to complete the autopsy, and of Frazier, who had resorted to the fantasy that Oswald had "created a sonic boom firing his weapon," Garrison termed the murder of John F. Kennedy "the most terrible moment in the history of our country." The jury could "cause justice to happen for the first time in this matter."

Judge Haggerty read the conspiracy statute to the jury, reminding them that anything done in furtherance of the conspiracy counted, not only an unlawful act, but even a lawful one. Nor was it necessary for the defendant to be present at the time of the commission of the crime. Only "common intent" (such as that expressed at Ferrie's gathering) was required, not a formal agreement. Nor even did the conspirators have to state expressly the terms of their common understanding: A "tacit, mutual understanding and the willful, intentional and knowing adoption by two or more persons of a common design" was enough. When Dymond asked that the jury be informed of "the general reputation of the accused for honesty, truthfulness, peace and quiet," Judge Haggerty denied this request.

It was after midnight. "March 1st" would be written on the verdict forms. Fifty-four minutes after they were sent to deliberate, the verdict was announced: "We the Jury find the defendant not guilty."

Nearly five years later, Clay Shaw came as close to a confession as he dared, setting him apart from the many CIA employees, from Lawrence Houston to David Atlee Phillips to Richard Helms, who carried their silence to the grave. Near death from lung cancer, Shaw was visited at the Ochsner Foundation hospital by longtime acquaintance and neighbor George Dureau, a New Orleans painter and photographer.

As Dureau remembers, Shaw said, "You know, I wasn't guilty of what Garrison charged. But Garrison had the right idea. He was almost right. Someone like me, with a background in army intelligence and with post-war intelligence connections, very well might have been asked to meet with someone like Oswald or Ferrie, to give them a package or some money or whatever, and I would have faithfully done it without ever asking what I was doing it for." That "package" recalls "Donald" P. Norton's testimony that Shaw gave him a suitcase of money to deliver to Oswald in Monterrey.

As for whether Shaw's government service extended into the 1960s, one day Shaw, who lived a block away, walked up to Dureau and said, "Would you like to go to Spain with me?"

Dureau was bisexual, "across the board," as he puts it. But Shaw's impromptu invitation did not appeal to him. Dureau found an excuse. "Oh, I couldn't go to Spain," he said. "I don't have a passport."

"Silly boy, you don't think I could get you a passport in one day?" Shaw said.

JUST ANOTHER DAY AT TULANE AND BROAD

20

Clarence Darrow lost the Scopes trial—who knows it?
—Jim Garrison

"**J**UST ANOTHER DAY AT Tulane and Broad," Garrison quipped as soon as he learned that Clay Shaw had been acquitted. Then in an ironic paraphrase of Lee Harvey Oswald, he added, "Now everyone will know who I am." He was not emotional, unlike the two of his assistants who had broken down. He spoke, instead, of his sympathy for President Kennedy: "If you happen to get elected president, you must not get the idea that you can with equanimity try to end an eighty billion dollar a year warfare operation." Kennedy had been "taking steps to end the Cold War," Garrison believed. Nor was the culprit the CIA alone. In implementing the assassination, the CIA was functioning as "the clandestine arm of the warfare interests in the United States government."

The investigation had cost, by his records, $99,488.96, of which he had personally donated $15,875.

The jury told Mark Lane they had agreed that there had been a conspiracy, with the United States government a participant. There was a good chance of Clay Shaw's having been involved. But there was also reasonable doubt. The two alternates said they would have voted to convict. Garrison concluded that it was not possible to expose "a sophisticated clandestine operation in an Anglo-Saxon courtroom." It had been like "trying to carry water in a sieve."

Jokingly, he said he had been "rudely interrupted by the jury's verdict," only for a reporter to write that he had criticized the jury. Garrison then wrote a letter of appreciation to each jury member.

He was sensitive to criticism that he had violated Clay Shaw's rights. He had not mentioned Shaw's name in the intervening two years, he said. He had allowed nothing about Shaw's personal life to arise at the trial.

"Garrison should resign," the *States-Item* blared. Garrison laughed. His office had never lost a major case in six and a half years, "and, darn it, we lose one case and the next morning I'm called on to resign!" The *New York Times* wrote he was unfit for public office.

Clay Shaw filed a $5 million lawsuit accusing Garrison, along with Perry Russo and the Truth and Consequences backers, of violating his constitutional rights. It was against the law to sue a prosecutor if you had been indicted by a grand jury. But Shaw was no ordinary defendant. The wife of Federal Judge Herbert Christenberry sent Clay Shaw a congratulatory letter, speaking as "we." During the investigation, Christenberry had informed on the Shaw case to the FBI.

Two days after the verdict, Garrison charged Shaw with two counts of perjury: that he had never met Lee Harvey Oswald, that he had never met David Ferrie. "He was lying to the jury," Judge Haggerty said publicly. "I think Shaw put a good con job on the jury . . . I believe he was lying to the jury on a number of things." Undistracted by Spiesel's peculiarities, Haggerty believed his testimony, impressed that Spiesel had been able to identify the building Shaw had once renovated, which was right next to one Shaw owned.

Pleading double jeopardy, Shaw and his lawyers marched over to the office of U.S. Attorney Louis LaCour. The perjury case landed on the lap of Federal Judge Herbert Christenberry.

Hunter Leake conveyed the news to Langley: "The *bête noir* has become a phoenix. Certainly Garrison must consider himself a miraculous bird to arise, in the face of widespread public indignation and hostility, from his own ashes." Leake had hoped that Garrison "had been consumed, in fire, by his own act." The CIA had planned to close down their "communications installation" on Garrison on April 28th. Now they had to maintain their surveillance. CIA continued its monitoring. Memos flew between the Office of General Counsel, and the St. Louis field office.

In the absence of a Louisiana law against obstruction of justice, Garrison charged Tom Bethell with "unlawful use of movable property for allegedly showing the state's trial memorandum in the Shaw case to a Shaw attorney." Dean Andrews was charged again with perjury, for lying on the stand at the Shaw trial. In the middle of the month, a "Proclamation" went out to Garrison's staff: "Because of the solemnity of this occasion and because so many of you worked overtime in the recent case, St. Patrick's Day will be a half-holiday." It was signed "Jim Garrison (of the McFerrins and Chapmans from County Monahan)."

Then Jim Garrison began to investigate the Kennedy assassination all over again. "I have just begun to fight," he announced. Lou Ivon thought it was time to go back to the office, and to politics, but Jim "just kept it up, kept it up." Summarizing as yet undeveloped leads, Garrison ordered red and yellow folders. He and Alcock shared one set of files, Sciambra, Alford and Ivon another. "The Murret Lead" reflected that Jim Garrison was not overlooking the Mafia connections of Oswald or anyone else. He learned that, some time after September 24, 1963, a man Oswald's aunt Mrs. Murret identified as Clay Shaw appeared at her home.

A man named Lopez said he went to Cuba with Clay Shaw. A chemistry professor said he met Thornley and Oswald together in New Orleans. The federal government listed a "Suggs" file as secret, as Garrison began to lift the corner of Jack Martin's CIA history. A Banister employee named Bob Guzman spotted Oswald at Thompson's Cafe where Tommy Beckham had met him. Bootsie Gay now came forward, her testimony further confirmed by Al Clark. David Gentry claimed he saw Shaw visit Oswald's house and was given a polygraph.

The investigation drew closer to Woodrow Hardy: Garrison interviewed Mrs. Esther Stein, who had worked at Shaw's house when Oswald visited, and chatted with the carpenter. A painter named George Clark saw Oswald playing cards with another man at Shaw's house: they were "friends of the owner," they said. Clark identified Oswald and Shaw, who had come in, talked briefly to the young men, and left.

Richard Burnes now represented Dick Wight, the vice-president of Freeport Sulphur, and agreed to bring him to the office. A cab driver had taken Shaw to Ferrie's apartment on numerous occasions. The office reexamined a Bertrand library card that had been discounted because the telephone number on it was wrong, although the lead had come through a Library Board member. They reinterviewed Mr. and Mrs. Eames, whom Ferrie had visited to ask "what library card Oswald was using at the time Mr. Eames saw him in the main library," believing it might be his.

Old friends helped. Pudgie Miranne suggested that Mr. C. Earl Colomb, a former vice president of the International Trade Mart, might clarify "Shaw's hidden intelligence connections with the federal intelligence apparatus." At the New Orleans Athletic Club, Harry Daniels suggested they talk to David Cotter, a close friend of Shaw's, who left New Orleans abruptly when the investigation began. They returned to the Ryder Coffee House because Garrison had never been satisfied with proprietor Jack Frazier's evasions.

Garrison wanted Henry Lesnick to persuade David Logan to come forward "this time." Eddie Porter said he met Oswald in the Penny Arcade of the 100 block of Royal in the company of a male prostitute; Oswald had told Francis Martello that this "John" was a member of the Fair Play for Cuba committee.

Local law enforcement was no more cooperative than it had ever been. With the assistance of New Orleans police intelligence, the Louisiana State Police had prepared a forty-one-page report on Oswald and Ferrie at the request of the Warren Commission; ten pages remained classified. No copies materialized.

At the end of April, Garrison's investigators located Allen and Dan Campbell. Allen could testify to relationships between Banister and G. Wray Gill, as well as between Banister and A. Roswell Thompson. He could also confirm that Ferrie had flown to Dallas the week of the assassination. He knew how well Banister knew Shaw and was aware of Banister's CIA connections. Dan Campbell had seen Oswald at Banister's office.

Wary, Garrison asked people to write to him in care of Judge Matthew Braniff, who owed Garrison his judgeship, which he had recommended on the condition that Braniff stop drinking. Never a man to hold grudges, Garrison ran into reporter Jack Dempsey and extended "his big right paw." He welcomed John Volz back into the office and Volz worked on the perjury case against Shaw.

Garrison ran for reelection in the autumn of 1969. "I did not fight the federal government two and a half years just to resign because the newspaper says I should," he declared. Hardy Davis sought revenge by implying that there had been corruption in the office's failure to collect forfeited bail from the Maryland National Insurance Company. It had been Charlie Ward's responsibility, but Garrison took the blame, calling it his "one serious mistake" in seven years in office.

When two vacancies opened up on the Criminal Court, Garrison reneged on his promise to Charlie Ward and proposed Al Oser and Israel Augustine, who would be the first African-American judge "in modern times." When Ward resigned from the district attorney's office, Jimmy Alcock became chief assistant, and Moo Moo Sciambra, executive assistant. "Now the top command is entirely made up of men who fought that fight with me," Garrison said.

Charlie Ward ran against him, declaring that he, unlike Garrison, would have charged student demonstrators at Fortier High School and Southern University for taking down an American flag and raising a black liberation flag. But Garrison defended even the right to display a Confederate flag on your license plate. This, too, represented protected speech. Even Rosemary James had to admit that Garrison had been "extremely fair with Negroes, uncommonly so for a Louisiana district attorney."

Among Garrison's opponents was Harry Connick, who attacked him for an increase of crime in New Orleans.

"In cities where I'm not district attorney, [crime] is spiraling," Garrison said dryly. He was unique in making no personal attacks on his opponents. Always he defended the Shaw case. "History will show that we were not wrong," he told one audience. "Just be patient. When it's over, you'll be proud of your DA."

He still had an aversion to fund-raising and money in general. Buck Kreihs, who ran a marine repair company, knowing Jim Garrison would never bother to collect a campaign contribution, sent his friend Vic Carona to Garrison's house with the money. There Carona suffered a brain hemorrhage and died. A bar owner friend of Moo Moo's said if Garrison would just walk into his saloon and shake his hand, he would make a $5,000 contribution. Garrison never bothered to make the time to do it. He hated to campaign so much that reporter David Snyder wrote that Garrison was "the Howard Hughes of New Orleans . . . harder to find than a Saints' victory." The *States-Item* and the *Times-Picayune* endorsed Harry Connick.

A mysterious poll suddenly surfaced. It claimed that 45 percent of voters favored Harry Connick, with 28 percent for Garrison. The poll turned out to be fraudulent, a product of "Eugene Newman's Mid-South Opinion Surveys," operating out of Little Rock. It received wide exposure from, among others, WDSU. When the Associated Press could not locate Newman, the Connick campaign insisted they had not "commissioned, sponsored or initiated the survey."

Although Connick spent $250,000 on his campaign to Garrison's $20,000, Garrison won handily in the first primary. Among the defeated was his former assistant Ross Scaccia, who came in last.

Depressed, sitting at home alone in his den on election night, Scaccia took a telephone call.

"Is this 'landslide Scaccia?'" Moo Moo said.

"Jim will hate me forever," Scaccia said. But Moo Moo invited him to headquarters: "Jim wants to see you." There Garrison made certain to shake hands with Scaccia as the cameras rolled. Years later when Garrison was a judge and Scaccia was cited for contempt in his divorce hearing, Garrison was sympathetic. "You never did know any law," Garrison told Scaccia, deadpan. Then he added, "I'll take care of it," and did.

Garrison also stood up for Judge Haggerty when he was caught in a scandal that cost him his judgeship. He called Haggerty's work on the Shaw case "the most distinguished work on the part of a District Judge that I have ever seen since I've been a lawyer." Garrison went on to recommend Jimmy Alcock for Haggerty's seat.

As the CIA watched angrily, Garrison's reelection allowed him to proceed with his Kennedy investigation. "Not only is subject case not dead, it is not even moribund," John Schubert complained to the head of the Domestic Contact Service as he reported on the $100-dollar-a-plate dinner sponsored by Cecil Shilstone to retire Garrison's campaign debt. "The CIA killed John Kennedy," Garrison told the guests, vowing to continue his investigation. "I won't compromise. And there's nothing they can do to stop me because I know who did it." He believed that "not much more evidence was really necessary."

He published a book about the case called *A Heritage of Stone,* distinguishing it from the work of other critics, whom he dubbed "the Baker Street Irregulars" who "meet annually at Sylvia Meagher's." (Meagher had written a congratulatory letter to Clay Shaw.) "We are all in accord that the earth is round," he said. The issue was no longer flaws in the Warren Commission, but who planned the crime.

Agent Max Gartenberg had brought the manuscript to feisty Arthur Fields at G. P. Putnam's Sons.

President Kennedy was not "just another escalating president," but was "blocking any further expansion in Indo-China," Garrison explained, warning Fields, "The people we are dealing with do not follow the Marquis of Queensburg's [sic] rules."

"I hate it but I'm going to publish it," Fields said. Because the perjury case was still pending, Clay Shaw's name is not mentioned in *A Heritage of Stone.* Garrison speaks of his odyssey, how he discovered that the CIA operated within the borders of the United States, and how it took the CIA six months to reply to the Warren Commission's question of whether Oswald and Ruby had been with the Agency. He enlisted his favorite conundrum: "Treason doth never prosper. What's the reason? For if it prosper, none dare call it treason." The final chapter, "The War Machine," connects the intelligence agencies with the military that they serve.

In response to *A Heritage of Stone,* the CIA rounded up its media assets. Jerry Cohen, who with Lawrence Schiller had attempted to prevent Loran Hall and Lawrence Howard from talking to Jim Garrison, panned it in the *Los Angeles Times. Life* dismissed the book as "smoke." Wegmann confidante, lawyer Elmer Gertz, who represented Gordon Novel in his libel case against Jim Garrison, in a flagrant conflict of interest, panned *A Heritage of Stone* in the *Chicago Sun Times.* In the *Washington Post,* George Lardner, the last person to see David Ferrie alive, writes, inaccurately, that the author Clay Shaw had in fact commissioned, James Kirkwood, had just appeared and wrote his book because he was "intrigued by the case after a chance meeting with Shaw."

John Leonard's *New York Times* review went through a metamorphosis. The original last paragraph challenged the Warren Report: "Something stinks about this whole affair," Leonard wrote. "Why were Kennedy's neck organs not examined at Bethesda for evidence of a frontal shot? Why was his body whisked away to Washington before the legally required Texas inquest? Why?"

This paragraph evaporated in later editions of the *Times.* A third of a column gone, the review then ended: "Frankly I prefer to believe that the Warren Commission did a poor job, rather than a dishonest one. I like to think that Garrison invents monsters to explain incompetence."

On WVUE television, Alec Gifford offered a rave. "If he had not become a lawyer," Gifford said, "he could certainly have earned his living as a writer." No sentence could have pleased Jim Garrison more. Lou Ivon thought Garrison's greatest joy was in his writing.

Resting in Palm Springs on his book tour, checked in as "Lamont Cranston" ("The Shadow"), Garrison wrote to Fields, his "Maxwell Perkins," signing his letters "B. Traven" and "L. Tolstoi." He then turned to fiction, studying *The Maltese Falcon, The Thin Man* and *The Day of the Jackal.* His next work, *The Star-Spangled Contract,* would be a novel, its hero bearing a variation on one of Garrison's family names, "McFerran."

The government's attempt to thwart Jim Garrison had included an attempt to charge him with tax fraud, an effort that had begun at least a month before Walter Sheridan's "White Paper." On tape, on May 25, 1967, George Wyatt remarks to Sheridan's assistant

Richard Townley, "I thought you were going to get him on income tax evasion."

Three years of investigating Jim Garrison's finances had not produced a case for the IRS. Working with the U.S. Attorney's Office, Aaron Kohn offered "detailed information," such as that the furnishings in the Garrison home were lavish, although the only valuable antiques had come from Liz Garrison's family, she says. Even Orestes Peña learned that IRS agents were inquiring about how Garrison could afford his house.

When Kohn could find no financial irregularities, he suggested that the government attack Garrison for tolerating pinball gambling. Although it was illegal for bars to pay off on pinball games with a gadget attached to the machine, no district attorney had ever been able to prosecute the elusive owners of these pinball machines. The gambling device was always added later, after the machines had left their hands.

In the company of Justice Department lawyer Mike Epstein, no longer bothering to call himself a television producer, Walter Sheridan visited Pershing Gervais at the Fontainebleau Motor Hotel. *Your taxes are being investigated*, Sheridan told Pershing. Owing back taxes of $8,000, Pershing had the choice of either helping them to nail Jim Garrison or going to jail himself for "three years."

Although Pershing had informed on Jim Garrison to the CIA and FBI on the Shaw case, this particular scheme promised little profit and Pershing had no taste for it. Jim Garrison was "an individual who did not care too much about becoming wealthy," Pershing told the IRS agents assigned to him in May 1968. If Garrison owed back taxes, it was "because of Mr. Garrison's carelessness." Any mistakes Garrison made were likely to be "in favor of the government." Garrison himself had told the IRS agents, "I guarantee you'll end up paying me when you finish your investigation." Pershing doubted if Garrison even knew the interest rate on his mortgage.

Pershing knew that Mike Epstein, working closely with Walter Sheridan on this effort, was about himself to be indicted. Yet, Pershing was surprised to discover, the government was not afraid that this irregularity might jeopardize its determined attempt to destroy Jim Garrison, no matter even that Epstein, already in trouble, and Sheridan were employing blackmail.

By January 1969, even before the Shaw case had gone to trial, Pershing was making secret tape recordings to incriminate Jim Garrison. All the while he complained to anyone who would listen that the government was trying to "use him to get to Garrison."

Sheridan, in concert with lawyer Edward Baldwin, had threatened him if he didn't cooperate, Pershing charged, pleading to be left alone. On March 12th, he appealed to IRS Special Agent Walter G. Gibson, reporting that Sheridan had threatened to have his income tax returns investigated if he didn't help them to implicate Garrison. Pershing also telephoned Senator Russell Long and requested his help. But Long was not powerful enough to fight Walter Sheridan, who operated as a law unto himself.

In May 1969, the Intelligence Service of the IRS met with Pershing and hammered out a final deal. Pershing would provide information on payoffs to Garrison. His own identity would not be disclosed. He would not have to testify in court. No information he volunteered could be used against him in a criminal case. The government's case against Garrison would rely solely on Pershing Gervais. They could find not a single other witness or any physical evidence that he had accepted bribes from the pinball owners.

Much of what Pershing reported had no value, such as that Garrison had purchased a piece of property with Dr. William Fisher—Garrison's mother had provided the money. Pershing claimed that Garrison had told the office to go easy on the pinball owners, although John Volz and Jimmy Alcock were to deny that this was so. Pershing charged that John Aruns Callery had paid Garrison $2,000 to lay off pinball machines, with Pershing keeping $500 for himself, but no one who knew Pershing would believe that particular distribution of the spoils. When Garrison's son Jasper fell off his bicycle and suffered a cerebral hemorrhage, Pershing told the federal agents that Garrison was "deeply distraught." Garrison did not care about the issues at hand, "one way or the other." He was an easy mark.

In June 1969, in a whispering campaign, Garrison was accused of sexually molesting a thirteen-year-old boy at the New Orleans Athletic Club. The scenario was orchestrated by Layten Martens, who "spun it to Walter Sheridan," claims Gordon Novel, no friend of Jim Garrison's. The boy's name was Pierre Bezou. His uncle was Monsignor Henry Charles Bezou, superintendent of the Catholic Schools; his father, James F. Bezou, was chancellor of the Belgian consulate at the International Trade Mart and a good friend of Clay Shaw's.

Garrison, James Bezou and two of Bezou's sons were in the "Slumber Room" of the NOAC, where cots were lined up for men to nap after swimming in the saltwater pool and enjoying their massages. According to Pierre Bezou, Garrison lifted Pierre's blanket and lightly flicked his genitals. He did not grab Bezou. He did not arouse him. He did not fondle him. Bezou contends that this occurred twice.

At the age of thirteen, Pierre Bezou admits, so repressive was the environment of his upbringing that he didn't even masturbate. That Garrison would have molested a child in the presence of his father and older brother strains credulity.

Garrison at once told Bezou senior, "There's a misunderstanding here." No charges were ever brought, and his monsignor uncle, according to Pierre Bezou, urged his father to back off. A week later, an NOAC member named Lamar Chavin reportedly observed Garrison having a drink with James Bezou at the Old Absinthe House, the two chatting amiably. A short time later, according to Numa Bertel, another of Pierre's brothers, Jacques, applied to Jim Garrison for a job as an assistant district attorney, hardly the action of a family member who believed Jim Garrison had really molested the boy.

One day at the Orleans Parish grand jury, a member named Velman demanded, "When are we going to hear these charges against Garrison at the NOAC?" He was so vehement that foreman William Krummel felt obliged to take it up. The only media person to cover the story was Jack Anderson—on February 23, 1970, eight months after the event was said to have taken place. Anderson wrote, obviously utilizing an inside source, that the grand jury was investigating. Anderson added, erroneously, that at the Shaw trial Garrison had "made much of Shaw's alleged homosexuality"; Shaw's sexuality had not been mentioned once.

The adviser to the grand jury was William Alford. Jimmy Alcock told Alford not even to tell Jim Garrison that the Bezou issue had come up. But Alford trooped up to Garrison's bedroom where he was confined with extreme back pain. Garrison insisted upon getting out of bed and meeting with Krummel. The Bezous never came forward to testify, even before the secret proceedings of the grand jury. When Velman again raised the issue, Krummel demanded, "If you're going to leak a story to Jack Anderson, but when it comes to ball cutting time nobody shows up, as far as I'm concerned, it never happened."

Aaron Kohn wrote Krummel that Garrison had "twice fondled" the boy, a gross exaggeration, one even Pierre Bezou never employed. When five years later James Bezou committed suicide, Coroner Frank Minyard ruled the death "accidental" since it was "witnessed by no one." Jim Garrison made no comment. It was a full decade later that William Gurvich claimed he had obtained affidavits from

James Bezou, Pierre and his brother, affidavits that have never surfaced.

Aware that Pershing Gervais could not be trusted, Sheridan sought others he might force to implicate Jim Garrison. One day in the summer of 1969 Ross Scaccia, now an assistant U.S. attorney, was at an LSU football game when he was summoned to report to security. Fearing that one of his children was hurt, he rushed over, only to be met by a Justice Department lawyer named Lee Leonard.

"We want you to come to Washington," Leonard said. "We want to know everything you know about Jim Garrison." Irritated, Scaccia complied, traveling to Silver Spring, Maryland, where, in a stately mansion, thirty people grilled him about Jim Garrison. Why had Scaccia quit Garrison's office? What did he know about Garrison's connections? Did he know anything about Pershing's partner, Red Strate? Was Jim Garrison in with the pinball people?

"There isn't anything to say about Jim," Scaccia said. Yes, he had heard about kickbacks. Yes, he had heard about the incident at the New Orleans Athletic Club.

"I don't believe any of that," Scaccia said.

"You work for us," a Justice Department lawyer said. Scaccia decided that being a federal prosecutor had lost its savor. He resigned and went into private practice.

On June 1, 1970, a Justice Department Strike Force opened for business in New Orleans. Pinball gambling stood at the top of its list of criminal activity in Louisiana. Some noise issued about Carlos Marcello and organized crime. The sole purpose of the "Strike Force," however, was to bring down Jim Garrison.

Pershing proceeded with his taping. He taped Garrison so persistently that once, suspecting they were being taped, Steve Bordelon joked, with a reference to the Bezou rumors, "I got a young boy in the car!" Bordelon had driven Garrison for years and never once had Garrison revealed any homosexual or pedophile proclivities. He knew Garrison did not take money because he emptied Garrison's pockets every night.

Pershing tried to cobble together a case for the government. Garrison, separated from Liz now, kept a room at the Fontainebleau. He was not a domestic man—his fatherless childhood with a controlling mother had all but precluded that—nor a faithful husband. "I couldn't take it any more," Liz had said, finally. "I just couldn't put up with that anymore."

Now Pershing offered to help him pay his Fontainebleau bill

with a "little cash." On one occasion, as soon as Bordelon paid, Pershing rushed over to the cashier to retrieve his marked bills. Pershing promised an ex-convict named Robert Murray $300 to hand Garrison an envelope while pictures would be snapped. But Murray reported him to assistant district attorney Byron P. LeGendre.

The government harassment had taken its toll as the seasons of tragedy rolled by. On a 1971 trip to Miami, Garrison insisted that he be met at the airport by Richard Gerstein's chief investigator, Martin F. Dardis. It was late. As the two proceeded through the deserted Eastern Airlines terminal, Garrison glanced at two black janitors mopping the floor.

They're FBI agents," Garrison said. "They're everywhere. You don't know how they operate."

Unaware of what Garrison had been through and was continuing to endure, irritated because he had tickets for a Dolphins' game that night, which he was missing, Dardis could not resist a sarcastic comeback.

"They don't have any black guys," Dardis said with his customary harsh realism. "The only black guy in the FBI is the one emptying J. Edgar Hoover's wastebasket!"

Three years passed. Pershing grew adept at manipulating the tapes. On February 25, 1971, Pershing seemingly gives Garrison $1,000. On the tape, Gervais makes it seem as if Garrison grabbed the envelope, crying, "You burned my fingers!" Garrison talks about legalizing pinball, but the context is McKeithen's self-interest, not Garrison's. If McKeithen supported banning the gadget that permitted pinball gambling, Garrison jokes, "Carlos Marcello will be the next Senator from New Orleans." Later he would tell William Alford to go easy on pinball owners whom Alford had personally subpoenaed to the grand jury. It came at that moment when Garrison wanted to help McKeithen in his race for the Senate by opposing the law making the knock-off device on the pinball machines illegal. Soon, disillusioned, Alford resigned from the office.

On the March 9, 1971 tape, Garrison asks Gervais what he wants to see him about. "The money," Gervais says. "Oh," Garrison says. On that same day, Gervais says, "The boys are talking of running you for governor." "Gee, that's great," Garrison says. On the doctored tape, Gervais says, "The boys have agreed to pay us $1,000 every two months," and Garrison replies, "Gee, that's great." Gervais is then heard to reply, "No, there's a thousand every two months," a non sequitur demonstrating that the tape machine had been turned off, and then on again. The conversation makes no sense.

On another tape, when Gervais states that Boasberg and Nims sent him $1,000, Garrison replies, "Don't get greedy. That's what always catches these bastards," another incoherent moment. On heavy painkillers, and distracted, Jim Garrison says of police investigator Frederick Soule, "oh, he's not with me any more," although Soule was in fact very much entrenched at Tulane and Broad.

One of those ultimately indicted, Louis Boasberg of New Orleans Novelty, confided to his lawyer, Jim McPherson, that Jim Garrison had never asked for bribes nor had he ever given him any bribes. One day Sharon Herkes took an anonymous call. "We've given the envelopes, so what's the problem?" the caller said. But those envelopes had not gone to Jim Garrison. He received a warning telegram, signed by "Impeccable Washington Source, S." "Watch out for 'friend' conversing about your finances," it read. "He's bugged to frame you for lay fraud." Still, Garrison did not suspect Pershing, whom he called his "closest friend."

On May 28, 1971, Herbert Christenberry dismissed the perjury charges against Clay Shaw on the ground that Garrison's investigation had been funded by a private organization, although four years earlier Louise Korns had determined that the Truth and Consequences contributions were entirely legal. In a press release, Garrison called Oswald "a low-level intelligence employee of the United States government." The assassination "was carried out by the domestic espionage apparatus of the United States government." He hoped to continue to educate the public about how the intelligence agencies had been "in the business of assassination—both foreign and domestic—for a number of years." Those involved were people engaged in cover occupations, well regarded in their communities, like Clay Shaw, and did not wear "black capes nor villains' mustaches."

A month later the government made its move. On June 26th, Gervais drew sketches for the federal agents of the layout of Garrison's house, remarking that Garrison often put money in the desk drawer in his study. Three days later, bearing a cheesecake, Pershing paid his final visit to the Garrison home. Garrison was, as usual, upstairs in bed. Outside, the federal agent assigned to Gervais, Arlie Puckett, sat in a surveillance truck, listening as the tape recorder clicked on and off.

Pershing has brought more than a cheesecake. He carries as well a plain white envelope with $1,000 in fifty-dollar bills, dusted with fluorescent powder. The bedroom is scented with Ben-Gay. Jim asks Liz for hot chocolate, but Pershing declines, Pershing is in a hurry. He needs a favor, he says. He wants Jim to hold some money for a few days. Put the money in the desk, Garrison says. He trusts Pershing to do it himself, since he knows the house well. Downstairs, Pershing puts the envelope in the middle drawer of the desk, locks the drawer, pockets the key and vanishes into the night.

"So perish all enemies of this country," Pershing whispers into his microphone, paraphrasing John Wilkes Booth as he drew his weapon to kill Abraham Lincoln.

The next morning, a small army of federal agents armed with a search warrant entered the house on Owens Boulevard, trooped upstairs and arrested Jim Garrison. Later Federal Prosecutor Eric Gisleson, playing out some imaginary scenario, said, they had "two teams stationed outside to protect his wife"; they were "fearful of what he would do to his wife." They demanded that Jim Garrison empty his pockets, but the fifty-dollar bills in his wallet did not match the serial numbers on their list. There was a metal box in the dresser, but it was empty.

Downstairs, the agents marched to the desk and demanded the key. Garrison looked at them blankly. He might have a spare in the office, he remarked. Revealing they knew perfectly well that he had no key—Pershing had taken it—the agents had come equipped with an eighteen-inch screwdriver. An agent jimmied open the desk and there was the money.

"A friend came by last night and left it," Garrison said. He was going out of town and had asked Garrison to hold it for his return. These serial numbers did match.

"How much is in the envelope?" Garrison asked. Later the agents lied and said Jim Garrison wouldn't tell them where the key was. They insisted he had put the money in the drawer. They said they found tiny traces of the fluorescent power on his fingers.

As far as I'm concerned, Jim Garrison said on the day he was arrested, "It's just another day at Tulane and Broad." Even vice squad officer Mike Seghers, who was helping Pershing all along, says that Garrison was being punished for the Shaw trial. (A total stranger to loyalty, Pershing had told the government that Seghers was "too rough on some violations and does nothing on others.")

Garrison blamed the CIA. "Congress doesn't control the country anymore," he said that night on television. "Neither does the president, really." The arrest was his reward for the Shaw case where he "communicated not wisely but too well." Shakespeare was ever his solace.

There would be nine defendants, but the trial was all about Jim Garrison. Even before he was formally indicted, in an astonishing breach of ethics, the government released to the press a 113-page affidavit of the charges against him. Appalled, F. Lee Bailey offered to represent Garrison for no fee. Pershing was now swept off to Canada and a witness protection program, where for $22,000 a year he need do nothing for his employer, General Motors. So General Motors functioned as a government proprietary.

The CIA gloated. "Looks like Mr. Garrison is on the ropes and will have all he can do to keep the hornets away," Jake Murphy of the Dallas field office wrote to the director of the Domestic Contact Service. When the government delayed in charging Garrison, his lawyer, Lou Merhige, came up with the strategy of having the case tried in state court. The special prosecutor would be Benjamin Smith, one of the Dombrowski defendants—three lawyers charged with "subversion" for helping to finance the integration efforts of Dr. Martin Luther King Jr., Smith, Garrison and Merhige assumed, would be someone likely to be vigilant in the safeguarding of a defendant's rights. The charges would be the same as those listed on the federal affidavit. Simultaneously, Smith would ask Judge Malcolm O'Hara for a change of venue.

In a meeting with Merhige, Smith agreed to prosecute in state court. Then, in a double-cross, Smith walked into court and said there was no evidence, despite the outlining of evidence in the federal affidavit. Smith charged Garrison only with malfeasance, a charge Malcolm O'Hara at once dismissed. The civil rights lawyer had behaved like a hired hand of the federal government.

On December 3, 1971, Jim Garrison was finally indicted by a federal grand jury of conspiracy to obstruct law enforcement and for fraud and false statements on his income taxes, including failure to report $48,000 in gambling protection money, the bribes. "Had I chosen to be crooked," Garrison said, "I easily could have made more than that." The IRS indicted him separately in March.

Assistant Attorney General Henry E. Petersen wrote to Richard Helms. Had any of the individuals under indictment been subjected to electronic surveillance "of any type, lawful or unlawful, by your agency?" There is no available record of Helms' reply. In a moment of confusion, while he waited for the case to come to trial, Garrison qualified for the State Supreme Court, then withdrew.

In May, languishing in Canada, Pershing telephoned his favorite New Orleans reporter, Rosemary James. He had something important to tell her, Pershing said. James flew to Vancouver where Pershing declared he was ready to tell the truth. "They wanted to 'get' Jim Garrison," Pershing confessed. Walter Sheridan had told him he would unleash the IRS against him. "I was forced to work for them," Pershing said. "But more than that. I was forced to lie for them."

"Are you saying that you participated in a deliberate frame of Jim Garrison and a whole bunch of pinball executives at the direction of the federal government?" James said.

"Without a doubt. I'm saying that unequivocably [sic]," Pershing said. "I was convinced I was going to jail. Jim Garrison never, ever, ever, fixed a case for me. Not ever." While pretending to be interested in the Mafia, the Strike Force was really interested in only "one man, Jim Garrison . . . they wanted to silence Jim Garrison."

Previously, Pershing had denied that he was being paid by the federal government.

"How many years do you know me, darling?" Pershing said. "I never did anything for nothing in my whole life." Pershing admitted that there was not "a single thing" that the Justice Department said "that was true . . . it was a total, complete, political frame-up." James asked whether Garrison had given Pershing money on a recent trip he had made to New Orleans.

"Mr. Garrison ain't got thirty cents," Pershing Gervais said. The government's only witness against Jim Garrison had rendered himself useless.

POTOMAC TWO-STEP 21

Nobody there really wants the truth.
—Richard Case Nagell

T HE TRIAL OF *United States of America v. Jim Garrison et al.* opened on August 20, 1973. U.S. Attorney Gerald Gallinghouse already feared the worst. The evidence you sent over was weak, Gallinghouse complained to Aaron Kohn. Even after the trial had begun, Kohn continued to search for information to incriminate Jim Garrison. All they had to connect Garrison and the pinball racketeers came through Pershing Gervais and, perhaps, a pinball owner named John Aruns Callery. The federal prosecution hoped that the defense would not be able to prove that Garrison had ever loaned Pershing any money, although Sharon Herkes could testify that one day Garrison had told her that Gervais had repaid him; "I never thought I would get this money back," Garrison had said.

During the *voir dire,* prospective jurors were asked if they knew who Jim Garrison was. Not a single hand went up. Eric Gisleson passed a note to fellow prosecutor, Michael Ellis: "We just lost the case."

How does it feel to be on trial? Rosemary James asked Garrison.

"It's considerably below an orgasm and considerably above a cremation," Garrison said. Wearing horn-rimmed glasses, he sat at the defense table and read David Halberstam's *The Best and the Brightest,* looking like a man "in his living room going through the mail." Presiding was—Herbert Christenberry. "You can bet it's not by accident," Pershing had said as soon as Christenberry's name was announced.

The climax of the trial came when one of the defendants, police officer Frederick Soule, that officer still, indeed, attached to Garrison's office, confessed to taking pinball bribes. Soule produced the contents of a pickle jar he had buried in his wife's garden: $63,000. He had warned bar owners in advance when the pinball machines would be checked, Soule admitted. Then he testified that "the man at the top" at Tulane and Broad had received a considerable cut of the money. This man was not Jim Garrison, however, but Superintendent of Police, Joseph Giarrusso, a fact since confirmed by both Mike Seghers and Joe Oster.

Every Friday afternoon, Seghers later confided to the head of the police union, Irvin L. Magri Jr., the bread stuffing was removed from a "po' boy" sandwich and hundred-dollar bills put in its place. Then this po' boy would be delivered to Giarrusso at his home on Cameron off Robert E. Lee in the Gentilly section of New Orleans, courtesy of the pinball owners. Sometimes Seghers delivered the po' boy, sometimes Chris ("Bozo") Vodanovich did it. Suddenly the trial was not about Jim Garrison, but his longtime adversary, Joe Giarrusso.

Under oath, John Callery, Lawrence Lagarde and John J. Els Jr. of TAC Novelty all confirmed that "the big man on Tulane Avenue" was Giarrusso. Lagarde said he never gave Garrison any money. Els admitted to sending Garrison a $1,000 or $1,500 campaign contribution, but he had also given a contribution to Charlie Ward. Louisiana law permitted the perpetual collection of political contributions. Gallinghouse had no choice but to invite Joseph Giarrusso to visit a federal grand jury.

Gallinghouse wanted to subpoena William Alford, but Alford had no desire to testify against Jim Garrison. He engineered what he called a "Gervais," after the master, and qualified to run for district attorney against Garrison in his coming reelection campaign. Now there would be a conflict of interest in Alford's testifying. "You've ruined yourself as a witness!" Gallinghouse sputtered. Precisely, Alford thought.

After the altered tapes were played in open court, Judge Christenberry, eschewing impartiality, told the jury that there was abundant evidence to support a guilty verdict for all the defendants. Given the shoddiness of the proceedings, Lou Merhige was reluctant to put Jim Garrison on the stand. But if he dismissed his lawyers and represented himself, Garrison would make the closing argument, which was as good as testifying, and he could not be cross-examined.

"Are you receiving legal aid since releasing Barnett [F. Lee Bailey's associate] and Merhige?" Christenberry demanded, as Garrison assumed the role of defense attorney. "I'm already receiving assistance from Captain America," Garrison replied, "but I believe it is unintentional assistance." He was referring to Gallinghouse.

Lynn Loisel testified that he had learned Gervais was taking pinball bribes, and that he heard Jim Garrison say frequently that Gervais owed him money. Lou Ivon added that the amount was $5,000 or $6,000. Gervais had been fired, Ivon testified, because he took a $3,000 bribe from Burton Klein to fix a case, and Klein had filed an affidavit to that effect.

Having run the office now for several years, John Volz testified that Jim Garrison never interfered with the prosecution of pinball gambling cases. No one could buy Jim Garrison, he said, if only because he was "too undependable." Although Garrison did not support him actively in his effort to retain his judgeship, generously Jimmy Alcock testified for him. The pinball owners could not be prosecuted successfully because the state lacked the power to grant any one of them immunity—they always took the Fifth Amendment—Alcock explained. Warren Commission lawyer and former New Orleans district attorney Leon Hubert also stood up for Jim Garrison. Defense expert witness Louis Gerstman called the tapes a "fraudulent fabrication."

The government had no choice but to bring in Pershing Gervais as a rebuttal witness. Pershing claimed that Jim Garrison had corrupted *him*, and that it was Denis Barry who filtered bribes to Garrison to the tune of $150,000. Before it was over, Pershing admitted to a meeting between himself, Garrison and a lawyer, Russell Schonekas, where Pershing had requested $50,000 to write the script for the trial.

"My God, Pershing," Schonekas said, "are you offering to perjure yourself?"

"I don't believe in God," Pershing said. He pointed upward. "You, God! If you're up there, strike me dead!"

Just before he began his closing argument, Jim Garrison learned that his mother had suffered a heart attack. Often Jane had exasperated him and often he had evaded her, not taking her calls, failing to appear at lunches they had arranged and resenting her interference in his life. Yet always he admired his mother and was grateful to her; *The Star-Spangled Contract* is dedicated to "Jane Garrison Gardiner." The news was shattering.

Liz and the five children sat in the front row. "It might hurt your dad if we're divorced," Liz had told the children. She had postponed the coming inevitable divorce proceedings.

Garrison spoke for three hours, his subjects justice, the system of law and what constituted patriotism. Defining the "Declaration of Independence" as a document designed "to protect the individual from the government," he requested that the jury stand as a shield, protecting him from the federal government, which had made a systematic effort to frame him.

A "small army of federal secret police" had been pursuing him, he said. In that secret meeting at the office of Russell Schonekas, Pershing had asked for $100,000, not $50,000, to help him. "Can you trust the word of such a man, whose only God by his own word is money?" he asked. He admitted that he was not without flaws: "It has been nearly 2,000 years since the last perfect man was on earth."

He spoke of how for two years he had to bear the knowledge that his children "must have some doubts about my innocence." His voice cracked as he choked back tears. Quoting the English poet, Robert Browning, he hoped the jury would not permit "an innocent man to be convicted: One more devil's triumph and sorrow for the angels, one more wrong to man." Two black jurors wept. Even his Uptown detractor, Judge Tom Wicker, had to admit that Jim Garrison's closing argument was "brilliant."

Only one ballot was taken. The vote acquitting Jim Garrison was unanimous on the first ballot. F. Lee Bailey says that "the jury would have let him go even if he had confessed in open court because the judge was so rude." Having failed to convict Jim Garrison, the Strike Force, forgetting about organized crime and Carlos Marcello, packed up and left Louisiana. John Wall, its leader, resigned.

In two months, Jim Garrison had to stand for reelection. To mount any campaign at all, he had to borrow money from loan shark "King Solomon," who hesitated. Jim Garrison was a financial risk. Finally the loan shark agreed to take a second mortgage on Garrison's house at an interest rate of 12 or 13 percent.

Garrison was exhausted and did almost no campaigning. He did not make an appearance even in Algiers where the assessor James Smith's daughter had been murdered by a man who had a prior charge reduced. A longtime Garrison supporter, Smith couldn't even reach Garrison, who owed him, at the very least, condolences, if not an explanation for why his office had chosen on that earlier occasion to treat his daughter's future murderer with leniency. Smith also expected that Jim Garrison would reassure him that the man this time would face the ultimate penalty. Because Garrison did not make contact with Smith, at once he lost Smith's support, and the Algiers vote.

Black organizations traditionally expected money for their endorsement, but not from Jim Garrison. All they wanted was a handshake. Garrison did not show up for a meeting with BOLD, one of the leading African-American groups. While BOLD leaders sat cooling their heels at Tulane and Broad, John Volz tried to reach Jim Garrison. Finally, Garrison called Volz, only, unperturbed, to say casually, that he had forgotten that he had an appointment with BOLD. At one television debate, Garrison was represented by an empty chair.

On election day, he didn't even bother to vote for himself. Then, when Harry Connick beat him by 2,221 votes, he demanded a recount. Leaving office, Garrison talked about what mattered to him most. The day would come, he predicted, when it would be recognized that "we were not wrong in our inquiry into President Kennedy's assassination."

Garrison had to stand trial once more, on March 18, 1974, for not paying taxes on the pinball bribes for which he had already been acquitted of accepting. He represented himself and sat reading the newspaper at the defense table. "As a bookkeeper, I'd probably be a better garbage man," he acknowledged. In his closing, he compared the ill-fated Louisiana Loan and Thrift to a "Chinese laundry in the middle of a thunderstorm." It took the jury less than an hour to acquit him.

His career shattered, his marriage finally over and his health questionable, at the age of fifty-two Jim Garrison had to begin life over again. In a desultory way, he practiced law with Russell Schonekas, mostly providing referrals. For a generous fee, he represented Gordon Novel, who had been accused of conspiracy to fire bomb the United Federation of Churches building on St. Charles Avenue during Mardi Gras. Only later would Garrison and prosecutor and former Garrison assistant, Lawrence Centola Jr., learn that there was a moratorium on the demolition of buildings on St. Charles Avenue. "Including those you yourself owned," Centola says with Garrison-like sardonic humor. Novel and his partner had planned a development on the site.

Novel wanted Garrison to introduce the CIA into the case, since Novel had been in touch with them. The Agency, fearing that "the Kennedy probe would be reinvigorated," at once dissociated itself from Gordon Novel. One Agency document, denying they knew Novel, has the word "employed" by the CIA in quotation marks, suggesting the reverse. But when the new resident agent in New Orleans, Peter Houck, in court to testify against Novel, looked into Garrison's eyes, he observed "a rather detached air."

"We don't want to get into that, Gordon," Garrison said. "We want to win this case." Although Novel's partner was acquitted and the charge was conspiracy, Novel gained only a hung jury. "It takes two to tango," Garrison had argued—in vain.

All that interested Jim Garrison was the Kennedy case. At the office, he screened the Zapruder film for his colleagues. His secretary, Pat Morvant, was wary as he spoke of telephone security. But one day there was a phone call about checking the equipment, although nothing was wrong. The next morning three men arrived. When they departed, the door to the phone equipment box was open and the contents of Morvant's desk were in disarray. Garrison put a device on the telephones. If you heard clicking, it meant the phones were tapped. Morvant heard the clicking.

In 1974, he ran for the State Supreme Court. How would the founders of America feel being "bugged by most of sixteen federal intelligence agencies?" he asked, hoping voters did not want "silent men in the final bastion for the protection of your rights." He had fought the Federal government, "the most powerful force on the face of the earth—based on personal conviction." This time he failed even to make the run-off.

"Let me tell you about this person I loved," he would say years later to another blonde who attracted him, the writer Christine Wilkes. He married Phyllis in 1976, finally. "A man will cheat on his wife, but never on his type," he had promised her; even so, the marriage would be brief. He tired easily now and complained about his heart. "You have the heart of a hundred-year-old person," his doctor told him.

There were foreign editions of *The Star-Spangled Contract* and he was invited to Norway, Russia and France, but he refused to go, despite Phyllis' entreaties. He remained so indifferent to money that when his mother died and he had the key to her safe deposit box, he asked a bank employee to open it for him; the man said it was empty. Then, not wanting to be bothered, he sold Jane Gardiner's house for a fraction of its worth.

Only the Kennedy case aroused him. Mark Lane discovered an FBI receipt for a "missile removed by Commander James J. Humes" at the autopsy. Garrison nicknamed it "Bullet #399.5, brother of the notorious Magic Bullet 399" that had supposedly run through the bodies of both President Kennedy and Governor Connally. Had the FBI named it "John Edgar Junior?" Garrison joked, since the director appeared to have "adopted it?" He embroidered the conceit until the bullet "may have been removed from Commander Hume's leg. This could be checked out by a reexamination of Specter's computations—provided he hasn't burned his notes by now."

In 1978, Garrison ran for the Louisiana Court of Appeal, Fourth Circuit, mortgaging the property he owned with Dr. Fisher to finance his campaign. Alone of the old crowd loyal, Lou Ivon helped him. He defeated his former law partner Denis Barry, who spent $100,000 to Garrison's $40,000. The black organizations supported Barry, but the black voters went for Garrison. "Rumors of my death were greatly exaggerated," he said, quoting Mark Twain.

Word came to him that his father had died. Under "family" on Earling Garrison's death certificate, it said "none." Reading that, Jim Garrison burst into tears, the wound as fresh as the day Jane had seized the children and left Iowa for good.

He was childlike in his pleasure at being a judge. Always he supported the underdog, no matter that the record might not support an appeal. He ruled for a grandmother seeking parental rights; for a boy on crutches who fell at the Schwegmann Brothers supermarket; and for a young woman paralyzed for life in an accident as she exited a friend's car. She will not ever have children, Garrison wrote, "and will never experience sexual fulfillment."

"You're a damned Robin Hood," said Judge James C. Gulotta, once his Tulane classmate and now chief judge of the court and his closest friend.

"I thought you had empathy for people," Garrison rejoined. His opinions were not predictable. In a case of police brutality, he ruled for the police. Once he sided with an oil company. When his old adversary Rosemary James came before the court to appeal a contempt citation, Garrison favored throwing out the case against her. It was a freedom of speech issue and he was always resolute on that principle. His sense of humor did not fail him. He voted to reverse the conviction of a man impersonating a lawyer and accepting a bribe from the family of an Angola inmate, a case that had been presided over by Jerome Winsberg, who had defeated Jimmy Alcock and cost him his judgeship. "This is the most pitiful and ridiculous decision I have seen in my entire life," Winsberg wrote Garrison.

"I think you should know that some idiot has written a letter to me and is using your name," Garrison replied.

He wrote two brilliant opinions. One was on behalf of a firefighter named Patrick M. Callaghan, who refused both to apologize to a superior whom he accused of abandoning his men in a burning building, and to work without pay. Callaghan's speech was protected under the First Amendment, Garrison wrote. As for the apology, "such matters are better left to the province of Amy Vanderbilt and Emily Post."

Even more imaginative was his invocation of the Thirteenth Amendment outlawing slavery in his defense of Callaghan's reluctance to work without being compensated. "We are somewhat surprised," Garrison wrote, "to learn that the Fire Department and the Civil Service Commission regard involuntary servitude as still in existence in the U.S. We thought the issue had been resolved some time ago." He copied the Thirteenth Amendment to the U.S. Constitution into his opinion.

After thirteen years of service, Vincent Bruno was fired by the police department, ostensibly for disobeying sick leave regulations. In fact, as president of the policemen's union, PANO, Bruno had infuriated his superiors by calling a strike leading to the cancellation of Mardi Gras. The court affirmed the lower court's decision, only for Garrison to dissent in his most passionate opinion, which he titled "The Grinch Who Stole Mardi Gras."

He noted that Bruno had been fired the day after PANO affiliated with the national AFL-CIO. Breaking the union was the real motive behind Bruno's dismissal. Garrison's opinion quotes Kafka, *Alice in Wonderland* and P. G. Wodehouse and compares the sick leave rules to the "much vaunted 'crime of the century,'" in an oblique reference to the Kennedy assassination. "They couldn't break the union, so they broke the union leader," Garrison concludes, calling the court system a "secret officials" club.

One day Bruno received a telephone call from Garrison friend and public relations aide, Silvio Fernandez, requesting that they meet at La Louisiane, still Garrison's favorite restaurant. When Bruno arrived, Jim Garrison was waiting for him.

"You lost your case, Vincent," Garrison said. "We had a meeting and we decided to put you back to work. We were going to rule in your favor." Then, Garrison revealed, that decision was reversed 2 to 1. Mayor Dutch Morial had telephoned all three judges on the panel to ensure that Bruno would not be reinstated. Judge Israel Augustine was planning to run for Congress and required Morial's support (he got it, only to lose anyway). Judge Charles Ward required Morial's help in retiring his campaign debt.

"Two of us capitulated," Garrison said. He wanted to hold a press conference, but Fernandez and Bruno talked him out of it. It would ruin his judgeship and nothing could be done for Bruno now anyway.

A single day did not go by without his mentioning the Kennedy assassination or the CIA. His clerk Sallee Boyce thought his hero worship of the Kennedys was like his admiration for the novels of F. Scott Fitzgerald. Julie Sirera, skeptical of his view that, had Kennedy have lived, he would have ended the Vietnam war, thought Garrison's opinion of John F. Kennedy was idealized. To his clerks, he described what he had seen at Dachau, adding he never wanted to return to Europe.

When in the spring of 1976 he learned that the government was planning another investigation of the Kennedy assassination, Jim Garrison was dubious. He didn't believe any congressional committee had "that much courage." He changed his mind when he met Gaeton Fonzi, then working with Pennsylvania senator Richard Schweiker.

Fonzi arrived in New Orleans believing that Jim Garrison had "minimized the relationship between organized crime and the intelligence community." But Garrison was nothing like what the media made him out to be. Garrison in fact acknowledged at once that organized crime was a "key part of the assassination conspiracy."

Describing his own investigation as only a beginning, Garrison stated that he did not want personally "to get into the act." He hoped to help Fonzi "avoid the mistakes" he had made, to "separate out the false leads and identify the Greek coming in with the gifts." He was particularly bitter about Bill Turner who, "using false statements," and a "totally false picture," had led him to charge Edgar Eugene Bradley mistakenly.

Fonzi had his own doubts once Turner told him about a supposed meeting between Enrique ("Harry") Ruiz Williams, E. Howard Hunt and Richard Helms in a CIA safe house in Washington D.C., on the very morning of the assassination as they planned a second Bay of Pigs. It seemed to Fonzi that Turner was directing him back to a CIA story discarded even by the Warren Commission, that Fidel Castro had ordered the assassination.

Fonzi confirmed many of Jim Garrison's suspicions. Seth Kantor, a journalist who studied Jack Ruby, suggested that Fonzi visit the Royal Street gallery of one E. Lorenz Borenstein. Up a "junk-strewn winding stairway" Fonzi trudged. Then he pushed open a door only to discover a "stoop-shouldered, bald-headed little man with a drooping gray mustache and thick glasses perched at the end of a bulbous nose."

Six months to a year before the assassination Ruby had bought a "vulgar water color scene," Borenstein told Fonzi. It had been CIA operative William Gaudet, working simultaneously for the FBI, who had told the Bureau of Ruby's visit.

Ruby had revealed that his real name was Rubenstein," Borenstein said. His own uncle was Lev Bronstein, Leon Trotsky, he claimed. ("I've never heard of him," laughs Esteban Volkov, Trotsky's grandson, who would be Borenstein's relative, if Borenstein was in fact Trotsky's nephew. "How many people have claimed to have a family relationship to the Old Man!").

"A pleasant enough slob," Borenstein remembered Ruby.

"I didn't know I sold paintings to Jack Ruby until the FBI told me," Borenstein had confided to his old friend Mary Ferrell.

Now Borenstein shared his opinion on who killed President Kennedy with Gaeton Fonzi.

"The CIA did it," Borenstein said.

"Larry, did you ever do any work for the CIA?" Mary, ever sharp, asked him one day.

"In any port city, businessmen are asked to do things for our government," Borenstein said.

The HSCA investigation sparked new public interest in Jim Garrison. He told *New Orleans* magazine in June 1976 that the involvement of the "federal intelligence community" in the murder of John Kennedy was so obvious that it was as if "I were to get into the habit of giving interviews to explain that the sun rises in the east." Had the entire Agency been involved? he was asked. Those involved were not underlings, he replied, but "powerful elements," which was why the assassination had to be "ratified by the entire Agency . . . as a policy."

Three CIA components reacted to this article: the Chief of Domestic Collection (formerly Domestic Contact Service); the Office of General Counsel; and the Deputy Chief of Operations (formerly Plans), the clandestine services. A memo from J. Walton Moore in Dallas is titled, "Request For Guidance In Responding To News Media Inquiries."

HSCA was headed by distinguished former Philadelphia prosecutor Richard A. Sprague and a brilliant prosecutor out of Frank Hogan's New York office, Robert K. Tanenbaum. Sprague at once set down guidelines. He would hire no one connected to the FBI,

CIA or any federal agency because "to do a thorough investigation, those agencies' actions would be part of the investigation." He would "delve deeply into the methods of the FBI and CIA." Richard Helms at once began to lobby the Kennedy family not to cooperate with the Committee. When Sprague called Edward Kennedy, he refused to come to the telephone. Bobby, of course, had already silenced the family, for all time, it would seem.

Sprague subpoenaed CIA records. They never arrived. Representative Henry Gonzalez himself, chairman of the committee, told the CIA just to ignore the subpoenas. When the CIA demanded security checks on everyone looking at the few materials it did supply, along with confidentiality agreements, Sprague refused. "I'll be damned if they'll investigate us before we investigate them," Tanenbaum said. The CIA retaliated by marshalling its media and congressional assets to accuse Sprague of trampling on people's rights, the same false charge they had leveled against Jim Garrison.

Like Fonzi, Tanenbaum was at first wary of Garrison. Then he was shown a list of CIA plants in Garrison's office, a list also witnessed by researcher Eddie Lopez and by Louisiana investigator, L. J. Delsa. There were at least nine names: Among them were Raymond Beck, William Martin, Gordon Novel, Thomas Bethell, William Gurvich, Bill Boxley and Pershing Gervais.

Tanenbaum also found a companion document, an internal memo from Richard Helms' office. It revealed how the CIA had followed, harassed and attempted to intimidate Jim Garrison's witnesses. When Jim Garrison had complained of CIA sabotage of his investigation, it had been true.

A Team #3 was created to investigate the Louisiana leads. Homicide detective L. J. Delsa, a burly ex-Marine with flashing green eyes enlisted Robert Buras, soft-spoken and introspective; Buras had once investigated radical groups for New Orleans police intelligence. L. J. was flamboyant, his language salty; Buras, conservative and religious, remained determined to withhold judgment on Jim Garrison. Fonzi dubbed them "the odd couple." Their involvement led Jim Garrison to believe that a genuine homicide investigation of the president's death had begun. Speaking in May 1977 at Fort Sill, Oklahoma, where he was elected to the Officer Candidate School Hall of Fame, Garrison said he hoped for arrests "before the year is out."

Sprague was soon fired. Former Supreme Court Justice Arthur Goldberg was willing to replace him under the condition of full CIA cooperation, which he explained in a telephone call to CIA director

Stansfield Turner. Silence filled the airwaves. Goldberg repeated his concerns.

"I thought my silence was my answer," Turner said coldly.

Sprague was replaced by G. Robert Blakey, an "expert" in organized crime, a man who had never seen the inside of a homicide investigation. Blakey was making his third appearance in Jim Garrison's story. At once Blakey cut a deal with the CIA. Larry Strawderman, the CIA's Information and Privacy Coordinator, on July 27, 1977, wrote out the terms of the CIA's control of Blakey's investigation. "Certain areas relating to the assassination of President Kennedy," he decreed, "should be entirely disregarded based upon our contention that they are without merit or corroboration." It was as if the CIA were judging the evidence before the Committee even collected any.

Blakey capitulated to every Agency demand, about "sanitized materials," about documents kept "top secret" and "eyes only," and about no notes or copies being made during those rare moments when investigators could, in a locked room at CIA headquarters, be permitted to view some CIA documents. A nondisclosure agreement would silence House investigators and lawyers "in perpetuity." Blakey further promised to "protect Agency sources and methods." He permitted the CIA to decide whether and how it wished to comply with any and all of the HSCA's requests. The CIA went on to control exactly what questions the Committee could ask of CIA assets like Bernardo de Torres, Lawrence Howard, Loran Hall and William Gaudet.

In the year 2003 Blakey would complain that the Agency did not reveal to Congress the role of George Joannides, the CIA's liaison to the HSCA, in the events of 1963, events which had included Joannides' encouraging the DRE to expose Oswald's supposed pro-Castro activities. Helms' choice of Joannides compromised the committee's investigation, Blakey protested. But it was Blakey himself who had compromised the investigation from the start. Richard Helms did not require the assistance of George Joannides to inflict CIA domination on the HSCA. Blakey had accomplished that himself.

Unaware of Blakey's agreement with the CIA, taking premature comfort in Blakey's having kept on some of Sprague's staff, Jim Garrison allowed himself to believe that in the Committee's final report, "my office is going to be vindicated." He made the error of sending memos of undeveloped leads to lawyer Jonathan Backmer, instead of handing them directly to Delsa and Buras, who remained incorruptible and independent. It was Blackmer whom Garrison asked to determine whether Fred Lee Crisman was a "domestic intelligence operative." Blackmer ignored him. It was Blackmer whom he asked to look into "Shaw and CMC activity." It was not done.

In some venues it was already too late. Delsa requested of the Dallas police that he be permitted to read the notes taken when Oswald was questioned; he was incredulous when he was told that there were none. "You were sitting with a guy suspected of killing the president and you didn't even write his name on a matchbook? How could you run a check on him?" Delsa demanded. In New Orleans, Francis Martello, with whom Buras had served on police intelligence, revealed his bitterness about the Warren Report, calling it a "travesty." Dubious about any federal investigation, Martello concealed from Robert Buras that Oswald had ordered him to telephone the FBI field office and say that someone they knew, Lee Oswald, was there with him.

Yet Delsa and Buras begin to vindicate Jim Garrison and add to his evidence. Jack Martin, now working as a night watchman at an old age home where in priest's robes he listened to confessions, introduced them to William Dalzell, who described making drops of medical supplies into Cuba with David Ferrie; Dalzell had driven Sergio Arcacha Smith to a training camp near Slidell. From Joe Oster, they confirmed that Banister talked with the CIA on the telephone often.

L. J. flew to California where he asked Kerry Thornley how he came to learn Spanish in the Marines, as he drew close to Thornley's own CIA connection. When, exactly in 1963, had Thornley returned to New Orleans? Delsa asked. They agreed to meet the next day, only for Thornley to fail to show up.

"This kid's running on me," L. J. told the Los Angeles police, who were willing to search for the missing witness. But the HSCA suddenly changed L. J.'s assignment. L. J. was ordered to abandon the Thornley lead and instead investigate a supposed photograph of Oswald, Che Guevara and Castro's mistress Marita Lorenz in a safe at the Russian embassy at Ottawa, a futile distraction. Thornley escaped. It was clear to L. J. that the HSCA did not want Thornley's associations penetrated and that he himself had drawn too close to the CIA's involvement in the assassination.

L. J. tracked down Lawrence Howard in El Monte, California. If he had worked for the CIA, Howard said, it would have been "indirectly." He had been in Dallas only for five days, from the end of September until October 4th. Shown a photograph of Thomas Edward

Beckham, Howard said he "looked familiar." Delsa concluded that Howard was an "interesting person," one who "could have fired the shots that changed history for the whole century."

Back in New Orleans, Buras interviewed Delphine Roberts, who now recounted Banister's remark about Oswald's use of "544 Camp Street" on his leaflet: "How is it going to look for him to have the same address as me?" Still she was not yet ready to admit she had seen Oswald in person.

The HSCA refused to authorize Buras and Delsa to investigate Oswald's appearance at the East Louisiana State Hospital at Jackson. Buras was permitted to talk only to the Clinton witnesses who had already been interviewed by Francis Fruge, Anne Dischler and Moo Moo Sciambra. Nor were Buras and Delsa permitted to go to Clinton and Jackson together. Instead, a Committee bureaucrat, Patricia Orr, came to Louisiana to accompany Buras to East Feliciana Parish. Orr carried the specific list of Clinton people Buras was authorized to interview. He was not sent the earlier statements of these witnesses so he could compare them with what the witnesses said now.

On the drive to Clinton, Orr told Buras she believed in the single bullet theory.

"Don't tell me this bullet did all that up and down and came out in pristine condition," Buras said.

"You don't know what you're talking about," Orr said. "You're just a cop. These people are ballistics experts."

"They're not experts. They're liars," Buras answered.

Blakey and Cornwell could not entirely stifle the Louisiana investigation. Interviewed by Buras, Henry Earl Palmer remembered the doctor with "a Spanish surname" with whom Oswald said he was living. But Dr. Frank Silva was not on Patricia Orr's list and Buras was not permitted to meet with him. Nor could he contact Ronald Johnston, the Baton Rouge private investigator who had telephoned the Committee saying he knew two separate people who had seen Oswald and Clay Shaw together at the Clinton courthouse, as well as at the hospital. Nor was Buras permitted to investigate any 1963 contacts between Guy Banister and Henry Earl Palmer, to corroborate Palmer's assertion that he knew Banister and that Banister had definitely not appeared in Clinton.

Buras was forbidden to examine any possible contact between Banister and Alvin and Lloyd Cobb. He could not investigate Marydale Farms and whether Ferrie, Shaw and Oswald had been seen there together. He could not inquire into whether John Henry Shipes had been correct in connecting Shaw with the East Feliciana Klan. He could not explore the appearance of someone calling himself "Oswald" at the Lafayette Holiday Inn. He could not look into the connection between Ruby, Oswald and Gladys Palmer. It was soon apparent to Buras and Delsa that they were being paid *not* to investigate what Oswald's residence in Louisiana revealed about the assassination.

In New Orleans, Delsa interviewed Warren de Brueys. Delsa now knew that John Quigley had consulted de Brueys before visiting Oswald in jail.

"I'd like to see your notes," Delsa said. He had no notes, de Brueys said. Besides, he had never met Lee Harvey Oswald.

Garrison's grand jury transcripts now sat in Harry Connick's filing cabinets. Connick and his assistant, Bill Wessell, insisted, "all grand jury records are destroyed after being held for ten years." Alive and well, the transcripts would become part of the National Archives owing to the courage of a police investigator attached to Connick's office named Gary Raymond.

Upon taking office, Connick began to burn Jim Garrison's records. When it came to the grand jury transcripts connected to the Clay Shaw trial, Raymond, whom Connick had put in charge of the incinerations, had demurred.

"It's not exactly John Brown killing Jim Smith here," Raymond said.

"Was Shaw convicted?" Connick argued. There was no appeal pending. When Raymond still hesitated, arguing that there was an "ethical or moral obligation" to hold onto these records, Connick became angry.

"I told you to burn it! Burn it all!" Connick ordered. Believing that "nothing in the law required me to follow an order I interpreted as illegal, immoral or unethical," Raymond held onto the transcripts.

By the time Buras visited Jack Rogers, he did not even bother to ask to see Rogers' files. Buras knew he was not supposed to request documents that might uncover new evidence. It would not please Blakey and his deputy, Gary Cornwell were he to validate Jim Garrison's work. The HSCA never obtained Jack Rogers' files on the assassination and preferred it that way.

So, too, no evidence reached Washington when Frank Bartes, that cousin of Dr. Frank Silva and Oswald cohort, showed Buras a photograph taken in Cuba. Beside an airplane stood Fidel Castro, Bartes himself and a tall gray-haired man whom Bartes easily identified from the photo book as #5, Clay Shaw: Buras did not bother to take that photograph with him. Clay Shaw, above all, was someone whose role in the assassination Buras and Delsa were not to explore.

As often as they could, Blakey and Cornwell separated Buras and Delsa. Buras had to take Harold Leap, the CIA's man on the Committee, with him when he interviewed former FBI clerk William Walter and the CIA's William Gaudet. As Walter discussed a report written by Warren de Brueys, which established that de Brueys had contacted Oswald as an FBI security informant, Leap repeatedly interrupted him. Irritated by Leap's attempts to prevent him from talking, Walter was indignant. "I know what I know and I know what I saw," he said angrily. Oswald had "an informant's status with our office." Other agents besides de Brueys had contacted Oswald. Later, testifying in Washington, Walter had to endure repeated insinuations by Committee lawyers that he was lying.

At the interview of William Gaudet, Leap made certain that Gaudet would not be asked why his name, just before Oswald's, was obliterated from the list of people getting Mexican tourist cards that had been sent to the Warren Commission. (The Commission had not called Gaudet.) Gaudet in turn kept silent about his relationship with the FBI and denied that he was the informant who had told the FBI that Jack Ruby had appeared at Larry Borenstein's gallery.

There were some weeks when Delsa and Buras were given no assignments at all. Yet within the small window of time in which they moved freely, they succeeded in developing a key assassination witness, Thomas Edward Beckham. "I was never able to do much with him," Garrison had written to Blackmer, but he was a "subject worthy of inquiry. He was a protégé of F. Lee Crisman and part of the Banister cell." Beset by "prevaricators, poultroons and opportunists of the lowest order," Garrison had allowed Beckham to elude him.

Garrison wondered whether Beckham had been set up as an "alternative patsy in case of a last minute problem with Lee Harvey Oswald."

On July 28, 1977, Delsa and Blackmer interviewed Beckham in Mobile, Alabama. Beckham admitted he knew Lee Harvey Oswald and had seen him at Banister's office. Oswald, Beckham said, had been involved with "a group of ex-CIA members who plotted, [and] carried out the assassination," then framed him. Beckham described meetings he had attended with David Ferrie and Shaw, Luis (whom he still called "Lucious") Rabel, G. Wray Gill, Grady Durham and Sergio Arcacha Smith.

On August 9th, Delsa and Blackmer interviewed Beckham again.

He had been a "runner" for Banister's group, Beckham explained. He had seen Ferrie in green fatigues returning from a training camp. He was certain Oswald was working for the government. He believed Banister had been murdered. He revealed how he had been dispatched to Dallas with that package of maps, photographs and diagrams handed to him by G. Wray Gill and David Ferrie. He had delivered them to Lawrence Howard in Dallas outside the Executive Inn motel. Delsa flew to Dallas and interviewed the manager of what had been the Executive Inn, but was now a Best Western. No 1963 records had survived.

When these extraordinary interviews were described to Jim Garrison, he formulated a new set of questions to be put to Beckham. Meanwhile Delsa and Buras should investigate Fred Lee Crisman, whom Garrison was more certain than ever was a "cutout or go-between at a very high level."

On October 1st, free of Blackmer, Delsa and Buras interviewed Beckham at the Holiday Inn in Jackson, Mississippi. Now Beckham outlined two specific meetings at which he had been present, and the assassination discussed. One was at Algiers, the other at the Marcello-owned Town and Country Motel in Jefferson Parish. He repeated how he had taken the drawings and maps of Dallas buildings to Lawrence Howard. He revealed now that Fred Lee Crisman had ordered him to lie to the Garrison grand jury. He explained Crisman's close connection to Offutt Air Force base in Omaha.

At this interview, Beckham was alternately remorseful and frightened. He was "wishing I hadn't done it," he said. He wondered who in the New Orleans police department still knew Jack Martin, whom he called "a very dangerous man." You'll never get anything on Fred Lee Crisman or Jack Martin, Beckham predicted. "They're too big."

He was right.

The next step, Buras and Delsa decided, was to test Beckham's credibility with a lie detector test.

THE DEATH OF JIM GARRISON: VALE 22

*I don't know if I would do it again because of the emotional price
I paid.*

—Jim Garrison

I N WASHINGTON, ROBERT BURAS and L. J. Delsa received permission for the polygraph of Thomas Edward Beckham. Only
then did they bring Beckham to New Orleans. On March 8th
and 9th, 1978, Richard Hunter of the New Orleans police department, and a former partner of Buras, as a favor, did the polygraph.
There was no cost to the Committee.

Buras put the requisite amount of pressure on Beckham, knowing that those most habituated to lying have the best chance of beating the machine. "Don't shade it," Buras told Beckham. "Give it your
best shot."

"Was he being truthful?" Buras and Delsa asked Hunter as soon
as it was over. Delsa had believed Beckham because he always made
distinctions and when he didn't know something, he said so. With
liars, Delsa had discovered from years in homicide, "water swells
over the levee without control." Beckham says he told Buras and
Delsa the truth.

After two days, Hunter revealed his conclusion. He had discovered no deception. Asked whether Fred Lee Crisman had conveyed
him into secret areas where you needed security clearance, Beckham said that he had. The machine revealed no deception. Did
Crisman bring him onto Offut Air Force Base? Beckham said yes,
and there was no sign of deception.

"This guy is amazing," Hunter said. Despite Beckham's lack of
any formal education whatsoever, he was a very intelligent man.

Beckham resembled no liar Hunter had ever encountered. He was telling the truth. Like Oswald, Buras and Delsa concluded, Beckham had been a young, uneducated kid grabbed up by intelligence.

The next day, March 10th, Delsa and Buras were summoned to Washington by their immediate superior, Cliff Fenton. They were questioned separately, then charged with conducting an unauthorized polygraph. They had questioned an important witness with CIA connections, zeroing in on truths that the compromised, CIA-controlled Committee could not tolerate.

Deeply religious, firm in his principles, Buras did not take lightly challenges to his rectitude.

"I looked you right in the eye and requested permission for the polygraph," Buras told Gary Cornwell.

"Did I give you a specific reply?" Cornwell shot back. "Would it be fair to say that by not replying, while I looked right at you, that you took that as tacit approval?" Cornwell denied he ever heard the request for permission to administer a polygraph to Beckham. When Delsa supported Buras, Cornwell scanned the horizon for a suitable scapegoat.

"Blackmer gave you permission, didn't he?" Cornwell said. Delsa noted that Blackmer had of late gotten dangerously close to Jim Garrison and might have become a Cornwell target.

"Bobby, they're afraid of what the polygraph showed," Delsa said. "They're looking for a scapegoat so it could be written off as a mistake."

There would be no investigation of Fred Lee Crisman, who had died in 1975. Buras concluded that if they could have connected Beckham and Crisman "to some guy with the vowels 'a' or 'o' at the end of their names," Blakey would have permitted them to continue. But in approaching those who had planned the assassination, Buras and Delsa had gone far beyond any role organized crime might have played in its implementation.

Buras and Delsa were punished with two-week administrative suspensions. Blackmer was also suspended. Grudgingly, on March 13th, 1978, the Committee constructed an after-the-fact paper authorization of the polygraph so that Buras and Delsa could be reimbursed for their air fares in bringing Beckham to Louisiana.

Team #3 had been effectively destroyed. Orestes Peña was deposed by Martin Daly, an ex-cop from New York, and William Brown, who knew next to nothing about the Louisiana evidence. When John Manchester appeared in Washington before an Executive Session, which meant that his testimony would be sealed, Buras and Delsa were not invited, although they alone knew what had happened in Clinton and Jackson.

Buras located a distraught Francis Fruge at home in Basile. Having lost all respect for the "federal people," Fruge was bitter about how the HSCA had treated him, bitter that the FBI had failed to pursue the leads he had developed from the Rose Cheramie story. He had told Mike Ewing, a Cornwell deputy, about the sudden suicide in jail of Andrew Dunn, but Ewing had not authorized an investigation.

Now Buras and Delsa were explicitly forbidden from following up on any of Jim Garrison's leads. "We're not interested in Garrison. Stay away from his stuff," they were ordered. "We were tadpoles in a sea of sharks and never knew it," Delsa concluded. "We didn't have a chance."

"Judge, I'm going to break your heart," L. J. told Jim Garrison. "This is gone. This is over. This country shouldn't spend one more copper penny on an assassination investigation out of Washington. They could offer me $200,000 and I wouldn't go back." Garrison urged Buras and Delsa to keep their jobs as long as they could. The truth will come out, he said. As always, he took the long view.

The final interviews of the Louisiana witnesses reveal the HSCA's bad faith. An Al Maxwell found Corrie Collins living in Highland Park, Michigan. Collins remained a man who did not suffer fools gladly. When Maxwell assumed, incorrectly, that Collins had worked at East, he remained silent, as he did when Maxwell asked what questions were on Henry Earl Palmer's voter registration test, an irrelevancy. Maxwell had no idea that Collins had identified Clay Shaw and David Ferrie as being in Clinton together. Collins did not bother to enlighten him.

"Are you sure the man you saw was Oswald?" Maxwell did ask.

"Yes, I'm sure," Collins said.

In May 1978, Thomas Edward Beckham was deposed at the federal courthouse in New Orleans. Robert Buras was present, but not invited to speak. His choice of questions reveals that lawyer James E. McDonald's purpose was not to learn anything new about the assassination, but to prove that this inconvenient witness was a liar, and unreliable.

McDonald attempted to discredit Beckham's statement that Clay

Shaw knew Jack Ruby. "Exactly how" was Beckham introduced to Ruby, what was he first doing?" McDonald asks in an obvious attempt to embarrass the witness, and to suggest that he might be homosexual, the theme of the entire interview. If Beckham was acquainted with Clay Shaw, McDonald attempted to suggest, it could only have been because Beckham, too, was homosexual, and a Shaw sexual partner.

"Would you consider yourself to be a friend of his?" McDonald asked. Did Beckham know Shaw's occupation?

"I never really seen him work," Beckham said. Then he added, "he had a nickname." Determined to avoid yet another identification of Clay Shaw as Clay Bertrand, McDonald quickly changed the subject.

Beckham remarked that Oswald was not a Communist: "He was one hundred percent American." Oswald and Arcacha had argued, but it wasn't because on one essential point they were not in agreement: they both were anti-Castro.

In this interview, Beckham establishes his bona fides in a host of ways. He knows that Arcacha called himself "Dr." He knows that Luis ("Lucious") Rabel ran a "cleaner's." He knows Banister habitually threw Jack Martin out of his office. The date of the Algiers meeting where the talk was of how "Kennedy ought to be assassinated" allows for Arcacha's presence. Oswald was then in the Soviet Union; Beckham does not place him at this meeting. Beckham discusses the package he carried to Dallas. For a moment, he seems to have trapped himself, saying he delivered it to a man named "Hall." Then he corrects himself. It was "Howard."

Beckham admits that he lied to Jim Garrison's grand jury. He says he was told they had an "in" planted in Garrison's office, ensuring that "the investigation would be ran the opposite direction, so for me not to worry." Fred and Jack Martin were CIA "operatives," Beckham says, performing "services for government agencies."

McDonald ridicules this witness repeatedly. He asks Beckham what the "C" in "Mark C. Evans" stood for. Unflappable, Beckham replies that it stood for "country." He admits his formal education ended at the third grade. McDonald then devotes considerable time to extracting from Beckham all his phony degrees, only to return to the subject of homosexuality. If Oswald was a homosexual, McDonald says, might not "these church groups [be] nothing more than a homosexual-type society or organization?"

Beckham laughs. "Not everybody connected with it was homosexual, you know," he says. "You don't have to be homosexual to like money."

Listening, Buras reflected: Beckham with his false religious and educational degrees had been made impeachable by the Agency. That was how he survived. In this he resembled Oswald, who was completely impeachable.

Some CIA-connected witnesses defied the CIA. Lawyer Robert Genzman fed William Gaudet the question of whether his CIA relationship, like Shaw's, was "purely informational," a question that contained the answer Gaudet was obviously expected to give. No, Gaudet said, he did "certain chores for them which were not informational." Then Gaudet exploded once more the CIA's persistent lie on its documents with respect to the end-dates of the service of its agents. Some CIA records state that Gaudet's service concluded in 1961. This time Gaudet did not offer 1969 as the end date of his CIA service. "I never did end my relationship with CIA," Gaudet remarked. Both CIA and FBI had insisted that Gaudet not be called before the Warren Commission. HSCA deposed Gaudet as a "protected witness," with the Committee being instructed by the CIA's Frank C. Carlucci on what they could and could not ask.

Late in July 1978, ex-CIA officer Victor Marchetti telephoned the HSCA. An old friend at the Agency had told him that the Committee was "getting close to the buried bodies." Gary Cornwell leaped into his car and drove to Marchetti's home in Vienna, Virginia. Marchetti refused to reveal the name of his CIA source, except to say that he was with Counter Intelligence. This source had told him that the CIA "had agreed to a limited hang out policy" for the HSCA. In a memo, James Angleton and Richard Helms had placed E. Howard Hunt in Dallas on November 22nd.

CIA has "decided to give up E. Howard Hunt as part of the limited hang out," Marchetti said. When he published this information in *Spotlight* magazine, Hunt sued him. In fact, Marchetti had been fed partial disinformation. There would be a person sacrificed by the CIA as a limited hang out. But it would not be E. Howard Hunt. Rather, the CIA's newest scapegoat was a certain gray-haired gentleman prominent in New Orleans society. As the final HSCA report reveals, the Agency sacrificed Clay Shaw. The report calls Shaw a "limited hang out, cut out" to play a role in the conspiracy, the very terms Marchetti had been told were being applied to Hunt.

Shaw had to be sacrificed for several reasons. Many witnesses by now had revealed how the CIA and FBI had concealed evidence from the Warren Commission. Even J. Lee Rankin, the senior counsel for the Warren Commission, told the HSCA he regretted he had taken the CIA's word that Oswald "was never a CIA agent." Was the HSCA investigating whether the people involved in the CIA cover-up were involved in the assassination as well? Rankin wanted to know. He received no reply.

Acoustic evidence arriving late in the HSCA investigation and revealing that there had been more than three shots fired at Dealey Plaza, eliminated the possibility that Oswald had acted alone. Richard Billings, who worked closely with Blakey, says that Blakey would never have conceded that there had been a conspiracy at all had the motorcycle dictabelt not been discovered recording what appeared to contain an audio transcript of the shots being fired in Dealey Plaza. It was in this context that the Committee sacrificed Shaw, who had died of lung cancer in 1974.

Shaw, the Committee decided, was "possibly one of the high level planners, or 'cut out' to the planners of the assassination." History replies to Helms' question, "are we doing enough for that guy down there?" in the negative. The CIA treated its asset Shaw with shameful indifference. Impoverished, Shaw was left to fend for himself. Shaw's friends blamed Jim Garrison, but it was the CIA that was responsible for Shaw's humiliation and for the depletion of his resources.

Meanwhile, with Oswald forever gone as the "lone assassin," Blakey and Cornwell decided to focus on organized crime as the real power behind the plot. Desperate for any kind of evidence that the Mafia was behind the assassination, Gary Cornwell interviewed Aaron Kohn in New Orleans. It was a "gross oversimplification" to say that the Bourbon Street clubs that violated the law had been controlled by Carlos Marcello, Kohn said. The public officials Marcello corrupted were primarily in Jefferson, not Orleans Parish, just as Jim Garrison had always said.

If Cornwell hoped to connect Oswald to organized crime through his uncle, Charles "Dutz" Murret, and then vilify Jim Garrison for not pursuing the connection, Kohn had to dash this expectation. Murret paid federal taxes on his wagering operation, Kohn pointed out. Nor had Kohn ever proved that Murret worked for Marcello cohort Sam Saia. Uncle Dutz had even repudiated illegal gambling in 1959! Another Oswald relative, Kohn remarked, Eugene Murret, was a "highly regarded" former professor of law at Loyola.

When Cornwell attempted to blame Regis Kennedy for the lack of enthusiasm of the New Orleans FBI field office in investigating Carlos Marcello, Kohn stopped him in his tracks. Regis Kennedy had always fought against crime, organized or otherwise, Kohn said, revealing how distasteful he found the crude implication that Regis Kennedy lacked integrity.

During this trip, Cornwell, with Mike Ewing in tow, met Jim Garrison. Garrison allotted him thirty minutes. The FBI and CIA had been able to "control and evade the investigative resources of any other body," Garrison said. He assumed the same thing had happened to the House Select Committee. In his memo of the encounter, Ewing complains about Garrison's "long monologue" about the CIA.

Many of your key witnesses had been employed by Carlos Marcello, Cornwell states, inaccurately.

If I had found anything relating to Marcello, Garrison says patiently, I "would definitely have pursued it." If I had taken bribes from Marcello, or was even linked to such bribes, I "would have retired on the money long ago." He knew Marcello, of course. He hoped, Garrison added, that the House Select Committee would pursue the role of Fred Lee Crisman, who was "an important figure." Forty-five minutes had passed. Garrison then asked Cornwell whether he would like another copy of *A Heritage of Stone.*

"It is important to know who killed Jack Kennedy and why," Garrison tells Cornwell and Ewing as he bids them an overdue farewell.

Subsequent documents have revealed that it was CIA counter intelligence chief James Angleton who was in bed with the Mafia, not Jim Garrison. In his HSCA testimony, John Whitten, Angleton's colleague, reveals he had been appalled to discover Angleton protecting his own Mafia assets and their numbered bank accounts in Panama. "He would not want to double cross them," Whitten observed.

Having first assigned Whitten to investigate the assassination for the CIA, Richard Helms had changed his mind, turning the matter back to Angleton and his right-hand man, Birch O'Neal. Jim Garrison's Alice-in-Wonderland metaphor was apt: it was the CIA who was shielding the Mafia, not Jim Garrison. It was Walter Sheridan who bribed and intimidated witnesses, not Garrison.

Delsa and Buras preferred that their names not be included on the HSCA final report. They knew the report was a "fix," even as they lacked the CIA memos later to become available at the National Archives, which reveal persistent demands that Blakey alter the text. There remains as well a paper trail of complaints from the CIA that

HSCA investigators went too far in their exploration of the role of the CIA in the assassination.

On September 27, 1978, CIA's Scott Breckinridge, writing on behalf of the Director of Central Intelligence, wrote a five-page, single-spaced letter to Blakey complaining about the HSCA's questioning of Richard Helms. Irregularities in the CIA's 201 file of Lee Harvey Oswald had led to questions, not least why no file was seemingly opened for Oswald for fourteen months after his October 1959 defection to the Soviet Union. The CIA had received a cable from the American consulate in the Soviet Union about a man who had threatened to commit espionage and give away military secrets to the Soviets. Yet no file was extant.

Hoover had sent the CIA a clipping from the *Washington Star* about a Marine who had defected to the Soviet Union, inquiring whether they knew about it. "Tell him we don't have anything on it," CIA ordered. Even when Oswald's name appeared in the spring of 1960 on a list of 200 people whose mail the CIA had ordered opened, no file was opened, if one were to believe CIA. The CIA cover sheet on the file of December 1960 reflected Oswald still being in the Marine Corps, even after his defection to the Soviet Union (Radar Operator, U.S. Marine Corps, as of 1960). CIA's behavior for the written record conveys a deliberate attempt to suggest that his defection was of no moment, or not real.

Helms had been questioned by HSCA lawyer Michael Goldsmith, inspiring the agency's fury that Blakey's staff should not honor Helms' plausible deniability. "A man of such senior position in a large organization would obviously be unfamiliar with the sort of details asked him," Breckinridge writes in a hectoring letter. His subtext is that Blakey had better get his staff under control. Breckinridge insists that there are "reasonable and convincing explanations" for the oddities in the Agency's records on Oswald.

"I find the nature of the questioning disturbing," he writes, as if HSCA were under CIA jurisdiction. "Mr. Goldsmith's performance on these points was tendentious at best. He introduced material into the record that we knew—or that he had reason to know—to be different from the way he elected to present it. This careful construction of a flawed record cannot serve the purpose of an objective investigation." Repeatedly attacking the HSCA's young investigators, the Agency demanded that Blakey accept its denials, while claiming simultaneously that the CIA was offering "cooperation."

Blakey had provided CIA with several drafts of his final report. In a sixteen-page memo to Blakey, again on behalf of the Director of Central Intelligence, Breckinridge proposes changes to a second draft. In this memo, Breckinridge's tone is arrogant and dismissive. He terms the report "incorrect," and attacks scornfully the investigator of Oswald's Mexico City visit, who was Eddie Lopez. Over and over Breckinridge defends the Agency against the charge that it had not informed the Warren Commission of what it knew. He serves up a plethora of excuses, including that it was the FBI that was charged with reporting to the Commission. "What the Agency did was to supply material that was deemed relevant," Breckinridge insists. He attacks the draft for "unsupported assertions," calling it "badly confused in its treatment of facts and sources." When he cannot refute the facts, he terms the report "unbalanced."

Breckinridge reserves special contempt for the CIA's John Whitten, the one officer who had spoken frankly to the HSCA regarding the Agency's maneuvers with respect to the assassination. Whitten's recollection was "wrong," Breckinridge says in one place. In another he charges that Whitten's "report" [his quotation marks] was "incorrect." Breckinridge also objects to the "unusual space" Whitten's testimony was given in the report. "This is not because he knew anything," Breckinridge claims, "but must be because he was prepared to speak about things he did not know."

Breckinridge insists upon one deletion after another, some on the basis of protecting sources, others for no stated reason at all. "We would prefer no reference in an unclassified report to what is in the Calderon 201 file," he writes, referring to the Mexico City material and Luisa Calderon. He objects to references even to the AMLASH trial in 1965, demanding that they be deleted: "Reportedly, Castro told the HSCA that he knew that AMLASH was Cubela; that is not for us to confirm." He writes as if CIA and HSCA were the same entity, with common interests.

In a March document, Breckinridge responds to a request made by Blakey that CIA "review inserts for the HSCA draft report on [Antonio] Veciana." CIA obliged, going on to accuse the HSCA "investigator," obviously Gaeton Fonzi, of misrepresenting "both the relationship of CIA with the man described generally as an 'asset' in the proposed inset, and what that man's relationship was with Veciana."

He denies that Veciana had any tie with the CIA through "Bishop," insisting that Maurice (Morris) Bishop "was not of, from, or with CIA." Breckinridge argues no less vehemently that Bishop was not David Atlee Phillips, no matter that Fonzi was able to accumulate a wealth of corroborating evidence, some from CIA officers themselves, that he was. Veciana was "an asset of another U.S. government agency," Breckinridge claims, accusing Fonzi of having "irretrievably botched the investigation."

"I have deleted the section on this because it is so flagrantly in error," Breckinridge writes. Then he reveals how Blakey had contacted CIA every step of the way. "You planned to contact us early this week to have a substantive exchange on the final draft report," he writes, as if for the record. "We are available at your convenience."

Less than two weeks later, CIA reviewed the HSCA's draft paper on "Evolution and Implications of the CIA-Sponsored Assassination Conspiracies Against Castro." Here Breckinridge is emboldened to "raise a personal question" on the very first paragraph; then he complains that there is more "simplistic rhetoric" than "mature moral principle."

Arguing that the writings of church philosophers have distinguished "between different kinds of homicide," Breckinridge invokes the red herring of whether Adolf Hitler should have been assassinated. Always he presents the CIA as morally impeccable, its concerns, "narrowly, protection of intelligence sources and methods." Predictably, he claims that the devastating conclusions of the Church Committee were "erroneous." There is no record that Blakey did anything but comply.

Jim Garrison praised the Church Committee, which discovered that the CIA "had installed permanent machinery for accomplishing assassinations." But the HSCA was "a solid cover-up as soon as Blakey got in there. Every time they came up with something good, it was blunted or turned aside by Blakey."

The HSCA Report calls the Clinton witnesses "credible and significant." CIA would not approve, so a qualification had to be affixed: "while there were points that could be raised to call into question their credibility, it was the judgment of the committee that they were telling the truth as they knew it." The "Summary Memorandum," from which the Report was drawn, and more honest, states that "Oswald must have been present at least two days in the Clinton-Jackson area." It grants that he did fill out an application at East. There was "clear indication" that Clay Shaw and David Ferrie were with him.

Blakey and Cornwell had insisted that Garrison's leads be ignored, treating his investigation as worthless. Yet, between 1995 and 1997, documents reveal Robert Blakey writing to the Assassination Records Review Board requesting any information it could supply on two incidental Garrison witnesses, Layton Martens and Alvin Beaubouef.

"I am writing from the Bench," Jim Garrison informed his editor. He was devoting weekends, evenings, and even idle moments when the court was in session, to telling the story of his investigation. "I am going to get this book published if it's the last thing I do," he vowed. His law clerks were enlisted: Julie Sirera to check on the date of Guy Banister's death; Ann Benoit to locate a safe house on Napoleon Avenue and to look up Mayor Earle Cabell. Garrison mulled over titles: *The Execution; The War Machine; A Game of Kings; Coup D'Etat; A Farewell to Justice.*

Between 1982 and 1986, *A Farewell to Justice* was rejected by nineteen publishers. Finally Prentice-Hall gave Garrison a contract, only to back out. They had chosen as outside reader Sylvia Meagher, who had been wide-eyed in her support of Clay Shaw. Garrison replied with courtesy, praising Meagher's book, *Accessories After the Fact,* as "excellent." To his agent, he was more blunt. "Score one for the CIA," he wrote bitterly, "resulting from its control of a large part of the publishing industry."

In Zachary Sklar at Sheridan Square Press, he found an open-minded editor. Sklar suggested that he convert the book into a memoir, his personal story, an idea Garrison had resisted when Ralph Schoenman had first suggested it to him. Years earlier Garrison had argued that the story was not about him, but about President Kennedy. "The truly new material," Sklar now persuaded him, was his own story.

Garrison wrote *On the Trail of the Assassins* in his characteristic sardonic voice, relying on memory because even he was unable to gain access to the Orleans Parish grand jury transcripts held in thrall by Harry Connick. He particularly wanted to reexamine Kerry Thornley's testimony. There are some inaccuracies. Garrison persists in the story that Russell Long awakened him to the case. He denies that he ever met Carlos Marcello, and that the *Paese Sera* articles came to him after the Shaw trial, an obvious memory lapse. Near the end of the editing process, he wrote to Sklar: "You must be some editor if you can cause me to weep at my own stuff."

On the Trail of the Assassins discovered a ready audience, selling 32,000 copies in its first five months. When the distributor declared bankruptcy, a federal court injunction froze Garrison's royalties. Nothing mattered but getting out the truth as he borrowed ten thousand dollars "with appropriate interest" from Lou Wolfson for some "effective advertising in this area." One ad quoted Norman

Mailer, who praises the book as "the most powerful case yet" that the assassination "was the work not of the Mob but the CIA."

Grateful, Garrison called Wolfson "the only American I know who went out of his way to do something for Jack Kennedy and that makes you one of my heroes." The widowed Mrs. Willard Robertson, whose Volkswagen dealer husband had been a founder of "Truth and Consequences," wrote she would never forget how Garrison "stood alone in the end, never giving up hope." The United States Supreme Court had ruled in Willard Robertson's favor in *Shaw v. Robertson*, Shaw's attempt to accuse Robertson of depriving him of his civil rights.

University courses in "The Crime Of The Century" placed *On the Trail of the Assassins* on their reading lists. "See," Garrison told Phyllis, whom he loved still, "I told you I would get out of that hole. You wouldn't wait!"

With Rosemary James, Jack Wardlow had coauthored a hasty Garrison attack in 1967 called "Plot or Politics." Now, in a *Times-Picayune* review, Wardlow wrote that *On the Trail of the Assassins* was "rife with paranoia." Yet, in the same paper Iris Kelso found Garrison's book "riveting," and "told in a well-modulated, wry and witty style that is Garrison at his best." Kelso closed: "Along the way the judge has turned into an accomplished writer." Garrison was disappointed that he could not get a hearing on a single major talk show. He told Wolfson he was even willing to go on the *Larry King Show!*

At the book party at the Columns Hotel, attended by two hundred people, mystery writer Joe Bosco came up to Garrison and observed "a great sadness behind his eyes." Bosco complimented Garrison on how well he had run the district attorney's office, and how he had drawn from Garrison's methods for his own fiction. "I appreciate it. That's nice of you," Garrison said. He was the shy and humble man his son Eberhard remembers.

At the New York book party, Garrison remarked that the stories of John F. Kennedy's affairs were FBI propaganda, to skeptical looks. When the musicians began to play Gershwin, he demanded that all chatter cease. There they were, his two great passions: the Kennedy assassination and the music of his youth.

In an elevator in Havana, his publisher Ellen Ray ran into a movie director and sold him the rights to *On the Trail of the Assassins.* Oliver Stone was a "man of unusual insight and courage," Garrison soon wrote Wolfson. It did take great courage in 1991 to treat Jim Garrison's investigation with respect. "Why didn't you tell me so many people hated Jim Garrison?" Stone demanded of Ellen Ray, tongue-in-cheek, when *JFK* was already in production. Fresh from the successes of *Platoon* (1986) and *Born on the Fourth of July* (1989), Oliver Stone worked unimpeded by censorship from Warner Brothers. "I was a hot director then," he says wistfully. The attacks on Stone and *JFK* would persist into the millennium. Like Richard Billings before him, Stone was punished for his association with Jim Garrison, who brought news the government even now wanted suppressed.

Never having heard of Kevin Costner, Garrison wished he could have been played by Robert Mitchum, or, at the very least, Harrison Ford. Dr. Frank Minyard, a tall, defiantly handsome man addicted to cowboy boots and cowboy shirts, a jazz musician, hoped to play the part of the Orleans Parish coroner.

"We could never pass you off as a doctor," Stone said. Jim Garrison, his hair dyed black, played Chief Justice Earl Warren. His health was failing and there were days he could not meet a call to the set. If it had not been for the movie *JFK*, Sallie Boyce thought, Jim Garrison would have died sooner.

He had never been a businessman; he had never been motivated by money. He granted his editor Zach Sklar 10 percent of his own royalties, and cut the publishers in on the film deal. When they insisted on renegotiating certain rights, he acquiesced. Snapper was now a young lawyer. Snapper objected. His father was being excessively generous.

"Son," Garrison said, "these people did me a favor. They published my book when no one else would."

With the money from the film option and the $50,000 consulting fee from Stone, Jim Garrison at last paid off the mortgage on the Occhipinti-constructed house on Owens Boulevard. The taxes were unpaid, and Liz had put the house up for auction without telling him. But Jim McPherson discovered a tiny sheriff's posting in the newspaper. On his own initiative, McPherson attended the auction and came away with the property for Jim Garrison.

During his last years, Garrison lived alone in the family house with his cat "Maximilian Big Paws Garrison." His private number was affixed to Max's collar, and Max was so faithful in greeting Garrison every evening when he returned from court that his United Cab driver was alarmed when one night Max did not appear at the door. "That son of a bitch is around here somewhere," Garrison said.

He trusted fewer people now. His driver, Steve Bordelon, thought the CIA had so pursued him as to "overload his circuits." Judge Edmund Reggie, father-in-law of Edward M. Kennedy, and Garrison's

Tulane classmate, urged him to attend their fortieth reunion: "We need you. Surely you miss us just a little, and if only to see how badly we've aged." Jim Garrison did not attend. But with Jimmy Gulotta, with whom he made another odd couple, one tiny, the other towering over him, he was always ready to debate the Kennedy assassination.

"Jim, this theory you have. The CIA, the FBI, a conspiracy, I don't see . . . ," Gulotta began.

"Jim, you don't understand," Garrison said, and Gulotta thought he could have walked out of the room, and Jim Garrison would still be talking.

He drew closer to his children, weeping in the limousine on the way to the church for Elizabeth's wedding. "It's not too late to change your mind," he said. She was marrying a man named "Fallen," and so he called her a "fallen angel." With his sons, he discussed the Kennedy case. "When you believe in something like this," he told Snapper, "You never give up. You'd be killing something inside yourself."

"When that bullet went through Kennedy's head, it was not the same country," he told Eb. He also recounted to Eb how Moo Moo had once asked him whether he really believed he could beat the federal government. Yes, he had said. "I never had the slightest doubt about it. I thought the truth could do it."

"Well, you know better now," Moo Moo had said.

"Yes, I do," Garrison said.

He began again to write fiction. Having debated CIA asset Melvin Belli at a 1987 testimonial dinner, he produced a brilliant spoof. Innovative in challenging the boundaries of the conventional short story, the piece is in the form of an "Affidavit." The author's name appended is not "Jim Garrison," but one Robert L. Russell, "also known as James Alexander II."

Russell is a "wealthy oil man" working undercover for Robert F. Kennedy. He swears under oath that he attended a 1964 meeting with Guy Banister, "known to me at that time as an employee of the CIA." The murder of Jack Ruby is planned by a method that will be "both undetectable and beyond suspicion of foul play."

In "Affidavit," Dr. Mary Sherman passes information from her cancer researches to David Ferrie, known to "Russell" as "a CIA contract employee." Sherman had created live cancer cells that were injected into Ruby's feet with a long needle between his toes. Ruby was finished off before he could talk, as history reveals he longed to do near the end, and as one of Bobby Kennedy's closest people suggests he did.

In fiction, Garrison can include details he suspected but could never prove: that Ruby knew Oswald; that Ruby had transported "at least one gunman" to the grassy knoll, the Julia Ann Mercer testimony. In a jibe at James Phelan, Garrison uses hypnotism and sodium pentothal to render Ruby passive. The motive for Sherman's unsolved murder, he suggests, was the need to keep a secret associated with the assassination. The planner of Ruby's murder was Dr. West, "who did his best to help people and to work for the security of the United States." West, of course, is a thinly disguised Dr. Alton Ochsner, who decrees that Ruby must die because if he won his trial, "he would hurt many people, open old wounds." The witness to the "Affidavit" bears the names of both Garrison's most virulent antagonist, Walter Sheridan, and his assistant, Richard Townley: "Richard Sheridan."

Garrison studied the "narrative lines" of the films of Alfred Hitchcock, and how he created suspense and manipulated point of view in *The Man Who Knew Too Much* through "the innocent bystander who accidentally learns that an assassination is scheduled to take place in London." He liked how in *Frenzy* the point of view shifted from that of the scapegoat to that of the police inspector.

He tried out his fictional ideas on Jimmy Gulotta. One story was called "King of the Grasshoppers." Another was about an Army colonel and a lieutenant and the detrimental effect they had on one another—done in slapstick, complete with a banana peel routine, even as it echoes Garrison's long-ago ambiguous friendship with Pershing Gervais. Another plot featured a drive-in funeral parlor with elevated caskets where you can pay your respects as you would purchase fast food.

He had not ceased to enjoy being in the company of beautiful women, in particular, those who were his "type," as Phyllis had put it. A film producer named Stephanie Brett Samuel was a petite, "bleached" blonde, by her own description, a film producer whose mother, Martha, Garrison had dated forty years ago when they both lived at Fanny Campbell's boardinghouse. Stephanie Samuel was thirty-five; he was nearing seventy. Over dinner, they would talk about Robert Penn Warren, Hemingway and Fitzgerald, the Fugitive Poets, and Thomas Wolfe's *Look Homeward, Angel.*

Samuel was in awe. She thought Jim Garrison had lived one of the fascinating American lives of the century. She introduced him to a friend and the man said he felt as if he had just met Thomas Jefferson; they both saw Jim Garrison as an American patriot.

He was flirtatious, and gallant, a quite decrepit older gentleman wanting to feel vital and male. After dinner, a United Cab would drive him home, and then he would telephone Stephanie and read aloud to her from the "Forum" letters in *Penthouse* magazine. She found it frisky and sweet, a substitute erotic moment. When he begged her to marry him, this, too, seemed part of his effort to feel young, although he could scarcely walk.

Another of the young women of his acquaintance was Monique Poirrier, a friend of William Walter. Poirrier and Walter were both young and blonde and very attractive. Together one evening the three were more than intoxicated. Together they wound up in bed.

"The least you could have done was give me a blow job," Walter said when it was over.

"Bill, a lot of people have talked about it. I've got to tell you, I've never been that way," Garrison said. He was neither homosexual nor bisexual, he added. Denis Barry, who participated with Garrison in the escapades of their youth, is certain. "If there were homosexual feeling, I would have spotted it."

Walter persisted. "But you invited us both up . . . ."

"That was the only way I could make her feel comfortable," Garrison confessed. "You were the kind of guy that would go along with it." Over the years, awkward in his approaches, he had made overtures to many women. He was unsuccessful in his advances more often than not.

Dr. Donald Richardson urged that he exercise, but all he did was walk around the block in his blue blazer and loafers, winding up at Gulotta's house. An ice storm hit New Orleans late in 1989. It was the last working day before Christmas, but Garrison insisted on going to work. Then he took a nasty spill and broke his collarbone. At one point, the ambulance stretcher slipped and he went sliding down Poydras Street, calling out for clerk Danielle Schott to "Enjoy your Christmas!" He was in his second term as an appeals court judge, and balked at the mandatory retirement age of seventy; he didn't want people to know his age.

In 1990, a series of hospital stays began. For a while Judge Gulotta, now retired, took his place on the bench. Garrison was unable to walk. His heart was enlarged. It became difficult for him to get out of bed. Then he refused to get out of bed.

Snapper discovered that his father had more than $85,000 from *JFK* in a non–interest-bearing account and suggested that he move that money. When Garrison ignored him, Snapper enlisted Jimmy Gulotta. "You ought to invest it," Gulotta began. "At least let Snapper put it in an interest-bearing account."

"I'm not interested in interest," Garrison said. He named Gulotta his executor. Later, quietly, Gulotta turned the role over to Snapper.

It was the idea of Judge David R. M. Williams that Garrison re-marry Liz so that the generous court pension payable only to a widow not be wasted. Liz had stood by him "in spite of his propensities." In 1978 and 1982 wills he had named her his "administrator."

"Do something good for a change," Gulotta told him. It took a year and a half, but he finally agreed. He was not always clear now, and so Judge Thomas Early, tapped to perform the ceremony, in-sisted that if Garrison were not lucid, he would walk out. Early asked him questions and made sure that no duress had been put on him by the children. Garrison replied with dry humor.

Liz was tense as she stood by the bed. As Early spoke the words binding them in marriage once more, Liz and Jim Garrison held hands.

Liz had been there for him and was now, sleeping in the down-stairs library should he need her. Nurses were present around the clock. Only two visitors were admitted, Gulotta and Louie Ivon, who with his affectionate heart still called Garrison "boss."

Denis Barry had visited during Garrison's final hospital stay. He was all skin and bones, weighing less than ninety-five pounds. Black sores popped out of his legs in which he no longer had any feeling. His heart could no longer pump fluids through his body.

"Lyle," Garrison said, using Barry's nickname. "You're going to be in my will. You know the penile implant. I told Frank to give it to you as a souvenir. The catch is that it's the biggest in the state of Louisiana and yours is too small."

"The least you can do is tell me who killed Kennedy," Barry re-joined. "I won't tell a soul."

Garrison just smiled.

"Buck, did you see the movie?" Garrison asked Ivon one day. When a cassette of *JFK* finally arrived, Garrison tried to watch it, but his attention wandered. Jimmy Gulotta looked over and he was not absorbed, he was not watching. It was too late.

"Are you coming back tomorrow?" Garrison asked Gulotta each day. He had been an atheist and was not about to change his beliefs now. Death, he had told Numa Bertel, was "the big sleep."

It was an excruciating death. The scabs on the infected bedsores had to be pulled off to make them bleed. One was so bad that the bone in his back was exposed. He contracted blood poisoning. Liz called Dr. Minyard and told him that Jim should be in a hospital.

"Whatever you do," Jim Garrison ordered the children, "Don't let him in!"

All five children sat on the steps of 4600 Owens Boulevard waiting for Dr. Minyard.

Suddenly Minyard stood at Jim Garrison's bedside.

"Who let you in the house?" Garrison demanded.

"I found an open door," Minyard said.

"I'll be OK," Garrison said. He would not permit Minyard to touch him.

On the last day of his life, all five children stayed the night, taking turns sitting with him. They slept on the floor, not even willing to be as far away as upstairs. Each had a moment alone with their father. They told him how proud they were of him, and how much they loved him.

"You know I love all five of you," he said.

Jim Garrison died on October 21, 1992. He was seventy years old.

The children had agreed that they would call Louie Ivon when their father died. Louie alone could be trusted to honor their wishes. Their father, they said, did not want an autopsy, having regretted the autopsy of his second child, John Lyon, who had died in infancy. Minyard insisted. Jim Garrison was a public figure; the press might ask questions. The death certificate reads, "Congestive Heart Failure," although the autopsy revealed that technically he died not of his heart illness, but of septicemia, blood poisoning from the unhealed bedsores.

"It was Kennedy that killed him," Dr. Minyard said. The investigation had robbed him of his energy and his spirit. Garrison left what he had, the house on Owens, some oil interests left by Jane Gardiner, and royalties, most of which would prove impossible to extract from Hollywood, to his "five beloved children."

Jimmy Gulotta read the eulogy at a funeral attended by many of the United Cab drivers who had come to know Jim Garrison. In several obituaries, Frank Mankiewicz, once Bobby Kennedy's press secretary, was quoted as saying, "Every American owes him a debt of gratitude. He kicked open a door that had been closed too long."

At the burial, John Volz, serving as a pall bearer, reprimanded

Garrison's officious son-in-law for chasing away the *Times-Picayune* photographer. "Let me tell you something," Volz said. "Jim Garrison never ran from a photographer in his life." Jim Garrison did not dedicate his life to the investigation of the murder of President Kennedy because he was lured by a lust for publicity. But the press had played its role in the dance.

"We darn near got the Agency by the big toe," Garrison said, close to the end.

Jim Garrison's headstone at the cemetery in Metairie is embossed with the scales of justice. Unlike those ornately decorated vertical tombs, overflowing with cherubs and statuary so common in watery New Orleans, it is plain and rests close to the ground. The legend reads: "Let Justice Be Done, Though the Heavens Fall."

RABBI

It's a big operation. It's predictable that a little bit of it would come up here and there.
　　　　　—Jim Garrison.

How many more Oswalds did they have out there, ready to go?
　　　　　—Gordon Novel

Allen Dulles, Richard Helms, Carmel Offie and Frank Wisner were the grand masters. If you were in a room with them you were in a room full of people that you had to believe would deservedly end up in hell. I guess I will see them there soon.
　　　　　—James Angleton

"**Y**OU'VE GOT YOUR OWN mailbox now," Jack Martin told Tommy Beckham late in 1962. Now if they wanted him to run an errand, or to pay him, or to send instructions, they would use the Old Post Office across from Guy Banister's office. Sometimes during the summer of 1963 Tommy would run into Lee Oswald at the post office. One day, Tommy found Jack in the company of two strangers.

"You know what CIA means?" Jack had laughed, trying, it seemed to Tommy, to impress the two men in suits. "Caught in the Act!" It is a phrase used by another CIA operative in this story, Richard Case Nagell.

One day in 1963—Beckham remembers it as late spring—Tommy opened his post office box and there was an airplane ticket with instructions that he proceed to the CIA training installation, Camp Peary near Williamsburg, Virginia, also known as "The Farm."

In Virginia, he is subjected to tests. They are named Rorschach and Minnesota Multifasic. He is shown three pictures projected on a screen, then asked what he remembers. Which picture stood out from the others? In one image, a man wears a hat perched at an odd angle. Tommy remembers that detail. Thomas Edward Beckham during his CIA training duplicates a scene described by Loran Hall to the House Select Committee. During Hall's military intelligence training, he, too, was bombarded with pictures flashing on a wall.

Tommy is shown the faces of heads of state: Mao-tse-Tung and Khrushchev. "These are leaders who at some time in the future might possibly have to be hit," Tommy is told. He will spend four weeks at Camp Peary.

In another phase of his training, he is pushed through a labyrinth of rooms. He is told to look carefully into each room. Then he is asked to describe in detail how the last person he saw was dressed. He is asked about the first room, which, by the end of the exercise, he scarcely remembers. What pictures were on the wall? He is taught how your voice can give you away. He is taught how the way you walk can give you away. He is taught never to leave anyone with anything by which they might remember you. He is forbidden to smoke his pipe because it leaves traces by which you could be identified. You must never carry identification. He is taught how not to leave a paper trail. He is taught how to create fake identification. He learns how, rapidly, to identify serial numbers on paper currency. He is taught how to create false information.

He is instructed never to volunteer an opinion on any issue. He must never brag about anything he has done. He must never talk about anything he has done in the past. He is taught to have only short conversations with people. This is difficult for him because, having grown up without learning how to read or write, he is a verbal person and loquacious. He must live as if he were a dead man, which is something E. Carl McNabb, "Jim Rose," also learned from the Agency, until it literally came true and he read in a newspaper his own obituary, under the name "Carl Davis."

Then he is taught how to use weapons. He is taught how to be an assassin. He wonders how long the CIA had been looking at him, recruiting him, grooming him for he knows not what. Years later Fred Lee Crisman, his handler, the man HSCA refused to investigate, a man they were willing to scuttle the entire Louisiana investigation to protect, although he was already dead anyway, bestowed upon Thomas Edward Beckham a government document meant never to be seen.

Fred gave it to him because it is difficult not to like Tommy. The document explains why Tommy was commandeered by Langley, why he was chosen and for what he had been trained.

The letterhead is not that of the CIA, but "United States Army Air Defense Command," suggesting that many elements of President Eisenhower's "military industrial complex" contributed to a collaborative effort to murder John F. Kennedy, an effort in which the CIA stood in the front line. Tommy has never served in the military. But a number connoting his military service name is on this document, along with his correct social security number.

The document describes Thomas Edward Beckham's "intelligence service from October 27, 1963," under "Gov Control Fact Finding Missions." "Army Rank Commissioned Officer," it says, but "not assig. to any Military Service."

Thomas Edward Beckham has a police record, the document declares: "Knife fighting, two counts of attempted murder." This information is false, Beckham says, but a false police record can be utilized or expunged, as necessity decrees. He was never involved in violent crimes. "Number of items cleansed as of 3-8-63," the document reads.

Thomas Edward Beckham is one of five sons, the document continues. He is expendable. "Has no personal feelings as to killing and or death, see Psychological Report," the document adds, as it sums up the training with which he has been provided at "The Farm," "Advanced and Special Training":

> Hand-to-hand combat special training, special firearms course, CIA field training, Advanced Medical and Psychological. . . .

He has also had "Special Mind Search IQ training, ETQ and TD-35, Army Field Officers Tr. Cour."

The document concludes with "Psychological Data: Subject gets upset with people and pulls away. Drinks and smokes (pipe), likes to study people. No psy. as to guil. on killing. Not married. 5 ft 7, 157, White Male."

This revelatory and never-before-seen document reveals how military intelligence, the Army, and the CIA, working in concert, had set up a scapegoat. Should Oswald have broken away or turned, they had Beckham groomed and waiting in the wings as an alternative scapegoat to take the blame for the murder of John F. Kennedy. Beckham was a man who would not mind killing, they had determined. He was similar in appearance to Lee Harvey Oswald, small, brown-haired, nondescript-looking. He had even more scant formal education than Oswald.

As Jim Garrison had surmised, Beckham's ultimate role in the assassination, should Lee Harvey Oswald not cooperate, was to be an alternative scapegoat. To play that part, he had to be young, uneducated, impressionable and eager. He had to be a virtual blank slate, whose identity could be created if he had to be placed in harm's way. Tommy was already a man gifted at reinventing himself.

This government document about Thomas Edward Beckham is rendered further credible by its remarkable similarity in both language and philosophy to a CIA report describing "the agent or asset ROGUE" whom the Agency had enlisted in its plan to assassinate Prime Minister Patrice Lumumba in the Congo. In a secret document conveyed to the Church Committee, the chief of the CIA's African Division, who at the time was Bronson Tweedy, wrote:

> He is indeed aware of the precepts of right and wrong, but if he is given an assignment, which may be morally wrong in the eyes of the world, but necessary because his case officer ordered him to carry it out, then it is right and he will dutifully undertake appropriate action for its execution without pangs of conscience. In a word, he can rationalize all actions.

The CIA determined that Thomas Edward Beckham was another such man, as was its first choice, Lee Harvey Oswald. With his Marxist self-invention and seeming Soviet defection, and his heterosexuality shadowed by occasional homosexual experiences, Oswald was the more desirable alternative should the government follow its original plan of blaming Fidel Castro for the assassination. So CIA planned to secure for the military—and the corporations that profited from its efforts—a long-desired ground war in Cuba.

Beckham was their second choice. His being groomed by the CIA for that role places the murder of the president at the highest levels of intelligence. Beckham's experience demonstrates that Oswald certainly did not plan the assassination of President Kennedy, nor did he operate at any time "alone," just as Jim Garrison had claimed all along.

Those with foreknowledge of the assassination, like Gerald Patrick Hemming, were well aware that alternative scapegoats were being put into place in 1963. Hemming has contended that Roy Hargraves, who accompanied him to Jim Garrison's office, was also in Dallas on November 22nd, in a "fallback position," even as the fake

Secret Service credentials Hargraves carried that day suggest that he was not merely another potential patsy, but an operative, a participant. Shortly before his death, Hargraves confirmed these facts in a taped interview with author Noel Twyman. Hargraves admits to being in Dallas, playing a role alongside people he had long known, people Jim Garrison had interrogated.

Beckham's document demonstrates that the government created an appropriate scapegoat to assume the blame for a murder committed by people in the government itself. It reveals ample foreknowledge of the assassination by government intelligence agencies. It demonstrates that the same people who murdered the president had, long before the heinous crime, begun the process of blaming some innocent man. Jim Garrison had uncovered a corner of that effort in Jackson and Clinton, Louisiana.

Thomas Beckham never forgot his CIA training. When Robert Buras interviewed him, Beckham looked at him hard, focusing on Buras' one white eyebrow. He needs to dye it, Tommy thought, because it's a dead giveaway, something people could remember him by. Buras had long distinguished himself in intelligence work, even with the white eyebrow, but Tommy was remembering his own intelligence training.

When Beckham requested his CIA files under the Freedom of Information Act, CIA claimed it had no records naming him; he received not a single piece of paper, not even those files referred to on the document Fred gave him as "not for public release." The file number even appears on the document: HQ-4567G2-File.

After that grueling appearance before the Orleans Parish grand jury in February 1968, Tommy had gone home to his mother's house. A. Roswell Thompson went with him. Rozzy would not let him out of his sight.

The telephone rings. It is Jim Garrison. Tommy is alarmed.

"What's happened now?" he blurts out.

"You know, we gave you immunity," Jim Garrison begins. "Why not tell the truth?"

"Yeah," Tommy says, remembering Fred's threat that he would kill him if Fred were subpoenaed, implicated in any way. Tommy knows he has immunity for anything he might have done prior to the assassination. But there is no immunity for murder.

"I know you know more than you're saying," Garrison says. "Off the record, you do know Jack Martin. . . ." At the close of his testimony, Tommy had even denied that he knew Jack, although earlier he had mentioned Jack's knowing about a German ship bound for Cuba.

"I know *Joe* Martin," Tommy repeats, referring to the man who had shielded him in an Iowa safe house, the man who was kidnapped from that Omaha radio station never to be the same again. Tommy had also denied knowing Clay Shaw, Jack Ruby and Lee Harvey Oswald. He had denied ever having met Lawrence Howard. He had even denied knowing Fred. Of course, he knew them all.

Jim Garrison runs down a list of names one last time, but Tommy remains silent.

"You're not going to tell me anything, are you?" Garrison says finally.

"I don't have nothing to tell you," Tommy says.

"Well, if I were you, I'd leave town," Garrison says.

"Are you threatening me?" Tommy says.

"You think I'm your enemy, but I'm not," Garrison says.

Long ago having sacrificed false pride, humbly, the district attorney of Orleans Parish has a last question for Thomas Edward Beckham, who would be twenty-eight years old on the following December 9. With the help of CIA operatives Jack Martin and Fred Lee Crisman, Beckham has defied the system of justice successfully, with apparent impunity. Still, Garrison must try again.

"Tom," Jim Garrison says, "Let me ask you one thing. Have I touched on anything? Am I close?"

The terrified witness has no room for registering Jim Garrison's sincerity now.

"I don't know if you are or not," Tommy says. "How am I to know?" Then he turns silent. He replaces the receiver.

"See how they are!" Rozzy gloats. "They'll get you one way or another." Rozzy tries to calm Tommy down because he is now very upset, very nervous.

"They're going to discredit him," Rozzy promises, his contempt for Jim Garrison intact. "He's going to look like a fool. We'll make him a nut. Nothing will happen."

Twenty years later, in the late 1980s, Tommy confronts Herman Keck, head of the "World Wide Church" in Springfield, Missouri, and another of the Agency people in his life over the years. "CIA can do a lot under cover," Tommy remarks. He is still trying to figure out how he had been drawn in, how he had been involved and in what. Keck affirms that Fred Lee Crisman was with the Agency.

"You were too," Keck says.

Tommy wants only to forget. He has asked a hypnotist to erase from his mind the memories of those years, to no avail. He receives a telephone call from New Orleans. A woman asks whether he will speak to Jim Garrison.

"You know, he's a judge now," she says. "You do know Jim Garrison?"

"I never heard of that man in my life," Tommy says. "Ma'am, you've got the wrong Beckham. I never heard of that guy in my life." Still, he is not ready.

At the turn of the 1990s, Oliver Stone's people track him down.

"Am I going to be a star?" Tommy says, the same defense he had used when police officers Buras and Delsa came too close. "Now I'll set up a table and take calls," he had told them, as if he were ready to reap the rewards of publicity. Rather, he wanted nothing more than to disappear, and when he learned that Crisman, and then Jack Martin, were dead, he felt a measure of relief. His next question, to this author, was whether Colonel Lawrence Lowry remained alive.

Beckham's testimony for this book points to the CIA's organization of the assassination, and to Clay Shaw's role in readying Oswald to take the blame for a crime he did not commit as Garrison had thought. Beckham connects Shaw to Ruby and Ruby to Oswald. He places Howard in Dallas. He places Ferrie in the midst of the planning of a crime "formulated in New Orleans." He knows that organized crime was kept informed of the plans to kill President Kennedy, that a "Marullo" or a "Marcello" was present at each meeting, both at Algiers, where they discussed how Kennedy had dispatched his school friend, William Attwood, to come to an agreement with Castro, and at the Town and Country Motel. A "tagalong," someone no one particularly noticed, Beckham was observant. He spotted Sergio Arcacha Smith in New Orleans in 1963, which vindicates David Lewis. Arcacha and "Lucious" Rabel behaved "as if they were glued together," Beckham remembers.

Beckham vindicates Jim Garrison, rendering him correct in his insight that Guy Banister was at the nexus of the transition from Operation Mongoose, the plot to murder Fidel Castro, to the assassination of the president. He exposes Fred Lee Crisman as a link between the planners of the crime and those enlisted to implement it, as Crisman organized Tommy's trip for CIA training. He reveals how Jack Martin, another Agency asset in New Orleans, had begun to prepare him for his role as possible scapegoat with the falling downstairs incident at Morrison's cafeteria, which had so perplexed him.

Martin's preparation of Beckham included his voluntary commitment to the mental hospital at Mandeville. Two young men were prepared to take the blame as "lone nuts" in an identical manner. Oswald had been led to the East Louisiana State Hospital at Jackson. Like Oswald, Tommy later could be dismissed as unstable, irresponsible.

That Jack Martin had betrayed Thomas Edward Beckham is revealed in the FBI's informant files where Jack S. Martin "advise[s]" that Tommy, "age seventeen . . . was in California allegedly passing fraudulent checks on father's account," and how in 1958 he had been "subject of an interstate transportation of stolen property investigation."

The CIA had vetted Tommy. That he was later utilized in the planning of the assassination belies the view that rogue operatives, or low level ex-agents, had on their own plotted the assassination of the president. Tommy passed the test. The CIA concluded that he was the kind of person who "has no personal feelings as to killing and or death . . . understands orders and has top leadership ability." Jim Garrison believed that Oswald had "acquired in the Marines the military habit of responding to orders without any questions." Tommy was an Oswald double.

Beckham was not needed, and so he was consigned to other duties, like the delivery of the maps and diagrams to Lawrence Howard, waiting for him in Dallas. The meetings Tommy attended in Algiers mirror the gathering described by Perry Russo at which David Ferrie and Clay Shaw revealed accurately what their alibis for November 22nd would be. Garrison's first suspect, David Ferrie, had indeed been deeply involved in the implementation of the assassination. Garrison's development of Ferrie's role in itself consigned to oblivion the Warren Report, whose conclusion was that Oswald acted alone.

Angelo Kennedy, once Angelo Murgado, was born in Havana, then moved to New York when he was nine years old. Now sixty-six and grizzled, if still slim and lithe, a dark-skinned, gray-haired man, he warns with a smile against the distraction of his considerable affability. "I was an assassin," he says pointedly, his target then the same Fidel Castro whom the great Cuban novelist Guillermo Cabrera Infante, residing in gloomy exile in London, compared to Adolf Hitler.

Angelo resides in what was once his parents' home, an elegant one-story house in the "Sweetwater" section west of Miami. His mother's collection of Lladro porcelain figurines and Limoges china adorns the spacious rooms tiled in rosy squares. The crystal chandelier sparkles. The table is perpetually set.

The father of six children, Angelo now lives alone. "I choose to be isolated completely," he says. His vices are Marlboros, smoked out on the porch, and Budweiser beer, "the people's drink." Material possessions hold no appeal, and service, neither to the CIA nor to Robert F. Kennedy, brought him no riches. One of his passions is cooking. He improvises a superb supper of pork chops, red beans and rice, salad and bread sprinkled in its basket with plantain chips, followed by a thickly rich thimble-sized jolt of Cuban coffee. He will move soon, he says, perhaps to within sight of the sea where he can indulge another passion, fishing. He is not anxious to reminisce about his years in close association with Bobby Kennedy, a man he still admires and loves. He remembers Bobby's perpetual boyish gesture, always running his hand through his hair. "We will always have Camelot," his thirteen-year-old daughter wrote on her 2005 Father's Day card.

Near the close of the evening, Angelo disappears only to emerge with a large, elaborately framed color photograph of three brothers, taken in 1960. The largest figure, the one closest to the camera, is on the left. It is John F. Kennedy, as we knew him. At the center of the composition is Bobby, smiling shyly, he who did so much of the work of the presidency, anxious always to smooth the way for his brother. A very young Teddy is at the right, engulfed in laughter. The world is all before them.

By 1963, Bobby Kennedy had gathered around him that brain trust of loyal Cubans. Among those closest to him were Manuel Artime, Manolo Reboso, who has moved to Nicaragua and married into the very rich Somoza family, and Angelo Murgado. After Bobby's death, Angelo became a U.S. citizen, and changed his surname to "Kennedy."

The responsibilities of this group were twofold: to help devise for Bobby a plan and a method of assassinating Fidel Castro and to protect his brother from the murderous impulses of some hot-headed Cuban incensed over Kennedy's failure to ensure the military success of the invasion of Cuba at the Bay of Pigs. Like other figures in this story, Bernardo de Torres ("Benny" to Angelo) and Alberto Fowler, Angelo, too, was a veteran of the Bay of Pigs disaster.

At their meetings, Bobby would read to them from an intelligence report supplied to him by the CIA, and by other sources. Then he would tear it up. There would be no paper trail. They were "invisible men," Angelo says, both supervising Bobby's assassination plots and attempting to protect the president. In this capacity, they made contact with many of those embedded in the Cuban exile community, from Sylvia Odio, who was visited in Dallas in late September by two men she was never to identify and Lee Harvey Oswald, to Sergio Arcacha Smith. Bobby's group grew close, as well, to Oswald himself, keeping Oswald under constant surveillance.

They focused on the Cubans residing in New Orleans, moving among Castro's agents, double agents and Cubans working for the CIA as they sought to neutralize a future assassin. By the summer of 1963, Angelo reports, Oswald had swum into their ken. They knew of his antics in New Orleans, his pretending to be a Castro sympathizer with his Fair Play for Cuba leaflets. They knew of his visit to Miami that summer of 1963, where he was observed as well by Edward I. Arthur, another soldier of fortune training in Florida under the umbrella of the Agency as part of Commandos L. Arthur remembers seeing Oswald in Miami that summer. He was warned by his CIA controller: "This guy, Oswald. If you come across him, stay away!" Another CIA colleague remarked to Ed Arthur that summer, "Kennedy's not long for this world." In some circles, if not in Bobby's, the impending assassination was a very open secret.

According to Angelo, he and the others monitored Oswald's movements so closely that they believed there was no one with whom Oswald was closely associated of whom they were not aware. Told of Oswald's being sighted with "Juan Valdes," Angelo laughs. He is amused by the obviously fake name, then suggests that the source, Victoria Hawes, could only have been a plant, a purveyor of disinformation, since had Oswald been seen with customs broker Valdes they would certainly have known about it. Bobby's men knew that despite Oswald's dispensing of pro-Castro leaflets, he was part of the anti-Castro community, as Dr. Frank Silva discovered. They knew about Oswald's relationship with Clay Shaw and that Shaw was "longtime CIA." They had only contempt for the corrupt Sergio Arcacha Smith.

During one briefing, Bobby was even shown a photograph of Lee Harvey Oswald. He was someone they kept bumping into, Angelo says. Who was he? There were so many coincidences. They grew even closer to Oswald, although, to Angelo's knowledge, Bobby Kennedy was never to meet Oswald "personally."

Others trying to help John F. Kennedy thwart the CIA's efforts against him, like Howard K. Davis, loyal to the president, worked with wealthy Kennedy backer, Theodore Racoosin, as they sought to penetrate what the Agency was up to.

Bobby learned that Oswald worked for the FBI. "If the FBI is controlling him," Bobby concluded, "he's no problem." Having studied Oswald, having focused on preventing the death of the president, his people underestimated Oswald's position and ceased to make him a major "target" of their interest.

Trained to watch for "indicators," these CIA-trained Cubans, devoted to Bobby now, did discover that "something was cooking in New Orleans." Bobby urged caution. "We were lost," Angelo says. "We knew something was cooking, but we didn't know how to proceed. We knew it was out of New Orleans." That Oswald was being set up was known to people closest to this group, like Bernardo de Torres, but not to them. "Smelling blood," as Angelo puts it, Bobby's team tried to find out what was going on. They visited with Sergio Arcacha Smith because he knew Oswald and was connected to the FBI. Thus they made that error of perceiving Oswald solely as a creature of Hoover, ignoring that he might be used by other agencies and subscribing to the myth that the FBI was in conflict with other national security interests. To spite Hoover, they even considered eliminating Oswald. But then, he seemed so insignificant, so like a "peon," with an IQ not much greater than his age, Angelo says, that they left him alone. But the elimination of Bobby's brother would have proceeded even had Oswald been "sanitized." There were those other Oswalds waiting in the wings, Oswalds who had been prepared and were ready to go, as Gordon Novel suggests.

It was at this time, Angelo says, that he drove to Dallas from New Orleans in the company of the man who identified himself to Odio as "Leopoldo" but who, in fact, was Bernardo de Torres. As far as Angelo knew, "Benny" was respectable; he was a fellow veteran, whose brother was running for mayor of Miami. When they were invited into Odio's home, there sat, to Angelo's surprise, according to Mr. Murgado, Lee Harvey Oswald. That de Torres and Murgado both knew Oswald prior to this occasion is undeniable.

Odio was to testify to the Warren Commission that the three drove to Dallas together, that all three of her visitors drove up in a car from New Orleans. Angelo says that this was not the case, that Oswald was already there when he arrived. After the assassination, Odio would identify the figure who had been called "Leon" as Lee Harvey Oswald, the man seen on television. Although she knew their identities, Mrs. Odio has never brought herself to identify Leon's companions. It may seem odd that she would identify Oswald for the Commission, yet lie about having known him prior to the visit, as opposed to not identifying Oswald at all.

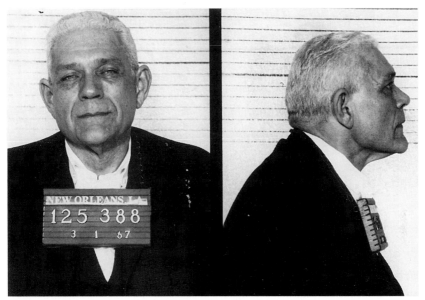

Clay Shaw is arrested, March 1, 1967: "Through the famous Looking Glass, the black objects can appear to be white and the white objects can appear to be black."

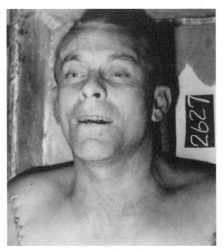

French Quarter chanteuse Barbara Bennett: "There's Clay Bertrand!" *(photograph courtesy of Barbara Bennett).*

Robert Lee Perrin after his autopsy (photograph courtesy of J. Gary Shaw Collection).

The Garrison family in 1967: From left, Virginia, Eberhard, Mrs. Liz Garrison, Elizabeth, Snapper (front), and Jasper *(photograph by Lynn Pelham)*.

Garrison with the author, 1969 *(photograph courtesy of Joan Mellen)*.

Shaw (center) as aide-de-camp to General Thrasher (left): "worse than the former German concentration camps."

Shaw with fellow CIA asset Dr. Alton Ochsner (*photograph courtesy of the New Orleans Public Library*).

Ferenc Nagy: "A cleared contact of the International Organizations Division of the Agency."

Perry Raymond Russo with Jim Garrison: "As far as I'm concerned, Bertrand and Shaw are the same" *(photograph by Lynn Pelham)*.

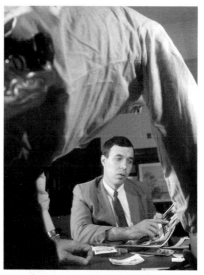

Garrison with Perry Raymond Russo: It didn't matter whether "Leon" was "the Oswald that showed up in Dallas," or was someone posing as Lee Harvey Oswald who "wanted to be remembered in that place at a certain time" *(photograph by Lynn Pelham)*.

James Phelan with Clay Shaw: "a casebook in the obstruction of justice."

(Donald) P. Norton: "Harvey Lee" told Norton he was from New Orleans *(photograph courtesy of Donold P. Norton)*.

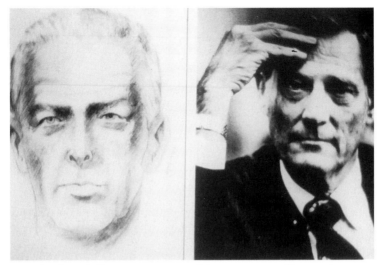

David Atlee Phillips: "I was one of the two case officers who handled Lee Harvey Oswald…"

Marlene Mancuso: "They're trying to destroy you and I'm not going to be part of anything like that" *(photograph courtesy of Marlene Mancuso)*.

Francis Fruge: "I've got your lady friend here in jail" *(photograph courtesy of Anne Dischler)*.

The East Louisiana State Hospital at Jackson: "Do you know this is a mental hospital?" *(photograph courtesy of Eric J. Brock).*

Dr. Frank Silva in 2000. Dr. Silva was medical director of the East Louisiana State Hospital in Jackson during the summer of 1963: "I've come to get a job at the suggestion of Dr. Malcolm Pierson," Oswald says *(photograph by Joan Mellen).*

Henry Earl Palmer, registrar of voters for East Feliciana Parish during the summer of 1963: "Look, this is where Oswald registered..." *(photograph courtesy of Margaret Harvey).*

Lea McGehee in his Jackson barbershop. "Hoping for a juicy argument, McGehee turned Oswald's chair so that he stared directly into the face of Martin Luther King, Jr. *(photograph courtesy of Lea McGehee).*

Anne Dischler at the time of the Garrison investigation: "We're trying to find out what happened to our President" *(photograph courtesy of Anne Dischler).*

Jack Rogers, counsel for the Louisiana Un-American Activities Committee. Rogers also believed he had made a major discovery.

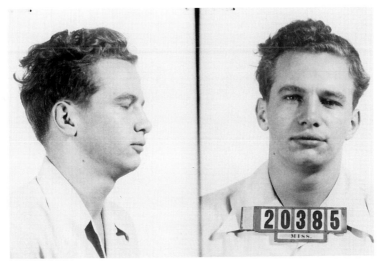

The Reverend Clyde Johnson: "As the Bible says, no man is as blind as the man that don't want to see."

Gerald Patrick Hemming: "One or more of Bobby's boys gone bad."

"Jim Rose" (E. Carl McNabb): "My next assignment is to fly arms into a little revolution in Biafra" *(photograph courtesy of AARC).*

Thomas Edward Beckham as Mark Evans: an infinite capacity to reinvent himself *(photograph courtesy of Thomas Edward Beckham).*

Kerry Thornley: a course in "Atomic, Biological and Chemical Warfare" *(photograph courtesy of the J. Gary Shaw Collection).*

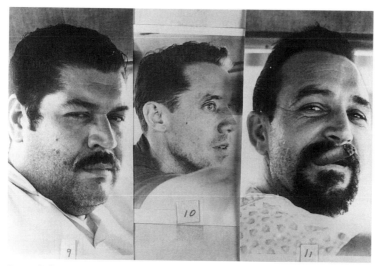

From left, Lawrence Howard, William Seymour and Loran Hall: "Jackals for the CIA" *(photograph courtesy of Christopher Sharrett).*

Lawrence Howard.

Free Lee Crisman: "Fred, I know you're a government agent."

William Wood ("Bill Boxley"). The CIA had been "keeping an eye on him" *(photograph courtesy of the J. Gary Shaw Collection)*.

Clay Shaw: "Have you ever worked for the Central Intelligence Agency?" "No, I have not."

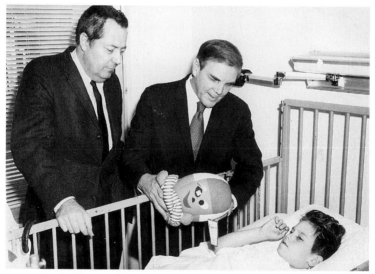

Garrison and Governor John J. McKeithen visit Jasper in the hospital, 1970 *(photograph by J.W. Guillot, The Times-Picayane, courtesy of Lyon Garrison)*.

Garrison lecturing on the Presidential motorcade route before members of PANO, the policemen's union, 1970s *(photograph courtesy of Irvin L. Magri. Jr.)*.

Garrison at his wedding to Phyllis Weinert, 1976 *(photograph courtesy of Phyllis Weinert)*.

Garrison honored at Fort Sill, Oklahoma, 1977. From left, Jasper, Garrison, Eberhard and Snapper *(photograph courtesy of Phyllis Weinert).*

Thomas Edward Beckham as a practicing Rabbi *(photograph courtesy of Thomas Edward Beckham).*

Signing "On The Trail Of The Assassins," 1989 *(photograph copyright Donn Young Photography)*.

Signing "On The Trail Of The Assassins," 1989, at another venue *(photograph copyright Donn Young Photography)*.

Garrison as judge on the Louisiana Fourth Circuit Court of Appeal
(photograph courtesy of Lyon Garrison).

It may seem that Mr. Murgado is distancing himself from Oswald, whom he acknowledges, however, that he had under surveillance. But whether Oswald traveled to Dallas with Bernardo de Torres and Angelo Murgado or was already there in Odio's apartment when they arrived, the meaning of the incident remains the same.

It was out of Angelo's hearing that the next day Leopoldo telephoned Odio and remarked that "Leon" had talked about how after what happened at the Bay of Pigs, some Cuban should kill John F. Kennedy. So later, it could be claimed that it was Oswald who had killed the president, Oswald who had acted against the president with premeditation. By dangling Oswald so close to Bobby Kennedy that he appeared to be traveling with one of Bobby's men, by placing him in the company of Angelo Murgado, those who set Oswald up sought to ensure Robert Kennedy's silence. For Angelo at the time, it seemed as if it were a coincidence, his calling on Odio and suddenly there was Oswald with "Benny." The CIA had placed Oswald with Angelo, one of those closest to Bobby, rendering Angelo a seeming if not real participant in the setting up of the man to be accused of the assassination. The CIA was setting up, no less, a man of whom the president's brother was already aware, information that came to the Agency from Benny. So Bobby's seeming complicity would even inspire someone in anti-Castro circles to remark, "goddamn Bobby's got his brother killed!" When Oswald was arrested as the assassin of President Kennedy, Angelo's reaction was visceral. He said he vomitted.

CIA tradecraft not only engineered the framing of Oswald through the Odio incident, but simultaneously silenced the one person in a position and with the motivation to expose the plot. The Odio incident explains why Bobby would later, on more than one occasion, claim that he would expose what had happened to his brother—only after he became president. Today Angelo says, "I hate everything I have done." Checkmated, "neutralized," by the Agency, waiting for the presidency that would never come, Bobby lost the opportunity to reveal what he knew.

During Jim Garrison's investigation, Bobby Kennedy fought hard to maintain the secret of his having known about Lee Harvey Oswald in advance of the death of his brother. To ensure the possibility of his becoming president, he had, no less, to keep secret his own involvement in plots to murder Fidel Castro. Focusing on the Cubans, aided by well-connected Alberto Fowler and knowing, as Bobby did, that Oswald did not kill John Kennedy, Garrison was a threat to Bobby's planned agenda.

One of the Cubans whom Garrison had targeted, and was attempting to extradite from Dallas, Sergio Arcacha Smith, knew that Bobby's people were aware of Oswald. So Bobby unleashed Walter Sheridan to ensure that his two secrets be kept: that he was attempting, independently of the CIA, the avowed enemy of his brother, to assassinate Fidel Castro and that Oswald had come to his attention. Governor Connolly then did his part and Arcacha was not extradited to Louisiana.

Destroying Garrison's investigation became Bobby's obsession. He kept a dossier on Garrison. After Alberto Fowler, in his innocence, brought Bernardo de Torres to work in the Garrison office, "Benny" reported not only to the CIA, but, separately, to Bobby's group. Now working as a private investigator, de Torres moved even among the friends of Garrison's lover, Phyllis Weinert. To Bobby's people, de Torres revealed the shape of Garrison's genitalia, one very large testicle hanging much lower than the other. Macho to a man, the Cubans chuckled.

Today Angelo remarks that they thought they knew enough about Oswald to be certain that Oswald was involved only in assassination plots to murder Fidel Castro, that to Oswald's knowledge he had nothing to do with the murder of the president. As for Garrison's investigation, Angelo Kennedy says, "we tried to control it, sanitize it."

Garrison's oft-voiced admiration of John F. Kennedy was not enough to earn him Bobby's endorsement: too much else was at stake. So public was Garrison's affection for the fallen president, affection he expressed on national television, on "Issues and Answers," "Mike Wallace At-Large," and "The Tonight Show," that only the secret of Bobby's awareness of Lee Harvey Oswald and how closely his group drew to Oswald, explains his vehemence regarding Garrison.

By the summer of 1963 Bobby suspected that a plot against the life of his brother was emanating out of New Orleans, as Jim Garrison concluded two years later. Today Angelo offers his own, which was also Bobby Kennedy's real assessment of Garrison's work. "On a scale of 0 to 100," Angelo says, "Garrison got to 92. He almost got the whole nine yards."

"Jim Garrison was closer to the truth about the conspiracy than anybody has ever been," agrees Donold P. Norton, the "Donald" P. Norton of Garrison's investigation and another witness Garrison did not utilize. Dr. Robert McClelland, who also was not brought to New

Orleans, observed that the back of Kennedy's skull had been blown out and that he could only have been shot from the front; he concludes that the assassination was "a high level plot to kill the president by the CIA and FBI, at the upper and middle levels. A lot of people in the CIA and FBI thought their fortunes were not attached to the Kennedys." These included those corporations for whom a burgeoning national deficit was a small price to pay for the revenues that would roll in once oil, helicopters, airplanes and other war materiel went streaming toward Vietnam. Even David Ferrie's friend Alvin Beaubouef now says, "I think the hit on Kennedy was government done."

Asked to speculate on the peculiar absence of CIA documents mentioning his DRE handler, George Joannides, DRE military strategist Isidro Borja concludes, "The CIA had to be involved in the assassination of President Kennedy." The DRE had met with Richard Helms and sensed that the assassination issued from a faction inside the government, where it was decided that "we can't let that man remain in power." The lax security at Dallas police headquarters alone told you that. As for the DRE, it was not in their interest that John F. Kennedy should die.

Borja's colleague, José Antonio Lanuza, concurs. "After a while, I thought it could be the CIA," he says. "Who can cover their rear ends so well? Castro could not. The Mafia could not. Who has a reason to kill him? Who is trying to cover up? I would say very high up in government." Oswald, Lanuza speculates, was a plant in the Soviet Union, "then deactivated, like many CIA agents and assets who keep their contacts later." Lanuza points to Watergate.

That CIA was in the murder business there is no doubt. Watergate conspirator James McCord was with the CIA's Office of Security in 1963. "When you have violated every federal statute up to and including murder," he told Martin F. Dardis, "what's breaking into a doctor's office?" a reference to the break-in of Daniel Ellsberg's psychiatrist.

Warren Commission historian Mary Ferrell reflected near the end of her life: "I had such contempt for Garrison, and now, as the years pass, he was so close and they did everything in the world to him."

The CIA's efforts in the cover-up continue. At the millennium a committee of archivists and librarians was convened by the National Archives. Its purpose was to examine some sealed records relating to the Kennedy assassination and to recommend whether they should be opened to the public. Before the group could make any determinations, they were visited by a man identifying himself as a representative of the CIA. He warned them that under no circumstances must they ever reveal to anyone what they had viewed in those documents. His visit was perceived as a threat by them all. No one talked.

In the final year of his life, bedridden, Jim Garrison continued to write. A "Scenario for Possible Docu-Drama" opens at Morrison's cafeteria. Tommy appears, along with Sergio Arcacha Smith, Arcacha's public relations contact [Ronnie Caire], and Rozzy. The scene shifts to the Habana Bar, where Oswald, Shaw, Arcacha, and Beckham chat companionably.

"How did things go in Mexico?" someone asks Oswald, referring to that summertime trip exposed by both Beckham and Richard Case Nagell.

A third scene takes place in Algiers. Shaw and Charlie Marullo are present, along with Anna Burglass, representing her friend Guy Banister. An unidentified Cuban listens in. "Lucious" Rabel arrives with his shadow, Arcacha—and Tommy. On this night they discuss the assassination.

Other scenes are at the Mission on North Rampart to which Shaw has a key, but not Oswald, which is accurate. Cubans in fatigues hold containers filled with money, the containers supplied by Continental Can. The industrial complex is everywhere in this story, from General Motors providing Pershing Gervais with a fake job in Canada to Continental Can in New Orleans assisting in anti-Castro efforts. Yet another scene takes place at the Town and Country Motel where Carlos Marcello discusses the assassination with Clay Shaw, Ferrie, Arcacha, Jack Martin and G. Wray Gill.

The final scene is set at Gill's office, two weeks before the assassination. Shaw and Arcacha, Ferrie, Rozzy and Jack Martin stand around as Tommy is handed the package to take to Lawrence Howard in Dallas. Rozzy drives Tommy to the airport.

In an essay he called "Power," Jim Garrison defined Oswald's role. "The scapegoat in a *coup d'état* is presumed guilty because of his weakness," he writes. "Those who question his guilt are presumed mentally unbalanced because of their irrelevance, and the government is presumed innocent because of its power."

"The Agency, when it was all over, they knew they'd been danced with," Garrison said as his life ran out.

Years passed. Living what he calls a lifetime of worry, "about something you can't put your finger on," Thomas Edward Beckham returned to the traditions of his origins. He studied to be a rabbi, never forgetting that his mother had longed for one of her sons to practice her faith. He was a field supervisor for the Southern Baptist Theological Seminary. Messianic Judaism attracted him with its belief that Jesus dwelled among us in fulfillment of God's plan.

He is the father of eight children, all of whom play musical instruments, the legacy of the perfect pitch and musical talent of "Mark Evans." Even when he was unable to read or write, Tommy could pick up any instrument and play it well. His oldest child is his daughter with the Cuban woman introduced to him by Clay Shaw. Having become a father for the first time when he was in his teens, he is a grandfather several times over. He flashes a gold ring with the Star of David on his finger. A shining mezzuzah hangs from his neck.

He resumed his singing career, featured as the "King of Hillbilly." In his repertoire are songs he wrote himself, like "It's Love," and Hank Williams' classics like "Your Cheating Heart" and "Beautiful Brown Eyes." He is a gray-haired, Kenny Rogers look-alike in miniature now.

To meet him is to like him, as once Guy Banister had warmed to his open personality. Beckham spent years looking over his shoulder, but does so less frequently now.

Thomas Edward Beckham remembers Jim Garrison and admits that Garrison "knew the whole thing; he had the right people." Many of those on whom Garrison focused—David Ferrie, Lawrence Howard, Kerry Thornley and Clay Shaw—had played roles in the implementation of the assassination. Some people, like Jack Martin, fed Garrison accurate information, Beckham acknowledges. Martin was "a double agent, and a good one." Others spread lies and deceived him.

Thomas Edward Bekcham is now in his sixties and ailing, suffering from diabetes and heart trouble. He describes himself as a person who has fled from publicity all his life and desires none now. He does wish there could have been another chance for him to tell the truth to Jim Garrison. He wishes he could return to that moment in February of 1968 after the grand jury when Jim Garrison called him up and asked, did Beckham think Garrison had uncovered anything true about the conspiracy to murder President Kennedy?

Jim Garrison had pleaded with this recalcitrant witness: "Am I right? Have I touched on anything? Am I close?"

Beckham wishes he could tell Jim Garrison what he knew then, and is as certain of now. "Yes, you were." Over the years he considered calling Garrison, then thought, why stir up something more?

"I believe in my heart that he knew the whole thing. He got it where it started and no one else came close," Beckham says. "I wish I could have told him."

NOTES

FREQUENTLY CITED ABBREVIATIONS:

AARC   Assassinations Archives and Research Center
ARRB   Assassination Records and Review Board
CAP   Civil Air Patrol
DRE   Revolutionary Student Directorate
FOIA   Freedom of Information Act
JMWAVE   CIA office in Maimi
MCC   Metropolitan Crime Commission
NARA   National Archives and Records Administration
NOAC   New Orleans Athletic Club
NODA   New Orleans District Attorney's office
NOPL   New Orleans Public Library
HSCA   House Select Committee on Assassinations
OAS   Organisation Armée Sécrète
ONI   Office of Naval Intelligence
SAC   Special Agent In Charge
SSCIA   Senate Select Committee On Intelligence Activities (Church Committee)
WC   Warren Commission

CHAPTER 1

p. 1, line 4: trip to Shreveport: Interviews with John Volz, May 21, 1998; May 12, 2000. Macdonald: "A Critique of The Warren Report," *Esquire* (March 1965), p. 59ff.

p. 1, line 24: Herbert J. Miller Jr. in Dallas. See "Texas To Hold Inquiry Court," *Times-Picayune,* November 26, 1963, Section 1, p. 14; Miller destroys the idea: Tapes of Herbert J. Miller Jr. 543 FOUR 24, reels 1–23; ARRB (Assassination Records and Review Board). August 7, 1997; see also Miller interview, August 7, 1997. NARA.

p. 2, line 6: "I would hope that none of these records are circulated": *The Freedom of Information Act and Political Assassinations,* ed. David R. Wrone. Volume I. The Legal Proceedings of Harold Weisberg v. General Services Administration, together with the January 22 and 27 Warren Commission Transcripts. (University of Wisconsin, Stevens Point, Wisconsin: Foundation Press, Inc, 1978). p. 236.

p. 2, line 10: "one man could not have fired": Boggs confided the same point to Edward Jay Epstein. Conversation with Edward Jay Epstein, April 17, 2001.

p. 2, line 11: no notes, no transcription: "Back Up Material For *On the Trail of the Assassins,*" June 27, 1989. AARC.

p. 2, line 15: It was Hale Boggs: Interview with Phyllis Kritikos, January 11, 2000. Kritikos was Garrison's second wife.

p. 2, line 34: "messianic": David W. Ferrie, "Suicide Note A." NODA. NARA.

p. 3, line 1: "my jurisdiction": Interview with Jim Garrison in *Beyond JFK.* Documentary film by Danny Schecter and Barbara Kopple.

p. 3, line 5: "not my affair": "Insert A" of draft of a letter regarding charges made by reporter James Phelan. *Garrison Family Papers*. NARA.

p. 3, line 11: "rather eccentric": Carl D. Lynch to Mrs. Alfred Garrison, October 25, 1964. Appendix to A Short History of the Garrison Family of North Carolina and Their Descendants. Courtesy of Lyon Garrison.

p. 3, line 16: the Robinson boys: Fragment of a history of the Robinson Family, pp. 32-33. The Garrison Family Papers. NARA.

p. 3, line 21: stark naked: Pearl Rank Heiden to Mrs. Ethel Thompson, March 8, 1967. Courtesy of Lyon Garrison.

p. 3, line 24: he could read. Interview with Mrs. Liz Garrison, January 11, 1998.

p. 3, line 30: "Oh, you mean Jimmy": Interview with Elizabeth Garrison, January 11, 1998.

p. 4, line 2: unable to afford a bicycle: Interview with Dr. Bernard Jacobs, April 14, 2000.

p. 4, line 4: "too much blue": Interview with the late Walter Gemeinhardt, May 31, 2000.

p. 4, line 8: ate lunch by himself: Interview with John Clemmer, June 1, 2000.

p. 4, line 11: parking violations: Interview with Alvin Gottschall, March 6, 1998.

p. 4, line 13: the Big Bands and Peggie Baker: Interviews with Peggie Baker and Wilma Baker, May 26, 1996.

p. 4, line 27: "Roger The Dodger": See, "A Piper Cub Over Germany," in *New Orleans: An Oral History of New Orleanians During World War II* comp. Brian Altobello (1990), pp. 134–136. (The Williams Research Center, 410 Charters Street, New Orleans, Louisiana, 70130.) See also: Memorandum. January 16, 1984. To: Stadiem. From: Garrison. Re: Characteristics of the Grasshopper (with regard to the Initial Combat Scene). Courtesy of Lyon Garrison. On Dachau: see "Foreword— A Heritage of Stone," in *Crime, Law and Corrections,* ed. Ralph Slovenko (Springfield, Illinois: Charles C. Thomas, 1966), pp. xx, xxi.

p. 4, line 30: "has haunted me": *Playboy.* Vol. 14, No. 10 (October 1967), p. 178.

p. 4, line 35: "afraid of people": Interview with Judge James C. Gulotta, January 9, 1998.

p. 4, line 35: never mentioned that he had been at Dachau: Interviews with Warren Garfunkel, June 14, 2000, and Rene Lehmann, June 16, 2000.

p. 4, line 37: he was bored with the law: Interview with Jay Teasdel, January 16, 2000.

p. 5, line 1: stealing a book: Interview with Jack Benjamin, May 31, 2000.

p. 5, line 5: Nazi ticket: Interview with Wilmer Thomas, March 7, 2001.

p. 5, line 6: mockery of the Louisiana political system: Interview with Wilmer Thomas, July 24, 2000.

p. 5, line 8: "Hotsy, totsy": Interview with Rosemary Pillow, April 23, 2000.

p. 6, line 2: "decidedly promising": A. L. Fierst to Jim Garrison. July 23, 1952. The Garrison Family Papers. NARA.

p. 6, line 9: blue denim trousers: *The Taming of the Shrew,* original script by Jim Garrison. Courtesy of Don Howell.

p. 6, line 12: dinner at Antoine's: Interview with H. Jackson Grayson Jr. January 16, 2000.

p. 6, line 25: "I'll get her to the head of the line." Interview with Mickey Parlour Bremermann, July 30, 1999.

p. 6, line 27: "I want to be district attorney": Interview with Numa Bertel, October 9, 2000.

p. 6, line 29: "just close the door": Interview with the late Herman Kohlman, May 19, 1998.

p. 6, line 34: "one man's dramatic involvement": Jot pad for notes and questions. Notes re: Jury Trials. The *Garrison Family Papers*. NARA.

p. 6, line 40: Marc Antony's arrest: interview with Joyce Wood, June 10, 2000.

p. 7, line 3: Marc Antony a Kohn informant: Investigative Report— Confidential. October 14, 1957. MCC (Metropolitan Crime Commission).

p. 7, line 7: little black book: Interview with Barbara Barry Ward, July 11, 2001.

p. 7, line 14: post additional signs: Milton Brener, *The Garrison Case: A Study in the Abuse of Power* (New York: Clarkson N. Potter 1969), p. 3.

p. 7, line 16: "posters don't vote":

Interview with Robert Haik, January 9, 2000.

p. 7, line 21: frequent the racetrack: Interview with G. Harrison Scott, June 9, 2000. Interview with Warren Garfunkel, June 2, 2000.

p. 7, line 22: in his seat: Interview with Garfunkel.

p. 7, line 28: disturbing the peace: "Picketers Arrested in N.O.," *Times-Picayune,* August 29, 1961, section 1, p. 12; "Bucaro Defers Trial of Three," *Times-Picayune,* August 30, 1961, section 1, p. 8; "Picketing Case Suspect Freed," *Times-Picayune,* September 1, 1961, section 3, p. 8; "Two Get 90-Day Jail Sentences," *Times-Picayune,* September 9, 1961, section 1, p. 7.

p. 7, line 40: "catches more oysters": "Verbal Blasts Mark D.A. Race," *Times-Picayune,* December 28, 1961. Section 1, p. 5.

p. 7, line 41: Haik approaches Schiro on Garrison's behalf: Aaron M. Kohn Interview with Robert Haik. Investigative Report. May 31, 1962. MCC.

p. 8, line 4: half-drunk: Interview with Judge Adrian Duplantier, February 6, 2001.

p. 8, line 13: "we will do no favors": Interview with the late Vance Gilmer, January 4, 2001.

p. 8, line 14: "tolerance of the status quo . . . smog": Richard N. Billings interview with Jim Garrison. Undated. 94 pages. Papers of Richard N. Billings. Special Collections. Georgetown University, Washington, DC.

p. 8, line 17: no one was above the law: Interview with John Volz, March 13, 2001.

p. 8, line 19: "Chinese whorehouse": Jim Garrison, *Coup D'Etat.* Unpublished manuscript, p. 3 of 1. AARC.

p. 8, line 25: law books: Interview with Louis Ivon, January 8, 1998.

p. 8, line 28: commanding officer: *Coup D'Etat,* p. 10 of 3.

p. 8, line 40: "Just another day": Interview with Louis Ivon and Frank Minyard, January 8, 1998.

p. 9, line 7: "You're hired": Interview with Ross Scaccia, January 6, 2000.

p. 9, line 9: first in her class: Interview with Louise Korns, July 13, 2001.

p. 9, line 30: a bank charter: Interview with Numa Bertel, October 9, 2000; interview with Phyllis Kritikos,

February 6, 2002; "Obtaining a Charter for a State Bank," Memo by Louise Korns, August 16, 1965. Courtesy of Lyon Garrison.

p. 9, line 40: uncashed national guard paychecks: Interview with Dr. Frank Minyard, January 8, 1998.

p. 9, line 41: a gambler named Jules Crovetto: Interview with Louis Crovetto, February 6, 2002.

p. 10, line 19: crackdown of Bourbon Street: Interview with Barbara Bennett, February 6, 2001; interview with William Livesay, March 24, 2001.

p. 11, line 7: charges would be reduced: Interview with William Alford, May 28, 1998.

p. 11, line 10: temper justice with mercy: Interview with William Porteous, July 15, 2000.

p. 11, line 14: no jail time: Interview with Judge Louis P. Trent, October 8, 2000.

p. 11, line 15: armed robbery: Interview with Ray McGuire, March 2, 2001.

p. 11, line 26: "I don't want them charged": Interview with John Volz, June 13, 2000.

p. 11, line 33: medical school professor: Interview with Ralph Slovenko, April 5, 2001.

p. 11, line 35: a hurricane, a cyclone: Interview with Numa Bertel, June 5, 2000.

p. 12, line 9: safe crackers: Interview with Denis A. Barry, May 17, 1998.

p. 12, line 13: long belly: description provided by Raymond Comstock, May 29, 1998.

p. 12, line 17: "the Devil incarnate": Interview with John Volz, January 15, 2000.

p. 12, line 19: card games: Notes of Jack N. Rogers. June 14, 1963. Papers of Jack N. Rogers. These papers are in the custody of Rogers' daughter.

p. 12, line 22: he kept dossiers: Interview with the late Frank Meloche, June 11, 2000.

p. 12, line 30: Gervais a Kohn informant: Interview with Louis Ivon, October 9, 2000.

p. 12, line 33: "those who have money": Interview with Burton Klein, April 5, 2001.

p. 12, line 39: collecting that much: The source is Denis Barry. Investigative Report. October 5, 1964; information received October 2, 1964. MCC.

p. 12, line 41: escaped the Bourbon Street crackdown: Interview with John Volz, July 17, 2001.

p. 13, line 6: Pershing also controlled the vice squad: Interview with Frank Meloche, June 11, 2000.

p. 13, line 6: everyone feared him: Interview with Meloche.

p. 13, line 7: skull cap: Internal *Newsweek* Memo: Garrison Backgrounder. February 24, 1967. NARA.

p. 13, line 19: "a man that don't take money": interview with Ross Scaccia, April 5, 2001.

p. 13, line 39: $1500: See Christine Wiltz, *The Last Madam: A Life in the New Orleans Underworld* (New York: Faber and Faber, 2000), p. 128.

p. 14, line 3: "the real character and purposes of people": Investigative Report. July 21, 1966. Date information received June 10, 1966, conversation between Aaron M. Kohn and Dalton Williams. MCC.

p. 14, line 10: Eventually Frank Klein resigned, unable to co-exist with Pershing: See "DA Fired Gervais For 'Shakedowns,'" by Lanny Thomas and Allan Katz. *Times-Picayune,* September 13, 1973, Section A, p. 2. See also. Memorandum. May 4, 1965. Date of Information, May 3, 1965. Reported by Aaron M. Kohn. MCC.

p. 14, line 11: for the Hardy Davis-William Livesay story, see: William Hardy Davis, *Aiming for the Jugular in New Orleans* (Port Washington, New York: Ashley Books Inc., 1976), p. 26; Interviews with William Livesay, December 20, 31, 2000; January 14, 15, 16, 2001. That Jim Garrison did not know about the setting up of Davis: Interview with Lester Otillio, December 10, 2002. Opposing a reduction in Livesay's sentence: "Garrison Hits Jail Term Cut," *Times-Picayune,* November 21, 1963, Section 1, p. 29. "A Gervais operation": Interview with Louis Ivon, May 28, 2002. "Clearly violated" Davis' constitutional rights: Campaign advertisement: "What About O'Hara's Ghost Stories?" *Times-Picayune,* October 30, 1965, Section 1, p. 20.

p. 15, line 29: "shakeup": "2 Assistant DA's Quit in Shakeup." *States-Item,* May 19, 1965. See also Jim Garrison to Aaron Kohn, May 18, 1965.

p. 15, line 32: Kay Roberts: FBI. Memorandum to Director. From: SAC, New Orleans. Subject: Dissemination of critical information to other agencies. New Orleans Division AR. Criminal Influence in Local Agencies. September 22, 1965. 66-6353-2874. 4 pages. "This information was not disseminated to Jim Garrison," the document reads.

p. 15, line 39: "paddling upstream": Jim Garrison to Aaron Kohn. Personal and Confidential. May 18, 1965. MCC.

p. 16, line 4: Jimmy Moran gave up sending bills: Interview with the late Walter Hammer, March 4, 2001.

p. 16, line 8: "never learned to slap": Jim Garrison to Louis Wolfson, August 24, 1989. Courtesy of Lyon Garrison.

CHAPTER 2

p. 17, Epigraph: "There is no final answer": Jim Garrison, "When Business Leaders Think of Crime and Politics," fragment of a play, *The Garrison Family Papers.*

p. 17, line 13: the judges had their own hands in the till: Interview with Donald V. Organ, January 10, 2000.

p. 18, line 2: Judge Cocke had run the Dowling office: Interview with Numa Bertel, February 6, 2001.

p. 18, line 5: "the white man should know better": Interviews with Judge Louis Trent and Walter Hammer.

p. 18, line 10: "the sacred cows of India": "Prison Crowding Laid to Judges," *States-Item,* October 31, 1962, p. 1.

p. 18, line 18: Carlos Marcello wanted Garrison out of office: Interview with McKeithen associate John Tarver, January 31, 2000.

p. 18, line 22: "put it in a law book": Interview with Tarver.

p. 18, line 25: a sex deviate: Report of Frank Manning to the FBI. March 6, 1967.

p. 18, line 34: *King James The First.* Investigative files received from New Orleans district attorney Harry Connick. NARA.

p. 19, line 36: "you lost": Interview with Robert Haik. Haik is also the source of the Gervais quotation.

p. 20, line 1: *Garrison v. Louisiana:* Supreme Court of the United States. No. 4, October Term, 1964. *Jim Garrison, Appellant, v. State of Louisiana.* On Appeal from the Supreme Court of Louisiana. Reargued October 19, 1964. Decided November 23, 1964. 379 U.S. 64.

p. 20, line 9: "filthy": *Times-Picayune,* June 21, 1963, Section 1, p. 7. For the history of James Baldwin's book being seized, see also: "Book Charges Refused by DA," *Times-Picayune,* June 19, 1963; "Offer in Novel's Case Pondered," *Times-Picayune,* June 26, 1963; "Citizens Group Raps Garrison," *Times-Picayune,* June 20, 1963, section 1, p. 30; "Case Dismissed Involving Book," *Times-Picayune,* September 11, 1964, Section 1, p. 4.

p. 20, line 34: choice between remaining with the Bureau: Interview with H. John Bremermann, July 30, 1999.

p. 20, line 37: "just couldn't make it": Medical Report by Marshall L. Fowler. 1st Lt. MC. Garrison, James C. Captain. 0-1165863 (1951). AARC.

p. 20, line 38: "I know this sounds crazy." Ibid. Fowler report.

p. 21, line 1: flying toward the enemy: "Memo to: Stadiem. From: Garrison. January 16, 1984.

p. 21, line 6: Dr. Matthews: Military Records: Garrison, James C. Captain.

p. 21, line 12: "neurasthenia, or a hypochondriasis": Douglas J. Page, Colonel. ARTY-RA President. Appended to FBI document 89-69-3250, Agency file: 124-10251-10247.

p. 21, line 13: "over-solicitous mother": Fowler report.

p. 21, line 18: he did not reply: Jane Garrison Gardiner to Robert Haik. Undated. Courtesy of Lyon Garrison.

p. 21, line 23: the heroine of a woman's film reminded Jim Garrison of his mother: Interview with Lyon Garrison, October 8, 2001.

p. 22, line 4: "I consider him very dangerous": Investigative Report. July 3, 1965. Date information received: July 1, 1965. Reported by Aaron M. Kohn. MCC. See also: "Resume of Conversation—General Pauley and Colonel Garrison—September 18, 1965. Courtesy of General Erbon W. Wise.

p. 22, line 8: his mother pressured

him to marry: Interviews with Jay Teasdel, Vance Gilmer.

p. 22, line 13: orgies: Interview with Denis Barry.

p. 22, line 21: "how do you know if you're in love?" Interview with Peggie Baker, June 6, 2000.

p. 22, line 32: "I belong up there": Interview with Robert Haik. "Get out of my way": Interviews with Haik and Barbara Barry Ward.

p. 23, line 3: "Sex has nothing to do with morality": Interview with John Volz, July 31, 2001.

p. 23, line 4: like a little pixie: Interview with Lenore Ward, August 8, 2000.

p. 23, line 6: he adored his children: Interview with Patricia Chandler, May 22, 1998.

p. 23, line 7: "we're going to have a Snapper": Interview with Mrs. Liz Garrison, January 11, 1998.

p. 23, line 14: "A Heritage of Stone," *Crime, Law and Corrections,* ed. Ralph Slovenko (Springfield, Illinois: Charles C. Thomas, 1966), pp. xvii-xxv.

p. 23, line 24: *Commentary* magazine: James H. Brown Jr. to Jim Garrison, October 2, 1966; Warner J. Dannhauser to Jim Garrison, October 25, 1966. Garrison papers at the New Orleans Public Library, hereafter NOPL.

p. 23, line 28: "all that he did": Louis Ivon interviewed in John Barbour's documentary film, *The Garrison Tapes.*

p. 24, line 4: "don't mess with him": Interview with the late Linda Brigette, July 28, 2001.

p. 24, line 11: "use your influence": Louis P. Trent to Jim Garrison, September 8, 1966. NARA.

p. 24, line 15: a private party: Robert Buras to Joan Mellen, April 21, 2004; conversation with Buras, May 28, 2004.

p. 24, line 24: "obviously I was paid": Interview with John Volz, April 18, 2001.

p. 24, line 29: "economic importance of Linda Brigette": MCC telegram to Governor John McKeithen, September 27, 1966.

p. 24, line 30: Carlos Marcello is behind Lamarca: MCC Memorandum, September 29, 1966.

p. 24, line 32: Core another Kohn

informant: Conversation with Mike Seghers, January 6, 2000.

p. 24, line 33: "a dancer could be important": Investigative Report. October 10, 1966. Date information received: October 7, 1966. Reported by Aaron M. Kohn. MCC.

p. 24, line 37: "Flat Earth Society": Press Release. New Orleans District Attorney's Office. September 21, 1966. MCC.

p. 25, line 8: a mortgage loan: "Denis A. Barry to Aaron M. Kohn, September 26, 1966. See also Aaron M. Kohn to Denis A. Barry, September 29, 1966. MCC.

p. 25, line 20: Bugsy Schwartz: "Jury Calls MCC Chief, Evidence on Organized Crime Is N.O. Aim," *Times-Picayune,* September 27, 1966, Section 1, p. 1.

p. 25, line 22: "Put up or shut up!": "Put Up Or Shut Up, DA's Word to Kohn": *Times-Picayune,* September 25, 1966, Section 1, p. 1.

p. 25, line 24: Kohn testified for three hours: See videotaped Kohn statement for WDSU-TV, September 24, 1966, and press release of the same date. MCC.

p. 25, line 28: return to sender: Memorandum. December 27, 1966. To: All Members of the Staff. From: Jim Garrison, District Attorney. Re: Mail from M.C.C. NOPL.

p. 25, line 30: Kohn had praised his office: "Garrison Given Praise by Kohn," *Times-Picayune,* August 25, 1962, Section 3, **p. 23.**

p. 26, line 5: "We got avenues": Interview with L. J. Delsa, January 12, 2000.

p. 26, line 12: "the Mafia angle": Memo. 3/20/77. To: Tanenbaum. From: Fonzi. Courtesy of Gaeton Fonzi.

p. 26, line 17: a shoplifting incident: Interview with William Walter, January 5, 2000. As FBI night clerk, Walter had access to the New Orleans field office files, and Beck had asked him to check on Beck's own secret file.

p. 26, line 17: Raymond Beck informs on Garrison: FBI Memorandum, December 24, 1966. 89-69-1484. See also: To: Director, FBI. From: SAC, New Orleans. December 23, 1966. 62-109060-4366. NARA. See also: Memorandum. To: Mr. Callahan from J. B. Adams. Subject: Aaron M. Kohn, Former Special Agent. SERVICE RECORD

INQUIRY. September 29, 1966. Identifying numbers illegible. Beck's name is redacted but the reference, "retired former Special Agent, now employed by District Attorney's Office," leaves no doubt as to his identity. Beck tells Walter the FBI sent him to spy: Interview with William Walter, January 5, 2000.

p. 26, line 18: Pershing Gervais "is advising Garrison": FBI Memorandum. To: Director, FBI. From: SAC, New Orleans. January 4, 1967. 89-69-1376. 4 pages. NARA.

p. 26, line 21: "expose errors in the Warren Report": FBI Memorandum. To: Director. From: New Orleans. February 23, 1967. 124-10241-10096. NARA.

p. 26, line 28: repaid his entire debt: Richard N. Billings, "The Case for a Conspiracy: The Garrison Hypothesis," March 1 and March 13, 1967. Papers of Richard N. Billings.

p. 26, line 42: Oswald's training: testimony of Colonel Allison G. Folsom. Volume VIII, p. 307.

p. 27, line 5: "my dog is really stupid": Jim Garrison interviewed in *Beyond JFK.*

p. 27, line 15: telephone records of Jack Ruby: Notes of Romney Stubbs. Stubbs viewed the document in the Hale Boggs Papers at the Special Collections at Tulane University. It is no longer there. Curator Bill Meneray says that one day FBI agents arrived, declared that they had the permission of Mrs. Lindy Boggs, and removed most of the material from the Boggs papers relating to his work on the Warren Commission. A freedom of information request to the Department of Justice has failed to produce these documents.

p. 27, line 21: "pouring out of the crematorium": Jim Garrison interviewed by the BBC. 1967. Transcript at NARA.

p. 27, line 23: bolt-action rifle: Discussion of Oswald and his rifle. Taped telephone conversation. Office of the District Attorney. Tape 541-HC-36. NODA. NARA.

p. 27, line 26: Jim Garrison marked the moment: Conversation with Jim Garrison. House Select Committee on Assassinations, November 26, 1978. NARA.

p. 27, line 33: "a little like Pershing": Interview with Herman Kohlman, May 17, 2001.

p. 27, line 35: "unstable": See: FBI Memorandum. From: W.A. Branigan to W. C. Sullivan. March 6, 1967. 124-10042-10456. 52-109060-4678. NARA.

p. 27, line 36: the same term used by the Secret Service: Robert Oswald, *Lee: A Portrait of Lee Harvey Oswald* (New York: Coward McCann, 1967), p. 156.

p. 27, line 41: Andrews told the Secret Service: Dean Andrews' statements to the FBI and the Secret Service during the weekend of the assassination and the week following can be found in Special Agent Warren C. de Brueys' Commission Document 75, December 2, 1963. File No. 100-10461. NARA.

p. 28, line 2: "frequent the Gaslibt Bar": Warren Commission Exhibit 3104. Vol. 26, pp. 732-733.

p. 28, line 6: "homosexual clique": Davis, *Aiming for the Jugular in New Orleans,* p. 25.

p. 28, line 14: Andrews told his clients he could be reached at Hotel Dieu: FBI Investigative Files on Lee Harvey Oswald. 180-100-301-0064. Box 2, Section 9. HSCA. NARA.

p. 28, line 18: "become famous": Dean Andrews interviewed for Walter Sheridan's "White Paper." Interview No. 2. NARA.

p. 28, line 19: Eva Springer: Memorandum. To: Jim Garrison. From: Sgt. Tom Duffy. Re: Miss E. H. Springer - Interview of (Former Secretary of Dean Andrews). Interviewed by: Sgt. Duffy, Sgt. Sedgebeer and Officer Navarre. April 13, 1967. NODA. Garrison's office also interviewed Prentiss Davis: March 9, 1967.

p. 28, line 38: Comstock telephones Regis Kennedy: FBI Memorandum. To: SAC. From: Jean B. Hearn. Subject: Lt. Raymond Comstock, information concerning. December 10, 1971. 89-69-3004A. NARA.

p. 29, line 4: "pushing me pretty hard": Andrews' interview for Walter Sheridan.

p. 29, line 12: thirty and forty men: Dean Andrews on WDSU radio, quoted in FBI teletype: To: Director and Dallas. From: New Orleans. Re: Action by Orleans Parish Grand Jury. 124-10237-10225. 89-69-1722. NARA.

p. 29, line 37: lunch: Jim Garrison's lunch with Andrews is described

in *On the Trail of the Assassins: My Investigation and Prosecution of the Murder of President Kennedy* (New York: Sheridan Square Press, 1988), pp. 79–83.

p. 30, line 7: "never intended": "Back Up Material for *On The Trail,*" June 27, 1989, p. 8.

p. 30, line 17: "playing out his assignment": "Notes re Oswald in '63." NODA. NARA.

p. 30, line 22: "doesn't yet know what can't be done": Interview with Mark Lane, January 15, 1998.

p. 30, line 23: Moo Moo might be aggressive: Interview with Numa Bertel, February 6, 2001.

CHAPTER 3

p. 31, Epigraph: "The key to the whole case": Jim Garrison interviewed by *WIN* magazine. 1 February 1969. "Garrison's Investigation, 1964-1969," p. 30.

p. 31, line 1: for an account of Garrison's trip to New York with Rault and Long, see "The Garrison Investigation: How and Why It Began," *New Orleans* magazine. April 1967, pp. 8, 50-51. See also: *On the Trail of the Assassins,* p. 13.

p. 31, line 6: "chewed my ear off": Conversation with Audra McCardell, granddaughter of Russell Long, April 20, 1999.

p. 31, line 8: "always thought": "Believes Two Riflemen Involved In Kennedy Assassination—Long," *Times-Picayune,* November 22, 1966, Section 1, p. 1.

p. 31, line 13: Charlie Ward handled the routine duties: To: Ward. Scribbled on a January 17, 1967, note to Jim Garrison from Charlie Ward. NOPL. See also the evidence of how many engagements Garrison turned down: Joe Humble to Mr. Jim Garrison, October 27, 1966. See also from the NOPL papers: S. R. Abramson to Jim Garrison, March 10, 1967; Irving Ward-Steinman to Jim Garrison, March 20, 1967; Boyce Holleman to Honorable Jim Garrison, March 22, 1967; Jim Garrison to Steven R. Plotkin, December 1, 1966; Steven R. Plotkin to Jim Garrison, November 29, 1966; Jim Garrison to George Muhs, December 1, 1966; The Exchange Club of New Orleans to Jim

Garrison, November 19, 1966; Jim Garrison to Honorable Edward J. Boyle, December 1, 1966; Jim Garrison to Honorable Lansing Mitchell, December 1, 1966; Jim Garrison to Frank R. Barnett, December 1, 1966; Charles Moore to Mr. James "Jim" Garrison. October 24, 1966. NOPL.

p. 31, line 16: "nothing else matters": CIA: From C/CI/R & A. Transcript. March 26, 1968. Memo: Garrison TV Interview At The Hague on 11 February 1968. 104-10435-10004. Agency file: RUSS HOLMES WORK FILE. NARA.

p. 31, line 10: "or the mob": Richard N. Billings, "The Case for a Conspiracy: The Garrison Hypothesis." March 1 and March 13, 1967. Papers of Richard N. Billings.

p. 32, line 14: "nothing to it": Investigative Report. March 23, 1967. Date of information: February 27, 1967. Reported by Aaron M. Kohn. MCC.

p. 32, line 25: he called the boys "Dad": Interview with Alvin Beaubouef, January 4, 2000.

p. 32, line 30: Eric Michael Crouchet extortion: Police Report of the Juvenile Bureau, February 18, 1962. Item B-7904-62. To: Joseph I. Giarrusso, Superintendent of Police. From: Major Adolph Mayterhafer, Supervisor, Juvenile Bureau. Subject: Investigation of Extortion, allegedly committed by David W. Ferrie, WM, 41, of 331 Atherton Drive, Metairie, Louisiana. NARA.

p. 32, line 34: Al Landry runs away from home: See Juvenile Bureau. To: Joseph I. Giarrusso. From: August C. Lang. August 18, 1961. Item H-8307-61. Subject: Contributing to the delinquency investigation, resulting from the runaway of Alexander Landry Jr., WM, age 15, of 5221 Arts Street. The subject alleged to be contributing is Dave Ferrie, WM, adult, residing at 331 Atherton Drive in Metairie, Louisiana.

p. 32, line 36: "I wouldn't screw her": Interview with Morris Brownlee, June 2, 2000.

p. 32, line 42: "little swatches of carpet": Aaron Kohn Deposition before the House Select Committee on Assassinations. November 7, 1978. 013261. NARA.

p. 33, line 10: parasites could en-

ter: Interview with Morris Brownlee. No expertise in science: Interview with Dr. Martin Palmer, May 9, 1999.

p. 33, line 13: Ferrie a police informant: Interview with Irvin L. Magri Jr., February 17, 2002.

p. 33, line 15: Dave's connections: Interview with Alvin Beaubouef, March 12, 2002.

p. 33, line 28: Tampa, the Keys: Memorandum. July 12, 1967. To: Jim Garrison. From: Robert E. Lee. Re: David W. Ferrie. NODA. NARA. Ferrie had honed his skills at the Sunnyside Flying School in Tampa, where years later Middle Eastern terrorists went themselves to train.

p. 33, line 28: Venice, Florida: Memorandum to Jim Garrison. From: Tom Bethell. Re: Information from Martin Waldron, *New York Times.* October 5, 1967. NODA. NARA.

p. 33, line 32: Del Valle set up training camps: Headquarters of the Army Office of the Assistant Chief of Staff for Intelligence. July 25, 1962. Memorandum for: Director, Federal Bureau of Investigation. Att'n: Mr. Patrick D. Putnam. Subject: Anti-Castro Guerrilla Training Camps in the U.S. (U). 2-1622-159. From: Claude D. Barton, Colonel, GS Chief, Security Division. Courtesy of Gordon Winslow.

p. 33, line 33: Ferrie's missions tracked by Cuban intelligence: See Transcript of Proceedings Between Cuban Officials and JFK historians. Document 0027-4. Cuban Information Archives. Nassau Beach Hotel, 7/9 December 1996. Tape #4. Available at cuban-exile.com.

p. 33, line 36: Marchetti confirms that Ferrie was employed by CIA: Marchetti interview with Bernard Fensterwald, April 22, 1975. Papers of the Citizens' Commission of Inquiry. AARC.

p. 33, line 41: the School of the Americas and Robert Kennedy: Richard Reeves, *President Kennedy: Profile of Power* (New York: Simon & Schuster, 1993), p. 268.

p. 34, line 3: your security clearance was so high: Interview with E. Carl McNabb, June 13, 1999.

p. 34, line 6: a "nigger lover": Jimmy Johnson, "New Orleans Story." Interview with an unnamed questioner. NARA.

p. 34, line 7: screwed up the Bay

of Pigs: Memorandum. To: Jim Garrison. From: Andrew J. Sciambra. Interview with Al Landry. March 23, 1967. NODA. NARA.

p. 34, line 10: Kennedy of making a deal: Interview with Alvin Beaubouef.

p. 34, line 16: a seashell rigged with explosives: See "booby-trapped sea shell": CIA Inspector General's Report on Attempts to Kill Fidel Castro. May 1967. p. 77.

p. 34, line 17: midget submarine: Interview with Carlos Quiroga, January 14, 2000. See also: Memorandum. To: Jim Garrison. From: Frank Klein. Re: Interview of Carlos Quiroga, January 13, 1966. Papers of Richard N. Billings, Box 2, Folder 24.

p. 34, line 30: "skinny, messy little guy": Interview with Sharon Herkes, January 14, 2000.

p. 34, line 33: subsisted on bad coffee: Description of Jack Martin courtesy of Thomas Edward Beckham, March 30, 2002.

p. 34, line 36: intelligence ties to Latin America: Joseph A. Oster interviewed by L. J. Delsa and Robert Buras. January 27, 1978. HSCA 005207. NARA.

p. 34, line 38: a "con man": Medical records of Jack Martin, Charity Hospital. NARA.

p. 34, line 41: "a type of Ferrie": e-mail from Robert Buras, September 21, 2002.

p. 34, line 42: "highly intelligent": Interview with Robert Buras, May 23, 2002. Buras interviewed Martin for the HSCA in 1977 and 1978.

p. 35, line 2: crime against nature: Interview with Joseph A. Oster, July 3, 2000.

p. 35, line 6: first name basis: See Russell Long to J. S. Martin Sr., August 8, 1961, and September 1, 1961. NARA.

p. 35, line 10: Jack Martin has filed a petition on the instructions of Mr. Leander Perez: From: S.A.—n— 4951. Louisiana State Police. Subject: General Edward [sic] Walker. NARA.

p. 35, line 16: Dalzell a CIA operative: HSCA 180-10070-10358. Agency file: 008269. (PT 18). Memorandum: October 30, 1968. To: Jim Garrison. From: Andrew J. Sciambra. Re: Interview with Vernon Gerdes. NARA. See also: Dalzell works under

cover as a petroleum consultant: FBI. To: Director. From: New Orleans. November 3, 1967. 124-10071-10326. 89-69-3575. NARA. And: William Dalzell admits he worked for the Central Intelligence Agency: Select Committee on Assassinations. Interview with William Dalzell. 064559. December 9, 1977. NARA. See also: HSCA re-interview of Dalzell, January 26, 1978, by William Brown. NARA.

p. 35, line 17: Newbrough with CIA: L. J. Delsa and Robert Buras interview with Jack S. Martin.

p. 35, line 18: supervised the clandestine services: CIA admits to the fact that the Domestic Contact Service and the clandestine services were one and the same in New Orleans. See Russ Holmes Work File, Memo Number 8. Agency: CIA. Record Number 104-10435-10009. From: DDO/PIC. To: CI Staff. Title. Official Routing slip with Attached Resanitized Copy of Memo #8 of the Garrison Package. 26 pages. Date: January 12, 1968: "Since 19 November 1964 contacts for the DDP have been handled by the DCS."

p. 35, line 20: Dalzell's criminal charges: The Department of Justice does not prosecute Dalzell: FBI AIRTEL. May 22, 1967. To: Director. From: SAC, WFO. 124-10259-10090. 89-69-3103. NARA. See also: Regarding Ferrie's acquaintance with Dalzell: see note appended to an article on cancer research found at David Ferrie's apartment: Memorandum For: Lead File. Re: Notes Made By David Ferrie. Signed by Jim Garrison. NODA. NARA. The note reads: "man— Bill Dazell [sic]: '(Billie Littlehorse).' Some of B's microfilm was sent to Atlanta right-wingers—many of original files are at Guy Banister's."

p. 35, line 22: Dalzell has "top secret clearance": Interview with William Dalzell with Robert Buras and L. J. Delsa. December 9, 1977. HSCA 180-10103-10258. Numbered files. 004559. Tabbed CIA 94-1. Box 94. NARA.

p. 35, line 23: FBI through Warren de Brueys and CIA through Hunter Leake shared information about Dalzell: FBI teletype. To: Director. From: New Orleans. May 7, 1967. 124-10237-10413. 89-69-2088. NARA. See also: FBI. To: Director, FBI. From:

Deputy Director for Plans. Subject: Friends of Democratic Cuba. 30 March 1961. 2 pages. C.S. & I. 3/764414/.CIA immediately informed the FBI about the Friends of Democratic Cuba incorporators Grady Durham, Guy Banister, Martin L. McAuliffe, Gerard O. Tujagues and Alfred Chittenden.

p. 35, line 30: Martin served with military intelligence: Select Committee on Assassinations. Interview with Jack S. Martin by L. J. Delsa and Robert Buras. December 5, 1977. 005212. NARA.

p. 35, line 32: Jack Martin's hidden history as a CIA operative: CIA 104-10515-10045. 80T01357A. From: Stevens, M. D. To: D/C Security Research. Memo: Joseph James Martin #43847. April 6, 1967. 8 pages. NARA. See also: CIA 104-10515-10047. Title: Processed Package on Joseph James Martin. 62 pages. NARA. This material was withheld by CIA until August 29, 2002. See also: one of Jack Martin's CIA files is under "Suggs." Routing Slip: CIA Title: Routing and Record Sheet: Insufficient Bio Data. Subjects: Johnson, Persac. To: CI/R & A. From: RID/201 104-10170-10225. NARA. To anyone who asked the Agency about Martin, the reply was to be "noncommittal": Headquarters. Attn: Office of General Counsel. Title: Lawrence J. Laborde and Jack Martin. Phone Calls. 104-10189-10371. 89T01357A. NARA.

p. 36, line 15: he had asked Stanley to consecrate him as a bishop to go to Cuba: FBI. February 28, 1967. Louisville. SA George W. Hutchison. Sergeant Herman Mitchell. Detective Larry Byrd, Louisville. LS 105-620.

p. 36, line 30: "Jack" Martin took off alone for several months every year: CIA. Thru: Deputy Chief, SRS. Chief, FIOB/SRS. M. D. Stevens. The Oswald Case. Jack S. Martin aka John J. Martin (?). 5 April 1967. NARA.

p. 36, line 34: Jack Martin's foreknowledge of the kidnapping of Carlos Marcello: Joseph Newbrough interviewed by William Davy. April 3, 1995. Courtesy of Mr. Davy.

p. 37, line 1: a crowd of spectators: "Two Police Officers Are Among 10 Arrested," *Times-Picayune,* July 1, 1971, Section 1, p. 1.

p. 37, line 9: Jack Martin discredited by the FBI on purpose: Hoke May interview with Don Lee Keith, c. 1979.

Papers of Don Lee Keith. Courtesy of Teresa Neaves.

p. 37, line 12: Martin told Pershing: Interview with Pershing Gervais, December 13, 1966. The next day Martin met with Jim Garrison.

p. 37, line 17: "the government" was paying for the gas: Statement of Herbert R. Wagner Jr. December 6, 1967. NODA.

p. 37, line 37: eight to ten years: United States Secret Service, Treasury Department. December 13, 1963. CO-2-34, 030. Investigation made by Special Agent Anthony E. Gerrots and Special Agent in Charge, John W. Rice. NARA.

p. 37, line 39: "in the last fifteen years": NO 44-2064. RLK/ush. December 10, 1963. Warren Commission (WC) document #205.

p. 38, line 1: scenes of the Wilsons with Jim Lewallen and David Ferrie: Interviews with John Wilson, October 27, November 3, November 12, 2000.

p. 38, line 40: Gill instructs Ferrie to rent an airplane: Tape of L. J. Delsa and Robert Buras interview with Thomas Edward Beckham, October 7, 1977.

p. 39, line 12: Wagner was a fellow CIA asset: Interview with Wagner's daughter, Sheila Breaux, March 6, 2002.

p. 39, line 23: Allen Campbell confirms that Ferrie flew to Dallas: Interview with Allen Campbell, June 10, 2002.

p. 39, line 30: Air Worthiness Certificate: Statement of Herbert R. Wagner Jr., President of Herb Wagner Finance Service, 1905 Airline Highway, Kenner, Louisiana. December 6, 1967. NODA. NARA.

p. 39, line 35: Ferrie admits to the FBI that the plane was not airworthy: FBI Interview with David William Ferrie. 11/27/63. By SA Ernest C. Wall Jr. & Theodore R. Vaiter. Commission Document 75. The HSCA cites the FBI Interview with Melvin Coffey, November 30, 1963, stating that the plane had not been airworthy for some time; Coffey last heard of its being used in February 1963; Ferrie told the FBI the plane had not been airworthy since the spring of 1962. Jack Martin in an FAA document insists that the plane was airworthy as of July 1963, "or, at least that a Stinson aircraft was available to Ferrie at that time," a partial variation. See Memo to the File, July 18, 1963, FAA. Vol. 1. This is HSCA document 014904.

p. 40, line 10: "here in front of my eyes was the proof": Interviews with Roger Johnston, February 19 and 22, 2002.

p. 40, line 15: Gurtner: Norbert A. Gurtner flew with Ferrie and Oswald and Shaw to Dallas "approximately one week prior to the JFK assassination": To: SAC, New Orleans. From: SA J. R. MacDonald February 17, 1984. NARA. Courtesy of Malcolm Blunt.

p. 40, line 30: Ferrie "never loaned his library card to Lee Harvey Oswald": CD 75. 199/201. David William Ferrie. Report of Special Agent Warren C. de Brueys dated 12/2/63, at Dallas, Texas. Re: LEE HARVEY OSWALD. Agency: WC (Warren Commission). Record number: 179-40005-10179 08: numbered Commission Documents (Interview of David Ferrie by Special Agents Ernest C. Wall Jr., and Theodore Viater. November 27, 1963. ("Ferrie stated he has never loaned his library card to LEE HARVEY OSWALD or to any other person at any time. . . .")

p. 40, line 34: Ferrie asks Mrs. Eames "whose library card Oswald had": Memorandum. To: Jim Garrison. From: Andrew J. Sciambra. Re: David Ferrie. March 1, 1968. NODA. NARA.

p. 40, line 36: they found my library card on Oswald: Ferrie visits Mrs. Lena Garner. Testimony before the Select Committee on Assassinations. May 5, 1978. 45 pages: 180-10104-10364. 009392. NARA.

p. 40, line 38: no evidence linking a library card: CIA. Memo: Garrison TV Interview at the Hague on 22 February 1968. March 26, 1968. Transcript. 104-10435-10004. RUSS HOLMES WORK FILE. NARA.

p. 40, line 41: "bearing the name 'George Washington'": Jim Garrison, *A Heritage of Stone*. (New York: G. P. Putnam's Sons, 1970), p. 103.

p. 41, line 12: "it was a certainty": Jerry Paradis: Telephone conversation with Mike Ewing. December 15, 1978.

p. 41, line 13: Ferrie told James Lewallen: Memorandum: To: Jim Garrison. From: James L. Alcock. Re: James R. Lewallen. NODA. NARA.

p. 41, line 18: "a nose too big for

his face": Interview with John Ciravolo, June 27, 2001.

p. 41, line 24: John Wilson sees Oswald at Ferrie's apartment: Interview with John Wilson, October 31, 2000.

p. 41, line 26: Thomas Lewis Clark heard Dave talk about Oswald: Statement of Thomas Lewis Clark, March 15, 1967. Office of the District Attorney. NARA.

p. 41, line 29: September of 1959: Chronology of Lee Oswald provided by the late Mary Ferrell. Mrs. Ferrell is also the source of the Marilyn Murret quotations.

p. 42, line 1: Van Burns meets Oswald and Ferrie: Interview with Van Burns, May 23, 2001.

p. 42, line 17: Oswald bought his mother a parakeet: Jean Stafford, *A Mother in History* (New York: Bantam Books, 1966), p. 23. In this supercilious book, with which she was helped by FBI and CIA asset Hugh Aynesworth of the *Dallas Morning News*, Stafford ridicules the senior Mrs. Oswald mercilessly, to no apparent end but to undermine her character and credibility. Stafford has Mrs. Oswald saying, "On some Mother's Day I think it would be wonderful for the United States to come out and say my son was an agent," on p. 18. Note the acknowledgement to Aynesworth.

p. 42, line 23: Minox: Anonymous lead to Jim Garrison's office. NODA. NARA.

p. 42, line 40: Loyola University tuition: Handwritten notes found in Sal Scalia file. Harry Connick collection of the papers of Jim Garrison. NARA.

p. 42, line 41: "secret orders": Outside Contact Report. Interview with Mr. Robert Boylston. October 17, 1978, by L. J. Delsa and Robert Buras. HSCA. NARA.

p. 43, line 10: "taking care of something": ibid., Delsa and Buras interview with Mr. Robert Boylston.

p. 43, line 13: "David Lee Oswald": Historian Larry Haapanen discovered this form in the Warren Commission findings. See Warren Commission XVI. Commission Exhibit 99, p. 435. See also Patricia Johnson McMillan, *Marina and Lee*. (New York: Harper and Row, 1977).

p. 43, line 29: "the covert operations division of the Office of Naval Intelligence": "Back Up Material for *On the Trail.*" June 27, 1989. AARC.

p. 43, line 32: "your son was working for the C.I.A.": Jim Garrison to Marguerite Oswald, June 12, 1968. NOPL.

p. 43, line 35: David Lewis: Sworn statement of David F. Lewis Jr. December 15, 1966. NODA. NARA.

p. 43, line 38: he did not hand out any leaflets: Interview with Thomas Edward Beckham, March 31, 2002.

p. 43, line 39: Beckham and Oswald were only casually connected: Interview with Thomas Edward Beckham, March 31, 2002.

p. 44, line 1: Jack Martin immediately tells Regis Kennedy that he has been interviewed by Jim Garrison: FBI Memorandum. To: SAC. From: Regis L. Kennedy. December 24, 1966. 89-69-1484. NARA.

p. 44, line 7: Beckham "was associated with Oswald": FBI Memorandum. To: Director. From: SAC, New Orleans. January 17, 1967. 62-109060-4407. NARA. See also: FBI. To: Director. From: New Orleans. February 20, 1967. 124-10256-10167. 89-69-1425. NARA.

p. 44, line 25: "at least a week in advance": Interview with Alvin Beaubouef. December 28, 1966, with Louis Ivon and John Volz. Statement of Alvin R. Beaubouef, December 28, 1966. NODA. NARA.

p. 44, line 42: "come out publicly against anti-Castro raids": Memorandum. To: Jim Garrison. From: John P. Volz. December 14, 1966. NODA. NARA.

p. 45, line 10: "acquainted with" Oswald: Interview of David Ferrie by John Volz at the District Attorney's Office, Thursday, December 15, 1966. NODA. NARA.

p. 45, line 12: archenemy Jack Martin: David Ferrie hired Jack Martin: to contact the witnesses in the Eastern Airlines case. Southern Research Report for Eastern Airlines. November 19, 1962, **p. 33.**

p. 45, line 20: Chuck Rolland contradicts Ferrie's statement that they had discussed the operation of an ice-skating rink: FBI. To: SAC, New Orleans. From: Stephen M. Callender. AFO. February 24, 1967. NARA.

p. 45, line 25: Ferrie lied to Frank Klein about the guns: Jim Garrison, *Coup D'Etat,* chap 1, pp. 5-6.

p. 45, line 26: Ferrie admitted to Brownlee he lied about the guns: Interview with Morris Brownlee, June 2, 2000.

p. 45, line 28: Ferrie told Beaubouef to lie: Interview with Alvin Beaubouef, January 4, 2001.

p. 45, line 33: Brownlee had broken with Ferrie: Interview with Morris Brownlee.

CHAPTER 4

p. 46, line 5: Cesario Diosdado works for both CIA and Customs, between 1957 and 1968: Memorandum. To: Robert K. Tanenbaum. From: Kenneth D. Klein. May 23, 1977. Re: Interview with Cesario Diosdado. 180-10105-10297. 014534. NARA. Diosdado had an "operational" relationship with JMWAVE, the CIA station in Miami: Lawrence R. Houston. Memorandum For: Deputy Director for Plans; Director, Domestic Contact Service; Director of Security. 2 February 1967. OGC 67-0181. Subject: Masferrer Prosecution, Miami, Florida. NARA.

p. 46, line 8: Oswald's customs' connections emerge at Levee Board headquarters: FBI facsimile. ARRB release of informant reports of #1309-C, Joseph A. Oster. 62-109060-4607. JFK Task Force. Courtesy of Joseph A. Oster.

p. 46, line 13: Orestes Peña testimony released in 2000: HSCA 180-10075-10167. Agency file: 010136. Sworn testimony of Orestes Peña. June 23, 1978. 36 pages. NARA. The cancellation of the deposition: HSCA 180-10093-10004. Agency file; 008948. One page. These documents were withheld with 256 restrictions. Regarding FBI informants meeting at the Habana Bar and the Customs House, see Memorandum: To: Paul Wallach. cc: Rick Inderfurth and Elliot Maxwell. From: Dwyer/Greissing. Re: Senator Schweiker's Review of Selected Warren Commission Archives. September 29, 1975. NARA.

p. 46, line 20: Orestes Peña's files destroyed by the FBI: the Bureau destroyed the document irrespective of whether "identity of source will be revealed if document made public."

Federal Bureau of Investigation. Communications Section. January 15, 1976. Teletype. Marked Urgent. To Director, From Legat Rome (105-5212). FBI 62-109060-641. NARA. Courtesy of Malcolm Blunt.

p. 47, line 9: Peña talked to Jim Garrison at length: New Orleans conference. September 21, 1968. Round Table Discussion, p. 32. This was a conference convened by Jim Garrison and included both independent researchers and Garrison investigators.

p. 47, line 41: Smith was "involved in CIA operations": FBI To: Director, FBI. Attention: Intelligence Division, W. O. Cregar. From: SAC, San Juan. United States Senate Select Committee (SSC) On Intelligence Activities. Re: Interview of SAC Warren C. de Brueys by SSC Staff members and Senator Richard S. Schweiker. Observations and Comments of SAC de Brueys. January 20, 1976. FBI. 124-10273-10172. HQ. 62-116395-1300X. 20 pages. NARA.

p. 47, line 18: Roache admits he knew de Brueys: Ibid. To: Files. From: Paul Wallach. December 3, 1975. Telephone Conversation with Wendall C. Roache.

p. 47, line 19: Church Committee summary: Theophais E. Pappelis: Attached to SSCIA 147-10011-10101. Affidavit of Theophanis Pappelis. Two pages. SSCIA Box 337, Folder 5 (VI-C-3-W) (Pappelis). NARA.

p. 47, line 23: Wendall C. Roache is investigating David Ferrie in 1961. His name on this FBI document appears as "Windle G. Rosch." Urgent. February 20, 1967. Teletype. To: Director and SAC-S Dallas and Miami. From: New Orleans. 105-8342-519.

p. 47, line 21: De Brueys had "a working relationship with the New Orleans INS office": SSCIA. Record number; 157-10011-10101. Affidavit of Theophanis Pappelis. 12/12/75. Two pages. SSCIA Box 337, Folder 5 (VI-C-3-W) (Pappelis). NARA. This is a 3/30/05 release.

p. 47, line 28: "Garrison had something": Memorandum To Files. From: Paul Wallach. Date: December 3, 1975. Re: Telephone Conversation With Wendall Roache. NARA.

p. 47, line 34: "I've been waiting twelve years": Memorandum. To: Files. From: Paul Wallach. Date: December

2, 1975. Re: Telephone conversation with Wendall C. Roache. SSCIA. 157-10005-10009. 2 pages. NARA.

p. 48, line 1: Oswald claims to be Cuban: To: Files. From: Paul Wallach. Date: December 9, 1975. Re: Ronald L. Smith. NARA.

p. 48, line 3: some time before April 10th: SSCIA. 157-10014-10138. Miscellaneous Records of the Church Committee: 07-M-43A. Title: Committee Report: The Intelligence Agencies and the Assassination of President Kennedy. 00/00/75. Classified "Top Secret," this report has been released only in part; it runs to 170 pages. The Defense Intelligence Agency in 2000 indicated that it had no objection to declassification. There was no New Orleans Police Department record of Oswald's arrest, although there should have been unless he was in on a "drunk charge". Smith testified that he would not have interviewed Oswald if he merely was drunk, however.

p. 48, line 6: New Orleans INS surveilled Cuban groups: To: Files. From: Paul Wallach. Date: December 3, 1975. Re: Telephone conversation with Wendall Roache. NARA.

p. 48, line 16: Robert K. Tanenbaum sees footage of a training camp in which Oswald, Ferrie and Phillips appear together: Interview with Robert K. Tanenbaum, August 14, 2000. See also: Testimony of Robert K. Tanenbaum, September 17, 1996. ARRB. NARA. Others who saw this footage were HSCA staffer Jackie Hess, and one Colonel William Bishop, who had served as a military intelligence aide on the staff of General Douglas Macarthur during the Korean war. Bishop said he had seen Oswald in a film of a training camp that summer. See also Tanenbaum's novel, *Corruption of Blood* (New York: Signet Books, 1996), which he says offers an all-but-documentary description of that footage.

p. 48, line 28: "maintained extensive relations": Arcacha and Customs: CIA 100-200-17. May 2, 1967. Secret. JMWAVE 6938. Priority: Director. This JMWAVE document misspells de Brueys as "De Bruce." NARA.

p. 48, line 33: "pertinent intelligence information": Lawrence R. Houston to Honorable J. Walter Yeagley. 16 December 1966. OGC 66-2615. NARA.

p. 48, line 37: customs house broker: Valdes so listed his occupation in his application to the rental agents Latter and Blum for his apartment at the Patios. The date was August 13, 1962. Courtesy of Don Lee Keith.

p. 48, line 42: "BC": Interview with Chuck Schulze, June 21, 2001. Schulze admired Valdes' orchids.

p. 49, line 8: Gretchen Bomboy: Interview with Gretchen Bomboy, December 29, 2002.

p. 49, line 14: for portraits of Mary Sherman, see the obituary in *The Journal of Bone and Joint Surgery,* Vol. 46-A, No. 8, December 1964 and Michael Bonfiglio, "In Memoriam: Mary Stults Sherman, M.D., *Journal of Surgical Oncology* 9:1-14 (1977).

p. 49, line 19: Alton Ochsner a longtime CIA asset in New Orleans: See, for example, CIA. 31 May 1968. Subject: Ochsner, Edward William Alton, aka Ochsner, Alton. 1998 CIA release. Other documents from CIA (HSCA 000072, for example) list Ochsner as a financial contributor to INCA.

p. 49, line 25: "like a little Jewish accountant": Interview with Victoria Hawes, January 15, 2000; December 8, 2001.

p. 50, line 27: Juan Valdes throws flowers over onto Mary Sherman's patio area: Interview with Don Lee Keith, December 13, 2002.

p. 50, line 28: "pest": Don Lee Keith interview with Larry Jennings. Notebook of Don Lee Keith.

p. 50, line 30: Mary Sherman's maid remembers Juan as a dinner guest: Don Lee Keith interview with Detective Robert Townsend, NOPD. June 15th and June 25, 1979. Papers of Don Lee Keith.

p. 50, line 35: that Valdes called the police seemed odd: Don Lee Keith Interviews with Detective Robert Townsend, June 15 and 25, 1979. Courtesy of Mr. Keith.

p. 50, line 35: for the best narrative of the bizarre murder of Mary Sherman, see "*A Matter of Motives: A Retrospective Autopsy of a Mystery Murder and the Investigation Thereinto*" by Don Lee Keith. (Unpublished). Courtesy of Mr. Keith.

p. 50, line 37: For the burns on Mary Sherman: See Autopsy Protocol. Orleans Parish Coroner's Office. No.

S64-7-288. Date & Time of Death: 7-21-64 at 5:25 A. M. Signed by Lloyd F. LoCascio, M.D., Assistant Coroner.

p. 50, line 38: a stub: Conversation with Teresa Neaves, August 1, 2004.

p. 51, line 4: a sex-related murder: According to Ralph Slovenko, the perpetrator was most likely a male: Slovenko told Keith: "I cannot recall ever having heard of a woman mutilating the genitalia of another woman": *A Matter of Motives* manuscript.

p. 51, line 7: Helen Wattley heard him come in: Report of Offenses Against Persons. Item No. G-12994-64. District No. Sixth. Date of Report: 7-23-64. Date Reported: 7-21-64. New Orleans, La. Department of Police. Courtesy of Don Lee Keith. The Hawes couple do not appear on the police report as residents, nor does Tulane department of psychiatry secretary, Irene Dempsey, who also lived there. And of course nowhere does the word "Ochsner" appear. A lesbian angle was pursued, but Hayward later changed his mind: "But, you know, I was wrong on something else, about us having the proof on the victim being a lesbian. Funny, I've spent all these years positive that we had come up with cold, hard facts on that matter. Why, in my head there wasn't any doubt at all. That was one of the aspects of this case that has stayed with me in my mind the strongest. But I checked and checked, and apparently we never did turn up anything that could substantiate that she was."

p. 51, line 20: Valdes fails to show up for his polygraph: Don Lee Keith interview with Detective Frank Hayward, June 1979.

p. 51, line 35: for speculation about the Public Health Service hospital and an accident which may have befallen Mary Sherman there, see Edward Haslam, *Mary, Ferrie & The Monkey Virus: The Story of an Underground Medical Laboratory* (Albuquerque, New Mexico: ordsworth Communications, 1995, 1997), p. 42, and especially p. 109.

p. 51, line 41: she worked at laboratories until midnight: Don Lee Keith interview with Allan Davis, public relations man for the Ochsner foundation and clinic. June 3, 1979. Courtesy of Don Lee Keith.

p. 52, line 12: a blank vaccination card: See International Certificate of Vaccination or Revaccination Against Smallpox. June 8, 1963. Cadigan exhibit No. 23. Warren Commission Volume XIX, p. 296. The FBI interview with Dr. Charles A. Stern regarding this vaccination card yielded no insight. Commission Exhibit No. 2012. November 25, 1963. Warren Commission Volume XXIV, p. 429.

p. 52, line 18: David Chandler confirms she was doing cancer research: Notebook of Don Lee Keith.

p. 52, line 22: valuable drugs: Don Lee Keith interview with Chris Blake. 1979. Courtesy of Mr. Keith.

p. 52, line 29: Dr. Sherman knew Dr. Martin Palmer: Gurvich Conference. August 29, 1967. Tape #2, p. 9. Papers of Edward F. Wegmann. NARA.

p. 52, line 34: "I'll never forget him": Sylvia Gilliam interview with Mr. Quartler, June 25, 1979. Papers of Don Lee Keith.

p. 53, line 7: "Latin playwright": "Valdes Called in Plot Probe": *Times-Picayune*, May 25, 1967.

p. 53, line 10: William Martin interviews Juan Valdes at Tulane and Broad: Memorandum. July 28, 1967. To: Jim Garrison. From: William R. Martin. NODA. NARA.

p. 53, lie 27: the FBI does a name check on Juan Valdes: FBI. 124-10039-10143. Agency file number: 62-109060-5306. From: Director, FBI. To: Subjects: Valdez, Juan M. Plotkin-Alvarez, Sapir, Name Checks. Undated. Two pages. NARA.

p. 53, line 37: Butler mentions that he knew Valdes: Don Lee Keith interview with Allan Davis.

p. 53, line 38: Mary Sherman contributed to INCA: See "A Matter of Motives." Keith quotes "an older physician" who remarks, "some of us didn't mind our names being connected with INCA . . . including Dr. Mary Sherman."

p. 53, line 40: Mary Sherman donated money to a training camp: Interview with Jim Olivier, October 6, 2000. Based on an interview between Garrison and Olivier.

p. 53, line 41: Mary Sherman took care of the trainees: Marc St. Gill interview with Ricardo Davis. Diary of Richard N. Billings. AARC.

p. 53, line 5: Ferrie worked on medical briefs: Suzanne Ormond interview with Ferrie family friend Jack Nelson. c. 1979. Papers of Don Lee Keith.

p. 54, line 10: Ferrie's mice: Memorandum. 15 February 1967. To: Jim Garrison. From: William Gurvich. Subj: David William Ferrie—1957 Incident. NODA. NARA.

p. 54, line 22: Mary Sherman and David Ferrie have a close personal connection: Hoke May interview with Don Lee Keith, c. 1979.

p. 54, line 25: rumors that Ferrie had killed Sherman: Notes of Don Lee Keith, "Agency-inspired."

p. 54, line 26: Garrison wonders if Sherman's death is connected to her association with David Ferrie: *Playboy* interview: Jim Garrison, *Playboy,* vol. 14, no. 10 (October 1967), p. 176.

p. 55, line 15: "the Cuban threat runs so clearly": Jim Garrison to Richard N. Billings. December 26, 1966. Available both at AARC and NARA.

p. 55, line 17: "in the picture": Interview with Cubans by Mr. Jim Garrison, Mr. Fowler, et al.,December 26, 1966. Harry Connick collection of the papers of Jim Garrison at NARA.

p. 55, line 22: CIA claimed to have "conceived, created and funded" DRE. In fact, CIA only funded the DRE; if to the tune of about $50,000 a month. CIA money poured freely into their hands, delivered in brown paper bags at $10,000 dollars a shot: See CIA. To: Director. Memo: Garrison's Charges Against CIA. September 15, 1967. 104-10435-10025. Russ Holmes Work File. NARA.

p. 55, line 25: *Washington Post* reporter Jefferson Morley has written on Joannides: See *Miami New Times.* "Revelation 19.63." Available at http://www.miaminewtimes. com/issues/2001-04-12/feature.html.

p. 55, line 33: Lee H. Oswald to V. T. Lee: Oswald's letter to Vincent T. Lee is in Warren Commission Report, pp. 407-8. Warren Commission Hearings Vol. X, 90-1; Vincent T. Lee Exhibit, No. 5, No. 9. Warren Commission Hearings, Vol. XX, 524, 533.

p. 56, line 4: Luis Fernandez-Rocha quickly discerned: Interview with Dr. Fernandez-Rocha, January 7, 2004.

p. 56, line 16: fellow FBI informant: Arnesto Rodriguez is an FBI informant: FBI. To: Director. From: SAC. NO. March 3, 1967. 124-10253-10075. 89-69-1568. NARA. Oswald visits Arnesto Rodriguez: Rodriguez conversation with Earl Golz of the *Dallas Morning News,* March 7, 1967. Transcript of tape. AARC. Rodriguez denies he made a tape: Warren Commission exhibit (CE) 2121.

p. 56, line 17: Arnesto Senior's CIA operating approval was issued in 1960. See Audio Surveillance Project. NARA. Emilio worked alongside Desmond Fitzgerald at JMWAVE.

p. 56, line 18; AMJUTE: Memo for Chief Security Support Division. April 7, 1960. Subject; Rodriguez (y Gonzalez), Arnesto Napoleon #214833. OA [Operational Approval] B/3. "For use in Audio Surveillance Work in Cuba by WH Divison Under Project JMARC." Signed Fred Hall for Director of Security. NARA.

p. 56, line 21: "Emilio": Intelligence Medal of Merit. Medal of Merit: See personnel file of Emilio Rodriguez. Document ID number: 1993.07.21. 16:40:55:900280. Recseries; JFK. Agfileno: 80T01357A. JFK Box # JFK45. Vol/Folder: F17. Title: Withheld. Document date: 7/10/1978. Number of pages: 60. "When diplomatic relations between the U.S. and Cuba were broken subject was on vacation in the United States," the CIA document describing his award reads. "He immediately left for Cuba to assume his duties, knowing that the risk was even greater now, but he was aware that his services at this point were very important. He arrived in Cuba the following day. He was harassed numerous times and lived under continuous strain subject to arrest by the Cuban G2. On four different occasions he was actually taken into custody by the Cuban authorities and questioned at length. Despite this danger and risk he remained until June 1961 and did an outstanding job. The request for award is based particularly on his successful activity during this period on our behalf and under extreme hazardous conditions."

p. 56, line 37: Bringuier as a CIA and FBI informant: a frequent FBI informant: See NO 100-166-1. December 17, 1963. Report of Special Agent John T. Reynolds. Sending a memo to

Jim Garrison, he simultaneously furnished it to the Bureau. This memorandum is attached to FBI Airtel February 21, 1967. To: Director, FBI. From: SAC, New Orleans. 124-10256-10180. 89-69-1437A, 1438, 1439. NARA. Bringuier also reported to CIA: See: "Soviets Are Spying on Alaskan Pipeline," The *Miami Herald.* May 17, 1976, p. 7-A. As late as October of 1968, Bringuier was reporting to the Bureau: FBI. To: Director, FBI. From: SAC, New Orleans. October 11, 1968. 124-10246-10434. 89-69-4171, 4172. NARA.

p. 56, line 37: de Brueys remembers Bringuier: Warren de Brueys testimony before HSCA in Executive Session.

p. 57, line 1: what leftist: Interviews with Bob Heller, June 28, 2002; Hugh Murray, June 27, 2002.

p. 57, line 14: the FBI already had a copy of the pamphlet: FBI. To: Director. From: SAC, New Orleans. 124-10248-10191. 89-69-138. NARA.

p. 57, line 16: the FBI Cuban informants do not report on Oswald's "pro-Castro" activity: See: FBI From: SAC, NO. To: Director, FBI. November 15, 1963. Record Number: 124-10220-10324. HQ. Agency file number: CR 105-107224-159. two pages. NARA. Yet the Bureau and Special Agent Warren de Brueys in particular were ever on the watch for pro-Castro groups: FBI. To: Director, FBI. From: SAC, New Orleans. Subject: Nationality Group Coverage—Cuba. January 29, 1963. 105-99459; 210-119. See also: To: Director, FBI. From: SAC, New Orleans. July 27, 1962. Record number: 124-10220-10316. HQ. Agency file number: CR 105-97459-210-71. NARA. This latter document lists the names of the FBI's informants in New Orleans, those in charge of pro-Castro, and those involved in anti-Castro matters. The FBI had watched for the establishment of a branch of Fair Play "on a continuing basis": FBI. To: Director, FBI. From: SAC, New Orleans. Subjects: Nationality Group Coverage, Summary, ACA, FB, BKG, Assoc Polit Act. Record number: 124-10220-10328. HQ. CR 105-97459-210-119. NARA.

p. 57, line 24: "large quantities of propaganda": FBI. To: Mr. D. J. Brennan. From: Mr. S. J. Papich. 9/13/63.

Subject: Fair Play for Cuba Committee. IS—Cuba. 97-4196-861. NARA.

p. 57, line 26: Joseph Burkholder Smith: Memorandum. May 8, 1978. To: G. Robert Blakey. From: Gaeton Fonzi. Re: Interview with JOSEPH BURKHOLDER SMITH. Memo courtesy of Gaeton Fonzi.

p. 57, line 26: CIA admits it infiltrated Fair Play for Cuba: CIA. Record Number 104-10310-10152. Record series; JFK-MISC. Agency file: CIA-DDP Files. NARA.

p. 57, line 31: "Dave Phillips ran that for us": Deposition of E. Howard Hunt. November 3, 1978. HSCA #180-10131-10342. Agency file: 014872. 87 pages. NARA.

p. 57, line 33: Veciana knew Phillips as "Maurice Bishop": Miami HSCA investigator Gaeton Fonzi confirmed this identification through interviews with Phillips' CIA associates, among them Ross Crozier, a CIA DRE handler, prior to Joannides. "Bishop" was indubitably David Atlee Phillips: To: Bob Blakey. From: Gaeton Fonzi & Al Gonzales. Re: Interview with Ross Crozier. Re: DRE. Courtesy of Gaeton Fonzi.

p. 58, line 6: CIA had Oswald under surveillance: Interview with Isidro Borja, January 5, 2004.

p. 58, line 13: "a sort of PR operation": Interview of William George Gaudet, May 13, 1975, in Waveland, Mississippi, by Bernard Fensterwald and Allan Stone. AARC. Gaudet was open about being a CIA asset: See, for example, John William Miller Interview with William George Gaudet. CD 558. Here Gaudet confides in the Bureau. His FBI affiliation appears only in pencilled notes on documents collected by the ARRB. Gaudet was also a PCI, Potential Security Informant, for the FBI. So the notation appears on Draft 1/03/96. January—1996. ARRB Note sheet. Re: Assassination Records Designations. To: John A. Hartingh, Inspector-In-Charge. JFK Task Force, Federal Bureau of Investigation. From: David G. Marwell, Executive Director. These are source files for New Orleans FBI field office informants. See p. 2: 134-649A (-27). 3/12/68 (Gaudet-PCI), the latter in right margin. Under the list of serials for NO 1213-S, who was Arnesto Rodriguez. Document courtesy of Malcolm Blunt.

Gaudet was both a CIA and an FBI agent: Peña confirms that Gaudet is a "CIA-FBI agent": Interview of Orestes Peña with Martin J. Daly and William Brown. January 20, 1978. HSCA 014118. NARA.

p. 58, line 17: Matt O. Wilson: Transcript of interview with Matt O. Wilson. 30 January 1968. The interviewer is Stanley R. Primmer. Courtesy of Lyon Garrison. DRE filed a report to its CIA sponsors on the incident: Memorandum. February 21, 1978. To: Blakey. From: Fonzi and Gonzales. Re: Isidro Borja—military leader DRE. Courtesy of Gaeton Fonzi.

p. 58, line 24: "same job as I was": Undated telephone call from Harry Dean to the district attorney of Orleans Parish. NODA. See also letter to Jim Garrison from Harry Dean, February 20, 1967. NODA. NARA.

p. 58, line 28: FBI taking photographs: Summary. HSCA. Orestes Peña. January 20, 1978. Interview by Martin J. Daly and William Brown. 180-10097-10491. 014118. 10 pages. NARA.

p. 58, line 38: "being used by these people": Department of Police. Interoffice Correspondence. To: Major Presley J. Trosclair Jr. From: Sgt. Horace J. Austin & Patn. Warren Roberts. Subject: Interview of four male subjects at the First District Police Station, on Friday, August 9, 1963, after their arrest from Canal Street. CE 1413.

p. 58, line 41: Bringuier asks Kent Courtney for legal advice: Interview with Carlos Bringuier, January 5, 2000.

p. 59, line 4: Oswald did: Testimony of Professor Revilo Pendleton Oliver. Warren Commission Hearings. Volume XV, p. 720.

p. 59, line 6: Oswald in Baton Rouge with Kent Courtney:
See Michael L. Kurtz, *Crime of the Century: The Kennedy Assassination from a Historian's Perspective* (Knoxville: The University of Tennessee Press, 1982), p. 203. Details are scant in this account.

p. 59, line 7: "Leon": Courtney introduces Oswald as "Leon": Michael Kurtz, "Lee Harvey Oswald In New Orleans." *Louisiana History* (Winter 1980), p. 17.

p. 59, line 13: Kent Courtney to Hon. J. Edgar Hoover. Subject: The

assassination of President Kennedy—
A Telephone Call from Mrs. Marguerite
Oswald to Kent H. Courtney. October
28, 1964. Northwestern State University at Natchitoches. Watson Library.
Cammie G. Henry Research Center.
Courtney collection. 3-I-1.

p. 59, line 8: "the entire matter of
the assassination is very serious":
FBI. To: Director. From: SAC, Miami.
March 10, 1967. 124-10167-10201.
89-69-1659. NARA.

p. 59, line 20: "no quarrel with
Jim Garrison": Interview with Juan
Manuel Salvat, November 16, 1999.

p. 59, line 31: "you have Lee Oswald": Interview with Irvin L. Magri
Jr., July 15, 2002. Magri was present
at the Larry Howard taping of Lt.
Francis Martello, who then made this
revelation. This Howard was working
at the turn of the 1990s as a researcher for filmmaker Oliver Stone.
Interviews with Bill Rester, July 15
and July 16, 2002. Both Magri and
Rester were present at the interview
where Martello relayed the story of
the note to Howard. According to Magri, Martello said he would release the
original of the note in exchange for a
brand-new Lexus automobile.

p. 59, line 33: Oswald asks to see
Warren de Brueys: Interviews with
William Walter and L. J. Delsa, January 12, 2000.

p. 59, line 36: William Walter took
the call: Interview with William Walter, January 5, 2000. See also William
Walter's testimony before the Select
Committee on Assassinations, March
23, 1978. 5542345. 70 pages. Box
249. Agency file: 14029. NARA. See
also: Affidavit from Mark Lane before
the Orleans Parish District Attorney,
January 30, 1968. NODA. Outside
Contact Report, November 10, 1977.
Jim Garrison interviewed by Robert
Buras and Lawrence Delsa. 005193.
HSCA.

p. 60, line 5: "for some security
purpose": Interview with William Walter, August 13, 2001.

p. 60, line 10: to attend a barbecue: Interview with Robert Buras, December 13, 2002. De Brueys
eventually conceded that the length of
Quigley's conversation with Oswald
demonstrated that the FBI had "an official interest" in Oswald and that he
was a "security subject" but denied

that he himself knew Oswald: HSCA
testimony of Warren C. de Brueys.
189-101117-10136. 014716. Box 280.
March 3, 1978. 94 pages. Executive
Session. NARA. In exchange for his
loyalty, the FBI reprimanded de
Brueys for revealing Orestes Peña's
name as an FBI informant to HSCA.
Harold N. Bassett, Assistant Director,
Records Management Division to Mr.
Warren C. de Brueys. June 23, 1978.
FBI 124-10273-10188. 62-117290-
1024X1. NARA. Ungrateful to the FBI,
CIA counter intelligence chief James
Angleton disingenuously testified to
the Church Committee of his distress
that the Bureau had failed to turn its
Oswald files over to the local police before the assassination: Senate Select
Committee to Study Governmental
Operations with Respect to Intelligence Activities. June 19, 1975. Testimony of James Angleton. SSCIA.
157-10014-10005. 01-H-05. NARA.

Warren de Brueys denies that he
knew Lee Harvey Oswald: Interview
with Warren de Brueys, January 15,
2000. See also: To: Director, FBI (Attention: Intelligence Division, W. O.
Cregar). From: SAC, San Juan. United
States Senate Select Committee on Intelligence Activities. Re: Interview of
SAC Warren C. de Brueys by SSC Staff
Members and Senator Richard S.
Schweiker. Observations and Comments of SAC de Brueys. FBI. 124-
10273-10172. HQ. 62-116395-1300X.
NARA. See also as above HSCA testimony of Warren C. de Brueys. See
also: CBS REPORTS: "The American
Assassins," Part II.

p. 60, line 19: Lieutenant Francis L.
Martello is interviewed in Volume X of
the Warren Commission hearings.
Martello insists that he gave the note
which he, in fact, kept, to Mr. Vial of
the Secret Service. Commission Exhibit No. 827, however, is not the note
Oswald gave Martello, but a facsimile,
and somewhat inaccurate. Copy of the
original note, courtesy of Lieutenant
Martello's son.

p. 60, line 21: "no mentality at
all": Jim Garrison at the New Orleans
conference. September 1968.

p. 60, line 32: "Harvey Lee Oswald," a transposition used by Army
and Naval intelligence: see Peter Dale
Scott, *Deep Politics II: The New Revelations in U. S. Government Files, 1994-*

1995 (Dallas: Lancer Publications, 1996), p. 88.

p. 61, line 1: Carlos Bringuier learns of Jim Garrison's investigation from David Ferrie: Interview with Carlos Bringuier by Robert A. Wilson at the office of Southern Research Company. March 31, 1967. Papers of Edward F. Wegmann. "This is a free country": Carlos Bringuier to Mr. E. Willis, Chairman, House Committee on Un-American Activities. April 2, 1967. FBI 89-69-2001. NARA.

p. 61, line 7: Ferrie carries a loaded rifle: From: Billings to Haskell. February 14, 1967. "David William Ferrie." Box 4, folder 48. Papers of Richard N. Billings. Georgetown.

p. 61, line 10: the FBI refuses to give Garrison its 1963 reports on Ferrie: See FBI. From: Director. To: SAC, New Orleans. 62-109060-4344. December 23, 1966. NARA. The government file on Ferrie revealed he had violated the Neutrality Act flying missions into Cuba.

p. 61, line 12: "mention or overhear": FBI. From: Director, FBI. To: SAC, BU. 124-10264-10286. HQ. 62-116395-1102. November 25, 1975. 2 pages. NARA.

p. 61, line 16: FBI installs a wiretap: Interview with William Walter, January 3, 2000.

p. 61, line 23: "outside the Bureau": Memorandum. To: Director, FBI. From: SAC, Dallas. Subject: Lee Harvey Oswald aka (Deceased) December 15, 1966. NARA.

p. 61, line 26: "bright blue eyes": Jim Brown, *Central Intelligence Assassination* (Unpublished). pp. 209-209. AARC.

p. 61, line 27: "the real Oxford": Interview with Patricia Chandler, May 22, 1998.

p. 61, line 29: Bethell had in fact been in New Orleans during the summer of 1963: Jim Brown interview with Bernard Fensterwald, November 23, 1970. AARC. The Tom Bethell Diary for February 9, 1968 (excerpts from a "Diary Kept While Working in the District Attorney's Office during the Investigation of Kennedy's Assassination"). AARC.

p. 61, line 34: government-subsidized shipping: Interview with Numa Bertel, May 19, 1998; Interview with William Alford, May 28, 1998.

p. 61, line 36: "unscrupulous rascal": FBI. To: Mr. Wick. From: M. A. Jones. February 28, 1967. 124-10047-10089. 62-109060-4586. NARA.

p. 61, line 39: "character assassins and black-mailers": To: Lang for Billings. From: Byers (in New Orleans). March 6, 1967. Papers of Richard N. Billings. Box 4, folder 49. Georgetown University, Washington, DC.

p. 62, line 1: Gurvich provides phone numbers: Jim Garrison interviewed by Jonathan Blackmer. 1977. HSCA.

p. 62, line 3: "like a Greek bearing gifts": Jim Garrison describes the arrival of William Gurvich in *Playboy*. Vol. 14, No. 10. October 1967, p. 68.

p. 62, line 4: Garrison allows Gurvich to use his own private office: Gurvich Conference. August 29, 1967. Tape 2. Papers of Edward F. Wegmann. NARA.

p. 62, line 7: "I don't trust Gurvich": Roundtable discussion, September 1968. pp. 35-36.

p. 62, line 10: "You're making a big mistake": Interview with Joe Oster, June 30, 2000. Gurvich was a plant: Interview with William Alford, May 28, 1998.

p. 62, line 16: Billings flies to New Orleans: Interview with Richard N. Billings, August 2, 2000. See also Diary of Richard N. Billings. AARC.

p. 62, line 28: Garrison writes to Billings back in New York: Jim Garrison to Richard N. Billings, December 26, 1966. AARC.

p. 62, line 33: Ferrie had flown Oswald to Cuba: Memo from David Chandler to Richard N. Billings. Undated. ARRC.

p. 62, line 35: Jim Garrison is studying Gill's telephone records: Richard N. Billings, *The Case for a Conspiracy (V): The Anatomy of the Investigation*. Papers of Richard N. Billings. Georgetown.

p. 62, line 39: telephone matches between Oswald, Ruby and Ferrie: See Garrison memo: "Time, Place and Number Correlations (Ruby, Ferrie, Oswald and Shaw)." NODA. NARA. See also: Memorandum. April 18, 1967. To: Special Investigation File. From: Jim Garrison. Re: Long Distance Calls—Ruby. NODA. NARA.

p. 63, line 23: "Oswald was there!"

Interview with Dr. Harold Lief, May 25, 1999.

p. 63, line 32: a biography of Lee Harvey Oswald: See "Notes re: Oswald in '63." Handwritten by Jim Garrison. NARA.

p. 63, line 28: "play the infiltrator": Interview of William E. Wulf. March 1, 1968. 3:00 p.m. by Gary Sanders. Transcribed March 6, 1968. NODA. NARA.

CHAPTER 5

Title: "Menagerie" is Jim Garrison's term: See "Banister Menage & Cubans," written in ink at the top of a December 18, 1967 memo, "Interview with 'BP' in Re: Friends of Democratic Cuba." NODA. NARA.

p. 65, Epigraph: "What number Camp?": Interview with Cubans by Mr. Jim Garrison, Mr. Fowler, et al., December 26, 1966. Harry Connick collection of the papers of Jim Garrison. NARA.

p. 65, line 4: "Where is Clay Bertrand?" Re: Smith Case #1. General Questions. NODA. NARA.

p. 65, line 14: "That's Clay Shaw": p. 36, line 11: David Chandler identifies Clay Shaw: Notes of Richard Popkin. AARC. See also: Memorandum: July 9, 1971. Richard Popkin, "Re: Matters Concerning the Garrison Investigation." AARC.

p. 65, line 14: "a bit of an agent provocateur": Interview with Gordon Novel, January 16, 2000.

p. 65, line 18: Shaw was actually well known to have frequented Cosimo's: among those who witnessed Shaw going in and out of Cosimo's was a Mrs. Jeanne Kelton: Memorandum. April 11, 1968. To: Louis Ivon. From: Gary Sanders. Re: Mrs. Jeanne Kelton. Subject: Lee Harvey Oswald and Clay Shaw. NODA. NARA. Dan Campbell, working as a bartender at Cosimo's, recalls how boys would come over from Shaw's house at 1313 Dauphine, a stone's throw away, and carry back a pitcher of whiskey sours.

p. 65, line 25: "drinks and a chess game": Statement of Layton Patrick Martens, W/M, December 23, 1966. NODA. NARA.

p. 66, line 2: Moo Moo was now faced: Memorandum. To: Jim Garrison. From: Andrew J. Sciambra. Re: Smith Investigation. My interview with

Clay Shaw, 12/23/66. Memorandum is dated February 9, 1967. NODA. NARA.

p. 66, line 18: Shaw jokes about being a suspect: Garrison Series III January 30, 1969. "Garrison vs. Shaw: The Big Melodrama in New Orleans" by Hugh Aynesworth. Newsweek Feature Service. Papers of Edward F. Wegmann. NARA.

p. 66, line 21: Dauenhauer reveals that Shaw lied: Memorandum. February 10, 1967. To: Jim Garrison. From: Andrew J. Sciambra. Re: Smith Investigation—Interview with Mr. J. B. Dauenhauer, Director of the Trade Mart. NODA. NARA.

p. 66, line 25: Marochini, Lewallen and Propinquities: See: Memorandum. March 6, 1967. To: Jim Garrison. From: James L. Alcock and Richard V. Burnes. Re: Dante A. Marochini. NODA. NARA. See also: "CAP and ITM correlations": Handwritten note by Jim Garrison in "Garrison (II): The Power of Public Disclosure," by Richard N. Billings. AARC. See also: Memorandum. March 6, 1967. To: Lou Ivon. From: James L. Alcock. Re: Truth verification of Dante Marochini's Statement. NODA. NARA.

p. 66, line 34: For the story of Alberto Fowler: Interview with Antonio Navarro, June 16, 2001. For a portrait of the young Alberto, see Antonio Navarro, *Tocayo* (Westport, Connecticut: Sandown Books, 1981). He had even given Castro permission to build a tank on the family estate: Interview with George Fowler, January 4, 2000. Fowler is Alberto's nephew. See also: "Cuban Blames Stevenson for Bay of Pigs Disaster," *Times-Picayune*, April 18, 1971, Section 1, p. 72; see also: Prisoners tell . . . the real story of the Bay of Pigs," *U.S. News & World Report*. January 7, 1963, p. 39; Burton Hersh, *The Old Boys: The American Elite and the Origins of the CIA* (New York: Charles Scribner's Sons, 1992), pp. 432-433.

p. 66, line 34: "legitimate Cuban": Richard N. Billings diary. Notes 444. AARC. See also: Jim Garrison to Richard N. Billings, December 28, 1966.

p. 67, line 5: "something other than it appears to be": Notes from Alberto Fowler. Written in Jim Garrison's handwriting. Undated. NARA.

p. 67, line 6: Tony Varona is the source for the CIA intending to appoint Alberto head of the CRC in New Orleans: New Orleans conference, September 21, 1968, p. 32.

p. 67, line 9: "Jim, I didn't kill him": Interview with George Fowler, January 4, 2000.

p. 67, line 11: "hardly pro-Castro": The Clay Shaw diary. March 24th, p. 2. Papers of Clay Shaw. NARA.

p. 67, line 13: Fowler calls Jim Garrison "Big Jim": Interview with Alberto Antonio Fowler, December 9, 1999.

p. 67, line 24: "one of my great discoveries": Jim Garrison interviewed by Jonathan Blackmer, Gaeton Fonzi, and L. J. Delsa, July 1977. Available on cassettes from NARA.

p. 67, line 30: Post Office boxes: See: Memorandum. To: Archives (Indicated Files). From: Jim Garrison. Re: Post Office Boxes (Undated). NODA. NARA.

p. 67, line 37: "he's not with anybody who's not with the CIA": "The Spy Who Was Left Out in the Cold: Was Jim Garrison Right After All?" by Joe Manguno. *New Orleans* magazine. June 1976, p. 28.

p. 67, line 38: Oswald's Marine records: Unit Diary. 1498. 4 Sep 59. Diary No. 240-59. NARA. 247-59, 11 Sep 59. 1512. 975. 13 May 57; Diary no. 62-57, etc.

p. 68, line 5: "cooperative contact": CIA Record Number 104-10069-10051. Agency file: 80T01357A. July 28, 1970. Title: Information on Edward Scannell Butler, III. NARA.

p. 68, line 7: leave Free Voice of Latin America. William R. Klein to Jim Garrison. May 4, 1967. Papers of Richard N. Billings. Box 2, folder 24. Georgetown University, Washington, DC.

p. 68, line 12: Marinus Van der Lubbe: Eugene A. Sheehan, "Oswald: Prelude to Assassination," *New Orleans* magazine. January 1967, p. 24.

p. 68, line 20: Joseph Rault and CIA: See CIA. To: Chief, WH. From: Chief of Station, JMWAVE. Subject: TYPIC. Contact Report—IDEN *A. Signed Andrew K. Reuteman. May 19, 1965. 104-10104-10107. 80T01357A. See also: To: Director, Domestic Contact Service. Att'n: Operational Support Staff (Musulin). From: Chief, New

Orleans Office. June 27, 1967. Subject: Case 49364—Garrison Investigation. Ref: DC/CI/R & A. Memorandum dated 19 June 1967. NO 249-67. Signed. Lloyd A. Ray. NARA.

p. 68, line 34: "it's almost semantics": Jim Garrison at the New Orleans Conference. September 21, 1968. Round Table Discussion, p. 87.

p. 68, line 39: a conduit for company money: Joseph Newbrough interview with Bernard Fensterwald, August 16, 1978. AARC. See also Joseph Newbrough interviewed by William Davy.

p. 68, line 41: money flowed: Anthony Summers interview with Delphine Roberts, Banister's mistress and secretary, in *Not in Your Lifetime: The Definitive Book on the J.F.K. Assassination* (New York: Marlowe & Company, 1998), p. 230.

p. 68, line 42: Banister sends Tommy Beckham to the camps: HSCA Notes. sub. Office New Orleans. NARA.

p. 69, line 5: Banister is close to the CIA field office: Interview with Allen Campbell, June 10, 2002.

p. 69, line 7: "foreign positive intelligence": CIA. Memorandum For: File. Subject: The Lee Harvey Oswald Case. 8 March 1967. Document number: 1338-1052. NARA.

p. 69, line 8: Banister's cohort were all CIA-connected: See Chapter Three: Newbrough was with CIA. L. J. Delsa and Robert Buras interview with Jack S. Martin; Dalzell is CIA: HSCA 180-10070-10358. Agency file: 008269. (PT 18). Memorandum: October 30, 1968. To: Jim Garrison. From: Andrew J. Sciambra. Re: Interview with Vernon Gerdes. NARA. Regarding Dalzell working under cover as a petroleum consultant: FBI, To: Director. From: New Orleans. November 3, 1967. 124-10071-10326. 89-69-3575. NARA. William Dalzell admits he worked for the Central Intelligence Agency: Select Committee on Assassinations. Interview with William Dalzell. 064559. December 9, 1977. NARA. See also: HSCA re-interview of Dalzell, January 26, 1978, by William Brown. NARA.

p. 69, line 12: jeeps to Cuba: Information Report: Office of Naval Intelligence. 2 September 1960. 110-6-210-58. From: Office In Charge: DIO, 8ND. topic: Economic Matters—Cuba. Document prepared by James S. Jack Jr. NARA.

p. 69, line 15: cleared them first with Guy Johnson: Banister clears the hiring of Bergeron with Guy Johnson: Guy Banister to Guy Johnson, January 5, 1959. AARC.

p. 69, line 16: "intelligence for sale": Dan Campbell interviewed by James DiEugenio. September 9, 1994. Courtesy of Mr. DiEugenio.

p. 69, line 17: Guy Johnson brought Sergio Arcacha Smith: Robert Buras and Lawrence Delsa, Interview with Jack S. Martin. Re: Association with Mr. Sergio Arcacha Smith. December 5, 1977. HSCA 005211. NARA.

p. 69, line 22: Phillips' role in the Houma operation is described by Gordon Novel in his deposition for his libel suit against Jim Garrison and *Playboy* magazine. Novel was among those who were involved in the Schlumberger burglary. AARC.

p. 69, line 25: David Atlee Phillips fears that Jim Garrison will discover that CIA is behind the Belle Chasse training camp: Memorandum For Chief, CI/ R & A. Subject: Garrison investigation: Belle Chasse Training Camp. Reference: CI/R & A Memorandum Dated 26 October 1967. WH/C 67-336. 104-10170-10261. Agency file: 80T01357A. NARA.

p. 69, line 30: Banister chats with Hoover: Robert Buras and L. J. Delsa, interview with Joe Oster. January 27, 1978. HSCA. NARA.

p. 69, line 31: Regis Kennedy visits Banister: Undated notes of Hoke May. AARC.

p. 69, line 32: Banister is very close to G. Wray Gill: Interview with Allen Campbell, July 4, 2002.

p. 69, line 36: Jack Martin has introduced George Lincoln Rockwell to Guy Banister: Interview with Thomas Edward Beckham, corroborated by Vernon Gerdes. Memorandum. October 30, 1968. To: Jim Garrison. From: Andrew J. Sciambra. Re: Interview with Vernon Gerdes. NODA. NARA.

p. 69, line 39: Thompson drives up to Banister's in his black Cadillac: Interview with Allen Campbell, June 10, 2002; Allen Campbell interviewed by Jim DiEugenio.

p. 70, line 1: little detective work: Interview with Lawrence Guchereau, June 2, 2000. After the assassination,

Banister had trouble paying his rent: Joe Newbrough interview with Bernard Fensterwald, August 14, 1978.

p. 70, line 8: Clay Shaw in full female drag: Delphine Roberts interview with HSCA. August 27, 1978.

p. 70, line 10: Banister meets frequently with Clay Shaw: Interview with Allen Campbell, June 10, 2002.

p. 70, line 12: the file on Oswald is kept isolated: Delphine Roberts interview with Robert Buras and L. J. Delsa, July 6, 1978. HSCA. NARA.

p. 70, line 18: "Allen, don't worry": Interview with Allen Campbell, June 10, 2002.

p. 70, line 19: Dan Campbell sees Oswald at Banister's: Dan Campbell interviewed by Jim DiEugenio; Memorandum. May 14, 1969. To: Jim Garrison. From: Andrew J. Sciambra. Re: Shaw Leads II (Dan Campbell. NODA. NARA. See also: Memorandum. May 14, 1969. To: Jim Garrison. From: Andrew Sciambra. Re: Shaw Leads II (Al Campbell). NODA. NARA. Allen Campbell's memo confirms that the Campbell brothers were at the Bethlehem Orphans Home at the same time as Oswald. Allen, never called "Al," laughs and says that Moo Moo told him far more than he revealed himself.

p. 70, line 23: Gaudet saw Banister and Oswald deep in conversation: Buras and Leap interview Gaudet: HSCA 180-10070-10274. 004826. January 18, 1978.

p. 70, line 25: Gaudet was persuaded that the Agency knew Lee Harvey Oswald: Interview with William Gaudet by Bernard Fensterwald and Allan Stone. May 13, 1975. AARC. HSCA's five page interview with Gaudet at Waveland would be restricted until 1996, when it was finally declassified by the Assassination Records and Review Board.

p. 70, line 28: Peña saw Oswald enter the building: Interview of Orestes Peña by Martin J. Daly and William Brown. January 20, 1978. 180-10097-10491. HSCA 014118.

p. 70, line 29: Delphine Roberts remembered: Delphine Roberts finally talked—to Robert Buras for the House Select Committee, and to authors Anthony Summers and Earl Golz.

p. 70, line 34: checked this man out: Delphine Roberts interviewed by Buras and Delsa, July 6, 1978.

p. 70, line 36: "he's with us": Summers, p. 229.

p. 70, line 38: Delphine suspects that Oswald has a relationship with the FBI: Anthony Summers' interview notes with Delphine Roberts, AARC.

p. 70, line 39: George Wilcox: Wilcox recognized that it was Oswald he had seen after the assassination. He recognized Ferrie after Jim Garrison's investigation became public. Later he spoke to historian Michael Kurtz. Interview with Michael Kurtz, February 5, 2001.

p. 71, line 6: Banister and Oswald appear at LSU: Interview with Michael Kurtz, February 5, 2001. See also: Testimony of Dr. Michael Kurtz, June 28, 1995, ARRB. Kurtz, *Crime of the Century: The Kennedy Assassination from a Historian's Perspective* (Knoxville: The University of Tennessee Press, 1982), pp. xxxix, 203. The perspective of this book is actually the one CIA first considered using for the cover-up: that Fidel Castro organized the murder of President Kennedy.

p. 71, line 14: Mary Banister saw Oswald's leaflets in Guy Banister's possession: Ross Banister interviewed by Bernard Fensterwald, August 11, 1978. AARC.

p. 71, line 16: "rather stupid": Bernard Fensterwald interview with Ross Banister, August 11, 1978. AARC.

p. 71, line 18: "Oswald worked for Banister": Tommy Baumler interviewed by Bernard Fensterwald and Gary Shaw. December 30, 1981. AARC.

p. 71, line 19: Vernon Gerdes has seen Oswald, Ferrie and Shaw together: Only when he went to work as an investigator for Steven Plotkin would Gerdes admit he saw Oswald, Ferrie and Banister together: Memorandum on the letterhead of Steven Plotkin. April 7, 1967. Memo begins, "On April 7, 1967, Plotkin was interviewed in Morrison's Cafeteria by Mr. Salvatore Panzeca and Robert A. Wilson. . . ." Papers of Edward F. Wegmann. The Wegmann papers. NARA.

p. 71, line 26: "one of them is mine": Memorandum. George Higginbotham. 4-12-68; 4-16-68. Signed Barbara Glancey Reid. NODA. NARA. "Close-mouthed": Garrison appended these lines to his copy of Reid's memo of her meeting with Higginbotham.

p. 71, line 32: "you must have seen Oswald up there": Jim Garrison in telephone conversation with Sam Newman. Reported by William Gurvich to Clay Shaw's lawyers. Tape #3. Gurvich Conference. August 29, 1967. Papers of Edward F. Wegmann. NARA. For the tangle of Newman's conflicting stories, see Memorandum. November 7, 1967. To: Jim Garrison. From: Tom Bethell. Re: Unidentified Men at 544 Camp Street. NODA. NARA.

p. 71, line 35: "some prior knowledge": HSCA. April 6, 1978. Brengel was originally interviewed for Jim Garrison by Cliency Navarre & Kent Simms. Re: Interview Mrs. Mary Helen Brengel. To: Louis Ivon. June 1, 1967. NODA. NARA.

p. 71, line 41: no ordinary citizen: Interview with Robert Buras, May 29, 2002.

p. 72, line 1: police report on the pistol-whipping: "Detailed Report." Item No. K-12634-63. Signed by Lieutenant Francis Martello. NARA. See also Garrison's notations on the police report dated July 12, 1969. "Who was attorney?" Garrison writes beside Guy Banister's statement that his attorney told him not to comment. NODA. NARA.

p. 72, line 5: "god damned lie": Jim Garrison, *Coup D'Etat,* chap. 3, p. 6. AARC.

p. 72, line 9: "Now all we have to do is kill Earl Warren": Joseph Newbrough interviewed by William Davy, April 3, 1995. Courtesy of Mr. Davy.

p. 72, line 12: "I wonder why Bobby wasn't included": Jack Martin and David Lewis affidavit to Jim Garrison. February 20, 1968. NODA. NARA.

p. 72, line 12: "I'm glad": Brengel became a Garrison source as she spoke to Cliency Navarre & Kent Simms, Garrison investigators: See Memorandum. June 1, 1967. To: Louis Ivon, Chief Investigator. Re: Interview Mrs. Mary Helen Brengel. NODA. See also Letter by Mary Helen Brengel, May 14, 1967. Available as HSCA document 007546. Originator: Citizen. From: Brengel, Mary H. To Daly, Martin. 5 pages. NARA.

p. 72, line 15: "Guy Banister is a key": Memorandum. October 28, 1968. To: Jim Garrison. From: Andrew J. Sciambra. NODA. NARA.

p. 72, line 20: Banister's obituary: "Banister Found Dead at Home," *Times-Picayune,* June 7, 1964. Section 1, p. 1.

p. 72, line 21: "natural causes": Police Report is signed by Sgt. C. L. Drumm and Det. David Kent. 06-06-64. Item #F3764-64. It was also signed by the platoon commander, James Kruebbe. Available as HSCA document 005966.

p. 72, line 22: "if I'm dead in a week": GUY JOHNSON. May 21, 1969. Interview with Bernard Fensterwald. AARC.

p. 72, line 26: the shots came in through the window: Interview with Allen Campbell, June 10, 2002.

p. 72, line 28: Allen Campbell removes files: Interview with Allen Campbell, July 10, 2002. Interview with Daniel Campbell, June 8, 2002.

p. 72, line 31: "Guy's been shot": Interview with Phyllis Kritikos, June 29, 2001. Lichtblau immediately called Phyllis' mother, Mrs. Trudy Weinert.

p. 72, line 34: Delphine believes "Guy Banister and David Ferrie were murdered": Report by Robert Buras. Interview with Delphine Points Roberts. August 27, 1978. 12:30 P.M. "It was made to look like a natural death," Roberts told Earl Golz. Interview with Golz. December 20, 1978. AARC. Jim Garrison reserved his judgment: "I must emphasize that . . . this is hearsay," he wrote to Jonathan Blackmer on August 16, 1977. "As a former D.A. in this Parish, I personally would have to give the deciding weight to the written version of the Coroner's office." Then he added, it was the same Coroner's office which ruled that David Ferrie died of natural causes. HSCA 013523. Kent Courtney's view: Interview with Guy Johnson by Bernard Fensterwald, May 21, 1969. AARC.

p. 72, line 42: Bolton Ford and Dumas Chevrolet: the Bolton Ford and Dumas Chevrolet sightings: Memorandum. May 9, 1967 To: Jim Garrison. From James L. Alcock. Re: Fred A. Sewell, Interview With. May 2, 1967 at 4:15 A.M. NODA. NARA. See also CD 75, p. 677, 678. November 25, 1963. Interview of Oscar W. Deslatte with Special Agents William F. McDonald and W. J. Danielson Jr. at New Orleans. See also: Memorandum. February 14, 1968. To: Louis Ivon? From:

Kent Simms. Re: Interview one FRED SEWEL [sic] Fleet & Truck Manager, Stephens Chevrolet, 840 Carondelet Street. NODA. NARA. For Oswald's attempts to purchase a car at Dumas and Milnes Chevrolet. United States Department of Justice, FBI. Report of SA Leonard F. Johnson. December 14, 1963. Commission No. 179. Bureau file No. 105-82555. See also: To: GF from JG: Re: New Orleans Activities Re: "Oswald" in 1961 and 1962. Courtesy of Gaeton Fonzi. See also: anonymous letter beginning, "In early January of 1961 I went to New Orleans. . . ." NODA. NARA.

p. 73, line 5: the vice president of Bolton Ford called the Bureau: FBI. To: SAC, New Orleans. From: Supvr. Paul R. Alker. November 25, 1963. Re: Lee Harvey Oswald. 89-69-94. NARA.

p. 73, line 18: "Betty Parrott's" description of Joseph Moore: For description of "Joseph Moore": Memorandum. December 18, 1967. To: Jim Garrison. From: Andrew J. Sciambra. RE: INTERVIEW WITH "BP". IN RE: FRIENDS OF DEMOCRATIC CUBA. NODA. NARA. "BP" is "Betty Parrot," who lived with William Dalzell, and was a Regis Kennedy informant. Betty tells the FBI that Sciambra has contacted her: FBI teletype. To: Director. From: New Orleans. Urgent. May 9, 1967. 124-10237-10438. 89-69-3018. NARA.

p. 73, line 25: No "Mr. Call" existed at the Bureau: Interview with Warren de Brueys, July 14, 2001.

p. 73, line 26: McAuliffe denies to Jim Garrison that he ever heard of the incident: Statement and Interrogation of Martin L. McAuliffe Jr. in the office of the District Attorney on Tuesday, May 9, 1967. NODA. NARA.

p. 74, line 10: Jack Martin was treated at Baptist Hospital: Police Report signed by Lieutenant Francis Martello. Item No. K-12634-63.

p. 74, line 16: "Do you have many girlfriends?" Scene at Guy Banister's office, and its aftermath, interview with Thomas Edward Beckham, March 31, 2002. Unless otherwise indicated, statements from the point of view of Thomas Edward Beckham are from interviews, March 30 and 31, 2002.

p. 75, line 4: desecrated the Jewish cemetery: Beckham interview. See also Rough Notes of Interview with Jules Kimble: "Head of Ku Klux Klan

Intelligence Bureau for the state of Louisiana." Transcript is signed "Charlie." Courtesy of Joseph A. Oster.

p. 75, line 12: Shaw sets Tommy up with a Cuban girl: Interview with Robert Buras, April 15, 2002.

p. 75, line 16: Batista is a part-owner: Memo Written by David Chandler. 4 pages. Undated. AARC.

p. 75, line 28: Rockwell will be seen at Dixie's Bar of Music: E-mail from Daniel Campbell, December 1, 2002.

p. 76, line 4: "only for short periods": Jack Martin interview with L. J. Delsa and Robert Buras.

p. 76, line 30: Howard works for the CIA: Interview with Gerald Patrick Hemming, June 2, 2002.

p. 76, line 33: Pancho Villa: HSCA description. 006058. From: Palmer, Betsy.

p. 77, line 29: Oswald's summer trip to Mexico City: Interview with Thomas Edward Beckham. Other evidence includes a reference by Dean Andrews to Oswald's "Mexican whore," included in a Harold Weisberg memorandum, and the testimony of two Australian women on a bus from Monterey to Mexico City, to whom, on September 26, 1963, Oswald recommended the Hotel Cuba as a comfortable place where he had stayed "several times before." Warren Commission. Volume XXV, Commission Exhibit No. 2194, p. 21. Interview by FBI of Miss Patricia Clare Resheligh Winston. December 18, 1963. There are also references to Oswald's having been in Mexico City in July in the files of Richard Case Nagell.

p. 78, line 1: Oswald has written to Governor Connally: Lee H. Oswald to Secretary of the Navy, John B. Connally Jr. January 30, 1961. Warren Commission Hearings, Volume XIX, p. 248.

p. 78, line 14: Thomas Edward Beckham is corroborated in his seeing Oswald at Thompson's restaurant: Memorandum. May 28, 1968. To: Jim Garrison. From: Andrew J. Sciambra. Re: Interview with Paul Taylor. NODA. NARA.

p. 78, line 33: de Brueys stands just inside the doors of the International Trade Mart: "Jesse Core and Alberto Fowler." Memorandum by David Chandler. Papers of Richard N. Billings. Box 4, folder 59. Georgetown University, Washington, DC.

p. 78, line 34: After handing out leaflets in front of the International Trade Mart, Lee Harvey Oswald enters the building and walks past the elevators to the rear of the building: Memorandum February 14, 1967. To: Jim Garrison from Andrew J. Sciambra. Re: Interview with Mrs. Carlos Márquez. NODA. NARA.

p. 78, line 39: Jack Dempsey offers Oswald a beer: Interview with Jack Dempsey, May 20, 1998.

CHAPTER 6

p. 79, Epigraph: "I knew I was dancing": Joe Manguno, "Was Jim Garrison Right After All?" p. 28.

p. 79, line 14: Banister sent Burglass in his place: Interview with Allen Campbell, July 10, 2002.

p. 79, line 27: Ruby is a regular at the Monteleone: Memorandum: From: Regis L. Kennedy. Subject: Betty Parent. November 26, 1963. 89-69-131. Ruby file: 44-2064. NARA.

p. 79, line 27: hotbed of international intrigue: Interview with Daniel Campbell, June 8, 2002.

p. 80, line 10: Ruby is treated for cancer at the Ochsner clinic: Interview with then St. Landry Parish assistant district attorney, Morgan Goudeau, August 5, 2003. Goudeau had been campaign manager for John F. Kennedy in Southern Louisiana.

p. 82, line 12: one of the maps Tommy took to Dallas is found in Oswald's room: "Handful Views Oswald Burial" by Jules Loh. *Times-Picayune*, November 26, 1963, Section 1, p. 8.

p. 82, line 22: "was going to kill the bastard": See LHN Church of God of Light. Signed: Rev. Ray Broshears; Interview of Raymond Broshears, Conducted by Steve Jaffe, James Alcock, and Louis Ivon. No date. NODA. NARA; Memorandum To: Jim Garrison. From: Steven J. Burton. Subject: Rev. Raymond Broshears. March 21, 1968; Thomas Edward Beckham to Brother Ray, July 6, 1968. NODA. NARA.

p. 82, line 33: Civello close to Patrick T. Dean: See John H. Davis, *Mafia Kingfish: Carlos Marcello and the Assassination of John F. Kennedy* (New York: McGraw, Hill Publishing Company, 1989), p. 207, 527. Interview with Thomas Angers, May 6, 2003. Interview with Morgan Goudeau, August 5, 2003.

p. 82, line 38: Campisi had bragged: Conversation with Morgan Goudeau, August 19, 2003.

p. 83, line 15: a diagram: Jimmy Johnson, "New Orleans Story." Interview with an unnamed questioner. NARA.

p. 83, line 21: "a building ten stories high": Walter Sheridan interview with Jimmy J. Johnson. Index 37. NARA.

p. 83, line 35: Bootsie Gay at the office of G. Wray Gill: Mrs. Clara Flournoy Gay to F. Edward Hebert. 13 pages. Tulane University Library. Papers of Clara Flournoy Gay. See also: Bootsie Gay to F. Edward Hebert, April 22, 1963; F. Edward Hebert to Mrs. Clara Gay, May 2, 1963; Memorandum. April 24, 1969. to: James L. Alcock. From: Captain Frederick A. Soule Sr. Re: Interview with Clara Flournoy "Bootsie" Gay. Under Item #2. Al Clark Interview. NODA. NARA. See also: To: Jim Garrison. From Harold Weisberg. Re: Interview with Al Clark and Clint Bolton, Dixieland Hall. NODA. NARA. See also: Jim Garrison, Memorandum to L. J. Delsa and Bob Buras. Re: Material allegedly seen at Wray Gill's office following assassination." October 20, 1977. NARA.

Bootsie Gay visited Gill's office on Tuesday, although she told Garrison investigator Frederick Soule it had been the Saturday after the assassination. In a letter to Congressman Hebert, however, Gay writes that she went to Gill's after she read in the newspapers that the district attorney's office was holding David Ferrie for the FBI and the Secret Service.

p. 85, line 1: "we have just come from New Orleans": Warren Commission. Vol. XI, p. 372.

p. 85, line 20: Jack Martin a "nut": FBI. To: SAC. From: SA Regis L. Kennedy. November 25, 1963. 89-69-167. NARA.

p. 85, line 20: Nelson Delgado: Mark Lane describes how the FBI attempted to undermine Nelson Delgado's testimony: *Rush to Judgment: A Critique of the Warren Commission's Inquiry into the Murders of President John F. Kennedy, Officer J. D. Tippit and Lee Harvey Oswald* (New York: Holt, Rinehart and Winston, 1966), p. 389. See also: FBI Memorandum. To: Mr. W. C. Sullivan. From: Mr. W. A. Branigan. Subject: Mark Lane. Security Matter—C. August 22, 1966. NARA. Under FBI pressure, Delgado changed his story, now insisting that Oswald "must have qualified" on the rifle range, even as, earlier, he had said Oswald had falsified his score; Nelson Delgado recants: FBI. To, Director, FBI. From: Murphy, John T. February 11, 1964. 124-10025-10160. Agency file: 105-82555-1873. NARA. Delgado, the FBI wrote for the record, was "exaggerating his acquaintanceship" with Oswald: Memorandum. To: W. C. Sullivan. From: W. A. Branigan. Subject: Lee Harvey Oswald. Internal Security—Russia—Cuba. June 16, 1964. 124-10034-10263. 105-82555-4154. NARA.

p. 85, line 25: "crying need for recognition": James J. Rowley, Treasury Department, US Secret Service, May 5, 1964 to Mr. J. Lee Rankin. RE: Rev. Walter J. McChann Interview. Commission No. 854. April 23-24, 1964. File No. Co-2-34-030, 100-10461-7749. Origin: Chief's Office. NARA.

p. 85, line 26: Garrison was a "nut": Interview with Warren de Brueys, January 15, 2000.

p. 85, line 29: having accused the FBI of persecuting her: Memo. Report on Sylvia Odio. May 31, 1967. NODA. NARA. Odio concluded that the Warren Commission did not wish to believe her. Memo. 1/18/76 To: Dave Marston. From: Gaeton Fonzi. Courtesy of Mr. Fonzi.

p. 85, line 31: Jim Garrison's investigation: Odio would be interviewed by Gaeton Fonzi for the HSCA. She reiterated that she had seen "the real Oswald" on that Thursday, September 26th, 1963, and no double, no imposter: See: Memorandum. To: Troy. From: Gaeton. July 27, 1976. Courtesy of Gaeton Fonzi. See also: Memorandum—February 9, 1978. To: G. Robert Blakey. From: Gonzales & Fonzi. Subject: Sylvia Odio. Re: Photo Identification Book. Courtesy of Gaeton Fonzi.

Oswald's appearance in Mexico City is riddled with ambiguity. David Atlee Phillips had requested of his asset Antonio Veciana that Veciana's cousin Guillermo Ruiz, working for Cuban intelligence, state that he and his wife met Oswald in Mexico City on that date. Ruiz would be paid a large amount of money. Ruiz was on his way to Havana, and it remains unknown whether he would have complied. See Gaeton Fonzi, *The Last Investigation* (New York: Thunder's Mouth Press, 1994), p. 143.

p. 85, line 32: Augustin Guitart: "I do not feel that she is insane": Statement of Dr. Augustin Guitart. Dated January 1967. NODA. NARA.

p. 85, line 38: proof of the plot: Sylvia Meagher, *Accessories after the Fact: The Warren Commission, Authorities & The Report* (New York: Vintage Books, 1976), p. 376.

p. 85, line 41: "testimony of Sylvia O": FBI Memorandum. From: SA Hughes. February 23, 1967. 124-10167-19145. 89-69-1604. NARA.

p. 86, line 9: a permissive father: "What purpose did that serve?" Interview with Lyon Garrison, May 23, 1998. His daughter, Elizabeth, calls him a district attorney who did not believe in punishment: Interview with Elizabeth Garrison, January 5, 1998.

p. 86, line 26: "CIA had some knowledge": This document in de Torres' FBI file contains a list of those members of Brigade 2506 with whom CIA had a relationship: FBI. To: D. J. Brennan. From: W. O. Cregar. Subject: Cuban Prisoner Exchange ISA -Cuba. January 11, 1963. Subject: Bernardo Alvarez, Handling of Returned Playa Giron Prisoners. 124-90012-10009. HQ. Agency file: 105-99200-205. See also: FBI. To: Director, FBI. From: SAC, Miami. April 3, 1961, 124-90012-10013. HQ 105-89923-158 NARA. De Torres was also Military Affairs Secretary of an association of veterans of the Bay of Pigs (AVBC), not shy about pursuing acts of sabotage against Cuba: Report No. CS DB-312/01134-66. April 22, 1966. CIA. Released as FBI 124-90012-10022. HQ 105-121847-28. NARA. CIA is sharing its information reports with FBI here.

p. 86, line 27: the roster of those CIA supported: See: CIA To: Director, Federal Bureau of Investigation. Attention: Mr. S. J. Papich. From: Deputy Director (Plans). Subject: Transmittal of Consejo Revolucionario Cubano Personnel Roster. 124-90012-10015. HQ 105-107224-32. NARA.

p. 86, line 27: offered FBI information about members of Brigade 2506:

See: FBI. To: Director, FBI. From: SAC, Miami. Re: Cuban Prisoner Exchange. January 21, 1963. 124-90012-10011. HQ CR 105-99200-216. Subjects: Bernardo Alvarez, Cuban Prisoner Exchange. The FBI reveals here as well the mutuality of its exchanges of information with CIA, De Torres informs to the FBI about Luis Tornes: From: MM to HQ. September 23, 1963. 124-90012-10003. CR 2-1818-3. NARA.

p. 86, line 34: B-26 bomber: FBI. April 9, 1964. Subjects: Bernardo Alvarez. Mario Oscar Baldatti Brieba. 124-90012-10037. HQ 105-124552-3. NARA.

p. 86, line 35: CIA yawned: To: Mr. J. Walter Yeagley, Assistant Attorney General. From: Director, FBI. September 13, 1963. 124-90012-10014. HQ 105-121847-3. NARA.

p. 86, line 36: De Torres' own father: FBI. To: Director, FBI. From: SAC, Miami. January 20, 1964. Subject: Asociación de Vetranos de Bahía de Cochinos, Brigada 2506. 124-90012-10023. HQ 105-121847-8. NARA. The document reads: "MM T-2 is Bernardo de Torres Sr., the father of the Military Planner of the Organization." De Torres senior also informed about his son's involvement in a proposed attack on a Soviet ship in waters off the coast of Florida in August of 1966. See: FBI. August 20, 1966. Subjects: Bernardo Alvarez; Asociación de Vetranos de Bahía de Cochinos. 124-90012-10021. HQ 105-121847-35. NARA. By then, FBI and CIA were collaborating in protecting de Torres: when a CIA informant named Miguel Cruz wrote to CIA's Miami field office, saying he had "information on Bernardo Torres," the person investigated was not de Torres, but Cruz: See: Justin F. Gleichauf to Mr. Ernest Aragon, U.S. Secret Service. February 24, 1967. 62-109060-4658; Treasury Department, United States Secret Service. Office of the Director. To: Federal Bureau of Investigation. Attention: SA Orrin Bartlett. From: Director. Subject: Assassination of President John F. Kennedy. February 27, 1967. 62-109060-4658.

p. 86, line 41: "cannot and will not cease his efforts": FBI, April 9, 1964.

p. 87, line 1: Garrison sends Sergeant Thomas Duffy: Hearings before the Subcommittee on the Assassination of John F. Kennedy of the Select Committee on Assassinations. House of Representatives. May 2, 1978, p. 36 reveals the visit of Duffy to de Torres in Miami.

p. 87, line 8: Alvarado: See SSCIA. Testimony of Samuel Halpern. April 22, 1976. 157-10014-10008. 01-H-03. NARA.

p. 87, line 13: According to Hemming, Czukas arranged for the Odio visit: e-mail from Gerald Patrick Hemming, May 31, 2004.

p. 87, line 14: Surveillance of Oswald: This is the contention of Gerald Patrick Hemming. Interview with Hemming, April 19, 2002.

p. 87, line 16: De Torres talks with Jim Garrison in New Orleans: Tape of Bernardo de Torres and Jim Garrison. Undated. In Spanish with some English translation.

p. 87, line 23: "Matamoros a Communist": A note reads: "Bernardo says she is a Communist." (Smith Case).

p. 87, line 30: "Miami planning in the summer of 1963": Richard N. Billings recorded these words of de Torres: Diary of Richard N. Billings, Jan. 24. File 17 17.

p. 87, line 33: "under no circumstances" should any information: Investigative Assignments. Smith Case. January 7, 1967. From: Jim Garrison. NODA. NARA.

p. 87, line 35: "his reliability is not established": Garrison wrote on an unsigned document headed "(Smith Case)." The document is signed 0-0-0-0-0-0-0 and attempts to identify the Cubans in the photograph with Oswald.

p. 87, line 36: Pershing had begun to inform to the FBI: Interview with Raymond Comstock, May 29, 1998. Interview with L. J. Delsa. Pershing's name appears on a CIA list of plants in Garrison's office witnessed by Delsa in Washington, DC.

p. 87, line 39: Bernardo de Torres reports on the Garrison investigation to CIA: A substantial trace of the evidence has been released: CIA Memorandum. To: Chief, 10 Thru: To: Chief, 10 Thru: Chief, 0/1 from: 10/2 Gerald D. Faulanger. 30 September 1967. Subject: TYPIC/AMFAUNA/13/Operational Activities of the AVBC. Jesus Vazquez Borrero, member of the 2506 Brigade, Discussions with a Mr. FNU

Levinson, in Washington, D. C. 104-10170-10266. 80T01357A; From: Chief of Station, JMWAVE To: Chief, WHD [Western Hemisphere Division]. Title: Dispatch: Operational/Activities of the AVBC. Member of the 2506 Brigade. Discussions with a Mr. FNU. October 9, 1967. 6 pages. NARA. In later years de Torres would report to CIA on Cubans involved in narcotics traffic: CIA. to: Chief, Western Hemisphere Division. From: Chief of Station. Subject: PBRUMEN—Cuban exiles in Narcotics. July 3, 1972. 104-0070-10179. 80T01357A. Two pages. This report was made to ACROBAT-1. See also: To: Director. 4 December 1969. From: Withheld. To: Director. Title: Cable concerning telephone call. 104-10070-10180. 89T01357A INFO WH/MIAMI. LITEMP-12 received a cable from Bernardo de Torres, who identifies himself as "Pentagon Intelligence." Report is on a man involved in arms contraband. Who can discern how many masters this man served? See also: Counter intelligence checks with JMWAVE about Bernardo de Torres: WH/COG #67-302. 27 September 1967. Memorandum For: C/CI/R & A. Attention: Mr. Pratt. Subject: Transmittal of 201 files on Individuals Involved in Garrison Investigation. From: Nancy Gratz, WH/COG/CICS. NARA. For de Torres' firmly established CIA connections, see also: CIA, 27 October 1967. Subject: Torres, Bernardo, aka Gonzales (de) Torres Alvarez, Bernardo.

p. 87, line 41: "everybody is looking for me": FBI. To: D. J. Brennan Jr. From: S. J. Papich. March 3, 1967. Subject: Bernardo Gonzalez de Torres Alvarez. 124-90012-10049. HQ 105-124552-5. NARA.

p. 87, line 42: Hoover paused. FBI reacts to the news: FBI Airtel. To: Director, FBI. From: SAC, Miami. February 20, 1967. 124-90012-10042. HQ 105-124552-NR. NARA.

p. 88, line 2: "Don't use Torres": FBI. To: W. C. Sullivan. From: W. A. Branigan. February 20, 1967. 124-90012-10043. HQ 105-124552-NR. NARA.

p. 88, line 4: De Torres had never been one of their informants: FBI. To: SACs Miami and New Orleans. From: Director, FBI. BERNARDO DE TORRES ALVAREZ. INTERNAL

SECURITY—Cuba. February 23, 1967. 124-90012-10046. HQ 105-124552-4. NARA.

p. 88, line 6: De Torres comes up with the name "Eladio del Valle": Memorandum. February 26, 1967. To: Jim Garrison. From: Louis Ivon. Re: Telephone conversation with Alberto Fowler. NODA. NARA.

p. 88, line 11: De Torres used up half: Edward Jay Epstein, *Counterplot*, p. 195.

p. 88, line 15: Major Roberto Verdaguer as Bernardo de Torres' source: See Hans Tanner, *Counter-Revolutionary Agent: Diary of the Events Which Occurred in Cuba Between January and July 1961* (G. T. Foulis & Co. Ltd.: London, 1962), p. 70.

p. 88, line 27: Adames talks to Fonzi: Memo 6/17/77 To: Tanenbaum. From: Fonzi. Re: Juan Adames.

p. 88, line 28: de Torres knew Oswald: See: Memo to Tanenbaum. From: Fonzi. June 15, 1977. Re: Adames and Otero Interviews; Memo, June 17, 1977. To: Tanenbaum. From: Fonzi. Re: Juan Adames.

p. 88, line 32: "is going to be hit": MEMO-3/13/77 To: Cliff Fenton. From: Gaeton Fonzi. NARA.

p. 88, line 39: "it was a Cuban refugee group": Information from a Cuban government secretary to an intelligence officer at the Cuban embassy in Mexico City: FBI To: Director, FBI. From: SAC, Miami. March 14, 1967. Re: Lee Harvey Oswald—Internal Security—Russia—Cuba. FBI 124-10237-10240. 89-69-1755, 1756. 4 pages. The FBI's Miami informant has interviewed Ramiro Jesus Abreu Quintana, an intelligence officer holding the position of Third Secretary and Chief of Consular Section at the Cuban embassy in Mexico City. The FBI's source is Aracelli Mastrappa, Quintana's secretary.

p. 89, line 10: Cobos names de Torres: FBI. SA Vincent J. Marger and Raymond L. O'Mally. January 15, 1976. MM 174-940: "Cobos furnished the name Bernardo Torres . . . as the man to call with contacts on a high level with the CIA in Washington, D.C. De Torres advised Gonzalez that he contacted his source in the CIA and learned that the FBI is aware that Rolando Otero did commit the bombings. . . ." See also: To: Tanenbaum.

From: Fonzi. Re: Rolando Otero Leads. May 17, 1977. 014582. NARA.

p. 89, line 11: a 1969 document: CIA 104-10070-10180. 80T01357A. To: Director. Title: Cable concerning telephone call. 12/04/69. 1999 CIA Historical Review Program. NARA.

p. 89, line 15: Bernardo was involved in the assassination: Fonzi. Rough Notes—Interview with (redacted). 5/25/77. (arranged through . . .). Courtesy of Gaeton Fonzi. The redacted name is Juan Adames. See also Fonzi notes 10-3-77. Report of a meeting with Juan Adames.

p. 89, line 16: Otero talks to the FBI: Department of Justice 179-20003-10422. Classified. Subject file: 129-11. Official Mail Section 35. March 4, 1977. 10 pages.

p. 89, line 17: Otero talks to Fonzi: see Memo 3/20/77. To: Tanenbaum. From: Fonzi. Re: Interview with Rolando Otero.

p. 89, line 13: Otero's information about Sheridan is confirmed by Edwin Guthman: Conversation with Edwin Guthman, May 16, 2000.

p. 89, line 26: photographs taken at Dealey Plaza: Notes, 10-3-77. Courtesy of Gaeton Fonzi.

p. 89, line 40: Lopez complained to Blakey: Eddie Lopez. 2-28-93. Tatel (s2) 020 RE : DE TORRES. NARA.

p. 90, line 17: Request for Immunity Form: March 10, 1978. Submitted by wktriplett: Form suggests witness was apt to claim the Fifth amendment: "Within the scope of his anti-Castro Cuban activities and associations during the 1960's, Mr. de Torres may consider himself potentially subject to testimony which might tend to incriminate him. We are in possession of investigative information which indicates that Mr. de Torres may have been in Dealey Plaza at the time of the assassination, and, further, that he may have been involved in an assassination conspiracy." NARA. Note the "an," a second line of CIA defense, one used in the Shaw case as well: Jim Garrison was asked to prove that it was THE conspiracy, rather than one of many, in which the defendant was involved.

p. 90, line 19: "dapper and casual confidence": E-mail from Gaeton Fonzi. February 15, 2002. De Torres testimony on May 2, 1978. 118 pages. NARA.

p. 90, line 25: "I don't know how I was chosen by him": De Torres testimony, p. 76.

p. 90, line 28: De Torres lies about having worked for CIA: See, for example, de Torres call to CIA on March 3, 1967, about the Kennedy assassination: FBI document. To: Mr. D. J. Brennan Jr. From: S. J. Papich. Subject: BERNARDO GONZALEZ DE TORRES ALVAREZ. INTERNAL SECURITY—CUBA. 105-124552-5. FBI 124-9012-10049. 105-124552-5. NARA.

p. 91, line 10: "a known Cuban association with Oswald": Fonzi to Tanenbaum, May 10, 1977, "Need for Augmented Miami Office." Courtesy of Gaeton Fonzi.

p. 91, line 14: for descriptions of Gerstein, see Hank Messick, *Syndicate in the Sun* (New York: The Macmillan Company, 1968), p. 62. Also: Interviews with Martin F. Dardis, February 6, 2001; May 4, 2001.

p. 91, line 18: "he's a fellow district attorney": Interview with Seymour Gelber, November 17, 1999.

p. 91, line 21: "short, stocky Cuban": Diary of Richard N. Billings. Notes 888. AARC.

p. 91, line 23: "the other murderer": Dialogue between Jim Garrison and Alberto Fowler; Interview with Cubans by Mr. Jim Garrison, Mr. Fowler et al., December 26, 1966. Harry Connick collection of the papers of Jim Garrison.

p. 91, line 29: how CIA-sponsored Cubans received their checks: Interview with Martin F. Dardis, May 4, 2001. See also: Interview by Martin F. Dardis of Eduardo Fernandez. Metropolitan Dade County Justice Building. Office of the State Attorney. May 9, 1967. NARA.

p. 91, line 30: checks from Eastern Airlines: CIA/JMWAVE proprietaries in Miami included: boat shops, shipping lines, real estate firms, travel agencies, gun shops, detective agencies and department stores: Gibraltar Steamship Corporation; Double-Chek Corporation; Radio Americas; Intermountain Air Service; Southern Air Transport; American Doctor (AMDOC); VITA; Paragon Air

Service; Ayerventures; Caribbean Air Services; Caribbean Marine Services (CARAMAR); Mineral Carriers, Inc. Warehouse; Burdine's Department Store, and many more. Some of the names emerged in *United States of America v. Benjamin Franklin Thomas, Gerald Patrick Hemming, Joseph Thomas LNU and Jacob Cochran.* Motion for production of favorable evidence in the United States District Court In and For the Southern District of Florida, Miami Division. ARRC. See also: Taylor Branch and George Crille, III, "The Kennedy Vendetta," *Harper's* magazine. August 1975, p. 51.

p. 91, line 33: the local FBI: Inspector General's Survey of the Cuban Operation and Associated Documents." National Security Archive. The George Washington University. The Gelman Library. p. 69.

p. 91, line 39: Manuel García Gonzales: The FBI found him first. A Manuel García Gonzalez, born in Havana on March 27, 1938, had been picked up in the Gulf of Mexico as a refugee on February 5, 1964. His Bureau number was 105-2171. This was, however, a very common Cuban name: FBI. To: SACs, New Orleans, Miami. From: Director. February 27, 1967. 124-10241-10144. 89-69-1519. NARA.

p. 92, line 4: Dardis holds up a sign: Interview with Martin F. Dardis, January 13, 2001; February 10, 2001. See also: Memorandum. January 24, 1967. From: Detectives Lester Otillio and Douglas Ward. Subject: Activities while on investigation in Miami area. NODA. NARA. The reference to the "Red Book of the Greater Miami area" is belied by the fact that it was Dardis who did the investigating.

p. 92, line 10: the wrong man: Interview with Martin F. Dardis, November 28, 1999.

p. 92, line 12: Dardis contacts police intelligence: Miami Police Memo. To: Lieut. H. Swilley, Intelligence Unit. From. E. W. McCracken, Intelligence Unit. January 23, 1967. Subject: Assistance to Outside Agency. Available at www.cuban-exile.com, Gordon Winslow's Web site. See also: City of Miami, Florida. Inter-Office Memorandum. February 20, 1967. To: Lieut. H. Swilley, Intelligence Unit. From: Sgt.

Everett Kay, Intelligence Unit. Subject: Suspect in Presidential Assassination. www.cuban-exile.com.

p. 92, line 17: Alberto introduces Alcock to Laureano Batista: Memorandum. February 5, 1967. To: Jim Garrison. From: Jim Alcock. Re: Laureano Batista. NODA. NARA. See also Alberto Fowler's interview with Batista. Memorandum. February 3, 1967. NODA. NARA. See also Fowler statement dated January 28th.

p. 92, line 20: "from an office building with a high powered rifle": Memorandum For Reference. 8-385/7 No. 11. February 6, 1970. THE MIAMI POLICE TAPE. Richard E. Sprague Collection: Georgetown University. Box 6, folder 37. See also FBI interview with Milteer, December 1, 1963. File # Atlanta 105-3193. NARA. See also Commission document 1347, pages withheld 121. See also : Dan Christensen, "JFK, King: The Dade County Links," *Miami* magazine. September 1976.

p. 92, line 32: Bernardo de Torres counters the denials of the Secret Service that they were warned following Milteer's having been taped: Bernardo de Torres quoted in "JFK Death Probe Sees Conspiracy" by Carlos Martinez. *Miami Herald.* February 19, 1967, p. 1, 2A. FBI denial that they talked to de Torres: FBI. February 23, 1967. Subject: Bernardo Alvarez; Bernardo Torres. 124-90012-10051. H. 105-124552.-NR. NARA.

p. 92, line 33: the Secret Service denied they had been warned following Somersett's tape of Joseph Milteer: Interview with Seymour Gelber, November 1999; Seymour Gelber diary (courtesy of Judge Gelber).

p. 92, line 36: he's *simpático:* Interview with Alberto Antonio Fowler.

p. 92, line 37: Patricia Chandler asks Fowler for photographs: Memo from David Chandler. "Jesse Core and Alberto Fowler." Papers of Richard N. Billings. Box 4, folder 59. Georgetown University, Washington, DC.

p. 93, line 7: a brick crashes through the window at the Fowler home: Interviews with Alberto Antonio Fowler and Alexandra Fowler.

CHAPTER 7

p. 94, Epigraph: "a tiger by the tail": Teletype of George Lardner's article for

the *Washington Post.* February 22, 1967. Available in the papers of Richard N. Billings. To: Lang. For: Orshevksy. From: Angeloff, Washington. Rush Copy For *LIFE* Wednesday closing, Georgetown University, Washington, DC.

p. 94, line 4: Santana is interviewed at Tulane and Broad: See polygraph, conducted by William Gurvich and Roy L. Jacob. February 15, 1967. See also: Memorandum. February 13, 1967. To: Louis Ivon. From: Sgt. Fenner Sedgebeer. Re: Emilio Santana; Memorandum. February 15, 1967. To: Jim Garrison. From: James L. Alcock. Re: Interview of Emilio Santana, February 14, 1967. NODA. NARA. Santana is also described in the CIA Segregated File: 000066 Emilio Santana. Paragraph 7 C of reference memorandum. Santana had been recruited by JMWAVE in December of 1960 as a guide for an infiltration team. CIA terminated his involvement because of "untruthful reporting concerning aspects of Team operations."

p. 94, line 19: Santana is an associate of Sergio Arcacha Smith: This information emerged only in 1978 during Rabel's deposition before HSCA: Summary of Deposition. To: G. Robert Blakey. From: Jonathan Blackmer. June 13, 1978. Re: Summary of Luis Rabel Deposition taken May 11, 1978 in New Orleans, Louisiana.

p. 94, line 12: Arcacha's presence in New Orleans during the summer of 1963 is confirmed by Thomas Edward Beckham. Interview with Thomas Edward Beckham.

p. 94, line 16: Alberto Fowler aids in the polygraph of Santana: Carlos Bringuier interview with Aaron M. Kohn. June 1, 1967. MCC.

p. 94, line 21: Jean Vales-Juan Valdes: see diary of Richard N. Billings, pp. 82-83. AARC.

p. 94, line 25: "revolutionary actions with regard to Cuba": Memorandum. To: Jim Garrison. From: Douglas Ward. Re: CHECK ON ALL VISITORS TO MIGUEL TORRES IN PARISH PRISON FROM JANUARY 31, 1967, TO THIS DATE. NODA. Memorandum: January 11, 1967. To: Jim Garrison. From: Andrew J. Sciambra. Re: SMITH INVESTIGATION. NODA. NARA. See also: Memorandum. February 17, 1967. To: Jim Garrison. From: Lynn

Loisel. Re: QUESTIONS ASKED OF EMILIO SANTANA IN REGARD TO DECEPTIONS FOUND IN POLYGRAPH TEST. NODA. NARA.

p. 95, line 1: Miguel Torres also revealed a "deception" reaction on the question of whether he knew Clay Shaw. See also the Walter Sheridan interviews, #18. (MCC). Miguel Torres. Torres here admits to this deceptive reaction in his interview with NBC for Sheridan's "White Paper.'

p. 95, line 20: "I'm engaged in a conference right now": Conversation with Samuel Exnicios, January 8, 2002.

p. 95, line 29: "a citizen that believes in your case:" Anonymous letter available in NODA. NARA.

p. 95, line 31: Orestes Peña knows Santana as "Cabellero": Interview Summary. Select Committee on Assassinations. January 20, 1978, by Martin J. Daly and William Brown. HSCA 014118. Record number: 180-10097-10491. NARA.

p. 95, line 35: it wasn't a lie: US Government Memorandum. No. 133067. To: Director, Domestic Contact Service. From: Chief, New Orleans Office. Subject: District Attorney Garrison's Investigation into Alleged Conspiracy to Assassinate President Kennedy. NARA.

p. 96, line 1: Roger Craig's credibility would later come into question.

p. 96, line 11: Baumler provides information on Oswald and Ruby being acquainted: Memorandum. March 6, 1967. To: Jim Garrison. From: James L. Alcock. Re: Telephone call from Tommy Baumler on February 27, 1967. NODA. NARA.

p. 96, line 18: Oswald used Jack Ruby as a personal reference: FBI. From: SAC, New Orleans. To: Director, FBI. March 5, 1967. Record number: 124-10027-10214. HQ. Agency file number: 62-109060-4657. NARA.

p. 96, line 20: Here is but a sample of the sources suggesting that Oswald and Ruby knew each other: A Chicago gun runner named Eugene Sauner placed Oswald and Ruby together. So did a man named Wilber (Bob) Litchfield. Taxi driver Raymond Cummings had come forward.

The testimony in Dallas was even more definitive: It included a man who told his barber that one of the Lucase owners of the B & B Cafe had seen Ruby and Oswald there "on more than one occasion." The waitress, Mary Lawrence, confirmed this interview, adding that Oswald had told her he was waiting for Jack Ruby. She came forward despite an anonymous telephone threat. Dallas police criminal intelligence learned that Ruby was a homosexual who attended parties in Dallas with Oswald, who was considered "trade" by other homosexuals.

Among people who came forward who saw Oswald and Ruby together at the Carousel Club (see Steven J. Burton to Louis Ivon, April 8, 1968), was a Jackie Caddell of Dentport who said many of her parents' friends say they had seen the two together. "We must get some written statements on this," Garrison wrote onto the letter. He wanted Boxley to interview Caddell.

See also the report to Garrison from Matt Herron. September 18, 1967. To: Jim Garrison. From: Matt Herron: Report on Investigations into possible records of Phone calls between Oswald and Ruby. NODA. NARA. See also Statement of Eugene Sauner, February 24, 1967. NODA. Billings papers. Georgetown. Box 1, folder 11. See also August 27, 1967. From: Bill Turner. To: Jim Garrison. Subject: Possible Witness to Ruby-Oswald Link." NARA. See also Memorandum. Undeveloped Lead —Ruby Case. January 27, 1964 from Henry Wade; Captain W. P. Gannaway Through Lieutenant Jack Revill, Criminal Intelligence Section. 30 January 1964. Subject: Criminal Intelligence (6). Mary Lawrence. From: R. W. Westphal, Detective and P. M. Parks, Detective; 2 December 1963. Gannaway through Lt. Jack Revill. From: H. M. Hart, Detective, Criminal Intelligence Section. Subject: Criminal Intelligence (1). Jack Ruby w-m. Records of the Dallas Police Department, courtesy of Gary Shaw. There is as well the testimony of Thomas Edward Beckham, Bill Demar, Rose Cheramie, and others.

p. 96, line 26: Oswald was at a table: Interview with Bill DeMar, January 26, 2003.

p. 96, line 28: Volz is sent to Dallas: Memorandum. January 31, 1967. To: Jim Garrison. From: John Volz. Re: SPECIAL INVESTIGATION, DALLAS.

NODA. NARA. Interview with John Volz, May 21, 1998.

p. 96, line 42: Ferrie paid Arcacha: Handwritten notes of Jim Garrison. Courtesy of Lyon Garrison.

p. 97, line 1: concentrated on Arcacha and Shaw: Diary of Richard N. Billings. Notes 14 14. AARC.

p. 97, line 5: Arcacha maintains extensive relations with FBI, Immigration and Warren de Brueys: CIA 100-200-17. May 2, 1967. Secret. JMWAVE 6938. Priority, Director. See also: FBI. From: W. A. Branigan. To: W. C. Sullivan. May 2, 1967. Subject: Arcacha Smith. Record number: 104-10310-10150. Agency file: CIA-DDP-FILES. NARA.

p. 97, line 6: Both Carlos Quiroga and Carlos Bringuier warn Arcacha that Garrison's men are coming: Interview with Carlos Bringuier, January 5, 2000. Interview with Carlos Quiroga, January 14, 2000.

p. 97, line 10: "I had expected them earlier": To: Will Lang. From: Holland McCombs. 4 April 1967. For Richard Billings and Nancy Haskell. Office Memorandum. AARC.

p. 97, line 17: admitted that he had traveled to New Orleans: Conversation with Sergio Arcacha Smith, November 29, 1999.

p. 97, line 19: denied he knew Oswald: Conversation with Sergio Arcacha Smith.

p. 97, line 21: "nutty as a fruitcake": Interviews of Ronny Caire by Jim Brown, May 31, 1970, and November 19, 1970. See Brown, *Central Intelligence Assassination.*

p. 97, line 24: "a waste of time": Memo. February 14, 1977. From: Fonzi. To: Tanenbaum. Courtesy of Gaeton Fonzi.

p. 97, line 34: "sterilizing him": Memorandum. September 30, 1968. From: William C. Boxley. Re: Banister's Associations. NODA. NARA.

p. 97, line 39: "David Ferrie is capable of almost anything": Statement of Joseph S. Newbrough. December 19, 1966. NODA. NARA.

p. 98, line 1: Oster reported everything to Regis Kennedy: FBI. Memorandum. To: Director, FBI. From: SAC, New Orleans. January 4, 1967. 124-10256-10132. 89-69-1376. NARA.

p. 98, line 1: Ivon consulted Oster nonetheless: See: Memorandum.

March 6, 1967. To: File. From: Lou Ivon. Re: Information from Joseph Oster. NODA. NARA.

p. 98, line 6: "someone should do away with Kennedy": Memorandum. December 30, 1966. 11:30 a.m. To: Jim Garrison. From: Douglas Ward. NODA. NARA. The witness is named Emile Stopper.

p. 98, line 7: I. E. Nitschke: Statement and Interview with Mr. I. E. Nitschke in the office of Jim Garrison. Tuesday, January 17, 1967, at approximately 1:00 p.m. NODA. NARA.

p. 98, line 22: "world-wide intelligence network": Statement of Delphine Roberts. January 19, 1967. NODA. NARA.

p. 98, line 23: Mary Banister concealed: Memorandum. May 1, 1967. To: Jim Garrison. From: Andrew J. Sciambra. Re: Mrs. Mary Banister—Interview with. April 29th and 30th, 1967. NODA. NARA. Sciambra's interviews with Ross Banister: February 1 and 2, 1967. Sciambra also talked to Banister's mother: See diary of Richard N. Billings, file 23 23. Sciambra wrote no memo of this interview.

p. 98, line 27: Quiroga drove the arms to Miami: Interview with Quiroga, January 14, 2000. Some boxes of plastic explosives remained. These Arcacha loaded into Quiroga's car and he drove them to the house of Arcacha's successor, Luis Rabel. "You guys are now in charge of this revolution," Quiroga told Rabel and the group of Cubans gathered at his house. "Take these arms to Miami." A few hours passed and Quiroga's car was empty. Later Jim Garrison was told that these arms had been dumped into Lake Pontchartrain.

p. 98, line 31: studying Russian at Tulane: the best source for this is Quiroga's interview with Kent Courtney, September 23, 1967. Papers of Kent Courtney. Northwestern State University at Natchitoches. Watson Library. Cammie G. Henry Research Center. Folder: 1963, 3-I-2.

p. 98, line 35: "physically attack": Interview with Carlos Quiroga.

p. 98, line 37: reported the names of students: Interview with Carlos Quiroga, January 14, 2000.

p. 98, line 39: Quiroga as an FBI informant: Warren de Brueys would credit Quiroga as a "source" for Commission Document 75, his 790 page rendition of the assassination, released on December 2, 1963. On the page "Identity of sources," Quiroga is listed as "New Orleans T-5." FBI 100-6601. Dallas field office no. 100-10461. Bureau file number: 105-82555. 12/2/63. Report made by Warren C. de Brueys. Character of case: IS -R-CUBA. "He was a source, not an informant," de Brueys says, even as he contradicts himself in his House Select Committee testimony: "sources of information would apply to anybody that we had talked to more than once and was inclined to give us information. They wouldn't initiate it." By this standard, given that he did a good deal of the initiating, Quiroga was an "informant." See HSCA 014716. May 3, 1978. Executive Session. Testimony of Warren C. de Brueys.

p. 98, line 42: "apparent detective complex": Memorandum. SAC, New Orleans. From: SA Robert J. Heibel. Subject: Carlos Quiroga Info Concerning. February 20, 1967. 89-69-1559. NARA. See also: FBI Airtel To: Director, FBI. From: SAC, New Orleans. April 17, 1967. 124-10259-10230. 89-69-1999, 2000, 2001. NARA. "Quiroga was interviewed by Bureau Agents on 1/5/67, for the purpose of accessing him as a PSI but the interviewing Agents felt that Quiroga possessed a detective complex."

p. 99, line 7: "plenty scared": To: Jim Garrison. From: Frank Klein. Re: Interview of Carlos Quiroga. January 13, 1967. NODA. NARA.

p. 99, line 19: another round of questions: Transcript of Jim Garrison's January 21, 1967, interview with Carlos Quiroga is available at AARC. Quiroga's comments on this interview are contained in his "Appendix to Mr. Carlos Bringuier's Letter of March 29, 1967."

p. 99, line 24: evasive about Mancuso cafe: Diary of Richard N. Billings, File 777.

p. 99, line 38: Quiroga reports Garrison to the House Un-American Activities Committee: HUAC: FBI 89-69-1999,2000, 2002, 2002. Agency record: 124-10259-10230. To: Director, FBI. From: SAC, New Orleans. April 17, 1967.

p. 99, line 40: Quiroga calls de Brueys at home: Memo to SAC 1/24/67. SA Warren C. de Brueys. Carlos Quiroga, Information concerning. 89-69-13. NARA. De Brueys suggests that his memo "be routed to the agent who may possibly be conducting any inquiries relative to the District Attorney's investigation of the Kennedy assassination."

p. 100, line 11: At the grand jury, Quiroga would expose his lack of belief in the basic principles of American democracy. He admitted that he had called the FBI asking "how come they would allow Oswald to distribute that type of propaganda in the streets of this country here." He "got mad" when the FBI explained that this was not illegal, and tried to get satisfaction from New Orleans police intelligence. Oswald asked him for money to join the Fair Play for Cuba Committee, but he declined: "I know better about giving money to organizations without asking the authorities if I can join the organizations." He must have thought he had emigrated to Stalin's Russia.

Quiroga's grand jury testimony transcripts are available both at NARA and AARC.

p. 100, line 23: Jim Garrison wanted more evidence, and so was not ready to arrest David Ferrie: This information, and the account of Louis Ivon's encounters with Ferrie, is from interviews with Louis Ivon, January 8, 1998; January 12, 2000; October 9, 2000.

p. 100, line 26: At White Rock airport: Gurvich goes to every airport in the Dallas area: Memorandum. To: Jim Garrison. From: William Gurvich, Investigator. January 28, 1967. NODA. NARA.

p. 100, line 27: Fred Lenz identifies Ferrie: Memorandum. February 14, 1967. To: Jim Garrison. From: William Gurvich. Subj: David William Ferrie—I. E. Nitschke's Description of. NODA. Dick Billings had the Gurvich memorandum corroborated. See: Will Lang, *Life* Magazine. For Billings on Ferrie. February 27, 1967. Papers of Richard N. Billings. Holland McCombs provided the research.

p. 100, line 29: piloting a plane in and out of Dallas: Billings. Haskell. February 14, 1967. DAVID

WILLIAM FERRIE. Biography written by Richard N. Billings. Papers of Richard N. Billings. Box 4, folder 48. Lenz confirmed the identification of Ferrie for Holland McCombs, working on Richard Billings' *Life* magazine investigation.

p. 100, line 37: "I've got some interesting ideas": FBI Airtel. To: Director, FBI. From: SAC, New Orleans. January 4, 1967. 124-10256-10132. 89-69-1376. NARA.

p. 101, line 1: Max Gonzales would try to spend time with Ferrie by pretending that he was interested in purchasing an airplane: Memorandum. January 11, 1967. To: Louis Ivon. From: Lynn Loisel. Re: Phone call from Jimmy Johnson Regarding Ferrie and the Smith Case (January 10, 1967, 4:00 p.m.). NODA. NARA.

p. 101, line 3: Jimmy Johnson: Jim Garrison had Johnson checked out after the fact: Memorandum. March 3, 1967. To: Jim Garrison. From: Julian R. Murray Jr. Re: Kennedy Assassination Investigation. NODA. Mrs. William B. Jones in January of 1965 interviewed Johnson for the position of male nurse for her husband. On the basis of a recommendation from "either a psychiatrist or a psychologist whose last name was Ferrie and who lived on Louisiana Avenue Parkway," she hired him.

p. 101, line 6: "to keep myself out of trouble": Walter Sheridan interview with Jimmy J. Johnson. Index 37. NARA.

p. 101, line 8: Neither Beaubouef nor Brownlee: Interview with Alvin Beaubouef, January 4, 2000. Beaubouef affected surprise about Johnson when told he was working for Garrison; interview with Morris Brownlee, June 2, 2000.

p. 101, line 10: the surveillance of Ferrie: Jimmy Johnson picks up an envelope, etc. Johnson's and the following NODA memoranda are available at NARA. See in particular: Memorandum: January 11, 1967 To: Louis Ivon. From: Lynn Loisel. Re: Phone call from Jimmy Johnson Regarding Ferrie and The Smith Case (January 10, 1967, 4:00 PM); Memorandum January 16, 1967. To: Jim Garrison. From: Undercover Agent #1 (Jimmy Johnson). Re: Information on Dave Ferrie received 1-11-67, gath-ered by Undercover Agent #1; Memorandum. January 19, 1967. To: Jim Garrison. From: Investigator Lynn Loisel. Re: Telephone Conversation with Agent #1; NODA; Memorandum. January 23, 1967. To: Louis Ivon. From: Lynn Loisel. Re: Phone call from Agent One to L. Loisel. 1/23/67. 12:30 P.M. NODA; Memorandum. February 3, 1967. To: Jim Garrison From: Agent #1. Re: Smith Case. NODA; Memorandum: February 6, 1967. To: Jim Garrison. From: Kent Simms. NODA; Memorandum. February 6, 1967. To: Jim Garrison. From: Sgt. Tom Duffy. NODA; Memorandum. February 8, 1967. To: Louis Ivon From: Detective C. Jonau; Memorandum, February 9, 1967. To: Jim Garrison. From: Louis Ivon. Re: Surveillance of 3330 Louisiana Avenue — Residence of William D. Ferrie [sic] on February 5, 1967; Memorandum. February 10, 1967. To: Jim Garrison. From: Agent #1. Re: Smith Case; Memorandum. February 14, 1967. To: Jim Garrison From: Lynn Loisel. Re: Surveillance of 3330 Louisiana Avenue Parkway, Residence of David Ferrie, W/M, to observe actions and associates; Memorandum. February 15, 1967 to: Lewis [sic] Ivon. From: Kent Simms. Re: Stake-Out at 3330 Louisiana Avenue, home of David Farrie [sic].

p. 101, line 15: run guns: Memorandum. January 9, 1967. To: Louis Ivon. From: Lynn Loisel. Re: Smith Investigation. NODA. NARA.

p. 101, line 17: Ferrie didn't have a license: Statement of James R. Williams. Office of the District Attorney. March 20, 1967. Re: Conversation with Mr. Al Crouch. Papers of Richard N. Billings. Box 1, folder 5. Ferrie had been employed by Crouch, who owned Saturn Aviation, before he started his own school in 1966.

p. 101, line 17: burglarize. This was not the first time Ferrie requested that one of his young followers commit robbery. Another was Michael Otto Clyde Wakeling. Memorandum. February 15, 1967. To: Jim Garrison. From: William Gurvich. Subj: David William Ferrie—1957 incident. NODA. NARA.

p. 101, line 19: the "dear Bastard" letter is available in the Wegmann papers.

p. 101, line 29: "the police suspect

me": Jimmy reported David Ferrie's comments to his brother Charles: DOJ. 179-20002-10108. CLASSIFIED SUBJECT FILE 129-11, OFFICIAL MAIL SECT. 17A. FBI. From: Oklahoma City, Ok. March 7, 1967. 2 pages. NARA.

p. 101, line 39: Ferrie calls Reverend Broshears and says he fears he will be killed: Broshears quoted in Dick Russell, "The Vindication of Jim Garrison," *Harper's Weekly.* September 6, 1976. p. 33.

p. 102, line 13: "in his need to talk to Ivon": Jim Garrison interviewed in Richard Cohen and Carol Kachmer, *Rough Side of the Mountain,* an unfinished documentary about the events in Clinton and Jackson, Louisiana.

p. 102, line 16: Judge Thomas Brahney told Dempsey, "You'd better get off your big Irish bazoo": Interview with Jack Dempsey, May 20, 1998.

p. 102, line 37: "I'm a dead man": Interview with Allen Campbell, July 4, 2002.

p. 102, line 41: "big joke": quoted in Rosemary James and Jack Wardlow, *Plot or Politics? The Garrison Case & Its Cast* (New Orleans: Pelican Publishing House, 1967), p. 39.

p. 102, line 42: "get your licks in first": FBI. To: Director. From: SAC, New Orleans. February 20, 1967. 124-10256-10155. 89-69-1404. NARA.

p. 103, line 1: Ferrie telephones Snyder: "Sick Ferrie Felt Life Unjust," by David Snyder. *States-Item.* February 23, 1967. Ferrie told Snyder that acquaintances had told him that the DA had questioned them: "New Orleans DA Says His Investigation Shows Oswald Didn't Act Alone." *States-Item.* February 18, 1967.

p. 103, line 5: arrests are months away: "Confident He Can Show JFK Killing Was Plotted—DA." *Times-Picayune,* February 21, 1967. Section 1, p. 1.

p. 103, line 7: "Jim Garrison has some information": "Thinks DA Has Data—Long." *Times-Picayune,* February 22, 1967, Section 1, p. 1.

p. 103, line 22: "as the S. P. C. A": The news release is dated February 23, 1967.

p. 103, line 27: Ferrie lived at one of Shaw's French Quarter properties: Interview with John Wilson, December 13, 2003.

p. 103, line 29: Ivon and Sciambra visit Ferrie: Memorandum. February 28, 1967. To: Jim Garrison. From: Andrew Sciambra and Louis Ivon. Re: Interview with David Ferrie. NODA. NARA.

p. 104, line 35: Ferrie calls Lou Ivon and talks: Interviews with Louis Ivon, January 8, 1998; January 12, 2000; October 9, 2000. Ivon's handwritten notes of his meeting with Ferrie disappeared from Jim Garrison's records.

p. 105, line 5: "Shaw was involved with the CIA": Louis Ivon interviewed in *Beyond JFK.*

p. 105, line 9: CIA affiliated Schlumberger ammunition dump: The president of Schlumberger drilling company in the U.S., Milton E. Loy, had been granted a Covert Security Approval in 1965 as the buyer of a JMWAVE boat from a JMWAVE corporation that would then be sold to "an Agency proprietary corporation." In 1963, he had moved from New Orleans to Houston, Texas. The document, marked "Secret", and chronicling Loy's career, offers a rare revelation of how CIA operates within US borders. See: Memorandum: Subject: DCS Contacts with the Schlumberger Well Surveying Corporation and Its Subsidiaries. numbers obliterated. See also CIA. Subject: Loy, M. E. aka Loy, Milton E. August 7, 1968. Subjects: Garrison, James. 104-10515-10078. 80T01357A. NARA.

p. 105, line 12: checks from the White House: Interview with Layton Martens, January 16, 2000.

p. 105, line 16: "you guys don't know what you're dealing with": Interview with William Alford, May 28, 1998.

p. 105, line 22: Loisel went out for cigarettes: Interview with William Alford, May 28, 1998.

p. 105, line 27: Ferrie asks Orestes Peña about Arcacha and Mas: HSCA. Sworn Testimony of Orest Peña. June 23, 1978. 180-10075-10167. HSCA 010136. 36 pages. NARA.

p. 105, line 33: During that talk, Ferrie asked Bringuier to slow his steps: Carlos Bringuier interviewed by Kent Courtney. p. 37. Kent Courtney Collection. Northwestern State University at Natchitoches. Folder no. 9, 3-I-1.

p. 105, line 36: when the conspiracy started: Interview with Carlos Bringuier, January 5, 2000.

p. 106, line 3: harassed because he helped Marcello: Memorandum. March 29, 1967. To: Louis Ivon. From: Cliency Navarre. Re: Interview—Tom C. Brister—W/M 24 years. NODA. NARA.

p. 106, line 4: figured out that Jimmy Johnson had been spying on him: Jimmy Johnson interviewed by Walter Sheridan, Undated, c. May 1967.

p. 106, line 7: Ferrie tells Krasnoff he is going to kill himself: Conversation with Sanford Krasnoff, March 5, 2002.

p. 106, line 13: Ferrie tells Lardner he did not know Oswald: Statement of George Lardner. February 22, 1967. Questions are by William Gurvich. NODA. NARA. See, for example, the photograph of Ferrie and Oswald together at a CAP cookout and included in this book.

p. 106, line 24: David Ferrie's "suicide notes" are available in the Garrison papers. NARA.

p. 106, line 33: under the microscope: Richard N. Billings interview with Dr. Nicholas Chetta. March 2, 1967. AARC.

p. 106, line 34: Krasnoff was at the scene: Interview with Irvin L. Magri Jr. February 17, 2002.

p. 106, line 37: city dump: Conversation with Alvin Beaubouef, March 12, 2002.

p. 106, line 39: "the conditions under which the District Attorney of New Orleans": Memorandum. July 9, 1971. Re: Matters Concerning the Garrison Investigation by Richard Popkin. AARC.

p. 106, line 42: "poison! poison!" Interview with John Volz, May 21, 1998.

p. 107, line 4: "slipshod": Letter from Dr. Martin Palmer to Joan Mellen, June 18, 2001. Interview with Martin Palmer, August 9, 2002.

p. 107, line 7: Chetta reports to the FBI: FBI. To: SAC, NO. From: SA Donald L. Hughes. February 23, 1967. 89-69-1445. NARA.

p. 107, line 8: Jim Garrison wondered whether Ferrie committed suicide with PROLOID: Memorandum. December 11, 1967. To: Jim Alcock.

From: Jim Garrison. Re: Autopsy of David Ferrie. NODA. NARA.

p. 107, line 11: drugs could cause an aneurysm: Memorandum. April 7, 1967. To: File—Ferrie's Death. From: Jim Garrison. Re: New Drugs Which Can Cause an Aneurysm." NODA. See also: Memorandum to File: Ferrie's Death. April 7, 1967. From: Jim Garrison. Re: Physicians and Druggists. NARA.

p. 107, line 14: "all burned up": Interview with Dr. Frank Minyard, January 8, 1998. The autopsy protocol reads: "There is a small area of dryness of the inner aspect of the upper lip on the right side. This area measures 3/4 in. in length and is somewhat reddish brown in color. There is a less defined area on the lower lip immediately inferior to the lesion in the upper lip." Autopsy Protocol. Orleans Parish Coroner's Office. Name: David W. Ferrie. Date & Time of Death: 2-22-67 at 1:00 p.m. Date & Time of Autopsy: 2-22-67 at 3:00 p.m. Classification of Death: Natural. The protocol is signed by Ronald A. Welsh, M.D., Pathologist. Note the impossible time of death: Jimmy Johnson discovered Ferrie's body before noon.

p. 107, line 17: "traumatically inserted": Minyard makes this statement in Stephen Tyler's documentary, *He Must Have Something.*

p. 107, line 19: "eggshell cranium": Dan Campbell interviewed by Jim DiEugenio, September 19, 1994.

p. 107, line 21: "weakened arterie": To: Jim Garrison. From: Barbara Reid and Joel Palmer. Re: Conversation with Morris Brownlee. October 8, 1968. NODA. NARA.

p. 107, line 22: Dr. Dimitri Contostavlos: See Dr. Dimitri L. Contostavlos to Richard A. Sprague, November 18, 1976. HSCA 000479. Assistant medical examiner when Richard A. Sprague was Philadelphia district attorney, Contostavlos contacted Sprague about Ferrie when he became chief counsel of the House Select Committee. Also: Interview with Dr. Dimitri L. Contostavlos, August 19, 2001.

p. 107, line 28: before midnight: James and Wardlow, *Plot or Politics,* p. 40.

p. 107, line 32: "major inconsistency": as reported in the *Times-Picayune,* and in FBI report: To:

Director. From: New Orleans. February 23, 1967. 124-10256-1-188. 89-69-1448. NARA.

p. 107, line 34: Robert F. Kennedy telephones Dr. Chetta: See Edward T. Haslam, *Mary, Ferrie & the Monkey Virus*, p. 18.

p. 108, line 2: "gales of history": *Playboy* interview with Jim Garrison, **p. 176.**

p. 108, line 3: "I don't want to rule out anything": *Life* magazine dialogue at Garrison press conference on Ferrie death. February 22, 1967. Papers of Richard N. Billings, Box 4, folder 48.

p. 108, line 7: "a fun time for Dave": Interview with John Wilson, November 28, 2000.

p. 108, line 13: "natural causes verdicts" and Nicholas Chetta; "just like a prostitute": Tape of Jack Martin with L. J. Delsa and Robert Buras. February 25, 1978. Tape recording.

p. 108, line 33: the death of Del Valle: Memo 2/1476. To: Dave Marston. From: Gaeton Fonzi. Courtesy of Mr. Fonzi.

p. 103, line 33: Del Valle: FBI. To: Director, FBI. From: SAC, Miami. August 1, 1966. Subject: Eladio Ceferino del Valle Gutierrez. 100-27851-11-27. NARA. See also: "Friend of Murdered Miami Man Tells His Story Exclusively for *Enquirer* Readers" by Diego Gonzales Tendedera, and "Miami Murder Linked to JFK Plot" by Charles Golden, *National Enquirer.* Vol. 41, No. 34. April 30, 1967. See also James and Wardlow, p. 46.

p. 108, line 36: Kennedy "must be killed": "JFK & the Cuban Connection," by Dick Russell. Electronic Assassinations. Newsletter, Issue #2. Russell is quoting General Fabian Escalante in Cuba.

p. 108, line 38: promised to help Alberto Fowler: The message from del Valle to Jim Garrison came in a telephone call to Alberto Fowler from Bernardo de Torres: Memorandum. February 26, 1967. To: Jim Garrison. From: Louis Ivon. Re: Telephone conversation with Alberto Fowler. NODA. NARA.

p. 108, line 39: Houston suspected: Lawrence Houston ponders the death of del Valle: Lawrence R. Houston to Honorable J. Walter Yeagley. Re: United States District Court, Southern District, Florida. *United States v. Rolando Masferrer,* et al. AARC.

p. 109, line 3: General Escalante, Tony Cuesta and Del Valle: See Dick Russell, *The Man Who Knew Too Much* (New York: Carroll & Graf, 2003 (revised edition), pp. 458-460.

p. 109, line 13: Charlie Ward: Interview with Lou Ivon, May 27, 2001.

p. 109, line 29: "we don't have the wherewithal": Interview with John Volz, May 21, 1998.

p. 109, line 35: Memorandum for file: 8 February 1973. Subject: Ferrie, David W., signed Bruce L. Solie DC/SRS. Approved for release 1993/CIA Historical Review Program. NARA.

CHAPTER 8

p. 111, Epigraph: "He was hardly Joe Smith": Jim Garrison to Jonathan Blackmer, September 14, 1977. NARA.

p. 111, line 7: "substantial reward": "Long Proposes Federal Reward to Assist Probe." *Times-Picayune,* February 25, 1967, p. 6.

p. 111, line 9: almost thirty thousand dollars: See Bethell diary. Sunday, February 11th. AARC.

p. 111, line 16: Nor did Rault and Shilstone view their own CIA connections as a contradiction. Shilstone was a friend of Lloyd A. Ray and Hunter Leake: Memorandum To: Director, Domestic Contact Service. Att'n: Operational Support Staff (Musulin). From: Chief, New Orleans Office. Subject: Case 49364—Garrison Investigation. Ref: DC/CI/R & A. Memorandum dated June 19, 1967. NARA.

p. 111, line 17: a "civic effort": "The Garrison Investigation: How and Why It Began." *New Orleans* magazine, p. 50.

p. 111, line 18: "snow job": "Garrison's Financiers Tighten Purse Strings," *Los Angeles Times.* June 11, 1967. Section A, p. 18.

p. 111, line 21: Avery Spear sends a contribution: Avery Spear to Jim Garrison. March 3, 1967. NARA.

p. 111, line 21: McKeithen sent $5,000 from a special fund, and another $10,000 in January of 1968, requesting no accounting: "Governor Won't Query Garrison," *Times-Picayune,* February 1, 1971, Section 1,

p. 1. See also: Jim Garrison to Honorable John J. McKeithen, January 30, 1968.

p. 112, line 6: "murder of Martin Luther King": FBI memorandum. To: Director, FBI. From: SAC, New Orleans. Subject: MURKIN (code name for the murder of Martin Luther King). 124-10269-10044. 89-69-4032, 4033. NARA.

p. 112, line 7: Joseph Sylvester checks up on Joe Rault: April 13, 1967. Searched by Jean B. Hearn, Clerk. NARA.

p. 112, line 11: Korns checks the law with respect to Truth and Consequences contributions: Memorandum to Jim Garrison. From: Louise Korns. Undated. NOPL.

p. 112, line 16: "$9,032": "Garrison Spends $9,032 Donated by T and C Group," *Times-Picayune,* June 10, 1967. Section 1, p. 1.

p. 112, line 18: "they didn't meet anymore": Jim Garrison at the New Orleans conference.

p. 112, line 19: Raymond Cummings, testimony and polygraph: Memorandum. To: Jim Garrison. From: William Gurvich. Subject: Raymond Cummings—Interview With. Interviews were on February 25th and 26th, 1967. NODA. NARA.

p. 112, line 27: Jacob could not be trusted: Notes appended to memorandum. Subject: Raymond Cummings.

p. 112, line 29: "possibly good lead": Garrison's note is written on an Office of the District Attorney, Parish of Orleans Rackets Division cover sheet, attached to a copy of the Jacob polygraph. NODA. NARA.

p. 112, line 31: Clyde Malcolm Limbough: Memorandum. March 6, 1967. To: Jim Garrison. From: James L. Alcock. Re: Clyde Malcolm Limbough. NODA. Found in Papers of Richard N. Billings, Box 2, folder 29. Georgetown University, Washington, DC.

p. 112, line 37: E. Carl McNabb joins the Garrison investigation: Interview with E. Carl McNabb. See also: Notes: Bill Turner. 8/5/76 by Gaeton Fonzi. NARA.

p. 113, line 20: Ferrie demonstrates his acquaintance with Perry Russo: Statement of David William Ferrie. 10 pages. Pages of Richard N. Billings, Box 1, folder 3. Georgetown University, Washington, DC.

p. 113, line 27: Moo Moo was to write two memos of his interviews with Perry Russo. Moo Moo wrote up the memo of Russo taking sodium pentothal in New Orleans on February 27th, before he wrote his memo of the Saturday, February 25th, interview with Russo in Baton Rouge. The events described in the sodium pentothal session make it clear that Russo had already identified Clay Shaw from his photograph at the first meeting in Baton Rouge. The visit to Baton Rouge itself was written up by Sciambra out of chronological order, then backdated to Monday, February 27, 1967.

p. 114, line 3: "Your boy's been shot!" Perry Raymond Russo interviewed by William Davy, August 31, 1994.

p. 114, line 13: "I knew the guy": Perry Russo interviewed by Peter Whitmey. Taped Interview. August 6, 1990.

p. 114, line 28: Russo's timetable: 9:30 a.m. that Monday. See Perry Raymond Russo recorded interview on January 29, 1971, with William Gurvich. MCC.

p. 114, line 33: Buras sketches "Clem" Bertrand: Interviews with Robert Buras, January 24, 2002; January 28, 2002.

p. 115, line 7: "to add to what they already had": Interview with Louis Ivon. January 12, 2000.

p. 115, line 20: "there's not a chance at all": For Dr. Chetta's reactions to Russo's sodium pentothal session, see Billings' notes marked 1919 and 1515 as well as Dick/Nancy 222222. Papers of Richard N. Billings.

p. 115, line 25: Moo Moo drove Russo: as testified by Perry Raymond Russo at the Preliminary Hearing held on March 16, 1967.

p. 115, line 26: chiseled face: Perry Raymond Russo interviewed by William Davy, August 31, 1994.

p. 115, line 30: in bed with Shaw and Ferrie together: Interview with Perry Rousseau [sic] by Jack N. Rogers. June 10, 1967. Papers of Jack N. Rogers.

p. 115, line 31: Lewallen had denied that he had seen Shaw and Ferrie together: Memorandum. February 20, 1967. To: Jim Garrison. From: James L. Alcock. Re: James R. Lewallen. NODA. NARA.

p. 115, line 39: Oster found a levee

board policeman who saw Shaw and Oswald together: FBI Airtel. To: Director, FBI. From: SAC, New Orleans. March 2, 1967. 124-10253-10049. 89-69-1543. NARA.

p. 115, line 39: Oster told both Ivon and the Bureau that Shaw was Bertrand: FBI teletype. February 25, 1967. To: Director, FBI. From: SAC, New Orleans. Re: New Orleans teletype dated February twenty four nineteen sixty seven. 124-10241-10130. 89-69-1503. NARA.

p. 115, line 41: Shaw lies when he says he didn't know Dean Andrews: Memorandum. February 9, 1967. To: Jim Garrison. From: Andrew J. Sciambra. Re: Smith Investigation—My Interview with Clay Shaw 12/23/66. Interview with Gordon Novel, confirmed in Steve Plotkin: Interview on April 7, 1967, by Salvatore Panzeca and Robert A. Wilson. Papers of Edward F. Wegmann. NARA. Interview with Gordon Novel: Novel says he told Garrison that he and Andrews had met with Shaw.

p. 116, line 6: Mrs. Jeff Hug corroborates: FBI. To: Director and Dallas. From: New Orleans. May 7, 1967. 124-10237-10414. 89-69-2089. NARA.

p. 116, line 18: "lone, grim, meditative figure": See *Traffic Manager* ("The Shipper's Guide"). Vol. 42, No. 11. November 1967, p. 27.

p. 116, line 24: "detonate a chain reaction": Richard N. Billings, "The Case for a Conspiracy (V): Anatomy of the Investigation. Papers of Richard N. Billings."

p. 116, line 27: Bernard Giquel's notes of his interview with Jim Garrison on February 28, 1967, are available in the papers of Richard E. Sprague, Special Collections, Georgetown University.

p. 116, line 33: "designated as a person not to be contacted": FBI Memorandum. To: All Agents. From: SAC, New Orleans. 89-69-1549. March 1, 1967. NARA.

p. 116, line 35: Division 5: Branigan of Division 5 enlists Bob Lenihan: FBI Memorandum. To: File. From: SAC. 89-69-1516. March 1, 1967. NARA.

p. 116, line 38: Shaw receives his subpoena: See *The Clay Shaw Diary*, "The Arrest." See also: Memorandum. March 1, 1967. To: Louis Ivon. From:

Detective Lester Otillio. Re: Clay Shaw. NODA. NARA.

p. 116, line 39 "for questioning": Interview with Lester Otillio, September 27, 2001.

p. 117, line 4: "very nervous": Interview with Lynn Pelham, September 16, 2001.

p. 117, line 6: "three witnesses proving you knew Dave Ferrie": *The Clay Shaw Diary*, "The Arrest."

p. 117, line 9: photographs of various Cubans: Interview with Salvatore Panzeca, June 4, 2000.

p. 117, line 12: not uncommon to offer a polygraph: Interview with John Volz, June 13, 2001.

p. 117, line 16: his homosexuality an open secret: Interview with Iris Kelso, May 19, 1998. Kelso was a *States-Item* reporter who knew Shaw socially.

The FBI had no difficulty in tracing Shaw's homosexuality back to when he was fifteen years old: FBI. HQ 124-10299-10023. Cr 190-5414.2. To: Mr. Powers. From: A. H. McCreight. Subject: FOIA Requests (51) of Dean G. Farrer. May 3, 1977. NARA. The report reads that Shaw had a "sadistic, masochistic and homosexual character": March 2, 1967. Radio teletype. To: Bureau/Dallas/New Orleans. From: San Antonio. 021926. Lee Harvey Oswald, AKA IS-R-Cuba. 00: Dallas. 89-69-1534. NARA. The Bureau also had a call from a busboy named Myron Shaw, who said Clay Shaw had whipped him on a number of occasions and was "queer for beatings." Memorandum to SAC. From: Roy Simon, Clerk. March 14, 1967. 89-69-1675. NARA.

p. 117, line 17: Shaw had assembled his lawyers long before his arrest on March 1st: Interview with Jack Dempsey, May 20, 1998.

p. 117, line 20: "Está maricón?" Interview with Salvatore Panzeca, June 4, 2000.

p. 117, line 32: Gurvich insists on making the announcement of Clay Shaw's arrest: Interview with Numa Bertel, October 9, 2000. "It's my birthday": Interview with Numa Bertel, May 19, 1998.

p. 117, line 37: Ivon uses information about Sciambra's first meeting with Russo in his search warrant, despite the fact that Sciambra's de-

NOTES

scription of that meeting had not yet been written. Author Joe Biles has noted this fact.

p. 118, line 4: Habighorst has never heard the name Clay Bertrand: Interview with Lou Ivon, May 27, 2001.

p. 118, line 10: "what names?": Office of the District Attorney. January 23, 1968. Statement of Aloysius J. Habighorst. Re: Fingerprinting and Facts Contained on Fingerprinting Card. (Bearing No. 125-388. New Orleans Police Department). NODA. NARA.

p. 118, line 21: pale green silk: description of Clay Shaw's house is from Richard N. Billings, 55555. . . . Shaw. AARC.

p. 118, line 27: many hands: Alford describes the scene in *"He Must Have Something."*

p. 118, line 30: the black gown bore whip marks: FBI teletype. To: Director. From: New Orleans. March 2, 1967. 62-169060-4654. NARA.

p. 118, line 32: "Let's dust and lift": Interview with William Alford, May 28, 1998.

p. 118, line 35: the list of items taken from Shaw's house on March 1st is available at NOPL.

p. 118, line 37: white satin linings that had never seen a pavement: Interview with Irene Dempsey, May 25, 1999. Dempsey was secretary to Dr. Robert Heath, head of the psychiatry department at Tulane.

p. 119, line 3: "sadistic, homosexual abnormality": Interview with Dr. Robert Heath, May 25, 1999. Jim Garrison repaid Heath for the favor, and when Heath wanted to study the effect of marijuana on the brains of monkeys, Garrison secured the marijuana for research on human subjects. Heath was experimenting with injecting the blood of schizophrenics into sane people with electrodes on their heads to measure the reaction, in an effort to determine whether and to what degree mental illness was physically based, rather than environmentally induced. Garrison contacted Attorney General Jack P. F. Gremillion and helped Heath gain access to volunteers from Angola. Heath was well-respected, and Russell Long called him for help with his uncle, Earl Long, when Long had taken to sleeping with a gun under his pillow and urinating

in an empty soft drink bottle on the floor of the state legislature.

p. 119, line 4: "I don't want that factor": Interview with Numa Bertel, February 6, 2001.

p. 119, line 5: "Phi Beta Kappa sadist": Notes of Richard N. Billings, 17 17 17.

p. 119, line 12: "the mysterious death or killing" Griscom Morgan to Tom Bethell. January 28, 1967 [the context suggests 1968, however]. NARA. Regarding the *LIFE* investigation: "a queer was flogged to death:" To: Dick Billings, *LIFE* From: Ben Cate, Houston. March 31, 1967. Papers of Richard N. Billings. Box 2, folder 21.

p. 119, line 17: "using wine bottles": Memorandum. March 6, 1967. To: Louis Ivon. From: Al Oser. Re: Investigative Leads. NODA. NARA.

p. 119, line 18: among the first people Shaw notified: Letter to Jim Garrison. January 1968. Anonymous. Crisman has the same sexual preference as Shaw: Memorandum. February 19, 1968. To: Jim Garrison. From: William Boxley. Re: Interview with Bob Lavender. NODA. NARA. That Crisman was in New Orleans twenty-four times, that Crisman was the person Shaw did indeed call when he realized he was in trouble, has been confirmed by Thomas Edward Beckham.

p. 119, line 26: "a terribly cynical and corrupt man": *Playboy* (October 1967), p. 68.

p. 119, line 30: "I have more in common with Clay Shaw": Interview with Joseph Wershba, July 14, 2000.

p. 119, line 36: "fruit fly": To: Jim Garrison. From: Robert Head. Re: The House of Bultman. Barbara Glancey Reid. 5568. NARA.

p. 119, line 40: "Is this another Wilmer?" Interview with H. John Bremermann, July 30, 1999.

p. 120, line 2: "personal fear": Notes on Clay Shaw. Barbara Reid file of the papers of Jim Garrison. Harry Connick files. NARA.

p. 120, line 3: David Chandler invents a story about Donald V. Organ calling Clay Shaw: Lang for Haskell for Billings. From: Chandler, New Orleans. "FYI only, his attorney—Don Organ—the day after Shaw's arrest informed Shaw he would be pleased to defend Shaw, free of charge": Papers of Richard N. Billings, Box 2, folder 14.

The story is false: Interviews with Donald V. Organ.

p. 120, line 16: "a one-eyed nigger Jew:" Interview with Mrs. Lenore Ward, August 7 and August 8, 1967.

p. 120, line 29: "I saw him throw a glass of wine": "of 'Not Guilty,'" by Rosemary James. *New Orleans* magazine. March 1971, p. 60.

p. 120, line 29: "I know you're the District Attorney": Interview with Liz Garrison, May 28, 1998.

p. 120, line 42: numbered Pershing Gervais: See February 21, 1967. Memo: to Billings, from Chandler. Papers of Richard N. Billings.

p. 121, line 2: Mrs. Brennan denies that she was at Clay Shaw's table: Conversation with Mrs. Ella Brennan, September 27, 2001. In general for this incident: Interviews with Mrs. Liz Garrison, May 28, 1998, and Mrs. Lenore Ward, August 7 and August 8, 2000; October 4, 2001.

p. 121, line 4: the wine landed on Shaw's white linen suit: Interview with Wilmer Thomas, March 7, 2001.

p. 121, line 7: In Jack Sawyer's memory: Interview with Jack Sawyer, May 24, 1998. The story of Shaw and Garrison at Brennan's runs through the bowels of the FBI: FBI 124-10251-10211. 89-69-3209, 3210. To: Director, FBI. From: SAC, New Orleans. June 21, 1967. This report by FBI informant Betty Parent (No. 949-C) came to Regis Kennedy in June of 1967. Parent stated "this was no personal information." She admitted that she was only passing on a rumor.

p. 121, line 9: Schiller reported three homosexual sources: Regarding Lawrence Schiller's reports to the FBI about "three homosexual sources. . . .": FBI, To: Director, FBI. From: SAC, Los Angeles. 124-10259-10152. 89-69-1897, 1898. March 23, 1967. NARA. Regarding "code name": FBI. To: Director, FBI. From: SAC, Los Angeles. 62-109060-5420. June 19, 1967. NARA.

p. 121, line 15: handwriting comparisons: diary of Richard N. Billings, p. 35.

p. 121, line 16: CIA would create a document: See William Davy, *Let Justice Be Done,* **p. 197.**

p. 121, line 20: Barbara Bennett: Interview with Barbara Bennett, February 6, 2001. Another who knew Shaw as Bertrand, was of course,

Daniel Campbell: Interview with Daniel Campbell, June 8, 2002. See also Daniel Campbell interviewed by Jim DiEugenio, September 14, 1994; and Memorandum. May 14, 1969. To: Jim Garrison. From: Andrew J. Sciambra. Re: Shaw Leads II (Interview with Dan Campbell). NODA. NARA.

p. 121, line 22: Shaw a frequent visitor to Pat O'Brien's: Memorandum. November 29, 1967. To: Jim Garrison. From: Andrew Sciambra. Re: LEE OSWALD. NODA. NARA.

p. 121, line 28: "We were intelligent women": interview with Rickey Planche, May 21, 2005.

p. 121, line 31: Fred Leemans Jr. saw "Clay Bertrand": Statement and Interrogation of Fred Hendrick Leemans Jr. in the Office of the District Attorney, Parish of Orleans, on Friday, May 5, 1967. Leemans was questioned by Robert E. Lee. NODA. NARA. Leemans then repudiated his statement: Re: Clay L. Shaw. May 24, 1967. Statement to the file by F. Irvin Dymond. NARA. See also: Memorandum. To: Charles R. Ward. From: Robert E. Lee. June 19, 1967. Re: Fred Leemans. NODA. NARA. Leemans' final word was on January 6, 1969, Statement to the district attorney, Orleans Parish.

p. 121, line 34: Virginia Johnson: Virginia Johnson saw a letter: Memorandum. To: Louis Ivon. From: Gary Sanders. Subject: Virginia Johnson—Clay Shaw's Maid. January 15, 1968. NODA. NARA.

p. 121, line 37: Valentine Ashworth: See Ashworth to Jim Garrison, July 19, 1967. Interview with Valentine Ashworth by Richard V. Burnes and Sergeant Sedgebeer. September 7, 1967. Lake Charles Parish Prison. Ashworth calls the FBI and says he's connected to the Garrison investigation, see: To: SAC. From: William H. Deily Jr. Subject: Valentine Ashworth. February 20, 1968. 89-69-3874. NODA. NARA. Valentine Ashworth identifies a photograph of Shaw as Bertrand: Memorandum. To: Jim Garrison. From: Richard V. Burnes. Re: Valentine Ashworth. September 8, 1967. NODA. NARA. The Agency checks into Ashworth: see 3 January 1968. Memorandum For: DC/CI/R & A. Subject: Valentine Ashworth. NARA.

p. 121, line 40: Steve Bordelon

found a witness: Interview with Steve Bordelon, June 14, 2000.

p. 121, line 42: Greg Donnelly: Greg Donnelly's statement came to Jim secondhand from Dr. Jacob Harold Kety: Memorandum. To: Louie Ivon. From: Gary Sanders. Re: Dr. Jacob Harold Kety. February 14, 1968. NODA. NARA.

p. 122, line 3: Thomas Breitner meets Clay Bertrand: See Notes of Richard Popkin, August 15, 1968, p. 31.

p. 122, line 9: "disciplinary crew of queers": Interview with Charles W. Frank Jr. May 11, 2000.

p. 122, line 12: dressed as a French executioner: Memorandum: November 28, 1967. To: Louis Ivon. From: C. J. Navarre. Re: LEAD FILE UNIT #23. NODA. NARA.

p. 122, line 16: "See Clay Shaw for prices": Memorandum. February 14, 1968. To: Louis Ivon. From: Gary Sanders. Re: Dr. Jacob Harold Kety. NODA. NARA.

p. 122, line 20: Pope Clement shields homosexuals in the fourteenth century: Sophia Menache, *Clement V., Cambridge Studies in Medieval Life and Thought* (Cambridge: Cambridge University Press, 1998), pp. 20-34; Guillaume Mollat, *The Popes of Avignon* 1305-1378. Translated by Janet Love (London: Thomas Nelson and Sonsn, 1963), pp. 3-8; Fernand Mourret, *History of the Catholic Church.* Eight Volumes. Translated by Newton Thompson (London: B. Herder Book Company, 1930, 1955), Volume Five. pp. 48-65.

p. 122, line 24: the FBI learns that Shaw and Jones have rented an apartment: FBI. From: New Orleans. To: Director, FBI. March 21, 1967. 89-69-1778, 1779. 4 pages. NARA. See also: FBI. 124-10053-10100. 62-109060-4925. March 21, 1967. NARA.

p. 122, line 36: Evelyn Jahncke hears about a postal carrier: Memorandum. To: Jim Garrison. From: Andrew J. Sciambra. February 19, 1968. NODA. NARA.

p. 123, line 40: Ferrie introduces Broshears to Shaw as "Clara": Interview of Raymond Broshears—conducted by Steve Jaffe, James Alcock, Louis Ivon. No date. NODA. NARA. The presence of Jaffe places the inter-

view in 1968. See also: Memorandum. To: Jim Garrison. From: Steven J. Burton. Subject: Rev. Raymond Broshears. NODA. NARA.

p. 123, line 5: "I know his slender hips": Broshears quoted at the New Orleans conference by Moo Moo Sciambra, September 1968.

p. 123, line 7: "one of the best cops": Reverend Raymond Broshears to James Alcock, August 16, 1968. NODA. NARA.

p. 123, line 15: Ferrie has privileged access into Shaw's office: FBI teletype marked URGENT. To: Director. From: New Orleans. March 4, 1967. 89-69-1569. NARA.

p. 123, line 18: "a big fellow who walked with a very slight limp": Statement of Herbert R. Wagner Jr. president of Herb Wagner Finance Service. December 6, 1967. NODA. NARA.

p. 123, line 20: L. P. Davis provides information on Shaw, Ferrie and the fishing camp: Memorandum. March 27, 1967. To: James L. Alcock. From: Charles R. Ward. Re: Special Investigation. NODA. NARA.

p. 123, line 22: Ferrie flies Shaw to a fishing camp: Memorandum. To: Jim Garrison. From: William Gurvich, Special Aide. April 5, 1967. Subject: Freemason Island Fishing Camp. NODA. NARA.

p. 123, line 23: Owners identified: Nat Milligan identifies Clay Shaw from his photograph: Memorandum. April 5, 1967. To: Jim Garrison. From: William Gurvich, Special Aide. Subject: Freemason Island Fishing Camp. NODA. NARA.

p. 123, line 25: Carroll S. Thomas: FBI. To: SAC. From: SA John Henry Love Jr. March 16, 1967. Interview with Carroll S. Thomas. 89-69-1780. NARA.

p. 123, line 29: Oswald knew someone named "Clay": Interview with Layton Martens. March 12, 1967. NODA. NARA.

p. 123, line 33: Henry Lesnick persuades David Logan: Interview with Henry Lesnick, October 12, 2001. Interview with Mary Lesnick, October 14, 2001.

p. 123, line 37: Barbara Bennett saw Oswald at Dixie's: Interview with Barbara Bennett, February 6, 2001.

p. 123, line 38: Oswald is at Dixie's Bar of Music, seems to want to associate with "gay guys": Memorandum. November 29, 1967. To: Jim Garrison. From: Andrew Sciambra. Re: Lee Oswald. NODA. NARA.

p. 123, line 39: David Logan: What survives in the files is a transcription of a telephone conversation between Logan and Jimmy Alcock. April 13, 1968. See also: *On the Trail of the Assassins*, p. 119.

p. 124, line 2: on glass: Jim DiEugenio interview with Art Kunkin. June 23, 1994.

p. 124, line 6: "for sexual purposes": Interview with William A. Morris by William Boxley and William Martin. July 12, 1967. Transcribed July 14, 1967. NODA. NARA.

p. 124, line 18: Betty Parrott confirms part of D'Avy's story: Memorandum. December 18, 1967. To: Jim Garrison. From: Andrew J. Sciambra. Re: Interview with "BP" In Re: Friends of Democratic Cuba. NODA. NARA.

p. 124, line 19: only in the late 1970s: Leander D'Avy interviewed by the House Select Committee. Interview by Belford Lawson and Jack Moriarty. June 23, 1977. 001685. NARA.

p. 124, line 21: was a Clay Bertrand working there?: Memorandum. December 5, 1967. To: Jim Garrison. From: Andrew Sciambra. Re: Interview of Leander D'Avy. NODA. NARA. See also: Memorandum. August 14, 1967. To: Jim Garrison. From: Andrew J. Sciambra. Re: Telephone Conversation with Mr. Leander D'Avy. NODA. NARA.

p. 124, line 30: "Clay Shaw's alleged homosexuality": Jim Garrison to Ted Gandolfo. April 14, 1986.

p. 124, line 40: Ronald R. Raymond "did not want to be involved": Statement of Ronald R. Raymond. Office of the District Attorney. Confidential. NODA. NARA.

p. 125, line 2: Jessie Parker comes forward: Her Affidavit for the Shaw trial is dated January 29, 1969. NODA. NARA.

p. 125, line 6: seamstress for a family Numa Bertel knew: Interview with Numa Bertel, October 9, 2000.

p. 125, line 11: photographs of the guest book: Memorandum. September 20, 1967. To: Louis Ivon. From: Cliency Navarre. Re: Photographs Taken at Moisant Airport of a Clay Bertrand Signature. NODA. NARA.

p. 125, line 16: Moran became a DD/P asset on or about 15 December 1962: See: CIA. Memorandum For: Director, Domestic Contact Service. Attention: Mr. George S. Musulin. Subject: Garrison Investigation of Kennedy Assassination: Alfred J. MORAN, 201-776772. 24 November 1967: From: Donovan E. Pratt, DC/CI/R & A. Record number: 104-10170-10154. NARA.

p. 125, line 19: a contact of JMWAVE: JMWAVE 0425, 100-300017. Miami station reports their last contact with Moran was on November 19, 1967. REF: Director 55441.

p. 125, line 31: "positive Shaw was not at the airport: Memorandum. November 17, 1967. To: Jim Garrison. From: Jim Alcock, Sgt. Tom Duffy. Re: Mr. Alfred Moran. NODA. NARA.

p. 125, line 32: he disliked him: Memorandum. November 17, 1967. To: Jim Garrison. From: Jim Alcock, Sgt. Tom Duffy. Re: Mr. Alfred Moran. NODA. NARA.

p. 126, line 1: Moran "objected strenuously but in vain to Clay Shaw's appointment as managing director": Lloyd Ray to Headquarters. Att'n: Office of General Counsel. December 13, 1967. Reference your 506 and our 007. Subject: Case 49364—Garrison Investigation. NODA. NARA.

p. 126, line 4: "ironclad case": Ray writes to Headquarters: NO-406-67. 15 November 1967. To: Director, Domestic Contact Service. Att'n: Operational Support Staff (Musulin). From: Chief, New Orleans Office. Subject: Case 49364—Garrison Investigation. OGC 67-2195. See also: Memorandum Number 8: Garrison and the Kennedy Assassination. January 11, 1968. 25 pages. 104-10435-10009. RUSS HOLMES WORK FILE. From: DDO/PIC To: CIA Staff. Title: official routing slip with attached resanitized copy of Memo #8 of the Garrison Package. NARA.

p. 126, line 9: CIA runs a check on Moran: November 24, 1967. Memorandum For: Director, Domestic Contact Service. Attention: Mr. George S. Musulin. Subject: Garrison Investigation of Kennedy Assassination (Alfred J. Moran). Reference: Report of DCS office, New Orleans, file no. NO-406-67, 15 November 1967.

Subject: Case 49364—Garrison Investigation. Signed by Donovan E. Pratt, DC/CI/R & A. NARA.

p. 126, line 18: Lawrence Houston cleanses the record: 30 November 1967. To: New Orleans. From: Office of General Counsel. CITE: Headquarters 487 Ref: No-406-67. Signed by Lawrence Houston.

p. 126, line 35: a slipped disk sends Moran to bed: Headquarters: Attn: Office of General Counsel. Reference your 487 and our 006. "restricted handling supervisor only" and no signature on this cable. Sent by Lloyd Ray.

p. 127, line 4: Lloyd A. Ray reports back to Houston: December 13, 1967. Ray to Att'n: Office of General Counsel. Reference your 506 and our 007. Subject: Case 49364—Garrison Investigation.

CHAPTER 9

p. 128, Epigraph: "it is fair to conclude": Jim Garrison's Notes on PERMINDEX. NARA.

p. 128, line 6: Shaw's name came up: Cartha DeLoach briefs Ramsey Clark in the morning. Interview with Ramsey Clark, February 21, 2000. "Shaw's name had come up in our investigation": To: Mr. Tolson. From: C. D. DeLoach. 3/2/67. 62-109060-4635. NARA.

p. 128, line 8: a fragment: Report of the Latent Fingerprint Section. Your file number: 89-68. Re: Assassination of President John F. Kennedy. 11/22/63, Dallas, Texas. December 5, 1963. 89-69-1085.

p. 128, line 36: "Mr. Bertrand and Mr. Shaw were the same man": Ibid., "Clark Discounts a Shaw Conspiracy." See also: FBI Memorandum. To: Mr. Tolson. From: C. D. DeLoach. March 2, 1967. 62-109060-4628. NARA.

p. 129, line 1: the FBI had manipulated him: Interview with Ramsey Clark, February 21, 2000.

p. 129, line 2: Clark has been kept in the dark by Hoover and Helms: Interview with Gordon Novel, January 16, 2000. Hoover then directed that all inquiries on Shaw's having been cleared be sent directly to Ramsey Clark: FBI 124-10237-10347. 89-69-2007. NARA. Ramsey Clark asked Hoover for information on Jim Garrison, but was refused: "Information concerning these individuals is being furnished to the Department at Seat of Government," he said, "where warranted as developments occur involving them": To: SAC, New Orleans. From: Director, FBI. Personal attention. 89-69-1775. Clark's original request is: To: Director. Federal Bureau of Investigation. From: The Attorney General. March 13, 1967. 129-11. NARA.

See also FBI Record Number 124-10237-10254. Agency file number: 89-69-1774. To: Director, Federal Bureau of Investigation From: The Attorney General. Subject: Assassination of President John F. Kennedy, Warren Commission Records. March 13, 1967. 129-11. NARA. The reply from Hoover: To: SAC, New Orleans. From: Director, FBI. March 16, 1967. FBI Record Number: 124-10237-10255. Agency file number: 89-69-1775. NARA.

p. 129, line 4: denying that Shaw had been investigated: "FBI never Investigated Shaw—Clark," *States-Item.* June 3, 1967. p. 1.

p. 129, line 5: Shaw "involved in an FBI investigation": "Clark Discounts A Shaw Conspiracy," by Robert B. Semple Jr. *The New York Times,* March 3, 1967.

p. 129, line 9: "wound up as tight": *LIFE* magazine memo from Angeloff. April 5, 1967. Papers of Richard N. Billings. Box 2, folder 21. Georgetown University, Washington, DC.

p. 129, line 10: "quite calm and assured": US Government Memorandum. CIA. To: Director, Domestic Contact Service. From: Chief, New Orleans Office. No. 133-67. April 6, 1967. Signed by Lloyd A. Ray. NARA. Bringuier, informing to CIA, is quoting Fowler.

p. 129, line 15: "a great admirer of Kennedy": *Penthouse* interview: Clay Shaw. British Edition. September 1969. p. 28.

See also Shaw interviewed by Walter Sheridan. NARA. Undated. This is number 24 in the MCC collection of Sheridan interviews.

p. 129, line 18: Ralph Slovenko gives a talk at Tulane: Interview with Ralph Slovenko, April 3, 1998. Slovenko's speech was published in *Tulane Studies in Political Science* 4: 79, 1957, under the title, "Nationalization and Nasser."

p. 129, line 30: Shaw seen with anti-Castro Cubans: Diary of Richard N. Billings, File 51b. AARC.

p. 129, line 32: Shaw was "helping us": CIA 1424-492-S. Enclosure 15. Subject: S. M. Kauffroth. FBI document dated April 6, 1967. Houston, Texas. 5627. CIA disseminated FBI report DDB 77370. NARA.

p. 129, line 33: "unscrupulous adventurer": CIA memorandum #2. May 8, 1967. Subject: Garrison and the Kennedy Assassination. Reference: CI/R & A Memorandum of 26 April 1967, subject as above. Enclosure 4. NARA.

p. 129, line 35: his conversation: Interview with Jack Sawyer, May 24, 1998.

p. 129, line 42: "I believe in beauty and ecstasy": Interview with Donald Scheuler, May 23, 1998.

p. 130, line 3: the Fowlers would not have seen Clay Shaw socially: Interview with Elizabeth Swanson, July 12, 2001. Swanson is a niece of Alberto Fowler.

p. 130, line 5: "they say I'm an octoroon": Interview with Patricia Chandler, May 22, 1998.

p. 130, line 8: "the King of England": Jim Garrison to Zachary Sklar, August 9, 1988. AARC.

p. 130, line 13: Shaw's favorite New Orleans story: Interview with Jefferson Sulzer, January 15, 2000.

p. 130, line 16: Clay Shaw's grandfather: "Clay Shaw of New Orleans" by Dorothy Raymer. *Key West Citizen.* March 28, 1971, p. 3. For Clay Shaw's early life: Memo written by David Chandler. To: Lang for Billings, Newsfronts. Clay Lavergne Shaw. March 4, 1967. Papers of Richard N. Billings, Box 2, folder 21. Georgetown.

p. 130, line 20: "I wouldn't hurt a fly": Interview with Dr. Harold Lief, May 25, 1999.

p. 130, line 21: "If there were no guns": Memo written by David Chandler.

p. 130, line 37: "I didn't even know what a fracture was": Shaw Biography. For: Charles Ward. Re: Clay Shaw. NODA. NARA.

p. 131, line 4: Thrasher's cruelty: See James Bacque, *Other Losses: The Shocking Truth Behind the Mass Deaths of Disarmed German Soldiers and Civilians Under General Eisenhower's Command* (Roseville, CA: Prima Publishing, St. Martin's Press: 1991), pp. 91-92; 95-96.

p. 131, line 20: "principal backer and developer": CIA. March 18, 1969. To: Director. TYPIC AMWIDE. REF: WH/Miami 3223 (IN17231). Identity A: Mr. Lloyd J. Cobb. NARA.

p. 131, line 21: Lloyd Cobb's security clearance: CIA 18 March 1968. SUBJECT: COBB, Lloyd J. NARA.

p. 131, line 26: David Baldwin's history: Memorandum. May 24, 1967. To: Jim Garrison. From: William R. Martin. Subject: Central Intelligence Connections in the City of New Orleans. NODA. NARA.

p. 131, line 27: "own CIA connections": David G. Baldwin to Clay Shaw, May 31, 1967. Papers of Clay Shaw. NARA.

p. 131, line 29: "shoe leather": Stephen Tyler interview with Jesse Core, in *Shades of Gray: A New Orleans Native's Search for the Real Clay Shaw.* Unpublished proposal. Courtesy of Mr. Tyler.

p. 131, line 30: every consulate was bugged: Interview with Gordon Novel, January 16, 2000. Asked how he knew, Novel says, "I took it apart": Interview with Novel, June 12, 2000.

p. 131, line 37: "blond hair blowing in the wind": Billings, Haskell, Byers, Rowan, Orshefsky. From: Will Lang. *LIFE* magazine. March 5, 1967. Papers of Richard N. Billings, Box 2, folder 21.

p. 131, line 41: Shaw was paid one hundred dollars a month: HSCA interview with Ross Banister by Martin J. Daly. Subjects; Banister, Guy; Wilson, Mary Banister; Banister, Ross. February 20, 1978. 180-10082-10170. HSCA 005967. NARA.

p. 131, line 42: apartment house in Madrid: Bill Turner to Bud Fensterwald, December 14, 1967. AARC.

p. 132, line 3: for the preceding five years: Interview with Robert Buras, September 18, 2002.

p. 132, line 5: Gaudet laughed: See Norman Kempster, "Oswald, CIA Trails Crossed: Shadowy Figure Emerges," *Washington Star.* January 15, 1976.

p. 132, line 18: "the exposure of Shaw's connections": CIA. From: J. Walton Moore to Chief, Domestic

Collection Division. Attn: Deputy Chief of Operations (Ed Watts). June 3, 1976. NARA.

p. 132, line 20: "limited to Domestic Contact Service activities": Memorandum For: Deputy Director of Support. Subject: Claimed Agency Affiliation by Conspiracy Case Figures. May 1, 1967. 104-10106-10466. 80T01357A. NARA. CIA found what it wanted to find. At one point Donovan Pratt, working under Raymond Rocca, nicknamed "the Rock," could find no Agency records for Joseph Rault, who had at least two contacts a month with JMWAVE: See: Memorandum For: Director, Domestic Contact Service, attention: Mr. George Musulin. Subject: Garrison Investigation: Cecil Maxwell Shilstone. 19 June 1967. Signed by Donovan F. Pratt. DC/CI/R & A. NARA.

p. 132, line 26: the highest of six CIA categories: DCD-670/78. June 5, 1978. Memorandum for: DDO/ISS/IP/EIS. From: Ruth Ellif DCD/FIO/PAO. Subject: House Select Committee on Assassinations Request (OLC 78-1179/1). NARA.

p. 132, line 29: cleared for Project QKENCHANT: September 18, 1998. Memorandum for: Laura Denk, Executive Director, ARRB. From: J. Barry Harrelson JFK Project Officer, HRP/OIM. Subject: CIA-IR-06 QKENCHANT. NARA.

p. 132, line 30: J. Monroe Sullivan is utilized under Project QKENCHANT: Memorandum for: File. From: M. D. Stevens. Subject: Sullivan, J. Monroe. #280-207. March 16, 1967. 201-813493. NARA.

p. 132, line 37: "used for intelligence procurement: August 3, 1976. Memorandum for Associate Deputy Director for Administration. From: Robert W. Gambino, Director of Security. Subject: High Chisholm McDonald. NARA.

p. 133, line 2: QKENCHANT was an "operational project": The Directorate of Operations in reply to a FOIA request determined that "a disclosure of additional information (records) concerning QKENCHANT or ZRCLIFF would tend to identify the full meaning of the cryptonyms." CIA repeats: the records "would reside in the DO's operational files," which they were under no obligation to release": Memorandum for: Kathryn I. Dyer, Information Privacy Coordinator. Information: Office of General Counsel, from: Redictated. DO/IMS; Subject: F-1993-02469—Litigation—William A. Davy v. CIA Re: Request for Records Pertaining to and/or Captioned QKENCHANT and ZRCLIFF—Nine (9) Documents, Reference; IRG Taskings, 28 Sept. and 1 Nov. 2000, courtesy of James H. Lesar. This demonstrates that Clay Shaw was hardly one among thousands of businessmen routinely briefed by the Agency after travel: Priority Handling FOIA request. DDO/DDA/DST/DCI. Info re: PROJECT QKENCHANT and PROJECT ZRCLIFF. Date sent: 22 February 1994. Request number F93-2469; Confidential. Memorandum for: Chief, Information Privacy and Classification Review Division. Via: Eldon I. Hatch, DDA/IRO. From: Chief, Office of Personnel Security. Subject: Freedom of Request-William Davy (Requester) for "ZRCLIFF and QKENCHANT" (Subject). Reference: IP & CRD (F) 93-2469. The denial reads: "this request should be coordinated in full with the Directorate of Operations (DO) prior to any affected release."

p. 133, line 4: Shaw's QKENCHANT records reside in CIA's operational files: See Declaration by William H. McNair, Information Review Officer, Directorate of Operations, U. S. Central Intelligence Agency. Case No. 1:00CV02134 (RCL). May 22, 2002.

p. 133, line 9: "covert security approval": Memorandum For: Chief, Central Cover Staff, Corporate Cover Branch. Attention: Mr. Martin Lukoskio. Subject: Hunt, E. Howard. #23 500. Signed by Victor R. White, Deputy Director of Security (IOS). NARA.

p. 133, line 10: Richard Burnes telephones Shaw: "who are you from?": Memorandum. February 10, 1967. To: Jim Garrison. From: Richard V. Burnes. Re: Preliminary Report—Clay Shaw—1313 Dauphine Street, New Orleans, LA. NODA. NARA.

p. 133, line 17: a peculiar form of salutation: diary of Richard N. Billings.

p. 133, line 20: Banister recruited "for QKENCHANT purposes": CIA. 104-10109-10374. JFK. 80T01357A. From: Chief, CCD/NC. To: Chief, OS/SSD/I & S. Title: Memorandum: Request For Special Inquiry—Guy W.

Banister Associates—New Orleans. 08/26/60. Subjects: Banister, Guy. This is a 6/16/04 release. NARA. A formal investigative report vetting Banister was filed by the CIA's Los Angeles Field Office. (CIA. 104-10109-10379. JFK. 80TO1357A. From: Los Angeles Field Office. To: Headquarters. Date: 09/13/60. Pages: 16. Subjects: Investigation. Report. GWBA, Inc. NARA).

p. 133, line 36: "not a policy-making Agency": "CIA Must Keep Quiet—Cabell." *Times-Picayune,* May 10, 1961, Section 1, p. 3.

p. 133, line 38: no questions from the floor: NO 155-67. Att'n: Director, Domestic Contact Service, Operational Support Staff (Musulin). From: Chief, New Orleans Office. Case 49364—Garrison's Investigation into Alleged Conspiracy to Assassinate John F. Kennedy (formerly HH-18123). Ref: Your memorandum of 11 April 1967. Lloyd A. Ray. NARA.

p. 134, line 1: "as a CIA observer": Att'n: Chief, Contact Division. From: Chief, New Orleans Office. August 6, 1955. NARA.

p. 134, line 1: CIA pays Shaw to go to an exhibition in Czechoslovakia: Chief, Contact Division. Attn: McHugh. From: Chief, New Orleans Office. Case 18751. Signed by William P. Burke. August 8, 1955. NARA.

p. 134, line 2: Shaw's relations with Czech intelligence: CIA shared information with the FBI on this, as per the 1948 agreement: FBI To: Director, FBI. From: SAC, New York. 124-10167-10113. 89-69-1573. 62-109060-4663. NARA.

p. 134, line 13: Shaw spies on mercury producers: Chief, New Orleans Office. Attn: H. C. Leake. Chief, Contact Division (WE/N). Case 20791. June 4, 1956. From: E. M. Ashcraft. File: Clay Shaw: A12274. The International Trade Mart itself had a separate CIA designated number: A-13027. See also: Chief, Contact Division. Attn: WE/N Branch (Sommerville). Chief, New Orleans Office. May 25, 1956. Case: 20791. William P. Burke.

p. 134, line 35: Shaw is briefed in advance: Attn: Chief, Contact Branch. Operations Section. From: Chief, New Orleans Office. Case No. 1046. June 7, 1949. NARA. See also: Attn: Chief,

Contact Branch, Operations Section. From: Chief, New Orleans Office. Case No. 1646. Re: (a) New Orleans Office teletype NO 102. (b) Evans' memorandum of February 19, 1949. By 1949, Clay Shaw was speaking fluent Spanish.

p. 134, line 35: in each country to which he traveled: February 18, 1949. Memorandum to Chief, New Orleans Office. From Chief, Contact branch. Subject: Case 1646. Reference (a) New Orleans Office teletype no. 102 by Leake. SOUTH AMERICA—Economic, Political. NARA. Shaw's CIA records contain descriptions of each of these assignments in Latin America.

p. 134, line 40: Garrison concluded that Clay Shaw worked for CIA: Jim Garrison to Zach Sklar, August 9, 1988. AARC.

p. 135, line 7: Freeport Sulphur: See: "David Atlee Phillips, Clay Shaw and Freeport Sulphur" by Lisa Pease. *PROBE* magazine. Vol. 3, No. 3. March-April 1996. See also: Ken Elliot confirms Kimble's story about Shaw's flight to Canada for Freeport Sulphur with Ferrie at the helm: Memorandum. June 27, 1967. To: Jim Garrison. From: Sal Scalia. Re: Interview with Perry Russo. NODA. NARA. For the investigation into Shaw, Ferrie, Oswald and Freeport Sulphur see also: Memorandum. October 1, 1968. To: Jim Garrison. From: Andrew J. Sciambra. Re: Interview with James J. Plaine. NODA. Memorandum. October 9, 1968. To: Jim Garrison. From: Andrew J. Sciambra. Re: Clay Shaw; Memorandum. October 23, 1968. To: Jim Garrison. From: Andrew J. Sciambra. Re: Shaw—Ferrie & White [sic] (Freeport Sulphur). Undated memo beginning "In '63 or 64: Reported that Dick White [sic], Pres—1st Natl—Gretna. . . .".

p. 135, line 8: Ferrie pilots Shaw and a man from Freeport Sulphur: See Memorandum. October 9, 1968. To: Jim Garrison. From: Andrew J. Sciambra. RE: Clay Shaw & Mr. Plaine. NODA. NARA; Memorandum. October 23, 1968. To: Jim Garrison. From: Andrew J. Sciambra. Re: Shaw—Ferrie & White. [sic] NODA. NARA.

p. 135, line 16: For Kimble's relations with the Klan, See Hoke May, "Death and Terror Wear Klan Hood,"

States-Item. September 8, 1967. Section 1, p. 1.

p. 135, line 17: Kimble went on to report on Jim Garrison to Lloyd Ray: Memorandum for: The General Counsel. Subject: Garrison Investigation. Reference: OGC Memorandum 67-1811, 22 September 1967. Subject as above. September 26, 1967. Donovan E. Pratt, DC/CI/R & A. NARA.

p. 135, line 18: Kimble tells Lou Ivon he had done special assignments for CIA: Memorandum. September 6, 1967. To: Jim Garrison. From: Louis Ivon. Re: Conversation with Jules Ricco Kimble. NODA.

p. 136, line 1: James J. Plaine: Memorandum. October 1, 1968. To: Jim Garrison. From: Andrew J. Sciambra. Re: Interview with James J. Plaine. See also: Memorandum. October 9, 1968. To: Jim Garrison. From: Andrew J. Sciambra. Re: Clay Shaw & Mr. Plaine." See also Unsigned memo beginning "in '63 or '64. Reported that Dick White [sic], Pres. 1st Nat'l.-Gretna." NODA.

p. 136, line 16: the *Paese Sera* articles of March 4, March 6, March 11-12 and March 18th are available at NARA. See also Clark Blaise, "Neo-Fascism and the Kennedy Assassins," *Canadian Dimension,* and Louis Wiznitzer, "Will Garrison's Inquiry into Kennedy's Assassination Lead to Montreal?" *Le Devoir.* March 16, 1967.

p. 136, line 29: "most notorious fascist organizations in French history": James D. Le Sueur, *Uncivil War: Intellectuals and Identity Politics During the Decolonization of Algeria* (Philadelphia: The University of Pennsylvania Press, 2001), **p. 56.**

p. 136, line 34: "those who killed John F. Kennedy": Tommy Baumler, interviewed by Gary Shaw and Bud Fensterwald, December 30, 1981. AARC.

p. 136, line 38: "shady speculation": Foreign Service Despatch. From: American Consulate, Basel. To: The Department of State, Washington. Ref: Our D-55, April 8, 1958. D-63, May 21, 1958, November 7, 1958. Signed by Elias A. McQuaid, American Consul. AARC.

p. 137, line 5: ten million dollars of CIA money: Joseph Trento, *The Secret History of the CIA,* (Roseville, CA: Prima Publishing, Forum, 2001), p. 408.

p. 137, line 8: the French: Author Gary Aguilar has collected the French sources in an article on Max Holland available on the Internet. See also. Andrew Tully, *CIA—The Inside Story* (New York: William Morrow and Company, 1962), pp. 48, 53. See also James Reston, "Pentagon To Get Some C.I.A. Duties," The *New York Times,* April 29, 1961, p. 3.

p. 137, line 18: for the Hungarian political career of Nagy, see Jorg Hoensch, *A History of Modern Hungary: 1967-1994.* Thank you to John McAdams for suggesting this reference.

p. 137, line 29: "cleared contact": Memorandum For: Chief, CI/R & A. Subject: Trace Results on Persons Connected with Centro Mondiale Commerciale (World Trade Center). Reference: Our memorandum of 8 March 1967 on Italian aspects of the Clay Shaw affair. CIA 104-10181-10114. Date: March 24, 1967. NARA. ARRB release.

p. 137, line 32: Nagy is a CIA asset of Frank Wisner: CIA. 104-10213-10146. Title: Correspondence with FBI On CIA/FBI Liaison Agreement in 1948. 18 pages. One wag dubbed this set of documents a "treaty" between the FBI and CIA. In particular, see: 13 September 1948. Memorandum For: Admiral Sidney W. Souers, Executive Secretary, NSC. VIA. Admiral R. H. Hillonkoetter, Director of Central Intelligence. From: Frank G. Wisner, Assistant Director, CIA. Subject: Cooperation with FBI. NARA.

p. 137, line 35: Nagy contributed: Nagy contributes to Jacques Soustelle: See Paris Flammonde, *The Kennedy Conspiracy: An Uncommissioned Report on the Jim Garrison Investigation.* (New York: Meredith Press, 1969), pp. 216ff.

p. 137, line 38: all but identical to OAS: See, for example, Benjamin Stora, *La gangrene et l'oubli: La memoire de la guerre d'Algerie* (Paris: La Decouverte, 1991).

p. 138, line 1: advocated overthrowing De Gaulle: James D. Le Sueur, *Uncivil War,* p. 4.

p. 138, line 3: Delphine Roberts recognizes Ferenc Nagy: Robert Buras Interview with Delphine Roberts. 5 pages. August 27, 1978. 12:30 P.M.

p. 138, line 16: Seligman banking family: See Peter Seligman-Schurch to

Clay Shaw, May 2, 1960. Papers of Clay Shaw. Involved as well was the Schroder Banking Corporation: Memorandum Concerning The Permindex Project, January 15, 1957. Foreign Service Despatch. From: John A. Lehrs, American Consul. AARC.

p. 138, line 21: "widespread public suspicion": Foreign Service Despatch. From: Amconsul Basel To: The Department of State, Washington, April 9, 1958. Ref: Basel's D-32. October 8, 1957, and related correspondence. AARC.

p. 138, line 24: "insufficient confidence in the business integrity": Foreign Service Despatch. From: American Consulate, Basel. To: The Department of State, Washington, ref: Basel's D-37 of January 15, 1957. January 16, 1957. AARC.

p. 138, line 25: Spring of 1958: For E. Wegmann's file. Memo from Clay Shaw. Papers of Edward F. Wegmann.

p. 138, line 28: Shaw helps PERMINDEX gain credibility: See Enrico A. Mantello to Clay Shaw, May 31, 1960. Papers of Clay Shaw.

p. 138, line 30: "to strengthen US control": Foreign Service Despatch. From: AmEmbassy, Rome. To: The Department of State, Washington. Ref: Dept. Instruction CA-10596. July 18, 1956. AARC.

p. 138, line 34: Shaw is "delighted" to join PERMINDEX: Clay Shaw to Enrico Mantello. August 7, 1958. Papers of Clay Shaw.

p. 138, line 36: Mantello's urgings: George Mantello to Clay Shaw, November 18, 1958.

p. 138, line 38: "this shadowy organization": Arthur P. Leonard to Clay Shaw, December 8, 1958. LHM U. S. Department of Commerce, Field Services. New Orleans, Louisiana. Papers of Clay L. Shaw. NARA.

p. 138, line 42. CIA's Shaw files with PERMINDEX materials:

PERMINDEX-related materials surface in Shaw's CIA file three years before the Kennedy assassination. The CIA compiled a list which included a March 18, 1960,Memorandum regarding Ferenc Nagy and an 00-A-3, 154,897 1 April 1960 CIA Information Report regarding Enrico Mantello aka Imre Mandel [sic].

These items emerged in the March 24, 1967, memorandum cited above,

Subject: persons connected with Centro Mondiale Commerciale (World Trade Center), Italian subsidiary of PERMINDEX. Examining a document of March 16, 1967, Victor Marchetti deciphered the line 12haw has #402897-A."

p. 139, line 12: expelled from Italy: The demise of Centro Mondiale Commerciale was engineered by a member of its own Board of Directors named Mario Ceravolo, a Christian Democrat who had resigned because "it was no longer possible to understand the sources of great sums of money obtained abroad by Mr. Giovanni (Giorgio) Mantello, and the real destination of this money." Ceravolo, obviously invited onto the Board of Directors to provide it with some veneer of liberal cover, could get no reply when he asked where the money was going. He contacted *Paese Sera* after the appearance of its first article on March 4th, and became a source. The CMC attempted to bribe Ceravolo with a parcel of land, but he turned them down. At least since November 19th: Memorandum No. 8 is dated 1/11/68 and was prepared by the R & A division of Counter Intelligence.

p. 139, line 22: Working on it for months: Interview of Giorgio Fanti by Ralph Schoenman, July 18, 2002.

p. 139, line 37: New Orleans-Rome air tickets: *Paese Sera,* March 14, 1967.

p. 139, line 39: "there must have been blackmail": Interview with Patricia Chandler, May 27, 1998.

p. 140, line 5: Max Holland spreads the disinformation that Jim Garrison was the victim of KGB disinformation dispensed by *Paese Sera:* Holland's articles are: "The Lie That Linked CIA to the Kennedy Assassination" by Max Holland. Winter 2001. *Studies in Intelligence* available at the CIA website, cia.gov/csi/studies/fall_winter_2001/article02.html. "The Demon in Jim Garrison" appeared in *Wilson Quarterly.* Spring 2001, pp. 2-9. See also: "Was Jim Garrison Duped by the KGB?" by Max Holland. *New Orleans* magazine. Volume 36, number 5. February 2002. Holland changed publishers from Houghton Mifflin to the more distinguished Alfred A. Knopf, and won the prestigious Anthony J. Lukas memorial prize for an unpublished work. See also Holland's "How Moscow Undermined The Warren Commission," *Washington Post,* November 21, 2003, and Holland, "The Assassination Tapes," *The Atlantic Monthly,* June 2004, pp. 82–94. As if the destruction of Jim Garrison's work were his own life project, Holland here calls Garrison "a cunning demagogue the likes of which had not been seen since the days of Senator Joseph McCarthy."

p. 140, line 24: Helms charged, falsely: See Senate Judiciary Committee, Communist Forgeries (Washington, DC: Government Printing Office, 1961). See also "Preparato in accordo con Washington il colpo di stato militare in Algeria?" *Paese Sera,* 22-23 April 1961. By the late 1970s, Helms had been convicted in federal court as a perjurer, having lied about the CIA's role in the overthrow of President Salvador Allende in Chile. "You dishonored your oath and you now stand before this court in disgrace and shame," Judge Barrington D. Parker told Helms. See "Helms Is Fined $2000 and Given Two-Year Suspended Prison Term," The *New York Times,* November 5, 1977, p. 1. See also Mark Lane, *Plausible Denial: Was the CIA Involved in the Assassination of JFK?* New York: Thunder's Mouth Press, 1991), pp. 222-223.

p. 141, line 4: despised CIA and KGB equally: Interview with Jean-Franco Corsini, October 1, 2002. Corsini was on the *Paese Sera* staff at the time.

p. 141, line 6: Neither the Italian Communist Party, nor the KGB, had any influence on *Paese Sera:* Ralph Schoenman Interview with Edo Parpalione. February 23, 2002. Parpalione was with *Paese Sera* from 1949 to 1989.

p. 141, line 12: *Paese Sera* resembles *La Repubblica* today: Giorgio Fanti interviewed by Ralph Schoenman, July 18, 2002.

p. 141, line 16: "the usual manipulation of the CIA": Interview with Jean Franco Corsini, October 1, 2002.

p. 141, line 23: Europeans see the Kennedy assassination as an "internal plot within the United States government": See "De Gaulle Viewed Death of JFK as a Conspiracy," *International Herald Tribune.* October 26, 1967, p. A1. Hoover forwarded a

copy of this article at once to Cartha DeLoach.

p. 141, line 29: "Countering Criticism of the Warren Report": From: Chief (CA Staff) To: Chief, Certain Stations and Bases." Document ID number (NARA Identification Aid): 1993.06.18.17:48:53:180000. The document was created by CA staff and CIA's Counter Intelligence, Research and Analysis Division.

p. 142, line 3: "volunteered information to the CIA": Max Holland, "The Demon in Jim Garrison," *Wilson Quarterly.* Spring 2001, pp. 8-9.

p. 142, line 11: Clay Shaw at one time: See Patricia Lambert, *False Witness: The Real Story of Jim Garrison's Investigation and Oliver Stone's Film JFK* (New York: M. Evans and Company, 1998), p. 204.

p. 142, line 11: "routine information": *False Witness,* p. 204. The Phelan article was in the *Saturday Evening Post* of April 23, 1967, and was called "Rush to Judgment in New Orleans."

p. 142, line 15: Phelan is both an FBI and CIA informant: For CIA: "a sensitive SPS activity": Subject: Special Projects Staff matter. June 25, 1974. Mr. Paul Evans, Security Officer, Special Projects Staff/DD/SST requests that office of security records be checked regarding a Mr. James R. Phelan and Mr. Wallace Turner. CIA 104-10122-10141. JFK agency file: 80T01357A. From CIA to DCI, CIA title. Memo: Re: Relationship between CIA and Robert Maheu. Prepared for DCI. 01/01/75. NARA; Phelan an FBI informant: See for example, : FBI: From: R. E. Wick to Mr. DeLoach. April 3, 1967. Airtel To: Director, FBI. From SAC, New Orleans, April 19, 1967.

p. 142, line 17: "routinely debriefed": Phelan recites the litany: Shaw had been debriefed: See Eugene M. Ingram, Interview of James Phelan. January 15, 1991. NARA.

p. 142, line 19: distortion: *A Look over My Shoulder: A Life in the Central Intelligence Agency* (New York: Random House, 2003), pp. 288-289.

p. 142, line 33: "rarely proven to be basically wrong": To: Nancy Haskell.. Office Memorandum. March 24, 1967; To Lang for Billings. From: Cerabona, Rome. Re: Clay Shaw In Rome? April 14, 1967. AARC.

p. 142, line 36: "Cubans in exile":

"What Are the Sources of the CMC's Millions?" *Paese Sera.* March 18, 1967.

p. 143, line 5: "under an oath of secrecy": CIA. To: Director, Domestic Contact Service. From: Chief, New Orleans Office. March 3, 1967. b-67-73. No. 84-67. NARA.

p. 143, line 10: Clay Shaw has some connection with CIA: File. Deputy Chief, Security Research Staff. Shaw, Clay L. #402897. 6 April 1967.

p. 143, line 13: since May of 1956: Memorandum: No. 106-67. To: Director, Domestic Contact Service. Att'n: Operational Support Staff. From: Chief, New Orleans Office. 23 March 1967. Subject: HH-18, 123—Garrison Investigation into Alleged Conspiracy to Assassinate President Kennedy. Ref: Your Memorandum, 20 March 1967/Ray McConnell telephone conversation, 21 March 1967, same subject. NARA.

p. 143, line 13: CIA lies to the FBI: To: File. From: Deputy Chief, Security Research Staff. April 7, 1967. Subject: Shaw, Clay. NARA.

p. 143, line 13: Shaw's last contact was in 1965: Memorandum. 2 March 1967. Subject: Clay Shaw's Connection with CIA. Document number: 1587-1117. NARA.

p. 143, line 27: "John Scelso": CIA "agent" v. "employee": HSCA 014728. May 16, 1978. Transcript. Security Classified Testimony of John Scelso. NARA.

p. 143, line 36: Shaw's CIA involvement was in Counter Intelligence: Memo to the file: from Chief of FIOB/SRS, John P. Dempsey based on call from Arthur Dooley of the Counter Intelligence Staff advising details of Shaw's file on March 3rd. The date of the document is 3 March 1967. Handwritten instruction is: Office of Security File Check on Clay Shaw. NARA.

CHAPTER 10

p. 144, Epigraph: "Let Justice Be Done": Jim Garrison, 1967 BBC Interview, p. 11. NARA.

p. 144, line 1: "wracked by exhaustion": "Strange Cast Plays Roles in New Orleans DA's Assassination Inquiry" by Merriman Smith. The *Sunday Bulletin* (Philadelphia). March 5, 1967. Section 1, p. 24.

p. 144, line 4: "never heard of the guy": Interview with Lynn Pelham, November 17, 2001.

p. 144, line 11: David Chandler actually wrote "The Vice Man Cometh": James Phelan, "The Vice Man Cometh," *The Saturday Evening Post.* June 8, 1963. See: *LIFE* magazine internal memo. March 5, 1967. Lang for Rowan for Newsfronts, Billings, Copy TXT, Miami Bureau. The following note is appended by David Chandler: "I did a manuscript "Garrison: Demagogue or Crusader?" in 1963 which was subsequently used by *Saturday Post* under title "Vice Man Cometh" by James Phelan. Since the *Post* only changed about 500 words of the manuscript I suppose we are free to quote it. I can send the original manuscript if you prefer...."

p. 144, line 13: Jim Garrison provides Phelan with the Sciambra memos: James Phelan interview with Eugene M. Ingram and James Phelan to Richard E. Sprague, May 20, 1970. Papers of Richard E. Sprague. Georgetown University.

p. 144, line 14: appalled Ivon and Alcock: Interview with William Alford, May 28, 1998. Ivon was to call Garrison himself "the biggest leak" in the investigation. Louis Ivon interviewed in The Garrison Tapes.

p. 144, line 17: Maheu and Banister: See SSCIA testimony of Robert Maheu, July 30, 1975.

p. 144, line 20: Maheu's history with CIA: CIA 104-10122-10141. 80T01357A. To: DCI. CIA title: MEMO RE: RELATIONSHIP BETWEEN CIA AND ROBERT MAHEU PREPARED FOR DCI. (Director of Central Intelligence). January 1, 1975. 13 pages. NARA. The FBI had long known of Maheu's role in the assassination of Castro: For material on Maheu's role in the assassination plots to kill Castro, turn to the following: To: Director, FBI. From: SAC, Miami. October 21, 1960. Operations—Havana, Cuba. 62-707-54-263 or 266. See also: To: W. C. Sullivan From: W. R. Wannall. March 6, 1967: "we checked matter with CIA on 5/3/61 and learned CIA had utilized Maheu as intermediary with Sam Giancana relative to CIA's 'dirty business' anti-Castro activities." See also: Memorandum for Mr. Sullivan Re: Central Intelligence Agency's Intentions to Send Hoodlums to Cuba to Assassinate Castro.": "we learned on 6/20/63 from CIA that its contacts with John Roselli [sic] (Maheu's link with Giancana) had continued until that time, when they were reportedly cut off."

p. 144, line 20: "Rosselli": When Rosselli spells out his name for the Senate Select Committee, it is with one "s" yet on other occasions, it is "Rosselli."

p. 144, line 21: public relations cover: SSCIA testimony of Robert Maheu, July 30, 1975.

p. 144, line 23: Phelan made contact with Maheu: James R. Phelan to Jim DiEugenio. Undated. Courtesy of Mr. DiEugenio.

p. 145, line 1: Phelan hands over Moo Moo's memos: Sciambra's memos become FBI documents: See FBI. 124-10259-10223. 89-69-1990. April 5, 1967.

p. 145, line 4: remain secret: "I would never reveal the contents of any story, prior to its publication, to anyone, especially to anyone connected to any governmental agency": Interview of James Phelan with Eugene M. Ingram. January 15, 1991. NARA. For Phelan giving the FBI an advance copy, FBI: 89-69-1991. April 12, 1967. The article was to be published on May 6th. On April 18th, R. E. Wick told Deke that "Phelan again pointed out that his identity as the source of this material should be fully protected": Memorandum To: Mr. DeLoach. From: R. E. Wick. April 18, 1967. 62-109060-5113. NARA.

p. 145, line 7: Phelan admits to Matt Herron that he has returned to New Orleans to discredit Jim Garrison: Interview with Matt Herron, May 10, 1999.

p. 145, line 8: Phelan approaches Lane and Popkin: Interview with Richard Popkin, June 10, 1999. Interview with Lane is January 15, 1998.

p. 145, line 17: Maheu offers Rosselli $150,000: The Inspector General's Report. Memorandum for the Record. 23 May 1967. 80T01357A. Subject: Report on Plots to Assassinate Fidel Castro. J. S. Earman. 143 pages. pp. 118, 120.

p. 145, line 20: Rosselli used to smear Garrison: See Charles Rappleye and Ed Becker, *All American Mafioso:*

The Johnny Rosselli Story. (New York: Doubleday, 1991), p. 297.

p. 145, line 23: The Garrison-Roselli contact: 1967 Inspector General's Report, p. 127: "The Roselli-Garrison contact in Las Vegas in March is particularly disturbing. It lends substance to reports that Castro had something to do with the Kennedy assassination in retaliation for U.S. attempts on Castro's life. We do not know that Castro actually tried to retaliate, but we *do* know that there were such plots against Castro. Unhappily, it now appears that Garrison may also know this."

p. 146, line 6: "it might have been the lawyer. . . .": Senate Select Committee to Study Governmental Operations with Respect to Intelligence Activities. Testimony of Richard Helms. June 13, 1975. SSCIA. 157-10014-10075. 10-H-07. NARA.

p. 146, line 14: "seeing Garrison in person": Senate Select Committee to Study Governmental Operations with Respect to Intelligence Activities. Testimony of Robert Maheu. April 28, 1976. SSCIA. 157-10014-10088. 11-H-07. NARA.

p. 146, line 15: Rosselli denied meeting Jim Garrison: "I don't know Jim Garrison other than seeing him on TV": United States Senate. Report on Proceedings. Senate Select Committee to Study Governmental Operations with Respect to Intelligence Agencies. April 23, 1976. Testimony of John Roselli [sic]. SSCIA 157-10014-10000. 02-H-02. NARA.

p. 146, line 18: "I suppose it is an honor": Jim Garrison to Philip Pochoda, November 10, 1986. NODA. NARA.

p. 146, line 26: Schiller as FBI informant: Schiller sends Hoover a transcript of the Ruby family: 124-10031-10001. 62-109060-1st NR 4429. From: Schiller, Lawrence. To: Director, FBI. NARA. The transcript was a conversation between Jack Ruby, his attorney and members of Ruby's family. Schiller also had informed Hoover that Edward J. Epstein was writing an article on the Garrison case, but that the Bureau should trust Epstein, since he was an "advocate of viewpoint of Warren Commission and is opposed to irresponsible journalism of writers such as Lane": (To: Director. From: Los Angeles. March 22, 1967. 62-109060-4907). Schiller also told Hoover the lie that Dick Billings was working for Jim Garrison. This was never the case. Schiller in turn told Billings he himself was working for Jim Garrison, also a lie (Interview with Richard N. Billings, August 2, 2000). Mark Lane uncovered that Schiller has made himself Jack Ruby's "business agent": *A Citizen's Dissent* (New York: Holt, Rinehart and Winston, 1968), pp. 84-85. Even Shaw's attorney Edward Wegmann distrusted Schiller: Dick Billings/Nancy Haskell. Notes on phone conversation with H. McCombs. Tues. 3/7/67. AARC.

p. 146, line 34: "give the defendant every chance": *Playboy* (October 1967), p. 62.

p. 146, line 35: confidential informant: See, for example, "New Orleans Judge Expects Informant to Be Identified" by Theodore C. Link. St. Louis *Post Dispatch.* March 9, 1967. Joe Oster tried hard to get the name of Garrison's witness so he could report to the FBI: FBI. To: Director and Dallas. From: New Orleans. March 13, 1967. 124-10167-10205. 89-69-1662. NARA.

p. 146, line 38: witnesses no longer available: Press Rate Collect. Lang, TIMEINC, WUX Atlanta. Pro Billings. Haskell. Undated. Papers of Richard N. Billings, Box 4, line 4.

p. 147, line 4: common purpose: *Frohwerk v. United States.* Argued January 27, 1919. Decided March 10, 1919. No. 685.

p. 147, line 5: need not commit any specific alleged overt act: Rudolph J. Nassif v. United States of America, Appellee. United States Court of Appeals. Eighth Circuit. December 6, 1966.

p. 147, line 6: in itself wrong: See H. T. Jordon Jr., Appellant v. United States of America, Appellee. *Gervase A. Breyand, Appellant v. United States of America, Appellee.* Nos. 8450, 8451. United States Court of Appeals for the Tenth Circuit. December 5, 1966. Rehearing denied January 26, 1967.

p. 147, line 7: "combination of minds": *State v. D'Ingianni.* Supreme Court of Louisiana. June 30, 1950.

p. 147, line 12: Russo faces Roy

Jacob: Perry Russo interviewed by William Davy, August 31, 1994. For Russo facing the polygraph, see also Transcript of Perry Russo interview with the *Washington Post.* NODA. NARA. Richard N. Billings remembered the same thing: "He was so nervous that a positive reading could not be obtained": "Garrison (II): The Power of Public Disclosure." Papers of Richard N. Billings.

p. 147, line 18: unsuitable subject: Interview with John Volz, June 13, 2001.

p. 147, line 19: coldest eyes in New Orleans: Interview with John Volz. December 11, 2001. See: Sgt. Edward O'Donnell's Report to Jim Garrison. Subject: Perry Russo Interview, June 20, 1967. NODA.

p. 147, line 20: bitter Garrison enemy: Interview with Frank Meloche. June 11, 2000.

p. 147, line 20: close to the Gurviches: Interview with Numa Bertel, February 6, 2001.

p. 147, line 21: police brutality charges: Interview with William Porteous, III, December 19, 2001. All from the *Times-Picayune:* "Only One Juror Chosen in Case." November 27, 1962, Section 1, p. 7; "Jury Selected in Attack Case." November 29, 1962, Section 1, p. 6; "Victims Recall Attack by Four." November 30, 1962, Section 3, p. 9; "Death Penalty Asked for Four." November 28, 1962, Section 2, p. 2; "Police Quizzed at Rape Trial." December 1, 1962, Section 3, p. 1; "Forced to Sign, Says Baptiste." December 5, 1962, Section 1, p. 5; "DA Seeking Use of Confessions." December 2, 1962, Section 1, p. 18; "Judge Scolds Shea at Trial." December 4, 1962, Section 3, p. 22; "Defense Objects to 'Confessions.'" December 6, 1963, Section 1, p. 2; "Defense Rests in Rape Trials." December 7, 1962, Section 3, p. 26; "Jurors Long 'Locked Up' Get Exemption for Life." December 8, 1962, Section 1, p. 20; "Confessions of 4 Allowed.' December 9, 1962, Section 1, p. 23; "Defense to Act as State Rests." December 11, 1962, Section 1, p. 10; "Arguments End in 16-Day Trial." December 12, 1962, Section 3, p. 15; "Life Sentence Given In Rape." December 19, 1962, Section 4, p. 9; "Jury Convicts 4 In Rape Trial." December 13, 1962. Section 2, p. 11. See also: *State of Loui-*

siana v. Joshua Carter and Lawrence Baptiste. No. 47514. Supreme Court of Louisiana. June 7, 1965; *State of Louisiana v. Joshua Carter and Lawrence Baptiste.* No. 47514. Supreme Court of Louisiana. January 17, 1966.

See also: New Orleans *Times-Picayune:* "Two in Police Beating Case Rearrested." February 6, 1957, p. 24; "Earlier Prisoner Beating Report Probed." February 7, 1957, p. 7; "Youth's Release Leads to Ruling." February 16, 1967; "Quiz in Alleged Beating Begins," April 25, 1957, p. 27; "Six Policemen Fired after Being Indicted," July 31, 1957, p. 1.

p. 147, line 23: black victims were afforded the dignity of testifying before the grand jury: Interview with William Porteous III, December 18, 2000.

p. 147, line 27: "they cleared some cases": Interview with Frank Meloche, June 11, 2000.

p. 147, line 27: Wendall C. Roache mentions Edward O'Donnell: among his INS colleagues: Memo to Files: From: Dan Dwyer. Date: December 9, 1975. Re: Notes on Testimony of Wendall G. Roache, 12/9/75.

p. 147, line 28: O'Donnell worked for the INS: Memo to Files: From: Dan Dwyer. Date: December 9, 1975. Re: Notes on Testimony of Windel [sic] G. Roache, 12/9/75. "Mr. Roache suggested the names of some individuals who would have detailed knowledge of Cuban exile activities in New Orleans who we might want to contact. They are the following": The first name on the list is "1. Eddie O'Donnell—former member of the NOPD, polygraph section; presently head of security at the Roosevelt Hotel in New Orleans." It was established during the time of the Church Committee that the INS investigative section in New Orleans worked closely with the CIA and the FBI.

p. 147, line 30: O'Donnell reports on Russo's polygraph to the FBI: FBI 124-10054-10413. HQ. 62-109060-5483. June 22, 1967. Two pages. Subjects: Garrison, Jim, Investigation, Polygraph. NARA.

p. 147, line 34: "don't bug me": this telephone conversation was taped by Orleans Parish district attorney's office: Re: extradition of Sandra Moffett. NARA. A local district attorney named Donald Knowles negotiated for

Moffett with Garrison investigators, Charles Jonau and Kent Simms. She wanted twenty dollars and clothes. Finally the high priced attorney told her the officers had no legal papers and she should drive to Des Moines since Iowa did not subscribe to the Uniform Fugitive Law. Returning to Omaha, she was arrested. She had met David Ferrie only in 1965, Moffett said, so she could not have attended the party described by Russo.

p. 147, line 34: Moffet also claimed she was afraid to fly: Memorandum. March 12, 1967. To: Louis Ivon. From: Detectives Simms and Jonau. Re: Locate One Lilly Mae McMaines . . . Omaha, Nebraska, in an attempt to bring her back to this city. NODA. NARA. See also: To: Director, FBI. From: SAC, Omaha. March 10, 1967. 124-10167-10209. 89-69-1667, 1668. NARA. See also: Young, The Investigation: Where It Stands Today," *New Orleans* magazine, p. 56.

p. 147, line 42: "diversionary tactics": Proceedings of the preliminary hearing: Transcript is available at AARC: Criminal Court for the Parish of Orleans. State of Louisiana. No. M-703. Clay L. Shaw, Arrestee. Honorable Bernard J. Bagert, Honorable Malcolm V. O'Hara. Honorable Matthew S. Braniff, Judges Presiding.

p. 148, line 15: burning cigarette: Shaw began to smoke four to five packs a day: Interview with Jefferson Sulzer, January 15, 2000.

p. 148, line 20: two years": "He did Perry a discourtesy," was how Alford put it: Interview with William Alford, May 28, 1998.

p. 148, line 28: "pathological liar": "Difficult to Lie in Hypnotic State," *Times-Picayune,* March 18, 1967.

p. 148, line 34: Kruebbe: There is an account of Kruebbe's contradictory behavior regarding Bundy's polygraph in *False Witness,* p. 100.

p. 148, line 39: Quiroga misinterprets Ivon's call about the color of Oswald's leaflets: Interview with Carlos Quiroga, January 14, 2000.

p. 149, line 3: Bundy identifies the photograph of Oswald with the beard stubble: April 20, 1967. To: Jim Garrison. From: William Gurvich, Special Aide. Subj: Vernon William Bundy—Interview With, 16 March 1967. NODA. NARA.

p. 149, line 4: Evidence developed later confirmed both Russo and Bundy that Oswald was not always military neat: John L. Anderson says Oswald was dirty: HSCA Interview of John L. Anderson. January 20, 1978, by Harold Leap and Patricia Orr. Anderson had recognized Oswald as soon as he saw his photograph on television after the assassination. See also: Connie T. Kaye: Memorandum. April 23, 1968. To: Jim Garrison. From: James Alcock and Louis Ivon. Re: Connie T. Kaye. Connie Kaye had even helped Oswald hand out leaflets: Interview with Barbara Bennett, February 6, 2001; Barbara Bennett interviewed by William Livesay, December 25, 2001.

p. 149, line 7: "That's him!" Memorandum. March 17, 1967. To: Jim Garrison. From: John P. Volz. NODA. NARA.

p. 149, line 7: Vernon Bundy's prison interview: Interview: Vernon Bundy Jr. Colored male. age 29. March 16, 1967. 4:50 P.M. Orleans Parish Prison. Present: William Gurvich, Charlie Jonau, Cliency Navarre. NODA. NARA.

p. 149, line 10: limp: this was the result of Shaw's injury in basic training: See "Shaw's Army Record Shows Nothing Sinister," *States-Item*. April 25, 1967.

p. 149, line 10: "I've talked to a lot of liars": Interview with John Volz, January 15, 2000.

p. 149, line 36: Bundy puts his hand over Shaw's head: "a 29-year-old admitted narcotics addict": "Hand over Shaw's Head Was Hearing High Point," by Paul Atkinson. *Times-Picayune*. March 19, 1967. Section 1, p. 27.

p. 150, line 41: "you're not serious": Proceedings of the preliminary hearing.

p. 150, line 3: "the first judicial decision": Annotated notes by Jim Garrison on Billings' manuscript, "Garrison (II): The Power of Public Disclosure."

p. 150, line 5: Russo testifies before the Gurvich. Present: Messrs: Alvin V. Oser and James Alcock; Members of the Orleans Parish grand jury. March 22, 1967.

p. 150, line 5: Grand Jury: Gurvich was to charge that Jim Garrison had picked the grand jury "out of the

locker room" of the New Orleans Athletic Club, but it was not so. William Gurvich went before the grand jury of Orleans Parish on June 28, 1967. See also: Tape #3. Gurvich conference. 8/29/67. Papers of Edward F. Wegmann.

p. 150, line 7: "totally honest": Huff quoted in Investigative Report. May 31, 1967. Reported by Aaron M. Kohn. MCC. Years later grand jury member J. C. Albarado says he was impressed by the care with which Garrison and his assistant district attorneys handled the evidence and its presentation to us." J. C. Albarado to the *Times-Picayune,* June 15, 1991, Section 3, p. 6.

p. 150, line 9: LaBiche and Centola are close to DeLoach. FBI. To: Mr. Tolson. From: C. D. DeLoach: February 28, 1967. 124-10027-10216. HQ file. 62-109060-4649. NARA. Centola even took his son to meet Deke. Interview with Lawrence Centola Jr., June 14, 2000.

p. 150, line 15: "Wilson-Franklin Roosevelt persuasion": "An Affable Shaw Is Host To Press" by Gene Roberts. The *New York Times*. April 4, 1967.

p. 150, line 41: "two other occasions": Joe Biles notes this phrase in *In History's Shadow: Lee Harvey Oswald, Kerry Thornley & the Garrison Investigation* (Lincoln, NE: iUniverse, Inc., Writers Club Press, 2002), p. 45.

p. 151, line 11: "go to hell": Memorandum. To: Jim Garrison. From: Stephen Jaffe. Re: Reverend Raymond Broshears. NODA. NARA.

p. 151, line 30: "You could be the patsy": Interview between Phelan and Russo. May 24, 1967. Transcribed June 16, 1967. NODA. NARA. Tape is 541HC-91. NARA.

p. 151, line 33: Phelan: Phelan sends copies of his interviews with Russo to the FBI in Washington. FBI. Airtel. To: SAC, New Orleans. From: Director, FBI. 124-10259-10224. 89-69-1991. NARA.

p. 151, line 35: "a casebook in the obstruction of justice": Interview with Lou Ivon, October 9, 2000.

p. 151, line 37: "too close to Garrison": Interview with Richard N. Billings. August 2, 2000. See also, Dick Billings/Nancy Haskell. Notes on Phone Conversation with H.

McCombs. Tues. 3/7/67. AARC. Billings learned that *Life* correspondent Holland McCombs was helping Aynesworth in sabotaging the Garrison case: See Holland McCombs to Richard B. Swenson. May 13, 1967. NARA. When the DA of Dallas County, Henry Wade, remarked, "I have never felt . . . that Oswald acted alone . . . I haven't criticized Garrison any, because I know what he's up against," McCombs was indignant: "It's rather relieving to see that such a professional as the District Attorney of Dallas County, a man who has been involved in it all, can set aside facts and evidence and simply *feel* things": To: Billings and Haskell—*LIFE*—New York. From: Holland McCombs—Dallas. May 18, 1967. AARC.

p. 151, line 38: Aynesworth attempted to join the Agency: See: Director, Domestic Contact Service, Chief, Houston Field Office. 25 January 1968. Case 49364. Ref: Headquarters Memo 22 Jan 1968, same subject. Signed: Ernest A. Rische. 100-300-17. NARA. CIA discusses its relationship with Aynesworth: CIA Memorandum. To: Director, Domestic Contact Service. From: Chief, Houston Field Office. 25 January 1968. Subject: Case 49364. 100-300-17. NARA. See also: To: Chief, Contact Division Via Chief, Houston Office. From: Resident Agent, Dallas. 10 October 1963. Possibility of Hugh Grant Aynesworth Making Trip to Cuba. Signed by J. Walton Moore. CI "requested a brief summary of your relationship with Mr. Aynesworth," whose name "has been surfaced in connection with the Garrison investigation," the document reads.

p. 151, line 41: Aynesworth is stabbed in the neck and the report is placed in a Lee Harvey Oswald file: Memorandum. To: SAC. From: ASAC Kyle G. Clark. Subject: Lee Harvey Oswald, aka IS-R-CUBA. July 2, 1964. 100-10461-6985. NARA. This is a domestic security file (100). Clark is in the Dealey Plaza news photo where Buddy Walthers picks up the bullet. Kyle Clark bends over and looks at it. If this information went to an informant file, Aynesworth had to know a lot about Oswald prior to the assassination.

p. 152, line 1: informants in place

inside Jim Garrison's office: D. K. Rodgers, Criminal Intelligence Division to Captain W. F. Dyson, Administrative Services Bureau. Dallas Police Department. March 3, 1967. Int. 2965-80A. Courtesy of Gary Shaw.

p. 152, line 5: Aynesworth was working for the CIA: Lonnie Hudkins confided this to Harold Weisberg. Interview with the late Harold Weisberg, July 27, 2000.

p. 152, line 6: Aynesworth provides information to CIA about Brown and Root: CIA 104-10435-1001. Agency file: Russ Holmes Work File. From: C/Houston Office. To: D.DCS. Title: Memo: James Garrison/George Brown—Possible Attempt to Embarrass Agency. December 27, 1967. NARA.

p. 152, line 7: Aynesworth informs to the FBI about Jim Garrison: See URGENT. To: Director. From Dallas. 124-10237-10364. 89-69-2030. NARA. See also: Memorandum for: ADDP C.CI/R & A (Mr. Rocca). Subject: Garrison and The Kennedy Assassination. WH/COG 67-194. Reference: CI/R & A. Memorandum. Dated 26 April 1967. NARA.

p. 152, line 7: Aynesworth said he intended "to make a complete report of my knowledge to the FBI as I have done in the past": Western Union Press Message. Lyndon B. Johnson Library.

p. 152, line 14: they met at Aynesworth's Texas home: Edward Wegmann to Hugh Aynesworth, January 25, 1968. Papers of Edward F. Wegmann. Dymond even planned to use one of Aynesworth's articles to request a subpoena duces tecum: Investigative Report. June 12, 1967. Date information received: April 27, 1967. Reported by Aaron M. Kohn. MCC.

p. 152, line 15: "sex orgy": Report of Hugh Aynesworth to Edward Wegmann. April 12, 1967. Papers of Edward Wegmann.

Interview with Burton Klein, May 25, 1998.

p. 152, line 17: Aynesworth sends the Shaw lawyers Garrison's press releases: See Edward Wegmann to Hugh Aynesworth. February 8, 1968; January 19, 1968. Papers of Edward Wegmann.

p. 152, line 37: "closing thing to the key": Jim Garrison interviewed by

Dick Russell, *The Man Who Knew Too Much* (New York: Carroll & Graf, 1992), p. 650. For the full story of Nagell's career, see *The Man Who Knew Too Much.*

p. 152, line 41: "if you find out what I had to do with Oswald": Interview with Richard Popkin, June 10, 1999.

p. 153, line 13: Oswald under CIA surveillance, and the testimony of Jim Southwood: Russell, *The Man Who Knew Too Much* (revised 2003 edition), pp. 455-457. Russell added this new material to his revised edition.

p. 153, line 17: CIA recruits Nagell in 1955: Richard Case Nagell, "Man in the Middle: The Inside Story." Addendum to article in *Family* (Overseas). January 28, 1970. AARC.

p. 153, line 17: For Nagell's account of Oswald's CIA activities in Japan, see Memo of Conversation with Richard Case Nagell by Bernard Fensterwald. May 31, 1978. AARC.

p. 153, line 24: "Oswald's manager": Richard Case Nagell to Arthur Greenstein, September 30, 1967. AARC.

p. 153, line 28: "the Ferrie-Banister group": *The Man Who Knew Too Much,* p. 58.

p. 153, line 31: "Leopoldo" and "Angel": Nagell quoted in *Family* (Overseas) June 20, 1969 by Thomas Lucey. AARC.

p. 154, line 9: ruin Kennedy's rapprochement with Cuba: *The Man Who Knew Too Much,* p. 369.

p. 154, line 11: warn Oswald: whether Nagell actually warned Oswald is a point which Nagell himself contradicted on several occasions: See Richard Case Nagell to Bernard Fensterwald, August 12, 1974.

p. 154, line 11: "upset and visibly shaken": Richard Case Nagell to Bernard Fensterwald, August 12, 1974.

p. 154, line 13: "domestic-inspired, domestic-formulated": *The Man Who Knew Too Much,* p. 58.

p. 154, line 17: his CIA handler had vanished: *The Man Who Knew Too Much,* p. 438.

p. 154, line 18: the letter from Nagell to Hoover of September 17, 1963, is not extant. This description is from Dick Russell, *The Man Who Knew Too Much,* p. 442. Nagell's nota-

rized affidavit of 1967 describing his letter to Hoover appears in Russell, pp. 56-57.

p. 154, line 29: Oswald's social security card: Oswald's social security card and Uniformed Service identification are pictured in *The Man Who Knew Too Much.*

p. 154, line 39: "to Robert Kennedy": Richard Case Nagell to Senator Kennedy, January 8, 1967. AARC.

p. 154, line 42: "foreknowledge": letter of Richard Case Nagell to Milton Greenstein at *New Yorker* magazine). November 14, 1968. NARA.

p. 155, line 8: pronounced him crazy: Report of SA David Reid. February 4, 1964. Field Office File No. EP 65-951. Title: RICHARD CASE NAGELL. Character: ESPIONAGE—S. NARA.

p. 155, line 12: a letter from "Don Morgan": Office of the District Attorney from Don Morgan. March 23, 1967. NARA.

p. 155, line 21: Martin's history with the Agency: No-3-68. 3 January 1968. To: Director, Domestic Contact Service. Att'n: Operational Support Staff (Musulin). From: Chief, New Orleans Office. Subject: William Richard Martin. Signed by Lloyd A. Ray. NARA.

p. 155, line 25: "his hands full": Memorandum. April 18, 1967. To: Jim Garrison. From: William R. Martin. Subject: Richard Case Nagell. Federal Prisoner No. PMB-A-166006-H. Medical Center for Federal Prisoners, Springfield, Mo. NARA.

p. 155, line 3: "distorted memos": Richard Case Nagell to Bud Fensterwald, May 8, 1975. AARC.

p. 155, line 5: William Martin proved to be of no help: Interview with Louis Ivon, May 27, 1998.

p. 155, line 6: Martin had admitted: Martin's second visit to Richard Case Nagell: Memorandum. May 11, 1967 (transcribed). To: Jim Garrison. From: William R. Martin. Re: Richard Case Nagell. A-166-6-H. Medical Center for Federal Prisoners, Springfield Missouri. NODA. NARA.

p. 156, line 7: Martin told Nagell he was "a former CIA officer": *The Man Who Knew Too Much,* p. 644.

p. 156, line 8: Martin knew Fitzgerald and Barnes: Richard Case Nagell to Bernard Fensterwald, August 2, 1971, quoted in *The Man Who Knew Too Much,* p. 644.

p. 156, line 11: Martin's purpose was to learn what Nagell thought: *The Man Who Knew Too Much,* p. 424. The correspondence between Martin and Nagell is available at AARC. See: William Martin's conciliatory letter: William R. Martin to Richard Case Nagell, April 25, 1967. Nagell refuses all further communication: R. S. Nicholas, Chief, Classification & Parole, To William R. Martin, April 28, 1967.

p. 156, line 13: William Martin describes his failure to obtain the tape: William R. Martin to Richard Case Nagell, June 20, 1967. NARA. Ten days later Nagell replied to Martin: "since the physical evidence referenced therein is no longer available, for whatever cause, I see no purpose in continuing with the preparation of my case": Richard Case Nagell to William Martin, July 30, 1967. AARC. Martin replied on August 7th. AARC.

p. 156, line 15: the FBI had the correspondence in its possession: FBI 124-10228-10488. 105-15823-579-589. The date, June 20, 1967, is obviously incorrect on the riff: there is later correspondence represented in this 27-page document.

p. 156, line 16: Nagell eventually promised not to "panic" and permitted Martin to visit: Richard Case Nagell to William R. Martin, May 24, 1967; "visit me as soon as possible": Richard C. Nagell to William Martin, May 31, 1967. See also: William R. Martin to Richard Case Nagell, June 1, 1967.

p. 156, line 17: William Martin was a professional spy: Memorandum: July 9, 1971. Re: Matters Concerning the Garrison Investigation. AARC.

p. 156, line 24: willingness to cooperate: To: Director, Domestic Contact Service. Att'n: Operational Support Staff (Musulin). From: Chief, New Orleans Office (Lloyd A. Ray). 3 January 1968. William Richard Martin. 104-10515-10022. 89T01357A. NARA.

p. 156, line 27: "the ghoul": Richard Case Nagell to Arthur Greenstein, September 17, 1967. AARC.

p. 156, line 28: "Hairy de Fairy . . . Dirty Dick": Richard Case Nagell to Arthur Greenstein, October 8, 1967.

p. 156, line 30: Helms gave the order: Noel Twyman, *Bloody Treason: The Assassination of John F. Kennedy* (Rancho Santa Fe, California: Laurel Publishing, 1997), p. 639; Conversation with Gary Shaw.

p. 156, line 36: "Clay will be slurred as fruit": Richard Case Nagell to Arthur Greenstein, October 8, 1967.

p. 156, line 38: Shaw of more importance than Ferrie: Conversation with Bernard Fensterwald, December 5, 1973.

p. 156, line 42: "hated" John F. Kennedy: Richard Case Nagell to Arthur Greenstein, September 30, 1967.

p. 157, line 8: Nagell had met Lee Harvey Oswald in Mexico City in July of 1963: See Richard Case Nagell to Richard H. Popkin, June 30, 1975. NARA.

p. 157, line 12: Nagell was visited "by CIA agents": Department of State telegram. Madrid. 01109252147Z. March 1969. Subject: Nagell, Richard C. NARA. (A CIA release).

p. 157, line 16: Ronald Lee Augustinovich: Memorandum. January 2, 1968. To: Jim Garrison. From: Lynn Loisel. Re: Call from Private Detective Smedly with Information Regarding CIA. NODA, NARA. Augustinovich told his story to Jimmy Alcock. January 15, 1968. To: Jim Garrison. From: Jim Alcock. Re: Ronald Lee Augustinovich. See also Statement of Calvin Barton Bull. February 5, 1968. Re: Addendum to Original Statement. NODA. NARA. Bull provided a 160-page report supposedly kept under Augustinovich's mattress.

p. 157, line 21: "a pilot in New Orleans was silenced": Statement of Calvin Barton Bull. Re: Material in Plain Folder Owned by Ronald Lee Augustinovich. February 6, 1968. NODA. NARA.

p. 157, line 26: Alcock flew to Miami: Memorandum. April 15, 1968. To: Jim Garrison. From: Jim Alcock, Executive Assistant District Attorney. Re: Ronald Lee Augustinovich. NODA. NARA.

p. 157, line 38: Donald P. Norton. "Donold": Norton renders his name as "Donold," rather than "Donald," the spelling used by both the CIA and the Garrison office. See Interview in Jim Garrison's Office with Donald P. Norton. Notes taken by Richard N. Billings. Courtesy of Lyon Garrison. See also: Ten pages of handwritten notes written February 9, 2003,

Barnesville, Georgia. From: Donald P. Norton to Joan Mellen: "Personal Comments of Donold P. Norton Re: The "Billings Transcript of Notes of an Interview in Jim Garrison's office on July 16, 1967, with Donald P. Norton. See also: "CIA Link Claimed with Three in Garrison Probes," *The Montreal Star.* August 7, 1967, p. 5.

p. 157, line 42: CIA attempts to kill an article in the *Vancouver Sun:* To: Director, DCS Attn: OSS (Musulin). From: Chief, Seattle Office. Subject: D. T. Norton—Alleged CIA Man for the Garrison Investigation. Ref: Musulin/Bakony Telecon 10 August 1967. NARA. The article was: John Taylor, "Fantastic Tale Links CIA with Oswald, Clay Shaw," *Vancouver Sun.* August 5, 1967. p. 1.

p. 158, line 36: working at Leslie Welding. Daily chronology of Lee Harvey Oswald provided by Mary Ferrell. October 13, 2001.

p. 159, line 15: "a corner of the operation": "a corner of the operation . . . we don't need him": Jim Garrison at the New Orleans round table conference.

p. 159, line 21: "boiler plate denial": CIA denies knowing Norton: CIA 100-300-17. August 21, 1967. To: Nancy G. Gratz WH/COG/CIGS. JMWAVE document. See also: CIA 104-10435-10032. RUSS HOLMES WORK FILE, CIA. From: DC/CI/R & A. Title: Memo: Garrison investigation of Kennedy assassination: Donald P. (Or T.) Norton. August 14, 1967. Signed by Donovan E. Pratt. DC/CI/R & E. CIA stated: "we have searched our files exhaustively and we do not find that this man worked for us at any time and there's no sign": "Garrison's conspiracy Probe," *Morning Advocate* (Baton Rouge). May 22, 1967. p. 10-A.

p. 159, line 26: Dymond: Irvin Dymond contacts Lloyd A. Ray, who contacts the Director of the Domestic Contact Service regarding Donald P. Norton. CIA NO-342-67. OGC67-1795. September 7, 1967. To: Director, Domestic Contact Service. Att'n: Operational Support Staff (Musulin). From: Chief, New Orleans Office. Subject: Case 49364—Garrison investigation. NARA.

p. 159, line 30: "we have means of getting this information on to Dymond": Memorandum. 18 September

1967. OGC 67-1787. Memorandum For: Executive Director—Comptroller. Subject: Garrison Investigation. 104-10428-10024. JFK. Russ Holmes Work File. Signed Lawrence R. Houston. Six offices received copies of this memorandum, beginning with the DDP (Clandestine services).

p. 159, line 33: had ever worked: CIA Memorandum. Subject: Garrison Investigation of Kennedy Assassination: Donald P. (Or T.) Norton. 14 August 1967. From: DC/CI/R & A. 104-10435-10032. Russ Holmes Work File. NARA.

p. 159, line 39: Norton's bodyguard is assaulted: FBI. To: Director, FBI. From: SAC, Seattle. October 13, 1967. 124-10071-10314. 89-69-3549, 3550. Includes Reisig's statement to police officer John Fisk, September 20, 1967. FBI 124-10071-10320. 89-69-SEE COMMENTS. To: Director, FBI. From: SAC, Seattle. Includes Louis V. Ivon to Honorable J. J. Atherton. September 28, 1967 (89-69-3561).

p. 160, line 18: Nagell said he had written to Rankin: Richard Case Nagell to Richard H. Popkin, July 9, 1975. NARA.

p. 160, line 18: A copy of Nagell's letter to J. Lee Rankin appears in the revised edition of *The Man Who Knew Too Much,* p. 7.

p. 28, line 21: "purely social": Commission Document 197.

p. 28, line 23: why he was questioned: Jim Garrison, *On the Trail of the Assassins,* p. 183.

CHAPTER 11

p. 161, Epigraph: "those CIA bastards": "I've got to do something": Reeves, *President Kennedy: Profile of Power* (Simon & Schuster: New York, 1993), p. 103.

p. 161, line 3: Jim Garrison reads about the CIA in The *New York Times:* "C.I.A. Maker of Policy or Tool? Agency Raises Questions around World," *New York Times,* Monday, April 25, 1966, The phrase about splintering the CIA is on p. 20. Copy annotated by Jim Garrison courtesy of Lyon Garrison.

p. 161, line 5: profound warfare with the Agency: The following books were particularly helpful: David Kaiser, *American Tragedy* (Cambridge, MA:

Harvard University Press Belknap Press, 2000); Francis Winters, *Year of the Hare: America in Vietnam,* January 25, 1963–February 15, 1964 (Athens, Ga.: University of Georgia Press, 1999); John Newman, *JFK and Vietnam* (New York: Warner Books, 1992); Richard Reeves, *President Kennedy: Profile of Power;* May, Ernest R. and Philip D. Zelikow, *The Kennedy Tapes* (Cambridge, MA: Harvard University Press, Belknap Press, 1977); Taylor Branch, *Parting the Waters: America in the King Years 1954–63* (New York: Simon & Schuster, 1988); Arthur M. Schlesinger, *One Thousand Days* (Boston: Houghton Mifflin Company, 1965), and *Robert Kennedy and His Times* (New York: Ballantine Books, 1978); Seymour M. Hersh, *The Dark Side of Camelot* (New York: Little, Brown and Company, 1997); Richard J. Walton, *Cold War and Counterrevolution: The Foreign Policy of John F. Kennedy* (New York: Penguin, 1972); Evan Thomas, *Robert F. Kennedy: His Life* (New York: Simon & Schuster, 2000).

p. 161, line 19: President Truman . . . "operational": "U.S. Should Hold CIA to Intelligence Role," *Washington Post,* December 22, 1963, p. 1.

p. 161, line 21: "the State Department for unfriendly countries": Quoted in Michael R. Beschloss, *May-Day: Eisenhower, Khrushchev and the U-2 Affair* (New York; Harper & Row: 1986), p. 126.

p. 161, line 24: "malignancy" on the body politic: Arthur Krock, "In the Nation: The Intra-Administration War in Vietnam," *New York Times,* October 3, 1963, Op page, section one.

p. 162, line 15: first "solo flight": Senate Select Committee to Study Governmental Operations with Respect to Intelligence Activities. Testimony of Richard Helms, September 12, 1975, Record number: 157-10011-10058. SSCIA box 247, folder 3. 58 pages, NARA.

p. 162, line 16: President Eisenhower attempts to control the C.I.A.: See Burton Hersh, *The Old Boys,* p. 407.

p. 162, line 25: Bissell as Wisner's assistant: Senate Select Committee to Study Governmental Operations with Respect to Intelligence Activities." (SSCIA), June 9, 1975, Testimony of

Richard Bissell, 108 pages, Record number: 157-10011-10020, SSCIA box 231, folder 3- Transcript/Bissell, NARA.

p. 162, line 39: "failure was almost impossible": Quoted in Beschloss, p. 387.

p. 163, line 8: on the U-2: "Powers came down": L. Fletcher Prouty to Joan Mellen, July 3, 1999, and Interview with Fletcher Prouty. See also Francis Gary Powers with Curt Gentry, *Operation Overflight: The U-2 Pilot Tells His Story for the First Time* (New York: Holt, Rinehart and Winston, 1970). See also, L. Fletcher Prouty, *The Secret Team: The CIA and Its Allies in Control of the U.S. and the World* (Englewood Cliffs, N.J.: Prentice-Hall, 1973) and "The Sabotaging of the American Presidency—The U-2 Debacle" (available on the Internet). See also Michael R. Beschloss, *MAY-DAY: Eisenhower, Khrushchev and the U-2 Incident* (New York: Harper and Row, 1986), and Lawrence R. Houston in *Periscope: Journal of the Association of Former Intelligence Officers* XI (Summer 1986): 11. See also the obfuscating statements of Dino Burgioni quoted in Gus Russo, *Live by the Sword: The Secret War against Castro and the Death of JFK* (Baltimore: Bancroft Press, 1980), p. 102.

p. 165, line 17: "important information regarding the U-2 flights": CIA. Record number 104-10309-10022. Record series: JFK. Agency file number: LA DIV WORK FILE. Originator: FBI. Title: Jack Edward Dunlap. Date: 04/21/66. 5 pages. NARA. JFK-WF04: F161. 1998. 09.22.11:46:07:123128. NARA.

p. 165, line 41: on February 16, 1961: Memorandum for the Record. 16 February 1961, Subject: Meeting with (redacted) and his Cousin. This document is signed only by C/WH/3 (Chief, Western Hemisphere, number 3), 5 pages. Only on May 13, 1961 did CIA send a briefing paper to the White House, at the request of President Kennedy's aide, Richard Goodwin. In this paper, CIA lies about its knowledge of the use to which the submachine guns passed to the "dissidents" were put. CIA contended that they were "for their use in personal defense." At the request of the Church Committee, the CIA searched for documentation that the Department of State or the Special Group approved the transfer of the carbines to "dissidents" in the Dominican Republic. It could locate no such documentation. For a discussion of the arming of Trujillo's assassins and the attempts to assassinate Lumumba, see SSCIA Testimony of Richard Bissell, July 22, 1975, 221 pages, Record Number: 157-10011-10017, and testimony of Richard Bissell, September 10, 1975, 84 pages, Record number: 157-10014-10093, Agency file: 13-H-02. The September testimony is a 1998 ARRB release, one long in coming.

In the late 1970s, Frank Church would be indignant as information of how the CIA withheld information from John F. Kennedy emerged: "Again and again and again, whenever a time comes for telling the President or telling his assistant in the White House, or telling the Attorney General what is going on, it is never done . . . everything is related except the fact that there was a specific plan laid on to assassinate Trujillo, and it is not there at all." It happens "again and again," Church repeated, the CIA keeping the president in the dark, informing the State Department and the president's "Special Group" of its schemes only after the fact, if at all.

Church chastised the Agency, and Bissell in particular: "The fact is, you were in on it, and the Agency knew about it, the Agency was in on it, the Agency was considering supplying weapons for a known purpose, and this was never communicated to the President." Listening to Bissell, Helms, Angleton, Harvey, and Maheu, Senator Morgan of North Carolina feared that should the "concrete evidence" of "murder plots" become public, the Committee would "completely destroy the intelligence community." See SSCIA, Testimony of Robert A. Maheu, June 9, 1975, Record Number 157-10011-10046, SSCIA box 252, folder 3, 45 pages, NARA.

p. 166, line 2: "the overthrow of Trujillo": Testimony of Richard M. Bissell, June 11, 1975.

p. 166, line 10: The CIA operates domestically: See U.S. Government Memorandum, Secret, January 15, 1964, To: Mr. W. C. Sullivan, From: Mr. D. J. Brennan Jr. 62-80750-4196, 4 pages, Re: CIA OPERATIONS IN THE U.S.

p. 166, line 14: James Angleton admitted: Senate Select Committee to Study Governmental Operations with Respect to Intelligence Activities, Testimony of James Angleton, June 19, 1975.

p. 166, line 22: the Alibi Club an all-male hangout: Robert Littell, *The Company: A Novel of the CIA* (New York: Penguin Books, 2003), p. 272.

p. 166, line 24: liquid bacteria: See the Inspector General's Report on Plots to Assassinate Fidel Castro, J. S. Earman, Inspector General, May 23, 1967, NARA.

p. 166, line 27: "man-eating shark": Harris Wofford, *Of Kennedys and Kings: Making Sense of the Sixties* (New York: Farrar, Straus & Giroux, 1980), p. 358.

p. 166, line 29: "secret state of its own": Ibid., Wofford, p. 356.

p. 166, line 37: "did not appear on paper . . . never will. . .": SSCIA Testimony of Richard Helms, September 12, 1975.

p. 166, line 42: "last president to believe": Interview with Gerald Patrick Hemming, October 22, 1999.

p. 167, line 8: "any person who doesn't clearly understand. . . .": Quoted in Beschloss, p. 153.

p. 167, line 16: Eisenhower did Kennedy "a disservice by not firing Dulles": Quoted in Beschloss, p. 387.

p. 167, line 21: mayor of Dallas: Jim Garrison, conversation with the author, April 14, 1989. New Orleans.

p. 167, line 22: Bissell was banished from the clandestine services: Testimony of Richard Bissell, June 9, 1975.

p. 167, line 25: "onrushing train": Testimony of Richard Helms, September 12, 1975.

p. 167, line 30: John Whitten characterizes William Harvey: HSCA. Security Classified Testimony, May 16, 1978, 193 pages, 014728, Transcript, NARA. pp. 143-146.

p. 167, line 34: Helms ran the clandestine services: Testimony of William Harvey, June 25, 1975.

p. 167, line 36: Helms didn't debrief McCone: Senate Select Committee to Study Governmental Operations with Respect to Intelligence Activities, Afternoon Session, June 25, 1975, Testimony of William Harvey, Record number: 157-10002-10106. Agency file: R-398, box 245, folder 14. 96 pages, NARA.

p. 167, line 38: Lawrence Houston admits he did not always debrief Mc-Cone, and neither did Helms: The U.S. Senate, Report of Proceedings, June 2, 1975, Witness: Lawrence Reed Houston, SSCIA, 157-10005-10224, Agency file: R174, 111 pages, NARA.

p. 168, line 1: "under a law passed on 20 June:" Norman Polmar, *Spyplane: The U-2 History Declassified* (Osceola, WI: MBI Publishing Company), p. 49.

p. 168, line 7: Minutes of the meetings of the President's Foreign Intelligence Advisory Board are available at AARC.

p. 168, line 16: "resisting the pressure": Senate Select Committee to Study Governmental Operations with Respect to Intelligence Activities, Testimony of Richard M. Bissell, June 11, 1975, 135 pages, SSCIA Record Number: 157-10011-10018, SSCIA box 231, folder 5, NARA.

p. 168, line 26: Kennedy limits the CIA's powers to conduct covert operations: See Mark Lane, *Plausible Denial,* pp. 99–100, 100n.

p. 168, line 20: Strategic Air Command: Minutes of the President's Foreign Intelligence Advisory Board, November 20, 1962, AARC.

p. 168, line 29: CIA denies Kennedy information: *The Kennedy Tapes,* p. 65.

p. 168, line 36: General Cabell attempts to restrict distribution of the Inspector General's Report: Eyes Only, Secret memorandum dated 28 November 1961, The National Security Archive, The George Washington University, Gelman Library. After Cabell's departure, copies did go out: Memorandum For: Director of Central Intelligence, February 16, 1962, Subject: Inspector General Survey of the Cuban Operation (dated October 1961), Lyman B. Kirkpatrick,The National Security Archive.

p. 168, line 37: "those CIA bastards": Reeves, p. 345.

p. 169, line 6: "no limitations": SSCIA Testimony of Richard Helms, September 11, 1975, Record number: 157-10011-10060, SSCIA box 247, folder 4, 71 pages, NARA.

p. 169, line 12: "a broad economic sabotage program": Testimony of Richard Helms, September 11, 1975. See also Memorandum for the Record, Subject: Cuban Operations, 12 November 1963, description of a meeting "with higher authority" on the subject, signed by Paul Eckel, NARA.

p. 169, line 15: "sabotage operations": Minutes of the President's Foreign Intelligence Advisory Board, October 4, 1962.

p. 169, line 18: assassination contingency plans: Testimony of Richard Helms, September 16, 1975, SSCIA 157-10002-10008, Agency file: R-1330, 41 pages, box 73, NARA.

p. 169, line 19: "concrete action against Cuba": FBI Memorandum, To: Mr. Tolson, From: A. H. Belmont, Subject: Cuban Situation, November 8, 1961; FBI Memorandum, To: Mr. W. C. Sullivan, From: Mr. D. E. Moore, Subject: Cuban Situation, December 4, 1961. See also FBI Memorandum, To: Mr. R. O. L'Allier, From: S. J. Papich, Subject: the Cuban Situation, August 7, 1961.

p. 169, line 21: Ramsey Clark discovers Lansdale's memos on how to kill Castro in Bobby Kennedy's files: Interview with Ramsey Clark, February 21, 2000.

p. 169, line 26: "Executive Action capability": Inspector General's report, p. 37.

p. 169, line 32: Executive Action capability is generated "within the Agency": Senate Select Committee to Study Governmental Operations with Respect to Intelligence Activities, Testimony of Richard Bissell, SSCIA box 231, folder 4, July 22, 1975, Record number: 157-10011-10017, NARA.

p. 169, line 34: "unseat": CIA Helms Exhibit #3B-30, HSCA 01110, box 8 of 78 -B-455.

p. 169, line 36: "CIA contribution to the Inter-Agency Mongoose effort": SSCIA William Harvey testimony, afternoon session, June 25, 1975.

p. 169, line 40: "actively engaged in giving instruction": Senate Select Committee to Study Governmental Operations with Respect to Intelligence Activities, June 18, 1975, Testimony of Samuel Halpern, SSCIA, 157-10002-10087, R-352, NARA.

p. 170, line 1: "the question was never asked": Bissell before the Church Committee, June 9, 1975.

p. 170, line 2: "keep its hand

tightly": Memorandum for Record, Subject: Minutes of Special Group (Augmented) on PROJECT MONGOOSE, 5 March 1962, signed by Thomas A. Parrott, 06904 and 06905.

p. 170, line 2: Robert Kennedy is misled by the Agency: See testimony of William Harvey, afternoon session, and testimony of Richard Helms, September 16, 1975.

p. 170, line 5: they ignored Bobby Kennedy: Senate Select Committee to Study Governmental Operations with Respect to Intelligence Activities, July 18, 1975, Testimony of Richard Helms, Record Number: 157-10011-10056, SSCIA box 246, folder 8, 85 pages, NARA. See also "major operations going beyond the collection of intelligence" were to be "approved in advance by the Special Group": testimony of William Harvey, afternoon session, June 25, 1975.

p. 170, line 7: Lansdale informed the FBI: Memorandum To: Mr. Tolson From: A. H. Belmont, November 8, 1961, Subject: Cuban situation, 2 pages, document number illegible, NARA. This was no different from the CIA's James Angleton from 1959 informing to Hoover. See Memorandum For: Director Federal Bureau of Investigation, Subject: Anti-Fidel CASTRO Activities, Internal Security—Cuba, September 29, 1959, 189-584-397, From: James Angleton, NARA. See also for Lansdale's communication with the FBI that "the President had instructed that an operation of great concern to this country be instituted efficiently and quietly:" Memorandum to: Mr. W. C. Sullivan, From: D. E. Moore, Subject: Cuban Situation, December 4, 1961, 2 pages, 105-89923, NARA.

p. 170, line 9: "operational relationship": CIA. Title: Special Activities Report on a JMWAVE Relationship. Date: 03/19/64. 104–10072–10289. JFK 15: F38 1993.08.06.14:34:43:310028. 10 pages. Courtesy of Malcolm Blunt and Gordon Winslow.

p. 170, line 10: "we become prisoners of our agents": Testimony of Richard Goodwin, July 18, 1975.

p. 170, line 11: Richard Goodwin offers Hemming and his mercenaries the opportunity to run Radio Swan: Interview with Howard K. Davis, March 18, 2002; interview with Gerald Patrick Hemming.

p. 170, line 19: Hemming infiltrates the 26th of July and participates in firing squads: Interviews with Gerald Patrick Hemming, October 22–25, 1999.

p. 170, line 26: David Atlee Phillips is seen with Oswald: See Gaeton Fonzi, *The Last Investigation.* See also "Who Killed JFK?" by Gaeton Fonzi. *Washingtonian, November* 1980, pp. 157–237.

p. 170, line 27: Kennedy attempts to monitor CIA in Miami through William Baggs: FBI 105-110398, June 30, 1962, AARC.

p. 170, line 42: opposition to Castro within Cuba: The *Kennedy Tapes,* p. 74.

p. 171, line 2: Operation Forty: Arthur Schlesinger comments on this development in a June 10, 1961, Memorandum: Subject: CIA Reorganization, NARA.

p. 171, line 9: Veciana press conference—attempts to embarrass John F. Kennedy: See Gaeton Fonzi's two articles in *Washingtonian* magazine as well as *The Last Investigation.* Whether an alternate group to Veciana's, also calling itself "Alpha 66," actually committed these acts does not alter that the CIA used them to embarrass John F. Kennedy.

p. 171, line 16: "Dickie": Conversation with Mary Keating, July 6, 2000.

p. 171, line 20: "a tremendous error and a serious concession": *Congressional Record,* October 9, 1962.

p. 171, line 22: Keating is supplied with film by Loran Hall: Testimony of Loran Hall in Executive Session before the House Select Committee on Assassinations, October 6, 1977, Record number: 180-10117-10027, Agency file number: 014661, NARA. See also Notes from taped Discussions with Loran Hall, August 20, 1977, August 26, 1977, From: Bill Triplett, HSCA 002153.

p. 171, line 27: "if it's the last thing": Richard Reeves, *President Kennedy,* p. 345.

p. 171, line 31: McCone threatens to resign: Minutes of the President's Foreign Intelligence Advisory Board, March 8 and 9, 1963, Memorandum for the File: March 11, 1963.

p. 171, line 35: "gesture to establish communication": Carlos Lechuga, *In the Eye of the Storm: Castro, Khru-*

shchev, *Kennedy and the Missile Crisis* (Melbourne, Australia: Ocean Press, 1995), p. 207.

p. 171, line 37: Robert Kennedy, McCone and Lansdale work on a post-Castro program: "Guideline for a Post-Castro Political Program": Meeting of the President's Foreign Intelligence Advisory Board, July 12, 1963.

p. 171, line 39: "both courses at the same time": CIA record number: 104-10306-10015, JFK-MISC, CIA-DCI file, 16 April 1963, Subject: Meeting with the President—5:30—15 April 1963 in Palm Beach, Florida, NARA.

p. 172, line 4: CIA presses for a military invasion of Cuba: Memorandum For: Director of Central Intelligence, Through: Deputy Director (Plans), Subject: OPERATION MONGOOSE—Appraisal of Effectiveness and Results Which Can Be Expected from Implementing the Operational Plan Approved at the Meeting of the Special Group (Augmented) on 16 March 1962.

p. 172, line 5: "it be done by clandestine means": Testimony of William Harvey, afternoon session, June 25, 1975.

p. 172, line 7: Kennedy questions Ian Fleming about what James Bond would do: John Pearson, *The Life of Ian Fleming* (New York: McGraw-Hill, 1966), pp. 321–322.

p. 172, line 12: "the only real solution would be to assassinate Castro": Richard Goodwin is not certain whether it was McNamara who made the statement. No one disagrees. Testimony of Richard Goodwin, July 19, 1975, U.S. Senate, Select Committee to Study Governmental Operations with Respect to Intelligence Activities, SSCIA, 157-10002-10051, Agency file: R-610, NARA.

p. 172, line 18: John and Robert Kennedy organize for a sniper to go to Cuba to kill Castro: Interview with F. Lee Bailey, November 11, 1999.

p. 172, line 30: confounded the national interest: Quoted in Winters, *The Year of the Hare,* p. 193.

p. 172, line 33: Rosemary Kennedy at Angola: Interviews with John R. Rarick, December 27, 2001; January 2, 2002.

p. 173, line 1: "they're going to throw our asses out of there": Reeves, p. 484.

p. 173, line 4: one thousand soldiers: John Newman points out in his book *Kennedy and Vietnam,* p. 433, that at the meeting of Kennedy's advisers held in Honolulu at the time of his death, that number had already been whittled down to 284.

p. 173, line 16: McCone is the first person Bobby sees: Washington Merry-Go-Round, September 9, 1976, "CIA Hid Facts on JFK Death" by Jack Anderson and Les Whitten, United Feature Syndicate.

p. 173, line 17: "Did the CIA kill my brother?" Arthur M. Schlesinger attributes this quotation to CIA asset Walter Sheridan in a recorded interview by Roberta Greene, June 12, 1970, RFK Oral History Program. See Arthur Schlesinger, *Robert Kennedy and His Times,* p. 665.

p. 173, line 19: "one of your guys did it": Quoted in Evan Thomas, *Robert F. Kennedy: His Life,* p. 277.

p. 173, line 21: "did you think there might be?": Interview with Frank Mankiewicz, December 1, 1999.

p. 173, line 23: Bobby Kennedy sends Walter Sheridan to Dallas: Interview with Edwin Guthman, May 11, 2000.

p. 173, line 26: Bobby called Julius Draznin and learns that the mob was not behind the assassination: To: David Marwell/ARRB, From: Dave Montague/ARRB, January 6, 1997, Subject: Independent Investigations into the Assassination. Julius Draznin returned the ARRB's call on November 19, 1996, NARA, ARRB document, Author: Brian Rosen/ARRB, Date created: 11/19/96; Telephone conversation with Julius Draznin, August 21, 2002.

p. 173, line 33: close communication with Sheridan and Bobby: Draznin and Sheridan communicate during the week following the assassination. Conversation with Julius Draznin, August 21, 2002. See also Agency: WC. Record Number: 179-40004-10098, From: Cassidy, John, To: Sheridan, Walter, 11/29/63, 1 page, Subjects: Block; Platt. Cassidy at the Department of Justice reports to Walter Sheridan of a telephone call from Draznin referring to Draznin's having told him about communications he had with Sheridan about three people, NARA.

p. 173, line 35: Sheridan tells the Church Committee that the "mob" was behind the assassination: SSCIA, 157-10014-10060, Records Series. Hearings, Agency file number: 90-H-01, September 19, 1975, Senate Select Committee to Study Governmental Operations with Respect to Intelligence Activities, testimony of Walter Sheridan, 40 pages, NARA.

p. 174, line 3: "undercover intelligence assignments": Jim Garrison, "The Murder Talents of the CIA," *Freedom* (April–May 1987), p. 14.

p. 174, line 5: "he'd still be talking": Jim Garrison to Jonathan Blackmer, July 15, 1977.

p. 174, line 7: "major menace": See *States-Item,* May 5, 1967: "DA Will Show Oswald in CIA Undercover Role Here." The second edition headline read: "Oswald Agent for CIA, DA Will Seek tTo Prove."

p. 174, line 10: "if the CIA killed the President": William Alford interviewed in John Barbour, *The Garrison Tapes.*

p. 174, line 19: "some truth in the allegation": CIA NO-43-67, To: Director, Domestic Contact Service, From: Chief, New Orleans Office, 6 February 1967, NARA.

p. 174, line 20: "I think Garrison will expose": Memorandum To: Director, Domestic Contact Service, From: Chief, New Orleans Office (Lloyd A. Ray), March 28, 1967, NO-112-67, NARA.

p. 174, line 21: "agreement of liaison with FBI": CIA 104-10213-10146, JFK, 80T01357A, Title: Correspondence with FBI on CIA/FBI Liaison Agreement in 1948, 18 pages, NARA, courtesy of Malcolm Blunt.

p. 174, line 24: "irresponsible actions . . . no comment": To: New Orleans, From: Director, 89-69-1440, February 21, 1967.

p. 174, line 28: "Give Garrison nothing": Memo to file, February 23, 1967, 89-69-1490.

p. 174, line 33: "the only investigation the FBI is making is of Jim Garrison whom they hate with a intense passion": See *Playboy* deposition of Gordon Novel, May 23, 1969, pp. 964–966.

p. 174, line 33: The FBI investigated Jim Garrison: See To: Mr. Barefoot Sanders, From: Fred M. Vinson Jr., March 28, 1967, NARA.

p. 174, line 34: continuing to investigate . . . as they claimed they were doing: Interview with Joseph T. Sylvester, June 15, 2000. Sylvester lied in the friendliest of ways.

p. 174, line 35: John Alice can identify the figures in the photographs of Oswald: FBI, To: SAC, New Orleans, From: SA Stephen M. Callender, February 24, 1967, with Memorandum, 89-69-1603, NARA. There are dozens of incidents where the Bureau did not pass on leads that might have helped Jim Garrison.

p. 174, line 40: "Clay Shaw and Clay Bertrand": FBI, Memorandum, To: SAC, From: ASAC Sylvester, April 26, 1967, 89-69-2055, NARA. Pizzo apparently wrote as well to Congressman F. Edward Hebert, but the letter is no longer available in the Hebert papers at Tulane University.

p. 175, line 1: Oswald frequented the Mission: R. C. Cook Sr, To Mr. Ray Berg, *Papers of Joseph A. Oster.* Cook was president of a firm called R & S Research of Houston, Texas. Berg ran Pacesetter Publishing on Camp Street and accused Jack Martin of using his name without authorization. See also: To: Director, FBI, From: SAC, New Orleans, March 17, 1967, 62-109060-4959.

p. 175, line 7: failed to develop any evidence: Years later, lawyer Jerry Paradis told HSCA's Mike Ewing, with respect to witnesses who could testify that Ferrie knew Oswald: "I could have given them what they wanted": HSCA 014374, Mike Ewing interview with Jerry Paradis, December 15, 1978, NARA.

p. 175, line 17: Hosty ordered not to attend the November 22, 1963 luncheon: SSCIA, 157-10014-10014. Hearings, File number: 04-H-01, December 12, 1975, Testimony of James Hosty. 163 pages, box 2, NARA.

p. 175, line 18: Oswald's letter: "Oswald's Final Letter: How Did He Know?" by Bob Allen, Paul Scott. *Shreveport Times,* November 20, 1967.

p. 175, line 23: for more on Oswald's intelligence connections: Memo, 6/21/76, To: Dave Marston, From: Gaeton Fonzi, Re: Interview with Jim Garrison.

p. 175, line 27: "Oswald was allegedly linked with CIA": To: Chief, New Orleans Field Office, From: Director, Domestic Contact Service, OSS, 20 March 1967, REF: NO-84-57, dated 3 March 1967, Signed James R. Murphy, NARA. Three days later, Ray denied any contact with Shaw since May 1956 and denied any contact with anyone on the list Murphy had provided: W. Hardy Davis; Layton Martens; Rudolph Richard Davis; Carlos Coroga [*sic*]; Perry R. Russo; or Dean A. Andrews Jr.; Director, Domestic Contact Service: Att'n: Operational Support Staff, From: Chief, New Orleans Office, March 23, 1967, signed by Lloyd A. Ray, NARA. See also Diary [of James Murphy], 6 May 1967, NARA. See also Hoke May, "CIA's Warren Panel Testimony Is Disputed by DA," *States-Item*, May 6, 1967, p. 1. Commission Exhibit 237, a photograph of an obvious impostor, that stocky man who is definitely not Oswald, appears beside the article.

p. 175, line 29: Shaw was and still is a CIA agent: Notes of Hoke May, AARC.

p. 175, line 32: McCone repeated his denial: McCone quoted in "Oswald Depicted As CIA Agent; Sources Here Say," *Times-Picayune*, May 6, 1967, section 1, p. 3. The CIA had been denying that they knew anything about Oswald. Notes from Raymond Rocca to Richard Helms 23 March 1964, 201-289248, 618-793. See also Memorandum for the Record, CIA, Oswald, Lee Harvey, 20 February 1964, signed by Steven L. Kuhn, Deputy Chief/Personal Security Division, 1272-1028, NARA.

p. 175, line 33: James Angleton controlled what the CIA told the Warren Commission: Memorandum to: Mr. A. H. Belmont, From: Mr. W. C. Sullivan, May 13, 1964, Subject: JAMES ANGLETON CENTRAL INTELLIGENCE AGENCY (CIA), 105-82555-3689, HSCA number is 000229. Angleton enjoyed a "hot line" to the Bureau.

For connections between CIA and FBI, see SSCIA (Church Committee), interview with James Angleton, February 6, 1976, 71 pages, NARA. Angleton sends a memo to the Director based on information sent by Walter Sheridan: Memorandum For: Director, Federal Bureau of Investigation, Attention: Mr. S. J. Papich, Subject: Alvin R. Beaubouef, Reference: Memorandum from FBI Office, Houston,

Texas, 27 April 1967, Subject: Assassination of President John Fitzgerald Kennedy, November 22, 1963, Dallas, Texas, Miscellaneous, Information Concerning, CSCI-316-02153-67, May 9, 1967. Originated by: DC/CI/R&A, NARA. For more of Angleton's liaison with FBI, see 14 June 1967, Memorandum For: Director, Federal Bureau of Investigation, attention: Mr. S. J. Papich, Subject: Allegations of Unidentified Woman regarding "Mario Gracias," et al., Reference: FBI Memorandum of 10 April 1967, file number (S) 62-109060, signed: for the Deputy Director for Plans; James Angleton (A James R. Hunt signed this memo), NARA.

p. 175, line 37: "allay the story of CIA's possible sponsorship": CIA 618-793, March 23, 1964, NARA.

p. 175, line 42: "any other US Government agency had used him: Memorandum For: Chief, CI Staff, Subject: Allegations of Lee Harvey Oswald's Connection with the Agency, Reference: Memorandum of Conversation, Dan Rather/Les Midgley and the DCI, dated 6 December 1975, CIA 1188-1000, signed by Paul Hartman of CI/R & A staff.

p. 176, line 5: Siragusa is recruited by Angleton: See Memorandum—February 5, 1978, To: G. Robert Blakey, From: Fonzi & Gonzales, Re: Interview with CHARLES SIRAGUSA.

p. 176, line 9: "focal point": To: CIA task force, From: The Review Staff, Walter Elder, Subject: SSC/HSC Request, 76-0298, March 9, 1976, NARA.

p. 176, line 26: Casasin showed "operational intelligence interest" in Oswald: Memo by Thomas B. Casasin, December 16, 1963, CIA. From: COS, Paris to: Chief, SR info Chief, WE, 104-10429-10239, JFK Agency file: RUSS HOLMES WORK FILES, NARA.

p. 176, line 31: "this individual looks odd": CIA 435-173A. The author, whose name is redacted, was "Chief of the 6 branch." For the CIA denial, Memorandum For: Chief, CI/R & A. Subject: comment regarding article alleging Oswald was interviewed by CIA.employees, March 17, 1964, NARA (1993.07.21.15.32.47:340340.JFK, 80T01357A, JFK 27, folder F26).

p. 176, line 36: information about Oswald went to CI/SIG rather than to the Soviet Realities section: John Newman, *Oswald and the CIA* (New York: Carroll & Graf, 1995), p. 27.

p. 177, line 10: "Oswald sent to USSR": CIA 304-113, 4 December 1963, NARA.

p. 177, line 13: a document in Oswald's file in Mexico City about Transcontinental: CIA, October 12, 1961, 100-10461-1065, FBI number is 124-10002-10387, Subject: Activities of Transcontinental, NARA.

p. 177, line 29: the CIA sent names to the National Security Agency for its watch list: See, for example, SSCIA, 157-10014-10188, records series: Miscellaneous Records of the Church Committee, Agency file number: 07-M-95, four pages, interview with Mabel Hoover and Ervan Kuhnke, Office of Security, CIA, July 25, 1975. See also FBI, 124-10156-10005, HQ, 105-82555-132, From: Brennan, D. J, To Sullivan, W. C., one page, December 4, 1963, Subjects: LHO, NSA Project, NEG. See also FBI 124-10264-10216, HQ, 62-116395-944, SSCIA re: Deposition of Assistant Director W. Raymond Wannall, October 7, 1975. Most of this document is redacted.

p. 177, line 31: "a threat to the internal security of the country": FBI Memorandum, To: Mr. A. H. Belmont, From: Mr. W. C. Sullivan, Subject: Security Index, November 26, 1963, NARA. These intercepts would not be made available to scholars: Meeting Report, Author: Tim Wray/ARRB, January 30, 1996. Department of Defense, January 29, 1996.

p. 177, line 37: James Wilcott says that Oswald was debriefed at Atsugi: *"Declaración de James Wilcott ante el tribunal internacional, 'La Juventud Acusa al Imperialismo,' el 2 de Agosto de 1978 en La Habana, Cuba, NARA."* James Wilcott talks about Oswald's connection with CIA: James Wilcott, "The Kennedy Assassination," HSCA 105-70076, 013800, 21 pages, June 13, 1977. This is the most coherent among several statements made by Wilcott beginning in 1968. This article was written, Wilcott told the HSCA's CIA expert Harold Leap, not for publication, but to aid investigators. He wrote it, he said, after reading Jim Garrison's book, *A Heritage of Stone.* See also Transcript: Wilcott, James B. Testimony Before the Committee, 110

pages, 180-10116-10096, 014672, March 22, 1978, NARA; interview of Wilcott with Harold Leap and Betsy Wolf, January 28, 1978, 006446.

p. 178, line 23: HSCA attempts to discredit James Wilcott: HSCA 180-10142-10385. CIA Segregated Collection, Agency file, 24-2701. This document was made available with thirteen "postponements." Handwritten HSCA staffer notes titled: "Wilcott Allegation." See also HSCA 180-10143-10275, CIA Segregated Collection: 29\09\02, twenty-five "postponements." These are Harold Leap's handwritten notes.

p. 178, line 38: "Subject considered a very naive man": HSCA handwritten document, Marked "Secret," box 29, folder 9: 11110302.

p. 179, line 8: instrumental in the assassination of Martin Luther King: See William Pepper, *Orders to Kill: The Truth Behind the Murder of Martin Luther King* (New York: Carroll & Graf Publishers, Inc., 1995). See especially chapter 30, "Orders to Kill."

p. 179, line 13: "highly secretive operation": Pepper, p. 414.

p. 179, line 17: Veciana met Oswald with Bishop (Phillips): "Veciana Interviews," To: DM From: SW. 3?/22/76, CIA document. three pages, Miscellaneous Records of the Church Committee, Agency: SSCIA, 157-10014-10041, Agency file number: 06-M-22, NARA.

p. 179, line 18: *The Amlash Legacy:* courtesy of Anthony Summers and James H. Lesar. *The Amlash Legacy,* in the hands of Phillips' widow and writer Joseph C. Goulden has not, Goulden says, at the insistence of the widow, been made available to historians. According to Goulden, this decision has been made in the light of suggestions by authors that Phillips had something to do with the Kennedy assassination: Conversation with Joseph C. Goulden, July 30, 2003. Other of Phillips' papers are at the Library of Congress, but this manuscript has been withheld. Phillips' widow and his executor, Joseph Goulden, have sealed the full outline/manuscript.

p. 179, line 42: a CIA cable: To: DIRECTOR, From: JMWAVE, ACTION: WH 8.PRIORITY MEXI INFO DIR CITE WAVE 8065, DYVOUR PBRUMEN, NARA.

p. 180, line 8: "directly linked to the Mafia": Seymour M. Hersh, *The*

Price of Power: Kissinger in the Nixon White House (New York: Summit Books, 1983), p. 279.

p. 180, line 14: That David Atlee Phillips sometimes used the alias "Michael Choaden" is revealed in a CIA document dated 08/31/59. The text refers to Choaden's "Operations" deemed essential, and requests a "security review" in the light of his identity as a "PBPRIME INTELLIGENCE AGENT" having been leaked in Havana. The document went "To: Habana," From: Director, Conf: WH5. Its title reads: "CABLE: SECURITY REVIEW OF PHILLIPS . . . OPERATIONS DEEMED ESSENTIAL" (RECORD NUMBER 104-10128-10330, RECORD SERIES: JFK, AGENCY FILE NUMBER: 80TO1357A). Cable courtesy of Jim Lesar. For a discussion of Sforza/Sloman's CIA activities, particularly his role in the assassination of Gen. Rene Schneider in Chile, see also Peter Kornbluth, *The Pinochet File: A Declassified Dossier on Atrocity and Accountability* (New York: New Press, 2004).

p. 180, line 38: Shawn Phillips, James Atlee Phillips, and David Atlee Phillips: Interview with Shawn Phillips, January 23, 2005. See also: research notes of Dick Russell, courtesy of Mr. Russell.

p. 181, line 4: hung up: E-mail from Shawn Phillips to researcher Gary Buell. See <\<>http://www.jfk murdersolved.com/phillips.htm>.

p. 181, line 10: J. Garrett Underhill: "foreign positive intelligence": Memorandum, 30 June 1967, To: DC/CI/R & A, From: Director, Domestic Contact Service, Subject: Case 49,364—Garrison Investigation: John Garrett Underhill Jr., NARA. See also Memorandum, June 19, 1967, Subject: *Ramparts:* John Garrett Underhill Jr., Samuel George Cummings, and INTERARMCO, NARA.

p. 181, line 10: "a small clique in the CIA": John Donovan to Jim Garrison, April 29, 1967, NODA, NARA. Garrison's source was Donovan, a news editor at WPIX (channel 11) in New York.

p. 181, line 13: "blow the whistle on the CIA": Edward S. Cohen to Dear David, June 2, 1966, NARA.

p. 181, line 17: blown up a ship: JMWAVE 30 April 1962, 201-309125 (this is Gerald Patrick Hemming's 201 file number), 100-009-014, NARA.

p. 181, line 18: "trained CIA assassin": Interview with Gerald Patrick Hemming, October 22, 1999.

p. 181, line 21: provisional covert security approval: Memorandum For: Chief, LEOB/SRS Subject: Highlights on the Cast of Characters Involved in Garrison's Investigation, December 28, 1967, NARA.

p. 181, line 22: should he leave the country?: CIA Memorandum for the Record, May 11, 1967, Subject: Laborde, Lawrence J., born August 27, 1909, NARA.

p. 181, line 23: Laborde's files: CIA asks FBI to do a records check on Laborde: CIA Memorandum For: Chief, Security Support Division, From: Chief, Investigations Branch, Subject: Laborde, Lawrence J. #241598, PSCA IB/3, 20 March 1961, signed H. K. Clayton, NARA.

p. 181, line 24: never been paid directly: CIA Memorandum For: Deputy Director for Plans, Subject: Interlocking Relationships Between Brown/Slafter and Garrison, WH/C 67-313. Signed by William V. Broe. Chief, Western Hemisphere section; HSCA number is 000178, NARA.

p. 181, line 25: Ray ordered not to see him: Cable Re: Lawrence J. Laborde Call to Talk to Agent Handling Kennedy CA, Document id. 1993.08.10.16.38:55:590015, 80T01357A, NARA.

Laborde returns to CIA in September for instructions: Lawrence Houston to Honorable Walter J. Yeagley, October 20, 1967, OGC67-1993, NARA. See also Memorandum for Director, Domestic Contact Service, Subject: Lawrence J. Laborde, Reference: A. Memorandum from Director, Domestic Contact Service to C/CI/ R & A, dated 12 May 1967, Subject: DCS Case 49364—Lawrence Laborde—Claims Past Affiliation with CIA—Seeks Advice, etc., May 19, 1967, signed by Raymond G. Rocca, C/CI/R & A, NARA.

p. 181, line 34: a list of its New Orleans employees: Enclosure 28: "It has been determined that These Following Components and Individual Employees of CIA. . . .": 104-10013-10348, 201-289248, NARA. They then did traces on "key figures in case to date:" Memorandum no. 2, Subject: Garrison and the Kennedy Investigation, Reference: CI/R & a Memorandum of 26 April 1967, Subject as above, May 8, 1967, NARA.

p. 181, line 35: Carl Trettin: Memorandum for the Record, Subject: Possible DRE Animus towards President Kennedy, Reference: Memorandum 8 March 1967, same subject, Date of Document: 04/03/67, Subjects: AMSPELL. Record Number 104-10181-10113, Record Series: JFK, Agency file number: 80T01357A.

p. 181, line 41: CIA involvement with Cubans: Reference: Memorandum WH/COG—194 (not dated but forwarded by routing sheet dated 8 May 1967) to ADDP and C/CI/R & A, Subject: Garrison and the Kennedy Assassination, 104-10406-10022, RUSS HOLMES WORK FILE, NARA.

p. 182, line 1: CIA had a "target file": Memorandum. To: The File. From: Kenneth D. Klein. Date: July 1, 1977. Re: telephone conversation with Chester Vigurie. NARA.

p. 182, line 10: The Agency considers F. Edward Hebert as a source: Diary, 11 May 1967, Case 49364, GSM (Musulin), NARA.

p. 182, line 14: a thousand dollar suit: Interview with Mark Lane, March 17, 1998.

p. 182, line 15: Lawrence Houston writes directly to Judge Bagert: Lawrence R. Houston to Honorable Bernard J. Bagert, 16 May 1967, NARA. Judge Bagert had issued the subpoena. Judge Bagert denies the motion to quash Kennedy's subpoena, Re: Regis L. Kennedy, Special Agent, Federal Bureau of Investigation, in the Criminal Court for the Parish of Orleans, State of Louisiana: Reasons for Denial of Motion to Quash, signed: Bernard J. Bagert, NARA.

FBI considers going into federal court with a petition for removal: FILE, From: SAC, May 17, 1967, 124-10259-10063, 89-69-3071, NARA.

p. 182, line 18: Jim Garrison subpoenas Allen Dulles: From: Bress, David, USA, To: Burnes, Richard V. Title: Memo: Re: Allen W. Dulles, March 13, 1968, Agency file: 80T01357A, record number 0-0-0, NARA.

p. 182, line 19: Dulles went on television: James Alcock at the New Orleans conference.

p. 182, line 22: de Brueys has been transferred: FBI To: Director, FBI.

From: SAC, New Orleans, May 7, 1967, 124-10237-10412, 89-69-2086, 2087.

p. 182, line 27: Garrison charges CIA was paying the lawyers: "Probe Figures' Lawyers Paid by CIA, says DA," *States-Item*, May 11, 1967. See also William Martin tells Jim Garrison that one Stephen B. Lemman handled CIA's clandestine payroll in New Orleans: Memorandum, May 24, 1967, To: Jim Garrison, From: William Martin, Subject: Central Intelligence Agency Connections in the City of New Orleans, NODA, NARA.

Burton Klein denied he knew Lemman: Interview with Burton Klein, March 3, 2002.

p. 182, line 32: "federal agents involved are taking the fifth amendment: See FBI To: Director, From: SAC, New Orleans, quoting the *States-Item* of May 10, 1967, 124-10259-10022, 89-69-3027, NARA.

p. 182, line 35: "interested Agency components": Speed letter: Case 49, 634: Garrison Investigation Newspaper Articles, signed George J. Musulin, From: Operational Support Staff, NARA.

p. 182, line 35: "Ray's Clip Joint": NO 218-67. 31 May 1967. To: Director, Domestic Contact Service, Attn: Services Division (Vaughan), From: Chief, New Orleans Office, Subject: Monthly Man-Hour Report, NARA.

p. 182, line 38: Regis Kennedy's reports are sealed: FBI. To: SAC, From: ASAC Sylvester, May 10, 1967, 89-69-3028, NARA.

p. 182, line 38: efforts to keep Regis Kennedy from going before the grand jury: LaCour immediately files a motion to suppress the subpoena served on Regis Kennedy, and Kennedy's affidavit: FBI, To: Director, From: SAC, New Orleans, May 9, 1967. 124-10237-10433, 89-69-3012, NARA.

p. 182, line 40: Ramsey Clark sends Big Regis a telegram: May 16, 1967, NARA. See also SAC Rightmyer, From: Clerk Clay Poche, Subject: Subpoena of SA Regis L. Kennedy, May 16, 1967, 89-69-3060, NARA.

p. 183, line 3: "use his own judgment": FBI. To: Director, From: New Orleans, May 17, 1967, 124-10259-10064, 89-69-3072, NARA.

p. 183, line 4: on the stand: Big Regis testifies to the Orleans Parish grand jury: Special Investigation, May 17, 1967. Present are Garrison, Oser, Alcock, Sciambra, Burnes and William Martin, NARA.

p. 183, line 16: attacked by Fred Vinson: "of serious concern to the Bureau": Director, Federal Bureau of Investigation, From: Fred M. Vinson Jr., Assistant Attorney General, Criminal Division, NARA.

p. 183, line 16: Ramsey Clark backs up Vinson: To: Director, Federal Bureau of Investigation, From: Attorney General. 179-11, undated, NARA. Robert Rightmyer defended Kennedy, and pointed to the "variance of instructions."

p. 183, line 19: "executive privilege": Official routing slip, September 18, 1967, From: Lawrence Houston, NARA.

p. 183, line 21: Rightmyer defends his agent: FBI, To: Director, FBI, From: SAC, New Orleans, May 18, 1967, 124-10259-10078, 89-69-3086, 3087, NARA.

p. 183, line 22: Bureau furnishing CIA with "data concerning several of the individuals of current interest to CIA": To: Director, FBI, From: SAC, New Orleans, (Rightmyer), May 5, 1967, 89-69-2066. Reply is: To: SAC, New Orleans, From: Director, FBI, May 8, 1967.

p. 183, line 23: Jack Rogers reports to the CIA: Angleton then reports to Hoover based on Jack Rogers' information to the CIA office in New Orleans: Memorandum For: Director, Federal Bureau of Investigation, Attention: Mr. S. J. Papich, Subject: Garrison Investigation: Mr. Jack N. Rogers, June 19, 1967, 105-82-555-NR5584, NARA.

p. 183, line 29: Rogers confides in the CIA about what he learned at Garrison's office: CIA. To: Director, Domestic Contact Service, Att'n: Operational Support Staff (Musulin), From: Chief, New Orleans Office, 5 June 1967, Subject: Case 49364—Garrison Investigation—Jack N. Rogers, NO-230-67, signed by Lloyd A. Ray, 104-10189-10042, 80T01357A, NARA. (Rogers had security status of MI(b) dating back from February 1960 with the Office of Security and had been involved in Domestic Contact Cases; he was the source of contact on twelve reports acknowledged by June of 1967.)

See also for Jack Rogers' activities as a CIA asset, Document ID number: 1993.07.15.18.59.17:120630, JFK, 80T01357A, JFK box #: JFK 16. Vol/folder: F67, Office Memorandum, U.S. Government, 3/12/62, From: Wm. P. Burke, C/New Orls. Office, To: Chief, Contact Division, Support BR, 3 pages, NARA.

p. 183, line 34: "two Americas": Jim Garrison, *The War Machine* (unpublished), AARC.

p. 183, line 36: WWL-TV: The transcript of Jim Garrison on Channel 4 (WWL-TV) is #22 in the file of Walter Sheridan manuscripts of interviews available at NARA. Or: HSCA 180-10099-10333, 004634, 15-page transcript.

p. 184, line 1: "Bay of Pigs sector": Jim Garrison in John Barbour, *The Jim Garrison Tapes*.

p. 184, line 6: "on solid ground": Minutes, June 5, 1967, MCC Executive Committee Meeting. By: Aaron Kohn, Managing Director, MCC.

p. 184, line 7: "hostile viewpoint": FBI Memorandum, To: Mr. Tolson, From: C. D. DeLoach, April 4, 1967, 62-19060-5075, NARA. (Jack Anderson visits Cartha DeLoach at the FBI upon his return from New Orleans.)

p. 184, line 14: "sitting duck" for "Garrison's wild accusations": FBI, To: Mr. W. C. Sullivan, From: Mr. W. A. Branigan, April 26, 1967, 62-109060-5139, NARA.

p. 184, line 25: the Agency formula for describing Jim Garrison: CIA, Memorandum, April 26, 1967, 104-10404-10448, RUSS HOLMES WORK FILE, 49 pages, NARA.

p. 184, line 31: "more vehemently, viciously, and mendaciously": CIA Memorandum For: General Counsel, Via: ADDP, Subject: Garrison TV Interviews of 21 May 1967 and 28 May 1967, 6 June 1967, Signed: Raymond G. Rocca, Chief, CI/R & A, NARA.

p. 184, line 38: an agency policy: "Was Garrison Right After All?" Ibid. *New Orleans* magazine, June 1976, p. 31.

CHAPTER 12

p. 185, Epigraph: "They didn't want to just discredit": William Alford quoted in *The Garrison Tapes*.

p. 185, line 11: Sheridan enlists Gordon Novel: Interview with Gordon Novel.

p. 185, line 13: the day he knocked on Clay Shaw's door: See the Clay Shaw Diary.

p. 185, line 1: "security approval": Sheridan was "security approved": CIA document, 1 December 1967, Subject: Sheridan, Walter James, NARA.

p. 185, line 21: using blackmail: for the illegal means by which Sheridan pursued Jimmy Hoffa, see three articles by Fred J. Cook in *The Nation* magazine: "The Hoffa Trial," April 27, 1964; "The Hoffa Decision," January 2, 1967; and "Anything to Get Hoffa," February 20, 1967. Cook was unique: few in the media dared to expose Sheridan's methods. Sheridan denied knowing of wiretapping, only for a retired police detective named Herman A. Frazier to trap him by introducing onto the wire a fake name "Armentrout." When Sheridan asked Frazier about "Armentrout," it was of course clear that he had listened to the tap. Frazier refused to submit to blackmail and was indicted; it took three trials before he could clear himself. An FBI employee named Bud Nichols swore Sheridan had hired him on two occasions to bug Hoffa's suite and his attorney's suite at the Patton Hotel. He identified Sheridan from his photograph. As Bobby Kennedy demanded one wiretap after another, even Ramsey Clark tried to stop him, (interview with Ramsey Clark, February 21, 2000). Deke admitted to conservative William Loeb of the *Manchester Union-Leader* that Sheridan headed Bobby Kennedy's wiretapping unit and that Kennedy had authorized the IRS to tap wires. When Loeb made that public, DeLoach denied it, but you could see Deke gritting his teeth. Sheridan also utilized the Internal Revenue Service, forgiving Partin thousands of dollars of back taxes.

When the Hoffa case came up for review before the U.S. Supreme Court, Ramsey Clark's father, Justice Tom Clark, at once disqualified himself. Hoffa lost, but foremost in dissent was Chief Justice Earl Warren. "An invasion of basic rights made possible by prevailing upon friendship with the victim is no less proscribed than an invasion accomplished by force," Justice

Warren wrote. He found Sheridan's methods "offensive to the fair administration of justice in federal courts," his behavior an "affront to the quality and fairness of federal law enforcement." Warren concluded his dissent by accusing Walter Sheridan of "obstructing justice." Earl Warren's dissent, see *Hoffa v. United States*. no. 32, Supreme Court of the United States, 383 U.S. 293; 87 S. Ct. 408; 17 L Ed 2d 374; 1966, U.S. Lexis 2778, October 13, 1966, argued, December 12, 1966, Decided.

p. 185, line 41: Partin reported to Herbert J. Miller Jr.: Partin's "JJC" reports to Herbert J. Miller, Memorandum January 16, 1967, Jeremy Gunn Records Collection, NARA.

p. 186, line 1: "You won't sue me": Interview with Lou Merhige, June 8, 2000.

p. 186, line 4: "Lotus Ford": Interview with Jim McPherson, January 9, 2000. McPherson represented Partin in seven of his trials.

p. 186, line 6: Sheridan asks Ramsey Clark to intervene: "Information from Walter Sheridan, Re: Affidavit to be filed either January 24 or January 25, 1967," Herbert J. Miller file, Jeremy Gunn Records Collection.

p. 186, line 8: Sheridan had put the Shaw defense team in touch with Herbert J. Miller Jr.: Interview with Gordon Novel, May 31, 2000. For Herbert J. Miller Jr.'s involvement with the Garrison investigation, see Nicki Kuckes to T. Jeremy Gunn, General counsel, Assassination Records Review Board, June 17, 1997, NARA and T. Jeremy Gunn to Nicki Kuckes, Re: Interview with Herbert J. Miller Jr., June 9, 1997. Submitting to a taped interview, Miller refused to discuss his role in sabotaging the Garrison investigation, claiming privilege since he had been Walter Sheridan's attorney.

p. 186, line 10: Herbert J. Miller Jr., sends briefs from the Shaw defense team to CIA on a regular basis: See Herbert J. Miller Jr., To Richard H. Lansdale, March 21, 1968; March 26, 1968; May 31, 1968; June 27, 1968, for example. "Enclosed are the briefs in the Shaw case which I mentioned to you on the telephone," is all Miller writes on June 27th. The March briefs deal with Novel, the May and June with Shaw. Shaw defense briefs go from Edward Wegmann to Herbert J. Miller Jr., to Richard Lansdale at CIA: May 31, 1968 and June 27, 1968, LHMs, NARA.

p. 186, line 12: Lawrence Houston's efforts to help the Shaw defense team: 30 November 1967, To: New Orleans, From: Office of General Counsel, Cite: Headquarters 487, Ref: NO-406-7, signed by Lawrence R. Houston. See also Memorandum, To: Director, Domestic Contact Service, Att'n: Operational Support Staff (Musulin) 15 September 1967, From: Chief, New Orleans Office, Subject: Case 49364—Garrison investigation, Ref: Your memorandum dated 12 September 1967/our memorandum No-342-67, dated 7 September 1967. See also CIA from DCS/Operational Support Staff to Office of General Counsel, Title: Memo—Garrison Investigation—attached are copies of memorandum from our New Orleans office, September 18, 1967, 104-10189-10049, Agency file: 80T01357A. These are but traces of what is obviously a copious correspondence between New Orleans and CIA headquarters in the CIA's effort to aid Clay Shaw. See also 18 September 1967, Memorandum For: Executive Director-Comptroller, Subject: Garrison Investigation, signed by Lawrence R. Houston, NARA.

p. 186, line 10: Miller communicated information from Sheridan to Lansdale: Memorandum for the Record, May 8, 1967, Subject: Further on the Garrison Investigation Matter, NARA.

p. 186, line 19: "disposed over the personnel": Hougan, *Spooks: The Haunting of America—The Private Use of Secret Agents* (New York: William Morrow, 1995), p. 128. 124ff.

p. 186, line 23: "his almost angelic appearance": Robert F. Kennedy, *The Enemy Within* (New York: Da Capo Press, 1994), p. 174.

p. 186, line 27: Internal Revenue capabilities: Sheridan doubles as an IRS agent again: Memorandum to File; January 22, 1969, in re: Pershing Gervais, Naurbon L. Perry, Supervisor, Group III, NARA.

p. 186, line 28: Federal agents posing as journalists: See "Protest in Feds Posing As Reporters" by David Ho, September 7, 2000, United Press copyrighted story. See also Norman Kempster, "Oswald, CIA Trails Crossed: Shadowy Figure Emerges," *Washington Star,* January 16, 1976.

p. 186, line 31: four times: Sheridan is quoted referring to "an old urge to become a journalist": "NBC's Supersleuth," *Newsweek,* October 23, 1967, p. 16.

p. 186, line 35: Garrison perceived "the major opposition" to his investigation as coming from Bobby Kennedy: Jim Garrison on *Nine at Noon,* September 22, 1967, Radio-TV Reports, Inc., NARA. Garrison made similar comments on *Page One* and other programs, *Page One,* September 24, 1967, WABC-TV and the ABC-TV Network, Radio TV Reports, Inc., NARA.

p. 186, line 36: "If my brother were killed": Jim Garrison interviewed by Joseph Wershba. *Mike Wallace At Large,* September 26, 1967, NARA.

p. 187, line 2: "never really wanted": Harris Wofford, *Of Kennedys and Kings: Making Sense of the Sixties* (New York: Farrar, Straus & Giroux, 1980), p. 414.

p. 187, line 4: Edwin Guthman says that Miller sent Sheridan to New Orleans: Conversation with Edwin Guthman, May 16, 2000.

p. 187, line 8: Sheridan pretended to investigate the Kennedy assassination: Jim Garrison, *On the Trail of the Assassins,* p. 166.

p. 187, line 8: Richard N. Billings introduces Sheridan to Garrison: Interview with Richard N. Billings.

p. 187, line 11: "artillery": Jim Garrison, *Coup d'Etat,* unpublished. Chapter 9, pp. 1–2 of 9. See also *A Farewell to Justice,* unpublished. Both manuscripts are available at AARC.

p. 187, line 13: "to spike Garrison": Bud Fensterwald notes on meeting with Guy Johnson, August 24, 1967, AARC.

p. 187, line 14: "bury" Jim Garrison: "bury . . . a wild and dangerous man": Memorandum for the Record, Subject: Further on the Garrison Investigation Matter, 8 May 1967, b-68-101, From: Richard H. Lansdale, Associate General Counsel, NARA. The notion that Garrison was "crazy" was repeated to the author by the local FBI in New Orleans, Interview with Warren de Brueys, January 15, 2000.

p. 187, line 21: "Garrison's schemes": Memorandum for Executive Director—Comptroller, Subject, Garrison Investigation, May 11, 1967, Signed Richard H. Lansdale, NARA.

p. 187, line 25: "under any terms we propose": Memo from Richard H. Lansdale to Mr. Houston, May 11, 1967, copies went to Mr. Goodwin, Asst., To DCI, and Mr. Rocca, CI Staff, Director of Security, 67-2420, NARA.

p. 187, line 32: Miller represented the Sheridan family in keeping Sheridan's papers from scholars: The family emerged with the papers in its possession.

p. 187, line 38: Sheridan sends the Agency Emilio Santana's file: Memorandum, 15 June 1967, Subject: Garrison Investigation: Emilio SANTANA Galindo, signed: Raymond G. Rocca, Chief, CI/R & A, NARA.

p. 187, line 39: Rocca decides that Sheridan should not use Santana: Ibid., Memorandum, 15 June 1967, NARA.

p. 188, line 5: "I can make a lot of statements he can't": Conversation between Rick Townley, John George, and Morris Brownlee, May 22, 1967, transcription of a taped telephone call made on May 21st, NODA, NARA.

p. 188, line 8: "a squad of federal marshals": Conversation between Morris Brownlee and Richard Townley, May 22, 1967, taped for the office of the District Attorney of Orleans Parish.

p. 188, line 12: "shoot him down": FBI. To: Director, From: New Orleans, May 18, 1967, 89-69-2075. Sheridan himself was not shy about admitting his purpose was to destroy Jim Garrison, see CIA Memo From: Ray Rocca to ADDP, May 12, 1967, NARA.

p. 188, line 15: "would destroy the credibility": FBI teletype, To: Director, From: New Orleans, May 12, 1967, 124-10259-10045, 89-69-3053A, NARA.

p. 188, line 17: "a reporter named Ainsworth [sic]": Investigative Report, May 31, 1967, Reported by Aaron M. Kohn, MCC.

p. 188, line 21: It was not determined by Jim Garrison whether Morrison and Dayries were indicted:

interview with Judge Adrian Duplantier, February 6, 2001.

p. 188, line 23: Sheridan wants Kohn to go before the NBC cameras: Investigative Report, May 31, 1967, reported by Aaron M. Kohn, MCC.

p. 188, line 26: "no such credit had been established": Investigative Report, June 15, 1967, MCC.

p. 188, line 28: Kohn sends Sheridan to Pershing Gervais: Investigative Report, August 23, 1967.

p. 188, line 29: Sheridan meets with Zachary ("Red") Strate: "Testified Sheridan Offered Deal To Discredit Garrison," *States-Item,* August 19, 1967. See also Orleans Parish grand jury, August 9, 1967, testimonies of Zachary A. Strate Jr., Malcolm O'Hara; Edward Baldwin, NARA.

p. 189, line 14: through the sound room of the FBI: FBI, To: SAC, From: SA Edward J. Carney Jr., August 25, 1967, 89-69-3464, NARA.

p. 189, line 17: "That's a damned lie": FBI Memorandum, To: Mr. Tolson, From: C. D. DeLoach, April 24, 1967, 124-10043-10456, 62-109060-5154, NARA.

p. 189, line 18: ten and fifteen agents: Interview with William Walter, January 5, 2000; interviews with Louis Ivon.

p. 189, line 20: Hoover sends a daily report to Lyndon Johnson: The source is William Turner. He says an aide to Robert Kennedy's 1968 presidential campaign, Richard Lubic, related that Hoover sent a daily report, "Progress of the Garrison Investigation." Interview with William Turner, December 3, 2001.

p. 189, line 21: Gordon Novel: Perspective of Gordon Novel comes from a series of interviews with Novel beginning on January 16, 2000. See also Testimony before the grand jury, Orleans Parish, Rancier Ehlinger, August 16, 1967, AARC.

p. 189, line 22: to debug Garrison's office: See Novel, *Playboy* deposition. p. 1520, AARC.

p. 189, line 28: FBI informant: for some of this history of Novel and the FBI, see FBI AIRTEL, To: Director, FBI, From: SAC, New Orleans, March 30, 1967, 124-10259-10170, 89-69-1922, NARA. See also FBI, To: Director, From: New Orleans, February 23, 1967, 124-10256-10186, 89-69-1446, NARA.

p. 189, line 30: robbery at the Schlumberger ammunition dump: Later, in Ohio, Novel told his lawyer, Jerry Weiner, he had picked up the Houma ammunition at the request of his "CIA contact." Novel, *Playboy* deposition, p. 1245.

p. 189, line 31: Banister and Novel: Interview with Gordon Novel, May 31, 2002.

p. 189, line 34: bolt cutters: Interviews with Marlene Mancuso, June 16, June 28, 2000. See also the testimony of Rancier Ehlinger before the Orleans Parish grand jury on August 16, 1967, Ehlinger talked about the key as well in the office on March 30th: See memorandum, To: Jim Garrison, From: William Gurvich, Special Aide, Subject: Rancier Blaise Ehlinger—Interview with on March 30, 1967, 2:35 P.M., NODA, NARA. See transcript of interview. Present are Louis Ivon, Jim Alcock, and Gurvich. Available from HSCA files as Exhibit no. 7. "A lot of what Gordon says is so rife with untruth that it is hard to separate one thing from another; it's impossible," Ehlinger told the grand jury.

p. 189, line 35: it was Sheridan who sent Novel into Garrison's office: Interview with Marlene Mancuso, July 6, 2002. See also Interview with Gordon Novel, January 16, 2000. See also *Gordon Novel, Plaintiff v. Jim Garrison and HMH Publishing Co.*, Incirca no. 67C 1895, Answers to interrogatories propounded by Defendant HMH Publishing Co., Inc., To Plaintiff, March 4, 1968, a CIA release. See also "I'm a former chief investigator": Novel *Playboy* deposition, p. 1042.

p. 190, line 1: Novel reported to the FBI on the day he entered Garrison's office: FBI, SA J. Peter Chase and SA Max M. Marr, February 21, 1967, 124-10241-10084, 89-69-1456, NARA.

p. 190, line 5: Novel tells the Bureau that Garrison believes that Clay Shaw is Clay Bertrand: FBI, To: SAC, New Orleans, From: SA Robert J. Heibel, February 22, 1967, 89-69-1460, NARA.

p. 190, line 5: Novel informed on the 23rd as well: AIRTEL, To: Director, FBI, From: SAC, New Orleans, February 23, 1967, 124-10256-10190, 89-69-1450, NARA. Varying versions of the information in this memo are in

interviews with Novel, and in the *Playboy* deposition.

p. 190, line 7: "find the loop holes": To: SAC, New Orleans, From: Director, FBI, February 28, 1967, 124-10241-10149, 89-69-1525, NARA.

p. 190, line 8: "Mafia look like altar boys": Interview with Gordon Novel, January 16, 2000.

p. 190, line 9: Luis Angel Castillo: See ARRB. Agency: FBI, Record Number: 124-10187-10208, Record Series: HQ, Agency File Number: CR 100-446775-60, From: Deputy Director for Plans, To: Director, FBI, 05-09-67, 16 pages, Subjects: DF, interrogations, Castillo, Luis Angel, NARA.

p. 190, line 27: "Novel tells the FBI that Garrison is exploring whether Marcello is connected to the assassination": FBI, To: SAC, From: SA J. Peter Chase, March 28, 1967, 89-69-1907, NARA.

p. 190, line 30: Garrison planned to indict Marcello: FBI, To: Director, From New Orleans, March 28, 1967. The original went from Mr. DeLoach to Director, 89-69-1907. The internal document was FBI To: SAC, From: SA J. Peter Chase, as above.

p. 190, line 31: Novel steals memos from Garrison's office: See Gordon Novel, *Playboy* deposition, p. 1085. Novel also gave copies of lie detector tests administered to Garrison witnesses to Sheridan: FBI teletype, To: Bureau, Dallas, From: New Orleans, March 27, 1967, FBI, 124-10237-10297, NARA. Here Novel reports to Regis Kennedy.

p. 190, line 39: letters were sent by the FBI to the members of Truth and Consequences: Interview with William Walter, January 5, 2000.

p. 190, line 42: Kohn requested that Dr. Lief call Jim Garrison a "paranoid schizophrenic": To: Irvin Dymond: Investigative Report: Confidential, April 19, 1967, Date information received: April 7 and 10, 1967, MCC. See also Memorandum for File, July 28, 1967, Reported by Aaron M. Kohn, MCC. Lief says "none of it is true." Interview with Dr. Harold Lief, November 13, 2001.

p. 191, line 6: Novel sells the photograph to Sheridan: Interview with Gordon Novel, January 16, 2000. See also *Playboy* deposition.

p. 191, line 19: "everybody is going

down": Interviews with Marlene Mancuso, June 28, 2000; August 23, 2001.

p. 191, line 28: a job on the "Tonight Show": Interview with Marlene Mancuso, June 28, 2000.

p. 191, line 35: Garrison violated no one's rights: Interview with John Volz, June 13, 2000.

p. 192, line 10: "behaved like gentlemen": Interview with Marlene Mancuso, June 10, 2000. See also Interview of Marlene Mancuso by Jim Garrison and Louis Ivon, May 20, 1967, NODA, NARA. Affidavit by Marlene Mancuso, May 20, 1967, courtesy of Marlene Mancuso.

p. 192, line 12: Jules Ricco Kimble and Sheridan: Statement of Jules Ricco Kimble, October 10, 1967, Office of the District Attorney, NODA, NARA.

p. 192, line 18: Sheridan persuades Kimble to stop talking to Jim Garrison: William Turner, "The Garrison Commission," *Ramparts*, vol. 6, number 6, January 1968, p. 68. Joe Oster eventually tracked Kimble down in Canada: interview with Joe Oster, October 11, 2001.

p. 192, line 22: Williams didn't trust Sheridan: Interview with Fred Williams, July 22, 2002.

p. 192, line 26: "on the wrong team": Nina Sulzer interferes with witness Vernon Bundy, Statement of Samuel Michael Davis Jr., May 22, 1967, Statement of Arthur King, May 22, 1967, NODA, NARA.

p. 192, line 32: "extortion": Statement of Jack Martin, June 5, 1967, NODA, NARA.

p. 192, line 33: "if you say it was a hoax": Jack Martin with Richard Townley on May 28, 1967, transcribed June 2, 1967, NODA, NARA.

p. 192, line 36: "Marcellos had nothing to do with the assassination": Tape transcription of conversation between Jack Martin and Richard Townley, June 1, 1967, transcribed June 16, 1967, NODA, NARA.

p. 192, line 42: "why don't you quit working with the CIA": Taped conversation between Jack Martin and Aaron Kohn, June 11, 1967, NODA, NARA.

p. 192, line 2: "excellent pipeline": Richard Townley interviewed by Robert A. Wilson of Southern Research, April 19, 1967, *Papers of Edward F. Wegmann.*

p. 193, line 6: Townley visited Russo three times: See Memorandum, June 19, 1967, To: Jim Garrison, From: Andrew J. Sciambra, Re: Conversations between Perry Russo, Richard Townley of WDSU television, Walter Sheridan of NBC News and James Phelan of the *Saturday Evening Post, NODA*, NARA. See also Memorandum, June 14, 1967, To: Louis Ivon, From: Sal Scalia, Re: Conversation between Perry Russo and Richard Townley, NODA, NARA. Perry Russo's affidavit is dated June 21, 1967, NODA, NARA. Townley also contacted Russo's cousin, Jerl Kershenstine: Signed affidavit by Jerl Kershenstine, State of Louisiana, Parish of Orleans, June 21, 1967, NODA, NARA.

p. 193, line 7: "tremendous amount of pressure": Perry Russo interviewed by the *Washington Post.* The interview is by their Atlanta correspondent. Russo was also wired for this interview, NODA, NARA.

p. 193, line 10: "ruined for life": Memorandum, June 14, 1967, To: Louis Ivon, From: Sal Scalia, Re: Conversation Between Perry Russo and Richard Townley, NODA, NARA.

p. 193, line 13: "I want you to understand": Dialogue courtesy of the NODA tape. Russo was wired.

p. 194, line 4: CIA was working closely with the Shaw defense team: Interview with Jefferson Sulzer, January 15, 2000. Sulzer's statement that the CIA was helping Clay Shaw is corroborated by Helms' former executive assistant, Victor Marchetti. Marchetti testified to Helms' question to Karamessines, "Are we giving that guy down there all the help he needs?" under oath, From: Snyder, William A. K. Jr., To: Office of General Counsel, Title: Federal Express: Letter: Dear Lee: July 10, 1984, and CIA 104-10412-10022, RUSS HOLMES WORK FILE, Transcript of Proceedings, Deposition of Victor L. Marchetti, *E. Howard Hunt Jr. v. Liberty Lobby,* Case no. 80-1121-Civ-JWK, July 9, 1984.

p. 194, line 5: Russo defended himself in an interview on WWL-TV, and in other venues. HSCA 004634, 180-10099-10354, NARA.

p. 194, line 15: "setting up chickens": AIRTEL to Director, From: SAC, New Orleans, March 22, 1967, appended to a Domestic Intelligence Division Informative Note, March 31, 1967, NARA. The report itself is dated March 27, 1967.

p. 194, line 18: the wedding of David Ferrie and Perry Russo: Interviews Regarding Oswald's Neatness, undated, *Papers of Edward F. Wegmann.*

p. 194, line 21: "absolutely correct": A candidate for this anonymous caller is Richard Murphy of Mobile, Alabama, whose family was connected with the United Fruit Company. Murphy had keys to Shaw's house and often stayed there. His lover, Charles Liner, also visited. Both knew Shaw and Ferrie. The FBI knew that when Shaw was arrested, Murphy "allegedly became excited . . . and received two or three telephone calls." They were "extremely close": Memorandum by Jim Garrison of the telephone call from Ellen Ray, Papers of Jim Garrison, NARA. The FBI knew of Richard Murphy (FBI, February 27, 1967). But this document was obviously completed after March 1st, since it refers to the arrest of Clay Shaw, 89-69-113, NARA.

p. 194, line 31: "what do you expect from a pig?" Interview with Eberhard Garrison, January 9, 1998.

p. 194, line 34: "lair of the CIA": Quoted in "The Investigation: Where It Stands Today" by Roger Young. *New Orleans* magazine, July 1967, p. 55.

p. 194, line 35: Novel's lie detector test: Testimony of Les Whitten, in the Court of Common Pleas of Franklin County, Ohio, In Re: Grand Jury Investigation of Conspiracy To Murder John F. Kennedy, Bill of Exceptions, NARA. In Novel's suit against *Playboy* and Garrison, Whitten invoked the "Newsmen's Privilege Act," exempting him from disclosing any information he had obtained from Novel.

p. 194, line 39: Novel tells the Bureau they can always reach him through Walter Sheridan: FBI, To: Bureau and Dallas, From: New Orleans, March 27, 1967, 124-10237-10297, 89-69-1829, NARA.

p. 194, line 40: "I was doing everything in my power": Interview with Gordon Novel, January 30, 2000.

p. 194, line 41 on behalf of the Shaw defense team, Salvatore Panzeca and Robert A. Wilson visit Novel: "Gordon Novel, Columbus Ohio," *Papers of Edward F. Wegmann.* Also, Interview with Salvatore Panzeca, June 4, 2000.

p. 195, line 2: According to Novel, Mr. Weiss was Director of Security at the State Department: Interview with Novel, January 30, 2000. Jim Garrison forwarded the letter to the Special Agent in Charge in New Orleans, Robert E. Rightmyer, and the FBI went on to check on Weiss: FBI, To: Director, From: Dallas. 124-10259-10094, 89-69-3108, NARA. He has "avoided one subpoena not to reveal Double-Chek [a CIA proprietary in Miami] activities," Novel writes, because he feared that Garrison "is aware of Double-Chek's involvement." The entire letter is adolescent gibberish, Novel as Tom Swift, or James Bond, even as he would call Jim Garrison "a Cajun James Bond": FBI, To: Director, FBI, From: SAC, Memphis, May 22, 1967, 124-10259-10097, 89-69-3111, NARA.

p. 195, line 11: According to CIA, Double-Chek, invoked by Novel, existed "for the sole purpose of making payments to widows: OGC 67-1085a. Lawrence R. Houston. Memorandum for C/CI/R & A, Subject: Garrison and the Kennedy Assassination: Gordon Dwane Novel, Reference 31 May 67 Memo for C/CI/R & A. Same subject. 104-10312-10017, Agency file: DDP Files, NARA.

p. 195, line 4: "That was cute": Interview with Gordon Novel, January 16, 2000.

p. 195, line 6: Novel files a damage suit against Jim Garrison: FBI, To: Director, From: SAC, New Orleans, May 10, 1967, 124-10259-10021, 89-69-3026, NARA.

p. 195, line 8: "a man of honesty": *States-Item,* May 24, 1967.

p. 195, line 9: James A. Comiskey refuses permission: "Novel Bids to Remain in Ohio for Suit," *States-Item,* June 7, 1967; "Court Rejects Novel Pleas," by Gordon Gsell. *Times-Picayune,* June 8, 1967.

p. 195, line 14: "supporting and financing Novel": CIA Memorandum, Subject: Garrison and the Kennedy Assassination: Gordon Dwane Novel, 104-10012-10028, Agency file: 201-289248, NARA.

p. 195, line 16: Walter Sheridan calls Governor Rhodes of Ohio: Interview with Victor Marchetti, May 15, 1998.

p. 195, line 18: "it would be deplorable": For the extradition of Gordon Novel, and the Department of Justice instruction to Louis LaCour to offer no assistance to Jim Garrison: FBI, March 27, 1967, To: Director, From New Orleans, 124-10237-10293, 89-69-1824, NARA. LaCour sent Joe Sylvester of the Bureau a copy of the Unlawful Flight Warrant sent to him by Jim Garrison: Louis C. LaCour to Joseph Sylvester, March 27, 1967, 89-69-1835, includes James L. Alcock to Honorable Louis LaCour, March 27, 1967, Re: Gordon Novel, Affidavit no. 198-066, Revised Statute; 15:257, NARA.

In Washington, discussion of ways and means of turning down Garrison's request proceeded for the extradition of Gordon Novel: FBI, Memorandum, To: Mr. Tolson, From: C. D. DeLoach, March 27, 1967, 62-109060-4921, NARA. See also To: Director, From: New Orleans, Urgent, 124-10167-10239, 89-69-1702, NARA. Ohio found the Louisiana extradition warrants irregular. See John McElroy, Assistant to the Governor, to the Honorable John J. McKeithen, May 29, 1967, NARA.

Novel in turn reassured the FBI: he was "solidly against Jim Garrison's hypocritical investigation": Memorandum to Mr. Tolson, From: C. D. DeLoach, March 27, 1967, 62-109060-4921, Refers to 62-109060-4932. See also FBI, To: SAC, From: SA J. Peter Chase, 89-69-1809, NARA.

p. 195, line 29: Martens had also told Jim Garrison that Ferrie was pro-Kennedy: Interview with Layton Martens, March 12, 1967. Present are Alvin Oser, Jim Alcock, Milton Brener, and Martens, Brener's client.

p. 195, line 33: "arrogant perfury": Jim Garrison to Jonathan Blackmer, November 8, 1977, HSCA.

p. 195, line 33: as he admitted to Sheridan. Tapes of Sheridan's interviews for the "White Paper" are available in the papers of the Metropolitan Crime Commission, NARA.

p. 195, line 35: there had been no "letters of marque": Martens went on to claim that Ferrie and Arcacha had used him, Memorandum, To: Louis Ivon, From J. S. (Jack) Martin, Subject: Investigation of Layton Martens, Thursday, 4th April 1968, NODA, NARA.

p. 195, line 38: Dean Andrews: Garrison persisted in attempting to extract the identity of Clay Bertrand from Andrews, who was interviewed both at Tulane and Broad and before the Orleans Parish grand jury on March 16, 1967, AARC. Present were James Alcock, Richard Burnes, and John Volz. See also: Memorandum, April 4, 1967, To: Jim Garrison, From: William Gurvich, Special Aide, Subject: Dean Andrews—Interview 3/2/67, NODA, NARA.

p. 196, line 8: Andrews talks to the FBI: FBI. To: Director, FBI, From: SAC, New Orleans, April 6, 1967, 124-10259-10197, 89-69-1958, 1959. See also To: Director, FBI, From: SAC, New Orleans, April 12, 1967, 62-109060-5090; To: Director, From: New Orleans, May 7, 1967, 124-10237-10414, 89-69-2089.

p. 196, line 10: "married and the father of four children": Memo of a meeting, April 19, 1967, between Robert A. Wilson, Dean Andrews, and Richard Townley at the Press Club, *Papers of Edward F. Wegmann*, NARA.

p. 196, line 13: "soft voice": To: Lang for Billings, From Byers (in New Orleans), March 5, 1967, *Papers of Richard N. Billings*, box 4, folder 47.

p. 196, line 16: Ferrie had sent Thomas Lewis Clark to Andrews: Statement of Thomas Lewis Clark, WM, age 19, March 15, 1967, NODA, NARA. See also Fenner O. Sedgebeer, grand jury testimony, March 16, 1967, and Thomas Lewis Clark, grand jury testimony, March 16, 1967.

p. 196, line 17: Prentiss Davis was familiar with the name "Clay Bertrand": Statement of Prentiles [*sic*] M. Davis, March 9, 1967, NODA, NARA.

p. 196, line 20: "If Giant gets past that": Harold Weisberg to Joan Mellen, October 18, 2001.

p. 196, line 21: he wanted "to live": Transcript of interview between Dean Andrews and Bob Scott, February 1967, WNAC, Boston, NODA, NARA.

p. 196, line 22: "I love to breathe": Quoted in Harold Weisberg, *Oswald in New Orleans* (New York: Canyon Books, 1967), pp. 138–139.

p. 196, line 23: Shaw was Bertrand: Interview with Harold Weisberg, July 27, 2000.

p. 196, line 25: "if I said anything": See Mark Lane, *A Citizen's Dissent* (New York: Holt, Rinehart and Winston, 1968), p. 56. See also "The Inquest" by William Turner, *Ramparts* 5, no. 12 (June 1967): 24. Here Andrews says, "They told me if I said anything I might get a bullet in the head."

p. 196, line 34: John Cancler: Cancler was a longtime FBI informant; his number was NO 1378-C. See AIRTEL, To: Director, From: SAC, New Orleans, April 14, 1967. Cancler's handler was Delbert W. Hahn. See also FBI, To: Director, FBI, From: New Orleans, August 30, 1967, 124-10236-10468, 89-69-3470, NARA.

p. 197, line 9: a denial he would later repudiate: Fred Leemans retracts his "White Paper" statements on January 6, 1969, NODA, NARA.

p. 197, line 19: Ivon went along: Interview with Louis Ivon, October 9, 2000. Ivon was "honorable": Interview with Gordon Novel, September 1, 2000. "I have no beef with him," Novel also remarked, interview with Novel, January 16, 2000.

p. 197, line 26: Lies were of no interest: "We would never suborn perjury," Garrison says in the *Playboy* interview, op. cit., p. 64.

p. 197, line 29: Loisel meets with Exnicios and Beaubouef: March 10, 1967, Partial transcript of the tape made by Exnicios, NARA.

p. 197, line 30: Exnicios: In his *Newsweek* story, Aynsworth suppressed his discovery that Exnicios had a history of the corrupt use of recorded conversations. Only the previous year Exnicios had threatened Frank Langridge, his opponent in the district attorney campaign in Jefferson Parish, with disclosure of a previously recorded conversation. Langridge recorded the threat. See also: "offered bribe": FBI, To: Director, From Dallas: 124-10237-10364, 89-69-2030, April 26, 1967, NARA.

p. 197, line 35: Dymond has the tape: Investigative Report—CONFIDENTIAL, April 19, 1967, date information received: April 7 and 10, 1967, MCC. Kohn makes no reference to the fact that Beaubouef has sworn out an affidavit repudiating the tape.

p. 197, line 38: Beaubouef would argue that he had signed the affidavit saying he had not been bribed only under duress. But Clyde Merritt, the lawyer who notarized Beaubouef's statement, reported that "at no time did he seem to be nervous": Clyde Merritt interviewed by Ross Yockey on the affidavit signed by Beaubouef, May 11, 1967, Notes of Ross Yockey, AARC.

p. 198, line 2: Klein and Beaubouef go to Washington courtesy of the CIA: Conversation between Morris Brownlee and Richard Townley May 22, 1967, taped for the district attorney of Orleans Parish, NODA, NARA.

p. 198, line 3: wasted trip: Beaubouef's Washington itinerary: Richard H. Lansdale, Associate General Counsel, 8 May 1967, Memorandum for the Record, Subject: Further on the Garrison Investigation Matter, NARA. Copies went first to the Counter Intelligence Staff, then to D/DCS (Domestic Contact); Director of Security; and Mr. Goodwin—Asst To DCI.

p. 198, line 11: The trajectory of information, from the FBI to Angleton: CIA, To: J. Edgar Hoover, From: James Angleton, Attn: Mr. S. J. Papich, Subject: Alvin R. Beaubouef, OGC60-0924, Reference: Memorandum from FBI Office, Houston, Texas, 27 April 1967. Subject: Assassination of President John Fitzgerald Kennedy . . . Miscellaneous Information concerning. . . . See also tape between Rick Townley, John George (George Wyatt), and Morris Brownlee, transcribed May 22, 1967, NODA, NARA.

p. 198, line 17: Klein was "either unwilling or unable" to offer specifics: To: Joseph I. Giarrusso, From: Presley J. Trosclair Jr. Subject: Reporting Information Gathered During an Inquiry into Allegations that Alvin Roland Beaubouef, WM, age 21 . . . was offered a bribe and subsequently threatened by Patrolmen Lynn Henry Loisel and Louis William Ivon, Office of the Deputy Superintendent, New Orleans Police Department, June 12, 1967, NARA.

p. 198, line 17: Beaubouef had called him: Burton G. Klein to Mr. Thomas O. Collins Jr., May 17, 1967, NARA. The third party had been Irvin Dymond: Interview with Burton Klein, May 25, 1998.

p. 198, line 26: "the whole conversation": Beaubouef interviewed by Presley Trosclair, June 2, 1967, Office of the Deputy Superintendent. Statement of Alvin Roland Beaubouef, NARA.

p. 198, line 36: the front page story: "DA's Men Cleared of Plot Case Bribe. Beaubouef Claim Refuted," *States-Item,* June 14, 1967, p. 1. See also "Pair Cleared in Bribe Probe" by Robert Ussery. *Times-Picayune,* June 15, 1967.

p. 198, line 36: Exnicios offered the tape to Sheridan for five thousand dollars: Investigative Report, June 5, 1967, MCC.

p. 198, line 39: Kohn in the office with Garrison, Alcock and Burnes, June 29, 1967. Tape is available at NARA.

p. 198, line 41: Liars wilted: Interview with Numa Bertel, August 5, 2002.

p. 199, line 7: Spindel was a "countermeasures technician," according to Jim Hougan: Interview with Jim Hougan, August 9, 2002. Spindel telephones Kohn: Investigative Report, July 16, 1967. MCC. References to tapes from Spindel: FBI. August 2, 1967. To: Director, From: SAC, New Orleans, 124-10236-10432. 89-69-3427, 3428. See also: To: Director, From: New Orleans, August 2, 1967, 124-10236-10395. 89-69-3384. NARA. Kohn informant Herbert Huber, running guns to Cuba, had already told Kohn, "Garrison is on the real track of them murderers of President Kennedy," but Kohn didn't want to hear that. See Investigative Report, May 31, 1967, etc. Investigative Report, May 31, 1967, Reported by Aaron M. Kohn, MCC.

p. 199, line 14: "convincing witness": "Garrison's Case" by Richard Popkin. *New York Review of Books,* September 14, 1967, **p. 21.**

p. 199, line 15: "sound": Gurvich praised the investigation, telling Ross Yockey it was "worth conducting," Ross Yockey before the Orleans Parish grand jury, July 12, 1967, AARC.

p. 199, line 18: Sheridan phones Gurvich in New York: Interview with Joe and Shirley Wershba, July 14, 2000.

p. 199, line 23: Moyers laughed:

Bill Moyers to the president, June 27, 1967, NARA.

p. 199, line 24: "Bobby was 'extremely grateful'": "Garrison's Chief Assistant Hints Investigation Lacks Substance," *Newsday,* June 16, 1967, p. 40B.

p. 199, line 34: "we'll shoot them with red pepper guns": Interview with Louis Ivon, January 12, 2000.

p. 199, line 38: Gurvich before the grand jury: June 28, 1967, and July 12, 1967, AARC.

p. 200, line 42: Baldwin and Gurvich visit Healy: Investigative Report, August 10, 1967, MCC.

p. 200, line 1: Healy and the FBI: See, for example, To: Director, FBI, From: SAC, New Orleans, April 14, 1967, Record number: 124-10048-10267, HQ, 62-109060-5061, 3 pages, NARA. Healy put the resources of the *Times-Picayune* at the disposal of the Bureau: FBI AIRTEL, To: Director, FBI, From: SAC, New Orleans, April 14, 1967, 124-10259-10221, 89-69-1988, NARA.

p. 200, line 3: Hoke May himself was an FBI informant: AIRTEL: To: Director, FBI, From: SAC, New Orleans, April 20, 1967, 124-10237-10354, 89-69-2016, 2017, NARA. See also Joe Sylvester reports that Hoke May told him to William Branigan: To: Mr. R. E. Lenihan, From: Mr. W. A. Branigan, April 21, 1967, 62-109060-5104, NARA. See also: To: ASAC Sylvester, April 20, 1967, 89-69-2015. For May's history with CIA: CIA. Chief, SRS. M. D. Stevens. Oswald Case, May, Hoke Smith, #167314, July 5, 1967, NARA.

p. 200, line 6: Louisiana would not have a specific statute forbidding the obstruction of justice until the 1980s. The statute is La. R.S. 14:130.1—Obstruction of Justice.

p. 200, line 14: Bobby Kennedy went public: *Washington Star,* July 19, 1967. See also "Sheridan Due Before Jury in 'Bribe' Quiz," *States-Item,* July 19, 1967.

p. 200, line 28: Hemming spins what amounts to a metaphor of a face-to-face meeting between Bobby Kennedy and Lee Harvey Oswald: Interviews with Gerald Patrick Hemming, November 15, 2000; June 5, 2005.

p. 201, line 19: compromising photographs of Jim Garrison: FBI, To:

SAC, From: SA Delbert W. Hahn, September 8, 1967, 124-10071-10263, 89-69-3483, NARA.

p. 201, line 25: Andrews returns to the grand jury: June 28, 1967, NODA, NARA.

p. 201, line 32: "we could subpoena you": Memorandum, August 3, 1967, To: Louis Ivon and James L. Alcock, From: Sal Scalia, Re: Highlights of taped conversation between J. Alcock and Wesley Liebeler on 8/2/67, NODA, NARA.

p. 201, line 34: Andrews names Eugene Davis as Clem Bertrand: Investigative Report, June 29, 1967, Reported by Aaron M. Kohn, MCC. Contains WWL-TV transcript of June 28th interview with Dean Andrews. Eugene Davis was himself a confidential informant of the FBI, and a Potential Criminal Informant beginning on April 28, 1960: To: Director, FBI and SAC, Dallas, From: SAC, New Orleans, June 21, 1967, 124-10251-10109, 89-69-3297, NARA. The New Orleans field office showed no alias for Davis, "and no information showing he utilized name Clem Bertrand," as indeed he had not. It was at this point that Davis told the FBI that a man named "Phil Schultz" was Bertrand: Memorandum to SAC, New Orleans, From: SA Kevin J. Harrigan, July 13, 1967, Subject: NO 1189-C. 89-69-3316, NODA, NARA. Davis called the identification of himself as Bertrand "false and malicious and damnable": Baton Rouge *Morning Advocate,* "C. Bertrand Label Denied by Orleanian," June 30, 1967. He also denied that he had ever heard the name "until this investigation": Interview with Eugene Davis, July 24, 1967, Office of the District Attorney, Interrogation by William R. Martin. Frank Meloche is also present, NODA, NARA. Davis met an untimely death, bludgeoned to death in his apartment: "Quarter Bar Owner Is Found Slain at Home," *Times-Picayune,* June 1, 1984, section 1, p. 17.

p. 202, line 3: "He is": Interview with Ross Scaccia, January 6, 2000. Eugene Davis *here confirms that Clay Shaw used the name Clay Bertrand.*

p. 202, line 6: Garrison demands equal time: Jim Garrison to Mr. William R. McAndrew, June 26, 1967, NOPL. See also Robert W. Lishman to Honorable Jim Garrison, June 19,

1967. Lishman was chief counsel of the congressional committee overseeing the FCC, NARA.

p. 202, line 7: "prosecution of an open case": "NBC Using Lies to Rap Case—DA," *States-Item,* June 20, 1967.

p. 202, line 9: "I will have to spend half my time": "Garrison Sets Up Conditions for TV," *New York Times,* July 5, 1967, p. 31.

p. 202, line 11: the Shaw defense attempts to enjoin Jim Garrison from appearing on television: To: Richard Billings & Nancy Haskell, From: Holland McCombs—Dallas, July 12, 1967, Re: Arcacha and Shaw, *Papers of Richard N. Billings,* box 4, folder 58.

p. 202, line 16: Jim Garrison compiled a list of those Sheridan attempted to bribe in the Hoffa case: Memorandum, July 17, 1967, To: Jim Garrison, From: Mike Karmazin, NODA, NARA.

p. 203, line 8: Lyndon Johnson is shown a Harris poll: Memorandum to the president, From: Fred Panzer, Subject: Advance Harris for Tuesday, September 19, 1967, NARA.

CHAPTER 13

p. 204, Epigraph: "Why was his name erased?" Interview with Anne Dischler, February 1, 2001.

p. 204, line 21: A. H. Magruder: February 23, 1967, To: Jim Garrison, From: Det. Frank Meloche and Sgt. Fenner Sedgebeer, Re: Statement of Mr. A. H. Magruder, NARA. See also Memorandum, February 25, 1967, To: Jim Garrison, From: Detective Frank E. Meloche, Re: Statement of Mr. A. H. Magruder, NARA.

p. 204, line 24: "East": "Insane Asylum of Louisiana at Jackson," *Times-Picayune,* October 18, 1963, section 1, p. 21. See also "Decay of Jackson Linked to East Louisiana Hospital. Once Center of Culture, Town Has Fallen," by Charles M. Hargroder. *Times-Picayune,* March 29, 1965, section 1, p. 1. The first of New Orleans' great cornet players, Buddy Bolden, beloved in Storyville, had spent the final twenty-four years of his life at "East."

p. 204, line 26: "involved with a group of men in the assassination": To: SAC, From: SA P. R. Lancaster,

November 23, 1967, 89-69-1480, NARA.

p. 205, line 15: "she's got something to share with us": Interview with Jim Olivier, July 17, 2001. Olivier videotaped Trooper Donald White.

p. 205, line 18: going to Dallas to kill President Kennedy: Deposition of Francis Louis Fruge, Interrogatories, April 18, 1978, House Select Committee on Assassinations, 49 pages, NARA. See also Interview by Robert Buras with Francis Louis Fruge, April 7, 1978, NARA.

p. 205, line 29: "this is when it's going to happen": Memorandum, May 22, 1967, To: Louis Ivon, From: Frank Meloche, NODA, NARA.

p. 205, line 33: Dr. Weiss hears her: Interview with Dr. Victor Weiss in *Rough Side of the Mountain.*

p. 205, line 38: Ruby and Oswald: Rose Cheramie is only one of many witnesses who place Ruby and Oswald together. See the notes for chapter 7.

p. 206, line 23: Jim Garrison called Fruge on February 25, 1967: Notes of Anne Dischler.

p. 206, line 26: Meloche, Dischler, and Fruge fly to Houston: Memorandum, March 13, 1967, To: Jim Garrison, From: Frank Meloche, Re: Rose Cheramie, NODA, NARA.

p. 206, line 28: Rose uses twenty aliases: Memorandum, March 28, 1967, To: Jim Garrison, From: William Gurvich, Re: Rose Cheramie, NARA.

p. 206, line 29: Rose Cheramie's name everywhere but in the Warren Commission archives: National Archives, March 29, 1967, T. Bethell, NODA, NARA.

p. 206, line 42: "accidental": April 4, 1967, State of Louisiana, Parish of St. Landry, City of Eunice, interview of J. A. Andrews by Francis Fruge, NARA.

p. 206, line 42: no record of the driver: Fruge checked on the driver who hit Rose: Outside Contact Report, telephone conversation with Francis Fruge, December 19, 1978, 015044, HSCA, NARA.

p. 207, line 5: direct knowledge of the assassination plot: *Comment Ça Va* by Matt Vernon, *Eunice News,* July 18, 1967, p. 1.

p. 207, line 7: The Silver Slipper: Commission Exhibit 3067, FBI interview 11/28/63 by SA J. Edward Kern. See also, "The Silver Slipper?" by Lisa Pease, *Probe,* July–August 1999, p. 4.

p. 207, line 8: "dapper, mustachioed": Nagell quoted in *The Man Who Knew Too Much,* p. 395.

p. 207, line 12: diagrams of the sewer system: Outside Contact Report, telephone conversation with Francis Fruge, December 19, 1978, 015044, HSCA, NARA.

p. 207, line 25: testimony of Cal Kelly: Interview with Mrs. Anne Dischler, Dischler Notes, courtesy of Mrs. Dischler.

p. 207, line 35: Investigation at the Holiday Inn, Lafayette: Dischler Notes.

p. 207, line 42: Alberto Fowler had met Angers: Memorandum, April 15, 1969, To: Andrew J. Sciambra, From: Alberto Fowler, Re: Telephone conversation of 4/14/69 with Harold Weisberg, NODA, NARA.

p. 208, line 4: "a Communist Louisiana": "Come to Louisiana: Cuban Council Envoy Is Heard," *Times-Picayune,* May 21, 1963, section 2, p. 3.

p. 208, line 5: "tight-lipped": Interview with Anne Dischler, February 4, 2002.

p. 208, line 10: criticizing the Kennedy family: Memorandum, July 13, 1967, To: Jim Garrison, From: Andrew J. Sciambra, Re: Information received from Lt. Fruge, July 11, 1967, NODA, NARA.

p. 208, line 23: Ernie Broussard Jr., of Abberville says the same man who had called himself "Lee Harvey Oswald" returned a few weeks after the assassination, Dischler Notes.

p. 208, line 30: "if you need anything, holler": Memorandum, April 6, 1967, To: Jim Garrison, From: Frank Meloche, Re: Telephone Call from Lt. Fruge, Lafayette, La. Op. 23, Lafayette, NODA, NARA.

p. 208, line 34: Cedric Rolleston telephones Frank Meloche: Memorandum, March 3, 1967, To: Jim Garrison, From: Frank Meloche, Investigator, Re: Lee Harvey Oswald and Clay Shaw in Alexandria, Louisiana, NODA, NARA.

p. 209, line 4: Corinne Verges Villard: Office of the District Attorney, February 28, 1967, Statement of:

Mrs. Corrine Verges Villard, Residing: 813 North Railroad Avenue. Morgan City, Louisiana, NODA, NARA.

p. 209, line 19: Barbara Messina knew Ruby and Oswald: Memorandum, October 21, 1968, To: Jim Garrison, From: Andrew J. Sciambra, Re: Travel to Monroe, Louisiana, NODA, NARA.

p. 209, line 26: "Lee Harvey Oswald" answers an advertisement for an apartment: Memorandum, July 29, 1968, To: Jim Garrison, From: Andrew Sciambra, Re: Interview of Aldeane Magee, 4360 Clayton Drive, Baton Rouge, Louisiana, NODA, NARA.

p. 209, line 29: all recorded by the state police: Interview with Anne Dischler, January 10, 2002.

p. 209, line 42: "he could have had a double": "Note" in *The Councilor* 4, (no. 19), 20 February 1967, **p. 3.**

p. 210, line 7: Judge Rarick gets a haircut: Interview with John R. Rarick, June 12, 2000. Regarding Oswald getting a haircut: interview with Lea McGehee, June 12, 2000.

p. 210, line 21: "a barber shop is a good place": Lea McGehee interviewed by Jim DiEugenio, August 26, 1994. McGehee remembers Oswald's line 24 "a barber shop is a good place for a haircut and information" in his HSCA interrogatories.

p. 210, line 25: "all or most everybody": Interrogatories, April 19, 1978, Testimony of Edwin Lea McGehee, Select Committee on Assassinations, Baton Rouge, Louisiana, NARA.

p. 210, line 37: ten Negroes: See "Voters Records of More Counties Are Called For" by Lewis Hawkins, *Times-Picayune,* May 24, 1960. section 1, p. 5.

p. 210, line 40: "I have no friends": Interview with Edwin Lea McGehee by Patricia Orr and Robert Buras, Select Committee on Assassinations, January 19, 1978, HSCA, NARA.

p. 210, line 2: "Oh!": Oswald is surprised when he learns that East is a mental hospital: Memorandum, July 26, 1967, To: Jim Garrison, From: Andrew J. Sciambra, Re: Interview with Lea McGee [*sic*] on July 17, 1967, NODA, NARA.

p. 211, line 2: "if you know somebody, you have a better chance": McGehee interviewed in *Rough Side of the Mountain.*

p. 211, line 13: the sanction of the right politician: "Decay of Jackson Linked to East Louisiana Hospital." Op. cit.

p. 211, line 21: Oswald departs in a large black car: It should be noted that McGehee first told Moo Moo Sciambra, tentatively, that Oswald had got into an old beat-up car, dark in color, a Nash or a Kaiser, with a young woman in the front seat and a basinette in back: Memorandum, June 26, 1967, To: Jim Garrison, From: Andrew J. Sciambra, Re: Interview with Mr. Lea McGee [*sic*] on June 17, 1967, NODA. To the House Select Committee in 1978, McGehee said he saw Oswald neither exit from the car or enter it upon his departure from the barber shop. By the time he turned around after washing his hands, the car was gone. Note that McGehee told Robert Buras and Patricia Orr, interviewing him on January 19, 1978, that "a big black car pulled away shortly after Oswald left." He continues to believe this is the car Oswald entered.

p. 211, line 27: Van Morgan plays "Tarzan": Interview with Van Morgan, June 11, 2000.

p. 211, line 27: "you have to see a politician to get a job": Reeves Morgan interviewed in the film, *Rough Side of the Mountain.*

p. 211, line 30: "a smart aleck white boy": Memorandum, January 23, 1968, To: Jim Garrison, From: Andrew J. Sciambra, Re: Interviews with people in Jackson and Clinton, Louisiana, NODA, NARA.

p. 211, line 39: the FBI called back and asked what Oswald had been wearing: *The Final Assassinations Report: Report of the Select Committee on Assassinations* (New York: Bantam Books, 1979), p. 170n. This detail represents an extraordinary indictment of the Warren Commission. As will later be shown, the FBI's behavior indicated that they did in fact receive the call from Reeves Morgan. Blakey's staff relegated this revelation—that the FBI had called Morgan back—to a footnote. That the FBI knew that Oswald had traveled to East Feliciana Parish in the company of Clay Shaw and David Ferrie could easily have been established had Blakey not pulled back from the Louisiana investigation.

p. 211, line 42: tough, "soldier-of-fortune type": McGehee interviewed by Patricia Orr and Robert Buras.

p. 212, line 7: McGehee identifies a photograph of Lawrence Howard: Memorandum: Summary of Deposition and Deposition of Edwin Lea McGehee, barber in Jackson, Louisiana, taken on April 19, 1978, at Baton Rouge, Louisiana.

p. 212, line 8: Blackmer's perfunctory depositions in Baton Rouge: Interrogatories, April 19, 1978, Baton Rouge, Lea MeGehee, 25 pages; Reeves Morgan: 008501, April 19, 1978, 23 pages; Henry Earl Palmer, 008499, April 19, 1978, 25 pages.

p. 212, line 34: Kilbourne and Rarick watch the black Cadillac: Interview with John R. Rarick, June 12, 2000. Description of Richard Kilbourne is by John R. Rarick.

p. 213, line 2: Manchester also reads gas meters: CORE papers, reel 4, frames 549–550.

p. 213, line 4: CORE records recount how strangers were stopped in Clinton on a regular basis: Congress of Racial Equality papers, Part 2, Southern Regional Office, 1959–1966, edited by August Meier and Elliot Rudwick, University Publications of America, Frederick, Maryland. Field Report, East Feliciana by Ed Vickery and Bill Brown, reel 3, frame 806.

p. 213, line 7: Manchester is proud to have been the one to arrest Mike Lesser: Memorandum from Sciambra to Garrison, July 18, 1967, NODA, NARA. Michael Lesser is arrested, FBI August 9, 1963, Report made by SA Michael Baron, Character of Case: CR, File #NO 44-1852, interview of Henry Earl Palmer by Michael Baron and Richard K. Tengstedt/bap, dictated, August 6, 1963, NARA.

p. 213, line 18: the White Camellia Organization was headed by Alvin Cobb: Report of Operator # X 65, June 25, 1965, Re: New Orleans Case # 486-65, *Papers of Jack N. Rogers.*

p. 213, line 25: "we pulled that guy over": Interview with John R. Rarick, who also reports on his conversation with Kilbourne.

p. 213, line 36: Jack Rogers hired private detective Mr. J. D. Vinson to develop information on Lee Harvey Oswald on November 22, 1963: FBI interview with Mr. J. D. Vinson, November 27, 1963, by SA John L. Quigley, FBI 124-10035-10368, agency file, 105-82555-3RDNR 454, NARA.

p. 213, line 41: in the *Councilor* Touchstone reported on the "pretty black Cadillac": Ned Touchstone, "The Truth About the Assassination," undated manuscript, p. 3, *Papers of Ned Touchstone,* Louisiana State University at Shreveport.

p. 214, line 5: a 1965 calendar: *Papers of Jack N. Rogers.* Material from Jack Rogers' files courtesy of his daughter.

p. 214, line 9: one of Jack Rogers "Operators," # X 10, learns about a photograph of Oswald and Ruby: March 11, 1964, Report of Operator # X 10. Re: New Orleans case # 220-63, *Papers of Jack N. Rogers.*

p. 214, line 15: Glady's maiden name was in fact Ragland, and they had another sister named Irene Ragland: Notes of Jack N. Rogers, March 11, 1967, *Papers of Jack N. Rogers.*

p. 214, line 18: Gladys worked for Jack Ruby at the Carousel Club: Interview with Billy Zachary, January 28, 2003. Zachary was a close friend of Matt Junior Palmer: Notebooks of Anne Dischler; Margaret Harvey interview with Billy Zachary, December 12, 2002.

p. 214, line 25: impeccably made-up: Interview with Margaret Harvey, December 12, 2002.

p. 214, line 25: "outspoken": Interview with Irene Lacoste, December 10, 2002.

p. 214, line 25: "noisy and boozy": Interview with Carl Bunch, January 2, 2002.

p. 214, line 27: Thomas Williams calls about Gladys Palmer: Memorandum, March 17, 1967, To: Louis Ivon, Chief Investigator, From: C. J. Navarre, Re: Information volunteered by Thomas Williams, Route 1, Box 8, Ethel, Louisiana, NODA, NARA; Billy Kemp, June 29, 1976, From: Jeff Gottlieb, interview with Billy Kemp, June 14, 1976, NODA, NARA.

p. 214, line 36: Lincoln: Jack Ruby also had a Cadillac: Testimony of Little Lynn Carlin, Warren Commission, Vol. XIII, pp. 213–214, taken at Fort Worth Post Office, April 15, 1964.

p. 215, line 38: "don't give her any money for the funeral": Interview with Josephine Palmer, January 31, 2002.
p. 215, line 2: Gloria Wilson was dating Lee Harvey Oswald: Interview with Lea McGehee, February 3, 2001.
p. 215, line 17: D. J. Blanchard saw Gladys with Lee Harvey Oswald: Dischler Notes.
p. 215, line 22: the FBI had interviewed Gladys: Henry Earl Palmer interviewed for the HSCA by Robert Buras, January 19, 1978.
p. 215, line 36: She did have her tape recorder: These tapes were in the custody of Francis Fruge, and disappeared after his death.
p. 215, line 42: Henry Earl was an "Exalted Cyclops": FBI, To: The Attorney General, From: Director, FBI, February 10, 1969, 180-10024-10264, 62-109060-6712, NARA. Hoover believed, cynically, that it might help the Shaw defense team should the Klan associations of some of the witnesses for Jim Garrison be made public.
p. 216, line 3: Henry Earl is suspicious of Judge Rarick: Interview with John R. Rarick, November 26, 2000.
p. 216, line 23: He was living with Dr. Frank Silva: Lynn Loisel drove up to Clinton and talked to Francis Fruge, who reported that Oswald had told Henry Earl Palmer that he was living with Dr. Frank Silva: *Diary of Richard N. Billings*, pp. 82–83.
p. 216, line 36: Manchester remembers there were three men in the car: Conversation of John Manchester with John R. Rarick, August 13, 2000.
p. 217, line 2: then they changed their minds: Interview with Anne Dischler, July 4, 2000.
p. 22, line 5: Henry Earl offered no explanation: This scene from interviews with Anne Dischler, January 31–February 2, 2001.
p. 217, line 32: "some damn state trooper": Interview with John R. Rarick, June 12, 2000.
p. 217, line 38: "Jim was always a finer man": John R. Rarick to Joan Mellen, March 6, 2000.
p. 217, line 42: Manchester knows that Oswald had registered to vote: Interview with Anne Dischler, January 3, 2002.
p. 217, line 7: "selling bananas": Affidavit of John Manchester, Town Marshal, Clinton, Louisiana, NODA, NARA.

p. 218, line 17: a witness named Henry Brown: Dischler Notes.
p. 218, line 22: "it's useless to try to register": Memorandum, January 17, 1968, To: Jim Garrison, From: Andrew J. Sciambra, Re: Interview with Melvin Morgan Ellis and John Ellis, Clinton, Louisiana—January 9, 1968, NODA, NARA. See also Estes Morgan talks to Oswald: Memorandum, January 23, 1968, To: Jim Garrison, From: Andrew J. Sciambra, Re: Interviews with people in Jackson and Clinton, Louisiana, NODA, NARA.
p. 218, line 31: "the 'i' in the word 'parish'": *Rough Side of the Mountain.*
p. 218, line 33: "Don't come thanking Jesus in here": *Rough Side of the Mountain.*
p. 219, line 1: Oswald takes his pre-employment physical: Interview with Maxine Kemp, June 12, 2000.
p. 219, line 10: "Dr. Silva is from Cuba": Interview with Dr. Frank Silva, October 7, 2000.
p. 219, line 20: Oswald applies for a job at the *States-Item:* Memorandum, October 18, 1967, To: Jim Garrison, From: Tom Bethell, Re: Oswald's Alleged Attempts to Find Work, NODA, NARA.
p. 219, line 28: *The Amlash Legacy.* Also quoted in Anthony Summers, *Not in Your Lifetime* (New York: Marlowe, 1998), p. 371.
p. 219, line 36: "father of psychiatry in Baton Rouge": Obituary, *Advocate* (Baton Rouge), October 15, 2004.
p. 219, line 39: second cousin. Their mothers were first cousins. Mrs. Silva had died when her son was born; she had chosen the name Francisco because she liked Bartes' name.
p. 219, line 39: Francisco Bartes Clarens: Among his complaints was that the views of the anti-Castro Cubans were not being heard, see *The Final Assassinations Report: Report of the Select Committee on Assassinations* (New York: Bantam Books, 1979), Introduction by G. Robert Blakey, Chief Counsel and Staff Director. See also Anthony Summers, *Not in Your Lifetime*, p. 231. Jim Garrison had assigned William Martin to interview Francisco Bartes Clarens: Memorandum: July 29, 1967, To: Jim Garrison, From: William R. Martin, Subject: Francisco (Frank) Bartes, NODA, NARA. Regarding the CIA con-

nections of Bartes Clarens, Martin sabotages Jim Garrison's investigation one more time here by neglecting to ask Bartes whether he had ever encountered Lee Harvey Oswald. Bartes had warned the FBI that Oswald was "a dangerous man," only a month later to say that Oswald was "unknown to him": Newman, *Oswald and the CIA*, p. 337. Martin tells Jim Garrison that "Mr. Bartes wants to be a friend of this office and do whatever he can to help us in our inquiry into the Kennedy assassination."

The Domestic Contact Service was kept in the dark about Frank Bartes: CIA Memorandum, November 20, 1967, Subject: Garrison Investigation of Kennedy Assassination, Francisco Antonio Bartes Clarens, 104-10106-10692, Agency file: 80T01357A, NARA: "It is requested that this inquiry be sent to the New Orleans office by a separate memorandum which omits all reference to the DD/P and to any association between Bartes and the Clandestine Services."

p. 219, line 41: Dr. Frank Silva met Frank Bartes only once, in New Orleans: Interview with Dr. Frank Silva, January 7, 2002.

p. 220, line 9: "I've come to get a job at the hospital at the suggestion of Dr. Malcolm Pierson": Interview with Dr. Frank Silva, October 7, 2000.

p. 220, line 20: "never seen or heard of Lee Harvey Oswald": Memorandum, August 21, 1967, To: Jim Garrison, From: Andrew J. Sciambra, Re: Trip to Jackson, Louisiana and subsequent interview with Dr. Frank Silva, NODA, NARA.

p. 220, line 25: Dr. Silva had the flu: Interview with Dr. Frank Silva, October 7, 2000.

CHAPTER 14

p. 221, Epigraph: "back in jail": Interview with Corrie Collins, June 13, 2000.

p. 221, line 18: Ned Touchstone confirms that Oswald applied for a job at East, his source a former Army intelligence officer: "Woman Who Told of Ruby-Oswald Link Found Dead," *The Councilor* 5 (no. 4), August 5, 1967, p. 1.

p. 221, line 21: Moo Moo interviews Reeves Morgan and Henry Earl

Palmer: June 1, 1967, To: Jim Garrison, From: Andrew J. Sciambra, Re: Interview with Mr. Reeves Morgan, Clinton, Louisiana, May 29, 1967, NODA, NARA, and Re: Mr. Henry Earl Palmer—Interview with Registrar of Voters, Clinton, Louisiana on May 29, 1967, NODA, NARA.

p. 221, line 23: Moo Moo talks to Henry Earl: Memorandum, To: Jim Garrison, From: Andrew Sciambra, Re: Mr. Henry Earl Palmer—Interview with Registrar of Voters, Clinton, Louisiana, May 29, 1967, NODA, NARA.

p. 222, line 22: Moo Moo tracked down Verla Bell: Interview with Verla Bell, January 17, 2002.

p. 222, line 23: Verla Bell had seen the black Cadillac: Memorandum, June 27, 1968, To: Jim Garrison and James L. Alcock, From: Tom Bethell, Re: Clay Shaw Case, NODA, NARA.

p. 222, line 28: Manchester: Affidavit of John Manchester, Town Marshal, Clinton, Louisiana, NODA, NARA.

p. 222, line 34: "in the scope of his employment": Memorandum, September 7, 1967, To: Jim Garrison, From: Andrew J. Sciambra, Re: Conversation with G. Wray Gill This Date, NODA, NARA.

p. 222, line 38: John Volz examined Shaw's appointment books: Memorandum, March 27, 1967, To: Jim Garrison, From: John P. Volz, Re: STATE versus CLAY SHAW, NODA, NARA.

p. 222, line 42: "well-dressed": Dischler Notes.

p. 223, line 3: Moo Moo meets Joseph Cooper: Memorandum, October 2, 1968, To: Jim Garrison, From: Andrew J. Sciambra, Re: Joseph Cooper, NODA, NARA. Based on Cooper's information, Moo Moo asks Palmer about Banister: Memorandum, October 9, 1968, To: Jim Garrison, From: Andrew J. Sciambra, Re: Interview with Henry O. [*sic*] Palmer, Clinton, La., NODA, NARA.

p. 223, line 21: Oswald as a naval intelligence agent: "The Tragic Career of William H. 'Joe' Cooper" by Claude B. Slaton, 16 December 1996, "Redacted" (Web site).

p. 223, line 19: Dunn with Fruge and Dischler: Dischler Notes.

p. 223, line 29: Moo Moo interviews Andrew H. Dunn: Memorandum, July 18, 1967, To: Jim Garrison, From: Andrew Sciambra, Re: July 17, 1967, Interview with Andrew H. Dunn, NODA, NARA.

p. 224, line 15: Gloria Wilson told Veda Freeman there were four men in the car: Memorandum, January 30, 1968, To: Louis Ivon, From: Frank Ruiz and Kent Simms, Re: Interview with Miss Veda Freeman on January 10, 1968, NODA, NARA.

p. 224, line 23: they blew up the photograph: Interview with Steve Bordelon, June 14, 2000.

p. 224, line 32: Kline talked to men in car": Dischler Notes.

p. 224, line 34: William Kline didn't see anything: Interview with William Kline, January 3, 2002.

p. 225, line 8: Jim Garrison thanks the Sovereignty Commission: Jim Garrison to Henry Sibley, August 21, 1967, NOPL.

p. 225, line 19: Martens had his mother committed: Memorandum, May 22, 1968, To: Louis Ivon, From: Gary Sanders, Re: Mrs. Marguerite Martens (Mother of Layton Martens), NODA, NARA.

p. 225, line 21: the FBI was questioning her: Memorandum, March 14, 1968, To: Jim Garrison, From: Andy Sciambra, Re: Beverly Farley, NODA, NARA.

p. 225, line 26: Mrs. Martens talks to Francis Fruge: HSCA. Francis Louis Fruge interviewed by Robert Buras, April 7, 1978, NARA. See also Interrogatories, HSCA, April 18, 1978, Baton Rouge, NARA. Regarding the statement of Mrs. Martens that "Clay Shaw, David Ferrie and Guy Banister" were in my home, see Memorandum, Summary of Deposition, To: G. Robert Blakey, From: S. Jonathan Blackmer, staff counsel, JFK, May 17, 1978, Re: Deposition of Francis Louis Fruge, Taken on April 18, 1978, in Baton Rouge, Louisiana, NARA.

p. 226, line 6: Moo Moo and Fruge interview Gladys Palmer: Memorandum, August 25, 1967, To: Jim Garrison, From: Andrew J. Sciambra, Re: Interview on August 22, 1967, of Gladys Palmer Wilson, 3554 Evangeline Street, Baton Rouge, Louisiana, NODA, NARA.

p. 226, line 17: Cal Kelly's daughter tells Moo Moo that she had heard Oswald had sought employment at East in the company of Gladys Palmer: Memorandum, August 31, 1967, To: Jim Garrison, From: Andrew Sciambra, NODA, NARA.

p. 226, line 26: Shaw and Oswald at the Clinton courthouse: Memorandum To: File, From: Kenneth D. Klein, April 4, 1977, Re: Phone conversation with Ronald L. Johnson, HSCA, 180-10076-10206, 008269, NARA.

p. 226, line 37: "suspicious of white people": Memorandum, August 23, 1967, To: Jim Garrison, From: Andrew J. Sciambra, Re: Results of CORE meeting in Clinton, Louisiana, NODA, NARA.

p. 226, line 42: "we don't know where our enemy is": These comments following the slide show appear in *Rough Side of the Mountain.*

p. 227, line 13: Henry Burnell Clark's sworn statement is HSCA 000019 and 000020.

p. 227, line 20: "One who may help you is Corrie Collins": Dischler Notes.

p. 227, line 24: details from the life of Corrie Collins: Interviews with Corrie Collins, June 13, 2000; February 3, 2001.

p. 227, line 25: for CORE demonstrations in East Feliciana Parish during the summer of 1963: "Judge to Hear Arguments on Core Ban," *Morning Advocate,* August 28, 1963. The rest are all from the *Times-Picayune:* "March Halted in Plaquemine," September 1, 1963, section 1, p. 4; "March Leaders Hit 'Brutality,'" September 2, 1963, section 1, p. 16; "Mayor Wires RFK for Help; Plaquemine Officials Ask for Federal Marshals," September 3, 1963, section 2, p. 2; "Farmer, Seven Others Are Found Guilty," September 4, 1963, section 3, p. 2; "Students Hold Demonstration," September 6, 1963, section 1, p. 12; "Judge refuses to Lift Order," September 7, 1963, section 3, p. 2; "CORE's Acts of Violence in Plaquemine Reported," September 8, 1963, section 2, p. 2; "Case Remanded to State Courts," September 14, 1963, section 1, p. 1; "Judge Studies Ban Injunction," September 20, 1963, section 4, p. 1; "Lift Ban, CORE asks Rarick," September 28, 1963, section 2, p. 5; "Order against CORE Still On," October 1, 1963, section 1, p. 16; "Judge Halts CORE Hearing," October 15, 1963, section 1, p. 6; "Hearing Friday Involves CORE," October 16, 1963, section 1, p. 5; "District Judge Assails Action by Appeals Court," October 25, 1963, section 1, p. 1; "LA. Sit-In Laws Target of Suit," November 5, 1963, section 1, p. 20; "Voter Records Photos Sought," November 13, 1963, section 1, p. 20; "Rarick Rejects CORE Protests," November 22, 1963, section 3, p. 13; "Delay in CORE Hearing Given," December 14, 1963, section 2, p. 2; "Dismissal Asked by Judge Rarick," December 17, 1963, section 1, p. 6; "McKeithen Lays Turmoil to JFK," September 22, 1963, section 1, p. 23. This is of course just a sample of the coverage of CORE in Louisiana during the late summer and early fall of 1963.

p. 228, line 3: "a Negro wearing a CORE T-shirt": "Rarick Rejects CORE Protest," *Times-Picayune*, November 22, 1963, section 3, p. 13. See also "Order against CORE Still On," *Times-Picayune*, October 1, 1963, section 1, p. 16.

p. 228, line 5: He would go down before he would give in: *Rough Side of the Mountain.*

p. 228, line 12: "by the time I get there": Interview with Corrie Collins, June 13, 2000.

p. 228, line 13: Corrie Collins knows when the Klan holds their meetings: Interview with Corrie Collins, February 3, 2001.

p. 228, line 18: "they knew better": Interview with Corrie Collins, February 3, 2001.

p. 228, line 20: "Barney": Interview with Corrie Collins, February 3, 2001. See also Corrie Collins, HSCA interview, October 24, 1978.

p. 228, line 25: did not equal the leave days: Congress of Racial Equality (CORE), Papers, Part 2, Southern Regional Office 1959-1966, Edited by August Meier and Elliot Rudwick, University Publications of America, Frederick, Maryland, reel 3, frame 825.

p. 228, line 31: four men in it: Interview with Corrie Collins, June 13, 2000.

p. 229, line 10: Maxwell interviews Corrie Collins: HSCA, Corrie Collins, October 24, 1978, interviewed in Highland Park, Michigan, NARA.

p. 229, line 1: Sciambra did not write this down: Interview with Corrie Collins, Memorandum, October 26, 1967, To: Jim Garrison, From: Andrew

J. Sciambra, Re: Interview with Corey [*sic*] Collins, NODA, NARA.

p. 229, line 19: Alcock and Sciambra interview Corrie Collins: Memorandum, January 31, 1968, To: Jim Garrison, From: Andrew J. Sciambra, Re: Clinton, Louisiana, NODA, NARA.

p. 229, line 25: Verla Bell also hears the line "trading with the enemy": Memorandum, March 14, 1968, To: Jim Garrison, From: Andy Sciambra, Re: Clinton, Louisiana, NODA, NARA.

p. 229, line 27: did Shaw wear a hat? Collins says he told Sciambra that Shaw was *not* wearing a hat, interview with Corrie Collins, June 13, 2000.

p. 229, line 35: Bobbie and her husband Joe: Dischler Notes.

p. 230, line 9: "we're short of people": Interview with Frank Meloche, June 11, 2000.

p. 230, line 30: state legislator demands money from Jim Garrison: "Mystery Investigation Expense Accounts Probed," by Bill Neikirk, *States-Item*, undated, and "State Police Aid in DA Probe Is Confirmed," *States-Item*, April 30, 1968, NARA.

p. 230, line 31: The Sovereignty Commission was accused of being "a junior Central Intelligence Agency": "Intelligence Unit Developed—Claim" by C. M. Hargroder. *Times-Picayune*, May 1, 1968, section 1, p. 1. See also "Garrison to Seek Early Trial in Shaw Case," *Times-Picayune*, May 1, 1968, section 1, p. 17.

p. 230, line 36: Sciambra receives disinformation from Pete Reech: Memorandum, January 22, 1968, To: Jim Garrison, From: Andrew J. Sciambra, Re: Pete Reech, Jackson, Louisiana, NODA, NARA.

p. 230, line 36: Pete Reech delivered Dr. Silva's newspaper: Memorandum, January 22, 1968, To: Jim Garrison, From: Andrew J. Sciambra, Re: Pete Reech, Jackson, Louisiana, NODA, NARA.

p. 230, line 38: false contention: Interview with Corrie Collins, June 13, 2000.

p. 230, line 39: emerged from a CORE meeting: Memorandum, January 22, 1968, To: Jim Garrison, From: Andrew J. Sciambra, Re: Henry Earl Palmer, Clinton, Louisiana, NODA, NARA.

p. 231, line 3: Andrew Dunn again identifies Guy Banister as a passenger: Memorandum, January 30, 1968, To: Louis Ivon, From: Frank Ruiz and Kent Simms, Re: Interview with Mr. Andrew H. Dunn, W/M General Delivery, Clinton, Louisiana on 1/10/68, NODA, NARA.

p. 231, line 5: Ruiz and Simms interview William Dunn: Memorandum, January 31, 1968, To: Louis Ivon, From: Frank Ruiz & Kent Simms, Re: Interview of William Dunn, 42, Box 793, Woodland, Louisiana, on January 17, 1968, NODA, NARA; William Dunn before the HSCA, April 18, 1978.

p. 231, line 10: Moo Moo interviews Ed Dwyer: Confidential Memorandum, April 2, 1969—Dictated and Transcribed, To: Jim Garrison, From: Andrew J. Sciambra, Re: Shaw in St. Francisville and Clinton, NODA, NARA.

p. 231, line 18: Jerry Sylvester dies in an airplane crash: "Further Feliciana Research" by Claude B. Slaton, June 24, 1997. Web site of "redacted." Other leads came from a judge named Ossie Brown. Brown told Jim Garrison he knew a young truck driver for the Holsum Bakery, who had told him he knew Ferrie and Oswald, and thought one day a black car had been following him on his bread route. When Ferrie's death was announced, the truck driver was deeply frightened. Richard Rolfe told Jim Garrison that "Shaw is much better known in Clinton than it would appear." Brown's is Number 95 of 100 open leads Jim Garrison amassed in the last months of his investigation. Courtesy of Lyon Garrison.

p. 231, line 22: a foreign lady in an old car: Jim Garrison to Jonathan Blackmer, July 15, 1977,

p. 231, line 22: same route: "Morgan City—late Sept?" "KT & LHO double," New Orleans District Attorney's Office List, undated, NARA.

p. 231, line 29: Moo Moo wrote to the FBI: Andrew J. Sciambra to Elmer Litchfield, January 22, 1968, 124-10264-10050, 89-69-3885. See also Gene S. Palmisano to Andrew J. Sciambra, February 14, 1968; Andrew J. Sciambra to Honorable J. Edgar Hoover, February 19, 1968; FBI, To: SAC, New Orleans, From: Director, FBI, Personal Attention, February 26, 1968; Robert E. Rightmyer to Louis C. LaCour, February 28, 1968, NARA.

p. 231, line 35: not to acknowledge the letter from Garrison's assistant: FBI, To: Attorney General, From: Director, FBI, January 25, 1968, 62-109060-6672.

p. 231, line 37: Branigan calls Sylvester: To: SAC, From: ASAC: Sylvester, 89-69-3805A, NARA.

p. 231, line 41: Litchfield contacts Rightmyer with his denial: FBI, To: SAC (New Orleans), From: SA Elmer B. Litchfield, January 25, 1968, 124-10258-10321, 89-69-3808B, NARA. See also To: SAC (New Orleans), From: SA Earl R. Petersen, January 25, 1968, 89-69-3809.

p. 232, line 4: Hoover ordered Ramsey Clark: FBI 62-109060-6672, NARA. Hoover's tone and method of address suggest a superior giving orders to an underling.

p. 232, line 11: Sciambra and Alcock visit Litchfield: FBI, January 31, 1968, To: Director, From: New Orleans, 124-10258-10329, 89-69-3817, NARA.

p. 232, line 15: "everything went through the Seat of Government": Interview with Elmer B. Litchfield, January 10, 2002.

p. 232, line 17: Branigan telephones Sylvester again and instructs that Litchfield be brief: FBI, To: SAC, From: ASAC Sylvester, February 1, 1968, 89-69-3819, NARA.

p. 232, line 34: "everything went through the Seat of Government": Sciambra now writes to Palmisano, and Palmisano replies: "We are sincerely attempting . . .": Andrew J. Sciambra to Gene S. Palmisano, March 29, 1968; To: Mr. Fred H. Vinson Jr., From: Director, FBI, April 22, 1968, 62-109060-6357, NARA.

p. 232, line 37: Branigan again telephoned Rightmyer: FBI, To: Supv. Wall, From: SAC Rightmyer, April 18, 1968, 89-69-4008, NARA.

p. 233, line 12: Merryl Hudson is visited by the FBI at the East Louisiana State Hospital at Jackson: Interview with Merryl Hudson, February 3, 2001.

p. 233, line 20: "I have some thoughts about who took it out": Interview with Maxine Kemp, June 12, 2000.

p. 233, line 29: "That must be where that guy thought he saw Oswald": Interview with Elmer B. Litchfield, January 30, 2002.

p. 233, line 35: the resident agent out of Lafayette took the knife and the bar slip signed "Hidell": Memorandum, July 13, 1967, To: Jim Garrison, From: Andrew J. Sciambra, Re: Information received from Lt. Fruge, July 11, 1967, NODA, NARA.

p. 233, line 36: follow up: Interview with Lou Ivon, October 9, 2000.

p. 234, line 8: "not necessary to correspond with Blakey": FBI. Record Number 124-10274-10196. File Number: 62-117290-997x2. From: legal counsel. To: assistant director. 06/19/78. Subjects: Notes, Blakey, G. R., Retained by FBI. NARA.

p. 234, line 19: Aynesworth and Manchester: See In Re: Grand Jury Investigation of Conspiracy to Murder John F. Kennedy, State of Louisiana, Parish of Orleans, Criminal District Court, Request for Attendance of Out-of-State Witness, To the Honorable Matthew S. Braniff, Judge of section 'B" of the Criminal District Court for the Parish of Orleans, State of Louisiana, signed by Assistant District Attorney Richard Burnes, NARA.

p. 234, line 33: "I advise you to leave the area": Aynesworth described the incident to Tom Bethell on his return to New Orleans, Tom Bethell *Diary.*

p. 235, line 11: He called James Leo Herlihy: Interview with Stuart Timmons, June 12, 1999.

p. 235, line 16: Kluger would never have published it: Conversation with Richard Kluger, October 8, 1998.

p. 235, line 17: Kirkwood goes to Clinton: James Kirkwood, *American Grotesque* (New York: Simon & Schuster, 1970), p. 222.

p. 235, line 20: "we shall overcome": Interview with Carl Bunch, January 2, 2002

p. 235, line 30: "bother me, not him": Interview with Corrie Collins, June 13, 2000.

p. 235, line 35: employed at East: The HSCA accepted as fact that Oswald had applied for a job at the East Louisiana State Hospital at Jackson: Summary Memorandum: Clinton, La., NARA.

p. 235, line 37: it would provide Oswald with a cover: Interview with Numa Bertel, February 6, 2001.

p. 236, line 4: "the crazed part would be accomplished at Jackson":

Jim Garrison interviewed in documentary film, *Rough Side of the Mountain.* (Work-in-progress) by Richard Cohen and Carol Kachmer.

p. 236, line 8: the turkey on Thanksgiving Day: Jim Garrison in *He Must Have Something* outtakes.

p. 236, line 14: "aggression beyond control": Jim Garrison interviewed in outtakes for *He Must Have Something.*

p. 236, line 16: "acting funny": Interview with Robert Buras, January 16, 2002.

p. 236, line 25: "establish meaningful relationships": Ibid. p. 423.

p. 236, line 26: "twisted": Chapter VII of the *Warren Commission Report:* Ibid, p. 375.

p. 236, line 27: a "troubled American citizen": Warren Report, Appendix XV, p. 778.

p. 236, line 31: "a rather disoriented individual": U.S. Senate Select Committee to Study Governmental Operations with Respect To Intelligence Activities (SSC), Re: Interview of FBI Special Agent in Charge (SAC) Warren C. de Brueys by SSC Staff Members, January 29, 1976, January 20, 1976, To: Director, FBI, Attention: Intelligence Division, W. O. Cregar, From: SAC, San Juan, Observations and Comments of SAC de Brueys. FBI 124-10273-10172, HQ, 62-116395-1300X, 20 pages, NARA.

p. 236, line 42: the Diary was gone: Interview with Anne Dischler, February 2, 2001.

p. 237, line 3: Andrew Dunn's suicide by hanging: "DA Witness Hanged Self, Clinton Records Confirm," *Times-Picayune,* January 27, 1971, section 1, p. 10.

p. 237, line 6: Salvatore Panzeca claims Shaw was not there: Interview with Salvatore Panzeca, June 4, 2000.

p. 237, line 11: Anne Dischler's statement of July 2000 repudiating Patricia Lambert, courtesy of Mrs. Dischler.

p. 237, line 22: Mary Ferrell linked telephone calls on David Ferrie's telephone to Clinton: See Critics Conference, September 18, 1977, HSCA, AARC; interview with Mary Ferrell, February 11, 2002.

p. 237, line 25: Alvin Beaubouef says the Clinton people have been bribed: Telephone conversation with Alvin Beaubouef, November 27, 1999.

p. 237, line 26: "just wasn't there": Interview with Rosemary James, May 22, 1998.

CHAPTER 15

p. 238, Epigraph: Humpty Dumpty: Jim Garrison on ABC television, *Issues and Answers*, Sunday, May 28, 1967, transcript at NOPL.

p. 238, line 3: an "army" of men: Anonymous letter May 22, 1967, Postmark is Dallas, Texas, To District Attorney Jim Garrison. The letter is signed Mr._____, NODA, NARA. The second letter is dated January 9, 1968, To: Mr. G.

p. 238, line 24: Wood as instructor for CIA: Memorandum, Subject: Garrison and the Kennedy Assassination, Reference: CI/R & A Memorandum no. 9, Subject: Garrison and the Kennedy Assassination, 5 June 1968, Paragraph 19 circa signed by Donovan E. Pratt, 104-10310-10253, Agency file: CIA-DDP-FILES, January 3, 1969, NARA.

p. 239, line 1: became one of his investigators: Boxley was taken on as a "special officer—without pay," Warrant of Appointment, May 4, 1967, William C, Boxley, document signed by Joseph I. Giarrusso, Superintendent of Police. Courtesy of Gary Shaw. Boxley at once ingratiated himself with Garrison with a memo outlining "CIA shop talk": "Jim—I have underlined in red authentic 'shop talk.'" AARC.

p. 239, line 3: failed his polygraph: In fact, it appeared that Boxley had "lied on every question," Wood interview with George E. Rennar.

p. 239, line 8: Garrison ignored the suspicions of his staff and defended Boxley, terming him "a man who had been with the intelligence agency but still cared about the United States": "Garrison claims Foreign Spy Link," *New York Times*, July 12, 1968, p. C35; see also FBI, Memorandum For: Director, Federal Bureau of Investigation, Attention: Mr. S. J. Papich, 15 July 1968, Subject: Garrison and the Kennedy Assassination: William Clarence Wood Jr., aka William Boxley, NARA.

p. 239, line 8: disappeared for weeks: Interview with Louis Ivon, January 12, 2000.

p. 239, line 9: Wood recounts how

Garrison gave him the name "Boxley": "Ex-CIA Agent Tells His Role in Garrison's Conspiracy Probe," *Tatler Investigative Special / National Tatler,* September 1975, pp. 4–5.

p. 239, line 10: maintained contact: Interview of William C. Wood, aka Bill Boxley by George E. Rennar, AARC (1971).

p. 239, line 12: Wood applies for reemployment: CIA requested a check from the FBI on Wood, and "adverse information" resulted in his not being formally rehired: CIA, Attn: Director, Domestic Contact Service, Deputy Director, DSC. 26 April 1968, HOU-80-68, Re: Bill Wood, Agent for Jim Garrison, Making Inquiries in Dallas, signed by Ernest A. Rische, NARA.

p. 239, line 14: "the color of thunderstorm clouds": Jim Brown, *Central Intelligence Assassination,* p. 203.

p. 239, line 15: "insurance adjuster": Tom Bethell, "Conspiracy to End Conspiracies," *National Review,* December 16, 1991. p. 48.

p. 239, line 16: twisted logic: Interview with Steve Bordelon; undated memos of Boxley, re: John "the Pirate" Rigsby and the National States Rights Party. See also Re: Jesse Curry, courtesy of Gary Shaw.

p. 239, line 17: Sea-land: Bordelon looked askance: Interview with Steve Bordelon, April 3, 2000.

p. 239, line 31: Boxley suggests that Oswald was an FBI penetration into the Soviet Union: Memorandum, February 23, 1968, To: Jim Garrison, From: William C. Wood (Boxley), Re: Penetration and Diversion of Clandestine Operations, NODA, NARA.

p. 239, line 39: Hemming claims he was the man at the gate: John Newman accepts Hemming's statement that it was he who went to see Oswald at El Toro, see *Oswald and CIA,* p. 105.

p. 239, line 40: Gerald Patrick Hemming was an asset of James Angleton and CIA Counter Intelligence: Interviews with Gerald Patrick Hemming. Hemming's close affiliation with Angleton was a persistent theme of these interviews.

p. 240, line 15: Giesbrecht identifies David Ferrie from his "bushy eyebrows . . . mustaches on top of his eyes": The latter comes from the *Na-*

tional Enquirer article by William Condie, William Dick, Iain Calder, Pearl Trachtenberg and Paul Feis, January 28, 1968.

p. 240, line 15: Giesbrecht had already provided his information to the FBI: See Report of Ewald I. Carlson, March 6, 1964, 124-10259, 89-69-1860. See also To: Director, FBI, From: SAC, Minneapolis, March 20, 1967, 124-10259-10118, 89-69-1861, NARA.

For further details about the Giesbrecht-Winnipeg Airport story, see Peter Whitmey, "The Winnipeg Airport Incident," *The Fourth Decade,* November 1995, pp. 22–25; and "The Winnipeg Airport Incident Revisited," *The Fourth Decade,* March 1999. I am indebted to Peter Whitmey for his help in unraveling the nuances of the Winnipeg Airport incident. See also the *National Enquirer* article, January 28, 1968. The Garrison files refer to Giesbrecht as "Mr. Richard": Memorandum, September 18, 1967, To: File: From: Louis Ivon, Chief Investigator, NODA, NARA. Regarding Garrison failing to receive a letter from Giesbrecht: See To: Boxley (The place in Canada file), October 30, 1968, handwritten, memo from Jim Garrison.

p. 240, line 21: "planted lead": "Time, Place and Number Correlations" (Ruby, Ferrie, Oswald and Shaw), undated memo, circa late 1967, NODA, NARA.

p. 240, line 25: "I got the distinct feeling": Memorandum, February 19, 1968, To: Jim Garrison, From: William Boxley, Re: Interview with Bob Lavender, NODA, NARA.

p. 240, line 40: Martin handles Boxley's expense requests: Memorandum, May 25, 1967, To: Charles R. Ward, From: William R. Martin, Re: William Boxley, Investigator. District Attorney's Staff: NODA, NARA. This one was for $200.

p. 240, line 40: a sketch of Ruby and Oswald: This telephone conversation between William Martin and Bill Boxley was taped and transcribed, July 20, 1967, NODA, NARA.

p. 241, line 11: Huff was a close friend of Guy Banister: Interview with Allen Campbell, June 10, 2002.

p. 241, line 14: Erbon W. Wise: See Erbon W. Wise, *My Military Years, 1941–1969* (Self-published, 2001).

The pages dealing with Jim Garrison are 161–162; 164–166.

p. 241, line 16: Wise made a sizable contribution to Governor McKeithen's campaign: Interview with John Tarver, June 15, 2000. A second source reporting that Wise became Adjutant of the Louisiana National Guard "as reward for his support" is Raymond Huff, in 1967 Regional Commissioner for the U.S. Customs Office, MCC Investigative Report, May 31, 1967, Reported by Aaron M. Kohn, MCC.

p. 241, line 23: Huff considers Wise "very weak and naive": Investigative Report, May 31, 1967, Reported by Aaron M. Kohn. Here Kohn interviews Raymond Huff, NARA.

p. 241, line 24: Garrison wanted to be a brigadier general: Interview with Erbon W. Wise, January 13, 2000.

p. 241, line 32: Huff attempts to collaborate with the FBI: To: Mr. W. C. Sullivan, From: D. J. Brennan Jr., April 12, 1967, Subject: James C. Garrison: Fraud against the Government, 124-10043-10396, 62-109060-5126, NARA.

p. 242, line 15: Statement of the Rev. Clyde Johnson, April 4, 1967, handwritten, April 4, 1967, typed version: April 5, 1967, Sworn statement witnessed by James Alcock and Louis Ivon, NODA, NARA.

p. 242, line 27: Johnson fears for his life: Interview transcript: Clyde Johnson and Sam Depino, June 14, 1967, NARA.

p. 242, line 29: Ed McMillan identifies Clay Shaw as having been in Clyde Johnson's room: Memorandum, April 11, 1967, To: Jim Garrison, From: Louis Ivon, Re: Statement of Edward McMillan, NODA, NARA. See also Clyde Johnson confirms Ed McMillan's statement: June 1, 1967, To: Jim Garrison, From: Dets. D. Ward & L. Otillio Jr., Re: Statement of Clyde Johnson residing at Box 327, Kentwood, La, NODA, NARA.

p. 242, line 32: Johnson was not an ideal witness. He didn't answer one of Garrison's subpoenas because of an outstanding bad check warrant: FBI, June 26, 1967, To: Director, FBI, From: SAC, New Orleans, 124-10251-10233, 89-69-3236, 3237, NARA.

p. 242, line 36: Jim Garrison was skeptical: See note by Jim Garrison appended to Statement of Edward James Whalen. The Whalen testimony is in Memorandum, September 18, 1967, To: Jim Garrison, From: James L. Alcock, Re: Edward James Whalen, W/M, 43, FBI #346-8982, NODA, NARA.

p. 243, line 5: "any time you step on a pig's tail": Memo from Yockey, interview with Clyde Johnson in room atop Tony's Bar, Kentwood, Louisiana, June 15, 1967, NARA.

p. 243, line 8: Gurvich stole Clyde Johnson's sworn statement: Transcription of taped conference with William Gurvich, 8/29/67, September 6, 1967, LHM Edward F. Wegmann, NARA. A snob, Gurvich called Johnson "Slidin' Clyde." Gurvich conference, August 29, 1967, p. 18. Gurvich also claimed that Johnson was available "for hire to anyone at a price": Re: Clay Shaw—7/6/67 Memorandum—Re: Clyde Johnson, Edward F. Wegmann, Papers of *Edward F. Wegmann*, NARA.

p. 243, line 15: the Wegmanns and Dymond flew to Dallas: John R. Nelms to F. Irvin Dymond, August 26, 1967, NARA.

p. 243, line 16: William Alexander helps the Shaw defense team: Edward F. Wegmann to William Alexander, September 1, 1967, NARA.

p. 243, line 18: Aynesworth continues to assist: Edward F. Wegmann to Hugh Aynesworth, September 12, 1967, NARA ("Please be reminded that I am still waiting for you to send me your expenses from our last trip to Dallas," Wegmann writes.)

p. 243, line 19: Depino was an FBI media asset under Joseph Sylvester: See FBI To: Director, From: SAC, New Orleans, November 4, 1966, 89-69-1355, 62-109060-4355, NARA. Depino asked only that "his identity be protected": AIRTEL to: Director, FBI, From: SAC, New Orleans, April 14, 1967, 124-10259-10228, 89-69-1996, 1997; this is a 44-page document. See also To: SAC, From: ASAC Sylvester, April 26, 1967, 89-69-2055, NARA.

p. 243, line 20: needed psychiatric help: Domestic Intelligence Division (5), June 16, 1967: "News articles have previously reported . . . ," NARA. A report of Depino's television performance is in FBI, To: Director, From: New Orleans, June 16, 1967, 124-10263-10044, 89-69-3190, NARA.

p. 243, line 23: Files were disappearing: Memorandum, November 2, 1967, To: Investigative Personnel, From: Tom Bethell, Re: Missing Files, NODA, NARA.

p. 243, line 24: the "Duncan Miller" letter: JOHN J. KING-OSWALD-GUNS-POST OFFICE BOX "FRAUDS," Marked King, John J, undated, a Boxley memo, NODA, NARA.

p. 243, line 33: twirling an Annapolis ring: Interview with Phyllis Kritikos, December 2, 2001.

p. 243, line 41: "there's nothing they could offer me": Jim Garrison at the New Orleans Round Table Conference, September 1968, p. 33, AARC.

p. 244, line 2: King is called "Miller": Although Garrison calls the man "John Miller," in *On the Trail of the Assassins*, he told Mary Ferrell it was John J. King, interview with Mary Ferrell, December 14, 2001. King's motives remain unclear. His son, John J. King Jr., told researcher Larry Haapanen that his father was apolitical, but believed there had been a conspiracy. How he could have obtained—if he did—authorization to offer Jim Garrison a judgeship is not known. He died in 1975: interview with Larry Haapanen, December 3, 2001. See also *On the Trail of the Assassins*, pp. 132–136. See also "A Barrel of Trouble" by Andy Van De Voorde, *Denver Westword*, magazine, vol. 17, no. 12, November 17–23, 1992, p. 22. The subject of this article is John J. King.

p. 244, line 10: A transcript of Jim Garrison's appearance on *The Tonight Show*, January 31, 1968, is available at the National Archives, transcribed February 1, 1968.

p. 244, line 25: "it's not going too well": Jim Garrison conversation with Robert Buras and L. J. Delsa, interview with Robert Buras, February 1, 2002.

p. 245, line 1: Carson stalked out: *Mirror* (Midlothian, Texas), March 21, 1968, Editorial.

p. 245, line 8: Carson is no Noel Coward: Jim Garrison to Zach Sklar, July 1, 1988, AARC.

p. 245, line 21: Bill Brazzil, vice president in charge of WTVJ, first wrote a thank-you letter to Jim Garrison, March 11, 1968, "I am deeply indebted and grateful to you for taking the time and trouble. . . ." Then he wrote to Helms, complaining about Jim Garrison: March 21, 1968, NARA. Lawrence Houston decided not to accept Brazzil's offer of help until they learned more about him, Official Routing Slip, April 1, 1968, D/DCS All key, signed by LR Houston.

p. 245, line 24: Gerstein asks Larry King to ask Louis Wolfson to help Jim Garrison: Interview with Seymour Gelber, November 17, 1999.

p. 245, line 34: Wolfson asks how much it would take to complete the investigation: Testimony in the Office of the States Attorney, September 15, 1971, Document 0071 <www.cuban-exile.com>.

p. 245, line 38: own troubles: King promised to write a column that would help Wolfson and to talk to John Mitchell on his behalf, for which Wolfson gave King $32,500. Then King lied to Wolfson about conversations he purportedly had with Mitchell and appropriated the $32,500: signed statement of Larry King.

p. 246, line 8: "the lowest person I've ever run into": Interview with Louis Wolfson, November 19, 1999.

p. 246, line 9: King arrested: "TV Personality Booked in Case," Times-Picayune, December 21, 1971, section 4, p. 16.

p. 246, line 12: for the Parrot Jungle incident: Sepe is told the Miami investigation is closed: FBI, To: Director, FBI, From: SAC, Miami, March 3, 1967, 89-69-1599, NARA. Sepe tells the FBI his inquiry is not related to the inquiry at New Orleans: AIRTEL, To: Director, FBI, From: SAC, Miami, March 3, 1967, 62-109060-4651, 89-69-1599. He had a friend named Lee: Memo: November 8, 1977, To: Bob Blakey, From: Fonzi & Gonzales, Re: Fauto Odon Alvarez—Aldo Vera Serafin, courtesy of Gaeton Fonzi. See also FBI interview with Mrs. Lillian Spingler, December 20, 1963, CD-246, pp. 3–15; interview on December 19, 1963 by Special Agent James J. O'Connor, File # Miami 105-8342, NARA.

Regarding Sepe wanting to continue the investigation of the Parrot Jungle incident: See: To: Richard E. Gerstein, From: Alfonso C. Sepe, Re: Assassination of President Kennedy, April 18, 1967. Sepe went ahead with his own super secret investigation: Dan Christensen, "JFK, King: The

Dade County Links," Miami magazine, September, 1976, p. 25. Regarding Alfonso Sepe's report on the Parrot Jungle incident, see April 18, 1967, Memo to: Richard E. Gerstein, From: Alfonso C. Sepe, Re: Assassination of President Kennedy, April 18, 1967, 5 pages, Marked: Close Investigation, NARA. Lillian Spingler's December 20, 1963 interview with SA James J. O'Connor is CD 246, which includes interviews with clerk Mrs. J. R. Trigg, who also saw Martinez Soto, interviews with ticket seller Mary Tyson, Mrs. Louise Rosher and the manager of the gift shop, Mr. William Vander Wyden.

p. 246, line 17: "forgetful": Interview with James Savage, January 5, 2001. See also "Wolfson Had Accused King in the Past, Gerstein Says," by James Savage. Miami Herald, December 22, 1971, p. 8C. See also Arvin K. Rothschild, Larry King: Brilliant Interviewer and Super Con-Man. manuscript.

p. 246, line 26: printed after the incident: Interview with Martin F. Dardis.

p. 246, line 30: King does not apologize to Wolfson: Interview with Louis Wolfson.

p. 246, line 32: for Savage's reporting, see "Wolfson: Give King Psychiatric Help," by James Savage. Miami Herald, December 24, 1971.

p. 246, line 34: talk only to Gene Miller: Interview with James Savage, July 30, 2002.

p. 246, line 38: Gerstein had been trying: "Garrison, Gerstein Talk about Donation, Gerstein Tells Why He Held $5,000, Has No Opinion on Garrison Probe," by James Savage and Gene Miller. Miami Herald, January 16, 1972, p. 1.

p. 247, line 8: "Garrison was something of an eccentric": Larry King by Larry King (New York: Simon & Schuster, 1982), p. 19.

p. 247, line 21: "I trust everyone": Jim Garrison to Zachary Sklar, June 1, 1988, AARC.

p. 247, line 23: Hemming at Tulane and Broad: Interviews with Gerald Patrick Hemming. Comments by Gerald Patrick Hemming are based on interviews with Gerald Patrick Hemming, October 22–25, 1999, Fayetteville, North Carolina, and numerous telephone calls and e-mails since. Information about Carl McNabb is from interviews with McNabb, June 13 and 14, 1999, and subsequent meetings and telephone calls. For Hemming at No Name Key, see "Hemming Wages Own War against Communist Cuba," by Larry Grove. *Dallas Morning News,* January 23, 1963.

p. 247, line 30: two heavy machine guns: "Adventurer Works Hard to Establish Anti-Castro Base Near Covington," by William Stuckey. *States-Item,* July 21, 1962. The source of this description was Luis Rabel.

p. 247, line 32: "deep beliefs in democratic principles": CIA 104-10273-10066, From: D/D Security, To: Chief, Contacts, Title: Memo: Hemming, Gerald P, Date February 21, 1962, RUSS HOLMES WORK FILE.

p. 247, line 38: "he is OK": Agency: Army, Record Number 198-10005-10014, Records Series: Califano Papers, Originator: OSD, From: Col. Patchell, To: Gen Lansdale, Date: 08/02/62, Subjects: Hemming, Jerry Patrick; Anti-Castro Cubans, Califano Papers, box 3, folder 1, NARA.

p. 248, line 5: "We're going to be indicted by Jim Garrison": Appendix A: Roy Hargraves tape 2, side A, 2001 Interview with Noel Twyman, in Larry Hancock, *Someone Would Have Talked: What We Know about the JFK Assassination after 40 Years* (Incirca Southlake, Tex.: JFK Lancer Productions & Publications, 2003), p. 276.

p. 248, line 15: "Hector" and "El Indio" are split into two separate "CIA officers" by David Atlee Phillips in his memoir, *The Night Watch* (New York: Atheneum, 1977), p. 49. Phillips describes both as having been involved in the overthrow of President Arbenz. Gaeton Fonzi has identified "El Indio" as David Sanchez Morales, see *The Last Investigation.*

p. 248, line 30: assassination training: Jim Garrison at the New Orleans conference.

p. 248, line 31: Jim Garrison's investigators are showing photographs of Hall, Howard and Seymour: Memorandum, To: Louis Ivon, From Kent A. Simms, Re: Four Pictures for Identification by Arestes [sic] Peña and Evaristo Rodriguez, June 5, 1967, NODA, NARA.

p. 248, line 32: Roy Hargraves: See "Greeting" dated 13 February 1963, signed "Away all boats, Gerry."

p. 248, line 34: CIA knows Hemming is there, but thinks Hargraves is Leroy Collins: 31 August 1967, Memorandum For: Director, Domestic Contact Service, Attn: Mr. George Musulin, Subject: Garrison and the Kennedy Assassination: Gerald Patrick Hemming Jr., 201-309125, reference: CI/R & A. Memorandum, subject; Memorandum no. 5: Garrison and the Kennedy Assassination, dated 7 August 1967, NARA.

p. 248, line 36: it is not true that Hemming has *Life* magazine credentials: Interview with Richard N. Billings, August 2, 2000.

p. 249, line 12: double-talk: Hemming attempts to confuse Jim Garrison: See Memorandum, September 18, 1967, To: Jim Garrison, From: Tom Bethell, Re: Visit of GERRY PATRICK HEMMING AND ROY HARGRAVES, NODA, NARA.

p. 249, line 17: Hemming did not share with Jim Garrison that Guy Banister had enlisted him to kill John F. Kennedy: Gerald Patrick Hemming, HSCA Interrogatories, March 21, 1978, 221 pages. Despite the efforts of the Assassination Records Review Board, there were 256 restrictions on this document, NARA. Hemming's own FOIA request mentions evidence of his meeting "with individuals threatening the life of President John F. Kennedy in 1962 and 1963," and refers to meetings in Florida, Texas and Louisiana: Gerald Patrick Hemming to Mr. Clarence Kelly, Director, FBI, 17 August 1975.

p. 249, line 33: nothing to do with the assassination: Tom Bethell would conclude the opposite, that Hemming spoke or revealed that Hall, Howard and Seymour were all guilty, Tom Bethell to Edward J. Epstein, July 25, 1967.

p. 249, line 36: "working Oswald on the assassination of Castro operation": Interview with Gerald Patrick Hemming, October 22, 1999.

p. 250, line 20: Hemming and Hargraves know that de Torres was working for CIA during the Garrison investigation: "Intrigue at No Name Key" by Tom Dunkin, *Back Channels,* Spring 1992. Available at <www.cuban-exile.com>. Technically, *Back Channels* was a "serial," since it appeared only irregularly.

p. 250, line 26: five foot eleven

inches tall: Memorandum, May 8, 1968, To: Jim Garrison, From: Steven J. Burton, Re: Interview of Gerald Patrick Hemming Jr., NODA, NARA.

p. 250, line 30: Hemming visits Gleichauf: CIA, March 17, 1967, Attn: John McConnell, Subject: Possible repercussions from Abortive Haitian Invasion, F-9-08-8.

p. 250, line 32: targeting his own assets: Memorandum For: Deputy Director for Plans, Subject: Interlocking relationships Between BROWN/ SLAFTER and GARRISON. WH/C 67-313, signed by William V. Broe, Chief, Western Hemisphere Division.

p. 250, line 33: Patrick was an informer for the CIA: June 5, 1968, Memo of Conversation with Manolo Aguilar—Also Present Sgt. Gus Zenoz of the Miami Police Force as Interpreter, Subject: Aguilar, Manuel (NMN), Date: 19 June 1970, File no. 062-28-2671. Aguilar appeared to be an associate of Loran Hall. From: G. Zenoz, policeman 1/c Intelligence Unit to: C. H. Sapp, Detective Sgt. Intelligence Unit, 11-1-63, Subject: Jerry Patrick.

p. 250, line 33: Hemming tells CIA he is with Naval Intelligence: Priority Contacts/Washington, Attn: OSS (Musulin), Subj. Case: 49364 (Garrison Case), Ref: Washington 77887 of 8 Sept 67 To: ODD (Musulin) from Lohmann. "Case 49364 (Gerald Patrick Hemming Jr., aka Jerry Hemming re: a call from Hemming 19 Jan 62 concerning a .45 automatic pistol confiscated by the sheriff's office. . . ."

p. 250, line 34: Hemming applies for regular employment with CIA and is turned down: Richard L. Rininger to Robert W. Rust, U.S. Attorney, Southern District of Florida, undated, 1977, "Mr. Hemming has been a voluntary informant for this Agency . . . our records do not reflect that Gerald Patrick Hemming was ever employed by the Central Intelligence Agency in any capacity, or that he was ever used as an agent or in similar capacity," HSCA 01007 OS7 0371-1. This, of course, was false: see Wesley G. Currier to Director, Central Intelligence Agency, January 19, 1977, Re: *U.S. v. Gerald Patrick Hemming:* Memorandum For: General Counsel, Attention: Mr. Richard L. Rininger, From: Edward Jones, Deputy Director of Security, Personnel Security and Investigations,

Subject: Gerald Patrick Hemming. 9 February 1977; Memorandum For: General Counsel, Attention: Edmund Cohen, From: Robert A. Barteaux, Chief, Information Processing Group, through O/SA/DO/0, Subject: Records Check in the Name Gerald Patrick Hemming, NARA; Frederick McCann. Memorandum For: O/SA/DO/), From: ISS/PICG (McCann), Subject: Gerald Patrick Hemming, Reference: OGC 77-1816. 21 March 1977.

p. 250, line 38: Hemming does not get the job with AID: FBI report of Norman E. Bliss. 9/14/67, Office: Miami, Florida, bureau file: 151-3208, field office file: 151–186. "The informant is MMT-1 (Howard K. Davis) and his source is Robert K. Brown, who had learned that Hemming had met with Dick Watley and Roy Hargreave [*sic*] and the three "reportedly got in touch with Jim Garrison."

p. 250, line 39: CIA, surveilling Garrison's office, checks up on Hemming, From: OSS (Musulin), To: Contacts Los Angeles/Miami, September 8, 1967, 104-10189-10053, 80T01357A, NARA. The visit to Garrison inspires the CIA to check out the entire INTERPEN group, Memorandum no. 5, Subject: Garrison and the Kennedy Assassination, 7 August 1967, Reference: CI/R & A memorandum of June 20, 1967, subject as above.

p. 251, line 1: Robert K. Brown: To Chief, WH Division, From: Chief of Station, JMWAVE, Subject: Garrison Investigation of Assassination, January 4, 1968, NARA.

p. 251, line 3: CIA admits to the Bureau that Hemming is a source: To: Chief, Personnel Security Division, OS, From: Chief, Contact Division, 00. 27 August 1964, Subject: Hemming, Gerald Patrick—Permission to Reveal Identity of a US citizen as a Source of this Agency to the FBI, signed James R. Murphy. CIA turned over to the FBI all reports of which subject was the source, 25 August 1964, at the request of FBI with the promise that the information will not be divulged w/o prior written consent of CIA. See also 4 October 1961, To: Director, Federal Bureau of Investigation, Attention Mr. S. J. Papich, From: Deputy Director (Plans), Subject: United States Citizens Who Wish To Volunteer for the Liberation of Cuba. Helms says: "They made the decision to fight for Cuba because they consider that the men directing the United States government are 'incompetent and incapable of action.'" Hemming's CIA contacts occurred both before and after the Bay of Pigs, CIA, 5 April 1961, Acting Chief, "contact division for chief, Los Angeles office: "His information in the past has been reasonable and he may have some pertinent comments on the current situation."

p. 251, line 3: the Director of Naval Intelligence inquires of Hoover what information he has on Hemming: FBI, November 2, 1961, To: Director of Naval Intelligence, From: John Edgar Hoover, Subject: Gerald Patrick Hemming, Internal Security-Cuba, 105-86406.

p. 251, line 4: Defense Investigative Program: Naval Intelligence Service, W. B. Jepson to Mr. Allen H, McCreight, Chief, Freedom of Information, Privacy Act branch, January 30, 1978, NARA.

p. 251, line 7: Michael Laborde's visit to Jim Garrison: See Memorandum For: Chief, LEOB/SRS, Subject: Highlights on the Cast of Characters Involved in Garrison's Investigation, December 28, 1967, NARA. Michael Laborde named Alberto Fernandez Hechavarria to Garrison: Memorandum For: Deputy Director for Plans: Subject: Interlocking Relationships between Brown/Slafter and Garrison, signed by William V. Broe, Chief, Western Hemisphere section, WH/C 67-313, NARA. Laborde tells Loisel and Ivon about Hemming: see Enclosure 14, Memo no. 5—Garrison and the Kennedy Assassination, August 7, 1967, 42 pages, 104-10404-10442, RUSS HOLMES WORK FILE, NARA. Garrison's investigators met with young Laborde four times: see FBI, To: Director, FBI, From: SAC, New Orleans, July 18, 1967, 124-10046-10313, 62-109060-5583, NARA.

p. 251, line 15: "do whatever he can to help you": Memorandum, July 29, 1967, To: Jim Garrison, From: William R. Martin, Subject: FRANCISCO (Frank) BARTES, NODA, NARA.

p. 251, line 19: "I created smoke myself": Fonzi Notes, taped interview—Gerry Patrick Hemming, 2/6/76.

p. 251, line 24: "add to the confusion": Memo 6/5/77 To: Tanen-baum, From: Fonzi, Re: Weberman/Hemming.

p. 251, line 36: William Cuthbert Brady: To: Jim Garrison, From: Bill Turner, Subject: Contact by Former CIA Agent, January 9, 1968. See also Memorandum, January 15, 1968, To: Louis Ivon, From: Jim Garrison, Re: CIA Aspects/William Cuthbert (or Cusbert) Brady, NODA, NARA.

p. 251, line 38: "proficient riflemen": Memorandum, January 26, 1968, To: Jim Garrison, From: Stephen Jaffe, Re: Interview with Jim Rose, Santa Barbara, Cal.—January 3, 1968.

p. 252, line 1: Rolando Masferrer is "the most dangerous man in the United States": Memorandum, January 26, 1968, To: Jim Garrison, From: Stephen Jaffe, Investigator, Re: Interview with Jim Rose, Santa Barbara, California, January 3, 1968, NODA, NARA.

p. 252, line 3: "his first choice": Memorandum, January 26, 1968, To: Jim Garrison, From: Stephen Jaffe, Re: Interview with Jim Rose, Santa Barbara, Cal.—January 3, 1968.

p. 252, line 9: "put on the next flight to New Orleans": Interview with E. Carl McNabb, July 10, 1999.

p. 252, line 11: AMCARBON-3: CIA had a number of media assets on the *Herald* and other papers, all with the cryptonym CARBON. If a *Herald* reporter was vehemently anti-Castro, the CIA would try to recruit him. As a former agent explained to Taylor Branch, the CIA would give these reporters "access to the station . . . feed them information and give them a career out of handouts. The guys learn not to hurt you. Only occasionally do you give them a big lie and then only for a good reason. The paper was always willing to keep things quiet for us": See "The Kennedy Vendetta" by Taylor Branch and George Crile III, *Harper's* magazine, August 1975, p. 53, 56.

p. 252, line 18: "confidential informant": CIA, Subject: Bohning, Donald Dean, 14 June 1968, CIA connections of Bohning, NARA, signed: Paul F. Gaynor, Chief, Security Research Staff/OS.

p. 252, line 19: Bohning is approved by the DDP on July 31, 1967: CIA, 104-10170-10160, JFK,

80T01357A, Title: Donald Dean Bohning, Postponement attached to April 2, 1967: Donald Dean Bohning, OS # 813 709, Release date of this document, handwritten, August 15, 2002.

p. 252, line 21: AMCARBON-3 reports on the visit: CIA, 104-10435-10003, RUSS HOLMES WORK FILE, From: JMWAVE, To: Director, March 29, 1968, Title: Cable: following information volunteered by AMCARBON-3, NARA.

p. 252, line 21: Rose visits Bohning: "This guy called me": Interview with Donald Bohning, November 16, 1999. It was indeed Bohning whom Jim Rose visited, see CIA, 104-10116-10119, 80T01357A. Memorandum no. 9 (Garrison and the Kennedy Assassination, June 5, 1968): "Bohning asserted he was contacted on 28 March 1968 by a Winston Smith who claimed to be investigating Rolando Masferrer for Jim Garrison." NARA.

p. 252, line 33: JMWAVE watches "Winston Smith" (Jim Rose): JMWAVE 1849, 100-300-17, 29 March 1968.

p. 252, line 34: Rose met with Lawrence Howard: Memorandum, March 20, 1968, To: Jim Garrison, From: Stephen Jaffe, Re: Interview with Jim Rose About His Anti-Castro Acquaintances, NODA, NARA.

p. 252, line 36: "he's too smart for that": To: District Attorney Jim Garrison, From: Bill Turner, February 28, 1968, Subject: Oswald—Florida Aspects, NODA, NARA.

p. 252, line 41: Garrison might find his "seven" Cubans among Masferrer's group: Lawrence R. Houston to J. Walter Yeagley, OGC 67-1993, 20 October 1967, Re: U.S. District Court, Southern District, Florida, *United States v. Masferrer, et al.,* NARA.

p. 253, line 1: Masferrer works with Rose: Memorandum, April 9, 1968, To: Jim Garrison, From: Gary Sanders, Re: Winston Smith, NODA, NARA.

p. 253, line 2: a mail drops in Austin, Texas: Memorandum: April 15, 1968, To: Jim Garrison, From: Gary Sanders, Re: Winston Smith, NODA, NARA.

p. 253, line 12: "CIA probably involved": Memo 12/8/75, To: Dave Marston, From: Gaeton Fonzi.

p. 253, line 19: a short, skinny guy: Interview with Gerald Patrick Hemming, August 16, 2002.

p. 253, line 21: Schlafter is the #2

man: Memorandum, April 22, 1968, To: Jim Garrison, From: Gary Sanders, Re: Winston Smith, Subject: Man arrested in Dealey Plaza on November 22, 1963, NODA, NARA.

p. 253, line 32: Masferrer identified the man with the scar: Memorandum, March 28, 1968, To: Jim Garrison, From: Gary Sanders, Re: W. Smith, Subject: Almondo [sic] Masferrer, NODA, NARA. One of the intermediaries between Rose and Masferrer was a Guatemalan named Major Nameo Elirque Bianchi: Memorandum, April 15, 1968, To: Jim Garrison, From Gary Sanders: Re: Winston Smith, Subject: The Man with the Scar, NODA, NARA.

p. 253, line 35: Jim Rose wants to go to New York to meet the "man with the scar": Memorandum, March 28, 1968, To: Jim Garrison, From: Gary Sanders, Re: W. Smith, NODA, NARA.

p. 253, line 35: Masferrer then hesitated: Memorandum, April 2, 1968, To: Jim Garrison, From: Gary Sanders, Re: Winston Smith, Subject: Status of Miami visit, NODA, NARA.

p. 253, line 38: "thick-necked Latin": Jim Garrison to Richard Gerstein, April 16, 1968, NARA.

CHAPTER 16

p. 254, Epigraph: "not very highly regarded by the Mafia": Jim Garrison Memorandum, April 17, 1968, To: Donald V. Organ, From: Jim Garrison, Re: *Life* magazine, NODA, NARA.

p. 254, line 4: "the director likes to do things for Sandy": Interview with Richard N. Billings.

p. 254, line 10: Richard Billings takes Smith to New Orleans: interview with Jim Garrison. Available at AARC.

p. 254, line 22: "never heard of him": Jim Garrison, *Coup d'Etat,* unpublished manuscript, pp. 16ff. Projected chapter on charges of a Mafia connection to the assassination.

p. 255, line 7: assistance of Aaron Kohn: As Kohn admitted, "We did assist *Life":* Memorandum, September 20, 1967, MCC.

p. 255, line 8: David Chandler then informed to the Bureau about Billings' interview with Garrison: August 23, 1967, SAC. SA Patrick J. Collins Jr., Carlos Marcello, aka AR, 89-69-3466.

p. 255, line 16: Bonoura and Giarrusso were partners in a security company: E-mail from Robert Buras, November 3, 2002.

p. 255, line 23: "Big John's already got his": Interview with John R. Rarick, February 3, 2001.

p. 255, line 29: Phelan helped in the effort: Phelan reports to Kohn about the $5,000 line of credit, Investigative Report, June 15, 1967, Reported by Aaron M. Kohn, MCC.

p. 255, line 33: Never any proof that he took the $5,000: Interview with Richard N. Billings, August 2, 2000.

p. 256, line 3: Smith refuses to name his sources: Interview with Richard N. Billings.

p. 256, line 5: "He's not in today": Interview with Richard N. Billings.

p. 256, line 8: close to Deke: DeLoach called Smith "a good friend of the Chicago office": FBI, To: Mr. Mohr, From: C. D. DeLoach, March 16, 1965, Subject: Proposed Article by William W. Turner for "*Playboy* Magazine" captioned "The FBI and Organized Crime" (C7-455829-502). Smith was also called "a great admirer of the Director": see FBI, March 16, 1965, To: Director, FBI, Attention: Asst. Director C. D. DeLoach, Crime Records Division, From: SAC, Chicago, Proposed Article by William W. Turner for "*Playboy* Magazine" captioned "The FBI and Organized Crime, 62-455829-5024, NARA.

p. 256, line 10: Media reports on the *Life* magazine charges: The *Clarion Herald* wrote that Garrison "had a $5,000 credit at the gaming tables," October 5, 1967. Another publication that took up the charge that Jim Garrison was protecting organized crime was the *Wall Street Journal:* see "DA on the Griddle; New Orleans Critics Say Garrison Neglects Fight against Rackets, Too Busy with JFK Murder," by Herbert Lawson and Dennis Farney, February 9, 1968, **p. 1.**

p. 256, line 18: "it has something to do with Sheridan": "Petition for O'Hara Ouster," *States-Item, September* 25, 1967.

p. 256, line 19: "Garrison and the Mafia": FBI Memorandum, June 10, 1967, 124-10263-10026, 89-69-3167, 3168. The source is Joe Holstead, news director of channel 3, KATC television.

p. 256, line 24: McKeithen blinks:

"McKeithen Vows Crime 'War' in Louisiana," *States-Item* September 27, 1967. See also McKeithen Begins Crime Crack Down," *State-Times* (Baton Rouge), September 27, 1967, p. 1. See also "Gambling in Louisiana Will Halt—McKeithen," *Times-Picayune,* September 28, 1967, p. 1.

p. 256, line 33: David Chandler seeks relief: See *David L. Chandler v. Jim Garrison, et al.* in the U.S. District Court for the Eastern District of Louisiana, New Orleans Division, NOPL. Chandler was interviewed by *The Driftwood,* the LSU student newspaper, "*Life* Reporter Chandler Speaks Out on Jim Garrison, Organized Crime," undated.

p. 256, line 34: "bribery": Chandler told Tom Bethell he had an assignment from *Esquire,* and that *Life* was planning another article, Memorandum, October 9, 1967, To: Jim Garrison, From: Tom Bethell, Re: David Chandler, NODA, NARA. Neither materialized.

p. 257, line 4: "let him sit out there": Interview with Sharon Herkes, June 10, 2000.

p. 257, line 5: Pershing testifies: "Bar Owner Testifies at Hearing on Crime," *States-Item,* September 21, 1967, p. 1.

p. 257, line 8: Novel informs to the FBI: FBI, October 13, 1967, To: Director, From: SAC, WFO (Washington field office), 124-10071-10315, 89-69-3551, 3552, NARA.

p. 257, line 12: ruling on the "electronic" slot machines: "'Big Tent' Held Gaming Device Slot Subject to Seizure, High Court Says," *Times-Picayune,* June 30, 1962, section 1, p. 3.

p. 257, line 15: Gervais had admitted that he lied: "Garrison Claims Gervais Admitted Lying in Probe," *Times* (Shreveport), November 28, 1967.

p. 257, line 22: "Mafia branch of the Agency": Jim Garrison to Jonathan Blackmer, July 15, 1977, HSCA.

p. 257, line 26: "beyond the bounds of reason": "The Murder Talents of the CIA," by Jim Garrison, *Freedom* (April–May 1967), p. 15.

p. 257, line 34: Mother Theresa and Pope Paul: Jim Garrison to Mr. Louis Sproesser, December 30, 1985, *Papers of Jim Garrison.*

p. 257, line 36: Blakey advises *Life:* Peter Dale Scott, *Deep Politics* and the Death of JFK (Berkeley and Los Angeles: University of California Press, 1993), p. 149.

p. 257, line 38: Would Organ help him to sue *Life* magazine? Jim Garrison Memorandum, April 17, 1968, To: Donald V. Organ, From: Jim Garrison, Re: *Life* magazine, NODA, NARA.

p. 258, line 4: a public figure suing: Interview with Donald V. Organ, August 29, 2000.

p. 258, line 16: "we know a good deal of this": Incident at *Look* was relayed by attorney and author William Pepper, September 6, 2001. Admittedly this story comes third-hand.

p. 258, line 18: "we know who the bastards are": Billings' *Diary*, p. 146.

p. 258, line 38: Garner rejects the advice of Aynesworth: Interview of Darrell Garner with Ken Elliott, June 27, 1967; interview with Darrell Wayne Garner by Mark Lane, December 14, 1967, NODA, NARA.

p. 258, line 39: Jim McPherson meets Dago Garner: Interview with Jim McPherson, January 9, 2000.

p. 259, line 14: Curtis Crafard: The name has been changed, so that it is now "Craford," interview with Curtis Craford, January 5, 2002, and Edward Craford, January 8, 2002. See also Memo on Crafard, 2 October 1968, To: Jim Garrison, From: Wm. C. Boxley, Re: Larry Crafard. See also Shirley Craford to Peter Whitney, April 19, 1989.

p. 259, line 23: check made out to Jack Ruby: Memo 9/9/76, To: Troy, From: Gaeton, NARA.

p. 259, line 24: "I think he's a professional killer": Notes-Garrison-Tatel, 6/28/76, by Gaeton Fonzi, NARA.

p. 259, line 26: "hit man": Curtis Crafard interviewed by Peter Whitney, December 8, 2001.

p. 259, line 27: "we get good leads": Jim Garrison at the New Orleans conference, September 1968.

p. 259, line 31: "light housekeeping": Jim Garrison to Gaeton Fonzi, June 28, 1976, NARA.

p. 259, line 34: "heavily involved": Interview with Edward Craford, January 8, 2002.

p. 259, line 41: Aynesworth reports to the Shaw defense team: Hugh Aynesworth to Edward F. Wegmann, August 22, 1967, *Papers of Edward F. Wegmann.*

p. 259, line 42: Garrison must be giving Garner money: Transcript of taped conference with William Gurvich 8/29/67, September 6, 1967, *Papers of Edward F. Wegmann.*

p. 260, line 1: "money don't mean that much to me": DA office taping of call from Dago Garner, NARA.

p. 260, line 27: "a totally honest person": Memorandum, January 13, 1968, To: Louis Ivon, From: Gary Sanders, Re: Richard Rolfe and June Rolfe (wife), NODA, NARA.

p. 260, line 29: Alcock meets Spiesel in New York: Memorandum, July 17, 1967, To: Jim Garrison, From: James L. Alcock, Re: Charles I. Spiesel, NODA, NARA.

p. 260, line 2: a double: See *Diary of Richard N. Billings*, pp. 126–128. Garrison revealed the specifics Alcock learned about Spiesel to Dick Billings over the telephone, interview with Richard N. Billings, September 12, 2002.

p. 261, line 7: Spiesel at CBS: Memorandum, August 14, 1967, To: Jim Garrison, From: Tom Bethell, Re: A. Phone call from Bob Richter, CBS-TV, August 11, 1967, B. De Mohrenschildt, NODA, NARA.

p. 261, line 14: Kern Stinson telephones the office of the district attorney: See *On the Trail of the Assassins*, pp. 217ff.

p. 261, line 25: a wrecker was needed: U.S. Department of Justice, FBI, March 23, 1964, Inspector J. Herbert Sawyer, Dallas Police, made available radio transmissions from Dallas Police Radio Station KKB-364, which reported at 11:07 that a police officer asked that a city wrecker be sent to the triple underpass just west of the underpass on Elm to clear a stalled truck. At 11:08 an officer asked that the call be disregarded. By 11:16 this was explained by the fact that a truck was there to push them out. The times of those calls are consistent with Julia Ann's Mercer's chronology of when she saw the truck with Ruby behind the wheel.

p. 261, line 26: Julia Ann Mercer was also interviewed on November 25th by SA Wallace R. Heitman, and on November 27th again.

p. 261, line 37: Ruby's alibi: See Jack Ruby, Warren Commission testimony, vol. V, p. 183; Hall Exhibit #2; vol. XX, p. 44, FBI report on an interview conducted with Jack Ruby on 11/25/63 by Special Agent C. Ray Hall; Hall Exhibit #3, vol. XX, p. 44, interview conducted with Ruby on 12/21/63 by C. Ray Hall and Manning C. Clements; FBI interview with Gladys Craddock, 11/27/63, CE 1479, XXII, p. 900; interview with Gladys Beal Ivey July 30, 1964, CE 2321, vol. XXV, p. 281; this is Craddock's new married name. See also John Wolks Newman, vol. XV, pp. 538–9; Billy Rea, vol. XV, pp. 573–75. Georgia Mayor's statement is in vol. XXV; Richard Saunders' testimony can be read at <http://www.jmas land.com/testimony/media/saunders .htm>. Saunders did not arrive at the paper until 12:40. He found Jack Ruby "very obviously shaken, and an ashen color—just very pale."

p. 262, line 7: Julia Ann Mercer tells her story to Jim Garrison, January 15, 1968: Note attached to FBI interview of 11/28 NODA, NARA.

p. 262, line 20: "this lady said": WC, vol. VII, pp. 332 ff.

p. 262, line 24: Statement of Julia Ann Mercer, NODA, NARA.

p. 262, line 27: promised not to subpoena her: Jim Garrison to Mrs. Kern Stinson, January 24, 1968, NODA, NARA.

p. 262, line 39: "no other witness so completely illuminated": *On the Trail of the Assassins,* p. 216.

p. 262, line 41: "a serious effort to protect her": Ibid., p. 219.

p. 263, line 21: "I don't care who the shooters were": Interview with Stephen Jaffe, June 10, 1999.

p. 263, line 21: paid about five hundred dollars a month: $510 or $520: Bradley could not remember the exact figure in his deposition in the suit and countersuit involving Carol Aydelotte, AARC.

p. 263, line 22: McIntire is admired by Jack N. Rogers: Jack N. Rogers to Dr. Carl McIntire, September 5, 1967, *Papers of Jack N. Rogers.*

p. 263, line 24: McIntire approved for CIA contact use: January 19, 1968, Subject: Bradley, Edgar Eugene. See also Bradley, Leslie Norman, NARA.

p. 263, line 26: Dr. Carl McIntire met with Guy Banister in Baton Rouge: Memorandum, May 13, 1968,

To: Jim Garrison, From: Andrew Sciambra, Re: Information on the N.S.R. P. and the American Nazi Party. The source is Joseph Cooper.

p. 263, line 40: Mafia contract in San Francisco: FBI, Urgent to Director, From Albuquerque, December 7, 1967, 124-10071-10355, 89-69-3618, NARA. See also FBI, December 14, 1967, To: Director, From: New Orleans, 124-10071-10353, 89-69-3616.

p. 263, line 41: "another diversionary tactic": General Investigative Division, December 15, 1967. Attached teletype concerns an alleged La Cosa Nostra (LCN) Plot to Assassinate Jim Garrison of New Orleans, 62-109060-5916.

p. 264, line 4: "paranoid garbage": See *On the Trail of the Assassins,* pp. 187–190 for this incident. See also *Coup d'Etat,* pp. 19-30, revised version. AARC, interview with Vincent Salandria (and Tom Katen),1972, tape.

p. 264, line 5: The death threats continued: "Garrison was next to be assassinated," they were told in January of 1968: George Eckert to Mr. William Boxley, January 31, 1968, NODA, NARA.

p. 264, line 7: "Garrison should be killed: FBI teletype, December 14, 1967, To: Director, San Francisco, Dallas and New Orleans, From: Albuquerque. 62-109060-5909, NARA. See also FBI December 14, 1967, 124-10071-10355, 89-69-3618 and 89-69-3621.

p. 264, line 8: "syndicate contract": See Memorandum. March 5, 1968, To: Jim Garrison, From: Gary Sanders, Re: Steve Jaffe, Subject: Syndicate Contract. Jaffe concluded that a West Los Angeles policeman, now retired, was "supposedly a friend of Eugene Bradley." See also Memorandum: March 30, 1968, To: Jim Garrison, From: Stephen Jaffe, Re: Dr. Richard Dudnick, NODA, NARA.

p. 264, line 36: CIA connections: MELVIN CRAIN-EDGAR EUGENE BRADLEY: CIA-FBI, Boxley Memo dated December 19, 1967. CIA denied knowing Bradley, but their denials, often false, have come to be a case of the boy who cried wolf: 21 December 1967, Memorandum, Subject: Garrison and the Kennedy Assassination, Edgar Eugene Bradley, signed, Donovan E. Pratt, DC/CI/ R & A.

p. 264, line 38: "self-avowed Minuteman": Ibid. MELVIN CRAIN-EDGAR EUGENE BRADLEY: CIA-FBI. See also Carol Aydelotte to "Mr. Boxley and Mr. Ivon," February 9, 1968, NARA: "The thing I find most alarming is that all Bradley's associates, the CIA-Minuteman types, had a very unpleasant common denominator: the continuous promotion of racial hatred, murder and violent revolution. If these CIA agents are agitating on both sides of the political spectrum, and that is possible, we will all awaken some morning to find full scale revolution waged in the streets of America."

p. 265, line 2: "government money": Carol Aydelotte to Louis Ivon, May 9, 1968, NODA, NARA.

p. 265, line 6: "he's in Dallas": Memorandum, February 16, 1968, To: Jim Garrison, From: Bill Turner, Re: Edgar Eugene Bradley, NODA, NARA.

p. 265, line 8: Bradley would never forgive Brice: Interview with Edgar Eugene Bradley, September 12, 2002.

p. 265, line 17: "That's Gene Bradley": Memorandum, February 16, 1968, To: Jim Garrison, From: Bill Turner, Re: Edgar Eugene Bradley.

p. 265, line 25: dressed in a Castro fatigue outfit: Memorandum, December 28, 1967, To: Jim Garrison, From: Andrew J. Sciambra, Re: Edgar Eugene Bradley, NODA, NARA.

p. 265, line 30: Alcock was not certain the evidence was there: Interview with Louis Ivon, January 12, 2000.

p. 266, line 6: Colonel Gale was a nut: Notes on Meeting. 12/28/67 by Art Kevin.

p. 266, line 12: Gugas had contacted HIM: Edgar Eugene Bradley on the radio with Joe Pyne, transcribed March 7, 1968, NODA, NARA.

p. 266, line 14: informed to the Los Angeles field office: FBI, To Director, From: Los Angeles, 124-10071-10372, 89-69-3642.

p. 266, line 17: "he is positive it is Edgar E. Bradley": Memorandum, December 26, 1967, To: Jim Garrison, From: Numa V. Bertel Jr., Re: Roger Craig Interview, NODA, NARA.

p. 266, line 21: light-colored Nash wagon: Memorandum, November 3, 1967, To: Jim Garrison, From: Mark Lane, Re: Interview with Roger Craig, October 25, 1967, Fontainebleau Hotel, New Orleans, Louisiana. Present: Roger Craig, Jim Garrison, Bill Boxley, Mark Lane, NODA, NARA.

That Craig said he had seen a Nash Rambler station wagon, and that Ruth Paine had a larger, if also square-cut, Chevrolet wagon, does not seem a sufficient discrepancy to undermine the basic facts of Craig's testimony. The heat of the moment—the murder of the Head of State—would have sufficed to blur the details—whether the automobile was white, as the Warren Commission and FBI insist Craig said—or light-colored—or green, which was the color of Paine's Chevrolet. Nor, given the monumental cover-up that had by then begun, was it persuasive that Craig was not in Captain Fritz's office, but only in the anteroom, and that Fritz later said he didn't remember Craig being in his office.

The Warren Commission insisted that Oswald had taken the bus, and had a bus transfer on him. But one witness, a Mrs. Bledsoe, had him in the shirt in which he was arrested, not the one he had on earlier, and the bus driver did not remember either Oswald or Bledsoe being on the bus. The timing suggests that he went by car.

That Ruth Paine owned a Chevrolet, not a Nash, also casts Oswald's reference to Paine's automobile into question.

p. 266, line 21: Jim Garrison welcomes Roger Craig, perhaps prematurely: Jim Garrison to Roger Craig, January 15, 1968, NOPL.

p. 266, line 24: "we were to take NO part": Roger Craig, *When They Kill a President*, unpublished manuscript, 1971.

p. 266, line 30: "'manufactured' a witness": FBI memorandum, To: Mr. W. C. Sullivan, From: Mr. W. A. Branigan, February 23, 1968, Record number 124-10061-10388, HQ, 62-109060-6208, 2 pages, NARA.

p. 266, line 37: "beyond any shadow of doubt": To: Mr. Louis Ivon, December 27, 1967, Report and Partial Memorandum on Dallas Visit of December 21, 1967 thru December 23, 1967, NODA, NARA.

p. 266, line 37: On the identification of Bradley as one of the tramps, see also Memorandum, June 23, 1968, To: Jim Garrison, From: Steven J. Burton, Subject: Photographs of Arrested Men in Dealey Plaza, NODA, NARA.

p. 266, line 40: Bradley had an operation: Richard E. Sprague to Fred Newcomb, January 9, 1969.

p. 267, line 2: Kevin informs to the Bureau; Alberto Fowler refuses to see him: FBI, To: Director, FBI, From: SAC, Los Angeles, March 7, 1967, 124-10167-10184, 89-69-1642, NARA.

p. 267, line 5: Art Kevin sends a reporter to Van Nuys Airport: To: Jim Garrison, From: Art Kevin, January 29, 1968, NODA, NARA.

p. 267, line 11: Hemming claimed to have known Burchette: Memorandum, May 8, 1968, To: Jim Garrison, From: Steven J. Burton, Re: Interview of Gerald Patrick Hemming, NODA, NARA.

p. 267, line 15: there are two available interviews with Margaret McLeigh: Interview regarding Edgar E. Bradley, December 29, 1967, transcribed May 3, 1968, NODA, NARA, and Interview with Margaret McLeigh, January 8, 1968, NODA, NARA. Art Kevin insisted that Margaret McLeigh was credible: Art Kevin to Lou Ivon, November 17, 1968.

p. 267, line 20: Jim Rose investigates Jim Braden: Date, January 6, 1969, To: Committee for the Investigation of Assassinations, c/o William W. Turner, From: West Coast investigator, code name "Rose." Subject: Office of JIM BRADEN, 280 South Beverly Drive, Beverly Hills, California, NODA, NARA. There is an earlier version of this memo: Date: November 3, 1968, To: Jim Garrison, From: Rosalie, Subject: Office of JIM BRADEN, NODA, NARA.

p. 267, line 23: Betty Helm will not give Bradley an alibi: FBI, January 9, 1968, Oklahoma City, 89-69-3750.

p. 267, line 33: On Stanley Drennan: See also Robert K. Brown talks to the FBI about Drennan, Commission Exhibit 3063, December 4, 1963.

p. 267, line 33: who wrote prescriptions: Carol Aydelotte to Mr. Boxley, January 2, 1968, NODA, NARA.

p. 267, line 34: Loran Hall met Bradley: Telephone conversation between May 2, 1968, between Louis Ivon and Stephen Jaffe, NODA, NARA.

p. 267, line 35: Kent Courtney was a friend of Bradley's: Memorandum, June 22, 1968, To: Jim Garrison, From: Steven J. Burton, Subject: Discussions with Carol Aydelotte and Dean Ray, NODA, NARA.

p. 267, line 37: Bradley contacts the Agency: CIA, 25 July 1968, Director, DCS for OSS (Musulin), Chief, Los Angeles Office, Case 49364, 100-300017, signed R. P. B. Lohmann.

p. 268, line 1: assisted by Hugh Aynesworth: George J. Jensen to Frank P. Hernandez, May 22, 1968,

p. 268, line 8: "set up" for failure: Edgar Eugene Bradley to Jim Garrison, May 22, 1969, in reply to Garrison's letter of April 24th, NARA; interview with Edgar Eugene Bradley, September 27, 2002.

p. 268, line 14: "Please Mr. Garrison": Edgar Eugene Bradley to Jim Garrison, September 17, 1969, NARA.

p. 268, line 17: formal exoneration: *The Garrison Papers*, NARA.

p. 268, line 33: meeting between Jim Garrison and Edgar Eugene Bradley: Interview with Edgar Eugene Bradley, September 10, 2002.

p. 269, line 6: "Bradley, we were both set up": Interview with Gene Bradley, *Contra Mundum*, no. 6, Winter 1993; Interview with Edgar Eugene Bradley, September 12, 2002.

CHAPTER 17

p. 270, Epigraph: "the failure to tell the whole truth": Press release, NODA, NARA.

p. 270, line 4: "before the Barrymores": Jim Garrison interview with Jonathan Blackmer, L. J. Delsa and Gaeton Fonzi for HSCA, 1977, tapes available from NARA.

p. 270, line 10: "entire fraudulent 'investigation'": NODA press release.

p. 270, line 11: Oswald's Marine Corps Unit: See: To: Mr. Winters, From: C/BSB, Title: Incident Report—Info from John E. Donovan, December 1, 1963, 4 pages, CIA 104-10300-10144, Record Series JFK, Agency file: 89T01357A. See in particular Telephone Call to the Agency from John E. Donovan. Document Number 1260-1033. Document courtesy of Malcolm Blunt.

p. 271, line 1: only if Thornley knew: See Jim Garrison to Gaeton Fonzi, September 23, 1976, NARA.

p. 271, line 9: "a rather short fellow": Jim Garrison interview with Jonathan Blackmer, L. J. Delsa and Gaeton Fonzi for HSCA. 1977, tapes available from NARA.

p. 271, line 14: "gold dust twins": Quoted in Memorandum to Jonathan Blackmer, Re: Kerry Thornley, From: Jim Garrison, HSCA, NARA.

p. 271, line 17: Brady left his belongings at the Ryder Coffee House when he took off for Canada: Memorandum, To: Louis Ivon, From: Jim Garrison, Re: CIA Aspects/William Cuthbert (or Cusbert) Brady, January 15, 1968. See also "Brady Named to Head Group" (Committee for State's Rights and Constitutional Action)," *Times-Picayune,* October 1, 1962, section 2, p. 8; "Free Cuba Unit Lauds Alpha 66," *Times-Picayune,* October 18, 1962. section 4, p. 10.

p. 271, line 22: Thornley's notarized statement about someone speaking Russian to Oswald is dated September 28, 1967, NODA, NARA.

p. 271, line 31: John René Heindel at the Grand Jury: John René Heindel's October 5, 1967, grand jury testimony is available both at AARC and NARA.

p. 271, line 38: "I'm glad": Memorandum, October 26, 1967, To: Jim Garrison, From: Andrew J. Sciambra, Re: Kerry Thornley, NODA, NARA. The same reaction is reported by Allen and Dan Campbell, who were with Thornley that night.

p. 271, line 39: "Have you heard the good news?": Memorandum, March 4, 1968, To: Louis Ivon, From: Gary Sanders, Re: Bernard Goldsmith, Subject: Kerry Thornley, William Brady. See also Memorandum, March 14, 1968, To: Jim Garrison, From: Andrew Sciambra. Repeat interview with Bernard Goldsmith, NODA, NARA.

p. 272, line 5: salary as a doorman: Jim Garrison, *Coup d'Etat,* p. 16 of 5, AARC.

p. 272, line 10: "the time of the Druids": Jim Garrison to Lou Ivon, January 19, 1968, Note handwritten appended to Memorandum, To: Louis Ivon, From: Jim Garrison, January 15, 1968, Re: CIA aspects/William Cuthbert (or Cusbert) Brady, NODA, NARA.

p. 272, line 22: Jones Printing Company: Garrison first sent Frank Meloche. Meloche visits Jones Printing, Memorandum, January 17, 1967, To: Jim Garrison, From: Frank Meloche, Re: Interview of employees at Jones Printing Company, NODA, NARA. Douglas Jones was interviewed

by Agent Donald C. Steinmeyer; Silver was interviewed by SA John M. McCarthy.

p. 272, line 29: bushy beard: Harold Weisberg to Joan Mellen, September 17, 2001. On February 13th, when Garrison investigators Simms and Sedgebeer visited Silver for a final confirmation, she was suddenly unable to identify a photograph of Thornley: See Memorandum, To: Louis Ivon, From: Detective Kent Simms and Sergeant Fenner Sedgebeer, February 14, 1968, NODA, NARA.

p. 272, line 34: Boxley insisted on accompanying Weisberg: Harold Weisberg to Joan Mellen, May 24, 2000.

p. 272, line 39: Jones and Silver identify Thornley: Harold Weisberg to Joan Mellen, October 18, 2001. See also Harold Weisberg Memo dated June 19, 1979, AARC.

p. 273, line 3: "a CIA agent": Thornley went on the radio, WLCY Radio, St. Petersburg, February 5, 1968: Kerry W. Thornley and Bob Ruark, transcribed May 16, 1968, NODA, NARA.

p. 273, line 4: Thornley fought the subpoena: "Hearing Set on Tampan's Subpoena from Garrison," by Thom Wilkerson. *Tampa Tribune,* January 19, 1968; "Thornley Must Go To New Orleans," by Thom Wilkerson. *Tampa Tribune,* January 23, 1968, p. 1. The district attorney's office taped Thornley's calls with Sciambra, February 1968, tape available at NARA. Memorandum, February 7, 1968, To: Jim Garrison, From: Andrew J. Sciambra, Re: Kerry Thornley, NODA, NARA.

p. 273, line 4: "formally extradited": "Ex-Marine Buddy of Oswald Is Subpoenaed," *Times-Picayune,* January 10, 1968, p. 1.

p. 273, line 7: in New Orleans, Barbara Reid was known as a writer on the history of witchcraft: Essays on witchcraft by Reid are available: NODA, NARA. Reid came forward in August of 1967, Memorandum, To: Tom Bethell, From: Jim Garrison, August 29, 1967, NODA, NARA.

p. 273, line 7: sworn statement: Sworn statement of Barbara Reid is dated February 19, 1968, NODA, NARA.

p. 273, line 18: Peter Deageano corroborates Reid: Memorandum, To: Jim Garrison, From: Andrew J. Sciambra, October 26, 1967, Re: Kerry Thornley, NODA, NARA.

p. 273, line 21: L. P. Davis saw Oswald and Thornley: Memorandum, January 30, 1968, To: File, From: Louie Ivon, NODA, NARA.

p. 273, line 24: Cliff Hall: Memorandum, January 30, 1968, To: Jim Garrison, From: Andrew J. Sciambra, Re: Kerry Thornley, NODA, NARA; Memorandum, To: Jim Garrison, From: Richard V. Burnes, January 11, 1968, Re: Kerry Thornley's Association with Lee Harvey Oswald in New Orleans in 1963, NODA, NARA.

p. 273, line 26: "Oswald did not do it alone": To: Jim Garrison, From: Bill Turner, Subject: Kerry Thornley, January 10, 1968, NODA, NARA.

p. 273, line 30: "Did I?": Interview with Barbara Reid, Outside Contact Report by Martin J. Daly and Robert Buras, January 21, 1978, HSCA.

p. 274, line 14: Marina and Orlov: See Memorandum, June 28, 1967, To: Jim Garrison, District Attorney, From: Bill Turner, Re: Investigation, NODA, NARA. See also Memorandum, July 28, 1967, To: Jim Garrison, From: Bill Turner, Re: Investigation. Turner reports on a call from an editor at the University of Michigan paper noting that an "Alexander Orlov" had been employed by the university simultaneously with Marina's being sent to the English Language Institute at Ann Arbor to learn English. The caller, "Steve Berkewitz" [sic] wonders whether "Orlov could be identical with the Colonel Orlov mentioned in the Warren Report as calling on Marena [sic] Oswald with George De Mohrenschildt."

p. 274, line 15: what he knew about Russian espionage: Allan Smith, Dean of the University of Michigan law school, quoted in Edward Gazur, *Alexander Orlov: The FBI's KGB General* (New York: Carroll & Graf, 2002), p. 359. The title is a bit of a misnomer: Orlov belonged no less to the CIA, although his defection itself occurred before the Agency came into existence.

p. 274, line 17: "a gentleman": Conversation with Marina Oswald, May 24, 2000.

p. 274, line 20: Marina claims that Oswald was innocent. Jennifer Gould, *Vodka, Tears and Lenin's Angel: My Adventures in the Wild and Woolly Former Soviet Union* (New York: St. Martin's Press, 1997), p. 201.

p. 274, line 38: "the sheer force of your personality": Ruth Paine to Jim Garrison, April 20, 1968, NODA, NARA. Orleans Parish Grand Jury testimony of Mrs. Ruth Hyde Paine, April 18, 1968.

p. 274, line 38: Jeanne Hack Napoli is surprised about Thornley's post office box: To: District Attorney Jim Garrison, From: Bill Turner, Subject: Jeanne Hack Napoli—Kerry Thornley Matter, February 27, 1968. This is their second interview. NODA, NARA.

p. 274, line 40: seen Kerry Thornley at the Oswald residence: John Schwegmann Jr., To Jim Garrison, February 22, 1968, NOPL.

p. 274, line 41: Mrs. LaSavia and Mr. LaSavia: Memorandum, To Jim Garrison, From: Andrew J. Sciambra, Re: Kerry Thornley, February 29, 1968.

p. 275, line 8: Dowell: Doris Dowell was interviewed by the district attorney's office on April 2, 1968.

p. 275, line 10: Thornley and Oswald in constant contact: Interview with Allen Campbell, July 4, 2002.

p. 275, line 11: Thornley impersonated Oswald in 1962: Jim Garrison to Zach Sklar, March 16, 1998.

p. 275, line 12: Thornley's affidavit: HSCA 180-10070-10297, 008269, PT, 16, Affidavit, From: Thornley, Kerry, February 16, 1976, NARA.

p. 275, line 13: Garrison had already investigated Clint Bolton: From: Jim Garrison. Memo Re: Clint Bolton and Other French Quarter Personnel, February 20, 1968, NODA, NARA.

p. 275, line 25: Fonzi reads the affidavit: Memo September 23, 1976, To: Troy, From: Gaeton, NARA.

p. 275, line 28: "a rather strained effort": Memo, August 17, 1977, To: Blackmer, From: Fonzi, Re: Kerry Thornley, NARA.

p. 275, line 33: "of recent date": County of Los Angeles Sheriff's Department, From: D. J. Cady, Lt. Norwalk Station Det. Bur, To: F. W. Rosenberg, Chief, Detective Division, November 26, 1963, File no. J-330, 89-75-190, Agency: FBI, 124-10270-10176, NARA.

p. 275, line 39: "atomic, biological and chemical warfare": Department of Defense—Files for Kerry Thornley, Reviewed May 9, 1978, DOD File Review, To: Patricia Orr. In particular, see Addendum—from "translation" of Thornley's file by DOD, pertinent part of file only. This is Judy Miller's Department of Defense summary of Kerry Thornley's files sent over to the HSCA. See also the Doug Horne files of the ARRB for Thornley's Marine Unit Diary, which also refers to his CIA Washington training.

p. 276, line 7: Rudy Vallee and Xavier Cugat: "DA Subpoenas 3 in JFK Slaying Probe," *States-Item, December 29, 1967.

p. 276, line 8: CIA says it has no connection with Howard: Memos, Hall, Loran Eugene and Howard, Lawrence J. aka Escurido Alonzo 104-10273-10012, RUSS HOLMES WORK FILE, January 9, 1968 See also Hemming, Gerald Patrick Jr. and Hall, Loran Eugene.

p. 276, line 13: "no comment": "Plot Suspect Denies Garrison's Charges," *Register,* January 12, 1968.

p. 276, line 16: Art Kevin says that Howard "can prove": Art Kevin, 1-11-68, NODA, NARA.

p. 276, line 20: Howard is interviewed by Steven J. Burton: Lawrence Howard: Memorandum, To: Jim Garrison, From: Stephen J. Burton, Subject: Interviews of Lawrence Howard, January 25, 1968; February 19, 1968.

p. 276, line 20: "That's Leon Oswald!" Note by Jim Garrison at the top of p. 2 of Memorandum, To: District Attorney Jim Garrison, From: Bill Turner, Subject: Oswald—Florida Aspects, NODA, NARA.

p. 276, line 24: Lawrence Howard at Tulane and Broad: Present at the February 25, 1968, interview of Lawrence Howard in New Orleans are Jim Garrison, Louis Ivon, Bill Boxley and Steven J. Burton.

p. 276, line 30: Hemming's liaison with Odio: Hemming says he had a flirtation with Sylvia Odio in Cuba, interview with Gerald Patrick Hemming. October 22, 1999.

p. 276, line 33: "There's no question": February 26, 1968, 86-page transcript of February 25th interview with Lawrence Howard in New Orleans.

p. 277, line 17: Schiller offers himself again to the Bureau: January 15, 1968, To: Director, From: SAC, Los Angeles. 124-10258-10307, 89-69-3798, NODA, NARA.

p. 277, line 26: Howard should have been followed up: Interview with Louis Ivon, January 12, 2000.

p. 277, line 29: Hall told Stephen Jaffe that both Cohen and Schiller tried to prevent him from going to New Orleans: Memorandum, To: Jim Garrison, From: Stephen Jaffe, March 20, 1968, NODA, NARA.

p. 277, line 34: Harold Weisberg's interview with Loran Hall is available in *The Garrison Papers*, NARA.

p. 277, line 38: Harry Dean: Conversation with Harry Dean, tape, Papers *of Richard N. Billings*, box 6, file 35A, Georgetown University, Washington, DC.

p. 277, line 39: Harry Dean . . . Special Agent Rapp: HSCA record number 180-10105-10298. Agency file; 01435. From: Klein, Kenneth to Tanenbaum, Robert K. Title: Interview with Harry Dean. Date: 05/23/77. 260-0. Box 260. NARA.

p. 278, line 3: Hall tells Jaffe a source saw Shaw enter Bradley's home: Memorandum, May 1, 1968, To: Jim Garrison, From: Stephen Jaffe, Re: Loran Hall, reinterviews following memo of March 20, 1968.

p. 278, line 9: Jack Huston says Hall knew Oswald in Dallas: See Jack Huston to Louis Ivon, February 21, 1968, NODA, NARA.

p. 278, line 9: Hall admits to Wiley Yates that he had been in New Orleans: Wiley Yates to Jim Garrison, June 28, 1967.

p. 278, line 22: "clammed up": Charles N. Phillips, 11th MI Group (III), CIA, From: Department of the Army, To: CIA, Liaison, Title: Army Document: Frente Revolucionaria Anti-Communista En Cuba, 104-10518-10322, August 7, 1970, NARA.

p. 278, line 26: for a report of the visit to Hall in jail in Dallas for the dexadrine pills: To: File, From: SAC J. Gordon Shanklin, December 27, 1967, 89-43-7726, NARA.

p. 278, line 26: "jackal[s] for the CIA": From Hall's testimony before the House Select Committee, Executive Session testimony of Loran Hall, October 5 and October 6, 1977, HSCA 014660 and 014661, 180-10117-10026, NARA.

p. 278, line 31: Jim Garrison interviews Loran Hall: May 6, 1968, transcribed May 8, 1968, NODA, NARA; or HSCA 002171.

p. 278, line 32: "you can make a great contribution": Jim Garrison to Loran Hall, January 29, 1968, NODA, NARA.

p. 278, line 33: Hall in Cuba: CIA document shared with FBI: 104-10103-10303, 80T01357A, August 14, 1964, Loran Eugene Hall.

p. 278, line 36: but not THE conspiracy: Interview with Stephen Jaffe, June 15, 1999.

p. 278, line 41: Crockett denies he had the 30.06 Johnson in his possession on November 22nd: Memo 5/11/76 To: Dave Marston, From: Gaeton Fonzi.

p. 279, line 3: José Duarte: See Dispatch. Chief, WOMUSE. Chief, WH Division. From: Chief of Station, Mexico City. Subject: RYBAT/MHCHAOS/ Revolutionary Guerrilla Training in Mexico. For Willard C. Curtis. HMMA 36214.

p. 279, line 5: "the big man": Skip L. E. Hall to Lou Ivon, July 15, 1968, NODA, NARA.

p. 279, line 7: statement exonerating Hall: "Hall Cleared by DA's Office," *Times-Picayune*, May 11, 1968, section 1, p. 8.

p. 279, line 17: Howard had been involved. Memo of Conversation with Manolo Aguilar, June 5, 1968, Sgt. Guz Zenoz of the Miami Police Force as interpreter.

p. 279, line 26: "not only rehearsed": Memorandum, To: Cliff Fenton, From: William K. Triplett, Martin J. Daly, August 26, 1977, Re: Interview of Loran Eugene Hall, HSCA 002154.

p. 279, line 37: "If I had to swim": Interview with L. J. Delsa, March 7, 2002.

p. 280, line 8: "quarters and canned goods": Dear Mr. Boxley, from Carol (Aydelotte). "Wednesday," NARA.

p. 280, line 15: Richard Magison's testimony about Lawrence Howard: HSCA, To: Kenneth D. Klein, From: Robert K. Tanenbaum, April 11, 1977, Re: March 29, 1977. Memo to me from Donovan Gay in regard to Mr. Magison testimony as JFK witness, Statement of Richard Magison, NARA. See also Memorandum, To: Robert K. Tanenbaum, From: Kenneth D. Klein, Date:

May 24, 1977, Re: Interview of Richard Magison, HSCA 001468.

p. 280, line 25: "work was disrupted": Interview of Lawrence Howard with Jim Garrison, February 25, 1968. See also Memorandum, To Jim Garrison, From: Stephen J. Burton, Subject: Interview of Lawrence Howard.

p. 280, line 27: "I was right on the job": Lawrence Howard testimony in Executive Session before the House Select Committee on Assassinations, June 1, 1978, 180-10105-10334, 014029.

p. 280, line 39: "I think Howard took a shot": Undated taped telephone conversation of Harry Dean, who has called Garrison's office. Dean is referred to as "man". His interviewer is "W". Available in Box 6, folder 35A. Papers of Richard N. Billings. Georgetown University, Washington, DC.

p. 280, line 42: "personal friends" of David Ferrie: Perry Russo interview with Jack N. Rogers, June 10, 1967, *Papers of Jack N. Rogers.*

p. 281, line 11: had taken to the road: Interview with Thomas Edward Beckham, August 29, 2002. This history of Thomas Edward Beckham is based in part on interviews with Thomas Edward Beckham, March 30th and 31st and April 3, 2002.

p. 281, line 26: Beckham and Crisman in business: This research was done by Edd A. Jeffords of the Tacoma *News Tribune* and passed on to Jimmy Alcock.

p. 281, line 37: Information about Herman Keck: Interview with Thomas Edward Beckham, June 5, 2005.

p. 282, line 25: Crisman showed his identification: Interview with Thomas Edward Beckham, February 1, 2003.

p. 282, line 36: CIA consults Lt. Col. Lowrie [*sic*]: From: Director, CIA to JMBAR, Title: Cable Re Interest in Acquiring Items, September 12, 1966, 104-10167-10406, JFK64-6:F14 1998.02.05.17:31:59:826031, NARA. JMBAR refers to CIA Maritime Covert Operations run out of Key West. The same cryptonym was also at times used for maritime covert operations out of New Orleans.

p. 283, line 3: Colonel Lawrence Lowry answers an advertisement: Interview with Colonel Lowry, October 6, 2002.

p. 22 line 16: he writes to the Reverend Raymond Broshears: July 6, 1968, NODA, NARA.

p. 283, line 24: The Inspector General investigates Lt. Colonel Lowry and Thomas Edward Beckham: USAF, From: Oullette, Paul A., January 12, 1968, FBI 124-10031-10197, HQ, 62-109060-6176, NARA, courtesy of Larry Haapanen.

p. 284, line 19: Ross Buckley and Thornley and Brady: Memorandum, March 6, 1968, To: Louis Ivon, From: Gary Sanders, Re: Jack Frazier—Owner of Ryder Coffee House, NODA, NARA.

p. 284, line 20: "Fair Cuba Committee": FBI AIRTEL, March 3, 1967, To: Director, FBI, From: SAC, New Orleans, 124-10253-10075, 89-69-1568, NARA.

p. 285, line 3: Jim Garrison searches for Thomas Edward Beckham: Memorandum, February 15, 1967, To: Lewis [sic] Ivon, From: Kent A. Simms, Re: Attempt to Locate One Thomas Edward Beckham, NODA, NARA.

p. 285, line 13: "CIA in Omaha?" "JFK and the CIA," Notes of Michael F. Starr, courtesy of Mr. Starr.

p. 285, line 17: When will he be back? Interview with Michael F. Starr, August 25, 2002.

CHAPTER 18

p. 286, Epigraph: "This is going to be a test of whether we really have justice": Jim Garrison tape transcript of press conference, December 11, 1968, available in Investigative Report, December 18, 1968, MCC.

p. 268, line 2: "late last year": "Witnesses Called in JFK Plot Probe, *Times-Picayune,* December 20, 1967, p. 10.

p. 268, line 8: Beckham and his brother are CIA agents: FBI 100-number illegible, February 7, 1968. August 15, 2002 release.

p. 268, line 8: Lewis raced over to Tulane and Broad with the news: Memorandum, February 16, 1968, To: Jim Garrison, From: Tom Bethell, Re: David Lewis and Thomas Edward Beckham, NODA, NARA.

p. 268, line 15: "we've got it covered": Interview with Thomas Edward Beckham.

p. 287, line 1: Grand jury: Grand

jury testimony of Thomas Edward Beckham, February 15, 1968, AARC.

p. 288, line 4: the "German ship" with narcotics: See "Cuba Is Seeking Judgment Void," *Times-Picayune,* April 12, 1962, section 2, p. 23; "Ship Line Sues Cuban Republic," *Times-Picayune,* November 16, 1962, section 1, p. 10.

p. 288, line 31: Beckham visited Eugene Davis three days before his grand jury testimony: Memorandum, February 12, 1968, To: Jim Garrison, From: Andrew J. Sciambra, Re: Gene Davis, NODA, NARA.

p. 288, line 35: Burnes' skepticism: Burnes didn't believe they had enough evidence: Interview with William Alford, May 28, 1998. Malpractice insurance: see interview with Alford, May 28, 1998.

p. 288, line 42: Sprague thinks Crisman is one of the tramps: "The old felt hat tramp . . . is Fred Lee Crisman": Richard E. Sprague to Fred Newcomb, January 9, 1969; Gary Schoener to Vincent Salandria, January 9, 1969. Larry Haapanen later established that Crisman had an airtight alibi for November 22nd; three of his colleagues at Cascade Union High School where he was teaching, said he was there that day.

p. 289, line 1: ten hundred dollar bills: Interview of William C. Wood, a/k/a Bill Boxley by George E. Rennar, August 30, 1971, AARC.

p. 289, line 2: Jim Rose in Tacoma: November 3, 1968, To: Chess Player, From: Rosalie, Subject: World Wide Advertising, NODA, NARA. See also "Watch Out for World Wide Advertising," transcription of notes by Better Business Bureau secretary, June 11, 1968, NODA. See also: Memorandum, June 14, 1968, To: Jim Garrison, From: William Boxley, NODA, NARA. Asked how he broke into Crisman's office, Rose said he just unscrewed the door, Jim Garrison said at the New Orleans conference, September 1968.

p. 289, line 12: Crisman is fired: "Teacher Hits Back in Cascade firing," Salem *Statesman,* April 21, 1966; "Fired teacher will Appeal Case," March 11, 1966.

p. 289, line 21: Crisman has been called because he knew Beckham: "JFK Plot Probe Subpoena Issued" by Clarence Doucet. *Times-Picayune,* November 1, 1968, section 1, p. 1.

p. 289, line 23: there was a conspiracy: "There Was Conspiracy, Crisman Believes" by Jack Wilkins. Tacoma *News Tribune,* November 2, 1968, NODA, NARA.

p. 289, p. 31: Crisman grand jury: Fred Lee Crisman Grand Jury Testimony, November 21, 1968, AARC.

p. 289, line 26: "bizarre cluster of 'Old Church' evangelical sects": To: Jonathan Blackmer, From: Jim Garrison, Re: Thomas E. Beckham, July 18, 1977, NARA.

p. 289, line 33: Joseph Newbrough applied to become a priest: James P. Dees to Joseph S. Newbrough Jr., August 4, 1966, NARA.

p. 289, line 36: "real courage": Archbishop Walter M. Propheta to Hon. James Garrison, September 12, 1967, NODA, NARA.

p. 289, line 401: Abundant Life Temple: Boxley was sent to Dallas: Memorandum: To: Jim Garrison, From: Wm. C. Boxley, 15 September 1967, NODA, NARA.

p. 290, line 4: "as a patsy": The Rev. Thomas A. Fairbanks to Harold Weisberg, January 9, 1969.

p. 290, line 5: "ordained" an Oswald double: Thomas A. Fairbanks to Bernard Fensterwald, July 5, 1977, AARC.

p. 290, line 9: "a Fagin to the Artful Dodger": Jim Garrison to Jonathan Blackmer, July 18, 1977, Re: Thomas E. Beckham, NARA.

p. 290, line 13: such churches had been utilized by O.S.S.: Jim Garrison, *Coup D'Etat,* page 18 of 8.

p. 290, line 21: breakfast meeting: Verbatim record by Fred Hammond, New Director, WWL radio, New Orleans, courtesy of Investigative Report, March 21, 1968, MCC.

p. 290, line 35: Hoover arranges that his award be presented on Friday: FBI, To: Mr. Bishop, From: M. A. Jones, March 18, 1968, 124-10031-10385, 62-109060-1st NR (94-43857-860), 6268, NARA.

p. 290, line 37: what would Garrison say: Interview with Numa Bertel, May 19, 1998.

p. 291, line 7: "French and Spanish influence": Jim Garrison interviewed by Zachary Sklar for the *JFK* screenplay. Courtesy of Mr. Sklar.

p. 291, line 9: the activities of Lyndon Johnson: Press Release District Attorney, Orleans Parish, March 16, 1968, NODA, NARA.

p. 291, line 14: "there will be no banquet": See "Garrison Stops D.A. Banquet," *Times-Picayune,* March 17, 1968, section 1, p. 1.

p. 291, line 21: Blakey stood by in silence while *Miranda v. Arizona* was attacked: "Crime May Top War—Governor," *Times-Picayune,* March 14, 1968, section 1, p. 5.

p. 291, line 25: "You can sue me in federal court": Interview with Martin F. Dardis, January 3, 2001. Dardis attended with Richard Gerstein.

p. 291, line 34: "you can't do that": Interview with Liz Garrison, May 28, 1998.

p. 291, line 38: "How many witnesses have you intimidated?" Depositions for Civil Action NO. 68-1063 are available at NARA. See U.S. District Court Eastern District of Louisiana, New Orleans Division, Clay L. Shaw, Plaintiff versus Jim Garrison individually, and as District Attorney for the Parish of Orleans. Ward and Alcock are also named, Civil Action, NO. 68-1063, section B, June 13, 1968.

p. 291, line 40: list of potential witnesses: Bethell collects the addresses of potential Dealey Plaza witnesses: See Memorandum, September 1, 1967, To: Tom Bethell, From: Richard V. Burnes; Memorandum, September 7, 1967, To: Richard V. Burnes, From: T. Bethell, Re: Dealey Plaza Witnesses, NODA, NARA.

p. 292, line 2: a volunteer named Jim Brown: See Jim Brown to Mr. Bethell, June 26, 1968, NODA, NARA.

p. 292, line 6: a memorandum of the trial witnesses: Memorandum, June 27, 1968, To: Jim Garrison and James L. Alcock, From: Tom Bethell, Re: Clay Shaw Case, NODA, NARA.

p. 292, line 23: Bethell confesses: "I gave Panzeca a copy of the trial file": Memorandum, May 6, 1969, To: Jim Garrison, From: Louis Ivon, Re: Confession of THOMAS BETHELL, NODA, NARA. See also Affidavit of Mr. Thomas Bethell, State of Louisiana, Parish of Orleans, January 16, 1969. The witness is Louis Ivon.

p. 292, line 34: Jim Rose goes to Mexico City: Interview with Jim Rose, June 13, 1999; interviews with William W. Turner; interview with

Stephen Jaffe. Turner describes the incident from Rose's point of view in *Rear View Mirror: Looking Back at the FBI, the CIA and Other Tails* (Granite Bay, CA: Penmarin Books, 2001).

p. 292, line 36: Rose meets two young women: Memo from Schoener on Nagell, Re: New Info in case of Richard Case Nagell, NODA, NARA.

p. 292, line 38: the person who financed the assassination: "The Gall of Gordon," *Newsweek,* February 5, 1968, p. 84.

p. 292, line 41: *Farewell America:* James Hepburn, *Farewell America* (Verviers, Belgium: Frontiers, 1968).

p. 293, line 20: Garrison requested the documentation, "any background material": Jim Garrison to Frontiers, May 10, 1968, NOPL.

p. 293, line 25: Herve Lamarre: Meeting with Representative of French Deuxième Bureau, June 21, 1968, Club Kama, Rue Dauphine, Stephen Jaffe, NODA, NARA. See also Jaffe memo, "Origin of the Book—*The Plot* by James Hepburn."

p. 293, line 37: Rothermel sent off the documents: See Paul Rothermel to J. Gordon Shanklin, January 6, 1969, an August 16, 2002, CIA release. The copy to Earle Cabell went out on the same day.

p. 293, line 41: "penetrated the assassination operation": "Foreign Group Has Facts—DA" by Clarence Doucet. *Times-Picayune,* July 12, 1968. See also the Peter Kihss article for the *New York Times,* published in the *Denver Post* as "Assassins—Spy Link Told," July 12, 1968, p. 13; "Foreign 'Ally' Confirms CIA JFK Link—DA," *States-Item,* July 12, 1968.

p. 294, line 6: "anti-Garrison propaganda": Fred Newcomb to Edd, George, Larry and Harold, January 15, 1969.

p. 294, line 11: Robert Lee Perrin and Nancy Perrin Rich: A sample of the documents reflecting Boxley's investigation of the Perrins with Joel Palmer are as follows: September 16, 1968, Interview of Nancy Perrin Rich by Joel Palmer; Joel Palmer interviewing Mrs. Hamilton (Nancy Perrin Rich Hamilton); Memorandum, September 25, 1968, from Boxley, re: interview with employees of Robert Perrin; To: Jim Garrison from Reid and Palmer re: Perrin and Ferrie, 1 page; September 26, 1968, to Jim Garrison from Boxley, interview with Preston Rar, regarding Robert Perrin, 2 pages; September 29, 1968, to Jim Garrison from Reid and Palmer; October 1, 1968, to Garrison from Boxley re: photos of Perrin; October 1, 1968, Memorandum, to Jim Garrison from Boxley, identification of Robert Lee Perrin, 2 pages; October 11, 1968, To: Jim Garrison from: Barbara Reid and Joel Palmer, Re: Interview with Lloyd Eagen of Lietz-Eagen funeral home concerning disposition of body of Robert Perrin; November 12, 1968, to Jim Garrison from Palmer; November 12, 1968, to Jim Garrison from Joel Palmer; November 12, 1968, discrepancies in morgue and police reports on Robert Perrin, 4 pages; November 13, 1968, to Jim Garrison from Boxley re: Perrin; November 13, 1968, to Jim Garrison from William C. Boxley; November 13, 1968, Nancy Perrin resume, 13 pages; November 13, 1968, Memorandum to Jim Garrison from William C. Boxley—Nancy Perrin resume; November 22, 1968, to Jim Garrison from Boxley re: arsenic death of Perrin November 22, 1968; To Jim Garrison from William C. Boxley—August 28, 1962, 7 pages; November 22, 1968, To: Jim Garrison from William C. Boxley Subject: Preliminary analysis of Nancy Perrin telephone calls; November 26, 1968, to: Jim Garrison from James L. Alcock, Re: Arthur E. Wise Jr., Lt. State Police, Re: Perrins; December 2, 1968, letter to Boxley from Mrs. Elmer Perrin; December 6, 1968, to: Sgt. Louis Ivon from: Frank Meloche, Re: Robert Perrin, w/m, Information received from Mrs. Cooksy of the Charity Hospital Record Division; December 9, 1968, Press release of the firing of Boxley; December 13, 1968, To: Jim Garrison, from Andrew Sciambra re: Mrs. Marianne Dereyna, 115 E. Avery Street, Pensacola, Florida re: Robert Perrin; December 13, 1968, to: Jim Garrison from Andrew J. Sciambra re: Interview with Mr. Schulmer, Cafeteria manager, Tulane University, regarding Mrs. James F. Cole, 1715 Calhoun Street, New Orleans, Louisiana; December 13, 1968, to: Jim Garrison from Andrew J. Sciambra re: Interview of the Kittess Family, 2522 York Street, New Orleans Louisiana regarding: Robert & Nancy Perrin; December 13, 1968, to: Jim Garrison from: Andrew J. Sciambra re: Interview with James F. Cole, 2108 Cedardale, Baton Rouge, Louisiana, regarding: Robert Perrin; December 13, 1968, to: Jim Garrison from: Andrew J. Sciambra re: Interview of: Mrs. Betty Miller, 1111 S. Dupre Street, New Orleans, Louisiana; December 13, 1968, to: Jim Garrison from: Andrew J. Sciambra re: Interview with Rev. A. Kruschevski, 4515 Galvez Street, New Orleans, La., 899-6378, Re: Robert Perrin; November 23, 1968, and November 25, 1968, Apartments on Calhoun Street; December 13, 1968, To: Jim Garrison, From: Andrew J. Sciambra re: Interview with James F. Cole, State Welfare Department, Third and Boyd Street, Baton Rouge, Louisiana re: Robert Perrin; December 13, 1968, to: Jim Garrison from Andrew Sciambra, Re: Robert Perrin, Deposition of legal action between Aydelotte and Bradley; December 2, 1968, to: Louis Ivon from Sgt. Fred Williams, Re: Occupants 1711-1717 Calhoun in 1962–63; December 13, 1968, To: Jim Garrison, From: Andrew Sciambra, Re: Interview with Ralph L. Barnett, 717–2nd Street, Gretna, Louisiana, Regarding Nancy Perrin; January 20, 1969, Affidavit from Joel Palmer in the matter of Boxley, Perrin and the E. E. Bradley charge, 3 pages. One of the witnesses to the statement is Penn Jones Jr.

p. 294, line 17: "solved the case": Re: William Boxley, From: Andrew Sciambra, December 6, 1968, NODA, NARA.

p. 294, line 35: Garrison allowed Boxley to remain: Interview with Louis Ivon, May 27, 2001.

p. 294, line 38: Jim telephoned Louie: Interview with Louis Ivon, May 3, 1999.

p. 294, line 40: Moo Moo and Ivon investigate: Memorandum, December 6, 1968, From: Andrew Sciambra, Re: William Boxley.

p. 295, line 22: "certain of the actions": Steven J. Burton to Jim Garrison, December 20, 1968, NODA, NARA.

p. 295, line 23: "Who was Clay Shaw?" Interview with Jim Rose, June 13, 1999.

p. 295, line 27: Elmer Robert Hyde: To: Andrew Sciambra, From: Bill Turner, Subject: Elmer Robert Hyde, November 25, 1968, NODA, NARA.

p. 295, line 33: "an edge of bitterness": E-mail from Ross Yockey, May 15, 2000.

p. 295, line 35: Turner told Boxley to get out of town: E-mail, Bill Turner to Joan Mellen, April 26, 2000.

p. 295, line 39: "request elucidation": CIA, From: Donovan E. Pratt, DC/CI/R & A, 104-10515-10040, 80T01357A, Memo: Garrison and the Kennedy Assassination: William Clarens Wood Jr., Alias William Boxley, January 3, 1969, 7 pages, NARA, Date of release: August 15, 2002. See also CIA, Memorandum For: Director, Domestic Contact Service, Subject: Garrison and the Kennedy Assassination, William Clarens Wood Jr., alias William Boxley, 201-83427, Reference: CI/R & A memorandum, subject as above, 3 January 1969, From: Donovan E. Pratt. DC/CI/R & A, 104-10189-10193, JFK, 89T01357A, NARA.

p. 295, line 40: they had been keeping an eye on him: See CIA, To: Director, Domestic Contact Service. Att'n: Deputy Director, DCS From: Chief, Houston Office. 26 April 1968, Subject: Bill Wood, Agent for Jim Garrison, Making Inquiries in Dallas, signed by Ernest A. Rische, 104-10189-10241, 80T01357A, NARA.

p. 295, line 42: Boxley asks Rothermel for a job: Re: Garrison file, January 29, 1969, AARC. Rothermel reports it to the FBI, Memo to J. Gordon Shanklin, January 6, 1969.

p. 296, line 3: Rothermel attempted to "guide" Jim Garrison's investigation: CIA, "Jim Garrison," January 26, 1968, 104-10515-10129, 80T01357A, Title: Report on Jim Garrison, NARA. Release date is August 16, 2002.

p. 296, line 5: Bradley lived across the street: CIA, Report: Garrison file, From: Paul Rothermel, January 29, 1969, CIA 104-10170-10480, NARA.

p. 296, line 15: Kohn's rumors: Investigative Report, July 18, 1968, MCC.

p. 296, line 20: sardonic irony: For a comprehensive summary and transcription of this December 11th press conference, see MCC Investigative Report, December 18, 1968, See also "Garrison Hits IRS Probe: 'Obvious Harassment,'" *Times-Picayune,* October 25, 1968, section 1, p. 22.

p. 296, line 26: Garrison in federal court on the medical evidence: Numa Bertel represented the office. See *United States of America ex rel. State of Louisiana, Petitioner, v. Dr. James B. Rhoads, Respondent,* Before: Judge Charles W. Halleck, January 31, 1969, Miscellaneous no. 825-69A.

p. 296, line 28: Garrison tries to get autopsy X-rays and photographs: New Orleans conference, September 1968, pp. 52–53, part II. See also "Garrison's Effort to Subpoena Kennedy Photos Faces Hurdles," *New York Times,* January 11, 1969; "A U.S. Judge Denies Kennedy Photos to Garrison," *New York Times,* January 18, 1968, p. 25. The Philadelphia *Inquirer* is less biased: "Garrison Links Case on Shaw to U.S. Held Data," *Philadelphia Inquirer,* January 18, 1960. p. 16. "Any and all documents": Reply to Major Contentions in Government's Pleading of January 16, 1969, *State of Louisiana v. Clay Shaw,* NO 825-68A.

p. 296, line 41: long since disappeared: Evidence that photographs were missing comes, according to Dr. Gary Aguilar, from Robert Knudsen, a former White House photographer who developed negatives and had been shown the complete photographic inventory. At least one image was not in the inventory he viewed for the HSCA in 1978. A former FBI agent named Francis X. O'Neill told T. Jeremy Gunn of the ARRB that one of the photographs "looks like it's been doctored in some way . . . it would appear to me there was a—more of a massive wound": Testimony before the ARRB, September 12, 1997. The other FBI agent present at the autopsy, James Sibert that also said the head wound "was more pronounced," and the photograph he viewed looked now "like it could have been reconstructed." Dr. Robert McClelland has been even more specific about President Kennedy's head wounds. See chapter eighteen.

Others spoke of a "large defect in the back side of the head" with "what appeared to be some brain hanging out of this wound" and "what appeared to be an exit wound in the posterior portion of the skull." This latter comes from a senior general surgery resident named Ronald Coy Jones. An anesthesiologist named Gene Aikin saw that "the right occipital/parietal region was the exit." These citations are courtesy of Dr. Aguilar. As Jim Garrison had said, there is always someone sitting under the oak tree. The three pathologists who performed President Kennedy's autopsy, Humes, Boswell and Finck united in what HSCA would call "gross errors."

p. 297, line 10: "Misprision of treason": Section 2382 of the Federal Criminal Code (Title 18 of the U.S. Code). The maximum punishment is seven years. The case law is scant to nonexistent. There were cases in the 1860s, one a jury charge trying to determine whether the Southern secession qualified as treason (January 14, 1861); another describes a mutiny involving government boats boats, an 1863 case: see 30 f.CAS. 1032 (1861): in re: Charge to Grand Jury; and 26 F.CAS. (18) (1863): *U.S. v. Greathouse.*

The law reads:

"Whoever, owing allegiance to the United States and having knowledge of the commission of any treason against them, conceals and does not, as soon as may be, disclose and make known the same to the President or to some judge of the United States, or to the governor or to some judge or justice of a particular State, is guilty of misprision of treason and shall be fined under this title or imprisoned not more than seven years, or both."

p. 297, line 21: "gunshot wound of the left temple": Commission Exhibit no. 392, November 22, 1963, 4:45 P.M. Doctor: Robert N. McClelland, "Statement Regarding Assassination of President Kennedy." For the description of Dr. McClelland's conversation with a Garrison assistant, See interview with Dr. Robert N, McClelland, December 31, 2003.

p. 298, line 12: the issue of Richard Case Nagell testifying: Jim Garrison, *On the Trail of the Assassins,* p. 183, 186, 229. See also *The Man Who Knew Too Much,* p. 664.

p. 298, line 17: "the most important witness": Dick Russell interview with Jim Garrison, October 16, 1975; *The Man Who Knew Too Much,* p. 47.

p. 298, line 18: "absolutely genuine": Jim Garrison at the New Orleans conference.

p. 298, line 20: CIA might try to "eliminate" him: FBI, To: Director, Federal Bureau of Investigation, Attention: Mr. S. Papich, From: Deputy Director for Plans, Subject: Richard Case Nagell, December 13, 1968, CSCI-316/ 04781-68. 62-109060-6624, NARA. Later Nagell said both that he had given Jim Garrison no information (Report of George R. Babineau, CPT. MC Psychiatrist, U.S. Army Hospital, Berlin, NARA), which was not true, and that he had been told by Garrison that his life was in danger, which was also not true: FBI, To: Director, FBI, From: Legat, Bern, June 7, 1968, 124-10269-10094, 89-69-4087, 4088, NARA.

p. 298, line 34: Thomas Breitner does not say Shaw was introduced as "Bertrand" in Turner's report: Interview Report—Assassination, March 17, 1967, Subject: Clay Shaw, Possible Contacts in Bay Area, NODA, NARA. Breitner tells Turner that Shaw introduced himself as "Clay Bertram" in a September 23, 1967, report. See also Notes of Richard Popkin, August 15, 1968.

p. 298, line 36: Norton was willing to testify: Interview with Donold P. Norton, February 4, 2003.

p. 298, line 37: Loran Hall was also another Bertrand witness: See Jack Huston to Jim Garrison, June 12, 1967, NODA, NARA. "That fruit, Shaw or Bertrand, whatever, is going to cause a hell'va lot of heat if someone doesn't get to him," Hall said.

p. 298, line 42: "who had been in trouble with the law": "Garrison Takes Blame for Trial," *Philadelphia Inquirer,* March 19, 1969, p. 20. See also "Garrison Says Evidence Rules Cost Him Verdict," *New York Times,* March 15, 1969.

p. 299, line 2: Edward James Whalen . . . to murder Jim Garrison: Memorandum, September 18, 1967, To: Jim Garrison, From: James L. Alcock, Re: Edward James Whalen, NODA, NARA.

p. 299, line 4: Girnus: Edward Girnus as witness: For Girnus' testimony about the station wagon: See: Conversation between James L. Alcock and an informant—Interview conducted Saturday, January 13, 1968, transcribed January 16, 1968, NODA, NARA. See also Memorandum,

December 7, 1967, To: Jim Garrison, From: James L. Alcock, Re: Edward Julius Girnus, Prison #A-90420-A, NODA, NARA; the flight plan is also available, NODA, NARA. See also: Edward J. Girnus to Sir: (Cliency Navarre), September 7, 1967, and Navarre to Girnus, August 31, 1967. There are also unsigned lead letters regarding Girnus.

p. 299, line 8: Broshears had been sent to an institution: Jim Garrison at the New Orleans conference, p. 149.

p. 299, line 20: Hicks would not be needed: See "Ex-Convict Awaits Call to New Orleans Trial," by Jack Taylor. Sunday *Oklahoman,* January 26, 1969, courtesy of Larry Hancock.

p. 299, line 23: "flying at night with no lights": Jim Garrison at the New Orleans conference, pp. 167–168.

p. 299, line 26: Lane lobbied hard: Interview with Stephen Jaffe, June 15, 1999.

p. 299, line 28: "with my luck": Interview with Mark Lane, February 6, 1998.

p. 299, line 30: "probably made a mistake": Jim Garrison to Jonathan Blackmer, July 15, 1977, AARC.

p. 299, line 31: "frozen with fear": Jim Garrison at New Orleans conference, September 1968. See also Jim Garrison to Mrs. Kern Stinson, January 24, 1968, NODA, NARA.

p. 299, line 34: the government stops William Walter from testifying: Interview with William Walter, January 3, 2000.

p. 300, line 1: "ace-in-the-hole": "Clyde Johnson Killed, Report," *Times-Picayune,* July 24, 1969, section 2, p. 3.

p. 300, line 10: "The CIA must have gotten to him": Interview with William Alford, May 28, 1998.

p. 300, line 15: Connally's animosity: Hugh Aynesworth to Edward F. Wegmann, January 30, 1969. This letter was on *Newsweek* letterhead.

p. 300, line 17: Shaw team worried: Document headed: "Jim Garrison," *Papers of Edward F. Wegmann.*

p. 300, line 29: Billings: *Life* lawyers told Billings to stay out of New Orleans: Interview with Richard N. Billings, September 12, 2002.

p. 300, line 33: have to be criminal: "not in itself have been wrong":

H. T. Jordan Jr. v. USA; Gervase A. Breyand v. USA. 8459, 8451, 10th circuit, December 5, 1966.

p. 300, line 35: as long as one of his coconspirators was involved: *Rudolph J. Nassif v. USA,* 8th circuit, December 6, 1966. Louisiana law mirrored the federal statutes: "Basically, there is very little to distinguish between these two statutes. Both require a conspiracy between two or more people to commit a crime and both provide that one of the parties to the conspiracy must do an act to effect, or in furtherance of the object of the conspiracy," Supreme Court of the United States, October term, 1968, no. *Clay L. Shaw v. Jim Garrison,* on Appeal from the U.S. District Court for the Eastern District of Louisiana, New Orleans Division, Jurisdictional Statement, p. 164.

p. 300, line 40: "I wasn't ready": Interview with William Walter, January 5, 2000.

p. 300, line 41: "let it go to trial": "I don't think it will ever come to trial": Jim Garrison interviewed by Mark Lane, August 1968, quoted in "Jim Garrison: It May Never Come to Trial," Los Angeles *Free Press.*

CHAPTER 19

p. 301, Epigraph: "I will not be able to produce any bank presidents": Jim Garrison interviewed by the BBC, March 1967, AARC. With the exception of the testimony of Vernon Bundy and Charles Spiesel, the transcript of *State of Louisiana v. Clay Shaw* is available at AARC or as "The Garrison Transcripts CD-ROM" <www.aarclibrary.org>.

p. 301, line 23: "talking about UFOs": Jim Garrison interviewed by Dick Russell, December 1980.

p. 301, line 12: Jim Garrison feels as if he is Santiago: *On the Trail of the Assassins,* p. 228.

p. 301, line 18: Alcock will prosecute: "Garrison Won't Head Shaw Prosecution," *States-Item,* January 14, 1969, section 1, p. 1.

p. 301, line 19: Hong Kong flu: Jim Garrison to Mr. Irwin E. Pilet, January 13, 1969, NOPL.

p. 302, line 4: "one of the most powerful men": Interview with Mark Lane, February 6, 1998.

p. 302, line 11: "erroneous game card": Memo to Jonathan Blackmer, Re: Statements of Perry Russo (made while under hypnosis) re: Clay Shaw, David Ferrie and Other Individuals, August 16, 1977, NARA.

p. 302, line 28: "put it all together": Kirkwood, *American Grotesque,* p. 223.

p. 302, line 39: never hospital whites, as he would confirm later: Interview with Corrie Collins, February 3, 2001.

p. 303, line 19: "our main case was the perjury case": Jim Garrison interviewed by Dick Russell, December 1980.

p. 303, line 24: "the one real piece of linkage": Interview with Richard Popkin, June 10, 1999.

p. 303, line 42: Dymond's attempt to impugn Bundy: January 15, 1969, *Cross-Examination of Vernon Bundy, State vs. Shaw, Papers of Edward F. Wegmann,* NARA.

p. 304, line 3: Russian roulette: That both Garrison and Alcock knew about Spiesel's eccentricities is irrefutable, interview with John Volz, May 21, 1999.

p. 304, line 11: Shaw had owned 906 Esplanade: Testimony of Arthur J. Bidderson before the Orleans Parish Grand Jury, January 9, 1969, NODA, NARA.

p. 304, line 15: did not identify the exact building: "New York Witness Fails to Find Shaw Apartment" by Gerald Moses. Baton Rouge *Morning Advocate,* February 9, 1969; "Shaw Witness Fails to Find Party Site," *Washington Post,* February 9, 1969.

p. 304, line 16: Spiesel had been investigated by Walter R. Holloway: FBI To: Director, FBI, From: SAC, Dallas, February 7, 1969, 62-109060-6715, NARA. This investigation was quite extensive. See also Statement of Tony Bacino, undated, *Papers of Edward F. Wegmann.*

p. 304, line 23: Boris Spiesel was a furrier: CIA, Memorandum for the Record, Subject: Spiesel, Charles I., #357204, Reference: *Washington Star* clipping dated 8 February 1969, 12 February 1969, NARA.

p. 304, line 31: "four minutes": Hugh Aynesworth on WDSU radio, March 3, 1969, "Press and Prejudice: The Clay Shaw Trial," moderated by Larry Johnson.

p. 304, line 33: "the Jack O' Diamonds was prepared": Jack Dempsey interviewed by Jim DiEugenio, September 2, 1994.

p. 305, line 5: "Spiesel was a set-up": Interview with Richard Popkin, June 10, 1999.

p. 305, line 8: "shooting a fish in a barrel": *On the Trail of the Assassins,* **p. 237.**

p. 305, line 12: "bunk": Memorandum, February 21, 1969, From: George Eckert, Re: Interview of Defense Witness, Frank Russo, NODA, NARA.

p. 305, line 29: "the Oswald that showed up": Peter Russo on tape for Peter Whitmey, September 9, 1990.

p. 305, line 32: Dymond had gotten nowhere: William Alford interviewed on *The Garrison Tapes.*

p. 306, line 19: clutching his cigarette: "Shaw Stands and Stares as Color Movie Is Shown," *Times-Picayune,* February 14, 1969, section 1, p. 14. See also "Shaw Trial Jury Shown Movie of JFK Death Frame by Frame," section 1, p. 1.

p. 306, line 21: the Zapruder film sent to universities: Jim Garrison to Zach Sklar, August 7, 1988.

p. 307, line 6: Wecht testified: Interview with Dr. Cyril Wecht: September 12, 2002.

p. 307, line 10: Wecht uneasy: Interview with Dr. Cyril Wecht, October 4, 2002.

p. 307, line 13: Nichols is investigated by CIA: 28 February 1969, Memorandum For; Director, FBI, Attention: Mr. S. J. Papich, Subject: Garrison and the Kennedy Assassination, Dr. John M. Nichols, for the Deputy Director for Plans, signed: James J. Angleton. But see also: Att'n: Chief, St. Louis Field Office, Kansas City R. A. (Direct), Director, Domestic Contact Service, OSS, 10 March 1969, Signed: James R. Murphy. Nichols had also written many letters to the FBI: March 7, 1969, To: Director, Central Intelligence Agency, Attention: Deputy Director, Plans, From: John Edgar Hoover. CIA 104-10515-10029, NARA.

p. 307, line 16: "flunked out": Memorandum for C/CI/R & A, attention: Mr. [03], Subject: John Marshall Nichols, M.D., 18 April 1969, Reference: Memo for DD/MS fr CI/R & A dated 10 April 69, Subject: Garrison and the Kennedy Assassination.

p. 307, line 22: CIA had been watching the Habighorst issue: 104-10189-10190, From: DCS/OSS to: Contacts/New Orleans, Title: TWX: Case 49364/ Suggestions Well Taken, August 13, 1968, NARA.

p. 307, line 30: Hunter Leake drives a truck filled with Oswald documents to CIA headquarters at Langley, Virginia: Michael Kurtz to Gary L. Aguilar, February 6, 2002.

p. 307, line 41: the "Haggerty bomb": Jim Garrison to Zach Sklar, August 9, 1988, AARC.

p. 308, line 11: "there was no way for Habighorst to come up with that name": Interview with Louis Ivon, May 27, 2001.

p. 308, line16: Butzman had not heard: January 30, 1969, Memorandum to: Mr. Edward Wegmann, From: Mr. Salvatore Panzeca, Re: Clay Shaw-Habighorst, *Papers of Edward F. Wegmann,* NARA.

p. 309, line 10: In *Escobedo v. Illinois* (1964), accused murderer Danny Escobedo made a damaging statement to the police in the absence of his lawyer, a statement not admitted on the ground that the police had refused to honor his request to talk to the lawyer. Clay Shaw made no such request.

p. 309, line 11: ruling was so capricious: "State Is Stunned by Judge's Ruling," *Times Picayune,* February 20, 1969, section 1, p. 1.

p. 309, line 14: Haggerty doesn't like the Habighorsts: Jack Dempsey interviewed by Jim DiEugenio, September 2, 1994.

p. 309, line 21: Ralph Whalen wrote a memo: Memorandum, To: Honorable Jim Garrison, From: Ralph Whalen, Re: Admissibility of Booking Document Containing Aliases. Courtesy of Mr. Whalen.

p. 309, line 39: "without having a relationship with the CIA": Interview with Gordon Novel, January 16, 2000.

p. 310, line 4: Colonel Finck: See Disposition Form, MEDEM-PF, Shaw Trial, New Orleans, 11 March 1969. Finck here traces the sequence of events of his testifying in New Orleans, document courtesy of Dr. Gary Aguilar.

p. 310, line 31: Boswell put on a plane when the Justice Department is "really upset": Boswell testified, finally, before the ARRB, February 26, 1996.

p. 311, line 8: "burn your notes": Al Oser cross-examining Dr. Pierre Finck at the trial of *State of Louisiana v. Clay Shaw.*

p. 311, line 18: strongest moments: Jim Garrison to Zach Sklar, August 15, 1988, AARC.

p. 311, line 25: "very very unhappy": Interview with Dr. Cyril Wecht, October 4, 2002.

p. 311, line 33: Andrews sued Garrison: "DA Is Perjurer, Says Andrews," *Times-Picayune,* June 3, 1969, section 4, p. 19.

p. 311, line 38: Charles Appel "proved" that Hauptmann wrote the Lindbergh ransom note: Curt Gentry, *J. Edgar Hoover: The Man and the Secrets* (New York: W. W. Norton, 1991), p. 46.

p. 312, line 21: he smiled slightly: "Conspiracy denied by Shaw as Defense Rests Its Case," *Philadelphia Inquirer,* February 28, 1969, p. 5.

p. 312, line 31: "not even concocted evidence": Gurvich conference, August 29, 1967, tape 3, p. 4. Gurvich adds: "But even old man Reily, a 79 year-old man, was a CIA agent, see?" In fact, recent CIA releases indicate that William Reily, too, was a CIA asset. Salvatore Panzeca insists that Shaw told his attorneys "everything."

p. 312, line 34: Dymond and Wegmann ask Justice for the CIA connections of a long list of people, including themselves: CIA, From: Headquarters, To: New Orleans, Title: Cable Re Clay Shaw Attorneys, September 26, 1967, 104-10189-10373, NARA. The New Orleans resident office of CIA obliged, see Headquarters, Att'n: Office of General Counsel, From: New Orleans, To: Headquarters, September 26, 1967, 104-10189-10372, NARA. See also From: New Orleans, To: Headquarters, Title: Cable Re CIA Connections, November 27, 1967, 104-10189-10374, NARA.

p. 312, line 36: Shaw had not told his lawyers of his Agency affiliation: CIA, From: Headquarters, To: New Orleans, Title: Cable Re Clay Shaw and CIA Connection, September 20, 1967, 104-10189-10369, NARA.

p. 312, line 38: no record of a secrecy agreement: From: New Orleans, To: Headquarters, Title: Cable Re Extent of Contacts by New Orleans Office with Clay Shaw, September 29, 1967, 104-10189-10368, NARA.

p. 312, line 40: "in attendance throughout": Max Holland, "The Lie That Linked CIA to the Kennedy Assassination," *Studies in Intelligence,* CIA Web site: <www.cia.gov/csi/studies/fall_winter 2001/article02.html>.

p. 312, line 42: "several Agency componants [*sic*]": 5 Jan 1968, Contacts Los Angeles From OSS (Musulin), Cable: re case 49, 364—Garrison Investigation of Kennedy Assassination, January 5, 1968, 104-10189-10056, NARA.

p. 313, line 2: William S. Block . . . an undercover agent for the government: Obituary of William S. Block, Federal Prosecutor. *Washington Post,* April 22, 2004, p. B6.

p. 313, line 12: lacked the resources: He didn't have the money or the staff, Jim Garrison interviewed by Zachary Sklar; e-mail from Sklar, May 7, 2001.

p. 313, line 13: Garrison "did not appreciate the fullness" of Shaw's involvement in CMC: "Was Jim Garrison Right After All?" p. 30.

p. 313, line 14: Garrison had discussed *Paese Sera* with Dick Billings: Interview with Richard N. Billings, September 24, 2002. Billings suggests too that neither of them registered the importance of the revelation of Shaw's participation in the Centro Mondiale Commerciale.

p. 313, line 15: we did not have any evidence: Jim Garrison to Zach Sklar, August 9, 1988.

p. 313, line 20: "taking the risk of leaving out motive": Jim Garrison interviewed by Dick Russell, December 1980, typed notes, courtesy of Dick Russell.

p. 313, line 22: "thanks to Victor Marchetti": "Was Garrison Right?" *New Orleans* magazine, June 1976, p. 30.

p. 313, line 35: the Tadins were more damaging: Interview with Salvatore Panzeca, June 4, 2000.

p. 313, line 36: they would never have lied: Interview with Frank Meloche, June 11, 2000.

p. 313, line 41: Alcock believed Shaw was guilty: Interview with John Volz, January 15, 2000.

p. 315, line 20: there were tears in Alcock's eyes: "Shaw Courtroom

Takes on Appearance of Art Gallery," *Times-Picayune*, March 1, 1969, section 1, p. 23.

p. 315, line 21: Alcock knew he was going to lose: Interview with Frank Meloche, June 11, 2000.

p. 316, line 18: "Garrison had the right idea": Interview with George Dureau, February 16, 2003. Dureau was taped for WYES television late in 2002 for a documentary on the history of the French Quarter. The interviewer was Peggy Laborde, courtesy of Steve Tyler.

CHAPTER 20

p. 317, Epigraph: Clarence Darrow: Jim Garrison to Zach Sklar, January 22, 1988, AARC.

p. 317, line 4: "Now everyone will know who I am": Interview with Vincent Salandria, April 30, 1999. Roger Craig had heard Oswald say, "Everyone will know who I am now."

p. 317, line 4: not emotional: Interview with Louis Ivon, January 8, 1998.

p. 317, line 13: $99,488.96: Brown manuscript, p. 219.

p. 317, line 15: Mark Lane talked to the jurors: Interview with Mark Lane, February 6, 1998.

p. 317, line 23: "rudely interrupted": "State AFL-CIO Retains Bussie: JFK Fight Just Begun, DA Tells Convention," *Times-Picayune*, April 4, 1969, section 1, p. 6; Jim Garrison to the Editor, *Times-Picayune*, April 7, 1969, NOPL.

p. 317, line 24: Garrison writes to each member of the jury: See, for example, Jim Garrison to Herbert John Kenison, April 7, 1968, NOPL.

p. 318, line 1: Shaw's rights: Jim Garrison to Eberhard Deutsch, April 9, 1969, NOPL.

p. 318, line 7: "we lose one case": Jim Garrison interviewed on WVUE-TV, March 13, 1969.

p. 318, line 7: "unfit for public office": "Justice in New Orleans" (Editorial). *New York Times,* Sunday, March 2, 1969, **p. E12.**

p. 318, line 13: the wife of Judge Christenberry sends Shaw a letter of "our most sincere congratulations": Caroline Christenberry to Dear Mr. Shaw, March 9, 1969, NARA.

p. 318, line 15: Herbert Christenberry is an FBI informant on the Shaw

case: See FBI, To: Director, From: New Orleans, March 22, 1967, 124-10237-10268, 89-69-1791, NARA.

p. 318, line 19: Haggerty says Shaw put on a con job: "Beyond JFK," Video by Barbara Kopple and Danny Schechter.

p. 318, line 24: Shaw visits La-Cour and the FBI: FBI, From: SAC, New Orleans, To: Director, FBI, 124-10089-10001, 44-41824-2, NARA.

p. 318, line 27: the *bête noir* has become a phoenix: CIA routing slip: To: Director, DCS Att'n: OSS (Musulin), March 4, 1969, HCLEAKE. no. NO-69-69, NARA, courtesy of Malcolm Blunt. The covering note was appended to a copy of the *Times-Picayune* of March 4, 1969, with its lead story, "Garrison Charges Shaw with Lying During Trial."

p. 318, line 31: "communications installation": Memorandum from John L. Schubert. No—120—69. 23 May 1969, To: Director, Domestic Contact Service, Att'n: Operational Support Staff (Musulin), Info: Executive Office, From: Chief, St. Louis Office. 104-10170-10449, 80T01357A, NARA.

p. 318, line 33: monitoring": March 4, 1970, New Orleans (Resident Agent), Director, Domestic Contact Service, New Case 54325 Clay Shaw/ Jim Garrison—Lawsuit for Damages, Reference: Leake/Musulin Telecom 2 March 1970, NARA.

p. 319, line 8: they summarized the list of undeveloped leads: Confidential Memorandum, March 20, 1969, To: James L. Alcock, Andrew J. Sciambra and Louis Ivon, From: Jim Garrison, Re: Shaw: Lead Summary. See, for example, Elmwood Plantation lead: Mr. Wence C. Cerne to William L. R. Alford Jr., June 17, 1969; Confidential Memorandum, June 20, 1969; To: Jim Garrison, From: William R. Alford Jr., Re: Lease of Elmwood Plantation Lead, NODA, NARA; To: Mr. Jim Alcock, From: Capt. F. A. Soule Sr., Subject: Names & Address given by arrested homosexuals who were attending a party for perverts on 2/25/62 at 3000 Edenborn Street, located in Jefferson Parish, April 7, 1969, NODA, NARA; Shaw in Clinton: Confidential Memorandum, April 3, 1969—dictated and transcribed, To: Jim Garrison, From: Andrew J. Sciambra, Re: Shaw in St. Francisville and Clinton, NODA,

NARA; Lynn Loisel to Captain Alvin Rankin, April 30, 1969; "Bayou Flying Club": Memorandum, March 25, 1969, To: Jim Garrison, From: Numa V. Bertel Jr., NODA, NARA; Memorandum, April 17, 1969, To: Sgt. Louis Ivon, From: Sgt. Fred Williams, Re: Golden Lantern Bar, NODA, NARA; Confidential Memorandum, March 31, 1969, Re: Shaw Leads Number II, To: Andrew J. Sciambra, William R. Alford, Louis Ivon and Garrison-Alcock, NODA, NARA; Jeanne Kelton: Confidential Memorandum, April 11, 1969, To: Jim Garrison, From: Andrew Sciambra, Re: Shaw Leads II, NODA, NARA; "Bill Gaudet Lead": Memorandum, April 22, 1969, To: Jim Garrison, From: Andrew J. Sciambra, Re: The New Shaw Lead File, NODA, NARA; To: Jim Garrison, From: Andrew Sciambra, Re: Shaw Leads II (Lakefront Airport), NODA, NARA.

See also Memorandum, April 18, 1969, To: Jim Garrison, From: Andrew J. Sciambra, Re: Shaw Leads II (Lakefront Airport). See also Memorandum, April 28, 1969, To: Jim Garrison, From: Andrew J. Sciambra, Re: Shaw Leads—2 (Lakefront Airport Lead), interview with Albert (Jeff) Jefferson; Memorandum, April 28, 1969, To: William R. Alford Jr. and Andrew Sciambra, From: Captain Fred A. Soule, Officer Kent A. Simms, Re: Shaw Leads II (Lakefront Airport); Memo, May 8, 1969, To: Mr. James Alcock, From: Mr. A. Sciambra & Capt. F. Soule, Subject: Shaw Case—Interviewing Witnesses that have frequented N.O. Airport, Lakefront; pool hall lead: To: Mr. James Alcock, From: Capt. Frederick Soule Sr., May 1, 1969, Item #13—Pool Hall, NODA, NARA.

Kloepfer and Shaw: To: Mr. James Alcock, From: Capt. F. A. Soule Sr., Subject: Point of Information in Re: Item 4 Fag Ball, May 2, 1969, NODA, NARA.

Oswald lies on one more job application: Memorandum, May 5, 1969, To: Jim Garrison, From: Andrew J. Sciambra, Re: Shaw Leads II File (Max Hill Lead), NODA, NARA.

"Oswald's alleged presence on the sixth floor": Jim Garrison to Mr. David Mills, May 9, 1969, NOPL. See also "SHAW LEADS -2": Confidential Memorandum, March 20, 1969, To: James L. Alcock, Andrew J. Sciambra and

Lou Ivon, From: Jim Garrison, Re: NEW SHAW LEAD FILE, NODA, NARA.

p. 319, line 8: red and yellow files: Confidential Memorandum, To: Messrs. Alcock, Sciambra, Alford and Ivon, From: Jim Garrison, Re: New File: Shaw II—Statements and Memos, NODA, NARA.

p. 319, line 13: Mrs. Murret identified one of them as Clay Shaw: March 25, 1969, Confidential. Shaw Leads II, To: Messrs. Alcock, Sciambra and Ivon, From: Jim Garrison, NODA, NARA.

p. 319, line 21: Guzman . . . Al Clark . . . James Lawrence: Confidential Memorandum, To: Jim Garrison, From: Andrew J. Sciambra, Re: The New Shaw Lead File, March 27, 1969, March 28, 1969 (transcribed), NODA, NARA. Finally, Guzman put them off: Memorandum, May 16, 1969, To: Jim Garrison, From: Andrew J. Sciambra, Re: Shaw Leads II, NODA, NARA.

p. 319, line 21: Al Clark is subpoenaed: Memorandum, April 15, 1969, To: Andrew J. Sciambra, From: Capt. F. A. Soule, Sr., Subject: Progress Report, NODA, NARA. Fred Soule interviews Al Clark, Memorandum, April 22, 1969, To: James L. Alcock, From: Captain Fred A. Soule, Senior, Re: Interview with Al Clark Item #2, NODA, NARA. Clark remains uncertain about whether Andrews introduced him to Oswald at Preservation Hall.

Bootsie Gay talks to Frederick A. Soule, Memorandum, April 24, 1969, To: James L. Alcock, From: Capt. Frederick A. Soule, Re: Interview with Clara Flournoy "Bootsie" Gay under Item # 2, Al Clark Interview, NODA, NARA.

p. 319, line 27: George Clark confirms he saw Oswald playing cards in Shaw's apartment: Confidential Memorandum, April 3, 1969—Dictated and transcribed, To: Jim Garrison, From: Andrew J. Sciambra, Re: Shaw Leads Number II (Mrs. Esther Stein Lead).

p. 319, line 38: Eames talks about Ferrie's visit about the library card: Confidential Memorandum, To: Jim Garrison, From: William R. Alford and Kent Simms, Re: Shaw Leads Number II ("4900 Magazine Street Lead"), (Mr. Jesse Garner), NODA, NARA.

p. 319, line 40: Earl Colomb: Confidential. Shaw Leads II To: Messrs. Alcock, Sciambra and Ivon, From: Jim

Garrison. Additional Leads, March 25, 1969.

p. 320, line 3: Ryder Coffee House . . . : Confidential Memorandum, March 31, 1969, From: Andrew J. Sciambra, Re: Shaw Leads Number II, NODA, NARA.

p. 320, line 6: Garrison wants to talk to Henry Lesnick: Confidential Memorandum, To: Messrs. Sciambra, Alford, Ivon and Garrison-Alcock, Re: Shaw Leads II, April 1, 1969, NODA, NARA.

p. 320, line 12: forty-one-page report: General Wade promises to get a copy: Memorandum, April 18, 1969, To: Jim Garrison, From: Andrew Sciambra, Re: Shaw Leads II (41-page report), NODA, NARA.

p. 320, line 14: classified pages: Confidential Memorandum, April 23, 1969, To: Jim Garrison, From: Andrew Sciambra, Re: Shaw Leads II (41-page Report Lead), NODA, NARA.

p. 320, line 16: Campbell brothers: Memorandum, May 14, 1969, To: Jim Garrison, From: Andrew Sciambra, Re: Shaw Leads II (Al Campbell), NODA, NARA. Allen Campbell's revelations: Interview with Allen Campbell, June 10, 2002; interview with Dan Campbell, June 8, 2002. See also Memorandum, May 14, 1969, To: Jim Garrison, From: Andrew Sciambra, Re: Shaw Leads II (Interview with Dan Campbell), NODA, NARA.

p. 320, line 23: "letters in care of Judge Matthew Braniff": Jim Garrison to Vincent Salandria, handwritten, undated.

p. 320, line 26: "big right paw": Jack Dempsey to Joan Mellen, March 27, 1998.

p. 320, line 30: "I did not fight": *New York Times,* March 15, 1969.

p. 320, line 34: "mistake": "Ga. Firm's Bonds to Be Rejected," *Times-Picayune,* August 2, 1969; for "one serious mistake": see "DA, Ward Views Differ on Bail Bonds Collection," *Times-Picayune,* August 6, 1969, section 1, p. 10. The city was out $317,412.50, see "Jim Garrison's Costly Mistake," *Times-Picayune* editorial, July 23, 1970, section 1, p. 8.

p. 320, line 319: "in modern times": "Augustine, Oser New N.O. Judges—McKeithen," *Times-Picayune,* June 18, 1969, section 1, p. 1. There is no doubt that this was Garrison's deci-

sion. Volz, who was present, says Garrison offered McKeithen two names, Oser's and Augustine's: Interview with John Volz, April 18, 2001; interview with Louis Ivon, January 12, 2000.

p. 321, line 17: Ward as Garrison's opponent: See "Ward Criticizes Two Opponents," *Times-Picayune,* October 1, 1969, section 4, p. 2; "Probe Blocked, Ward Charges," *Times-Picayune,* September 16, 1969, section 2, p. 2; Memorandum, July 30, 1969, To: William J. Stevens, Assistant Superintendent, From: Captain Frederick A. Soule, Re: Investigation into allegations made by Mr. Charles Ward, NODA, NARA. See also "Garrison Linked with 'New Left.'" *Times-Picayune,* September 30, 1969.

p. 321, line 29: Garrison had refused to allow Ward to prosecute the students: Investigative Report, July 21, 1969, Reported by Aaron M. Kohn, MCC.

p. 321, line 5: a Confederate flag: "Garrison Gives Ruling on Flag," *Times-Picayune,* May 16, 1969, section 1, p. 12.

p. 321, line 7: "fair with Negroes": Rosemary James, "The Dark Side of 'Not Guilty,'" *New Orleans* magazine, March 1971, p. 60.

p. 321, line 11: "in cities where I'm not district attorney": "Three Candidates for DA Again Attack Garrison," *States-Item,* August 1, 1969.

p. 321, line 14: "history will show we were not wrong": "Garrison Says Third Term Aim," *Times-Picayune,* May 15, 1969, section 1, p. 24.

p. 321, line 15: "you'll be proud": "DA Candidates Present Cases," *Times-Picayune,* October 8, 1969, section 1, p. 6.

p. 321, line 20: Carona delivers a check: Jim Garrison to Mr. Buck Kreihs, June 13, 1969, NOPL.

p. 321, line 22: a bar owner tries to give Jim Garrison a contribution: Andrew J. Sciambra interview with Zachary Sklar. E-mail from Sklar, April 10, 2001.

p. 321, line 25: "the Howard Hughes of New Orleans": "Garrison Image: Mystery Man," *States-Item,* November 1, 1969, p. 13. See also, with respect to the fraudulent poll, Jane Garrison Gardiner writes to the FCC, November 19, 1969.

p. 321, line 27: Both newspapers

endorse Connick: "Trying the District Attorney," *Times-Picayune,* November 6, 1969, section 1, p. 1; "What Kind of DA?" *States-Item,* November 6, 1969. But G. Wray Gill and many other lawyers supported Garrison: see Election Day advertisement for Jim Garrison, *Times-Picayune,* November 7, 1969, section 1, p. 21. Others supported him because he took a stand against Kohn: see Memorandum, September 17, 1969, To: Andrew J. Sciambra, From: Capt. Frederick Soule, Re: Interview with Alvin H. Cobb, NODA, NARA. The Crescent City Democratic Association supported Garrison as well: "Garrison Gets CCDA Support," *Times-Picayune,* October 9, 1969, section 1, p. 21. The bar association endorsed Connick: "Connick: A Boost from the Lawyers," *Times-Picayune,* October 18, 1969, section 1, p. 10.

p. 321, line 36: Garrison spent $20,000: Memorandum of Telephone Conversation, Date: November 12, 1969, Time: 10:15 A.M., To 10:35 A.M., Arlie G. Puckett interview with Pershing Gervais, Special Agent, courtesy of Lyon Garrison.

p. 321, line 36: Garrison won handily: "Orleans DA Tops Field," *Times-Picayune,* November 9, 1969, section 1, p. 1. See also "Garrison Winner in First Primary," *States-Item,* November 10, 1969.

p. 321, line 40: "Is this landslide Scaccia?": Interview with Ross Scaccia, January 6, 2000.

p. 322, line 9: "distinguished work": In re Judge Edward A. Haggerty, Jr., no. 50667. Supreme Court of Louisiana, November 23, 1970, Testimony before the Judiciary Commission.

p. 322, line 13: "not even moribund": Memorandum: to: Director, Domestic Contact Service, Att'n: Operational Support Staff (Musulin), From: Chief, St. Louis Office, Subject: Case 49364, NO-23-70, 26 January 1970, From John L. Schubert, 104-10170-10410, 80T01357A, Title: Memo: Case 49364—Garrison Investigation, NARA.

p. 322, line 16: "The CIA killed John Kennedy": "CIA Killed JFK, Says Garrison," *Times-Picayune,* January 21, 1970, section 1, p. 8.

p. 322, line 21: "not much more evidence": Jim Garrison to Vincent Salandria, undated.

p. 322, line 30: "just another escalating president": Jim Garrison to Arthur Fields, June 26, 1970.

p. 322, line 34: "I hate it but I'm going to publish it": Interview with Max Gartenberg, August 4, 2001.

p. 322, line 36: Putnam's lawyers wanted all references to Shaw removed: Arthur Fields to Jim Garrison, July 9, 1970.

p. 322, line 41: none dare call it treason: Garrison attributes this couplet to Michael Farrington, 16th-century poet.

p. 323, line 5: "smoke": "A Heritage of Smoke," by Donald Jackson, *Life,* December 4, 1970.

p. 323, line 8: Gertz reviews a *Heritage of Stone:* "Bizarre Happening Called the 'Clay Shaw Conspiracy Trial,'" by Elmer Gertz, Chicago *Sun-Times,* November 29, 1970. Reprinted in *The Philadelphia Inquirer,* December 13, 1970, as "2 Views of Grotesque Trial in the Assassination of JFK," p. 7.

p. 323, line 12: "intrigued by the case": "Jim Garrison: Far-Fetched," by George Lardner Jr., *Washington Post,* December 18, 1970, p. C4.

p. 323, line 13: John Leonard: John Leonard's review was titled "Who Killed John F. Kennedy?" *New York Times,* December 1, 1970, p. 49.

p. 323, line 24: Alec Gifford: tear sheets: WVUE-TV News Department, Story: Garrison/Gifford, courtesy of Max Gartenberg.

p. 323, line 32: *"The Maltese Falcon":* Jim Garrison to Max Gartenberg, April 15, 1973.

p. 323, line 33: *The Star-Spangled Contract:* Full-page ad for *The Star Spangled Contract, New York Times,* April 19, 1976, p. 18. A quarter of a page ad followed on April 30th, p. C17; Sunday *Book Review* full page ad: April 25, 1976. Garrison's novel was reviewed in the Sunday *Times* by Larry McMurtry.

p. 323, line 42: on income tax evasion: Transcript of tape of George Wyatt with Richard Townley, May 25, 1967, NARA.

p. 324, line 3: United States Attorney's office involved: Investigative Report, August 23, 1967, Reported by Aaron M. Kohn, MCC.

p. 324, line 5: the antiques came from Liz Garrison's family: Interview with Liz Garrison, May 11, 1999.

p. 324, line 7: even Orestes Peña knew: To: Jim Garrison, From: Harold Weisberg, April 12, 1968, Information from Orestes Peña, NODA, NARA.

p. 324, line 22: Pershing was a plant in Garrison's office: Interview with L. J. Delsa.

p. 324, line 22: "Garrison's carelessness": Memorandum of Interview in re: Jim Garrison, Date & time: Wednesday, May 1, 1968, Place: Empire Room, Fontainebleau Motor Hotel, Present: Pershing Gervais, Alexander C. Brodtmann Jr., Internal Revenue agent, and James L, McCormick, Special Agent, IRS documents, courtesy of Lyon Garrison.

p. 324, line 27: "you'll end up paying me": Jim Garrison at the New Orleans conference, September 1968, p. 30.

p. 324, line 30: Pershing learned that Mike Epstein was going to be indicted: Memorandum of Telephone Conversation, June 30, 1969, 3:09 P.M., To 3:21 P.M., Arlie G. Puckett Special Agent.

p. 324, line 30: "use him to get to Garrison": Memorandum of Interview, in re: Pershing O. Gervais, Date & Time: January 22, 1969, Present: Pershing O. Gervais, William G. Gibson, Norman Lanoix, IRS documents/Garrison papers.

p. 325, line 1: "Walter Sheridan and others": Telephone Conversation with Pershing O. Gervais, March 12, 1969, William G. Gibson. See also Memorandum of Meeting with Pershing O. Gervais, Date and time: April 18, 1969, Present: William G. Gibson and Norman Lanoix, IRS documents.

p. 325, line 9: Pershing hammers out the deal: In re: Pershing Gervais, From: Naurbon L. Perry, Supervisor, Group III, Memorandum to File, IRS documents/Garrison papers. See also Moore and Perry meet with Pershing, Affidavit of Floyd David Moore, June 1, 1972, IRS documents courtesy of Lyon Garrison.

p. 325, line 15: Gervais was the government's sole witness: Interview with K. Eric Gisleson, June 8, 2000. It was the best case he ever had, Gisleson insists, this despite its hanging on the slender reed of Ger-vais whose admitted lying destroyed his credibility, as Gervais obviously desired. On Gisleson's office wall is a commendation dated November 1973 from the Metropolitan Crime Commission for his prosecution of Jim Garrison. Kohn, at least, appreciated his effort.

p. 325, line 22: two thousand to Garrison: Memorandum for File, Arlie G. Puckett, July 18, 1969.

p. 325, line 27: "deeply distraught": Memorandum of Telephone Conversation, Date: January 12, 1970, time: 5:30 p.m.

p. 325, line 32: "Layton Martens spun it to Walter Sheridan": Interview with Gordon Novel, January 14, 2000.

p. 325, line 41: according to Bezou: Interview with Pierre Bezou, May 18, 1998.

p. 326, line 11: Garrison was having a drink: Gregory Burnham interview with Lamar Chauvin, December 6, 2000, courtesy of Mr. Burnham.

p. 326, line 14: a Bezou brother applies for a job at Tulane and Broad after the "incident": Interview with Numa Bertel, May 19, 1998.

p. 326, line 18: Velman: Interview with William Alford, May 28, 1998.

p. 326, line 37: "Garrison twice fondled": Aaron M. Kohn to Mr. William J. Krummel, November 5, 1969, MCC.

p. 326, line 39: committed suicide: Interview with Pierre Bezou; "Fall Is Blamed in Man's Death," *Times-Picayune*, August 23, 1974, section 4, p. 11.

p. 326, line 41: Jim Garrison made no comment: Interview with Numa Bertel, May 19, 1998.

p. 327, line 1: Gurvich had affidavits from the Bezou family: Interview with William Gurvich by Gary Cornwell, Mike Ewing and Robert Buras, November 7, 1978, HSCA.

p. 327, line 12: "everything you know about Jim Garrison": Interview with Ross Scaccia, January 6, 2000.

p. 327, line 26: the Strike Force opens for business: "Crime Office to Open Here," *Times-Picayune*, May 22, 1970, section 1, **p. 7.**

p. 327, line 28: placing pinball at the top of his list: To: Gerald J. Gallinghouse, From: Aaron M. Kohn, Subject: Recommendations for Inves-

tigative Development and Potential
Prosecutions by the Organized Crime
Strike Force, U.S. Department of Justice, May 15, 1970, MCC.

p. 327, line 34: "I got a young boy
in the car": Interview with Steve Bordelon.

p. 327, line 42: "I just couldn't put
up with that": Interview with Judge
James C. Gulotta, June 9, 2000.

p. 328, line 5: handing Garrison an
envelope: Robert P. Murray to Byron P.
LeGendre, August 23, 1971, NODA,
NARA.

p. 328, line 37: Alford resigns:
"DA's Office 'Fixes' Charged by Ex-
Aide," *Times-Picayune,* June 22, 1971,
section 1, p. 1. See also "Pressured by
DA Staff's 'Upper Echelon'—Alford,"
Times-Picayune, July 7, 1971, section
1, p. 3.

p. 329, line 15: Boasberg confides
in Jim McPherson: Interview with Jim
McPherson, January 9, 2000.

p. 329, line 23: the Shaw perjury
case draws to a close: Civ. A. no. 71-
135, *Clay L. Shaw v. Jim Garrison,* Individually and as District Attorney for
the Parish of Orleans, U.S. District
Court for the Eastern District of
Louisiana, New Orleans Division. 328f.
Supp. 390; 1971, U.S. Dist. Lexis
13079. See also "Temporary Order
Blocks Clay Shaw Perjury Trial," *Times-
Picayune,* January 20, 1971, section 1,
p. 1. See also "DA, Three More Will Be
Called," *Times-Picayune,* January 23,
1971, section 1, p. 3. Christenberry's
decision is Civ. a. no. 71-135. U.S.
District Court for the Eastern District
of Louisiana, New Orleans Division,
328. f. supp. 390, 1971, U.S. Dist.
LEXIS 13079, May 27, 1971, Opinion
by Christenberry, District Judge.

p. 329, line 27: Garrison's reaction to the dismissal of the perjury indictment: "Was 'Hardly Surprised' by
Decision—Garrison," *Times-Picayune,*
May 29, 1971, section 1, p. 10.

p. 329, line 27: Press Release,
May 31, 1971, NODA, NARA.

p. 330, line 4: envelope: Memorandum of Marking—U.S. Currency,
Tuesday, June 29, 1971, in re: Jim
Garrison, Freddie Soule, Robert Frey
et al., From: Irving J. Johnson, Special Agent.

p. 330, line 19: "two teams stationed outside": Interview with K. Eric
Gisleson, June 8, 2000.

p. 330, line 35: Garrison wouldn't
tell them where the key was: Interview with Steve Bordelon, June 14,
2000.

p. 330, line 40: he was being punished: Conversation with Mike Seghers,
January 6, 2000.

p. 330, line 42: "too rough on
some violations": Memorandum on
telephone conversation, Date and
time: July 26, 1969, 9:30 P.M., Arlie G.
Puckett.

p. 331, line 2: Congress doesn't
control: NBC Nightly News, Public Affairs Staff, June 30, 1971.

p. 331, line 4: "not wisely but too
well": "Gervais Framed Me—Garrison,"
Times-Picayune, July 6, 1971, section
1, p. 18.

p. 331, line 10: Bailey offers to
represent Jim Garrison: F. Lee Bailey
to Jim Garrison, July 16, 1971,

p. 331, line 14: "on the ropes":
CIA, Chief, Dallas Field Office, Att'n:
New Orleans Resident Agent, Director,
Domestic Contact Service, 6 October
1971, 14-79-55, Case 54326, NARA.

p. 331, line 19: Lou Merhig came
up with the strategy: Interview with
Lou Merhige, June 8, 2000; August
22, 2000.

p. 331, line 19: Having the case
tried in state court: "Garrison Directs
Own Indictment," *Times-Picayune,*
November 16, 1971, section 1, p. 1.
See also all from *Times-Picayune:*
"Motion on Venue Postpones Arraignment for Garrison," November 23,
1971, section 1, p. 1. and "Smith
Slaps Malfeasance Charge on DA
Garrison," November 25, 1971, section 1, p. 1; "Smith Declines Gaming
Count," November 27, 1971, section
1, p. 1; "DA's Malfeasance Charge
Ruled Null," November 30, 1971, section 1, p. 1; "Review of Charge against
Garrison Sought by Smith," December 2, 1971, section 1, p. 1; "Garrison
Case Dismissal Upheld by La. High
Court," December 14, 1971, section
1, p. 11. See also "Ben Smith Takes
on Garrison, No One Can Call It a
Mismatch," by Ray Lincoln. *States-
Item,* November 30, 1971, p. 1.

p. 331, line 31: Garrison indicted:
"Charges against DA Bared—By DA,"
Times-Picayune, December 3, 1971,
section 1, **p. 1.**

p. 331, line 35: "Had I chosen to
be crooked": "Garrison Hits Tactics of

IRS," *Times-Picayune,* March 14, 1972, section 1, p. 1. See also "DA didn't File $60,000 Income, U.S. Charges," *Times-Picayune,* March 12, 1972, section 1, p. 1.

p. 331, line 38: Petersen writes to Helms: March 13, 1972, CIA 104-10117-100069, NARA.

p. 332, line 1: Pershing recants: WWL-TV interview with Rosemary James, May 22, 1972, Transcript, NARA. "Trapped Garrison, Ex-Aide Declares," *Atlanta Journal,* May 23, 1972, p. 4A. "Gervais 'Forced to Entrap' DA," *States-Item,* May 23, 1972; WVUE-TV, June 6, 1972 with Alec Gifford and Richard Angelico.

p. 332, line 8: "I was forced to lie for them": Pershing Gervais interviewed by Rosemary James in Vancouver, WWL-TV interview with Rosemary James, May 22, 1972, Transcript, NARA.

CHAPTER 21

p. 333, Epigraph: The phrase "Potomac Two-Step": Robert Buras summing up his experience as an investigator with HSCA.

p. 333, line 8: "Nobody there really wants the truth": Nagell speaking of HSCA, quoted in *The Man Who Knew Too Much,* p. 367.

p. 333, line 6: As the trial began, Kohn was still looking for evidence against Jim Garrison. Memorandum for file, August 23, 1973, MCC.

p. 333, line 13: "I never thought I would get this money back": Interview with Sharon Herkes, January 14, 2000.

p. 333, line 25: "it's not by accident": Pershing Gervais on WVUE-TV, June 6, 1972.

p. 334, line 5: Soule had warned the bar owners: "Pinball Raids Tipped Off," *States-Item,* August 22, 1973, p. 1.

p. 334, line 9: the "big man" was Giarrusso: Interview with Irvin L. Magri Jr., March 3, 2002.

p. 334, line 19: the trial is about Giarrusso: "Trial Emphasis Marks Big Shift," *States-Item,* September 1, 1973.

p. 334, line 20: Lagarde implicates Giarrusso: "Lagarde Reports Paying ex-Police Chief $30,000," *States-Item,* August 30, 1973, p. 1; "Joseph Giarrusso Again Named As Getting Bribe,"

Times-Picayune, August 31, 1973, section 1, p. 11.

p. 334, line 30: Alford did not want to testify: Interview with William Alford, May 28, 1998.

p. 335, line 4: "assistance from Captain America": "Garrison Lawyers Out; He Begins Own Defense," by Don Hughes and John McMillan. *Times-Picayune,* September 13, 1973, p. 1.

p. 335, line 12: Burton Klein: See Memorandum, May 4, 1965, Reported by Aaron M. Kohn. Date of information, May 3, 1965. Klein tells Kohn he was "personally satisfied" that the Garrison office was "more corrupt than it ever was under Richard Dowling . . . cases can be fixed now with more ease and certainty." MCC.

p. 335, line 23: "he was too undependable": Interview with John Volz, June 13, 2000.

p. 335, line 24: Gerstman: "Voice 'Expert' Rejected," *States-Item,* September 18, 1973, p. 1.

p. 335, line 27: "fraudulent fabrication": "Voice of Garrison Said Spliced into Recording," *Times-Picayune,* September 19, 1973, section 1, p. 1.

p. 335, line 32: Garrison had corrupted *him:* "Garrison Received Daily Bribery Money—Gervais," *Times-Picayune,* September 20, 1973, section 1, p. 1.

p. 335, line 375: "My God, Pershing": "Lawyer: Gervais Tried to Auction Testimony" by Don Hughes and John McMillan. *Times-Picayune,* September 22, 1973, section 1, p. 1.

p. 335, line 37: Jim Garrison's Closing Argument: United States of America versus Jim Garrison et al., September 25, 1973, Case Number 71-542. See also "Jury Acquits Garrison, Nims, Callery in Pinball Bribe Case," by John McMillan and Don Hughes. *Times-Picayune,* September 28, 1973, section 1, p. 1. The jury found the tapes unconvincing: "DA Won on First Ballot; Jury 'Didn't Go on Tapes,'" *States-Item,* September 28, 1973, p. 1.

p. 335, line 38: his mother had had a heart attack: Jane Garrison Gardiner to Dear Margaret, April 17, 1974, courtesy of Lyon Garrison.

p. 336, line 2: "it might hurt your Dad": Interview with Lyon Garrison, October 9, 2000.

p. 336, line 23: two black jurors wept: Interview with Ralph Whalen, January 8, 2000.

p. 336, line 24: "brilliant": Interview with Judge Tom Wicker, June 5, 2000.

p. 336, line 28: "the jury would have let him go": Interview with F. Lee Bailey, November 11, 1999.

p. 336, line 30: Strike Force packs up: "N.O., May Lose Strike Force against Crime," *States-Item,* October 2, 1973.

p. 336, line 33: Numa Bertel approached loan shark "King Solomon": Interview with Numa Bertel, August 27, 2002.

p. 336, line 36: almost no campaigning: Interviews with: Silvio Fernandez, May 31, 2002; Ralph Capitelli and Lawrence Centola, January 11, 2000; Ralph Whalen, January 8, 2000; John Volz.

p. 337, line 11: "forgotten": Interview with John Volz, May 21, 1999.

p. 337, line 14: he didn't bother to go out and vote for himself: Interview with Steve Bordelon.

p. 337, line 15: Connick beats him: "Connick Defeats Garrison in Photo-Finish D.A. Election," December 16, 1973, section 1, p. 1.

p. 337, line 16: a recount: "Garrison Contests Results of Election" *Times-Picayune,* December 22, 1973, section 1, p. 1. See also "Garrison's Attorneys Claim Over 7,000 Irregularities," *Times-Picayune,* December 25, 1973, section 1, p. 23; "Vote Fraud Charges Up," *Times-Picayune,* December 27, 1973, section 1, p. 1.

p. 337, line 23: reading the newspaper: Interview with Lyon Garrison.

p. 337, line 24: "a better garbage man": "Government Guilty, Garrison Charges," *Times-Picayune,* March 18, 1974, section 1, p. 1. See also "Garrison Begins His Own Defense; U.S. Rests Case," *Times-Picayune,* March 23, 1974, section 1, p. 20.

p. 337, line 26: "Chinese laundry in the middle of a thunderstorm": "Garrison Alleges Misconduct of U.S.," by Ed Anderson and Gordon Gsell. *Times-Picayune,* March 26, 1974, section 1, p. 2.

p. 337, line 27: "acquit": "Garrison Acquitted" by Vincent Lee. *Times-Picayune,* March 27, 1974, section 1, p. 1.

p. 337, line 32: Garrison represents Gordon Novel: Novel says he chose Garrison for his high profile, Interview with Gordon Novel, January 16, 2000.

p. 337, line 36: there was a moratorium against dynamiting: Interview with Lawrence Centola Jr., June 14, 2000.

p. 337, line 13: CIA feared it would be introduced into the case as a smokescreen: Memorandum for the Record from Peter Houck, NO-147-76. 15 October 1976, Subject: Gordon Michael Dwane Novel, 18-52-10. CIA called Novel "one of the spookiest persons we have ever met," CIA 21 November 1975, MO 162-75, 104-10312-10084, DDP files, Title: Operational proposal by Gordon Novel and Associates, From: New Orleans resident office to OSG/OSB.

The Agency was clearly nervous about the alliance between Garrison and Novel: Memorandum for the Record. 21 October 1976, Subject: Discussions regarding DCD relationships with Gordon M. D. Novel, signed Jackson P. Horton, Chief, Domestic Collection Division. But the Agency would not bail out Novel: Memorandum for the Record Signed by Peter Houck. O-96-76- 28 May 1976, Subject: Gordon Novel, Reference: NO-95-76 dated 27 May 1976.

Peter Houck testified; Houck also gave an interview to the *Times-Picayune:* "CIA Official Says Fire Not in Novel Talk," March 5, 1976, section 1, p. 2.

p. 338, line 1: Houck had given Connick a certificate of "non-employment," repudiating Novel as an agency employee: OGC 76-6018. 29 October 1976, Memorandum for the Record: From: John K. Greaney, Associate General Council, Subject: Gordon Novel, NARA.

p. 338, line 2: "employed" by CIA is in quotation marks: Jackson P. Horton, Chief, Domestic Collection Division, 21 October 1976, Memorandum for the Record: Subject: Discussions Regarding DCD Relationships with Gordon M. D. Novel, 18-52-10, NARA.

p. 338, line 5: "a rather detached air": Peter Houck, Memorandum for the Record, 5 November 1976, NO-151-76, Subject: Gordon Novel's Arson Conspiracy Trial, References: Houck-

Greaney Telecons on 28 and 29 October 1976: Same Subject, NARA. See also "The Cloak and Dagger Trial of Gordon Novel," by Dalt Wonk. *New Orleans* magazine, November 1976. See also Peter Houck, Memorandum for the Record, No -166-76, 21 December 1976, Subject: Gordon Novel, NARA.

p. 338, line 13: a phone call about checking telephone equipment: Interview with Pat Morvant, May 30, 1998.

p. 338, line 21: "bugged by most of sixteen": "Garrison Gives Views on D. C," *Times-Picayune,* June 28, 1974, section 1, p. 18.

p. 338, line 26: "let me tell you": Interview with Christine Wiltz, February 10, 1999.

p. 338, line 28: for his life with Phyllis: Interviews with Phyllis Kritikos, May 29, 1998; January 11, 2000; June 16, 2000; October 9, 2000; February 6, 2002.

p. 338, line 42: "Bullet 399.5": FBI, 22 November 1963, From: Francis X. O'Neill Jr. Agent, FBI, James W. Sibert, Agent, FBI, To: Captain J. H. Stovar Jr. Commanding Officer, U.S. Naval Medical Center, Bethesda, Maryland: "We hereby acknowledge receipt of a missile removed by Commander James J. Humes, MC, USN on this date, signed Francis X. O'Neill Jr. and James W. Sibert, *Papers of Jim Garrison.*

p. 339, line 7: "Specter's computations": Jim Garrison to Vincent Salandria, April 2, 1977, *Papers of Jim Garrison.*

p. 339, line 12: Garrison defeated Barry: "Garrison Elected to Judgeship," *Times-Picayune,* May 28, 1978, section 1, p. 1.

p. 339, line 15: "rumors of my death": "Garrison, Prober of JFK Death, Elected to the Louisiana Bench," by John Pope. *Washington Post,* May 29, 1978, p. A2.

p. 339, line 17: Earling Garrison's death certificate: Interview with Phyllis Kritikos, May 29, 1998.

p. 339, line 23: a grandmother seeks parental rights: State of Louisiana in the Interest of the Minor Senedra Madrell Bartee, no. CA-1244, Court of Appeal of Louisiana, Fourth Circuit, 446 So. 2d 512; 1984 La. App. LEXIS 8063, February 13, 1984.

p. 339, line 24: a boy on crutches: *Ernest Thibodeaux v. Schewegmann*

Brothers *Supermarket,* no. 11488, December 9, 1980.

p. 339, line 26: paralyzed for life: *Armantine Smith v. Travelers Insurance Company,* Jerry Krushin, and Arthur Chester, as Representative for Certain Underwriters at Lloyd's, London, Subscribing to Certificate no. 31527, no. 11, 819.

p. 339, line 30: "I thought you had empathy for people": Interview with Judge James C. Gulotta, January 8, 1998.

p. 339, line 32: ruled for the police: Herbert and Huber and police brutality: *James A. Herbert v. Department of Police; David C. Huber v. Department of Police,* no. 9280, 9381, September 12, 1978.

p. 339, line 35: Rosemary James comes before the court: Interview with Rosemary James, May 22, 1998.

p. 339, line 37: impersonating a lawyer: *State of Louisiana v. Claude Robinson,* no. Ka 1780, January 11, 1985.

p. 339, line 42: "this is the most pitiful": Jerome M. Winsberg to Jim Garrison, February 6, 1985.

p. 340, line 2: "some idiot has written a letter to me": Jim Garrison to Jerome Winsberg, February 7, 1985.

p. 340, line 3: two brilliant opinions: *Patrick M. Callaghan v. Department of Fire,* no. 11068, May 13, 1980; *Vincent Bruno v. Department of Police,* no. 12506, June 29, 1983. on Rehearing, June 6, 1984.

p. 340, line 37: you lost your case, Vincent: Interview with Vincent J. Bruno, August 18, 2002.

p. 341, line 1: Judge Augustine was planning to run for Congress: Interview with Silvio Fernandez, August 18, 2002.

p. 341, line 8: a single day did not go by: Interview with Sallee Benjamin Boyce, May 27, 1998.

p. 341, line 10: hero worship of the Kennedys: Interview with Sallee Boyce Benjamin, May 27, 1998.

p. 341, line 10: Julie Sirera was skeptical: Interview with Julie Sirera, May 20, 1998.

p. 341, line 19: "that much courage": "Was Jim Garrison Right After All?" by Joe Manguno, *New Orleans* magazine, June 1976, pp. 26–31.

p. 341, line 24: "minimized the relationship": Memo 6/21/76, To: Dave

Marston, From: Gaeton Fonzi, Re: Interview with Jim Garrison, NARA.

p. 341, line 28: into the act: Garrison told Jonathan Blackmer the same thing; he was "not trying to get into the act," Jim Garrison to Jonathan Blackmer, August 25, 1977, NARA.

p. 342, line 12: "I've never heard of him": Telephone interview of Ralph Schoenman with Esteban Volkov, April 27, 2005.

p. 342, line 21: "The CIA did it": Memo 9/9/76 To: Troy, From: Gaeton.

p. 342, line 23: "Did you ever do any work for the CIA?": Interview with Mary Ferrell, May 24, 2001.

p. 342, line 27: Jim Garrison is interviewed in *New Orleans* magazine: "Was Jim Garrison Right After All?" by Joe Manguno, pp. 26–31.

p. 342, line 38: J. Walton Moore issues a cry for help: CIA, From: J. Walton Moore. Chief, Domestic Collection Division (Direct), Att'n: Deputy Chief of Operations (Ed Watts) w/attach., INFO: Chief of General Counsel (John Greaney) w/attach., Chief, Dallas Field Office (New Orleans Resident Office), NO-98-76. 3 June 1976. The response to Moore, dated 6/23/76, is on a Routing and Record Sheet. Its author is John Greaney of the Office of General Counsel.

p. 343, line 2: no one connected to the FBI: Interview with Richard A. Sprague. *Probe,* January–February 2000, p. 17.

p. 343, line 5: "deeply into the methods": Interview with Richard A. Sprague, Part II, *Probe,* March–April 2000, p. 18.

p. 343, line 20: Tanenbaum was wary of Jim Garrison: Interview with Bob Tanenbaum, August 14, 2000.

p. 343, line 21: a list of CIA plants: Interview with Jim DiEugenio, June 12, 1999, based on his conversations with Lopez. The figure of nine plants was reported by Bill O'Reilly on *Inside Edition,* February 5, 2001. Dr. Cyril Wecht confirmed it on Pacifica Radio. L. J. Delsa also witnessed this document.

p. 343, line 37: Buras withheld judgment on Garrison: E-mail from Robert Buras, May 19, 2002.

p. 343, line 37: the "odd couple": Recollections of Gaeton Fonzi, January 23, 2002. Quotes from Robert Buras and L. J. Delsa from extensive interviews with both between 2000

and 2005. See also L. J. Delsa interviewed by Jim DiEugenio, August 18, 1993, courtesy of Mr. DiEugenio.

p. 343, line 40: Fort Sill: See Numa P. Avendano to Colonel T. Barnard, 20 August 1976, courtesy of the staff at Fort Sill.

p. 343, line 42: "before the year is out": "Arrests Predicted in Kennedy Probe," by Mark Kingsolver. *The Lawton Constitution* (Oklahoma), May 6, 1977, p. 1. See also. "Hall of Fame Due New Members," by Paul McClung. *The Lawton Constitution,* May 6, 1977, section 2, p. 1.

p. 344, line 12: Letters between Robert Blakey and Larry Strawderman are available at NARA. See, for example, G. Robert Blakey to Larry Strawderman, Information and Privacy Coordinator, CIA, August 2, 1977, and Larry Strawderman to G. Robert Blakey, July 27, 1977. NARA.

p. 344, line 24: "protect Agency sources and methods": Office of Legislative Counsel Coordination and Review Staff, Mr. Douglas Cummins, Special Assistant to the DDO for External Oversight, From: B. Hugh Tovar, Chief, Counterintelligence Staff, Subject: Name Trace: Gerald Patrick Hemming, Reference: Memorandum for the Office of Legislative Counsel, dated 29 September 1977, same subject, #04489, NARA.

p. 344, line 29: Blakey in 2003: See "JFK's Assassination," *New York Review of Books,* December 18, 2003. p. 101. When CIA continued to refuse to release its Joannides' files, Blakey signed another letter of protest. See "Blocked," *New York Review of Books,* August 11, 2005, p. 65.

p. 344, line 39: Garrison takes premature comfort in Blakey's having kept on some of Sprague's staff: Taped telephone conversations between Jim Garrison and Ted Gandolfo, February 10, 1978, courtesy of Gaeton Fonzi.

p. 345, line 25: Buras and Delsa visit Joe Oster: January 27, 1978, HSCA 005207, NARA.

p. 345, line 41: L. J. Delsa tracks down Lawrence Howard: May 23, 1978, 008962. This report was cosigned by Martin J. Daly and sequestered from the public until it was liberated by the ARRB in 1996.

p. 346, line 6: Buras interviews Delphine Roberts, July 6, 1978, NARA.

p. 346, line 14: already interviewed by Francis Fruge: Buras interviewed William Dunn on January 19, 1978. The interviews of Reeves Morgan and Henry Earl Palmer by Patricia Orr and Robert Buras were also January 19, 1978. Dr. Frank Silva was not on Orr's list, Interview with Dr. Frank Silva, October 7, 2000.

p. 347, line 14: De Brueys denies he ever met Oswald: Interview with L. J. Delsa; interview with Warren de Brueys, January 15, 2000.

p. 347, line 15: Blackmer tries to obtain grand jury records: Jim Garrison tells Blackmer about the grand jury testimonies: Jim Garrison to Jonathan Blackmer, November 8, 1977, 03525, NARA; Blackmer wants to battle Connick: Memorandum, To: G. Robert Blakey, Gary Cornwell, Bill Triplett, Jim Wolf, From: Jonathan Blackmer, Date: February 13, 1978, Re: Garrison Grand Jury Minutes, NARA. See also Memorandum, July 12, 1995, To: Jeremy Gunn, From: Joe Freeman, Subject: HSCA Chronology, Re: Clay Shaw Grand Jury Minutes/Transcripts, NARA.

p. 347, line 31: "I told you to burn it": Notarized statement by Gary Raymond. Included in set of materials marked "Memorandum. To: Jeremy Gunn. From: Joe Freeman. June 7, 1995. Re: HSCA/Garrison Records." ARRB. NARA.

p. 347, line 35: Buras and Martin Daly visit Jack Rogers: HSCA 005964, Investigation Interview Schedule, February 22, 1978, HSCA 180-10082-10167, NARA.

p. 347, line 42: Frank Bartes showed Buras: March 15, 1978, NARA.

p. 348, line 9: Buras and Leap interview William Walter, February 27, 1978. Leap signed the report, 22 pages, NARA.

p. 348, line 23: Gaudet was not called before the Warren Commission: *Congressional Record*, House, September 17, 1976, H 10359. See also Bernard Fensterwald and Allan Stone, interview with William Gaudet, May 13, 1975, AARC; interview with Robert Buras, March 25, 2002; Buras and Leap interview Gaudet: HSCA 180-10070-10274. 004826, January 18, 1978; on Gaudet's denial that he had telephoned the FBI, see Draft of Report, HSCA 180-10141-10492, CIA

SEGREGATED COLLECTION, agency file: 22-04-01, January 23, 10976, 11 pages. The original FBI report is NO 44-2064, November 27, 1963, by SA John William Miller.

p. 348, line 31: Garrison's memo to Blackmer on Thomas Edward Beckham: To: Jonathan Blackmer, From: Jim Garrison, Re: Thomas E. Beckham, July 18, 1977, NARA.

p. 348, line 39: Interviews with Thomas E. Beckham: To: G. Robert Blakey, Ken Klein and Cliff Fenton, From: Jonathan Blackmer, August 18, 1977, Re: Interview of Thomas Edward Beckham, 014162, NARA; Memorandum to Chief Counsel G. Robert Blakey and Chief Investigator Cliff Fenton, October 7,1977. 005984.

p. 349, line 13: L. J. goes to Dallas: HSCA 003541. Outside Contact Report, interview with Ma/G. Kissell, November 11, 1977, NARA.

p. 349, line 17: a new set of questions for Beckham: "Memo to L. J. Delsa, Re Possible Questions for T. E. Beckham," NARA.

CHAPTER 22

p. 350, Epigraph: *Vale* means Farewell. This is the last word of *The History of That Ingenious Gentleman Don Quixote De La Mancha* by Miguel de Cervantes Saavedra.

p. 350, line 8: "the emotional price I paid": Jim Garrison interviewed in *The Garrison Tapes.*

p. 350, line 9: "Don't shade it": Interview with Robert Buras, December 15, 2003.

p. 350, line 1413: Beckham said he didn't know when he didn't: Interview with L. J. Delsa, April 8, 2002.

p. 351, line 4135: John Manchester goes to Washington: Executive Session, Tuesday, March 14, 1978, 008503, 39 pages, plus index, NARA.

p. 352, line 3: Buras visits Fruge: HSCA, April 7, 1978, signed by Robert Buras, 9 pages, NARA.

p. 352, line 4: Fruge had lost all respect for the federal people: Interview with Anne Dischler, February 12, 2001.

p. 352, line 35: Thomas Edward Beckham is deposed: HSCA 180-10104-10278, 014031, May 24, 1978, 82 pages, NARA.

p. 354, line 20: Marchetti telephones HSCA: HSCA 180-10099-10079, 010460, July 28, 1978. Outside contact report by Harold Leap: Victor Marchetti.

p. 354, line 31: Marchetti, Hunt and *Spotlight* magazine. Mark Lane's, *Plausible Denial* discusses Hunt's suit in great detail throughout.

p. 354, line 41: J. Lee Rankin: HSCA Outside Contact Report: J. Lee Rankin, June 1, 1978, 008815, NARA. Rankin's August 17, 1978, testimony is 014027.

p. 355, line 9: never have conceded: Blakey rejected all personal testimony as subjective: Interview with Richard N. Billings, August 2, 2000. Blakey had to accept there was a conspiracy: Interview with Gary Mack, March 4, 2002.

p. 355, line 21: For details of Clay Shaw's last days: New Orleans Department of Police, Report, August 28, 1974, Homicide detectives John Dillmann and Detective Fred Dantagnan, NARA. See *New York Times* obituary, August 16, 1974, p. 32: "Clay Shaw Is Dead at Sixty: Freed in Kennedy 'Plot,'" by David Bird. See also "Police 'Quietly' Probe Shaw's Death," by Kenneth A. Weiss. *Times-Picayune,* August 18, 1974. For Shaw's net assets, see Civil District Court for the Parish of Orleans, Succession of Clay Shaw, Descriptive List of Assets, 1975, undated, NARA. See also "The Strange Death of Clay Shaw," by Richard Boyle. *True* magazine, April 1975, vol. 56, no. 455, p. 55.

p. 355, line 26: Gary Cornwell interviews Aaron Kohn in New Orleans: HSCA 180-10087-10439, 013261, Deposition of Aaron M. Kohn, November 7, 1978,

p. 356, line 4: Cornwell and Ewing meet with Jim Garrison: November 26, 1978, HSCA.

p. 356, line 37: The Report was published as *The Final Assassinations Report: Report of the Select Committee on Assassinations.* U.S. House of Representatives. (New York: Bantam Books, 1979).

p. 356, line 40: Complaints from the CIA: See, for example, CIA. From: DCI. To: G. Robert Blakey. Title: letter Commenting on a Section of the Draft HSCA Report. 02/15/79. 16 pages. 104-10019. Agency file num-

ber: 80T01357A. NARA. The document is signed S. D. Breckinridge, Principal Coordinator. HSCA.

p. 357, line 26: "a man of such senior position": S. D. [Scott] Breckinridge, Principal Coordinator, HSCA to G. Robert Blakey, September 22, 1978, on Director of Central Intelligence, Office of Legislative Counsel letterhead. JFK Collection: HSCA (RG 233). Courtesy of Malcolm Blunt.

p. 357, line 42: Breckenridge proposes changes: CIA. From: DCI. To: G. Robert Blakey. Title: Letter Commenting on a Section of the Draft HSCA Report. 02/15/79. 16 pages. 104-10019. Agency file number: 80T01357A. NARA. The document is signed S. D. Breckinridge, Principal Coordinator. HSCA.

p. 358, line 32: "review inserts for the HSCA draft report": CIA. Document ID number: 1993.07.19.08:53:00:250620. Rec-series: JFK. Agfileno: 80T01357A. JFK Box # JFK21. Vol/Folder; F191. Title: Letter "Response to Your Request that We Review Inserts for the HSCA D". 03/03/79. From: Breckinridge, S. D., CIA. To: Blakey, G. Robert, HSCA. Originator: CIA. NARA.

p. 359, line 11: draft paper on "Evolution and Implications of the CIA-Sponsored Assassination Conspiracies Against Castro": CIA. Record Number: 104-10082-10034. Record Series: JFK. Agency file number: 80T01357A. From: Breckinridge, Scott D., OLC to C/Counsel, HSCA Blakey. Title: Comments on the Draft Paper on "Evolution and Implications of the CIA-Sponsored Assassination Conspiracies Against Castro". Date: 03/15/79. Pages: 8. NARA.

p. 359, line 42: Blakey was writing about Beauboeuf and Martens: G. Robert Blakey to David and Jeremy, received by ARRB May __ 1995 [date illegible], NARA. T. Jeremy Gunn to Professor G. Robert Blakey, February 11, 1997, NARA.

p. 360, line 1: "I am writing from the Bench": Jim Garrison to Zachary Sklar, March 8, 1988, AARC.

p. 360, line 5: "I'm going to get this book published": Jim Garrison to Vincent Salandria, July 14, 1987.

p. 360, line 16: "score one": Jim Garrison to Peter Miller, March 30, 1987.

p. 360, line 24: "the truly new material": Zach to Ellen, Bill, John, July 23, 1987, AARC.

p. 360, line 29: he wished he could have had access to Thornley's grand jury testimony: April 29, 1988, Notes re Chapters 4, 5 & 6, re-writes: To: Zach, From: Jim, AARC.

p. 360, line 35: "you must be some editor": Jim Garrison to Zach Sklar, July 1, 1988, AARC.

p. 360, line 37: 32,000 copies: Jim Garrison to Louis Wolfson, August 24, 1989.

p. 360, line 38: the distributor, Kampmann & Company, goes bankrupt: See "Small Publishers Struggling after Court Impounds Books," by Edwin McDowell. *New York Times,* June 29, 1989.

p. 360, line 42: Norman Mailer's blurb: *Times-Picayune,* January 23, 1989.

p. 361, line 8: Mrs. Willard Robertson: Marlin H. Robertson to Jim Garrison, January 16, 1989.

p. 361, line 18: "rife with paranoia": "Retrying a Losing Case" by Jack Wardlow, *Times-Picayune,* January 15, 1989, p. E-6.

p. 361, line 21: "the judge has turned into an accomplished writer":" Other Opinions: Columns, "Garrison's Book on JFK's Slaying" by Iris Kelso. *Times-Picayune,* January 12, 1989.

p. 361, line 23: major talk show: Jim Garrison to Bill/Ellen/Zach, February 15, 1989.

p. 361, line 24: he would have been happy to appear on the *Larry King Show:* Jim Garrison to Louis Wolfson, August 24, 1989.

p. 361, line 27: "a great sadness behind his eyes": Interview with Joseph Bosco, June 14, 1999.

p. 361, line 34: when the musicians began to play: Interview with Zachary Sklar, December 16, 1997.

p. 361, line 42: "so many people hated Jim Garrison": Interview with Ellen Ray, December 4, 1997.

p. 362, line 4: "I was a hot director then": Interview with Oliver Stone, June 6, 1999.

p. 362, line 21: he gave his editor ten per cent of his royalties: Zach Sklar to Jim Garrison, January 14, 1989.

p. 363, line 13: closer to his children: Interviews with Elizabeth Garrison: January 11, 1998, and May 28, 1998; Jasper Garrison: January 11, 1998; Eberhard Garrison: January 11, 1998, and May 23, 1998; Lyon Garrison: May 23, 1998, January 8, 2000, May 30, 2000, October 9, 2000, and numerous telephone conversations; Phyllis Kritikos: January 11, 2000, June 5, 2000, June 16, 2000, October 9, 2000, and telephone conversations.

p. 363, line 24: "I thought the truth could do it": 1977 tape with Ted Gandolfo.

p. 363, line 27: CIA asset Melvin Belli: See CIA Memorandum no. 9, Subject: Garrison and the Kennedy Assassination. This memorandum lists those who "have or have claimed to have a connection with the Central Intelligence Agency." Melvin Belli is the second person on the list: To: DCI, DDP and others, From: Kesler, J. W. CI/R & A, 104-10310-10251, Agency file number: CIA-DDP-FILES, NARA.

p. 363, line 30: "Affidavit": September 27, 1986, *Papers of Jim Garrison,* NARA.

p. 363, line 17: Garrison and Hitchcock: Occasional notes of Jim Garrison in *Garrison Family Papers.*

p. 365, line 12: "the least you could have done": Interview with William Walter, January 3, 2000; interview with Monique Poierrier, January 12, 2000.

p. 365, line 18: "I would have spotted it": Interview with Judge Denis A. Barry, May 17, 1998.

p. 365, line 27: walk around the block: Interview with Judge Tom Early, January 10, 1998.

p. 365, line 33: "Enjoy your Christmas!": Interview with Danielle Schott, May 19, 1998.

p. 365, line 39: he didn't want to get out of bed: Interview with Frank Minyard, January 8, 1998.

p. 366, line 6: idea of Judge David R. M. Williams: Interview with Judge Williams, June 16, 2000.

p. 366, line 9: Liz as his administrator: See handwritten wills, September 2, 1978 and November 28, 1982, courtesy of Lyon Garrison.

p. 366, line 10: "Do something good": Interview with Judge James C. Gulotta, June 9, 2000.

p. 366, line 30: "it's the biggest in the state of Louisiana": Interview with Judge Denis A. Barry, May 10, 1999.

p. 366, line 41: The death of Jim Garrison: See "La. Judge Jim Garrison Dies; 'JFK' Film Based on His Ideas," by J. Y. Smith. *Washington Post, October* 22, 1992, p. B6.

p. 366, line 42: the bed sores were on the pressure points of the bone: Interview with Dr. Frank Minyard, June 21, 1999.

p. 367, line 35: "five beloved children": Last Will, Handwritten, November 28, 1982, courtesy of Lyon Garrison.

p. 367, line 40: "every American owes him a debt of gratitude": "Conspiracy Theorist Garrison, 70," by Sean McNamara, *USA Today,* October 22, 1992, p. A2.

p. 368, line 6: "Agency by the big toe": Jim Garrison interviewed in Steve Tyler's *He Must Have Something.* See also Fred Powledge, "Is Garrison Faking? The DA, The CIA, and the Assassination," *New Republic,* June 17, 1967.

CHAPTER 23

All quotations from Thomas Edward Beckham come from interviews with Mr. Beckham.

p. 369, Epigraph: "big operation": Jim Garrison at the New Orleans conference, September 1968.

p. 369, Epigraph: "How many more Oswalds": Interview with Gordon Novel, September 1, 2000.

p. 369, Epigraph: "I guess I will see them there soon": Angleton quoted by Trento, *The Secret History of the CIA,* p. 479.

p. 369, line 1: "you've got a mailbox now": This chapter is based on interviews with Thomas Edward Beckham, March 30 and 31st and April 3, 2002.

p. 369, line 10: "caught in the act": State Department Memorandum, To: Director, O/SY thru: Chief, O/SY/E, Subject: Item in *East Village Other,* August 20, 1969, September 2, 1969, NARA.

p. 370, line 5: pictures flashing: Loran Hall describes his training with military intelligence: Loran Hall in Executive Session before the House Select Committee on Assassinations, October 5, 1977, 014660, NARA.

p. 370, line 39: a government document: U.S. Army Air Defense Command, Office of Commanding General, Ent Air Force Base, Colorado Springs, Colorado, Beckham, Thomas Edward, Unit Com. section: Field Code: T-Bird, The Republic of Vietnam, Biet Dong Quan, HQ-43567G2-File, courtesy of Thomas Edward Beckham.

p. 372, line 15: "He is indeed aware": This document is part of the Testimony of Richard M. Bissell before the Senate Select Committee to Study Governmental Operations with Respect to Intelligence Activities, June 11, 1975, Record Number: 157-10011-10018, 135 pages, SSCIA box 231, folder 5, NARA.

p. 372, line 41: "fallback position": Conversation with Gerald Patrick Hemming, August 18, 2003.

p. 373, line 4: Roy Hargraves admission: See Larry Hancock, *Someone Would Have Talked,* Appendix A, pp. 268-306.

p. 376, line 4: Jack Martin denounces Beckham to the FBI: FBI 124-10058-10072, HQ, 62-109060-4618, From: SAC, New Orleans, To: Director, FBI, February 20, 1967, 9 pages, NARA.

p. 376, line 17: "the military habit of responding to orders": Jim Garrison to Zach Sklar, March 16, 1988.

p. 376, line 28: "Angelo Kennedy . . .": Interview with Angelo Kennedy, Miami, June 27, 2005; telephone conversations, June 28, 2005; June 30, 2005; July 11, 2005.

p. 378, line 13: "If you come across him, stay away": Conversation with Edward I. Arthur, June 29, 2005.

p. 378, line 36: worked with wealthy Kennedy backer Ted Racoosin: Interview with Howard K. Davis, June 29, 2005.

p. 381, line 19: "Jim Garrison was closer to the truth": Interview with Donold P. Norton, January 24, 2003.

p. 381, line 28: "a high level plot": Interview with Dr. Robert N. McClelland, December 31, 2003.

p. 381, line 34: "the CIA had to be involved": Interview with Isidro Borja, January 5, 2004.

p. 382, line 3: "it could be the CIA": Interview with Jose Antonio Lanuza, February 5, 2004.

p. 382, line 9: "he was so close": Interview with Mary Ferrell, February 11, 2002.

p. 382, line 20: "No one talked":

The source for this information is employed by a major research library in
the United States and prefers to remain anonymous.

p. 382, line 23: Docu-drama: *Papers of Jim Garrison*, courtesy of Lyon
Garrison.

p. 382, line 24: "they knew they'd
been danced with": Jim Garrison in
The Garrison Tapes.

p. 384, line 47: "I wish I could
have told him": Conversation with
Thomas Edward Beckham, July 24,
2003.

ANNOTATED AND
SELECT JIM GARRISON
BIBLIOGRAPHY

Adams, Frank T. 1992. *James A. Dombrowski: An American Heretic, 1897–1983.* Knoxville: University of Tennessee Press.

Bacque, James. 1991. *Other Losses: The Shocking Truth behind the Mass Deaths of Disarmed German Soldiers and Civilians under General Eisenhower's Command.* Roseville, CA: Prima Publishing. Distributed by St. Martin's Press.

Badeaux, Hubert J. 1959. *The Underworld of Sex: A Documented Account of Organized Sexual Degeneracy.* Privately printed. New Orleans: Herald Press.

Bamford, James. 2001. *Body of Secrets: Anatomy of the Ultra-Secret National Security Agency.* New York: Doubleday.

Beschloss, Michael R. 1986. *May-Day: Eisenhower, Khrushchev and the U-2 Affair.* New York: Harper and Row.

———. 1991. *The Crisis Years: Kennedy and Khrushchev: 1960–1963.* New York: HarperCollins.

Bethell, Tom. 1988. *The Electric Windmill: An Inadvertent Autobiography.* Washington, DC: Regnery Gateway. Having worked for Garrison as his archivist, Bethel suddenly turned over the witness list for the trial to the attorneys of Clay Shaw.

Biles, Joe G. 2000. *The Arrogance of Ignorance: Essays on the HSCA and the Shaw Trial.* Processed.

———. 2002. *In History's Shadow: Lee Harvey Oswald, Kerry Thornley, and the Garrison Investigation.* Lincoln, NE: Writers Club Press: iUniverse.

Blain, Dr. Hugh Mercer. 1937. *Favorite Huey Long Stories.* Baton Rouge, LA: Otto Claitor.

Blakey, G. Robert, and Richard Billings. 1981. *The Plot To Kill the President: Organized Crime Assassinated J.F.K.–The Definitive Story.* New York: Times Books.

———. 1992. *Fatal Hour: The Assassination of President Kennedy by Organized Crime.* New York: Berkley Books. The new introduction, "Murder Will Out," is by Richard Billings.

Blum, William. 1995. *Killing Hope: U.S. Military and CIA Interventions since World War II.* Monroe, ME: Common Courage Press.

Branch, Taylor. 1988. *Parting the Waters: America in the King Years 1954–63.* New York: Simon and Schuster.

———, and Eugene M. Propper. 1982. *Labyrinth: How a Stubborn U.S. Prosecutor Penetrated a Shadlowland of Covert Operations on Three*

Continents To Find the Assassins of Orlando Letelier. New York: Viking Press.

Brener, Milton E. 1969. *The Garrison Case.* New York: Clarkson Potter. As an attorney, Brener represented several figures in this case, notably Walter Sheridan.

Bringuier, Carlos. 1969. *Red Friday: November 22nd, 1963.* Chicago: Chas. Hallberg.

Brown, Sarah Hart. 1998. *Standing against Dragons: Three Southern Lawyers in An Era of Fear.* Baton Rouge: Louisiana State University Press. See chapter 8 titled "They Were the Real Subversives. The Dombrowski Case and the Mississippi Crusade, 1963–1965."

Butler, Anne. 1983. *A Tourist's Guide to West Feliciana Parish.* St. Francisville, LA: Greenwood Press.

———. 2000. *Weep for the Living.* Philadelphia: Xlibris.

Butler, Ed., 1968. *Revolution Is My Profession.* Twin Circle Publishers. Distributed by Square Center, Los Angeles, CA.

Calder, Michael. 1998. *JFK VS. CIA: The Central Intelligence Agency's Assassination of the President.* Los Angeles: West LA Publishers.

Cook, Fred. 1967. "Anything To Get Hoffa." *The Nation.* February 20, 1967. Describes the illegal activities of Walter Sheridan in framing Jimmy Hoffa.

Corn, David. 1994. *Blond Ghost: Ted Shackley and the CIA's Crusade.* New York: Simon and Schuster.

Cornwell, Patricia. 1993. *Cruel* and *Unusual.* New York: Avon Books.

Corso, Col. Philip J. 1997. *The Day after Roswell.* New York: Pocket Books.

Davis, John. 1989. *Mafia Kingfish.* New York: McGraw-Hill.

Davis, William Hardy. 1976. *Aiming for the Jugular in New Orleans.* Port Washington, NY: Ashley Books.

Davy, William. 1995. *Through the Looking Glass: The Mysterious World of Clay Shaw.* Los Angeles: CTKA.

———. 1999. *Let Justice Be Done.* Reston, VA: Jordon Publishing. The first volume to examine the voluminous CIA archives on Jim Garrison's case against Clay Shaw, released under the 1992 JFK act.

DiEugenio, James. 1992. *Destiny Betrayed: JFK, Cuba, and the Garrison Case.* New York: Sheridan Square Press.

DiEugenio, James, and Lisa Pease, eds. 2003. *The Assassinations: Probe Magazine on JFK, MLK, RFK, and Malcolm X.* Los Angeles: Feral House.

Deutsch, Eberhard P. 1966. "From Zenger to Garrison: A Tale of Two Centuries." *New York State Bar Journal* 38, no. 5 (October 1966): 409–419.

Epstein, Edward Jay. 1992. *The Assassination Chronicles: Inquest, Counterplot,* and *Legend.* New York: Carroll and Graf.

Fairchild, Wayne. 1998. *Innocence of Oswald and the JFK Assassins.* Nashville: Research Publications.

Fetzer, James H., ed. 2000. *Murder in Dealey Plaza: What We Know Now that We Didn't Know Then about the Death of JFK.* Chicago: Catfeet Press.

Flake, Otto. 1931. *The Marquis de Sade with a Postscript on Restif De La Bretonne.* Trans. from the German by Edward Crankshaw. London: Peter Davies.

Flammonde, Paris. 1969. *The Kennedy Conspiracy: An Uncommissioned Report on the Jim Garrison Investigation.* New York: Meredith Press.

Fonzi, Gaeton. 1994. *The Last Investigation.* New York: Thunder's Mouth Press.

Franqui, Carlos. 1985. *Family Portrait with Fidel.* New York: Vintage Books. Don't miss the foreword by the great Cuban novelist Guillermo Cabrera Infante.

Fursenkso, Aleksandr, and Timothy Naftali. 1997. *One Hell of a Gamble: Khrushchev, Castro & Kennedy, 1958–1964.* New York: Norton.

Garrison, Jim. 1970. *A Heritage of Stone.* New York: Putnam.

———. 1976. *The Star-Spangled Contract.* New York: McGraw-Hill.

———. 1988. *On the Trail of the Assassins: My Investigation and Prosecution of the Murder of President Kennedy.* New York: Sheridan Square Press.

Gentry, Curt. 1991. *J. Edgar Hoover: The Man and the Secrets.* New York: Norton.

Gibson, Donald. 2000. *The Kennedy Assassination Cover-Up.* Commack, NY: Kroshka Books.

Gottschall, Alvin G. 1997. *Growing Up in New Orleans.* New York: Vantage Press. Gottschall went to high school with Jim Garrison and provides several amusing anecdotes about Garrison as a practical joker, friend and fraternity brother.

Gould, Jennifer. 1997. *Vodka, Tears, and Lenin's Angel: My Adventures in the Wild and Woolly Former Soviet Union.* New York: St. Martin's Press.

Grose, Peter. 1994. *Gentleman Spy: The Life of Allen Dulles.* Amherst: University of Massachusetts Press.

Haas, Edward F. 1974. *DeLesseps S. Morrison and the Image of Reform: New Orleans Politics, 1946–1961.* Baton Rouge: Louisiana State University Press.

Hancock, Larry. 2003. *Someone Would Have Talked: What We Know Forty Years after the Murder of President Kennedy.* Southlake, TX: JFK Lancer Productions and Publications.

Heath, Robert G. 1996. *Exploring the Mind—Brain Relationship.* Baton Rouge, LA: Moran Printing.

Helms, Richard. 2003. *A Look Over My Shoulder: A Life in the Central Intelligence Agency.* New York: Random House.

Hepburn, James. 1968. *Farewell America.* Verviers, Belgium: Frontiers.

Hersh, Burton. 1992. *The Old Boys: The American Elite and the Origins of the CIA.* New York: Scribner.

Hersh, Seymour M. 1997. *The Dark Side of Camelot.* New York: Little, Brown. The implication is that John F. Kennedy's profligate sexuality affected his decision making, a charge Hersh cannot substantiate.

Hinckle, Warren, and William Turner. 1992. *Deadly Secrets: The CIA— MAFIA War against Castro and the Assassination of JFK.* New York: Thunder's Mouth Press.

Holz, Denice, ed. 1981. *Conspiracy in Dallas.* Shreveport, LA: Fairchild Books, Research Division.

Hosty, James P. Jr. 1996. *Assignment: Oswald.* New York: Arcade.

James, Rosemary, and Jack Wardlaw. 1967. *Plot or Politics?* New York: Pelican Books. Breezily sarcastic, this book superficially covers Jim Garrison's early political career. Its bias is unrelentingly in favor of Clay Shaw. Information about Jim Garrison is drawn primarily from the public record.

Joesten, Joachim. 1964. *Oswald: Assassin or Fall Guy?* New York: Marzani and Munsell.

———. 1967. *The Garrison Enquiry.* London: Peter Dawnay.

The Joint Legislative Committee on Un-American Activities: State of Louisiana. 1963, 1964. Report No. 4. "Activities of the Southern Conference Educational Fund, Inc. in Louisiana." Part 1, November 19,

1963. Report No. 5. "Activities of the Southern Conference Educational Fund, Inc. in Louisiana." Part 2, April 13, 1964. Prepared and released by the Joint Legislative Committee on Un-American Activities, State of Louisiana. Old State Capitol. Baton Rouge, Louisiana.

Kaiser, David. 2000. *American Tragedy: Kennedy, Johnson, and the Origins of the Vietnam War.* Cambridge, MA: Belknap Press of Harvard University Press.

Kaiser, Robert Blair. 1975. "The JFK Assassination: Why Congress Should Reopen the Investigation." *Rolling Stone,* no. 185, April 24, 1975, pp. 27–28, 30–31, 33, 37–38.

Kantor, Seth. 1978. *Who Was Jack Ruby?* New York: Everest House.

Keefer, Edward C., Charles S. Sampson, and Louis J. Smith, eds. 1996. *Cuban Missile Crisis and Aftermath.* Foreign Relations of the United States, 1961–1963, Vol. XI. Washington, DC: U.S Government Printing Office.

Kiel, R. Andrew. 2000. *J. Edgar Hoover: The Father of the Cold War.* Lanham, NY: University Press of America.

King, Larry. 1982. *Larry King by Larry King.* New York: Simon and Schuster. King attempts to justify his purloining of money donated to the Garrison investigation by financier Louis E. Wolfson.

Kinoy, Arthur. 1983. *Rights on Trial: The Odyssey of a People's Lawyer.* Cambridge, MA: Harvard University Press. Contains an excellent account of the Dombrowski case.

Kirkwood, James. 1970. *American Grotesque.* New York: Simon and Schuster. When Clay Shaw, scanning the homosexual community, requested that James Herlihy write a positive book about him, and he declined, Herlihy enlisted Kirkwood to undertake the task. This book manages to describe the Shaw trial without a shred of political insight.

Kurtz, Michael L. 1982. *Crime of the Century: The Kennedy Assassination from a Historian's Perspective.* Knoxville: University of Tennessee Press.

La Fontaine, Ray, and Mary La Fontaine. 1996. *Oswald Talked: The New Evidence in the JFK Assassination.* Gretna, LA: Pelican Publishing. This book includes Mary Ferrell's discovery regarding the government Department of Defense card carried by Oswald after he left the service.

Lambert, Patricia. 1998. *False Witness: The Real Story of Jim Garrison's Investigation and Oliver Stone's JFK.* 1998. New York: M. Evans. A one-dimensional attack on Garrison, which includes a preposterous charge that Oliver Stone must have Nazi sympathies since he, like every film artist, admires the work of Leni Riefenstahl.

Lane, Mark. 1966. *Rush To Judgment.* New York: Holt, Rinehart and Winston. The landmark study by the originator of this field of research.

———. 1968. *A Citizen's Dissent: Mark Lane Replies.* New York: Holt, Rinehart and Winston.

———. 1991. *Plausible Denial: Was the CIA Involved in the Assassination of JFK?* New York: Thunder's Mouth Press.

Lewis, Ron. 1993. *Flashback: The Untold Story of Lee Harvey Oswald.* Roseburg, OR: Lewcom.

Le Sueur, James D. 2001. *Uncivil War: Intellectuals and Identity Politics During the Decolonization of Algeria.* Philadelphia: University of Pennsylvania Press. Relates some of the story of Jacques Soustelle.

Littell, Robert. 2003. *The Company: A Novel of the CIA.* New York: Penguin Books.

Macdonald, Dwight. 1965. "A Critique of the Warren Report." *Esquire.* March, pp. 59–67.

Mallon, Thomas. 2002. *Mrs. Paine's Garage and the Murder of John F. Kennedy.* New York: Pantheon Books.

Malone, Lee. 1989. *The Majesty of the Felicianas.* Gretna, LA:. Pelican.

Mangold, Tom. 1991. *Cold Warrior: James Jesus Angleton: The CIA's Master Spy Hunter.* New York: Simon and Schuster.

Marchetti, Victor, and Marks, John D. 1974. *The CIA and the Cult of Intelligence.* New York: Knopf.

Marcus, Raymond. 1995. *Addendum B: Addendum to the HSCA, The Zapruder Film, and the Single Bullet Theory.* Marcus did original photographic analysis, particularly on Mary Moorman's photograph taken at Dealey Plaza. MIT photographic laboratories confirmed that the figure of a man with a gun could be discerned to the front of the Kennedy motorcade.

Marks, John. 1979. *The Search for the Manchurian Candidate.* New York: Times Books.

The Marquis de Sade: The Complete Justine, Philosophy in the Bedroom and other writings. 1966. Comp. and trans. by Richard Seaver and Austryn Wainhouse. New York: Grove Press.

Marrs, Jim. 1989. *Crossfire: The Plot That Killed Kennedy.* New York: Carroll and Graf.

May, Ernest R., and Philip D. Zelikow. 1997. *The Kennedy Tapes: Inside the White House during the Cuban Missile Crisis.* Cambridge, MA: Belknap Press of Harvard University Press.

McClellan, Barr. 2003. *Blood, Money and Power: How L.B.J. Killed J.F.K.* New York: Hanover House.

McComb, John. 1968. *Stand Up! You Are an American.* Vienna, VA: Founders Press.

McMillan, Priscilla Johnson. 1977. *Marina and Lee.* New York: Harper and Row.

Meagher, Sylvia. 1976. *Accessories after the Fact: The Warren Commission, the Authorities and the Report.* New York: Vintage Books.

Melanson, Philip H. 1990. *Spy Saga: Lee Harvey Oswald and U.S. Intelligence.* Westport, CT: Praeger.

Messick, Hank. 1968. *Syndicate in the Sun.* New York: Macmillan.

Navarro, Antonio. 1981. *Tocayo: A Cuban Resistance Leader's True Story.* Westport, CT: Sandown Books.

Newman, John. 1992. *JFK and Vietnam: Deception, Intrigue, and the Struggle for Power.* New York: Warner Books.

———. 1995. *Oswald and the CIA.* New York: Carroll and Graf.

Oglesby Carl. 1976. *The Yankee and Cowboy War.* Kansas City, MO: Sheed, Andrews and McMeel. Oglesby attempts to find a motive for the murder of President Kennedy in a dispute between warring factions of capitalism.

Oswald, Robert. 1967. *Lee: A Portrait of Lee Harvey Oswald.* New York: Coward-McCann. There are interesting glimpses of Oswald in his boyhood. Discount all the attempts, obvious in their absurdity, to place guns in the hands of the young Lee, and the assumption, offered by ignoring the Zapruder film, that his brother acted alone in the murder of the President. Where Robert Oswald attempts to justify the conclusions of the Warren Report, he is embarrassing. Where he offers images of Lee navigating a childhood of neglect, his book is invaluable.

Pearson, John. 1966. *The Life of Ian Fleming.* New York: McGraw-Hill.

Phelan, James. 1982. *Scandals, Scamps, and Scoundrels: The Casebook of an Investigative Reporter.* New York: Random House. Posing as an independent reporter for the *Saturday Evening Post*, Phelan attempted to discredit Garrison's investigation on behalf of the FBI and the CIA. Memos of his numerous contacts with that agency, contacts originally initiated by Phelan himself, are available at the National Archives.

Philbrick, Herbert A. 1952. *I Led 3 Lives: Citizen, "Communist," Counterspy*. New York: Grosset and Dunlap. Philbrick was Oswald's hero—and his model.

Piper, Michael Collins. 1995. *Final Judgement: The Missing Link in the JFK Assassination Conspiracy*. Washington, DC: Wolfe Press.

Polmar, Norman. 2001. *Spyplane: The U-2 History Declassified*. Osceola, WI: MBI Publishing.

Popkin, Richard H. 1966. *The Second Oswald*. New York: An Avon Library New York Review Book.

Posner, Gerald. 1994. *Case Closed: Lee Harvey Oswald and the Assassination of JFK*. New York: Anchor Books, Doubleday. Edited by Robert Loomis, this book has been touted as the last word on the subject, despite its many factual errors. See William Turner, *Rear View Mirror*, for an account of how Random House editor Robert Loomis solicited Posner to write this book with the promise of full CIA cooperation.

Powers, Francis Gary, with Curt Gentry. 1970. *Operation Overflight: The U-2 Pilot Tells His Story for the First Time*. New York: Holt, Rinehart and Winston. Powers notes the presence of Lee Harvey Oswald in the Soviet courtroom where he stood trial.

Powers, Thomas. 1979. *The Man Who Kept the Secrets: Richard Helms and the CIA*. New York: Knopf.

Prochnau, William. 1995. *Once Upon a Distant War*. New York: Times Books. A source for John F. Kennedy's obsessive attacks on *New York Times* reporter David Halberstam.

project mk/ultra, The CIA's Program of Research in Behavioral Modification. 1977. Joint Hearing before the Select Committee on Intelligence and the Subcommittee on Health and Scientific Research of the Committee of Human Resources, U.S. Senate. Ninety-Fifth Congress. First Session. August 3. Washington, DC: U.S. Government Printing Office.

Prouty, L. Fletcher. 1973. *The Secret Team: The CIA and its Allies in Control of the United States and the World*. Englewood Cliffs, New Jersey: Prentice Hall.

———. 1992. *JFK, the CIA, Vietnam, and the Plot to Assassinate John F. Kennedy*. New York: Citadel Press.

Rappleye, Charles, and Ed Becker. 1991. *All American Mafioso: The Johnny Rosselli Story*. New York: Doubleday.

Ratcliffe, David T. 1999. *Understanding Special Operations and Their Impact on the Vietnam War Era*. Santa Cruz, CA: rat haus reality press.

Reeves, Richard. 1993. *President Kennedy: Profile of Power*. New York: Simon and Schuster.

Report of the President's Commission on the Assassination of President John F. Kennedy. 1964. United States Government Printing Office. Washington, D.C. The 26 volumes are available at *historymatters.com*.

Rodriguez, Juan Carlos. 1999. *The Bay of Pigs and the CIA*. Melbourne, Australia, and New York: Ocean Press. This is the official Cuban point of view regarding that event.

Rogers, Kim Lacy. 1993. *Righteous Lives: Narratives of the New Orleans Civil Rights Movement*. New York: New York University Press.

Russell, Dick. 1992. *The Man Who Knew Too Much*. New York: Carroll and Graf. "The man" is the ambivalent Richard Case Nagell. Russell's research is exhaustive. Second Carroll and Graf paperback edition, 2003.

Russo, Gus. 1998. *Live by the Sword: The Secret War against Castro and the Death of JFK.* Baltimore: Bancroft Press. Ignore Russo's conclusion and examine his interviews with Miami sources.

Sahl, Mort. 1976. *Heartland.* New York: Harcourt, Brace, Jovanovich. Many errors in the discussion of the Garrison investigation.

Salandria, Vincent J. 1971. "The Assassination of President John F. Kennedy: A Model for Explanation." *Computers and Automation,* December 1971, pp. 32–40.

Saunders, Frances Stonor. 1999. *The Cultural Cold War: The CIA and the World of Arts and Letters.* New York: New Press.

Scheim, David E. 1988. *Contract on America: The Mafia Murder of President John F. Kennedy.* New York: Shapolsky.

Schlesinger, Arthur M. Jr. 1965. *A Thousand Days: John F. Kennedy in the White House.* Boston: Houghton Mifflin.

———. 1978. *Robert Kennedy and His Times.* New York: Ballantine Books.

Schotz, E. Martin. 1996. *History Will Not Absolve Us: Orwellian Control, Public Denial, and the Murder of President Kennedy.* Kurtz, Brookline, MA: Ulmer and DeLucia.

Scott, Peter Dale. 1977. *Crime and Cover-Up: The CIA, the Mafia, and the Dallas-Watergate Connection.* Santa Barbara, CA: Open Archives Press. Some of the references to Garrison here are erroneous; sources for discussion of Garrison come from hostile FBI/CIA informants James Phelan and Walter Sheridan.

Seelig, Frederick. 1967. *Destroy the Accuser.* Miami: Freedom Press.

Sheridan, Walter. 1972. *The Fall and Rise of Jimmy Hoffa.* New York: Saturday Review Press. Sheridan here attempts to defend himself and asserts that he did not try to bribe Garrison witnesses for his NBC "White Paper." Since he fled the jurisdiction, rather than face charges of attempted bribery, the matter was never adjudicated. See "Anything To Get Hoffa," which exposes Sheridan's methods.

Simpson, Christopher. 1988. *Blowback: America's Recruitment of Nazis and Its Effect on the Cold War.* New York: Weidenfeld and Nicolson.

Slovenko, Ralph, ed. 1966. *Crime Law And Corrections.* Springfield, IL: Charles C. Thomas. For Jim Garrison's Foreword, "A Heritage Of Stone," pp. xvii-xxv.

Sonnenberg, Ben. 1991. *Lost Property: Memoirs and Confessions of a Bad Boy.* New York: Summit Books: Sonnenberg was cleared for CIA's Project QKENCHANT in 1959, and the clearance was renewed in 1965. During that period, he edited Mark Lane's *Rush To Judgment.* Sonnenberg reveals few of the details of his CIA service.

Sorensen, Theodore C. 1966. *Kennedy.* New York: Bantam Books.

———. 1969. *The Kennedy Legacy.* New York: Macmillan.

Sprague, Richard E., Thomas G. Whittle, and Kay Skinner. "The Ultimate Cover-Up: The CIA and the Killing of John F. Kennedy, Part II." Mimeographed. Available at the National Archives.

Sproesser, Louis, ed. 1999. *The Garrison Investigation: November 1966 to February 1968.* Sturbridge, MA: Southern New England Research.

———, ed. 1997. *Justice Denied: The Sirhan, Shaw, Ray Trials. A Chronology, January 1969 to December 1969.* Sturbridge, MA: Southern New England Research.

Stafford, Jean. 1966. *A Mother in History: Marguerite Oswald, The Mother of the Man Who Killed Kennedy.* New York: Bantam Books. A smug, heartless little book, simultaneously overwritten ("It sounded like catastrophe, and I was sorry to be in alien corn") and ignorant of the elementary facts, by the distinguished fiction writer and widow of stellar journalist A. J. Liebling who should have known better.

Summers, Anthony. 1980. *Conspiracy.* New York: McGraw-Hill.

———. 1998. *Not in Your Lifetime: The Definitive Book on the J.F.K. Assassination.* New York: Marlowe. Update of *Conspiracy,* 1980. Contains important original interviews.

Stone, Oliver, and Zachary Sklar. 1992. *JFK: The Book of the Film.* New York: Applause Books.

Tanner, Hans. 1962. *Counter-Revolutionary Agent: Diary of the Events which Occurred in CUBA between January and July, 1961.* London: G. T. Foulis.

Thomas, D. M. 1992. *Flying in to Love: A Novel.* New York: Carroll and Graf.

Thomas, Evan. 1995. *The Very Best Men: Four Who Dared: The Early Years of the CIA.* New York: Simon and Schuster.

———. 2000. *Robert F. Kennedy: His Life.* New York: Simon and Schuster.

Thomas, Kenn. 1999. *Maury Island UFO: The Crisman Conspiracy.* Lilburn, GA: IllumiNet Press.

Thornley, Kerry. 1965. *Oswald.* Chicago: New Classics House.

———. 1991. *The Idle Warriors.* Avondale Estates, GA: IllumiNet Press.

Toplin, Robert Brent, ed. 2000. *Oliver Stone's USA: Film, History, and Controversy.* Lawrence: University Press of Kansas.

Trento, Joseph J. 2001. *The Secret History of the CIA.* Roseville, CA: Forum, Prima Publishing.

Turner, William. 2001. *Rearview Mirror: Looking Back at the FBI, the CIA and other Tails.* Granite Bay, CA: Penmarin Books.

Twyman, Noel. 1997. *Bloody Treason: On Solving History's Greatest Murder Mystery: The Assassination of John F. Kennedy.* Rancho Santa Fe, CA: Laurel.

U.S. House of Representatives. 1979. *The Final Assassinations Report: Report of the Select Committee on Assassinations.* New York: Bantam Books.

Walton, Richard J. 1972. *Cold War and Counterrevolution: The Foreign Policy of John F. Kennedy.* New York: Viking Press.

Weisberg, Harold. 1965. *Whitewash: The Report on the Warren Report.* New York: Dell.

———. 1966. *Whitewash II: the FBI Secret Service Coverup.* Hyattstown, MD: Harold Weisberg.

———. 1967. *Oswald in New Orleans.* New York: Canyon Books.

———. 1967. *Photographic Whitewash: Suppressed Kennedy Assassination Pictures.* Hyattstown, MD: Harold Weisberg.

———. 1974. *Whitewash IV: JFK Assassination Transcript.* Hyattstown, MD: Harold Weisberg.

———. 1994. *Case Open: The Omissions, Distortions and Falsifications of Case Closed.* New York: Carroll and Graf.

Wilson, Jane. 1967. "Hurricane Garrison Flattens New Orleans." *Los Angeles Free Press,* October 20, 1967.

Wiltz, Christine. 2000. *The Last Madam: A Life in the New Orleans Underworld.* New York: Faber and Faber.

Winters, Francis X. 1999. *The Year of the Hare: America in Vietnam, January 25, 1963–February 15, 1964.* Athens: University of Georgia Press.

Wise, David, Ross Wise, and Thomas B. Wise. 1962. *The U-2 Affair.* New York: Bantam Books.

Woodward, Bob. 2005. *The Secret Man: The Story of Watergate's Deep Throat.* New York: Simon & Schuster.

Wrone, David R., ed. 1978. *The Freedom of Information Act and Political Assassinations. Vol. I. The Legal Proceedings of Harold Weisberg v. General Services Administration, together with the January 22 and 27 Warren Commission Transcripts.* Stevens Point, WI: Foundation Press, University of Wisconsin.

———. 2003. *The Zapruder Film: Reframing JFK's Assassination.* Lawrence: University Press of Kansas.

INDEX

School of the Americas, 33–34
Schubert, John, 323
Schulingkamp, Oliver, 18, 19
Schwegmann, John, Jr., 275
Sciambra, Andrew (Moo Moo), 30,
  65–66, 135, 321
  Ferrie and, 103–104
  memo about meeting with Russo
    and Ferrie, 150–151
  Oswald's presence in Louisiana
    and, 221–233
  Perrin and, 295
  Regis Kennedy and, 72
  Russo and, 113–115
  Shaw and, 117
  Shaw trial testimony of, 306–307
Security Homestead, 297
Seghers, Mike, 331, 335
Seligman-Schurch, Peter, 138
Sepe, Alfonso, 247
Sessions, Cliff, 128
Sewel, Fred, 73
Seymour, William, 249, 252, 281,
  291
Sforza, Anthony, 180
Shanklin, J. Gordon, 294
Shaw, Clay (grandfather), 130
Shaw, Clay Lavergne
  admission to Dureau, 317
  Andrews and, 14, 27–30
  arrest of, 116–120
  Banister and, 70, 75
  Beckham and, 75, 81
  Bethell divulges witness list of,
    292–293
  book of, 236
  charged with conspiracy, 150
  charged with perjury, 319
  CIA and, 131–143, 355–356
  as Clay Bertrand, 65–66, 121–127,
    202–203
  closing statements, 315–317
  defense case, 309, 310–314
  early life of, 130
  Ferrie and, 38, 39–40, 122–123
  grand jury testimony and, 287–289
  Hardy and, 95
  JFK X-rays and autopsy
    photographs and, 297–299
  JG and, 120–121, 318
  Johnson (Clyde) and, 243
  liberal faççade of, 129–130
  lies of, exposed, 115–116
  military service of, 130–131
  news reporting of, 307
  Norton's story and, 158–159
  opening statements, 303
  Oswald and, 27–30, 60, 122, 124
  photographed in Cuba, 349
  preliminary hearing, 146–150

prosecution case, 302–310
reactions to, 318–320
Shaw v. Robertson, 362
trial of, 301–316
trial testimony of, 312
Valdes and, 53
verdict, 317
witnesses unavailable to testify at,
  298–300
Shea, John, 15
Sheridan, Walter
  Carson and, 245
  charged with bribery, 200
  Gervais and, 332
  Gurvich and, 199
  Hoffa and, 185
  JG's finances and, 324–325, 327
  JG's witnesses and, 187–194, 357
  Red Strate and, 188–189
  RFK and, 89, 173, 186–188, 201,
    381
  "White Paper" of, 194–199, 202–203
Sherman, Mary, 49–55
Shilstone, Cecil, 111–112, 323
Shipes, John Henry, 347
Silva, Frank, 217, 220–221, 223,
  231, 300, 347, 379
Silver, Myra, 273
Simpson, Art, 278
Simpson, Robert, 278
Siragusa, Charles, 86
Sirera, Julie, 342, 361
Sklar, Zachary, 361, 363
"Sloman, Henry J.", 180
Slovenko, Ralph, 129
Smith, Benjamin, 332
Smith, David, 46, 47
Smith, James, 337–338
Smith, Joseph Burkholder, 57
Smith, Ron L., 47–48
Smith, Sandy, 255–257
Smith, Sergio Arcacha, 48, 67, 94,
  96–97, 231, 239, 346
  Manuel identifies, 208
  Martin (Jack) and, 55, 76
  RFK and, 382
Snipes, Vaughn, 155
Snyder, David, 102, 103, 321
Society for the Preservation of
  Southern Tradition, 287
Solie, Bruce L., 109
Somersett, Willie, 92
Somoza, Luis, 86
Sorrell, Forest, 263
Soule, Frederick A., 20, 330, 335
Soustelle, Jacques, 137–138, 140
Southwood, Jim, 153
Spadafora, Guterez di, 137
Spencer, James A., 73
Spiesel, Boris, 305

ABOUT THE AUTHOR

JOAN MELLEN is a professor of English and creative writing at Temple University in Philadelphia. In 2004, she received Temple's "Great Teacher" award. She has written seventeen books, ranging from film criticism *(Marilyn Monroe; Film Guide to The Battle of Algiers; Women And Their Sexuality in the New Film; The Waves at Genji's Door: Japan Through Its Cinema; Big Bad Wolves: Masculinity in the American Film)*, fiction *(Natural Tendencies)* and Latin American Studies to true crime *(Privilege)*, sports *(Bob Knight: His Own Man)*, and biography *(Kay Boyle: Author of Herself; Hellman and Hammett)*. She also writes for a variety of publications, among them the *New York Times*, the *Philadelphia Inquirer*, the *Los Angeles Times*, *Newsday*, the *Wall Street Journal* and the *Baltimore Sun*. She lives in Pennington, New Jersey.